PLA
FOOTL

2008–2009

61st edition

Editors: Glenda Rollin
and Jack Rollin

headline

Cover photographs Front and spine: Micah Richards (Manchester City) –
Richard Sellers/Sportsphoto; back: Roque Santa Cruz (Blackburn Rovers) –
Michael Mayhew/Sportsphoto.

ISBN 978 0 7553 1821 6

Typeset by Wearset Ltd, Boldon, Tyne and Wear

Printed and bound in Great Britain by Clays Ltd, St Ives plc

Headline's policy is to use papers that are natural, renewable and recyclable
products and made from wood grown in sustainable forests. The logging and
manufacturing processes are expected to conform to the environmental regulations
of the country of origin.

HEADLINE PUBLISHING GROUP
An Hachette Livre UK Company
338 Euston Road
London NW1 3BH

www.headline.co.uk
www.hachettelivre.co.uk

CONTENTS

European and International Football

Other Football

Information and Records

EDITORIAL

With the Euro 2008 finals reduced to a watching brief and making notes on future opponents in the 2010 World Cup qualifying competition, the inevitable discussion centred on the question of too many foreign players in the Premier League, stifling the growth of local talent and depriving the national team of a wider choice of first-class material.

To seek a satisfactory answer it is necessary to look back on the situation 50 years ago when the World Cup finals were held in Sweden. All four UK countries were among the 16 finalists, representing a quarter of the successful teams. On top of this, Sweden the host nation had an English born coach in charge, George Raynor!

In 2008 not even England has an English born coach, Steve McClaren being replaced by Fabio Capello of Italy. Ironically the same voices crying for fewer foreigners are content it seems to have yet another brought from abroad following the original appointment of Sven-Goran Eriksson who just about lasted a season back in club football in charge of Manchester City.

Of course in 1958 European cup football was still very much in its infancy. The European Cup of the Champions as it was known then, was virtually the preserve of one club Real Madrid, having won the first three and heading for a high five by 1960. There was also a complicated secondary tournament called the International Inter-Cities Fairs Cup, qualification for which was that it confined itself to cities where industrial fairs were held and thus enabling representative teams to be fielded.

As such London put a team into the competition and managed to reach the last stage. However, this long, drawn out affair had started in 1955! London beat Basle, Frankfurt and Lausanne to reach the final against Barcelona. The home leg was drawn 2-2, but the return match ended in a 6-0 thrashing, albeit with a weaker team lacking Jimmy Greaves and Johnny Haynes from the home game, but still with players of the calibre of Danny Blanchflower, Bobby Smith and Terry Medwin.

That was the past. In 2008 the Champions League final had two English teams, if not entirely stocked with home grown players. Manchester United and Chelsea had to resort to penalties to sort it all out and their meeting only served to underline the problems of club versus country when the foreign invasion is on everyone's mind.

Sepp Blatter at FIFA wants what he calls the 6-5 split to force clubs to field a split in the overwhelming foreign ranks. UEFA, on the other hand, mindful that the freedom of movement of labour in the European Union forbids any attempt at such restriction, consider a different option. This involves naming a set number of English born players among the 25 names nominated for European competitions, but with a guaranteed number for each match. This of course is OK for such games, the problem is domestic football.

However, will supporters of Manchester United and Chelsea, say, as the recent finalists in the Champions League, continue to be delighted if the players they are forced to put into the field are of lesser ability than previously, thus reducing their chances of similar trophies?

Everyone wants England to succeed at international level, but club football is the backbone of the game and always will be. If the average fan is asked whether he or she wants England or their own team to succeed, and must choose, the honest answer would frighten those in charge.

Of course no club is forced to sign foreign players. The quota system if applied would be in favour of English talent. The development of talent in this country must be given every opportunity to flourish until it reaches a level where it would be foolish to sign someone from across the sea of inferior quality. This is surely the way forward rather than a system which is being artificially forced onto the game, misguidedly with the best intentions but clearly entirely the wrong way in which to go about achieving it.

CLUB AND OTHER RECORDS DURING 2007–2008

Arsenal — Emmanuel Adebayor scored the club's 1000th Premier League goal v Reading on 12 November.

Birmingham City — Stephen Kelly is the only player in the Premier League to play in all 3420 minutes of the season.

Bradford City — Luke Medley scores with first touch on debut 25 August.

Carlisle United — Club record 12th successive home win on 8 March.

Charlton Athletic — Youngest League debutant Jonjo Shelvey, 16 years 59 days v Burnley 26 April 2008.

Chelsea — Frank Lampard scores his 100th and 101st goals for Chelsea on 16 February against Huddersfield.

Colchester United — Teddy Sheringham scores his 349th career goal.

Crystal Palace — John Bostock becomes club's youngest debutant at 15 years 287 days on 29 October.

Derby County — Finished the season with worst Premier League record with just one win, 20 goals, fewest points 11.

Everton — Club record sixth win in a row in the UEFA Cup on 13 February.

Gillingham — Luke Freeman becomes youngest FA Cup player at 15 years 233 days on 10 November and 14 days later is the club's youngest League debutant.

Hereford United — Trevor Benjamin becomes first fully capped player with two games for Jamaica.

Leyton Orient — Scored 5000th League goal v Carlisle United 1 September.

Liverpool — Scored 7000th League goal v Sunderland 25 August; break Champions League scoring record beating Besiktas 8-0 on 6 November; Fernando Torres becomes first club player to hit 20 League goals since 1995-96 and later equals Roger Hunt's feat of scoring in eight successive home League games.

Manchester United — Ryan Giggs scores his 100th League goal on 8 December v Derby County, makes his 100th European cup appearance on 20 January and catches up with Sir Bobby Charlton's 759th first team appearance in the Champions League final. Cristiano Ronaldo becomes the fifth to score 30 goals in the Premier League.

Portsmouth — Portsmouth 7 Reading 4 on 29 September breaks Premier League record aggregate.

Stockport County — Club record equalled with seven away wins on 1 March.

Swansea City — Club record 18th unbeaten match at Huddersfield on 1 March.

Tottenham Hotspur — Celebrate 125th anniversary by recovering from 4-1 down to draw v Aston Villa; Robbie Keane scores his 100th goal for the club v Sunderland on 19 January; Gilberto hits club's 500th home Premier League goal on 9 March.

Walsall — Tommy Mooney hits 200th and 201st career goals on 3 November.

England — David Beckham reaches his 100th full cap.

France — Thierry Henry reaches his 100th full cap.

Northern Ireland — David Healy breaks the European Championship goalscoring record with his 13th goal on 17 November.

Champions League — Manchester United v Chelsea final is the first with two English teams.

LEAGUE REVIEW AND CLUB SECTION

Just for a moment it seemed that the Cristiano Ronaldo-led Manchester United charge to another Premiership title was to be blunted in sight of the promised land when Chelsea beat them 2-1 at Stamford Bridge on 26 April. The Portuguese swashbuckler did not even start the game as a confident Sir Alex Ferguson indulged in a spot of tinkering with the team. It could have proved fatal. But while United recovered their poise, Chelsea had to be content with runners-up again and it added to the debit side of manager Avram Grant who had replaced Jose Mourinho earlier in the season and was to be forced to walk the plank.

Naturally in the context of the squad system, ever present players are a rare species. In 2007–08, the Premier League produced just 12 and amazingly just one of them, Stephen Kelly the Birmingham City full-back, succeeded in playing every one of the 90 minutes throughout the 38 matches.

Not surprisingly perhaps in view of the previous comments, Manchester United did not have one. Of the 25 different players called upon Wes Brown came nearest missing just two games, though two of his appearances were as a substitute. Rio Ferdinand turned out in 35 full matches while Ronaldo and Carlos Tevez, spirited away from West Ham United, both had 34 outings, including three from the bench.

Ronaldo with 31 League goals, and once again dual PFA and FWA player of the year as in 2006–07, was top scorer and only the fourth in the Premier League's short history to top the thirty goal mark. Tevez had 14 goals, Wayne Rooney who missed a number of matches with injury scored 12 goals himself from a total of 27 appearances.

Owen Hargreaves, prised out of Germany after many years, recovered from his broken leg and made an invaluable contribution in several midfield and defensive roles, the evergreen Ryan Giggs broke several personal records, not the least of them in the Champions League final when his substitute appearance eclipsed Sir Bobby Charlton's 758 first team games for the Old Trafford club.

By Arsenal standards third place was disappointing and such are the expectations in the top echelon, fourth for Liverpool was equally so, though they did pip Merseyside rivals Everton. At times Aston Villa looked capable of even better things as did Blackburn Rovers. Once they had reached the FA Cup final, Portsmouth seemed to lose concentration. Manchester City promised much earlier, faded and Sven-Goran Eriksson departed.

West Ham United looked mid-table most of the time, Tottenham Hotspur were erratic and Newcastle United improved enough with the return of Kevin Keegan. Wigan Athletic rallied well while both Middlesbrough and Sunderland kept out of trouble. Bolton Wanderers just escaped as did Fulham late on, but Reading, Birmingham City and Derby County breaking all the worst records went down.

For the first time 11 goals were scored in a Premier League game when Portsmouth beat Reading 7-4 and ten goals involved Reading, too, when they were beaten 6-4 by Tottenham Hotspur. Middlesbrough beat Manchester City 8-1 in another high scoring affair.

Automatic promotion came for West Bromwich Albion and Stoke City, Hull City via the play-offs. Down went Leicester City, Scunthorpe United and Colchester United. League One produced Swansea City and Nottingham Forest in first and second places, Doncaster Rovers through in the play-offs at the expense of points-penalised Leeds United while relegation was the lot for Bournemouth, Gillingham, Port Vale and Luton Town. Bournemouth and Luton had points deducted for going into administration, too.

Milton Keynes Dons, Peterborough United and Hereford United were the first-time teams promoted from League Two and were joined by Stockport County from the play-offs. For the first time since their introduction, the highest finishing team in all divisions were successful in this way. Wrexham and Mansfield Town were consigned to the Blue Square Premier replaced by two ex-League clubs Aldershot Town (after 16 years absence) and Exeter City.

FA Barclays Premiership

			Home					Away					Total					
		P	W	D	L	F	A	W	D	L	F	A	W	D	L	F	A	Gd	Pts
1	Manchester U	38	17	1	1	47	7	10	5	4	33	15	27	6	5	80	22	58	87
2	Chelsea	38	12	7	0	36	13	13	3	3	29	13	25	10	3	65	26	39	85
3	Arsenal	38	14	5	0	37	11	10	6	3	37	20	24	11	3	74	31	43	83
4	Liverpool	38	12	6	1	43	13	9	7	3	24	15	21	13	4	67	28	39	76
5	Everton	38	11	4	4	34	17	8	4	7	21	16	19	8	11	55	33	22	65
6	Aston Villa	38	10	3	6	34	22	6	9	4	37	29	16	12	10	71	51	20	60
7	Blackburn R	38	8	7	4	26	19	7	6	6	24	29	15	13	10	50	48	2	58
8	Portsmouth	38	7	8	4	24	14	9	1	9	24	26	16	9	13	48	40	8	57
9	Manchester C	38	11	4	4	28	20	4	6	9	17	33	15	10	13	45	53	–8	55
10	West Ham U	38	7	7	5	24	24	6	3	10	18	26	13	10	15	42	50	–8	49
11	Tottenham H	38	8	5	6	46	34	3	8	8	20	27	11	13	14	66	61	5	46
12	Newcastle U	38	8	5	6	25	26	3	5	11	20	39	11	10	17	45	65	–20	43
13	Middlesbrough	38	7	5	7	27	23	3	7	9	16	30	10	12	16	43	53	–10	42
14	Wigan Ath	38	8	5	6	21	17	2	5	12	13	34	10	10	18	34	51	–17	40
15	Sunderland	38	9	3	7	23	21	2	3	14	13	38	11	6	21	36	59	–23	39
16	Bolton W	38	7	5	7	23	18	2	5	12	13	36	9	10	19	36	54	–18	37
17	Fulham	38	5	5	9	22	31	3	7	9	16	29	8	12	18	38	60	–22	36
18	Reading	38	8	2	9	19	25	2	4	13	22	41	10	6	22	41	66	–25	36
19	Birmingham C	38	6	8	5	30	23	2	3	14	16	39	8	11	19	46	62	–16	35
20	Derby Co	38	1	5	13	12	43	0	3	16	8	46	1	8	29	20	89	–69	11

LEADING GOALSCORERS 2007–08

Players in this competition scoring eleven or more League goals are listed. Other leading scorers classified by total number of goals in all competitions. Only goals scored in the same division are included.

BARCLAYS PREMIERSHIP

	League	Carling Cup	FA Cup	Other	Total
Cristiano Ronaldo *(Manchester U)*	31	0	3	8	42
Fernando Torres *(Liverpool)*	24	3	0	6	33
Emmanuel Adebayor *(Arsenal)*	24	1	2	3	30
Roque Santa Cruz *(Blackburn R)*	19	3	0	1	23
Dimitar Berbatov *(Tottenham H)*	15	1	2	5	23
Robbie Keane *(Tottenham H)*	15	2	2	4	23
Ayegbeni Yakubu *(Everton)*	15	3	0	3	21
Benjani Mwaruwari *(Manchester C)*	15	0	0	0	15
(Includes 12 League goals for Portsmouth.)					
Carlos Tevez *(Manchester U)*	14	0	1	4	19
John Carew *(Aston Villa)*	13	0	0	0	13
Wayne Rooney *(Manchester U)*	12	0	2	4	18
Jermain Defoe *(Portsmouth)*	12	1	0	3	16
(Includes 4 League goals, 1 Carling Cup and 3 other goals for Tottenham H.)					
Steven Gerrard *(Liverpool)*	11	1	3	6	21
Nicolas Anelka *(Chelsea)*	11	0	0	1	12
(Includes 10 League and 1 other goal for Bolton W.)					
Michael Owen *(Newcastle U)*	11	1	1	0	13
Frank Lampard *(Chelsea)*	10	4	2	4	20
In order of total goals:					
Didier Drogba *(Chelsea)*	8	1	0	6	15
Cese Fabregas *(Arsenal)*	7	0	0	6	13

Other matches consist of European games, J Paint Trophy, Community Shield and Football League play-offs. Players listed in order of League goals total.

Coca-Cola Football League Championship

	P	W	D	L	F	A	W	D	L	F	A	W	D	L	F	A	Gd	Pts
		Home					Away					Total						
1 WBA	46	12	8	3	51	27	11	4	8	37	28	23	12	11	88	55	33	81
2 Stoke C	46	12	7	4	36	27	9	9	5	33	28	21	16	9	69	55	14	79
3 Hull C	46	13	7	3	43	19	8	5	10	22	28	21	12	13	65	47	18	75
4 Bristol C	46	13	7	3	33	20	7	7	9	21	33	20	14	12	54	53	1	74
5 Crystal Palace	46	9	9	5	31	23	9	8	6	27	19	18	17	11	58	42	16	71
6 Watford	46	8	7	8	26	29	10	9	4	36	27	18	16	12	62	56	6	70
7 Wolverhampton W	46	11	6	6	31	25	7	10	6	22	23	18	16	12	53	48	5	70
8 Ipswich T	46	15	7	1	44	14	3	8	12	21	42	18	15	13	65	56	9	69
9 Sheffield U	46	10	8	5	32	24	7	7	9	24	27	17	15	14	56	51	5	66
10 Plymouth Arg	46	9	9	5	37	22	8	4	11	23	28	17	13	16	60	50	10	64
11 Charlton Ath	46	9	7	7	38	29	8	6	9	25	29	17	13	16	63	58	5	64
12 Cardiff C	46	12	4	7	31	21	4	12	7	28	34	16	16	14	59	55	4	64
13 Burnley	46	7	9	7	31	31	9	5	9	29	36	16	14	16	60	67	-7	62
14 QPR	46	10	6	7	32	27	4	10	9	28	39	14	16	16	60	66	-6	58
15 Preston NE	46	11	5	7	29	20	4	6	13	21	36	15	11	20	50	56	-6	56
16 Sheffield W	46	9	5	9	29	25	5	8	10	25	30	14	13	19	54	55	-1	55
17 Norwich C	46	10	6	7	30	22	5	4	14	19	37	15	10	21	49	59	-10	55
18 Barnsley	46	11	7	5	35	26	3	6	14	17	39	14	13	19	52	65	-13	55
19 Blackpool	46	8	11	4	35	27	4	7	12	24	37	12	18	16	59	64	-5	54
20 Southampton	46	9	5	9	26	27	4	10	9	30	45	13	15	18	56	72	-16	54
21 Coventry C	46	8	8	7	25	26	6	3	14	27	38	14	11	21	52	64	-12	53
22 Leicester C	46	7	7	9	23	19	5	9	9	19	26	12	16	18	42	45	-3	52
23 Scunthorpe U	46	7	8	8	31	33	4	5	14	15	36	11	13	22	46	69	-23	46
24 Colchester U	46	4	8	11	31	41	3	9	11	31	45	7	17	22	62	86	-24	38

COCA-COLA FOOTBALL LEAGUE CHAMPIONSHIP

	League	Carling Cup	FA Cup	Other	Total
Sylvain Ebanks-Blake *(Wolverhampton W)*	23	1	1	0	25
(Includes 11 League, 1 Carling Cup and 1 FA Cup goal for Plymouth Arg.)					
Kevin Phillips *(WBA)*	22	0	2	0	24
James Beattie *(Sheffield U)*	22	0	0	0	22
Stern John *(Southampton)*	19	0	0	0	19
Kevin Lisbie *(Colchester U)*	17	0	0	0	17
Clinton Morrison *(Crystal Palace)*	16	0	0	0	16
Fraizer Campbell *(Hull C)*	15	0	0	0	15
(on loan from Manchester U)					
Ricardo Fuller *(Stoke C)*	15	0	0	0	15
Liam Lawrence *(Stoke C)*	14	0	1	0	15
Roman Bednar *(WBA)*	13	0	4	0	17
Andy Gray *(Charlton Ath)*	13	2	0	0	15
(Includes 11 League and 2 Carling Cup goals for Burnley.)					
Jamie Cureton *(Norwich C)*	12	2	9	9	14
Brian Howard *(Barnsley)*	13	0	1	0	14
Martin Paterson *(Scunthorpe U)*	13	1	0	0	14

Coca-Cola Football League Division 1

			Home						Away						Total					
		P	W	D	L	F	A	W	D	L	F	A	W	D	L	F	A	Gd	Pts
1	Swansea C	46	13	5	5	38	21	14	6	3	44	21	27	11	8	82	42	40	92
2	Nottingham F	46	13	8	2	37	13	9	8	6	27	19	22	16	8	64	32	32	82
3	Doncaster R	46	14	4	5	34	18	9	7	7	31	23	23	11	12	65	41	24	80
4	Carlisle U*	46	17	3	3	39	16	6	8	9	25	30	23	11	12	64	46	18	80
5	Leeds U*	46	15	4	4	41	18	12	6	5	31	20	27	10	9	72	38	34	76
6	Southend U	46	12	6	5	35	20	10	4	9	35	35	22	10	14	70	55	15	76
7	Brighton & HA	46	12	6	5	37	25	7	6	10	21	25	19	12	15	58	50	8	69
8	Oldham Ath	46	10	7	6	32	21	8	6	9	26	25	18	13	15	58	46	12	67
9	Northampton T	46	12	6	5	38	21	5	9	9	22	34	17	15	14	60	55	5	66
10	Huddersfield T	46	12	4	7	29	22	8	2	13	21	40	20	6	20	50	62	-12	66
11	Tranmere R	46	13	4	6	32	18	5	7	11	20	29	18	11	17	52	47	5	65
12	Walsall	46	7	9	7	27	26	9	7	7	25	20	16	16	14	52	46	6	64
13	Swindon T	46	12	5	6	41	24	4	8	11	22	32	16	13	17	63	56	7	61
14	Leyton Orient	46	9	6	8	27	29	7	6	10	22	34	16	12	18	49	63	-14	60
15	Hartlepool U	46	11	5	7	40	26	4	4	15	23	40	15	9	22	63	66	-3	54
16	Bristol R	46	5	10	8	25	30	7	7	9	20	23	12	17	17	45	53	-8	53
17	Millwall	46	9	4	10	30	26	5	6	12	15	34	14	10	22	45	60	-15	52
18	Yeovil T	46	9	4	10	19	27	5	6	12	19	32	14	10	22	38	59	-21	52
19	Cheltenham T	46	10	8	5	23	21	3	4	16	19	43	13	12	21	42	64	-22	51
20	Crewe Alex	46	8	6	9	27	33	4	8	11	20	32	12	14	20	47	65	-18	50
21	Bournemouth†	46	10	4	9	31	35	7	3	13	31	37	17	7	22	62	72	-10	48
22	Gillingham	46	9	9	5	26	22	2	4	17	18	51	11	13	22	44	73	-29	46
23	Port Vale	46	5	8	10	26	35	4	3	16	21	46	9	11	26	47	81	-34	38
24	Luton T††	46	10	5	8	29	25	1	5	17	14	38	11	10	25	43	63	-20	33

Leeds U deducted 15 points; † Bournemouth and Luton Town deducted 10 points.

LEADING GOALSCORERS 2007–08

COCA-COLA FOOTBALL LEAGUE DIVISION 1

	League	Carling Cup	FA Cup	Other	Total
Jason Scotland (*Swansea C*)	24	1	2	2	29
Jason Beckford (*Leeds U*)	20	0	0	0	20
Nicky Forster (*Brighton & HA*)	15	0	2	2	19
Simon Cox (*Swindon T*)	15	0	0	1	16
Danny Graham (*Carlisle U*)	14	1	0	2	17
Nicky Maynard (*Crewe Alex*)	14	0	0	0	14
Joe Garner (*Carlisle U*)	14	0	0	0	14
Rickie Lambert (*Bristol R*)	14	0	6	0	20
Adam Boyd (*Leyton Orient*)	14	1	2	0	17
Steven Gillespie (*Cheltenham T*)	14	0	2	0	16
Richard Barker (*Hartlepool U*)	13	0	2	1	16
Junior Agogo (*Nottingham F*)	13	0	0	0	13
Poul Hubertz (*Northampton T*)	13	0	0	0	13
Andy Kirk (*Yeovil T*)	12	1	2	0	15

(Includes 8 League, 1 Carling Cup and 2 FA Cup goals for Northampton T.)

| Jo Osei-Kuffour (*Bournemouth*) | 12 | 0 | 0 | 1 | 13 |

Coca-Cola Football League Division 2

			Home					Away					Total						
		P	W	D	L	F	A	W	D	L	F	A	W	D	L	F	A	GD	Pts
1	Milton Keynes D	46	11	7	5	39	17	18	3	2	43	20	29	10	7	82	37	45	97
2	Peterborough U	46	14	4	5	46	20	14	4	5	38	23	28	8	10	84	43	41	92
3	Hereford U	46	11	6	6	34	19	15	4	4	38	22	26	10	10	72	41	31	88
4	Stockport Co	46	11	5	7	40	30	13	5	5	32	24	24	10	12	72	54	18	82
5	Rochdale	46	11	4	8	37	28	12	7	4	40	26	23	11	12	77	54	23	80
6	Darlington	46	11	7	5	36	22	11	5	7	31	18	22	12	12	67	40	27	78
7	Wycombe W	46	13	6	4	29	15	9	6	8	27	27	22	12	12	56	42	14	78
8	Chesterfield	46	9	8	6	42	29	10	4	9	34	27	19	12	15	76	56	20	69
9	Rotherham U*	46	12	4	7	37	29	9	7	7	25	29	21	11	14	62	58	4	64
10	Bradford C	46	10	4	9	30	30	7	7	9	33	31	17	11	18	63	61	2	62
11	Morecambe	46	9	6	8	33	32	7	6	10	26	31	16	12	18	59	63	-4	60
12	Barnet	46	10	6	7	37	30	6	6	11	19	33	16	12	18	56	63	-7	60
13	Bury	46	8	6	9	30	30	8	5	10	28	31	16	11	19	58	61	-3	59
14	Brentford	46	7	5	11	25	35	10	3	10	27	35	17	8	21	52	70	-18	59
15	Lincoln C	46	9	3	11	33	38	9	1	13	28	39	18	4	24	61	77	-16	58
16	Grimsby T	46	7	5	11	26	34	8	5	10	29	32	15	10	21	55	66	-11	55
17	Accrington S	46	7	1	15	20	39	9	2	12	29	44	16	3	27	49	83	-34	51
18	Shrewsbury T	46	6	8	9	31	22	3	8	12	25	43	12	14	20	56	65	-9	50
19	Macclesfield T	46	6	8	9	27	31	5	9	9	20	33	11	17	18	47	64	-17	50
20	Dagenham & R	46	6	7	10	27	32	7	3	13	22	38	13	10	23	49	70	-21	49
21	Notts Co	46	8	5	10	19	23	2	13	8	18	30	10	18	18	37	53	-16	48
22	Chester C	46	5	5	13	21	30	7	6	10	30	38	12	11	23	51	68	-17	47
23	Mansfield T	46	6	3	14	30	39	5	6	12	18	29	11	9	26	48	68	-20	42
24	Wrexham	46	6	7	10	16	28	4	3	16	22	42	10	10	26	38	70	-32	40

Rotherham U deducted 10 points.

COCA-COLA FOOTBALL LEAGUE DIVISION 2

	League	Carling Cup	FA Cup	Other	Total
Aaron McLean (*Peterborough U*)	29	0	3	1	33
Scott McGleish (*Wycombe W*)	25	0	0	0	25
Jack Lester (*Chesterfield*)	23	1	1	0	25
Michael Boulding (*Mansfield T*)	20	0	3	0	23
Liam Dickinson (*Stockport Co*)	19	0	0	2	21
Andy Bishop (*Bury*)	19	0	5	1	25
Adam Le Fondre (*Rochdale*)	16	1	0	0	17
Ben Strevens (*Dagenham & R*)	15	1	3	1	20
Ben Wright (*Lincoln C*)	15	0	0	0	15
Peter Thorne (*Bradford C*)	14	0	1	0	15
Glenn Poole (*Brentford*)	14	0	0	0	14
Mark Wright (*Milton Keynes D*)	13	0	0	2	15
Theo Robinson (*Hereford U*)	13	1	2	0	16
(*On loan from Watford.*)					
Anthony Elding (*Stockport Co*)	13	1	0	1	15
(*Transferred to Leeds U January 2008.*)					

FA BARCLAYS PREMIERSHIP

HOME TEAM	Arsenal	Aston Villa	Birmingham C	Blackburn R	Bolton W	Chelsea	Derby Co	Everton	Fulham	Liverpool
Arsenal	—	1-1	1-1	2-0	2-0	1-0	5-0	1-0	2-1	1-1
Aston Villa	1-2	—	5-1	1-1	4-0	2-0	2-0	2-0	2-1	1-2
Birmingham C	2-2	1-2	—	4-1	1-0	0-1	1-1	1-1	1-1	2-2
Blackburn R	1-1	0-4	2-1	—	4-1	0-1	3-1	0-0	1-1	0-0
Bolton W	2-3	1-1	3-0	1-2	—	0-1	1-0	1-2	0-0	1-3
Chelsea	2-1	4-4	3-2	0-0	1-1	—	6-1	1-1	0-0	0-0
Derby Co	2-6	0-6	1-2	1-2	1-1	0-2	—	0-2	2-2	1-2
Everton	1-4	2-2	3-1	1-1	2-0	0-1	1-0	—	3-0	1-2
Fulham	0-3	2-1	2-0	2-2	2-1	1-2	0-0	1-0	—	0-2
Liverpool	1-1	2-2	0-0	3-1	4-0	1-1	6-0	1-0	2-0	—
Manchester C	1-3	1-0	1-0	2-2	4-2	0-2	1-0	0-2	2-3	0-0
Manchester U	2-1	4-0	1-0	2-0	2-0	2-0	4-1	2-1	2-0	3-0
Middlesbrough	2-1	0-3	2-0	1-2	0-1	0-2	1-0	0-2	1-0	1-1
Newcastle U	1-1	0-0	2-1	0-1	0-0	0-2	2-2	3-2	2-0	0-3
Portsmouth	0-0	2-0	4-2	0-1	3-1	1-1	3-1	0-0	0-1	0-0
Reading	1-3	1-2	2-1	0-0	0-2	1-2	1-0	1-0	0-2	3-1
Sunderland	0-1	1-1	2-0	1-2	3-1	0-1	1-0	0-1	1-1	0-2
Tottenham H	1-3	4-4	2-3	1-2	1-1	4-4	4-0	1-3	5-1	0-2
West Ham U	0-1	2-2	1-1	2-1	1-1	0-4	2-1	0-2	2-1	1-0
Wigan Ath	0-0	1-2	2-0	5-3	1-0	0-2	2-0	1-2	1-1	0-1

12

2007–2008 RESULTS

Manchester C	Manchester U	Middlesbrough	Newcastle U	Portsmouth	Reading	Sunderland	Tottenham H	West Ham U	Wigan Ath
1-0	2-2	1-1	3-0	3-1	2-0	3-2	2-1	2-0	2-0
1-1	1-4	1-1	4-1	1-3	3-1	0-1	2-1	1-0	0-2
3-1	0-1	3-0	1-1	0-2	1-1	2-2	4-1	0-1	3-2
1-0	1-1	1-1	3-1	0-1	4-2	1-0	1-1	0-1	3-1
0-0	1-0	0-0	1-3	0-1	3-0	2-0	1-1	1-0	4-1
6-0	2-1	1-0	2-1	1-0	1-0	2-0	2-0	1-0	1-1
1-1	0-1	0-1	1-0	2-2	0-4	0-0	0-3	0-5	0-1
1-0	0-1	2-0	3-1	3-1	1-0	7-1	0-0	1-1	2-1
3-3	0-3	1-2	0-1	0-2	3-1	1-3	3-3	0-1	1-1
1-0	0-1	3-2	3-0	4-1	2-1	3-0	2-2	4-0	1-1
—	1-0	3-1	3-1	3-1	2-1	1-0	2-1	1-1	0-0
1-2	—	4-1	6-0	2-0	0-0	1-0	1-0	4-1	4-0
8-1	2-2	—	2-2	2-0	0-1	2-2	1-1	1-2	1-0
0-2	1-5	1-1	—	1-4	3-0	2-0	3-1	3-1	1-0
0-0	1-1	0-1	0-0	—	7-4	1-0	0-1	0-0	2-0
2-0	0-2	1-1	2-1	0-2	—	2-1	0-1	0-3	2-1
1-2	0-4	3-2	1-1	2-0	2-1	—	1-0	2-1	2-0
2-1	1-1	1-1	1-4	2-0	6-4	2-0	—	4-0	4-0
0-2	2-1	3-0	2-2	0-1	1-1	3-1	1-1	—	1-1
1-1	0-2	1-0	1-0	0-2	0-0	3-0	1-1	1-0	—

COCA-COLA FOOTBALL LEAGUE

HOME TEAM	Barnsley	Blackpool	Bristol C	Burnley	Cardiff C	Charlton Ath	Colchester U	Coventry C	Crystal Palace	Hull C
Barnsley	—	2-1	3-0	1-1	1-1	3-0	1-0	1-4	0-0	1-3
Blackpool	1-1	—	1-1	3-0	0-1	5-3	2-2	4-0	1-1	2-1
Bristol C	3-2	1-0	—	2-2	1-0	0-1	1-1	2-1	1-1	2-1
Burnley	2-1	2-2	0-1	—	3-3	1-0	1-1	2-0	1-1	0-1
Cardiff C	3-0	3-1	2-1	2-1	—	0-2	4-1	0-1	1-1	1-0
Charlton Ath	1-1	4-1	1-1	1-3	3-0	—	1-2	4-1	2-0	1-1
Colchester U	2-2	0-2	1-2	2-3	1-1	2-2	—	1-5	1-2	1-3
Coventry C	4-0	3-1	0-3	1-2	0-0	1-1	1-0	—	0-2	1-1
Crystal Palace	2-0	0-0	2-0	5-0	0-0	0-1	2-1	1-1	—	1-1
Hull C	3-0	2-2	0-0	2-0	2-2	1-2	1-1	1-0	2-1	—
Ipswich T	0-0	2-1	6-0	0-0	1-1	2-0	3-1	4-1	1-0	1-0
Leicester C	2-0	0-1	0-0	0-1	0-0	1-1	1-1	2-0	1-0	0-2
Norwich C	1-0	1-2	1-3	2-0	1-2	1-1	5-1	2-0	1-0	1-1
Plymouth Arg	3-0	3-0	1-1	3-1	2-2	1-2	4-1	1-0	1-0	0-1
Preston NE	1-2	0-1	0-0	2-1	1-2	0-2	0-3	1-0	0-1	3-0
QPR	2-0	3-2	3-0	2-4	0-2	1-0	2-1	1-2	1-2	2-0
Scunthorpe U	2-2	1-1	0-1	2-0	3-2	1-0	3-3	2-1	0-0	1-2
Sheffield U	1-0	1-1	2-1	0-0	3-3	0-2	2-2	2-1	0-1	2-0
Sheffield W	1-0	2-1	0-1	0-2	1-0	0-0	1-2	1-1	2-2	1-0
Southampton	2-3	1-0	2-0	0-1	1-0	0-1	1-1	0-0	1-4	4-0
Stoke C	0-0	1-1	2-1	1-1	2-1	2-1	2-1	1-3	1-2	1-1
Watford	0-3	1-1	1-2	1-2	2-2	1-1	2-2	2-1	0-2	1-0
WBA	2-0	1-1	4-1	2-1	3-3	4-2	4-3	2-4	1-1	1-2
Wolverhampton W	1-0	2-1	1-1	2-3	3-0	2-0	1-0	1-0	0-3	0-1

CHAMPIONSHIP 2007–2008 RESULTS

Ipswich T	Leicester C	Norwich C	Plymouth Arg	Preston NE	QPR	Scunthorpe U	Sheffield U	Sheffield W	Southampton	Stoke C	Watford	WBA	Wolverhampton W
4-1	0-1	1-3	3-2	1-0	0-0	2-0	0-1	0-0	2-2	3-3	3-2	2-1	1-0
1-1	2-1	1-3	0-0	0-0	1-0	1-0	2-2	2-1	2-2	2-3	1-1	1-3	0-0
2-0	0-2	2-1	1-2	3-0	2-2	2-1	2-0	2-1	2-1	1-0	0-0	1-1	0-0
2-2	1-1	2-1	1-0	2-3	0-2	2-0	1-2	1-1	2-3	0-0	2-2	2-1	1-3
1-0	0-1	1-2	1-0	2-2	3-1	1-1	1-0	1-0	1-0	0-1	1-2	0-0	2-3
3-1	2-0	2-0	1-2	1-2	0-1	1-1	0-3	3-2	1-1	1-0	2-2	1-1	2-3
2-0	1-1	1-1	1-1	2-1	4-2	0-1	2-2	1-2	1-1	0-1	2-3	3-2	0-1
2-1	2-0	1-0	3-1	2-1	0-0	1-1	0-1	0-0	1-1	1-2	0-3	0-4	1-1
0-1	2-2	1-1	2-1	2-1	1-1	2-0	3-2	2-1	1-1	1-3	0-2	1-1	0-2
3-1	2-0	2-1	2-3	3-0	1-1	2-0	1-1	1-0	5-0	1-1	3-0	1-3	2-0
—	3-1	2-1	0-0	2-1	0-0	3-2	1-1	4-1	2-0	1-1	1-2	2-0	3-0
2-0	—	4-0	0-1	0-1	1-1	1-0	0-1	1-3	1-2	1-1	4-1	1-2	0-0
2-2	0-0	—	2-1	1-0	3-0	0-0	1-0	0-1	2-1	0-1	1-3	1-2	1-1
1-1	0-0	3-0	—	2-2	2-1	3-0	0-1	1-2	1-1	2-2	1-1	1-2	1-1
2-2	1-1	0-0	2-0	—	0-0	0-1	3-1	1-0	5-1	2-0	1-0	2-1	2-1
1-1	3-1	1-0	0-2	2-2	—	3-1	1-1	0-0	0-3	3-0	1-1	0-2	0-0
1-2	0-0	0-1	1-0	2-1	2-2	—	3-2	1-1	1-1	2-3	1-3	2-3	0-2
3-1	3-0	2-0	0-1	1-1	2-1	0-0	—	2-2	1-2	0-3	1-1	1-0	3-1
1-2	0-2	4-1	1-1	2-1	2-1	1-2	2-0	—	5-0	1-1	0-1	0-1	1-3
1-1	1-0	0-1	0-2	0-1	2-3	1-0	3-2	0-0	—	3-2	0-3	3-2	0-0
1-0	0-0	2-1	3-2	3-1	3-1	3-2	0-1	2-4	3-2	—	0-0	3-1	0-0
2-0	1-0	1-1	0-0	0-0	2-4	0-1	1-0	2-1	3-2	0-0	—	0-3	3-0
4-0	1-4	2-0	3-0	2-0	5-1	5-0	0-0	1-1	1-1	1-1	1-1	—	0-0
1-1	1-1	2-0	1-0	1-0	3-3	2-1	0-0	2-1	2-2	2-4	1-2	0-1	—

COCA-COLA FOOTBALL LEAGUE

HOME TEAM	Bournemouth	Brighton & HA	Bristol R	Carlisle U	Cheltenham T	Crewe Alex	Doncaster R	Gillingham	Hartlepool U	Huddersfield T
Bournemouth	—	0-2	2-1	1-3	2-2	1-0	0-2	1-0	2-0	0-1
Brighton & HA	3-2	—	0-0	2-2	2-1	3-0	1-0	4-2	2-1	1-1
Bristol R	0-2	0-2	—	3-0	2-0	1-1	0-1	1-1	0-0	2-3
Carlisle U	1-1	2-0	1-1	—	1-0	1-0	1-0	2-0	4-2	2-1
Cheltenham T	1-0	2-1	1-0	1-0	—	2-2	2-1	1-0	1-1	0-2
Crewe Alex	1-4	2-1	1-1	0-1	3-1	—	0-4	2-3	3-1	2-0
Doncaster R	1-2	0-0	2-0	1-0	2-0	2-0	—	2-1	2-0	2-0
Gillingham	2-1	1-0	3-2	0-0	0-0	0-3	1-1	—	2-1	1-0
Hartlepool U	1-1	1-2	1-0	2-2	0-2	3-0	2-1	4-0	—	2-1
Huddersfield T	1-0	2-1	2-1	0-2	2-3	1-1	2-2	1-3	2-0	—
Leeds U	2-0	0-0	1-0	3-2	1-2	1-1	0-1	2-1	2-0	4-0
Leyton Orient	1-0	2-2	3-1	0-3	2-0	0-1	1-1	0-0	2-4	0-1
Luton T	1-4	1-2	1-2	0-0	1-1	2-1	1-1	3-1	2-1	0-1
Millwall	2-1	3-0	0-1	3-0	1-0	2-0	0-3	1-1	0-1	1-2
Northampton T	4-1	1-0	0-1	2-2	2-1	0-0	2-0	4-0	1-1	3-0
Nottingham F	0-0	0-0	1-1	0-1	3-1	3-0	0-0	4-0	2-1	2-1
Oldham Ath	2-0	1-1	0-1	2-0	2-1	3-2	1-1	2-1	0-1	4-1
Port Vale	1-3	0-1	1-1	1-1	3-0	0-1	1-3	2-1	0-2	0-0
Southend U	2-1	2-0	0-1	0-1	2-2	3-0	3-2	3-0	2-1	4-1
Swansea C	1-2	0-0	2-2	2-1	4-1	2-1	1-2	1-1	1-0	0-1
Swindon T	4-1	0-3	1-0	2-2	3-0	1-1	1-2	5-0	2-1	3-2
Tranmere R	3-1	2-0	0-2	2-0	1-0	1-1	0-1	2-0	3-1	3-0
Walsall	1-3	1-2	0-1	1-1	2-0	1-1	1-1	2-1	2-2	4-0
Yeovil T	2-1	2-1	0-0	2-1	2-1	0-3	2-1	2-1	3-1	0-2

DIVISION 1 2007–2008 RESULTS

Leeds U	Leyton Orient	Luton T	Millwall	Northampton T	Nottingham F	Oldham Ath	Port Vale	Southend U	Swansea C	Swindon T	Tranmere R	Walsall	Yeovil T
1-3	3-1	4-3	2-0	1-1	2-0	0-3	0-1	1-4	1-4	2-2	2-1	1-1	2-0
0-1	1-1	3-1	3-0	2-1	0-2	1-0	2-3	3-2	0-1	2-1	0-0	1-1	1-2
0-3	2-3	1-1	2-1	1-1	2-2	1-0	3-2	1-1	0-2	0-1	1-1	1-1	1-1
3-1	1-0	2-1	4-0	2-0	0-2	1-0	3-2	1-2	0-0	3-0	0-1	2-1	2-1
1-0	1-0	1-0	0-1	1-1	0-3	1-1	1-0	1-1	1-2	1-1	1-1	1-2	1-1
0-1	0-2	2-0	0-0	1-0	0-0	1-4	0-2	1-3	2-2	0-0	4-3	0-0	2-0
0-1	4-2	2-0	0-0	2-0	1-0	1-1	2-1	3-1	0-4	2-0	0-0	2-3	1-2
1-1	3-1	2-1	1-1	0-1	3-0	0-0	1-2	1-1	1-2	1-1	0-2	2-1	0-0
1-1	1-1	4-0	0-1	0-1	0-1	4-1	3-2	4-3	1-3	1-1	3-1	0-1	2-0
1-0	0-1	2-0	1-0	1-2	1-1	1-1	3-1	1-2	0-1	1-0	1-0	2-0	1-0
—	1-1	1-0	4-2	3-0	1-1	1-3	3-0	4-1	2-0	2-1	0-2	2-0	1-0
0-2	—	2-1	0-1	2-2	0-1	1-0	3-1	2-2	0-5	2-1	3-0	1-0	0-0
1-1	0-1	—	1-1	4-1	2-1	3-0	2-1	1-0	1-3	0-1	1-0	0-1	1-0
0-2	0-1	0-0	—	2-0	2-2	2-3	3-0	2-1	2-2	1-2	0-1	1-2	2-1
1-1	2-0	2-1	1-1	—	1-2	2-0	2-1	0-1	4-2	1-1	2-1	0-2	1-2
1-2	4-0	1-0	2-0	2-2	—	0-0	2-0	4-1	0-0	1-0	2-0	1-1	3-2
0-1	2-0	1-1	1-1	0-1	0-0	—	1-1	0-1	2-1	2-2	3-1	0-2	3-0
3-3	2-1	1-2	3-1	2-2	0-2	0-3	—	1-2	0-2	2-1	0-0	1-1	2-2
1-0	1-2	2-0	1-0	1-1	1-1	0-1	1-1	—	1-1	2-1	1-2	1-0	1-1
3-2	4-1	1-0	1-2	3-0	0-0	2-1	2-0	3-0	—	2-1	1-1	1-0	1-2
0-1	1-1	2-1	2-1	1-1	2-1	3-0	6-0	0-1	1-1	—	1-0	0-3	0-1
1-2	1-1	2-1	2-0	2-2	0-2	0-1	2-0	1-0	0-1	2-1	—	0-0	2-1
1-1	0-0	0-0	3-0	0-2	1-0	0-3	0-0	0-2	1-3	2-2	2-1	—	2-0
0-1	0-1	0-0	0-1	1-0	0-3	0-0	1-0	0-3	1-2	0-1	1-1	0-2	—

COCA-COLA FOOTBALL LEAGUE

HOME TEAM	Accrington S	Barnet	Bradford C	Brentford	Bury	Chester C	Chesterfield	Dagenham & R	Darlington	Grimsby T
Accrington S	—	0-2	0-2	1-0	0-2	3-3	2-1	1-0	0-3	4-1
Barnet	2-2	—	2-1	1-2	3-0	3-1	0-2	3-1	0-0	0-3
Bradford C	0-3	1-1	—	1-2	1-2	2-1	1-0	0-2	0-0	2-1
Brentford	3-1	2-1	2-2	—	1-4	3-0	2-1	2-3	0-2	0-1
Bury	2-1	3-0	2-2	1-2	—	0-2	0-1	0-2	1-2	1-1
Chester C	2-3	3-0	0-1	0-2	2-1	—	0-0	4-0	2-1	0-2
Chesterfield	4-2	0-1	1-1	1-0	3-1	1-1	—	1-1	1-1	1-2
Dagenham & R	1-3	1-1	1-4	1-2	1-1	6-2	0-3	—	0-3	0-0
Darlington	1-0	1-0	1-3	3-1	3-0	1-0	0-0	2-3	—	3-2
Grimsby T	1-2	4-1	1-1	1-2	1-0	1-2	4-2	1-4	0-4	—
Hereford U	0-0	1-2	4-2	2-0	0-0	2-2	2-0	4-1	5-1	2-0
Lincoln C	2-0	4-1	1-2	3-1	1-1	0-1	2-4	2-0	0-4	1-2
Macclesfield T	2-1	3-0	0-1	1-0	2-2	1-2	1-0	1-1	0-0	1-2
Mansfield T	1-2	2-2	0-0	2-3	1-1	1-3	1-3	0-1	0-1	1-2
Milton Keynes D	5-0	0-1	2-1	1-1	1-2	1-0	1-2	4-0	1-0	2-0
Morecambe	0-1	0-0	2-1	3-1	2-1	5-3	1-1	1-0	0-3	0-4
Notts Co	1-0	0-0	1-3	1-1	1-3	1-0	1-0	1-0	0-1	1-1
Peterborough U	8-2	1-0	2-1	7-0	1-0	1-0	2-3	3-1	0-2	2-1
Rochdale	4-1	3-0	2-1	1-1	1-2	1-2	0-1	1-0	3-1	3-1
Rotherham U	0-1	1-0	1-1	1-2	2-1	1-1	2-1	2-1	0-2	2-1
Shrewsbury T	2-0	1-0	1-0	0-1	0-1	0-0	2-3	4-0	0-0	2-1
Stockport Co	2-0	2-4	2-1	1-0	1-2	1-2	2-2	1-0	1-0	1-1
Wrexham	1-3	0-2	1-1	1-3	2-1	2-2	0-4	0-0	2-0	0-0
Wycombe W	0-1	0-0	2-1	1-0	1-0	1-0	1-0	0-1	2-0	3-0

DIVISION 2 2007–2008 RESULTS

Hereford U	Lincoln C	Macclesfield T	Mansfield T	Milton Keynes D	Morecambe	Notts Co	Peterborough U	Rochdale	Rotherham U	Shrewsbury T	Stockport Co	Wrexham	Wycombe W
0-2	0-3	3-2	1-0	0-1	3-2	0-2	0-2	1-2	0-1	1-2	0-2	0-2	0-2
1-2	5-2	2-2	1-1	0-2	0-1	1-1	0-2	0-0	2-0	4-1	2-1	3-2	2-1
1-3	2-1	1-1	1-2	1-2	1-0	3-0	1-0	1-2	3-2	4-2	1-1	2-1	0-1
0-3	1-0	1-0	1-1	0-3	0-1	0-0	1-2	0-2	1-1	1-1	1-3	2-0	1-3
0-1	1-1	1-0	2-0	1-5	2-1	2-1	2-0	1-1	3-0	1-1	2-3	0-1	2-2
1-1	1-2	0-0	0-1	0-2	0-1	0-1	1-2	0-4	0-1	3-1	0-0	0-2	2-2
4-0	4-1	2-2	2-0	1-2	2-2	1-1	1-2	3-4	0-2	4-1	1-1	2-1	2-0
1-0	1-0	0-1	2-0	0-1	2-0	1-1	2-3	1-1	0-2	1-1	0-1	3-0	2-2
0-1	2-0	2-2	1-2	0-1	2-2	2-2	1-1	1-1	1-1	2-0	4-0	2-0	1-0
2-1	1-0	1-1	1-0	0-1	1-2	1-1	1-4	1-2	0-1	1-1	1-1	1-0	0-1
—	3-1	0-1	2-1	0-1	0-3	0-0	0-1	1-1	0-0	3-1	0-1	2-0	1-0
2-1	—	3-1	1-2	1-2	1-1	2-1	1-1	2-1	1-3	0-4	0-1	2-4	1-0
0-1	1-2	—	0-0	3-3	1-2	1-1	0-3	2-2	1-1	2-1	0-2	3-2	1-2
0-1	1-3	5-0	—	1-2	1-2	2-0	2-0	0-4	0-1	3-1	4-2	2-1	0-4
0-0	4-0	1-1	1-0	—	1-1	3-0	1-1	0-1	1-1	3-0	0-2	4-1	2-2
0-3	1-2	0-1	3-1	0-1	—	1-1	3-2	1-1	5-1	1-1	2-0	2-2	0-1
2-3	0-1	0-1	0-0	1-2	1-1	—	0-1	1-0	0-1	2-1	1-2	2-1	1-0
1-1	4-0	0-1	2-1	1-2	1-1	0-0	—	3-0	3-1	2-1	0-1	0-0	2-1
2-4	0-2	1-1	1-0	3-2	1-0	4-2	0-2	—	4-1	1-1	1-2	0-0	0-1
0-1	3-2	3-0	3-2	0-1	3-1	1-1	3-1	2-4	—	2-0	1-4	3-0	1-1
1-2	1-2	2-0	0-0	3-3	2-0	0-0	0-2	3-4	1-1	—	3-1	3-0	0-1
2-3	1-3	2-0	2-1	2-3	2-1	1-1	1-2	2-0	2-2	1-1	—	2-1	6-0
0-2	1-0	1-1	1-1	1-0	2-1	1-0	0-2	0-2	0-1	0-1	0-1	—	0-0
2-2	1-0	2-1	1-2	1-1	2-0	3-1	2-2	0-1	1-0	1-1	0-0	2-1	—

ACCRINGTON STANLEY · FL CHAMPIONSHIP 2

Player	Ht	Wt	Birthplace	D.O.B.	Source
Arthur Kenny (G)	6 3	13 08	Bellshill	7 12 78	Partick T
Carden Paul (M)	5 9	11 10	Liverpool	29 3 79	Peterborough U
Cavanagh Peter (D)	5 11	11 09	Liverpool	14 10 81	Liverpool
Craney Ian (M)	5 10	12 00	Liverpool	21 7 82	Swansea C
Dunbavin Ian (G)	6 2	10 10	Knowsley	27 5 80	Scarborough
Edwards Phil (D)	5 8	11 03	Kirkby	8 11 85	Wigan Ath
Grant Robert (M)	5 11	12 00	Blackpool	27 3 87	Scholar
Mannix David (M)	5 8	11 06	Winsford	24 9 85	Liverpool
Miles John (F)	5 10	10 08	Fazackerley	28 9 81	Macclesfield T
Mullin Paul (F)	6 0	12 01	Bury	16 3 74	Radcliffe Borough
Proctor Andy (M)	6 0	12 04	Lancashire	13 3 83	Gt Harwood T
Richardson Leam (D)	5 8	11 04	Blackpool	19 11 79	Leeds
Webb Sean (D)	6 2	12 04	Dungannon	4 1 83	Ross Co
Williams Robbie (D)	5 10	12 00	Liverpool	12 4 79	St Dominics

League Appearances: Arthur, K. 24; Bell, J. 2; Boco, R. 6(5); Branch, G. 19(3); Brown, D. 8(7); Carden, P. 4; Cavanagh, P. 19; Craney, I. 34; D'Sane, R. 18(4); Dennehy, B. 2(5); Doughty, P. 3; Dunbavin, I. 22(1); Edwards, P. 28(3); Grant, R. 5(2); Harris, J. 38(3); Kempson, D. 8; King, M. 4(2); Mangan, A. 3(4); Mannix, D. 9(3); McEvilly, L. 3(8); McGivern, L. 2(10); McGrail, C. (1); Miles, J. 12(4); Mullin, P. 43; Murphy, P. 2; Proctor, A. 40(3); Richardson, L. 33(4); Roberts, M. 33(1); Smith, A. (1); Thomas, A. 13; Todd, A. 14(7); Turner, C. (1); Webb, S. 18; Whalley, S. 14(17); Williams, R. 23(3).
Goals – League (49): Mullin 12, Proctor 10 (4 pens), Craney 7, D'Sane 7, Whalley 3, Thomas 2, Cavanagh 1, Edwards 1, Kempson 1, Mangan 1, McGivern 1, Richardson 1, own goals 2.
Carling Cup (0).
FA Cup (2): Cavanagh 1, Mullin 1.
J Paint Trophy (2): D'Sane 1, Proctor 1 (pen).
Ground: The Fraser Eagle Stadium, Livingstone Road, Accrington, Lancashire BB5 5BX. Telephone: 01254 356 950.
Record Attendance: 4368 v Colchester U, FA Cup 1st rd, 3 January 2004.
Capacity: 5,057.
Manager: John Coleman.
Secretary: Hannah Bailey.
Most League Goals: 96, Division 3 (N) 1954–55.
Highest League Scorer in Season: George Stewart, 35, 1955–56 Division 3(N); George Hudson, 35, 1960–61, Division 4.
Most League Goals in Total Aggregate: George Stewart 136, 1954–58.
Most Capped Player: Romuald Boco, (17), Benin.
Most League Appearances: Jim Armstrong, 260, 1927–34.
Colours: Red shirts, white shorts, red stockings.

ALDERSHOT TOWN · FL CHAMPIONSHIP 2

Player	Ht	Wt	Birthplace	D.O.B.	Source
Bull Nikki (G)	6 1	11 03	Hastings	2 10 81	Hayes
Chalmers Lewis (M)	6 0	12 04	Manchester	4 2 86	Altrincham
Charles Anthony (D)	6 0	12 00	Isleworth	11 3 81	Barnet
Day Rhys (D)	6 1	12 08	Bridgend	31 8 82	Mansfield T
Donnelly Scott (M)	5 8	11 10	Hammersmith	25 12 87	QPR
Elvins Rob (F)	6 2	12 04	Alvechurch	17 9 86	WBA
Gier Rob (D)	5 9	11 07	Ascot	6 1 80	Woking
Grant Joel (M)	6 0	11 01	Hammersmith	27 8 87	Watford

Grant John (F)	5 11	11 00	Manchester	9 8 81	Halifax T
Harding Ben (M)	5 10	11 02	Carshalton	6 9 84	Milton Keynes D
Hudson Kirk (F)	6 0	10 10	Rochford	12 12 86	Bournemouth
Hylton Danny (F)	6 0	11 03	London	25 2 89	Youth
Jaimez-Ruiz Michael (G)	6 1	12 00	Merida	12 7 84	Northwood
Mendes Junior (F)	5 10	11 04	Ballam	15 9 76	Notts Co
Newman Ricky (D)	5 10	12 06	Guildford	5 8 70	Brentford
Scott Ryan (M)	5 10	12 07	Aldershot	27 12 86	Youth
Smith Dean (D)	5 10	10 10	Islington	13 8 86	Chelsea
Soares Louis (M)	5 11	11 05	Reading	8 1 85	Barnet
Straker Anthony (D)	5 9	11 11	Ealing	23 9 88	Crystal Palace
Williams Ryan (M)	5 4	11 02	Chesterfield	31 8 78	Bristol R
Winfield Dave (D)	6 3	13 08	Aldershot	24 3 88	Youth

League Appearances: Bull, 44; Chalmers, 41(1); Charles, 35; Davies, 24(5); Day, 32(4); Dixon, 18(3); Donnelly, 2(6); Elvins, 29(8); Gier, 38; Grant, Joel 20(10); Grant, John 32(2); Harding, 46; Hudson, 18(17); Hylton, 9(14); Jaimez-Ruiz, 2(1); Mendes, 3(3); Newman, 14(13); Scott, 1; Simmons, 0(1); Smith, 6(2); Soares, 30(7); Straker, 43; Williams, 1; Winfield, 18(6).
Goals – League (82): Grant John 20 (3 pens), Davies 10, Dixon 7, Elvins 7, Hudson 7, Harding 5, Hylton 5, Grant Joel 4, Soares 4, Chalmers 3, Day 3 (2 pens), Newman 2, Charles 1, Donnelly 1, Mendes 1, Winfield 1, own goal 1.
FA Cup (3): Dixon 2, Soares 1.
Trophy (16): John Grant 5, Dixon 2, Hudson 2, Mendes 2, Charles 1, Davies 1, Harding 1, Soares 1, Winfield 1.
Ground: EBB Stadium at the Recreation Ground, High Street, Aldershot GU11 1TW. Telephone: 01252 320211.
Record Attendance: 19,138 v Carlisle U, FA Cup 4th rd (replay) 28 January 1970.
Capacity: 7,500.
Manager: Gary Waddock.
Secretary: Graham Hortop.
Most League Goals: 83, Division 4, 1963–64.
Highest League Scorer in Season: John Dungworth, 26, Division 4, 1978–79.
Most League Goals in Total Aggregate: Jack Howarth, 171, 1965–71 and 1972–77.
Most Capped Player: Louie Soares, 3, Barbados.
Most League Appearances: Murray Brodie, 461, 1970–83.
Honours – Blue Square Premier League: Champions 2007–08. **Setanta Shield:** Winners 2008.
Colours: All red with blue trim.

ARSENAL   FA PREMIERSHIP

Adebayor Emmanuel (F)	6 4	11 08	Lome	26 2 84	Monaco
Almunia Manuel (G)	6 3	13 00	Pamplona	19 5 77	Celta Vigo
Ayling Luke (D)			London	25 8 91	Scholar
Barazite Nacer (M)	6 2	13 01	Arnhem	27 5 90	Scholar
Bartley Kyle (D)			Manchester	22 5 91	Scholar
Bendtner Nicklas (F)	6 2	13 00	Copenhagen	16 1 88	Scholar
Blackwood Anton (D)			Edmonton	18 8 91	Scholar
Botelho Pedro (D)	6 2	12 00	Salvador	14 12 89	Salamanca
Clichy Gael (D)	5 9	10 04	Toulouse	26 7 85	Cannes
Cruise Thomas (D)			London	9 3 91	Scholar
Denilson (M)	5 10	11 00	Sao Paulo	16 2 88	Sao Paulo
Diaby Vassirki (M)	6 2	12 04	Paris	11 5 86	Auxerre
Djourou Johan (D)	6 3	13 01	Ivory Coast	18 1 87	Scholar
Dunne James (M)			Farnborough	18 9 89	Scholar
Eastmond Craig (D)			Wandsworth	9 12 90	Scholar

Eboue Emmanuel (D)	5 10	10 03	Abidjan	4 6 83	Beveren
Eduardo (F)	5 10	10 03	Rio de Janeiro	25 2 83	Dinamo Zagreb
Emmanuel-Thomas Jay (M)			Forest Gate	27 12 90	Scholar
Fabianski Lukasz (G)	6 3	13 01	Costrzyn nad Odra	18 4 85	Legia
Fabregas Francesc (M)	5 11	11 01	Vilessoc de Mar	4 5 87	Barcelona
Flamini Mathieu (M)	5 11	11 10	Marseille	7 3 84	Marseille
Fonte Rui (F)			Lisbon	23 4 90	Scholar
Gallas William (D)	5 11	12 10	Asnieres	17 8 77	Chelsea
Gibbs Kieran (M)	5 10	10 02	Lambeth	26 9 89	Scholar
Gilbert Kerrea (D)	5 6	11 03	Willesden	28 2 87	Scholar
Gilbert Kerrea (D)	5 6	11 06	Hammersmith	28 2 87	Scholar
Hleb Aleksandr (M)	5 10	11 07	Minsk	1 5 81	Stuttgart
Hoyte Gavin (D)			Waltham Forest	6 6 90	Scholar
Hoyte Justin (D)	5 11	11 00	Waltham Forest	20 11 84	Scholar
Lansbury Henri (M)			Enfield	12 10 90	Scholar
Mannone Vito (G)	6 0	11 08	Desio	2 3 88	Atalanta
Nordtveit Havard (D)			Vats	21 6 90	Vats 94
Ogogo Abu (D)			Epsom	3 11 89	Scholar
Perez Fran Merida (M)	5 11	13 00	Barcelona	4 3 90	Scholar
Randall Mark (M)	6 0	12 12	Milton Keynes	28 9 89	Scholar
Rodgers Paul (D)			Edmonton	6 10 89	Scholar
Rosicky Tomas (M)	5 11	11 06	Prague	4 10 80	Borussia Dortmund
Sagna Bakari (D)	5 10	11 05	Sens	14 2 83	Auxerre
Senderos Philippe (D)	6 1	13 10	Geneva	14 2 85	Servette
Silva Gilberto (M)	6 3	12 04	Lagoa da Prata	7 10 76	Atletico Mineiro
Simpson Jay (M)	5 11	13 04	London	1 12 88	Scholar
Song Bilong Alexandre (M)	6 4	12 07	Douala	9 9 87	Bastia
Steer Rene (D)			Luton	31 1 90	Scholar
Szczesny Wojciech (F)			Warsaw	18 4 90	Scholar
Toure Kolo (D)	5 10	13 08	Ivory Coast	19 3 81	ASEC Mimosas
Traore Armand (D)	6 1	12 12	Paris	8 10 89	Monaco
Van den Berg Vincent (M)			Holland	19 1 89	Heerenveen
Van Persie Robin (F)	6 0	11 00	Rotterdam	6 8 83	Feyenoord
Vela Carlos (F)			Mexico	1 3 89	Celta Vigo
Walcott Theo (F)	5 9	11 01	Compton	16 3 89	Southampton
Watt Sanchez (M)			London	14 2 91	Scholar

League Appearances: Adebayor, E. 32(4); Almunia, M. 29; Bendtner, N. 7(20); Clichy, G. 37(1); Denilson, 4(9); Diaby, V. 9(6); Diarra, L. 4(3); Djourou, J. 1(1); Eboue, E. 20(3); Eduardo, 13(4); Fabianski, L. 3; Fabregas, F. 32; Flamini, M. 30; Gallas, W. 31; Hleb, A. 29(2); Hoyte, J. 2(3); Lehmann, J. 6(1); Randall, M. (1); Rosicky, T. 15(3); Sagna, B. 29; Senderos, P. 14(3); Silva, G. 12(11); Song Billong, A. 5(4); Toure, K. 29(1); Traore, A. 1(2); Van Persie, R. 13(2); Walcott, T. 11(14).

Goals – League (74): Adebayor 24 (3 pens), Fabregas 7, Van Persie 7 (2 pens), Rosicky 6, Bendtner 5, Eduardo 4, Gallas 4, Walcott 4, Flamini 3, Hleb 2, Senderos 2, Toure 2, Diaby 1, Sagna 1, Silva 1, own goal 1.

Carling Cup (10): Eduardo 4, Denilson 2, Adebayor 1, Bendtner 1, Diaby 1, Walcott 1.

FA Cup (5): Adebayor 2, Bendtner 1, Eduardo 1, own goal 1.

Champions League (24): Fabregas 6, Adebayor 3, Eduardo 3, Bendtner 2, Diaby 2, Hleb 2, Van Persie 2, Walcott 2, Rosicky 1, own goal 1.

Ground: Emirates Stadium, Drayton Park, Islington, London N5 1BU. Telephone (0207) 704 4000.

Record Attendance: 73,295 v Sunderland, Div 1, 9 March 1935. **Capacity:** 60,361.

Manager: Arsène Wenger.

Secretary: David Miles.

Most League Goals: 127, Division 1, 1930–31.

Highest League Scorer in Season: Ted Drake, 42, 1934–35.

Most League Goals in Total Aggregate: Thierry Henry, 174, 1999–2007.
Most Capped Player: Thierry Henry, 81 (102), France.
Most League Appearances: David O'Leary, 558, 1975–93.
Honours – FA Premier League: Champions – 1997–98, 2001–02, 2003–04. **Football League:** Division 1 Champions – 1930–31, 1932–33, 1933–34, 1934–35, 1937–38, 1947–48, 1952–53, 1970–71, 1988–89, 1990–91. **FA Cup:** Winners – 1929–30, 1935–36, 1949–50, 1970–71, 1978–79, 1992–93, 1997–98, 2001–02, 2002–03, 2004–05. **Football League Cup:** Winners – 1986–87, 1992–93. **European Competitions: European Cup-Winners' Cup:** Winners – 1993–94. **Fairs Cup:** Winners – 1969–70. **Colours:** Red and white.

ASTON VILLA   FA PREMIERSHIP

Agbonlahor Gabriel (F)	5 11	12 05	Birmingham	13 10 86	Scholar
Barry Gareth (D)	5 11	12 06	Hastings	23 2 81	Trainee
Bevan David (G)	6 2	13 00	Cork	24 6 89	Scholar
Bouma Wilfred (D)	5 10	13 01	Helmond	15 6 78	PSV Eindhoven
Carew John (F)	6 5	15 00	Lorenskog	5 9 79	Lyon
Collins Jordan (F)	5 7	11 08	Birmingham	11 3 89	Scholar
Delfouneso Nathan (F)				2 2 91	Scholar
Forrester Harry (M)				2 1 91	Scholar
Gardner Craig (M)	5 10	11 13	Solihull	25 11 86	Scholar
Harewood Marlon (F)	6 1	13 07	Hampstead	25 8 79	West Ham U
Herd Chris (M)	5 9	11 04	Melbourne	4 4 89	Scholar
Hofbauer Dominik (M)			Eggenberg	19 9 90	Scholar
Hogg Jonathan (M)	5 7	10 05	Middlesbrough	6 12 88	Scholar
Knight Zat (D)	6 6	15 02	Solihull	2 5 80	Fulham
Laursen Martin (D)	6 2	12 05	Silkeborg	26 7 77	AC Milan
Lichaj Eric (M)			Denwers Grove	17 11 88	Chicago Magic
Lowry Shane (D)	6 1	13 01	Perth	12 6 89	Scholar
Lund Eric (D)	6 1	13 00	Gothemberg	6 11 88	Scholar
Maloney Shaun (M)	5 7	10 01	Sarawak	24 1 83	Celtic
McGurk Adam (F)	5 9	12 13	St Helier	24 1 89	Scholar
Mikaelsson Tobias (F)	6 3	11 04	Jorlanda	17 11 88	Scholar
Moore Luke (F)	5 11	11 13	Birmingham	13 2 86	Trainee
O'Halloran Stephen (D)	6 0	11 07	Cork	29 11 87	Scholar
Osbourne Isaiah (M)	6 2	12 07	Birmingham	5 11 87	Scholar
Petrov Stilian (M)	5 11	13 05	Montana	5 7 79	Celtic
Reo-Coker Nigel (M)	5 8	12 03	Southwark	14 5 84	West Ham U
Routledge Wayne (M)	5 6	11 02	Sidcup	7 1 85	Tottenham H
Salifou Moustapha (M)	5 11	10 12	Lome	1 6 83	FC Wil
Stiever Zoltan (M)	5 8	9 10	Savar	16 10 88	Scholar
Taylor Stuart (G)	6 5	13 07	Romford	28 11 80	Arsenal
Williams Sam (M)	5 11	10 08	London	9 6 87	Scholar
Young Ashley (F)	5 6	9 06	Stevenage	9 7 85	Watford

League Appearances: Agbonlahor, G. 37; Barry, G. 37; Berger, P. (8); Bouma, W. 38; Cahill, G. (1); Carew, J. 32; Carson, S. 35; Davies, C. 9(3); Gardner, C. 15(8); Harewood, M. 1(22); Knight, Z. 25(2); Laursen, M. 38; Maloney, S. 11(11); Mellberg, O. 33(1); Moore, L. 8(7); Osbourne, I. 1(7); Petrov, S. 22(6); Reo-Coker, N. 36; Routledge, W. (1); Salifou, M. (4); Taylor, S. 3(1); Young, A. 37.
Goals – League (71): Carew 13 (1 pen), Agbonlahor 11, Barry 9 (5 pens), Young 9, Laursen 6, Harewood 5, Maloney 4, Gardner 3, Mellberg 2, Bouma 1, Davies 1, Knight 1, Moore 1, Petrov 1, own goals 4.
Carling Cup (5): Maloney 2, Harewood 1, Moore 1, Reo-Coker 1.
FA Cup (0).
Ground: Villa Park, Trinity Road, Birmingham B6 6HE. Telephone (0121) 327 2299.
Record Attendance: 76,588 v Derby Co, FA Cup 6th rd, 2 March 1946.

Capacity: 42,640.
Manager: Martin O'Neill.
Secretary: Sharon Barnhurst.
Most League Goals: 128, Division 1, 1930–31.
Highest League Scorer in Season: 'Pongo' Waring, 49, Division 1, 1930–31.
Most League Goals in Total Aggregate: Harry Hampton, 215, 1904–15.
Most Capped Player: Steve Staunton 64 (102), Republic of Ireland.
Most League Appearances: Charlie Aitken, 561, 1961–76.
Honours – Football League: Division 1 Champions – 1893–94, 1895–96, 1896–97, 1898–99, 1899–1900, 1909–10, 1980–81. Division 2 Champions – 1937–38, 1959–60. Division 3 Champions – 1971–72. **FA Cup:** Winners – 1887, 1895, 1897, 1905, 1913, 1920, 1957. **Football League Cup:** Winners – 1961, 1975, 1977, 1994, 1996. **European Competitions: European Cup:** Winners – 1981–82. **European Super Cup:** Winners – 1982–83. **Intertoto Cup:** Winners – 2001.
Colours: Claret and blue shirts, white shorts, blue stockings.

BARNET   FL CHAMPIONSHIP 2

Adomah Albert (F)	6 1	11 08	Harrow	13 12 87	Harrow Borough
Akurang Cliff (F)	6 2	12 03	Histon	27 2 81	
Beckwith Rob (G)	6 1	13 12	Hackney	12 9 84	Luton T
Birchall Adam (F)	5 6	10 09	Maidstone	2 12 84	Mansfield T
Bishop Neil (M)	6 1	12 10	Stockton	7 8 81	York C
Carew Ashley (M)	6 0	11 00	Lambeth	17 12 85	
Devera Joe (D)	6 2	12 00	Southgate	6 2 87	Scholar
Gillet Kenny (M)	5 10	12 04	Bordeaux	3 1 86	
Hart Danny (M)	5 10	11 09	London	26 4 89	
Hendon Ian (D)	6 1	13 05	Ilford	5 12 71	Peterborough U
Leary Michael (M)	6 0	11 11	Ealing	17 4 83	Luton T
Porter Max (M)	5 10	12 04	London	29 6 87	Bishop's Stortford
Puncheon Jason (M)	5 10	11 02	Croydon	26 6 86	Milton Keynes D
St Aimie Kieron (M)	6 1	13 00	Brent	4 5 89	QPR
Yakubu Ishmail (D)	6 1	12 09	Nigeria	8 4 85	Scholar

League Appearances: Adomah, A. 22; Akurang, C. 17(4); Angus, S. 1; Beckwith, R. 9; Birchall, A. 36(6); Bishop, N. 39; Burton, S. 29(1); Carew, A. 18(15); Devera, J. 41; Gillet, K. 30(1); Grazioli, G. 2(9); Harrison, L. 37(1); Hart, D. (2); Hatch, L. 10(11); Hendon, I. 2(2); Leary, M. 19(3); Nicolau, N. 31(7); Norville, J. 5(3); O'Cearuill, J. 9(5); Parkes, J. 7(3); Porter, M. 26(4); Puncheon, J. 37(4); Seanla, C. 1(2); St Aimie, K. 5(5); Thomas, A. 14(12); Wright, J. 31(1); Yakubu, I. 28.
Goals – League (56): Birchall 11, Puncheon 10 (2 pens), Akurang 7 (1 pen), Hatch 6, Adomah 5 (1 pen), Thomas 4, Bishop 2, Nicolau 2, Yakubu 2, Burton 1, Carew 1, Leary 1, Norville 1, Porter 1, Wright 1, own goal 1.
Carling Cup (2): Birchall 1, Puncheon 1.
FA Cup (6): Birchall 2, Hatch 2, Yakubu 1, own goal 1.
J Paint Trophy (1): Birchall 1.
Ground: Underhill Stadium, Barnet Lane, Barnet, Herts EN5 2DN. Telephone 0208 441 6932.
Record Attendance: 11,026 v Wycombe Wanderers, FA Amateur Cup 4th Round 1951–52. **Capacity:** 5,568.
Manager: Paul Fairclough.
Secretary: Andrew Adie.
Most League Goals: 81, Division 4, 1991–92.
Highest League Scorer in Season: Dougie Freedman, 24, Division 3, 1994–95.
Most League Goals in Total Aggregate: Sean Devine, 47, 1995–99.
Most Capped Player: Ken Charlery, 4, St. Lucia.

Most League Appearances: Paul Wilson, 263, 1991–2000.
Honours – Football League: GMVC: Winners – 1990–91. **Football Conference:** Winners – 2004–05. **FA Amateur Cup:** Winners 1945–46.
Colours: Amber and black.

BARNSLEY   FL CHAMPIONSHIP

Anderson (M)	6 2	12 11	Sao Paulo	29	8 82	Everton
Atkinson Rob (M)	6 1	12 00	North Ferriby	29	4 87	Scholar
Butterfield Jacob (D)	5 10	11 00	Manchester	10	6 90	Scholar
Campbell-Ryce Jamal (M)	5 7	12 03	Lambeth	6	4 83	Southend U
Christensen Kim (F)	6 2	12 08	Frederiksvaerk	8	5 80	Odense
Coulson Michael (F)	5 10	10 00	Scarborough	29	4 87	Scarborough
Devaney Martin (M)	5 11	12 00	Cheltenham	1	6 80	Watford
Ferenczi Istvan (F)	6 2	13 10	Gyor	14	9 77	Zalaegerszeg
Foster Stephen (D)	6 0	11 05	Warrington	10	9 80	Burnley
Hassell Bobby (D)	5 10	12 00	Derby	4	6 80	Mansfield T
Heslop Simon (M)	5 11	11 00	York	1	5 87	Scholar
Howard Brian (M)	5 8	11 00	Winchester	23	1 83	Swindon T
Johnson Andy (M)	6 0	13 00	Bristol	2	5 74	Leicester C
Kozluk Rob (D)	5 8	10 02	Mansfield	5	8 77	Sheffield U
Leon Diego (M)	5 7	10 10	Palencia	16	1 84	Grasshoppers
Letheren Kyle (G)	6 2	12 00	Swansea	26	12 87	Swansea C
Macken Jon (F)	5 11	12 04	Manchester	7	9 77	Derby Co
Mattis Dwayne (M)	6 1	12 00	Huddersfield	31	7 81	Bury
Mostto Miguel (F)	5 10	11 11	Ica	11	1 79	Cienciano
Muller Heinz (G)	6 4	15 04	Frankfurt-on-Main	30	5 78	Lillestrom
Odejayi Kayode (F)	6 2	12 02	Ibadon	21	2 82	Cheltenham T
Potter Luke (D)	6 2	12 07	Barnsley	13	7 89	Scholar
Reid Paul (D)	6 2	11 08	Carlisle	18	2 82	Northampton T
Souza Dennis (M)	6 3	13 05	Sao Paulo	1	9 80	Charleroi
Togwell Sam (M)	5 11	12 04	Beaconsfield	14	10 84	Crystal Palace
Van Homoet Marciano (D)	5 9	11 11	Rotterdam	7	3 84	Sparta Rotterdam

League Appearances: Adam, J. (1); Anderson, 20; Butterfield, J. 1(2); Campbell-Ryce, J. 34(3); Christensen, K. (12); Colgan, N. 1; Coulson, M. 1(11); Devaney, M. 24(10); Ferenczi, I. 25(12); Foster, S. 41; Hassell, B. 17(3); Howard, B. 41; Johnson, A. 4; Kozluk, R. 24; Leon, D. 16(2); Macken, J. 28(1); Mattis, D. (1); McCann, G. 11(8); Mostto, M. 7(7); Muller, H. 28; Nardiello, D. 8(3); Nyatanga, L. 40(1); Odejayi, K. 23(16); Reid, P. 2(1); Ricketts, R. 2(8); Souza, D. 45; Steele, L. 14; Tininho, 3; Togwell, S. 10(12); Van Homoet, M. 17(2); Warner, T. 3; Werling, D. 16(1).
Goals – League (52): Howard 13 (7 pens), Macken 7 (1 pen), Ferenczi 5, Devaney 4, Campbell-Ryce 3, McCann 3, Odejayi 3, Nardiello 2, Souza 2, Christensen 1, Foster 1, Leon 1, Mostto 1, Nyatanga 1, Togwell 1, Werling 1, own goals 3.
Carling Cup (2): Ferenczi 1, Reid 1.
FA Cup (6): Foster 2, Campbell-Ryce 1, Coulson 1, Howard 1, Odejayi 1.
Ground: Oakwell Stadium, Grove St, Barnsley, South Yorkshire S71 1ET. Telephone (01226) 211 211.
Record Attendance: 40,255 v Stoke C, FA Cup 5th rd, 15 February 1936. **Capacity:** 23,176.
Manager: Simon Davey.
Secretary: Albert Donald Rowing.
Most League Goals: 118, Division 3 (N), 1933–34.
Highest League Scorer in Season: Cecil McCormack, 33, Division 2, 1950–51.
Most League Goals in Total Aggregate: Ernest Hine, 123, 1921–26 and 1934–38.
Most Capped Player: Gerry Taggart, 35 (50), Northern Ireland.
Most League Appearances: Barry Murphy, 514, 1962–78.

Honours – **Football League:** Division 3 (N) Champions – 1933–34, 1938–39, 1954–55. **FA Cup:** Winners – 1912.
Colours: Red shirts, white shorts, red stockings.

BIRMINGHAM CITY   FL CHAMPIONSHIP

Aluko Sone (F)	5 8	9 11	Hounslow	19 2 89	Scholar
Aydilek Semih (F)	6 1	11 13	Frankfurt	16 1 89	
De Ridder Daniel (M)	5 11	10 12	Amsterdam	6 3 84	Celta Vigo
Doyle Colin (G)	6 5	14 05	Cork	12 8 85	Scholar
Jaidi Radhi (D)	6 2	14 00	Gabes	30 8 75	Bolton W
Jerome Cameron (F)	6 1	13 06	Huddersfield	14 8 86	Cardiff C
Johnson Damien (M)	5 9	11 09	Lisburn	18 11 78	Blackburn R
Joyce David (D)	5 10	12 13	County Mayo	8 8 90	Scholar
Kapo Olivier (M)	6 1	12 06	Abidjan	27 9 80	Levante
Kelly Stephen (D)	6 0	12 13	Dublin	6 9 83	Tottenham H
Kingson Richard (G)	6 3	13 10	Accra	13 6 78	Hammarby
Krysiak Artur (G)	6 1	12 08	Lodz	11 8 89	UKS Lodz
Larsson Sebastian (M)	5 10	11 00	Eskilstuna	6 6 85	Arsenal
McFadden James (M)	6 0	12 11	Glasgow	14 4 83	Everton
McKerr Michael (D)	5 10	12 00	Craigavon	23 2 90	Glenavon
McPike James (F)	5 10	11 02	Birmingham	4 10 88	Scholar
McSheffrey Gary (M)	5 8	10 06	Coventry	13 8 82	Coventry C
Moses-Garvey Aaron (F)	5 8	11 13	Birmingham	6 9 89	Scholar
Muamba Fabrice (M)	6 2	12 04	DR Congo	6 4 88	Arsenal
Murphy David (D)	6 1	12 03	Hartlepool	1 3 84	Hibernian
Nafti Mehdi (M)	5 9	11 03	Toulouse	20 11 78	Santander
O'Connor Garry (F)	6 1	12 02	Edinburgh	7 5 83	
Parnaby Stuart (M)	5 11	11 00	Durham	19 7 82	Middlesbrough
Pearce Kaystian (D)	6 1	13 05	Birmingham	5 1 90	Scholar
Queudrue Franck (D)	6 1	12 01	Paris	27 8 78	Fulham
Ridgewell Liam (D)	5 10	10 03	Bexley	21 7 84	Aston Villa
Taylor Maik (G)	6 4	14 02	Hildeshein	4 9 71	Fulham
Taylor Martin (D)	6 4	15 00	Ashington	9 11 79	Blackburn R

League Appearances: Danns, N. (2); De Ridder, D. 6(4); Djourou, J. 13; Doyle, C. 3; Forssell, M. 21(9); Jaidi, R. 18; Jerome, C. 21(12); Johnson, D. 17; Kapo, O. 22(4); Kelly, S. 38; Kingson, R. 1; Larsson, S. 32(3); McFadden, J. 10(2); McSheffrey, G. 24(8); Muamba, F. 37; Murphy, D. 14; Nafti, M. 19(7); O'Connor, G. 5(18); Oubina, B. 1(1); Palacios, W. 4(3); Parnaby, S. 4(9); Queudrue, F. 14(2); Ridgewell, L. 35; Sadler, M. 3(2); Schmitz, R. 12(3); Taylor, Maik 34; Taylor, Martin 4; Zarate, M. 6(8).
Goals – League (46): Forssell 9, Jerome 7, Larsson 6, Kapo 5 (1 pen), McFadden 4 (2 pens), Zarate 4, McSheffrey 3 (3 pens), Muamba 2, O'Connor 2, Murphy 1, Ridgewell 1, own goals 2.
Carling Cup (2): O'Connor 1, McSheffrey 1.
FA Cup (1): O'Connor 1.
Ground: St Andrews Stadium, Birmingham B9 4NH. Telephone (0844) 557 1875.
Record Attendance: 66,844 v Everton, FA Cup 5th rd, 11 February 1939.
Capacity: 30,079.
Manager: Alex McLeish.
Secretary: Julia Shelton.
Most League Goals: 103, Division 2, 1893–94 (only 28 games).
Highest League Scorer in Season: Joe Bradford, 29, Division 1, 1927–28.
Most League Goals in Total Aggregate: Joe Bradford, 249, 1920–35.
Most Capped Player: Kenny Cunningham, 32 (72), Republic of Ireland.
Most League Appearances: Frank Womack, 491, 1908–28.
Honours – Football League: Division 2 Champions – 1892–93, 1920–21, 1947–48,

1954–55, 1994–95. **Football League Cup:** Winners – 1963. **Leyland Daf Cup:** Winners – 1991. **Auto Windscreens Shield:** Winners – 1995.
Colours: TBC.

BLACKBURN ROVERS   FA PREMIERSHIP

Arestidou Andreas (G)				6 12 89	Scholar
Bentley David (F)	5 10	11 03	Peterborough	27 8 84	Arsenal
Brown Jason (G)	5 11	13 03	Southwark	18 5 82	Gillingham
Bussmann Bjorn (G)	6 0	12 00	Germany	18 3 91	Scholar
Clarke Jamie (F)	5 10	11 11	Sunderland	11 9 88	Scholar
Derbyshire Matt (F)	5 10	11 01	Gt Harwood	14 4 86	Great Harwood T
Doran Aaron (M)			Ireland	13 5 91	Scholar
Dunn David (M)	5 9	12 03	Gt Harwood	27 12 79	Birmingham C
Emerton Brett (M)	6 1	13 05	Bankstown	22 2 79	Feyenoord
Fielding Frank (G)	5 11	12 00	Blackburn	4 4 88	Scholar
Flynn Jonathan (D)	5 8	11 00		18 11 89	
Friedel Brad (G)	6 3	14 00	Lakewood	18 5 71	Liverpool
Gallagher Paul (F)	6 1	12 00	Glasgow	9 8 84	Trainee
Griffiths Rostyn (M)	6 2	12 08	Stoke	10 3 88	Scholar
Hodge Bryan (M)	5 10	12 02	Hamilton	23 9 87	Scholar
Judge Alan (F)			Dublin	11 11 88	
Kane Tony (D)	5 11	11 00	Belfast	29 8 87	Scholar
Khizanishvili Zurab (D)	6 1	12 08	Tbilisi	6 10 81	Rangers
McCarthy Benny (F)	6 0	12 08	Cape Town	12 11 77	Porto
Mokoena Aaron (D)	6 2	14 00	Johannesburg	25 11 80	Genk
Nelsen Ryan (D)	5 11	14 02	New Zealand	18 10 77	DC United
Nielsen Gunnar (G)	6 3	14 00	Torshavn	7 10 86	Frem
Nolan Eddie (D)	6 0	13 05	Waterford	5 8 88	Scholar
O'Keefe Josh (M)	6 1	11 05	Whalley	22 12 88	Scholar
Olsson Martin (D)	5 7	11 00	Sweden	17 5 88	Hogaborg
Ooijer Andre (D)	6 0	12 00	Amsterdam	11 7 74	PSV Eindhoven
Pedersen Morten (F)	5 11	11 00	Vadso	8 9 81	Tromso
Peter Sergio (M)	5 8	11 00	Ludwigshafen	12 10 86	Scholar
Reid Steven (M)	6 0	12 07	Kingston	10 3 81	Millwall
Rigters Maceo (F)	5 10	14 07	Amsterdam	22 1 84	NAC Breda
Roberts Jason (F)	6 1	13 06	Park Royal	25 1 78	Wigan Ath
Samba Christopher (D)	6 5	13 03	Creteil	28 3 84	Hertha Berlin
Santa Cruz Roque (F)	6 2	13 12	Asuncion	16 8 81	Bayern Munich
Treacy Keith (M)	5 11	11 11	Dublin	13 9 88	Scholar
Tugay Kerimoglu (M)	5 9	11 07	Istanbul	24 8 70	Rangers
Vogel Johann (M)	5 10	11 03	Geneva	8 3 77	Betis
Warnock Stephen (D)	5 7	11 09	Ormskirk	12 12 81	Liverpool
Winnard Dean (D)	5 9	10 04	Wigan	20 8 89	

League Appearances: Bentley, D. 37; Berner, B. 2; Derbyshire, M. 4(19); Dunn, D. 25(6); Emerton, B. 31(2); Friedel, B. 38; Khizanishvili, Z. 10(3); McCarthy, B. 21(10); Mokoena, A. 8(10); Nelsen, R. 22; Olsson, M. (2); Ooijer, A. 23(4); Pedersen, M. 32(5); Reid, S. 20(4); Rigters, M. (2); Roberts, J. 11(15); Samba, C. 33; Santa Cruz, R. 36(1); Savage, R. 10(2); Tugay, K. 12(8); Vogel, J. 6; Warnock, S. 37.

Goals – League (50): Santa Cruz 19, McCarthy 8 (5 pens), Bentley 6, Pedersen 4, Derbyshire 3, Roberts 3, Samba 2, Tugay 2, Dunn 1, Emerton 1, Warnock 1.

Carling Cup (7): Santa Cruz 3, Bentley 1, Derbyshire 1 (pen), McCarthy 1, Pedersen 1.

FA Cup (1): Bentley 1.

Inter-Toto Cup (6): McCarthy 2, Derbyshire 1, Pedersen 1, Roberts 1, Samba 1.

UEFA Cup (5): Bentley 1, Derbyshire 1 (pen), Roberts 1, Santa Cruz 1, Warnock 1.
Ground: Ewood Park, Blackburn, Lancashire BB2 4JF. Telephone (0871) 702 1875.
Record Attendance: 62,522 v Bolton W, FA Cup 6th rd, 2 March 1929. **Capacity:** 31,154.
Manager: Paul Ince.
Secretary: Andrew Pincher.
Most League Goals: 114, Division 2, 1954–55.
Highest League Scorer in Season: Ted Harper, 43, Division 1, 1925–26.
Most League Goals in Total Aggregate: Simon Garner, 168, 1978–92.
Most Capped Player: Henning Berg, 58 (100), Norway.
Most League Appearances: Derek Fazackerley, 596, 1970–86.
Honours – FA Premier League: Champions – 1994–95. **Football League:** Division 1 Champions – 1911–12, 1913–14. Division 2 Champions – 1938–39. Division 3 Champions – 1974–75. **FA Cup:** Winners – 1884, 1885, 1886, 1890, 1891, 1928.
Football League Cup: Winners – 2002. **Full Members' Cup:** Winners – 1986–87.
Colours: Blue and white halved shirts.

BLACKPOOL   FL CHAMPIONSHIP

Barker Shaun (D)	6 2	12 08	Nottingham	19 9 82	Rotherham U
Bayliss Ashton (D)	6 0	11 06	Liverpool	15 5 90	Scholar
Burgess Ben (F)	6 3	14 04	Buxton	9 11 81	Hull C
Coid Danny (D)	5 11	11 07	Liverpool	3 10 81	Trainee
Crainey Stephen (D)	5 9	10 06	Glasgow	22 6 81	Leeds U
D'Agostino Michael (M)	5 9	11 08	Vancouver	7 1 87	Kentucky Univ
Evatt Ian (D)	6 3	13 12	Coventry	19 11 81	QPR
Fox David (M)	5 9	11 08	Leek	13 12 83	Manchester U
Gorkss Kaspars (D)	6 3	13 05	Riga	6 11 81	Ventspils
Green Stuart (M)	5 10	11 01	Whitehaven	15 6 81	Crystal Palace
Hoolahan Wes (M)	5 6	10 03	Dublin	10 8 83	Livingston
Jorgensen Claus (M)	5 10	10 06	Holstebro	27 4 76	Coventry C
Kay Matty (M)	5 9	11 00	Blackpool	12 10 89	Scholar
McPhee Stephen (F)	5 7	11 05	Glasgow	5 6 81	Hull C
Mitchley Danny (F)	5 10	10 08	Liverpool	7 10 89	Scholar
Morrell Andy (F)	5 11	12 00	Doncaster	28 9 74	Coventry C
Rachubka Paul (G)	6 2	13 04	California	21 5 81	Huddersfield T
Southern Keith (M)	5 10	12 06	Gateshead	24 4 81	Everton
Steinbors Pavels (G)	6 2	12 06	Riga	21 9 85	Jurmala
Taylor-Fletcher Gary (F)	5 11	12 06	Liverpool	4 6 81	Huddersfield T
Wiles Simon (M)	5 11	11 04	Preston	22 4 85	Scholar

League Appearances: Barker, S. 46; Burgess, B. 25(10); Coid, D. 9(4); Crainey, S. 37(3); Dickov, P. 7(4); Evatt, I. 27(2); Flynn, Michael 20(8); Forbes, A. (2); Fox, D. 16(12); Gorkss, K. 39(1); Green, S. 1(5); Hills, J. 1(3); Holt, G. (4); Hoolahan, W. 43(2); Jackson, Matt 2(1); Jackson, Mike 23(2); Jorgensen, C. 30(7); Martin, J. 1; McMahon, T. 2; McPhee, S. 16(3); Morrell, A. 23(15); Parker, K. 10(11); Rachubka, P. 46; Slusarski, B. 4(2); Southern, K. 29(1); Taylor-Fletcher, G. 40(2); Vernon, S. 6(9); Welsh, A. 3(18).
Goals – League (59): Burgess 9, Dickov 6, Taylor-Fletcher 6, Gorkss 5, Hoolahan 5 (4 pens), Morrell 5, Jorgensen 4, McPhee 4, Vernon 4, Michael Flynn 3, Southern 3, Barker 2, Crainey 1, Fox 1, Slusarski 1.
Carling Cup (5): Gorkss 2, Burgess 1, Hoolahan 1, Mike Jackson 1.
FA Cup (1): Fox 1.
Ground: Bloomfield Road, Seasiders Way, Blackpool FY1 6JJ. Telephone (0870) 443 1953.

Record Attendance: 38,098 v Wolverhampton W, Division 1, 17 September 1955.
Capacity: 9,731.
Manager: Simon Grayson.
Secretary: Matt Williams.
Most League Goals: 98, Division 2, 1929–30.
Highest League Scorer in Season: Jimmy Hampson, 45, Division 2, 1929–30.
Most League Goals in Total Aggregate: Jimmy Hampson, 246, 1927–38.
Most Capped Player: Jimmy Armfield, 43, England.
Most League Appearances: Jimmy Armfield, 568, 1952–71.
Honours – Football League: Division 2 Champions – 1929–30. **FA Cup:** Winners – 1953. **Anglo-Italian Cup:** Winners – 1971. **LDV Vans Trophy:** Winners – 2002, 2004.
Colours: Tangerine shirts, white shorts, tangerine stockings.

BOLTON WANDERERS   FA PREMIERSHIP

Al-Habsi Ali (G)	6 4	12 06	Oman	30 12 81	Lyn
Basham Chris (M)	5 11	12 08	Stafford	20 7 88	Scholar
Bogdan Adam (G)	6 4	14 02	Budapest	27 9 87	
Braaten Daniel (F)	6 0	13 05	Oslo	25 2 82	Rosenborg
Cahill Gary (D)	6 2	12 06	Dronfield	19 12 85	Aston Villa
Cohen Tamir (M)	5 11	11 09	Israel	4 3 84	Maccabi Netanya
Davies Kevin (F)	6 0	12 10	Sheffield	26 3 77	Southampton
Diouf El Hadji (F)	5 11	11 11	Dakar	15 1 81	Liverpool
Dzemaili Blerim (M)	5 10	11 07	Tetovo	12 4 86	Zurich
Fojut Jaroslaw (D)	6 2	13 00	Legionowo	17 10 87	Scholar
Gardner Ricardo (D)	5 9	11 00	St Andrews	25 9 78	Harbour View
Harsanyi Zoltan (D)	6 1	12 00	Bratislava	1 6 87	Senec
Helguson Heider (F)	5 10	12 09	Akureyri	22 8 77	Fulham
Hunt Nicky (D)	6 1	13 08	Westhoughton	3 9 83	Scholar
Jaaskelainen Jussi (G)	6 3	12 10	Mikkeli	19 4 75	VPS
McCann Gavin (M)	5 11	11 00	Blackpool	10 1 78	Aston Villa
Meite Abdoulaye (D)	6 1	12 13	Paris	6 10 80	Marseille
Nolan Kevin (M)	6 0	14 00	Liverpool	24 6 82	Scholar
O'Brien Joey (M)	6 0	10 13	Dublin	17 2 86	Scholar
O'Brien Andy (D)	6 2	11 13	Harrogate	29 6 79	Portsmouth
Samuel JLloyd (D)	5 11	11 04	Trinidad	29 3 81	Aston Villa
Sinclair James (F)	5 6	10 05	Newcastle	22 10 87	Scholar
Sissons Robert (M)	5 8	11 02	Stockport	29 9 88	Scholar
Steinsson Gretar (D)	6 2	12 04	Siglufjordur	9 1 82	AZ
Taylor Matthew (M)	5 11	12 03	Oxford	27 11 81	Portsmouth
Vaz Te Ricardo (F)	6 2	12 07	Lisbon	1 10 86	Scholar
Walker Ian (G)	6 2	13 01	Watford	31 10 71	Leicester C

League Appearances: Al-Habsi, A. 10; Alonso, M. 4(3); Anelka, N. 18; Braaten, D. (6); Cahill, G. 13; Campo, I. 25(2); Cid, G. 6(1); Cohen, T. 3(7); Davies, K. 31(1); Diagne-Faye, A. 1; Diouf, E. 30(4); Gardner, R. 25(1); Giannakopoulos, S. 1(14); Guthrie, D. 21(4); Helguson, H. 3(3); Hunt, N. 12(2); Jaaskelainen, J. 28; McCann, G. 21(10); Meite, A. 21; Michalik, L. 5(2); Nolan, K. 33; O'Brien, A. 31(1); O'Brien, J. 15(4); Rasiak, G. 2(5); Samuel, J. 14(6); Speed, G. 11(3); Steinsson, G. 16; Taylor, M. 16; Teimourian, A. 1(2); Vaz Te, R. 1; Wilhelmsson, C. (8).
Goals – League (36): Anelka 10, Nolan 5, Diouf 4, Davies 3, Taylor 3, Giannakopoulos 2, Helguson 2, Braaten 1, Campo 1, Cohen 1, McCann 1, Speed 1, own goals 2.
Carling Cup (2): Giannakopoulos 1, Guthrie 1.
FA Cup (0).
UEFA Cup (9): Diouf 2, McCann 2, Anelka 1, Davies 1, Gardner 1, Giannakopoulos 1, Meite 1.

Ground: The Reebok Stadium, Burnden Way, Lostock, Bolton, Lancashire BL6 6JW. Telephone Bolton (01204) 673 673.
Record Attendance: 69,912 v Manchester C, FA Cup 5th rd, 18 February 1933.
Capacity: 28,101.
Manager: Gary Megson.
Secretary: Simon Marland.
Most League Goals: 100, Division 1, 1996–97.
Highest League Scorer in Season: Joe Smith, 38, Division 1, 1920–21.
Most League Goals in Total Aggregate: Nat Lofthouse, 255, 1946–61.
Most Capped Player: Mark Fish, 34 (62), South Africa.
Most League Appearances: Eddie Hopkinson, 519, 1956–70.
Honours – Football League: Division 1 Champions – 1996–97. Division 2 Champions – 1908–09, 1977–78. Division 3 Champions – 1972–73. **FA Cup:** Winners – 1923, 1926, 1929, 1958. **Sherpa Van Trophy:** Winners – 1989.
Colours: White shirts, white shorts, white stockings.

AFC BOURNEMOUTH   FL CHAMPIONSHIP 2

Anderton Darren (M)	6 2	13 04	Southampton	3 3 72	Wolverhampton W
Bartley Marvyn (M)	6 1	12 04	Reading	4 7 86	Hampton & Richmond B
Bradbury Lee (F)	6 0	12 07	Isle of Wight	3 7 75	Southend U
Cooper Shaun (D)	5 10	10 05	Newport (IW)	5 10 83	Portsmouth
Cummings Warren (D)	5 9	11 08	Aberdeen	15 10 80	Chelsea
Garry Ryan (D)	6 0	11 05	Hornchurch	29 9 83	Arsenal
Gowling Josh (D)	6 3	12 08	Coventry	29 11 83	Herfolge
Hollands Danny (M)	6 0	12 00	Ashford	6 11 85	Chelsea
Moss Neil (G)	6 2	13 10	New Milton	10 5 75	Southampton
Osei-Kuffour Jo (F)	5 8	11 11	Edmonton	17 11 81	Brentford
Pearce Jason (D)	5 11	12 00	Hampshire	6 12 87	Portsmouth
Pitman Brett (M)	6 0	11 00	Jersey	31 1 88	St Paul's, Jersey
Vokes Sam (F)	6 1	13 10	Southampton	21 10 89	Scholar

League Appearances: Anderton, D. 20; Bartley, M. 14(6); Begovic, A. 8; Bradbury, L. 33(2); Christophe, J. 5(5); Cooper, S. 33(5); Cummings, W. 31(1); Finlay, M. (1); Forde, D. 11; Franks, B. 1; Garry, R. 6(2); Golbourne, S. 5; Gowling, J. 36(1); Gradel, M. 31(3); Henry, J. 8(3); Hollands, D. 37; Hutchings, S. (1); Karacan, J. 11(2); Lallana, A. 2(1); McQuoid, J. 2(3); Moss, N. 7; O'Connor, G. 5(1); Osei-Kuffour, J. 37(5); Partington, J. (6); Pearce, A. 11; Pearce, J. 30(3); Perrett, R. 10; Pitman, B. 14(25); Pryce, R. 2(2); Shimmin, D. 1(1); Stewart, G. 18; Telfer, P. 17(1); Tessem, J. 5(6); Vokes, S. 30(11); Wilson, M. 7; Young, N. 18(3).
Goals – League (62): Osei-Kuffour 12, Vokes 12, Gradel 9 (2 pens), Pitman 6 (1 pen), Henry 4, Hollands 4, Anderton 3, Bradbury 3 (1 pen), Cummings 2 (1 pen), Bartley 1, Christophe 1, Cooper 1, Karacan 1, Partington 1, Pearce J 1, own goal 1.
Carling Cup (0).
FA Cup (5): Cooper 1, Golbourne 1, Gradel 1 (pen), Hollands 1, Karacan 1.
J Paint Trophy (3): Bradbury 2, Osei-Kuffour 1.
Ground: The Fitness First Stadium at Dean Court, Bournemouth BH7 7AF. Telephone (01202) 726 300.
Record Attendance: 28,799 v Manchester U, FA Cup 6th rd, 2 March 1957.
Capacity: 10,375 (with temporary stand) 9,776 (without).
Manager: Kevin Bond.
Secretary: Neil Vacher (Football Administrator).
Most League Goals: 88, Division 3 (S), 1956–57.
Highest League Scorer in Season: Ted MacDougall, 42, 1970–71.
Most League Goals in Total Aggregate: Ron Eyre, 202, 1924–33.
Most Capped Player: Gerry Peyton, 7 (33), Republic of Ireland.
Most League Appearances: Steve Fletcher, 466, 1992–2007.

Honours – Football League: Division 3 Champions – 1986–87. **Associate Members' Cup:** Winners – 1984.
Colours: Red and black.

BRADFORD CITY   FL CHAMPIONSHIP 2

Ainge Simon (D)	6 1	12 02	Bradford	18	2 88	Scholar
Bower Mark (D)	5 10	11 00	Bradford	23	1 80	Trainee
Bullock Lee (M)	6 0	11 04	Stockton	22	5 81	Hartlepool U
Clarke Matthew (D)	6 3	12 07	Leeds	18 12 80		Darlington
Colbeck Joe (M)	5 10	10 12	Bradford	29 11 86		Scholar
Conlon Barry (F)	6 3	14 00	Drogheda	1 10 78		Mansfield T
Daley Omar (M)	5 7	10 03	Jamaica	25	4 81	Charleston Battery
Heckingbottom Paul (D)	6 0	13 01	Barnsley	17	7 77	Barnsley
Medley Luke (F)	6 1	13 03	Greenwich	21	6 89	Tottenham H
Nix Kyle (F)	5 6	9 10	Sydney	21	1 86	Sheffield U
O'Brien Luke (D)	5 9	12 01	Halifax	11	9 88	Scholar
Taylforth Sean (F)	5 11	10 03	Chester	10	3 89	Scholar
Thorne Peter (F)	6 1	13 13	Manchester	21	6 73	Norwich C
Topp Willy (F)	5 9	11 04	Temuco	4	3 86	Universitario
Wetherall David (D)	6 3	13 12	Sheffield	14	3 71	Leeds U

League Appearances: Ainge, S. (4); Bentham, C. (3); Bower, M. 25(2); Brown, D. (5); Bullock, L. 12; Clarke, M. 15(2); Colbeck, J. 27(6); Conlon, B. 21(21); Daley, O. 37(4); Evans, P. 19(6); Evans, R. 4; Harban, T. 6; Heckingbottom, P. 44; Johnson, E. 30(2); Joynes, N. 1(1); Law, N. 10; Loach, S. 20; Medley, L. 1(8); Moncur, T. 6(1); N'Dumbu Nsungu, G. 17(1); Nix, K. 31(9); O'Brien, L. 2; Penford, T. 13(2); Phelan, S. 8(5); Rhodes, Alex 11(17); Ricketts, D. 22; Starosta, B. 12(3); Taylforth, S. 1; Thorne, P. 31(2); Topp, W. 6(5); Wetherall, D. 46; Williams, D. 28.
Goals – League (63): Thorne 14 (2 pens), Conlon 7 (3 pens), Colbeck 6, N'Dumbu Nsungu 6 (1 pen), Nix 6, Daley 4, Johnson 4, Bower 3, Rhodes Alex 3, Law 2, Medley 2 (1 pen), Wetherall 2, Brown D 1, Bullock 1, Clarke 1, Penford 1.
Carling Cup (1): Nix 1.
FA Cup (1): Thorne 1.
J Paint Trophy (1): Nix 1.
Ground: Cral Window Stadium, Valley Parade, Bradford BD8 7DY. Telephone 01274 773 335.
Record Attendance: 39,146 v Burnley, FA Cup 4th rd, 11 March 1911. **Capacity:** 25,136.
Manager: Stuart McCall.
Secretary: Jon Pollard.
Most League Goals: 128, Division 3 (N), 1928–29.
Highest League Scorer in Season: David Layne, 34, Division 4, 1961–62.
Most League Goals in Total Aggregate: Bobby Campbell, 121, 1981–84, 1984–86.
Most Capped Player: Jamie Lawrence, (42), Jamaica.
Most League Appearances: Cec Podd, 502, 1970–84.
Honours – Football League: Division 2 Champions – 1907–08. Division 3 Champions – 1984–85. Division 3 (N) Champions – 1928–29. **FA Cup:** Winners – 1911.
Colours: Claret and amber.

BRENTFORD   FL CHAMPIONSHIP 2

Brown Simon (G)	6 2	15 00	Chelmsford	3 12 76		Colchester U
Charles Darius (M)	5 11	11 10	Ealing	10 12 87		Scholar
Connell Alan (F)	6 0	12 00	Enfield	5	2 83	Hereford U
Dickson Ryan (M)	5 10	11 05	Saltash	14 12 86		Plymouth Arg
Elder Nathan (F)	6 1	13 12	Hornchurch	5	4 85	Brighton & HA

Heywood Matt (D)	6 3	14 00	Chatham	26 8 79	Bristol C
Ide Charlie (M)	5 8	10 06	Sunbury	10 5 88	Scholar
Montague Ross (F)	6 0	12 11	Isleworth	1 11 88	Scholar
Mousinho John (D)	6 1	12 07	Buckingham	30 4 86	Univ of Notre Dame
O'Connor Kevin (F)	5 11	12 00	Blackburn	24 2 82	Trainee
Osborne Karleigh (M)	6 2	12 08	Southall	19 3 88	Scholar
Pead Craig (M)	5 9	11 06	Bromsgrove	15 9 81	Walsall
Poole Glenn (M)	5 7	11 04	Essex	3 2 81	Rochdale
Shakes Ricky (M)	5 10	12 00	Brixton	26 1 85	Swindon T
Smith Gary (M)	5 8	10 09	Middlesbrough	30 1 84	Milton Keynes D

League Appearances: Basey, G. 8; Bennett, A. 11; Brooker, P. (1); Brown, S. 26; Brown, W. 7(4); Charles, D. 8(9); Connell, A. 35(7); Dickson, R. 30(1); Elder, N. 16(1); Emanuel, L. 3; Hamer, B. 20; Heywood, M. 30(2); Ide, C. 16(3); Mackie, J. 14; Masters, C. (1); Milsom, R. 5(1); Montague, R. 7(3); Moore, S. 13(7); Mousinho, J. 13(10); O'Connor, K. 36(1); Osborne, K. 25(4); Parkes, J. (1); Pead, C. 27(5); Peters, R. (4); Pettigrew, A. 9(2); Poole, G. 42(3); Reid, R. 1(9); Sankofa, O. 10(1); Shakes, R. 25(14); Sinclair, E. 1(3); Smith, G. 26(3); Starosta, B. 20(1); Stone, C. 5(1); Thorpe, L. 17(2); Tillen, S. (1).
Goals – League (52): Poole 14 (2 pens), Connell 12, Elder 4, Thorpe 4, O'Connor 3 (1 pen), Shakes 3, Moore S 2, Mousinho 2, Bennett 1, Brown W 1, Heywood 1, Montague 1, Osborne 1, Reid 1, Smith G 1, own goal 1.
Carling Cup (0).
FA Cup (1): Ide 1.
J Paint Trophy (1): Shakes 1.
Ground: Griffin Park, Braemar Road, Brentford, Middlesex TW8 0NT. Telephone (0845) 3456 442.
Record Attendance: 38,678 v Leicester C, FA Cup 6th rd, 26 February 1949.
Capacity: 12,400.
Manager: Andy Scott.
Secretary: Lisa Hall.
Most League Goals: 98, Division 4, 1962–63.
Highest League Scorer in Season: Jack Holliday, 38, Division 3 (S), 1932–33.
Most League Goals in Total Aggregate: Jim Towers, 153, 1954–61.
Most Capped Player: John Buttigieg, 22 (98), Malta.
Most League Appearances: Ken Coote, 514, 1949–64.
Honours – Football League: Division 2 Champions – 1934–35. Division 3 Champions – 1991–92, 1998–99. Division 3 (S) Champions – 1932–33. Division 4 Champions – 1962–63.
Colours: Red and white striped shirts, black shorts, black stockings with red turnovers.

BRIGHTON & HOVE ALBION   FL CHAMPIONSHIP 1

Chamberlain Scott (M)	5 9	10 08	Eastbourne	15 1 88	Scholar
Cox Dean (M)	5 4	9 08	Haywards Heath	12 8 87	Scholar
Dixon Jonny (F)	5 9	11 01	Murcia	16 1 84	Aldershot T
El-Abd Adam (D)	5 10	13 05	Brighton	11 9 84	Scholar
Elphick Tommy (M)	5 11	11 07	Brighton	7 9 87	Scholar
Fogden Wes (F)	5 8	10 04	Brighton	12 4 88	Scholar
Forster Nicky (F)	5 9	11 05	Caterham	8 9 73	Hull C
Fraser Tom (M)	5 10	11 00	Brighton	5 12 87	Scholar
Gargan Sam (F)	6 2	13 01	Brighton	24 1 89	Scholar
Gatting Joe (D)	5 11	12 04	Brighton	25 11 87	Scholar
Hinshelwood Adam (D)	5 11	13 00	Oxford	8 1 84	Scholar
Kuipers Michels (G)	6 2	15 00	Amsterdam	26 6 74	Bristol R
Loft Doug (M)	6 0	12 01	Maidstone	25 12 86	Hastings U

Lynch Joel (D)	6 1	12 10	Eastbourne	3 10 87	Scholar
Martot David (M)	5 8	11 00	Fecamp	1 2 81	Le Havre
Murray Glenn (F)	6 1	12 12	Maryport	25 9 83	Rochdale
Robinson Jake (F)	5 7	10 10	Brighton	23 10 86	Scholar
Sullivan John (M)	5 10	11 04	Brighton	8 3 88	Scholar
Thomson Steve (M)	5 8	10 04	Glasgow	23 1 78	Peterborough U
Whing Andrew (D)	6 0	12 00	Birmingham	20 9 84	Coventry C

League Appearances: Bowditch, D. 5; Butters, G. 19(2); Chamberlain, S. ; Cox, D. 40(2); Dixon, J. 2(2); El-Abd, A. 31(4); Elder, N. 1(8); Elphick, T. 39; Fogden, W. 1(2); Forster, N. 39(2); Fraser, T. 15(9); Gargan, S. (1); Gatting, J. (9); Hammond, D. 24; Hart, G. 2(5); Hinshelwood, A. (1); Kuipers, M. 46; Loft, D. 1(12); Lynch, J. 18(4); Martot, D. 17(9); Mayo, K. 10(5); McFaul, S. (1); Murray, G. 20(1); O'Callaghan, G. 13(1); Racon, T. 8; Reid, P. 3(4); Rents, S. 4(1); Revell, A. 14(7); Richards, M. 28; Robinson, J. 16(18); Savage, B. 17(4); Thomson, S. 20; Westlake, I. 11; Whing, A. 42.
Goals – League (58): Forster 15 (3 pens), Murray 9, Cox 6, Revell 6, Hammond 5 (3 pens), Robinson 4, Savage 3, Elphick 2, Westlake 2, Butters 1, El-Abd 1, Elder 1, Lynch 1, Martot 1, own goal 1.
Carling Cup (0).
FA Cup (6): Forster 2, El-Abd 1, Hammond 1 (pen), Loft 1, Revell 1.
J Paint Trophy (6): Forster 2, Cox 1, Martot 1, Robinson 1, Savage 1.
Ground: Withdean Stadium, Tongdean Lane, Brighton, East Sussex BN1 5JD. Telephone (01273) 695 400 (admin offices 44 North Road, Brighton).
Record Attendance: 36,747 v Fulham, Division 2, 27 December 1958 (at Goldstone Ground).
Capacity: 8,850.
Manager: Micky Adams.
Secretary: Derek J. Allan.
Most League Goals: 112, Division 3 (S), 1955–56.
Highest League Scorer in Season: Peter Ward, 32, Division 3, 1976–77.
Most League Goals in Total Aggregate: Tommy Cook, 114, 1922–29.
Most Capped Player: Steve Penney, 17, Northern Ireland.
Most League Appearances: 'Tug' Wilson, 509, 1922–36.
Honours – Football League: Division 2 Champions – 2001–02. Division 3 Champions – 2000–01. Division 3 (S) Champions – 1957–58. Division 4 Champions – 1964–65.
Colours: Blue and white striped shirts, white shorts, white stockings.

BRISTOL CITY   FL CHAMPIONSHIP

Adebola Dele (F)	6 3	12 08	Lagos	23 6 75	Coventry C
Artus Frankie (M)	6 0	11 02	Bristol	27 9 88	Scholar
Basso Adriano (G)	6 1	11 07	Jundiai	18 4 75	Woking
Betsy Kevin (M)	6 1	12 00	Seychelles	20 3 78	Wycombe W
Brooker Stephen (F)	5 11	13 13	Newport Pagnell	21 5 81	Port Vale
Carey Louis (D)	5 10	12 09	Bristol	20 1 77	Trainee
Carle Nick (F)	5 9	12 04	Sydney	23 11 81	
Elliott Marvin (M)	6 0	12 02	Wandsworth	15 9 84	Millwall
Fontaine Liam (D)	5 11	11 09	Beckenham	7 1 86	Fulham
Henderson Stephen (G)	6 3	11 00	Dublin	2 5 88	Aston Villa
Johnson Lee (M)	5 6	10 07	Newmarket	7 6 81	Hearts
Keogh Richard (M)	6 0	11 02	Harlow	11 8 86	Stoke C
McAllister Jamie (D)	5 10	11 00	Glasgow	26 4 78	Hearts
McCombe Jamie (D)	6 5	12 05	Scunthorpe	1 1 83	Lincoln C
McIndoe Michael (M)	5 8	11 00	Edinburgh	2 12 79	Wolverhampton W
Murray Scott (M)	5 8	11 02	Aberdeen	26 5 74	Reading

Myrie-Williams	5 11	12 08	Lambeth	17 5 88	Scholar
Jennison (F)					
Noble David (M)	6 0	12 04	Hitchin	2 2 82	Boston U
Orr Bradley (M)	6 0	11 11	Liverpool	1 11 82	Newcastle U
Plummer Tristan (F)	5 6	10 07	Bristol	30 1 90	Scholar
Ribeiro Christian (D)	5 11	12 02	Neath	14 12 89	Scholar
Skuse Cole (M)	6 1	11 05	Bristol	29 3 86	Scholar
Sproule Ivan (M)	5 8	11 09	Castlederg	18 2 81	Hibernian
Trundle Lee (F)	6 0	11 06	Liverpool	10 10 76	Swansea C
Weale Chris (G)	6 2	13 01	Chard	9 2 82	Yeovil T
Wilson Brian (D)	5 10	11 00	Manchester	9 5 83	Cheltenham T
Wilson James (D)	6 2	11 05	Newport	26 2 89	Scholar

League Appearances: Adebola, D. 16(1); Basso, A. 44; Betsy, K. (1); Brooker, S. 1(3); Byfield, D. 17(16); Carey, L. 33; Carle, N. 14(3); Elliott, M. 44(1); Fontaine, L. 32(6); Henderson, S. (1); Jevons, P. (2); Johnson, L. 39(1); McAllister, J. 40(1); McCombe, J. 25(9); McIndoe, M. 45; Murray, S. 4(10); Noble, D. 16(10); Orr, B. 42; Russell, A. 1; Showunmi, E. 10(7); Skuse, C. 5(20); Sproule, I. 31(9); Trundle, L. 21(14); Vasko, T. 8(11); Weale, C. 2(1); Wilson, B. 16(2).
Goals – League (54): Byfield 8, Adebola 6, McIndoe 6 (1 pen), Elliott 5, Trundle 5 (1 pen), Orr 4 (1 pen), McCombe 3, Murray 3, Showunmi 3, Noble 2, Sproule 2, Brooker 1, Fontaine 1, Johnson 1, Vasko 1, Wilson B 1, own goals 2.
Carling Cup (4): Jevons 2, Elliott 1, Orr 1.
FA Cup (1): Fontaine 1.
Play-Offs (4): Carey 1, McIndoe 1, Noble 1, Trundle 1.
Ground: Ashton Gate Stadium, Bristol BS3 2EJ. Telephone (0871) 222 6666.
Record Attendance: 43,335 v Preston NE, FA Cup 5th rd, 16 February 1935.
Capacity: 21,804.
Manager: Gary Johnson.
Secretary: Michelle McDonald.
Most League Goals: 104, Division 3 (S), 1926–27.
Highest League Scorer in Season: Don Clark, 36, Division 3 (S), 1946–47.
Most League Goals in Total Aggregate: John Atyeo, 314, 1951–66.
Most Capped Player: Billy Wedlock, 26, England.
Most League Appearances: John Atyeo, 597, 1951–66.
Honours – Football League: Division 2 Champions – 1905–06. Division 3 (S) Champions – 1922–23, 1926–27, 1954–55. **Welsh Cup:** Winners – 1934. **Anglo-Scottish Cup:** Winners – 1977–78. **Freight Rover Trophy:** Winners – 1985–86. **LDV Vans Trophy:** Winners – 2002–03.
Colours: Red shirts, white shorts, white stockings.

BRISTOL ROVERS   FL CHAMPIONSHIP 1

Anthony Byron (D)	6 1	11 02	Newport	20 9 84	Cardiff C
Campbell Stuart (M)	5 10	10 00	Corby	9 12 77	Grimsby T
Clough Charlie (M)	6 2	12 07	Taunton	3 9 90	Scholar
Coles Danny (D)	6 1	11 05	Bristol	31 10 81	Hull C
Disley Craig (M)	5 10	10 13	Worksop	24 8 81	Mansfield T
Elliott Steve (D)	6 1	14 00	Derby	29 10 78	Blackpool
Fraser James (M)	5 9	12 07	Brighton	26 4 89	Scholar
Green Mike (G)	6 1	13 01	Bristol	23 07 89	Scholar
Green Ryan (D	5 7	10 10	Cardiff	20 10 80	Hereford U
Groves Matt (F)	5 8	11 07	Bristol	11 12 88	Scholar
Haldane Lewis (F)	6 0	11 03	Trowbridge	13 3 85	Scholar
Hinton Craig (D)	6 0	12 00	Wolverhampton	26 11 77	Kidderminster H
Jacobson Joe (D)	5 11	12 06	Cardiff	17 11 86	Cardiff C
Kite Alex (D)	6 0	12 05	Kent	7 3 89	Scholar
Klein-Davies Josh (F)	5 11	13 09	Bristol	6 7 89	Scholar

Lambert Ricky (F)	6 2	14 08	Liverpool	16 2 82	Rochdale
Lescott Aaron (M)	5 8	10 09	Birmingham	2 12 78	Stockport Co
Lines Chris (M)	6 2	12 00	Bristol	30 11 85	Filton College
Mahdi Adam (M)	5 8	11 00	London	2 12 89	Scholar
Parrinello Tom (D)	5 6	10 07	Parkway	11 11 89	Scholar
Phillips Steve (G)	6 1	11 10	Bath	6 5 78	Bristol C
Pipe David (M)	5 9	12 01	Caerphilly	5 11 83	Notts Co
Reece Charlie (M)	5 11	11 03	Birmingham	8 9 88	Scholar
Rigg Sean (F)	5 9	12 01	Bristol	1 10 88	Scholar
Walker Richard (F)	6 0	12 04	Sutton Coldfield	8 11 77	Oxford U
Williams Andy (F)	5 11	11 09	Hereford	14 8 86	Hereford U

League Appearances: Andrews, W. 1; Anthony, B. 19(1); Campbell, S. 46; Carruthers, C. 13(4); Clough, C. (1); Coles, D. 24; Disley, C. 41(3); Elliott, S. 33; Green, R. 12; Groves, M. (1); Haldane, L. 22(10); Hinton, C. 21(3); Igoe, S. 9(12); Jacobson, J. 34(6); Klein-Davies, J. 2(8); Lambert, R. 42(4); Lescott, A. 34; Lines, C. 25(2); Phillips, S. 46; Pipe, D. 37(3); Pulis, A. (1); Reece, C. (1); Rigg, S. 14(17); Walker, R. 12(12); Williams, A. 19(22).

Goals – League (45): Lambert 14 (3 pens), Disley 6, Walker 4 (4 pens), Williams A 4, Elliott 3, Lines 3, Hinton 2, Pipe 2, Anthony 1, Coles 1, Haldane 1, Jacobson 1, Klein-Davies 1, Rigg 1, own goal 1.

Carling Cup (2): Disley 1, Williams 1.

FA Cup (14): Lambert 6 (1 pen), Hinton 3, Coles 2, Disley 2, Williams 1.

J Paint Trophy (0).

Ground: The Memorial Stadium, Filton Avenue, Horfield, Bristol BS7 0BF. Telephone (0117) 909 6648.

Record Attendance: 9,464 v Liverpool, FA Cup 4th rd, 8 February 1992 (Twerton Park). 38,472 v Preston NE, FA Cup 4th rd, 30 January 1960 (Eastville). 11,433 v Sunderland, Worthington Cup 3rd rd, 31 October 2000 (Memorial Stadium). **Capacity:** 11,916.

Manager: Paul Trollope.

Secretary: Rod Wesson.

Most League Goals: 92, Division 3 (S), 1952–53.

Highest League Scorer in Season: Geoff Bradford, 33, Division 3 (S), 1952–53.

Most League Goals in Total Aggregate: Geoff Bradford, 242, 1949–64.

Most Capped Player: Vitalijs Astafjevs, 31 (142), Latvia.

Most League Appearances: Stuart Taylor, 546, 1966–80.

Honours – Football League: Division 3 (S) Champions – 1952–53. Division 3 Champions – 1989–90.

Colours: Blue and white quartered shirts, blue shorts, white stockings.

BURNLEY   FL CHAMPIONSHIP

Akinbiyi Ade (F)	6 1	13 08	Hackney	10 10 74	Sheffield U
Alexander Graham (D)	5 10	12 07	Coventry	10 10 71	Preston NE
Berisha Besart (M)	5 11	11 12	Pristina	29 7 85	Hamburg
Blake Robbie (F)	5 9	12 00	Middlesbrough	4 3 76	Leeds U
Caldwell Steve (D)	5 11	11 05	Stirling	12 9 80	Sunderland
Carlisle Clarke (D)	6 2	14 11	Preston	14 10 79	Watford
Duff Michael (D)	6 3	12 10	Belfast	11 1 78	Cheltenham T
Elliott Wade (M)	5 10	10 03	Southampton	14 12 78	Bournemouth
Gudjohnsson Joey (M)	5 9	12 04	Akranes	25 5 80	AZ
Harley Jon (D)	5 8	10 03	Maidstone	26 9 79	Sheffield U
Jensen Brian (G)	6 4	16 09	Copenhagen	8 6 75	WBA
Jones Steve (F)	5 10	10 05	Derry	25 10 76	Crewe Alex
Jordan Stephen (D)	6 1	13 00	Warrington	6 3 82	Manchester C
Kiraly Gabor (G)	6 3	13 06	Szombathely	1 4 76	Crystal Palace
Lafferty Kyle (F)	6 4	11 02	Belfast	21 7 87	Scholar

Mahon Alan (M)	5 8	12 03	Dublin	4	4 78	Wigan Ath
McCann Chris (M)	6 1	11 11	Dublin	21	7 87	Scholar
O'Connor James (M)	5 8	11 06	Dublin	1	9 79	WBA
Rodriguez Jay (F)	6 0	12 00	Burnley	27	7 89	Scholar
Unsworth Dave (D)	6 1	13 07	Chorley	16	10 73	Wigan Ath

League Appearances: Akinbiyi, A. 14(25); Alexander, G. 43; Blake, R. 4(4); Caldwell, S. 26(3); Carlisle, C. 32(1); Cole, A. 8(5); Duff, M. 8; Elliott, W. 45(1); Gray, A. 25; Gudjonsson, J. 13(15); Harley, J. 31(2); Jensen, B. 19; Jones, S. 1(16); Jordan, S. 20(1); Kiraly, G. 27; Lafferty, K. 34(3); MacDonald, A. 2(); Mahon, A. 13(13); McCann, C. 34(1); O'Connor, G. (1); O'Connor, J. 24(5); Randall, M. 2(8); Rodriguez, J. (1); Spicer, J. 9(15); Thomas, W. 1; Unsworth, D. 26(3); Varga, S. 10.
Goals – League (60): Gray 11 (4 pens), Blake 9, Akinbiyi 8, Cole 6, Lafferty 5, McCann 5, O'Connor J 3, Caldwell 2, Carlisle 2, Elliott 2, Alexander 1, Duff 1, Gudjonsson 1, Jones 1, Mahon 1, Unsworth 1, own goal 1.
Carling Cup (4): Gray 2, Akinbiyi 1, Blake 1.
FA Cup (0).
Ground: Turf Moor, Harry Potts Way, Burnley, Lancashire BB10 4BX. Telephone (0871) 221 1882.
Record Attendance: 54,775 v Huddersfield T, FA Cup 3rd rd, 23 February 1924.
Capacity: 21,973.
Manager: Owen Coyle.
Most League Goals: 102, Division 1, 1960–61.
Highest League Scorer in Season: George Beel, 35, Division 1, 1927–28.
Most League Goals in Total Aggregate: George Beel, 179, 1923–32.
Most Capped Player: Jimmy McIlroy, 51 (55), Northern Ireland.
Most League Appearances: Jerry Dawson, 522, 1907–28.
Honours – Football League: Division 1 Champions – 1920–21, 1959–60. Division 2 Champions – 1897–98, 1972–73. Division 3 Champions – 1981–82. Division 4 Champions – 1991–92. **FA Cup:** Winners – 1913–14. **Anglo-Scottish Cup:** Winners – 1978–79.
Colours: Claret and blue.

BURY   FL CHAMPIONSHIP 2

Adams Nicky (F)	5 10	11 00	Bolton	16 10 86	Scholar
Baker Richie (M)	5 7	11 10	Burnley	29 12 87	Preston NE
Barry-Murphy Brian (M)	6 1	13 01	Cork	27 7 78	Sheffield W
Belford Cameron (G)	6 1	11 10	Nuneaton	16 10 88	Coventry C
Bishop Andy (F)	6 0	11 00	Stone	19 10 82	York C
Buchanan David (M)	5 8	10 08	Rochdale	6 5 86	Scholar
Dorney Jack (M)	5 9	10 00	Ashton-under-Lyne	9 1 90	Scholar
Futcher Ben (D)	6 7	12 05	Manchester	20 2 81	Peterborough U
Haslam Steven (M)	5 11	10 10	Sheffield	6 9 79	Halifax T
Hurst Glynn (F)	5 10	11 05	Barnsley	17 1 76	Shrewsbury T
Morgan Paul (D)	6 0	11 05	Belfast	23 10 78	Lincoln C
Rouse Domaine (F)	5 6	10 10	Stretford	4 7 89	Scholar
Scott Paul (D)	5 11	12 00	Wakefield	5 11 79	Huddersfield T
Stephens Dale (M)	5 7	11 04	Bolton	12 12 87	Scholar

League Appearances: Adams, N. 41(2); Baker, R. 21(11); Barry-Murphy, B. 27(4); Belford, C. (1); Bennett, E. 18(1); Bishop, A. 37(7); Buchanan, D. 24(11); Bullock, L. 8; Challinor, D. 26; Dean, J. 3(1); Dorney, J. 3(4); Futcher, B. 40; Haslam, S. 37; Hughes, L. 1(3); Hurst, G. 29(13); Mangan, A. 7(13); Morgan, P. 20; Parrish, A. 17(9); Provett, J. 32; Randolph, D. 14; Richardson, M. 1; Rooney, A. 10(6); Rouse, D. (6); Scott, P. 40; Sodje, E. 16; Stephens, D. 4(2); Woodthorpe, C. 30(1); Yeo, S. (8).

36

Goals – League (58): Bishop 19 (5 pens), Adams 12 (3 pens), Hurst 6, Scott 6, Mangan 4, Rooney 3, Baker 1, Barry-Murphy 1, Bennett 1, Haslam 1, Parrish 1, Sodje 1, Stephens 1, Woodthorpe 1.
Carling Cup (0).
FA Cup (8): Bishop 5, Adams 1, Futcher 1, Scott 1.
J Paint Trophy (5): Hurst 2, Bishop 1, Futcher 1, Rouse 1.
Ground: Gigg Lane, Bury BL9 9HR. Telephone (0161) 764 4881.
Record Attendance: 35,000 v Bolton W, FA Cup 3rd rd, 9 January 1960. **Capacity:** 11,669.
Manager: Alan Knill.
Secretary: Mrs Jill Neville.
Most League Goals: 108, Division 3, 1960–61.
Highest League Scorer in Season: Craig Madden, 35, Division 4, 1981–82.
Most League Goals in Total Aggregate: Craig Madden, 129, 1978–86.
Most Capped Player: Bill Gorman, 11 (13), Republic of Ireland and (4), Northern Ireland.
Most League Appearances: Norman Bullock, 506, 1920–35.
Honours – Football League: Division 2 Champions – 1894–95, 1996–97. Division 3 Champions – 1960–61. **FA Cup:** Winners – 1900, 1903.
Colours: White shirts, royal blue shorts, royal blue stockings.

CARDIFF CITY   FL CHAMPIONSHIP

Blake Darcy (M)	5 10	12 05	New Tredegar	13 12 88	Scholar
Capaldi Tony (D)	6 0	11 08	Porsgrunn	12 8 81	Plymouth Arg
Feeney Warren (F)	5 8	12 04	Belfast	17 1 81	Luton T
Flood Willo (M)	5 7	10 05	Dublin	10 4 85	Manchester C
Johnson Roger (D)	6 3	12 02	Ashford	24 4 83	Wycombe W
Ledley Joe (M)	6 0	11 07	Cardiff	23 1 87	Scholar
Loovens Glenn (D)	6 2	14 00	Rotterdam	22 10 83	Feyenoord
McNaughton Kevin (D)	5 10	10 06	Dundee	28 8 82	Aberdeen
McPhail Steve (M)	5 10	13 03	Westminster	9 12 79	Barnsley
Parry Paul (M)	5 11	12 12	Newport	19 8 80	Hereford U
Purse Darren (D)	6 2	12 08	Stepney	14 2 77	WBA
Rae Gavin (D)	5 11	10 04	Aberdeen	28 11 77	Rangers
Ramsey Aaron (M)	5 9	10 07	Caerphilly	26 12 90	Scholar
Sak Erwin (G)	6 0	12 00	Lublin	15 2 90	Sokol
Scimeca Riccardo (D)	6 1	12 09	Leamington Spa	13 6 75	WBA
Thompson Steven (F)	6 2	12 05	Paisley	14 10 78	Rangers
Whittingham Peter (M)	5 10	11 06	Nuneaton	8 9 84	Aston Villa

League Appearances: Blake, D. 4(4); Brown, J. (2); Capaldi, T. 43(1); Enckelman, P. 15(1); Feeney, W. 1(4); Fowler, R. 10(3); Gunter, C. 11(2); Hasselbaink, J. 33(3); Johnson, R. 41(1); Ledley, J. 38(3); Loovens, G. 36; MacLean, S. 6(9); McNaughton, K. 35; McPhail, S. 42(1); Oakes, M. 11; Parry, P. 37(4); Purse, D. 12(6); Rae, G. 40(5); Ramsey, A. 11(4); Schmeichel, K. 14; Scimeca, R. 4(5); Sinclair, T. 14(7); Thompson, S. 17(19); Turnbull, R. 6; Whittingham, P. 25(16).
Goals – League (59): Ledley 10 (1 pen), Parry 10, Hasselbaink 7, Johnson 5, Thompson 5, Whittingham 5, Fowler 4 (2 pens), Rae 4, McPhail 3, MacLean 1, McNaughton 1, Purse 1, Ramsey 1, Sinclair 1, own goal 1.
Carling Cup (7): Fowler 2 (1 pen), Hasselbaink 1, Johnson 1, Purse 1, Sinclair 1, Whittingham 1.
FA Cup (10): Whittingham 3, Hasselbaink 1, Johnson 1, Ledley 1, McNaughton 1, Parry 1, Ramsey 1, Thompson 1 (pen).
Ground: Ninian Park, Sloper Rd, Cardiff CF11 8SX. Telephone (029) 2022 1001.
Record Attendance: 62,634, Wales v England, 17 October 1959. **Capacity:** 20,500.
Manager: Dave Jones.
Secretary: Jason Turner.

Most League Goals: 95, Division 3, 2000–01.
Highest League Scorer in Season: Robert Earnshaw, 31, Division 2, 2002–03.
Most League Goals in Total Aggregate: Len Davies, 128, 1920–31.
Most Capped Player: Alf Sherwood, 39 (41), Wales.
Most League Appearances: Phil Dwyer, 471, 1972–85.
Honours – Football League: Division 3 (S) Champions – 1946–47; Division 3 Champions – 1992–93. **FA Cup:** Winners – 1926–27 (only occasion the Cup has been won by a club outside England). **Welsh Cup:** Winners – 22 times.
Charity Shield: Winners 1927.
Colours: Blue shirts with yellow trim, white shorts with blue trim.

CARLISLE UNITED   FL CHAMPIONSHIP 1

Bridge-Wilkinson Marc (M)	5 6	11 00	Coventry	16 3 79	Bradford C
Campion Darren (D)	5 11	12 00	Birmingham	17 10 88	Scholar
Carlton Danny (F)	5 11	12 04	Leeds	22 12 83	Morecambe
Dobie Scott (F)	6 1	12 05	Workington	10 10 78	Nottingham F
Gall Kevin (F)	5 9	10 08	Merthyr	4 2 82	Yeovil T
Garner Joe (F)	5 10	11 02	Blackburn	12 4 88	Blackburn R
Graham Danny (F)	5 11	12 05	Gateshead	12 8 85	Middlesbrough
Hackney Simon (M)	5 8	9 13	Stockport	5 2 84	Woodley Sports
Horwood Evan (D)	6 0	10 06	Billingham	10 3 86	Gretna
Howarth Chris (G)	6 2	12 10	Bolton	23 5 86	Bolton W
Joyce Luke (M)	5 11	12 03	Bolton	9 7 87	Wigan Ath
Livesey Danny (D)	6 3	12 10	Salford	31 12 84	Bolton W
Lumsdon Chris (M)	5 11	10 06	Newcastle	15 12 79	Barnsley
Madine Gary (F)	6 1	12 00	Gateshead	24 8 90	Scholar
Murphy Peter (M)	5 10	12 10	Dublin	27 10 80	Blackburn R
Raven David (D)	6 0	11 04	Birkenhead	10 3 85	Liverpool
Smith Grant (M)	5 11	12 07	Irvine	5 5 80	Dundee U
Smith Jeff (M)	5 11	11 10	Middlesbrough	28 6 80	Port Vale
Taylor Cleveland (M)	5 8	10 07	Leicester	9 9 83	Scunthorpe U
Thirlwell Paul (M)	5 11	11 04	Springwell Village	13 2 79	Derby Co
Vipond Shaun (M)	5 11	11 04	Hexham	25 12 88	Scholar
Westwood Keiren (G)	6 1	13 10	Manchester	23 10 84	Manchester C

League Appearances: Anyinsah, J. 10(2); Aranalde, Z. 27; Arnison, P. 7(10); Bridge-Wilkinson, M. 44(1); Brittain, M. (1); Campion, D. 1(1); Carlton, D. 5(26); Dobie, S. 8(7); Gall, K. 10(11); Garner, J. 30(1); Graham, D. 39(6); Hackney, S. 39(4); Horwood, E. 19; Joyce, L. 1(2); Keogh, R. 7; Livesey, D. 45; Lumsdon, C. 38(2); Madine, G. 1(10); Murphy, P. 33(3); Raven, D. 43; Reid, P. 1; Smith, G. 15(1); Smith, J. 13(9); Taylor, C. 14(4); Thirlwell, P. 9(4); Westwood, K. 46; Worley, H. 1.
Goals – League (64): Garner 14, Graham 14 (2 pens), Hackney 8, Bridge-Wilkinson 6 (1 pen), Livesey 6, Dobie 4, Anyinsah 3, Murphy 3, Gall 1, Joyce 1, Raven 1, Smith G 1, Smith J 1, own goal 1.
Carling Cup (1): Graham 1.
FA Cup (1): Aranalde 1 (pen).
J Paint Trophy (4): Gall 2, Bridge-Wilkinson 1, Graham 1.
Play-Offs (2): Bridge-Wilkinson 1, Graham 1.
Ground: Brunton Park, Warwick Road, Carlisle CA1 1LL. Telephone (01228) 526 237.
Record Attendance: 27,500 v Birmingham C, FA Cup 3rd rd, 5 January 1957 and v Middlesbrough, FA Cup 5th rd, 7 February 1970. **Capacity:** 16,982.
Manager: John Ward.
Secretary: Sarah McKnight.
Most League Goals: 113, Division 4, 1963–64.
Highest League Scorer in Season: Jimmy McConnell, 42, Division 3 (N), 1928–29.

Most League Goals in Total Aggregate: Jimmy McConnell, 126, 1928–32.
Most Capped Player: Eric Welsh, 4, Northern Ireland.
Most League Appearances: Allan Ross, 466, 1963–79.
Honours – Football League: Division 3 Champions – 1964–65, 1994–95; Championship 2 Champions – 2005–06. **Auto Windscreen Shield:** Winners 1997.
Colours: Blue shirts, white shorts, blue stockings.

CHARLTON ATHLETIC   FL CHAMPIONSHIP

Ambrose Darren (M)	6 0	11 00	Harlow	29 2 84	Newcastle U
Arter Harry (M)	5 9	11 07	Sidcup	23 12 89	Scholar
Basey Grant (D)	6 2	13 12	Farnborough	30 11 88	Scholar
Bent Marcus (F)	6 2	13 03	Hammersmith	19 5 78	Everton
Bougherra Madjid (D)	6 2	14 02	Dijon	7 10 82	Sheffield W
Christensen Martin (D)	5 11	12 10	Ishoj	23 12 87	Herfolge
Dickson Christopher (F)	5 11	11 00	East Dulwich	28 12 84	Dulwich H
Elliot Rob (G)	6 3	14 10	Chatham	30 4 86	Scholar
Faye Amady (M)	6 0	12 03	Dakar	3 2 77	Newcastle U
Fofana Beko (F)			Ivory Coast	8 9 88	ASEC Mimosas
Fortune Jon (D)	6 2	12 12	Islington	23 8 80	Trainee
Gray Andy (F)	6 1	13 00	Harrogate	15 11 77	Burnley
Harkin Ruairi (M)	5 10	11 04	Derry	11 10 89	Don Boscos
Iwelumo Chris (F)	6 3	15 03	Coatbridge	1 8 78	Colchester U
Kouadio Konan (M)			Abidjan	31 12 88	ASEC Mimosas
McCarthy Patrick (D)	6 2	13 07	Dublin	31 5 83	Leicester C
McLeod Izale (F)	6 1	11 02	Birmingham	15 10 84	Milton Keynes D
Moutaouakil Yassin (D)	5 10	11 05	Nice	18 7 86	Chateauroux
Racon Therry (M)	5 10	10 02	Villen've-St-Georges	1 5 84	Guingamp
Randolph Darren (G)	6 2	14 00	Dublin	12 5 87	Scholar
Sam Lloyd (F)	5 8	10 00	Leeds	27 9 84	Scholar
Semedo Jose (D)	6 0	12 08	Setubal	11 1 85	Sporting Lisbon
Sinclair Dean (M)	5 10	11 03	St Albans	17 12 84	Barnet
Thomas Aswad (D)	5 11	12 08	Westminster	9 8 89	Arsenal
Thomas Jerome (M)	5 9	11 09	Brent	23 3 83	Arsenal
Varney Luke (F)	5 11	12 00	Leicester	28 9 82	Crewe Alex
Wagstaff Scott (F)	5 10	10 03	Maidstone	31 3 90	Scholar
Walker James (F)	5 10	11 10	Hackney	25 11 87	Scholar
Weaver Nick (G)	6 4	14 07	Sheffield	2 3 79	Manchester C
Wright Josh (M)	6 1	11 07	Tower Hamlets	6 11 89	Scholar
Youga Kelly (D)	5 11	12 06	Bangui	22 9 85	Lyon
Zhi Zheng (M)	5 11	11 11	Shenyang	20 8 80	Shandong Luneng

League Appearances: Ambrose, D. 29(8); Basey, G. 8; Bent, M. 3; Bougherra, M. 24(5); Cook, L. 4(5); Dickson, C. 2; Elliot, R. (1); Faye, A. (1); Fortune, J. 25(1); Gray, A. 10(6); Halford, G. 16; Holland, M. 28(3); Iwelumo, C. 32(14); Lita, L. 8; McCarthy, P. 27(2); McLeod, I. 2(16); Mills, D. 19; Moutaouakil, Y. 7(3); Powell, C. 16(1); Racon, T. 1(3); Randolph, D. 1; Reid, A. 21(1); Sam, L. 24(4); Sankofa, O. (1); Semedo, J. 28(9); Shelvey, J. 2; Sinclair, S. (3); Sodje, S. 20(7); Thatcher, B. 11; Thomas, J. 20(12); Todorov, S. 3(4); Varney, L. 23(16); Wagstaff, S. (2); Weaver, N. 45; Youga, K. 11; Zheng-Zhi, 38(4).
Goals – League (63): Iwelumo 10, Varney 8, Ambrose 7, Zheng-Zhi 7, Reid 5 (3 pens), Lita 3, Bougherra 2, Fortune 2, Gray 2, Halford 2, McCarthy 2, Sam 2, Sodje 2, Todorov 2, Basey 1, Bent 1, Holland 1, McLeod 1, Powell 1, own goals 2.
Carling Cup (7): Ambrose 1, McCarthy 1, Reid 1 (pen) Sam 1, Sinclair 1, Todorov 1, Zheng-Zhi 1 (pen).
FA Cup (3): Ambrose 1, Dickson 1, Zheng-Zhi 1.
Ground: The Valley, Floyd Road, Charlton, London SE7 8BL. Telephone (020) 8333 4000.

Record Attendance: 75,031 v Aston Villa, FA Cup 5th rd, 12 February 1938 (at The Valley). **Capacity:** 27,111.
Manager: Alan Pardew.
Secretary: Chris Parkes.
Most League Goals: 107, Division 2, 1957–58.
Highest League Scorer in Season: Ralph Allen, 32, Division 3 (S), 1934–35.
Most League Goals in Total Aggregate: Stuart Leary, 153, 1953–62.
Most Capped Player: Jonatan Johansson, 41 (88), Finland.
Most League Appearances: Sam Bartram, 583, 1934–56.
Honours – Football League: Division 1 Champions – 1999–2000. Division 3 (S) Champions – 1928–29, 1934–35. **FA Cup:** Winners – 1947.
Colours: Red shirts, white shorts, red stockings.

CHELSEA   FA PREMIERSHIP

Player						
Alex (D)	6 2	14 00	Niteroi	17 6 82	PSV Eindhoven
Anelka Nicolas (F)	6 1	13 03	Versailles	14 3 79	Bolton W
Ballack Michael (M)	6 2	13 05	Gorlitz	26 12 76	Bayern Munich
Belletti Juliano (D)	5 9	10 12	Casacvel	20 6 76	Barcelona
Ben Haim Tal (D)	5 11	11 09	Rishon Le Zion	31 3 82	Bolton W
Bertrand Ryan (D)	5 10	11 00	Southwark	5 8 89	Scholar
Boulahrouz Khalid (D)	6 0	12 11	Maassluis	28 12 81	Hamburg
Bridcutt Liam (M)	5 9	11 07	Reading	8 5 89	Scholar
Bridge Wayne (D)	5 10	12 13	Southampton	5 8 80	Southampton
Cech Petr (G)	6 5	14 03	Plzen	20 5 82	Rennes
Cole Ashley (D)	5 8	10 08	Stepney	20 12 80	Arsenal
Cole Joe (M)	5 9	11 07	Islington	8 11 81	West Ham U
Cork Jack (D)	6 0	10 12	Carshalton	25 6 89	Scholar
Cudicini Carlo (G)	6 1	12 06	Milan	6 9 73	Castel di Sangro
Cummings Shaun (F)			Hammersmith	25 2 89	Scholar
Di Santo Franko (F)			Mendoza	7 4 89	Audax Italiano
Drogba Didier (F)	6 2	13 08	Abidjan	11 3 78	Marseille
Essien Michael (M)	5 10	13 06	Accra	3 12 82	Lyon
Fabio Ferreira (M)			Barreiro	3 5 89	Sporting Lisbon
Fernandes Ricardo (M)			Portugal	20 4 78	Scholar
Hibbert Jordan (M)	5 10	11 05	Hampstead	25 10 90	Scholar
Hilario (G)	6 2	13 05	San Pedro da Cova	21 10 75	Nacional
Hutchinson Sam (D)	6 0	11 07	Slough	3 8 89	Scholar
Ivanovic Branislav (M)	6 0	12 04	Sremska Mitreovica	22 2 84	Lokomotiv Moscow
Kalou Salomon (F)	6 0	12 02	Oume	5 8 85	Feyenoord
Lampard Frank (M)	6 0	14 01	Romford	20 6 78	West Ham U
Magnay Carl (D)			Durham	27 1 89	
Makelele Claude (M)	5 7	10 08	Kinshasa	18 2 73	Real Madrid
Malouda Florent (M)	6 0	11 06	Cayenne	13 6 80	Lyon
Mancienne Michael (D)	6 0	11 09	Isleworth	8 1 88	Scholar
Mikel John Obi (M)	6 0	13 05	Jos	22 4 87	Lyn
Modubi Michael (M)			Polokwane	22 4 85	
Nielsen Morten (F)	6 3	13 12	Copenhagen	24 2 90	FC Copenhagen
Ntuka Pule (M)	6 3	13 00	South Africa	10 5 85	Westerlo
Ofori-Twumasi Nana (D)	5 8	11 09	Accra	15 5 90	Scholar
Paulo Ferreira (D)	6 0	11 13	Cascais	18 1 79	Porto
Pizarro Claudio (F)	6 0	12 06	Lima	3 10 78	Bayern Munich
Rajkovic Slobodan (D)	6 5	14 00	Belgrade	3 3 89	OFK Belgrade
Ricardo Carvalho (D)	6 0	12 04	Amarante	18 5 78	Porto
Sahar Ben (F)	5 10	12 05	Holon	10 8 89	Hapoel Tel Aviv
Sarki Emmanuel (M)			Nigeria	26 12 87	
Sawyer Lee (M)	5 10	10 03	Leytonstone	10 9 89	Scholar
Shevchenko Andriy (F)	6 0	11 05	Dvirkivshchyna	29 9 76	AC Milan

Sidwell Steve (M)	5 10	11 00	Wandsworth	14 12 82	Reading
Sinclair Scott (F)	5 10	10 00	Bath	26 3 89	Bristol R
Smith Jimmy (M)	6 0	10 03	Newham	7 1 87	Scholar
Stoch Miroslav (F)	5 6	10 01	Nitra	19 10 89	Scholar
Taiwo Tom (M)	5 8	10 07	Leeds	27 2 90	Scholar
Taylor Rhys (G)	6 2	12 08	Neath	7 4 90	
Tejera Rodriguez	5 11	10 10	Barcelona	28 5 90	Scholar
Sergio (M)					
Terry John (D)	6 1	13 08	Barking	7 12 80	Trainee
Van Aanholt Patrick (D)	5 9	10 08	S'Hertogenbosch	3 7 88	Ajax
Woods Michael (M)	6 0	12 07	York	6 4 90	Scholar
Wright-Phillips Shaun (F)	5 5	10 01	Lewisham	25 10 81	Manchester C

League Appearances: Alex, 22(6); Anelka, N. 10(4); Ballack, M. 16(2); Belletti, J. 20(3); Ben Haim, T. 10(3); Bridge, W. 9(2); Cech, P. 26; Cole, A. 27; Cole, J. 28(5); Cudicini, C. 10; Drogba, D. 17(2); Essien, M. 23(4); Hilario, 2(1); Johnson, G. 1(1); Kalou, S. 24(6); Lampard, F. 23(1); Makelele, C. 15(3); Malouda, F. 16(5); Mikel, J. 21(8); Paulo Ferreira, 15(3); Pizarro, C. 4(17); Ricardo Carvalho, 21; Shevchenko, A. 8(9); Sidwell, S. 7(8); Sinclair, S. (1); Terry, J. 23; Wright-Phillips, S. 20(7).
Goals – League (65): Lampard 10 (4 pens), Drogba 8, Ballack 7 (2 pens), Cole J 7, Kalou 7, Essien 6, Shevchenko 5 (1 pen), Alex 2, Belletti 2, Malouda 2, Pizarro 2, Wright-Phillips 2, Anelka 1, Cole A 1, Ricardo Carvalho 1, Terry 1, own goal 1.
Carling Cup (14): Lampard 4, Kalou 2, Shevchenko 2, Cole J 1, Drogba 1, Sidwell 1, Sinclair 1, Wright-Phillips 1, own goal 1.
FA Cup (6): Lampard 2, Anelka 1, Kalou 1, Wright-Phillips 1, own goal 1.
Champions League (20): Drogba 6, Lampard 4 (1 pen), Ballack 2, Cole J 2, Alex 1, Kalou 1, Malouda 1, Shevchenko 1, own goals 2.
Community Shield (1): Malouda 1.
Ground: Stamford Bridge, Fulham Rd, London SW6 1HS. Telephone (0871) 984 1955.
Record Attendance: 82,905 v Arsenal, Division 1, 12 October 1935.
Capacity: 41,841.
Manager: Luiz Felipe Scolari.
Secretary: David Barnard.
Most League Goals: 98, Division 1, 1960–61.
Highest League Scorer in Season: Jimmy Greaves, 41, 1960–61.
Most League Goals in Total Aggregate: Bobby Tambling, 164, 1958–70.
Most Capped Player: Marcel Desailly, 67 (116), France.
Most League Appearances: Ron Harris, 655, 1962–80.
Honours – FA Premier League: Champions – 2004–05, 2005–06. **Football League:** Division 1 Champions – 1954–55. Division 2 Champions – 1983–84, 1988–89. **FA Cup:** Winners – 1970, 1997, 2000, 2007. **Football League Cup:** Winners – 1964–65, 1997–98, 2004–05, 2006–07. **Full Members' Cup:** Winners – 1985–86. **Zenith Data Systems Cup:** Winners – 1989–90. **European Cup-Winners' Cup:** Winners – 1970–71, 1997–98. **Super Cup:** Winners – 1999.
Colours: Reflex blue shirts, reflex blue shorts, white stockings.

CHELTENHAM TOWN   FL CHAMPIONSHIP 1

Bird David (M)	5 9	12 00	Gloucester	26 12 84	Cinderford T
Brown Scott (G)	6 2	13 01	Wolverhampton	26 4 85	Bristol C
Brown Scott (M)	5 9	10 03	Runcorn	8 5 85	Bristol C
Caines Gavin (D)	6 1	12 00	Birmingham	20 9 83	Scholar
Connor Paul (F)	6 2	11 08	Bishop Auckland	12 1 79	Leyton Orient
Duff Shane (D)	6 1	12 10	Wroughton	2 4 82	Juniors
Finnigan John (M)	5 8	10 09	Wakefield	29 3 76	Lincoln C
Gallinagh Andy (D)	5 8	11 08	Sutton Coldfield	16 3 85	Stratford T
Gill Ben (M)	5 9	10 11	Harrow	9 10 87	Watford

Gill Jeremy (D)	5 11	12 00	Clevedon	8	9 70	Northampton T
Gillespie Steven (F)	5 9	11 02	Liverpool	4	6 84	Bristol C
Higgs Shane (G)	6 3	14 06	Oxford	13	5 77	Bristol R
Ledgister Aaron (M)	5 10	11 07	Hong Kong	15	11 88	Bristol C
Lindegaard Andy (M)	5 8	11 04	Taunton	10	9 80	Yeovil T
Puddy Will (G)	5 10	11 07	Salisbury	4	10 87	Scholar
Ridley Lee (D)	5 9	11 11	Scunthorpe	5	12 81	Scunthorpe U
Spencer Damien (F)	6 1	14 00	Ascot	19	9 81	Bristol C
Townsend Michael (D)	6 1	13 12	Walsall	17	5 86	Wolverhampton W
Vincent Ashley (F)	5 10	11 08	Oldbury	26	5 85	Wolverhampton W

League Appearances: Armstrong, C. 13(1); Bird, D. 46; Brooker, S. 14; Brown, S. 9(11); Caines, G. 22(6); Connolly, A. 3(12); Connor, P. 26(13); D'Agostino, M. 14(11); Duff, S. 30; Finnigan, J. 10; Gallinagh, A. 24(2); Gill, B. (2); Gill, J. 43; Gillespie, S. 35(2); Higgs, S. 46; Keogh, R. 10; Lindegaard, A. 31(10); Madjo, G. 2(3); Myrie-Williams, J. 7(5); Reid, C. 2(6); Ridley, L. 8; Russell, A. 12(1); Sinclair, D. 12; Spencer, D. 22(8); Townsend, M. 13; Vincent, A. 19(18); Wright, A. 33; Yao, S. (5).
Goals – League (42): Gillespie 14 (1 pen), Brooker 5, Bird 4, Connor 4, Spencer 3, Caines 2, Lindegaard 2, Russell 2, Vincent 2, Finnigan 1, Sinclair 1, Townsend 1 (pen), Wright 1.
Carling Cup (1): Finnigan 1.
FA Cup (2): Gillespie 2.
J Paint Trophy (4): Connor 1, Myrie-Williams 1, Reid 1, own goal 1.
Ground: Whaddon Road, Cheltenham, Gloucestershire GL52 5NA. Telephone (01242) 573 558.
Record Attendance: at Whaddon Road: 8,326 v Reading, FA Cup 1st rd, 17 November 1956; at Cheltenham Athletic Ground: 10,389 v Blackpool, FA Cup 3rd rd, 13 January 1934.
Capacity: 7,136.
Manager: Keith Downing.
Secretary: Paul Godfrey.
Most League Goals: 66, Division 3, 2001–02.
Highest League Scorer in Season: Julian Alsop, 20, Division 3, 2001–02.
Most League Goals in Total Aggregate: Martin Devaney, 38, 1999–2005.
Most Capped Player: Grant McCann, 7 (16), Northern Ireland.
Most League Appearances: Jamie Victory, 258, 1999–.
Honours – Football Conference: Champions – 1998–99. **FA Trophy:** Winners – 1997–98.
Colours: All red with white trim.

CHESTER CITY   FL CHAMPIONSHIP 2

Butler Paul (D)	6 2	13 00	Manchester	2	11 72	Leeds U
Danby John (G)	6 2	14 06	Stoke	20	9 83	Kidderminster H
Dinning Tony (M)	6 0	13 05	Wallsend	12	4 75	Stockport Co
Ellison Kevin (M)	6 0	12 00	Liverpool	23	2 79	Tranmere R
Holroyd Chris (F)	5 11	12 03	Macclesfield	24	10 86	Crewe Alex
Hughes Mark (M)	5 10	12 05	Dungannon	16	9 83	Stevenage B
Kelly Shaun (D)	6 1	11 04	Southampton	4	7 86	Scholar
Linwood Paul (D)	6 2	13 03	Birkenhead	24	10 83	Tranmere R
Lowndes Nathan (F)	6 0	11 10	Salford	2	6 77	Port Vale
McManus Paul (F)	5 6	10 00	Liverpool	22	4 90	Scholar
Murphy John (F)	6 2	14 00	Whiston	18	10 76	Macclesfield T
Newton Sean (D)	6 2	13 00	Liverpool	23	9 88	Scholar
Partridge Richie (M)	5 8	11 00	Dublin	12	9 80	Rotherham U
Roberts Kevin (D)	6 2	14 00	Chester	10	3 87	
Rutherford Paul (M)	5 9	11 07	Moreton	10	7 87	Greenleas
Vaughan James (D)	5 10	12 09	Liverpool	6	12 86	Tranmere R
Wilson Laurence (M)	5 10	10 09	Huyton	10	10 86	Everton

League Appearances: Bolland, P. 2; Butler, P. 35; Carroll, N. 1; Danby, J. 46; Dinning, T. 20; Ellison, K. 36; Grant, T. 15(4); Hand, J. (1); Holroyd, C. 14(11); Hughes, M. 39(4); Kelly, S. 7(3); Lindfield, C. 5(2); Linwood, P. 42; Lowndes, N. 8(4); Marples, S. 16; McManus, P. 9(10); Mitchell, A. (4); Murphy, J. 39; Newton, S. 2; Palethorpe, P. (1); Partridge, R. 34(2); Roberts, K. 30(7); Rule, G. 2(8); Rutherford, P. 10(13); Sandwith, K. 12(10); Vaughan, J. 29(1); Welsh, J. 6; Wilson, L. 40; Yeo, S. 7(14).

Goals – League (51): Ellison 11 (1 pen), Murphy 9, Partridge 5, Holroyd 4, Hughes 4, Yeo 4, Roberts 3, Butler 2, Dinning 2 (2 pens), Wilson 2, Grant 1, Linwood 1, McManus 1, Rutherford 1, Sandwith 1.

Carling Cup (0).

FA Cup (0).

J Paint Trophy (3): Partridge 2, Holroyd 1.

Ground: Deva Stadium, Bumpers Lane, Chester CH1 4LT. Telephone (01244) 371 376.

Record Attendance: 20,500 v Chelsea, FA Cup 3rd rd (replay), 16 January 1952 (at Sealand Road).

Capacity: 5,556.

Manager: Simon Davies.

Secretary: Tony Allan.

Most League Goals: 119, Division 4, 1964–65.

Highest League Scorer in Season: Dick Yates, 36, Division 3 (N), 1946–47.

Most League Goals in Total Aggregate: Stuart Rimmer, 135, 1985–88, 1991–98.

Most Capped Player: Angus Eve, 35 (117), Trinidad & Tobago.

Most League Appearances: Ray Gill, 406, 1951–62.

Honours – Conference: Champions – 2003–04. **Welsh Cup:** Winners – 1908, 1933, 1947. **Debenhams Cup:** Winners 1977.

Colours: Sky blue and white striped shirts, sky blue shorts, sky blue stockings.

CHESTERFIELD   FL CHAMPIONSHIP 2

Player						
Downes Aaron (D)	6 3	13 00	Mudgee	15	5 85	Frickley C
Fletcher Steve (F)	6 2	14 09	Hartlepool	26	7 72	Bournemouth
Kovacs Janos (D)	6 4	14 10	Budapest	11	9 85	MTK
Lester Jack (F)	5 9	12 08	Sheffield	8	10 75	Nottingham F
Leven Peter (M)	5 11	12 13	Glasgow	27	9 83	Kilmarnock
Lowry Jamie (M)	6 0	12 04	Newquay	18	3 87	Scholar
Niven Derek (M)	6 0	12 02	Falkirk	12	12 83	Bolton W
Picken Phil (D)	5 9	10 08	Droylsden	12	11 85	Manchester U
Robertson Gregor (D)	6 0	12 04	Edinburgh	19	1 84	Rotherham U
Roche Barry (G)	6 5	14 08	Dublin	6	4 82	Nottingham F
Ward Jamie (F)	5 6	9 04	Birmingham	12	5 86	Torquay U
Winter Jamie (M)	5 10	13 10	Dundee	4	8 85	Aberdeen

League Appearances: Algar, B. 1(1); Allison, W. (9); Barnes, M. 1(2); Bastians, F. 12; Cooper, K. 2(5); Davies, G. (1); Downes, A. 38(2); Dowson, D. 9(3); Dyer, B. (3); Fletcher, S. 23(15); Gray, K. 10(5); Hartley, P. 12; Hawkins, C. 5; Jackson, J. (4); Jordan, M. 1; Kerry, L. 8(5); Kovacs, J. 41; Lester, J. 35(1); Leven, P. 42; Lowry, J. 41(1); Moloney, B. 8(1); Niven, D. 38; O'Hare, A. 4(9); Owens, G. 2(2); Picken, P. 34(3); Robertson, G. 34(1); Roche, B. 45; Rooney, A. 11(11); Smith, A. 2(6); Travis, N. (2); Ward, J. 27(8); Winter, J. 20(5).

Goals – League (76): Lester 23 (1 pen), Ward 12, Rooney 7, Leven 6 (1 pen), Lowry 6, Fletcher 5, Dowson 3, Niven 3, Downes 2, Kerry 2, Kovacs 2, Bastians 1, Cooper 1, Moloney 1, Robertson 1, own goal 1.

Carling Cup (1): Lester 1.

FA Cup (1): Lester 1.

J Paint Trophy (1): Allison 1.

Ground: The Recreation Ground, Chesterfield, Derbyshire S40 4SX. Telephone (01246) 209 765.
Record Attendance: 30,968 v Newcastle U, Division 2, 7 April 1939. **Capacity:** 8,502.
Manager: Lee Richardson.
Secretary: Alan Walters.
Most League Goals: 102, Division 3 (N), 1930–31.
Highest League Scorer in Season: Jimmy Cookson, 44, Division 3 (N), 1925–26.
Most League Goals in Total Aggregate: Ernie Moss, 161, 1969–76, 1979–81 and 1984–86.
Most Capped Player: Walter McMillen, 4 (7), Northern Ireland; Mark Williams, 4 (30), Northern Ireland.
Most League Appearances: Dave Blakey, 613, 1948–67.
Honours – Football League: Division 3 (N) Champions – 1930–31, 1935–36. Division 4 Champions – 1969–70, 1984–85. **Anglo-Scottish Cup:** Winners – 1980–81.
Colours: Blue shirts, white shorts, white stockings.

COLCHESTER UNITED   FL CHAMPIONSHIP 1

Baldwin Pat (D)	6 3	12 07	City of London	12 11 82	Chelsea
Cousins Mark (G)	6 1	11 03	Chelmsford	9 1 87	Scholar
Coyne Chris (D)	6 2	13 10	Brisbane	20 12 78	Luton T
Duguid Karl (M)	5 11	11 06	Hitchin	21 3 78	Trainee
Elito Medy (M)	6 2	13 00	Kinshasa	20 3 90	Scholar
Gerken Dean (G)	6 1	12 08	Rochford	22 5 85	Scholar
Guy Jamie (M)	6 1	13 00	Barking	1 8 87	Scholar
Hammond Dean (M)	6 0	11 09	Hastings	7 3 83	Brighton & HA
Ifil Phil (D)	5 10	12 02	Willesden	18 11 86	Tottenham H
Izzet Kem (M)	5 7	10 05	Mile End	29 9 80	Charlton Ath
Jackson Johnnie (M)	6 0	12 08	Camden	15 8 82	Tottenham H
Lisbie Kevin (F)	5 10	11 06	Hackney	17 10 78	Charlton Ath
McLeod Kevin (F)	5 11	12 13	Liverpool	12 9 80	Swansea C
Platt Clive (F)	6 4	12 07	Wolverhampton	27 10 77	Milton Keynes D
Vernon Scott (F)	6 1	11 06	Manchester	13 12 83	Blackpool
Virgo Adam (D)	6 2	13 12	Brighton	25 1 83	Coventry C
White John (M)	5 10	12 01	Maldon	26 7 86	Scholar
Wordsworth Anthony (M)	6 1	12 00	London	3 1 89	Scholar
Yeates Mark (F)	5 8	13 03	Dublin	11 1 85	Tottenham H

League Appearances: Baldwin, P. 23(3); Balogh, B. 10(7); Connolly, M. 13(3); Cousins, M. (2); Coyne, C. 16; Davison, A. 6; Duguid, K. 37; Elito, M. 7(4); Elokobi, G. 17; Gerken, D. 40; Granville, D. 14(5); Guttridge, L. 5(9); Guy, J. (11); Hammond, D. 11(2); Heath, M. 5; Ifil, P. 20; Izzet, K. 35(4); Jackson, J. 46; Lisbie, K. 39(3); McLeod, I. (2); McLeod, K. 21(7); Platt, C. 34(7); Sheringham, T. 11(8); Vernon, S. 8(9); Virgo, A. 30(6); Watson, K. 7; White, J. 21; Wordsworth, A. 1(2); Yeates, M. 29.
Goals – League (62): Lisbie 17 (1 pen), Platt 8, Yeates 8 (1 pen), Jackson 7, Vernon 5 (1 pen), McLeod K 4, Sheringham 3 (1 pen), Connolly 2, Coyne 1, Elito 1, Elokobi 1, Izzet 1, Virgo 1, own goals 3.
Carling Cup (0).
FA Cup (1): Sheringham 1 (pen).
Ground: Colchester Community Stadium, United Way, Colchester, Essex CO2 7JJ. Telephone (0871) 226 2161.
Record Attendance: 19,072 v Reading, FA Cup 1st rd, 27 November, 1948.
Capacity: 10,000
Manager: Geraint Williams.
Secretary: Miss Caroline Pugh.

Most League Goals: 104, Division 4, 1961–62.
Highest League Scorer in Season: Bobby Hunt, 38, Division 4, 1961–62.
Most League Goals in Total Aggregate: Martyn King, 130, 1956–64.
Most Capped Player: Bela Balogh, 2 (9), Hungary.
Most League Appearances: Micky Cook, 613, 1969–84.
Honours – GM Vauxhall Conference: Winners – 1991–92. **FA Trophy:** Winners:
1991–92.
Colours: Royal blue and white striped shirts, royal blue shorts, royal blue
stockings.

COVENTRY CITY   FL CHAMPIONSHIP

Best Leon (F)	6 1	13 03	Nottingham	19 9 86	Southampton
Birchall Chris (M)	5 7	13 05	Stafford	5 5 84	Port Vale
Borrowdale Gary (D)	6 0	12 01	Sutton	16 7 85	Crystal Palace
Dann Scott (D)	6 2	12 00	Liverpool	14 2 87	Walsall
Doyle Micky (M)	5 8	11 00	Dublin	8 7 81	Celtic
Fox Daniel (D)	5 11	12 06	Crewe	29 5 86	Walsall
Gray Julian (M)	6 1	11 00	Lewisham	21 9 79	Birmingham C
Hall Marcus (D)	6 1	12 02	Coventry	24 3 76	Stoke C
Hughes Stephen (M)	5 9	12 12	Wokingham	18 9 76	Charlton Ath
Ireland Daniel (G)			Sydney	20 1 89	
Konstantopoulos	6 4	14 02	Kalamata	29 11 79	Hartlepool U
Dimitrios (G)					
Kyle Kevin (F)	6 3	12 00	Stranraer	7 6 81	Sunderland
Marshall Andy (G)	6 3	14 08	Bury St Edmunds	14 4 75	Millwall
McKenzie Leon (F)	5 11	12 11	Croydon	17 5 78	Norwich C
McNamee David (D)	5 11	11 02	Glasgow	10 10 80	Livingston
Mifsud Michael (F)	5 6	9 11	Pieta	17 4 81	Lillestrom
Osbourne Isaac (M)	5 9	11 11	Birmingham	22 6 86	Scholar
Simmonds Donovan (F)	5 11	11 00	Walthamstow	12 10 88	Charlton Ath
Simpson Robbie (F)	6 1	11 11	Poole	15 3 85	Cambridge U
Tabb Jay (M)	5 7	10 00	Tooting	21 2 84	Brentford
Thornton Kevin (M)	5 7	11 00	Drogheda	9 7 86	Scholar
Turner Ben (D)	6 4	14 04	Birmingham	21 1 88	Scholar
Ward Elliot (D)	6 2	13 00	Harrow	19 1 85	West Ham U

League Appearances: Adebola, D. 15(11); Andrews, W. (7); Best, L. 29(5); Birchall, C. 1; Borrowdale, G. 20(1); Cairo, E. 4(3); Dann, S. 14(2); Davis, L. 2(4); De Zeeuw, A. 16(1); Doyle, M. 42; Duffy, R. 2; Fox, D. 18; Gray, J. 20(6); Hall, M. 17(1); Hines, Z. (7); Hughes, M. 16(2); Hughes, S. 32(5); Konstantopoulos, D. 21; Kyle, K. 7(6); Marshall, A. 16; McKenzie, L. 9(2); McNamee, D. 12(1); Mifsud, M. 34(7); Osbourne, I. 37(5); Schmeichel, K. 9; Simpson, R. 10(18); Tabb, J. 40(2); Thornton, K. 9(10); Turner, B. 19; Ward, E. 35(2).
Goals – League (52): Mifsud 10, Best 8, Doyle 7 (2 pens), Ward 6 (5 pens), Tabb 5, Adebola 4, Gray 3, Kyle 2, McKenzie 2, Fox 1, Hines 1, Hughes S 1, Simpson 1, Thornton 1 (pen).
Carling Cup (8): Mifsud 4, Adebola 1, Best 1, Simpson 1, Tabb 1.
FA Cup (6): Mifsud 3, Adebola 1, Hughes S 1, Ward 1 (pen).
Ground: Ricoh Arena, Phoenix Way, Foleshill, Coventry CV6 6GE. Telephone (0870) 421 1987.
Record Attendance: 51,455 v Wolverhampton W, Division 2, 29 April 1967 (at Highfield Road). **Capacity:** 32,609.
Manager: Chris Coleman.
Secretary: Pam Hindson.
Most League Goals: 108, Division 3 (S), 1931–32.
Highest League Scorer in Season: Clarrie Bourton, 49, Division 3 (S), 1931–32.

Most League Goals in Total Aggregate: Clarrie Bourton, 171, 1931–37.
Most Capped Player: Magnus Hedman, 44 (58), Sweden.
Most League Appearances: Steve Ogrizovic, 507, 1984–2000.
Honours – Football League: Division 2 Champions – 1966–67. Division 3 Champions – 1963–64. Division 3 (S) Champions 1935–36. **FA Cup:** Winners – 1986–1987.
Colours: Sky blue and white striped shirts with navy sleeve and back, sky blue with navy side trim shorts, sky blue stockings with navy turn down and foot.

CREWE ALEXANDRA   FL CHAMPIONSHIP 1

Abbey George (D)	5 10	12 04	Port Harcourt	20 10 78	Port Vale
Bailey James (M)	6 0	12 05	Bollington	18 9 88	Scholar
Baudet Julien (D)	6 2	13 07	Grenoble	13 1 79	Notts Co
Bopp Eugene (M)	5 11	12 03	Kiev	5 9 83	Rotherham U
Carrington Mark (M)	6 0	11 00	Warrington	4 5 87	Scholar
Daniel Colin (M)	5 11	11 06	Crewe	15 2 88	Eastwood T
Jones Billy (D)	5 11	13 00	Shrewsbury	24 3 87	Scholar
Lowe Ryan (F)	5 10	12 08	Liverpool	18 9 78	Chester C
Maynard Nicky (F)	5 11	11 00	Winsford	11 12 86	Scholar
McCready Chris (D)	6 1	12 05	Ellesmere Port	5 9 81	Tranmere R
Miller Shaun (F)	5 10	11 08	Alsager	25 9 87	Scholar
Moore Byron (M)	6 0	10 06	Stoke	24 8 88	Scholar
O'Connor Michael (M)	6 1	11 08	Belfast	6 10 87	Scholar
O'Donnell Daniel (D)	6 2	11 11	Liverpool	10 3 86	Liverpool
Pope Tom (F)	6 3	11 03	Stoke	27 8 85	Lancaster C
Rix Ben (M)	5 9	11 05	Wolverhampton	11 12 82	Scholar
Roberts Gary (M)	5 8	10 05	Chester	4 2 87	Scholar
Schumacher Steven (M)	5 10	11 00	Liverpool	30 4 84	Bradford C
Tomlinson Stuart (G)	6 1	11 02	Chester	10 5 85	Scholar
Williams Owain Fon (G)	6 1	12 09	Gwynedd	17 3 87	Scholar
Woodards Danny (M)	5 11	11 01	Forest Gate	7 10 83	Exeter C

League Appearances: Abbey, G. 20(3); Anyinsah, J. 6(2); Bailey, J. (1); Bailey, M. (2); Barnard, L. 9(1); Baseya, C. 1(2); Baudet, J. 35; Bennett, E. 4(5); Bopp, E. 5(5); Boyle, P. 17; Brown, J. (1); Carrington, M. 3(6); Church, S. 11(1); Cox, N. 21(6); Daniel, C. (1); Dickson, C. 2(1); Gray, D. 1; Jones, B. 22; Jones, S. 2(2); Lowe, R. 16(11); Lunt, K. 14; Lynch, R. 1(1); Maynard, N. 25(2); McCready, C. 32(2); Miller, S. 5(10); Moore, B. 25(8); Morgan, D. 7(2); O'Connor, M. 17(6); O'Donnell, D. 19(8); Pope, T. 15(11); Rix, B. 21(4); Roberts, Gary M 4; Roberts, Gary S 40(2); Schumacher, S. 24(2); Vaughan, D. (1); Williams, B. 46; Woodards, D. 36.

Goals – League (47): Maynard 14, Pope 7, Roberts Gary S 6 (3 pens), Lowe 4, Barnard 3, Moore 3, Baudet 1, Bennett 1, Bopp 1, Church 1, Jones S 1, McCready 1, Miller 1, Morgan 1, O'Donnell 1, Schumacher 1.
Carling Cup (0).
FA Cup (2): Cox 1, McCready 1.
J Paint Trophy (1): Lowe 1.
Ground: The Alexandra Stadium, Gresty Road, Crewe, Cheshire CW2 6EB. Telephone (01270) 213 014.
Record Attendance: 20,000 v Tottenham H, FA Cup 4th rd, 30 January 1960.
Capacity: 10,046.
Manager: Steve Holland.
Secretary: Andrew Blakemore.
Most League Goals: 95, Division 3 (N), 1931–32.
Highest League Scorer in Season: Terry Harkin, 35, Division 4, 1964–65.
Most League Goals in Total Aggregate: Bert Swindells, 126, 1928–37.
Most Capped Player: Clayton Ince, 38(66), Trinidad & Tobago.
Most League Appearances: Tommy Lowry, 436, 1966–78.

Honours – **Welsh Cup:** Winners – 1936, 1937.
Colours: Red and white.

CRYSTAL PALACE   FL CHAMPIONSHIP

Butterfield Danny (D)	5 10	11 06	Boston	21 11 79	Grimsby T	
Craig Tony (D)	6 0	10 03	Greenwich	20 4 85	Millwall	
Danns Neil (M)	5 10	10 12	Liverpool	23 11 82	Birmingham C	
Dayton James (M)	5 8	10 01	Enfield	12 12 88	Scholar	
Derry Shaun (M)	5 10	10 13	Nottingham	6 12 77	Leeds U	
Fletcher Carl (M)	5 10	11 07	Camberley	6 4 80	West Ham U	
Flinders Scott (G)	6 4	13 00	Rotherham	12 6 86	Barnsley	
Fonte Jose (D)	6 2	12 08	Penafiel	22 12 83		
Freedman Dougie (F)	5 9	12 05	Glasgow	21 1 74	Nottingham F	
Hill Clint (D)	6 0	11 06	Liverpool	19 10 78	Stoke C	
Hills Lee (D)	5 10	11 11	Croydon	3 4 90	Scholar	
Hughes Jeff (D)	6 1	11 00	Larne	29 5 85	Lincoln C	
Ifill Paul (M)	6 0	12 08	Brighton	20 10 79	Sheffield U	
Kuqi Shefki (F)	6 2	13 13	Kosova	10 11 76	Blackburn R	
Lawrence Matthew (D)	6 1	12 10	Northampton	14 6 74	Millwall	
Morrison Clinton (F)	6 0	12 00	Tooting	14 5 79	Birmingham C	
Moses Victor (F)	5 10	11 07	Lagos	12 12 90	Scholar	
Scannell Sean (F)	5 9	11 07	Cork	21 3 89	Scholar	
Scowcroft James (F)	6 2	12 12	Bury St Edmunds	15 11 75	Coventry C	
Soares Tom (M)	6 0	11 04	Reading	10 7 86	Scholar	
Spence Lewis (M)	5 9	11 02	Lambeth	29 10 87	Scholar	
Speroni Julian (G)	6 0	11 00	Buenos Aires	18 5 79	Dundee	
Watson Ben (M)	5 10	10 11	Camberwell	9 7 85	Scholar	
Wiggins Rhoys (D)	5 8	11 05	Hillingdon	4 11 87	Scholar	
Wilkinson David (G)	5 11	12 00	Croydon	17 4 88	Scholar	

League Appearances: Ashton, N. 1; Bostock, J. 1(3); Butterfield, D. 25(5); Cort, L. 12; Craig, T. 13; Danns, N. 2(2); Derry, S. 30; Dickov, P. 6(3); Fletcher, C. 17(11); Fonte, J. 17(5); Freedman, D. 4(15); Grabban, L. 2; Green, S. 7(3); Hall, R. (1); Halls, J. 5; Hill, C. 28; Hills, L. 6(6); Hudson, M. 45; Hughes, J. 4(6); Idrizaj, B. 3(4); Ifill, P. 5(8); Kennedy, M. 8; Kudjodji, B. (1); Kuqi, S. 2(6); Lawrence, M. 36(1); Martin, D. 2(7); Morrison, C. 33(10); Moses, V. 9(4); Reid, K. (2); Robinson, A. (6); Scannell, S. 10(13); Scowcroft, J. 35(3); Sinclair, S. 6; Soares, T. 38(1); Songo'o, F. 9; Speroni, J. 46; Watson, B. 41(1).
Goals – League (58): Morrison 16, Scowcroft 9, Soares 6, Watson 5 (3 pens), Hill 3, Moses 3, Green 2, Hudson 2, Ifill 2, Scannell 2, Sinclair 2, Fletcher 1, Fonte 1, Freedman 1, Hills 1, Lawrence 1, own goal 1.
Carling Cup (1): Freedman 1.
FA Cup (0).
Play-Offs (2): Watson 2 (1 pen).
Ground: Selhurst Park, Whitehorse Lane, London SE25 6PU. Telephone (020) 8768 6000.
Record Attendance: 51,482 v Burnley, Division 2, 11 May 1979. **Capacity:** 26,297.
Manager: Neil Warnock.
Secretary: Christine Dowdeswell.
Most League Goals: 110, Division 4, 1960–61.
Highest League Scorer in Season: Peter Simpson, 46, Division 3 (S), 1930–31.
Most League Goals in Total Aggregate: Peter Simpson, 153, 1930–36.
Most Capped Player: Aleksandrs Kolinko, 23 (76), Latvia.
Most League Appearances: Jim Cannon, 571, 1973–88.
Honours – Football League: Division 1 – Champions 1993–94. Division 2 Champions – 1978–79. Division 3 (S) 1920–21. **Zenith Data Systems Cup:** Winners – 1991.
Colours: Red and blue striped shirts, red shorts.

DAGENHAM & REDBRIDGE   FL CHAMPIONSHIP 2

Benson Paul (F)	6 1	11 01	Rochford	12 10 79	White Notley
Boardman Jon (D)	6 1	12 01	Reading	27 1 81	Rochdale
Cook Anthony (D)	5 7	11 02	London	10 8 89	Croydon Ath
Erskine Emmanuel (F)	6 1	13 06	London	13 1 89	Wingate & Finchley
Foster Danny (D)	5 11	13 02	Enfield	23 9 84	Tottenham H
Gain Peter (M)	5 9	11 07	Hammersmith	11 11 76	Peterborough U
Graham Richard (M)	5 10	11 10	Newry	5 8 79	Barnet
Green Dominic (F)	5 6	11 02	London	5 7 89	Scholar
Griffiths Scott (D)	5 9	11 08	London	27 11 85	Aveley
Huke Shane (M)	5 11	12 07	Reading	2 10 85	Peterborough U
Nurse Jon (F)	5 9	12 04	Barbados	28 3 81	Stevenage B
Okuonghae Magnus (D)	6 3	13 04	Nigeria	16 2 86	Rushden & D
Patterson Marlon (D)	5 9	11 10	London	24 6 83	Yeading
Roberts Tony (G)	6 0	14 11	Bangor	4 8 69	QPR
Rochester Kraig (M)	6 1	13 01	London	3 11 88	Leicester C
Saunders Sam (M)	5 8	11 06	London	29 10 82	Thurrock
Southam Glen (M)	5 9	11 06	Enfield	27 8 80	Bishop's Stortford
Strevens Ben (F)	6 0	12 02	Edgware	24 5 80	Barnet
Taiwo Soloman (M)	6 1	13 02	Lagos	29 4 85	Sutton U
Taylor Jamie (F)	5 9	12 06	Crawley	16 12 82	Woking
Tejan-Sie Thomas (F)	5 6	1108	London	23 11 88	Wingate & Finchley
Uddin Anwar (D)	6 1	13 07	London	1 11 81	Bristol R

League Appearances: Arber, M. 16; Baidoo, S. 1(2); Benson, P. 19(3); Boardman, J. 22(5); Cook, A. (1); Foster, D. 31(1); Gain, P. 18; Goodwin, L. (1); Graham, R. 4(3); Green, D. 2(10); Griffiths, S. 41; Hall, R. 2(6); Huke, S. 31(5); Moore, C. 13(13); Nurse, J. 23(7); Okuonghae, M. 9(1); Patterson, M. 5(1); Rainford, D. 28(1); Roberts, T. 43; Saunders, S. 21(1); Sloma, S. 22(7); Smith, R. 23; Southam, G. 44(1); Strevens, B. 39(7); Taiwo, S. 4(6); Taylor, J. 2(10); Thompson, E. 3; Uddin, A. 40(1).

Goals – League (49): Strevens 15, Rainford 8 (5 pens), Benson 6 (1 pen), Hall 2, Huke 2, Moore 2, Sloma 2, Southam 2 (2 pens), Arber 1, Foster 1, Gain 1, Nurse 1, Smith 1, Taylor 1, Uddin 1, own goals 3.

Carling Cup (1): Strevens 1.

FA Cup (8): Benson 3, Strevens 3, Huke 1, Nurse 1.

J Paint Trophy (3): Moore 1, Saunders 1, Strevens 1.

Ground: London Borough of Barking and Dagenham Stadium, Victoria Road, Dagenham, Essex, RM10 7XR. Telephone (0208) 592 1549 or (0208) 592 7194.

Record Attendance: 5,949 v Ipswich T, FA Cup 3rd rd, 5 January 2002. **Capacity:** 6,087.

Manager: John L. Still.

Secretary: Terry Grover.

Most League Goals: 97, Ryman Premier, 1999–2000.

Highest League Scorer in Season: Paul Benson, 28 Conference 2006–07.

Most League Goals in Total Aggregate: 105, Danny Shipp, 1997–2004.

Most League Appearances: Jason Broom, 462, 1992–2003.

Honours – Conference: Champions – 2006–07. **Isthmian League (Premier):** Champions 1999–2000.

Colours: Red and blue striped shirts, white shorts, red stockings.

DARLINGTON   FL CHAMPIONSHIP 2

Abbott Pawel (F)	6 2	13 10	York	5 5 82	Swansea C
Austin Neil (D)	5 10	11 09	Barnsley	26 4 83	Barnsley
Blundell Gregg (F)	5 10	11 00	Liverpool	1 1 76	Chester C
Foster Steve (D)	6 1	13 00	Mansfield	3 12 74	Scunthorpe U
Hardman Lewis (D)	5 10	11 00	Sunderland	12 4 85	Scholar
Kazimierczak Prezemek (G)	6 0	12 02	Lodz	22 2 88	Bolton W
Liversedge Nick (G)	6 1	11 07	Huddersfield	18 7 88	Scholar
Miller Ian (M)	6 2	12 02	Colchester	23 11 83	Ipswich T
Oakes Andy (G)	6 3	12 04	Northwich	11 1 77	Swansea C
Purdie Rob (M)	5 9	11 06	Leicester	28 9 82	Hereford U
Ravenhill Ricky (M)	5 10	11 00	Doncaster	16 1 82	Grimsby T
Ryan Tim (D)	5 10	11 00	Stockport	10 12 74	Boston U
Stockdale David (G)	6 3	13 04	Leeds	20 9 85	York C
Valentine Ryan (D)	5 10	11 05	Wrexham	19 8 82	Wrexham
White Alan (D)	6 0	13 04	Darlington	22 3 76	Notts Co
Wright Tommy (F)	6 0	12 02	Leicester	28 9 84	Barnsley

League Appearances: Abbott, P. 16(8); Austin, N. 23(6); Barrau, X. (1); Blundell, G. 17(19); Brackstone, J. 3; Colbeck, J. 4(2); Cummins, M. 31(9); Foran, R. 11(1); Foster, S. 42; Gall, K. 7(1); Green, M. 3(1); Harty, I. (1); Hodge, B. 7; Joachim, J. 40; Kazimierczak, P. (1); Keltie, C. 21(6); Kennedy, J. 13; Main, C. (1); Mayo, P. 7; McBride, K. 3(3); Miller, I. 18(10); N'Dumbu Nsungu, G. 4(4); Nelthorpe, C. 4(3); Oakes, A. 6; Palmer, C. 4; Parker, B. 13; Purdie, R. 30(9); Ravenhill, R. 25(10); Reay, S. (1); Ridley, L. 6; Ryan, T. 13; Smith, J. 3; Smith, M. (4); Stockdale, D. 40(1); Valentine, R. 13(4); Wainwright, N. 5(9); White, A. 35; Wiseman, S. 2(5); Wright, T. 37(3).

Goals – League (67): Wright 13, Abbott 9 (1 pen), Blundell 6 (1 pen), Cummins 6, Joachim 6, Keltie 4 (4 pens), N'Dumbu Nsungu 3 (1 pen), Ravenhill 3, Austin 2, Colbeck 2, Foran 2, Foster 2, Kennedy 2, Miller 2, Mayo 1, McBride 1, White 1, own goals 2.

Carling Cup (1): Wright 1.

FA Cup (2): Blundell 1, Wright 1.

J Paint Trophy (0).

Play-Offs (3): Keltie 1 (pen), Kennedy 1, Miller 1.

Ground: Darlington Arena, Neasham Road, Hurworth Moor, Darlington DL2 1DL. Telephone (01325) 387 000.

Record Attendance: 21,023 v Bolton W, League Cup 3rd rd, 14 November 1960.

Capacity: 27,000.

Manager: Dave Penney.

Secretary: Lisa Charlton.

Most League Goals: 108, Division 3 (N), 1929–30.

Highest League Scorer in Season: David Brown, 39, Division 3 (N), 1924–25.

Most League Goals in Total Aggregate: Alan Walsh, 90, 1978–84.

Most Capped Player: Jason Devos, 3 (49), Canada and Adrian Webster, 3, New Zealand.

Most League Appearances: Ron Greener, 442, 1955–68.

Honours – Football League: Division 3 (N) Champions – 1924–25. Division 4 Champions – 1990–91. **GM Vauxhall Conference:** Champions – 1989–90.

Colours: Black and white hooped shirts, black shorts, white stockings.

Addison Miles (D)	6 2	13 03	Newham	7	1 89	Scholar
Barnes Giles (M)	6 0	12 10	Barking	5	8 88	Scholar
Beardsley Jason (D)	6 0	11 00	Burton	12	7 89	Scholar
Bywater Stephen (G)	6 2	12 08	Manchester	7	6 81	West Ham U
Camara Mo (D)	5 11	11 09	Guinea	25	6 75	Celtic
Carroll Roy (G)	6 2	13 12	Enniskillen	30	9 77	Rangers
Davis Claude (D)	6 3	14 04	Kingston	6	3 79	Sheffield U
Earnshaw Robert (F)	5 6	9 09	Mulfulira	6	4 81	Norwich C
Fagan Craig (F)	5 11	11 11	Birmingham	11	12 82	Hull C
Feilhaber Benny (M)	5 9	10 10	Rio de Janeiro	19	1 85	Hamburg
Hanson Mitchell (D)	6 1	13 07	Derby	2	9 88	Scholar
Jones David (M)	5 11	10 00	Southport	4	11 84	Manchester U
Leacock Dean (D)	6 2	12 04	Croydon	10	6 84	Fulham
Lewis Eddie (M)	5 10	11 02	Cerritos	17	5 74	Leeds U
McEveley James (D)	6 1	13 13	Liverpool	11	2 85	Blackburn R
Mears Tyrone (D)	5 11	11 10	Stockport	18	2 83	West Ham U
Miller Kenny (F)	5 10	10 09	Edinburgh	23	12 79	Celtic
Moore Darren (D)	6 2	15 07	Birmingham	22	4 74	WBA
Nyatanga Lewin (D)	6 2	12 08	Burton	18	8 88	Scholar
Pearson Stephen (M)	6 1	11 11	Lanark	2	10 82	Celtic
Price Lewis (G)	6 3	13 05	Bournemouth	19	7 84	Ipswich T
Richards Matthew (M)	5 9	11 07	Derby	1	12 89	Scholar
Savage Robbie (M)	5 11	11 00	Wrexham	18	10 74	Blackburn R
Sterjovski Mile (M)	6 1	12 08	Wollongong	27	5 79	Genclerbirligi
Stubbs Alan (D)	6 2	14 02	Kirby	6	10 71	Everton
Teale Gary (M)	5 9	11 04	Glasgow	21	7 78	Wigan Ath
Todd Andy (D)	5 11	13 04	Derby	21	9 74	Blackburn R
Villa Emanuel (F)	6 0	12 00	Capital Federal	24	2 82	Atlas

League Appearances: Addison, M. 1; Barnes, G. 14(7); Bywater, S. 18; Camara, M. 1; Carroll, R. 14; Davis, C. 19; Earnshaw, R. 7(15); Edworthy, M. 7(2); Fagan, C. 17(5); Feilhaber, B. 1(9); Ghaly, H. 13(2); Griffin, A. 13(2); Howard, S. 14(6); Johnson, M. 1(2); Jones, D. 11(3); Leacock, D. 22(4); Lewis, E. 22(2); Macken, J. (3); Malcolm, B. 1; McEveley, J. 21(8); Mears, T. 22(3); Miller, K. 30; Mills, D. 2; Moore, D. 29(2); Nyatanga, L. 2; Oakley, M. 19; Pearson, S. 23(1); Price, L. 6; Robert, L. 3(1); Savage, R. 16; Simmons, P. (1); Sterjovski, M. 9(3); Stubbs, A. 8; Teale, G. 9(9); Todd, A. 14(5); Villa, E. 9(7).

Goals – League (20): Miller 4, Oakley 3, Villa 3, McEveley 2, Barnes 1, Earnshaw 1, Howard 1, Jones 1, Mears 1, Nyatanga 1, Todd 1, own goal 1.

Carling Cup (2): Camara 1, Fagan 1.

FA Cup (4): Miller 2, Barnes 1, Earnshaw 1.

Ground: Pride Park Stadium, Derby DE24 8XL. Telephone (0871) 472 1884.

Record Attendance: Pride Park: 33,475 Derby Co Legends v Rangers 9 in a Row Legends, 1 May 2006 (Ted McMinn Benefit). Baseball Ground: 41,826 v Tottenham H, Division 1, 20 September 1969. **Capacity:** 33,540.

Manager: Paul Jewell.

Secretary: Clare Morris.

Most League Goals: 111, Division 3 (N), 1956–57.

Highest League Scorer in Season: Jack Bowers, 37, Division 1, 1930–31; Ray Straw, 37 Division 3 (N), 1956–57.

Most League Goals in Total Aggregate: Steve Bloomer, 292, 1892–1906 and 1910–14.

Most Capped Players: Deon Burton, 41 (51), Jamaica and Mart Poom, 41 (118), Estonia.

Most League Appearances: Kevin Hector, 486, 1966–78 and 1980–82.

Honours – Football League: Division 1 Champions – 1971–72, 1974–75. Division 2 Champions – 1911–12, 1914–15, 1968–69, 1986–87. Division 3 (N) Champions – 1956–57. **FA Cup:** Winners – 1945–46. **Texaco Cup:** Winners 1972.
Colours: White shirts, black shorts, white stockings.

DONCASTER ROVERS   FL CHAMPIONSHIP

Name			Birthplace	Birthdate	Previous club
Coppinger James (F)	5 7	10 03	Middlesbrough	10 1 81	Exeter C
Green Paul (M)	5 10	12 00	Pontefract	10 4 83	Trainee
Greer Gordon (D)	6 2	12 05	Glasgow	14 12 80	Blackburn R
Guy Lewis (F)	5 10	10 07	Penrith	27 8 85	Newcastle U
Hayter James (F)	5 9	10 13	Newport (IW)	9 4 79	Bournemouth
Heffernan Paul (F)	5 10	11 00	Dublin	29 12 81	Bristol C
Hird Samuel (D)	5 7	10 12	Askern	7 9 87	Leeds U
Lockwood Adam (D)	6 0	12 07	Wakefield	26 10 81	Yeovil T
McCammon Mark (F)	6 5	14 05	Barnet	7 8 78	Brighton & HA
McDaid Sean (D)	5 6	9 08	Harrogate	6 3 86	Leeds U
Nelthorpe Craig (M)	5 10	11 00	Doncaster	10 6 87	Scholar
O'Connor James (D)	5 10	12 05	Birmingham	20 11 84	Bournemouth
Price Jamie (D)	5 10	11 00	Normanton	27 10 81	Trainee
Roberts Gareth (D)	5 8	12 00	Wrexham	6 2 78	Tranmere R
Roberts Steve (D)	6 1	11 02	Wrexham	24 2 80	Wrexham
Smith Ben (G)	6 0	13 00	Newcastle	5 9 86	Stockport Co
Stock Brian (M)	5 11	11 02	Winchester	24 12 81	Preston NE
Sullivan Neil (G)	6 2	12 00	Sutton	24 2 70	Leeds U
Taylor Gareth (F)	6 2	13 07	Weston-Super-Mare	25 2 73	Tranmere R
Wellens Richard (M)	5 9	11 06	Manchester	26 3 80	Oldham Ath
Wilson Mark (M)	5 11	12 00	Scunthorpe	9 2 79	Dallas
Woods Martin (M)	5 11	11 13	Airdrie	1 1 86	Rotherham U

League Appearances: Coppinger, J. 31(8); Elliott, S. 1(9); Green, L. 26(12); Greer, G. 10(1); Guy, L. 13(16); Hayter, J. 21(13); Heffernan, P. 18(9); Hird, S. 3(1); Lee, G. (1); Lockwood, A. 39; McCammon, M. 23(9); McDaid, S. 14(10); Mills, M. 29(5); Nelthorpe, C. (2); O'Connor, J. 40; Price, Jason 18(11); Roberts, G. 35(2); Roberts. S. 20(5); Stock, B. 40; Sullivan, N. 46; Taylor, G. 4(8); Wellens, R. 45; Wilson, M. 23(8); Woods, M. 7(8).
Goals – League (65): Hayter 7 (2 pens), Heffernan 7 (2 pens), Price Jason 7, Guy 6, Wellens 6, Green 5, Stock 5 (2 pens), McCammon 4, Coppinger 3, Lockwood 3, Mills 3, Roberts G 3, Greer 1, McDaid 1, Taylor 1, Wilson 1, own goals 2.
Carling Cup (4): Hayter 1, Heffernan 1, McCammon 1, Wellens 1.
FA Cup (3): Hayter 2, McCammon 1.
J Paint Trophy (10): Guy 2, McCammon 2, Woods 2, Green 1, Heffernan 1 (pen), Price 1, own goal 1.
Play-Offs (6): Coppinger 3, Hayter 1, Stock 1 (pen), own goal 1.
Ground: Keepmoat Stadium, Stadium Way, Lakeside, Doncaster, South Yorkshire DN4 5JW. Telephone (01302) 764 664.
Record Attendance: 37,149 v Hull C, Division 3 (N), 2 October 1948. **Capacity:** 15,269.
Manager: Sean O'Driscoll.
Secretary: David Morris.
Most League Goals: 123, Division 3 (N), 1946–47.
Highest League Scorer in Season: Clarrie Jordan, 42, Division 3 (N) 1946–47.
Most League Goals in Total Aggregate: Tom Keetley, 180, 1923–29.
Most Capped Player: Len Graham, 14, Northern Ireland.
Most League Appearances: Fred Emery, 417, 1925–36.

Honours – Football League: Division 3 Champions – 2003–04. Division 3 (N) Champions – 1934–35, 1946–47, 1949–50. Division 4 Champions – 1965–66, 1968–69. **J Paint Trophy:** Winners – 2006–07. **Football Conference:** Champions – 2002–03.
Colours: Red and white hooped shirts, black shorts, black stockings.

EVERTON   FA PREMIERSHIP

Agard Kieran (F)			Newham	10	10 89	Scholar
Anichebe Victor (F)	6 1	13 00	Nigeria	23	4 88	Scholar
Arteta Mikel (M)	5 9	10 08	San Sebastian	26	3 82	Real Sociedad
Baines Leighton (D)	5 8	11 00	Liverpool	11	12 84	Wigan Ath
Barnett Moses (D)			London	3	12 90	Arsenal
Cahill Tim (M)	5 10	10 12	Sydney	6	12 79	Millwall
Carsley Lee (M)	5 10	12 04	Birmingham	28	2 74	Coventry C
Dennehy Darren (D)	6 3	11 11	Republic of Ireland	21	9 88	Scholar
Gosling Dan (M)	6 0	11 00	Brixham	2	2 90	Plymouth Arg
Hibbert Tony (D)	5 9	11 05	Liverpool	20	2 81	Trainee
Howard Tim (G)	6 3	14 12	North Brunswick	6	3 79	Manchester U
Irving John (M)	5 10	11 00	Liverpool	17	9 88	Scholar
Jagielka Phil (D)	6 0	13 01	Manchester	17	8 82	Sheffield U
Johnson Andrew (F)	5 7	10 09	Bedford	10	2 81	Crystal Palace
Jutkiewicz Lukas (F)	6 1	12 11	Southampton	20	3 89	Swindon T
Kissock John (M)			Fazackerley	1	12 89	Scholar
Krenn George (M)			Austria	4	10 90	Scholar
Lescott Jolean (D)	6 2	13 00	Birmingham	16	8 82	Wolverhampton W
Molyneux Lee (D)	5 10	11 07	Liverpool	24	2 89	Scholar
Neville Phil (M)	5 11	12 00	Bury	21	1 77	Manchester U
Nuno Valente (D)	6 0	12 03	Lisbon	12	9 74	Porto
O'Kane Eunan (M)			Co Derry	10	7 90	Scholar
Osman Leon (F)	5 8	10 09	Billinge	17	5 81	Trainee
Pienaar Steven (M)	5 10	10 06	Westbury	17	3 82	Borussia Dortmund
Rodwell Jack (D)	6 2	12 08	Birkdale	11	3 91	Scholar
Ruddy John (G)	6 3	12 07	St Ives	24	10 86	Cambridge U
Sheppard Karl (F)			Shelbourne	14	2 91	Scholar
Sinnott Cory (D)			Liverpool	31	8 90	Scholar
Spencer Scott (F)			Oldham	1	1 89	Scholar
Stewart Michael (M)			Warrington	3	1 91	Scholar
Stubhaug Lars (G)			Haugesund	18	4 90	Vard
Turner Iain (G)	6 3	12 10	Stirling	26	1 84	Trainee
Van der Meyde Andy (M)	5 10	12 04	Arnhem	30	9 79	Internazionale
Vaughan James (F)	5 11	12 08	Birmingham	14	7 88	Scholar
Yakubu Ayegbeni (F)	6 0	14 07	Benin City	22	11 82	Middlesbrough
Yobo Joseph (D)	6 1	13 00	Kano	6	9 80	Marseille

League Appearances: Anichebe, V. 10(17); Arteta, M. 27(1); Baines, L. 13(9); Cahill, T. 18; Carsley, L. 33(1); Fernandes, M. 9(3); Gravesen, T. 1(7); Hibbert, T. 22(2); Howard, T. 36; Jagielka, P. 27(7); Johnson, A. 20(9); Lescott, J. 37(1); McFadden, J. 5(7); Neville, P. 37; Nuno Valente, 8(1); Osman, L. 26(2); Pienaar, S. 25(3); Rodwell, J. (2); Stubbs, A. 7(1); Vaughan, J. (8); Wessels, S. 2; Yakubu, A. 26(3); Yobo, J. 29(1).
Goals – League (55): Yakubu 15 (1 pen), Lescott 8, Cahill 7, Johnson 6, Osman 4, McFadden 2, Neville 2, Pienaar 2, Anichebe 1, Arteta 1, Carsley 1, Jagielka 1, Stubbs 1, Vaughan 1, Yobo 1, own goals 2.
Carling Cup (7): Yakubu 3, McFadden 2, Cahill 1, Osman 1.
FA Cup (0).
UEFA Cup (23): Anichebe 4, Johnson 4, Arieta 3 (1 pen), Yakubu 3, Cahill 2, Lescott 2, Osman 2, Jagielka 1, McFadden 1, Vaughan 1.

Ground: Goodison Park, Goodison Road, Liverpool L4 4EL. Telephone (0870) 442 1878.
Record Attendance: 78,299 v Liverpool, Division 1, 18 September 1948. **Capacity:** 40,157.
Manager: David Moyes.
Secretary: David Harrison.
Most League Goals: 121, Division 2, 1930–31.
Highest League Scorer in Season: William Ralph 'Dixie' Dean, 60, Division 1, 1927–28 (All-time League record).
Most League Goals in Total Aggregate: William Ralph 'Dixie' Dean, 349, 1925–37.
Most Capped Player: Neville Southall, 92, Wales.
Most League Appearances: Neville Southall, 578, 1981–98.
Honours – Football League: Division 1 Champions – 1890–91, 1914–15, 1927–28, 1931–32, 1938–39, 1962–63, 1969–70, 1984–85, 1986–87. Division 2 Champions – 1930–31. **FA Cup:** Winners – 1906, 1933, 1966, 1984, 1995. **European Competitions: European Cup-Winners' Cup:** Winners – 1984–85.
Colours: Blue shirts, white shorts, white stockings.

EXETER CITY   FL CHAMPIONSHIP 2

Basham Steve (F)	5 11	12 04	Southampton	2 12 77	Oxford U
Carlisle Wayne (M)	6 0	11 06	Lisburn	9 9 79	Leyton Orient
Cozic Bertrand (M)	5 10	12 06	Quimper	18 5 78	Team Bath
Edwards Rob (M)	6 0	12 07	Kendal	1 7 73	Blackpool
Elam Lee (M)	5 8	10 12	Bradford	24 9 76	Weymouth
Friend George (D)			Barnstaple	19 10 87	
Gill Matthew (M)	5 11	11 10	Cambridge	8 11 80	Notts Co
Harley Ryan (D)	5 9	11 00	Bristol	22 1 85	Weston-Super-Mare
Jones Paul (G)	6 3	13 00	Maidstone	28 6 86	Leyton Orient
Logan Richard (F)	6 0	12 05	Bury St Edmunds	4 1 82	Weymouth
Marriott Andy (G)	6 2	11 00	Sutton-in-Ashfield	11 10 70	Boston U
Moxey Dean (D)	5 11	12 00	Exeter	14 1 86	
Richardson Jon (D)	6 1	12 02	Nottingham	29 8 75	Forest Green R
Saunders Neil (M)			Barking	7 5 83	Team Bath
Seaborne Daniel (D)			Barnstaple	5 3 87	
Sercombe Liam (M)			Exeter	25 4 90	
Stansfield Adam (F)	5 11	11 02	Plymouth	10 9 78	Hereford U
Taylor Andrew (M)	5 9	12 10	Exeter	17 9 82	Northwich V
Taylor Matt (D)			Ormskirk	30 1 82	Team Bath
Tully Steve (D)	5 9	11 00	Paignton	10 2 80	Weymouth

League Appearances: Artus, 8(2); Basham, 15(17); Carlisle, 24(8); Cozic, 10(5); Edwards, 46; Elam, 9(14); Friend, 27(3); Gill, 43; Harley, 9(3); Jones, 7; Logan, 28(13); Mackie, 21(3); Marriott, 39; Moxey, 43(2); Richardson, 15(4); Seaborne, 24; Sercombe, 4(3); Stansfield,36(5); Taylor, A. 19(1); Taylor, M. 40; Tully,38(1); Watson, 1(8).
Goals – League (83): Logan 18 (4 pens), Mackie 11, Stansfield 11, Moxey 9, Taylor M 9, Basham 5 (1 pen), Carlisle 4, Elam 3, Gill 3, Seaborne 2, Edwards 1, Friend 1, Harley 1, Watson 1, own goals 4.
FA Cup (7): Mackie 2, Taylor M 2, Basham 1 (pen), Carlisle 1, own goal 1.
Trophy (3): Basham 1, Mackie 1, Moxey 1.
Play-Offs (6): Carlisle 2, Edwards 1, Harley 1, Logan 1, Watson 1 (pen).
Ground: St James Park, Exeter EX4 6PX. Telephone: (0871) 855 1904.
Record Attendance: 20,984 v Sunderland, FA Cup 6th rd (replay), 4 March 1931.
Ground Capacity: 9,036.
Manager: Paul Tisdale.
Secretary: Sally Cooke.
Most League Goals: 88, Division 3 (S), 1932–33.
Highest League Scorer in Season: Fred Whitlow, 33, Division 3 (S), 1932–33.

Most League Goals in Total Aggregate: Tony Kellow, 129, 1976–78, 1980–83, 1985–88.
Most Capped Player: Dermot Curtis, 1 (17), Eire.
Most League Appearances: Arnold Mitchell, 495, 1952–66.
Honours – Division 3 (S) Cup: Winners 1934.
Colours: Red and white shirts, black shorts, black stockings.

FULHAM   FA PREMIERSHIP

Name			Birthplace			
Andreasen Leon (D)	6 1	13 03	Aidt Thorso	23	4 83	Werder Bremen
Ashton Nathan (D)	5 8	9 07	Plaistow	30	1 87	Scholar
Baird Chris (D)	5 10	11 11	Ballymoney	25	2 82	Southampton
Batista Ricardo (G)	6 2	12 06	Portugal	19	11 86	Vitoria Setubal
Bouazza Hameur (F)	5 10	12 01	Evry	22	2 85	Watford
Brown Wayne (M)			Surrey	6	8 88	Scholar
Bullard Jimmy (M)	5 10	11 05	Newham	23	10 78	Wigan Ath
Cook Lee (M)	5 8	11 10	Hammersmith	3	8 82	QPR
Davies Simon (M)	5 10	11 07	Haverfordwest	23	10 79	Everton
Davis Steve (M)	5 7	9 07	Ballymena	1	1 85	Aston Villa
Dempsey Clinton (M)	6 1	12 02	Nacogdoches	9	3 83	New England R
Hangeland Brede (D)	6 4	13 05	Houston	20	6 81	FC Copenhagen
Healy David (F)	5 8	10 09	Downpatrick	5	8 79	Leeds U
Hughes Aaron (D)	6 0	11 02	Cookstown	8	11 79	Aston Villa
John Collins (F)	5 11	12 13	Zwandru	17	10 85	Twente
Johnson Eddie (F)	6 0	12 02	Bunnell	31	3 84	Kansas City Wizards
Kallio Tony (D)			Tampere	9	8 78	
Kamara Diomansy (F)	6 0	11 05	Paris	8	11 80	WBA
Keller Kasey (G)	6 1	13 08	Washington	27	11 69	Tottenham H
Konchesky Paul (D)	5 10	11 07	Barking	15	5 81	West Ham U
Leijer Adrian (D)	6 1	12 08	Dubbo	25	3 86	Melbourne Victory
McBride Brian (F)	6 0	12 08	Chicago	19	6 72	Columbus Crew
Milsom Robert (D)			Redhill	2	1 87	Scholar
Moncur Tom (D)			Hackney	23	9 87	Scholar
Murphy Danny (M)	5 10	11 09	Chester	18	3 77	Tottenham H
Nevland Erik (F)	5 10	11 12	Stavanger	10	11 77	Groningen
Niemi Antti (G)	6 1	12 04	Oulu	31	5 72	Southampton
Omozusi Elliot (D)			Hackney	15	12 88	Scholar
Osei-Gyan King (M)	6 3	11 11	Ghana	22	12 88	
Owusu Daniel (M)	5 8	10 03	Ghana	13	6 89	
Seol Ki-Hyun (F)	6 0	11 07	South Korea	8	1 79	Reading
Smertin Alexei (M)	5 9	10 10	Barnaul	1	5 75	Dynamo Moscow
Stefanovic Dejan (D)	6 2	13 01	Belgrade	28	10 74	Portsmouth
Volz Moritz (D)	5 8	11 07	Siegen	21	1 83	Arsenal
Watts Adam (D)	6 1	11 09	London	4	3 88	Scholar
Zakuani Gabriel (D)	6 1	12 13	DR Congo	31	5 86	Leyton Orient

League Appearances: Andreasen, L. 9(4); Ashton, N. 1; Baird, C. 17(1); Bocanegra, C. 18(4); Bouazza, H. 15(5); Bullard, J. 15(2); Christanval, P. (1); Davies, S. 36(1); Davis, S. 22; Dempsey, C. 29(7); Diop, P. (2); Hangeland, B. 15; Healy, D. 15(15); Hughes, A. 29(1); John, C. (2); Johnson, E. 4(2); Kamara, D. 17(11); Keller, K. 13; Knight, Z. 4; Konchesky, P. 33; Kuqi, S. 3(7); McBride, B. 14(3); Murphy, D. 28(5); Nevland, E. 2(6); Niemi, A. 22; Omozusi, E. 8; Pearce, I. (1); Seol, K. 4(8); Smertin, A. 11(4); Stalteri, P. 13; Stefanovic, D. 13; Volz, M. 5(4); Warner, T. 3.
Goals – League (38): Dempsey 6, Davies 5, Kamara 5, Murphy 5 (2 pens), Healy 4, McBride 4, Bullard 2, Nevland 2, Bocanegra 1, Bouazza 1, own goals 3.
Carling Cup (2): Healy 1, Kamara 1.

FA Cup (2): Healy 1, Murphy 1.
Ground: Craven Cottage, Stevenage Road, London SW6 6HH. Telephone: (0870) 442 1222.
Record Attendance: 49,335 v Millwall, Division 2, 8 October 1938. **Capacity:** 25,478.
Manager: Roy Hodgson.
Secretary: Darren Preston.
Most League Goals: 111, Division 3 (S), 1931–32.
Highest League Scorer in Season: Frank Newton, 43, Division 3 (S), 1931–32.
Most League Goals in Total Aggregate: Gordon Davies, 159, 1978–84, 1986–91.
Most Capped Player: Johnny Haynes, 56, England.
Most League Appearances: Johnny Haynes, 594, 1952–70.
Honours – Football League: Division 1 Champions – 2000–01. Division 2 Champions – 1948–49, 1998–99. Division 3 (S) Champions – 1931–32. **European Competitions: Intertoto Cup:** Winners – 2002.
Colours: White shirts, black shorts, white stockings.

GILLINGHAM   FL CHAMPIONSHIP 2

Ba George (F)	6 1	13 05	Abidjan	24 1 79	
Bentley Mark (M)	6 2	13 07	Hertford	7 1 78	Southend U
Brown Aaron (M)	5 10	11 11	Bristol	14 3 80	Swindon T
Clohessy Sean (D)	5 11	12 07	Croydon	12 12 86	Arsenal
Crofts Andrew (D)	5 10	11 13	Chatham	29 5 84	Trainee
Cullip Danny (D)	6 0	12 12	Bracknell	17 9 76	QPR
Facey Delroy (F)	6 0	15 02	Huddersfield	22 4 80	Rotherham U
Fuller Barry (M)	5 10	11 10	Ashford	25 9 84	Stevenage B
Howard Charlie (M)	6 0	15 00	London	26 11 89	Scholar
Jackson Simeon (M)	5 10	10 12	Kingston Jam	28 3 87	Rushden & D
King Simon (D)	6 0	13 00	Oxford	11 4 83	Barnet
Lewis Stuart (M)	5 10	11 06	Welwyn	15 10 87	Stevenage B
Miller Adam (M)	5 11	11 06	Hemel Hempstead	19 2 82	Stevenage B
Mulligan Gary (F)	6 1	12 01	Dublin	23 4 85	Sheffield U
Nutter John (D)	6 2	12 10	Taplow	13 6 82	Stevenage B
Oli Dennis (F)	6 0	12 00	Newham	28 1 84	Grays Ath
Pugh Andy (F)	5 9	12 02	Gravesend	28 1 89	Scholar
Richards Garry (D)	6 3	13 00	Romford	11 6 86	Southend U
Royce Simon (G)	6 2	12 10	Forest Gate	9 9 71	QPR
Sodje Efe (D)	6 1	12 00	Greenwich	5 10 72	Southend U
Southall Nicky (M)	5 11	12 04	Stockton	28 1 72	Nottingham F
Thurgood Stuart (M)	5 8	12 03	Enfield	4 11 81	Grays Ath

League Appearances: Armstrong, C. 12(1); Ba, G. 1(3); Bentley, M. 32(1); Brown, A. 10(1); Bygrave, A. 13(2); Clohessy, S. 16(1); Cogan, B. 9(7); Cox, I. 20; Crofts, A. 41; Cullip, D. 11; Cumbers, L. 2(4); Dickson, C. 9(3); Facey, D. 27(5); Freeman, L. (1); Fuller, B. 9(1); Graham, D. 7(9); Griffiths, L. 4(20); Hamilton, M. 3(2); Howard, C. 1; Jackson, S. 14(4); Jupp, D. 2; King, S. 39(3); Lewis, S. 6(4); Lomas, S. 8; Maher, K. 7; Miller, A. 26(2); Mulligan, G. 15(15); Nowland, A. 4(1); Nutter, J. 23(1); Oli, D. 17(5); Pugh, A. (2); Richards, G. 12(2); Rocastle, C. 2; Royce, S. 33; Simmonds, D. (3); Sodje, E. 12(1); Southall, N. 31(2); Stillie, D. 13(1); Stone, C. 4(5); Thurgood, S. 11(1).
Goals – League (44): Dickson 7 (1 pen), Crofts 5, Mulligan 5 (1 pen), Jackson 4, Oli 4, Facey 3, Graham 3, Miller 3 (1 pen), Bentley 2, Griffiths 2, Brown 1, Cogan 1, Cox 1, Nutter 1, Richards 1, Southall 1.
Carling Cup (0).
FA Cup (1): Graham 1.
J Paint Trophy (9): Dickson 4 (1 pen), Armstrong 1, Bentley 1, Brown 1, Oli 1, Stone 1.

Ground: Priestfield Stadium, Redfern Avenue, Gillingham, Kent ME7 4DD. Telephone (01634) 300 000.
Record Attendance: 23,002 v QPR, FA Cup 3rd rd, 10 January 1948. **Capacity:** 11,440.
Manager: Mark Stimson.
Secretary: Gwendoline Poynter.
Most League Goals: 90, Division 4, 1973–74.
Highest League Scorer in Season: Ernie Morgan, 31, Division 3 (S), 1954–55; Brian Yeo, 31, Division 4, 1973–74.
Most League Goals in Total Aggregate: Brian Yeo, 135, 1963–75.
Most Capped Player: Mamady Sidibe 7 (8), Mali.
Most League Appearances: John Simpson, 571, 1957–72.
Honours – Football League: Division 4 Champions – 1963–64.
Colours: Blue with white insert.

GRIMSBY TOWN   FL CHAMPIONSHIP 2

Barnes Phil (G)	6 1	11 01	Sheffield	2 3 79	Sheffield U
Bennett Ryan (D)	6 0	13 02	London	4 8 85	Scholar
Bird Matthew (D)	6 0	11 07	Grimsby	31 10 90	Scholar
Bolland Paul (M)	5 10	10 12	Bradford	23 12 79	Notts Co
Bore Peter (M)	5 11	11 04	Grimsby	4 11 87	Scholar
Boshell Danny (M)	5 11	11 09	Bradford	30 5 81	Stockport Co
Butler Martin (F)	5 11	11 09	Wordsley	15 9 74	Walsall
Clarke Jamie (D)	6 2	12 03	Sunderland	18 9 82	Boston U
Fenton Nick (D)	6 0	10 02	Preston	23 11 79	Doncaster R
Hegarty Nick (M)	5 10	11 00	Hemsworth	25 6 86	Scholar
Hunt James (M)	5 8	10 03	Derby	17 12 76	Bristol R
Jarman Nathan (F)	5 11	11 03	Scunthorpe	19 9 86	Barnsley
Montgomery Gary (G)	5 11	13 08	Leamington Spa	8 10 82	Rotherham U
Newey Tom (D)	5 10	10 02	Sheffield	31 10 82	Leyton Orient
North Danny (F)	5 9	12 08	Grimsby	7 9 87	Scholar
Taylor Andy (M)	6 2	13 00	Grimsby	30 10 88	Scholar
Till Peter (M)	5 11	11 04	Birmingham	7 9 85	Birmingham C
Toner Ciaran (M)	6 1	12 02	Craigavon	30 6 81	Lincoln C

League Appearances: Atkinson, R. 24; Barnes, P. 42; Bennett, R. 28(12); Bird, M. (2); Bolland, P. 33(2); Bore, P. 4(13); Boshell, D. 38(2); Butler, M. 15(6); Clarke, J. 27(2); Fenton, N. 40(2); Hegarty, N. 27(3); Hird, S. 17; Hunt, J. 32(5); Jarman, N. 5(2); Jones, G. 15(21); Logan, S. 5; Montgomery, G. 4(1); Mulligan, D. 4(2); Newey, T. 42; North, D. 21(6); Rankin, I. 12(5); Taylor, A. 1(25); Till, P. 31(3); Toner, C. 25(5); Whittle, J. 14(4).
Goals – League (55): North 9 (1 pen), Boshell 6 (3 pens), Butler 6, Taylor 5, Bolland 4, Hegarty 4, Jones 4, Toner 3 (3 pens), Bore 2, Clarke 2, Fenton 2, Logan 2, Till 2, Atkinson 1, Bennett 1, Newey 1, Whittle 1.
Carling Cup (1): North 1.
FA Cup (2): Bolland 1, Jones 1.
J Paint Trophy (10): Till 2, Bolland 1, Boshell 1, Clarke 1, Fenton 1, Rankin 1, Toner 1, own goals 2.
Ground: Blundell Park, Cleethorpes, North-East Lincolnshire DN35 7PY. Telephone (01472) 605 050.
Record Attendance: 31,651 v Wolverhampton W, FA Cup 5th rd, 20 February 1937. **Capacity:** 10,033.
Manager: Alan Buckley.
Chief Executive: Ian Fleming.
Most League Goals: 103, Division 2, 1933–34.
Highest League Scorer in Season: Pat Glover, 42, Division 2, 1933–34.
Most League Goals in Total Aggregate: Pat Glover, 180, 1930–39.
Most Capped Player: Pat Glover, 7, Wales.

Most League Appearances: John McDermott, 647, 1987–2007.
Honours – Football League: Division 2 Champions – 1900–01, 1933–34. Division 3 (N) Champions – 1925–26, 1955–56. Division 3 Champions – 1979–80. Division 4 Champions – 1971–72. League Group Cup: Winners – 1981–82. Auto Windscreens Shield: Winners – 1997–98.
Colours: Black and white striped shirts, black shorts, white stockings with black trim.

HARTLEPOOL UNITED   FL CHAMPIONSHIP 1

Barker Richard (F)	6 0	14 06	Sheffield	30 5 75	Mansfield T
Boland Willie (M)	5 9	11 02	Ennis	6 8 75	Cardiff C
Brown James (F)	5 11	11 00	Newcastle	3 1 87	Cramlington J
Budtz Jan (G)	6 0	13 05	Denmark	20 4 79	Doncaster R
Clark Ben (D)	6 1	13 11	Shotley Bridge	24 1 83	Sunderland
Collins Sam (D)	6 2	14 03	Pontefract	5 6 77	Hull C
Foley David (F)	5 4	8 09	South Shields	12 5 87	Scholar
Humphreys Richie (M)	5 11	12 07	Sheffield	30 11 77	Cambridge U
Lee-Barrett Arran (G)	6 2	14 01	Ipswich	28 2 84	Coventry C
Liddle Gary (D)	6 1	12 06	Middlesbrough	15 6 86	Middlesbrough
Mackay Michael (F)	6 0	11 08	Durham	11 10 82	Consett
McCunnie Jamie (D)	5 10	10 11	Bellshill	15 4 83	Dunfermline Ath
Monkhouse Andrew (M)	6 2	12 06	Leeds	23 10 80	Swindon T
Nelson Michael (D)	6 2	13 03	Gateshead	15 3 82	Bury
Porter Joel (F)	5 9	11 13	Adelaide	25 12 78	Sydney Olympic
Robson Matty (D)	5 10	11 02	Durham	23 1 85	Scholar
Sweeney Anthony (M)	6 0	11 07	Stockton	5 9 83	Scholar
Young Martin (M)	5 11	11 07	Hartlepool	8 9 88	Scholar

League Appearances: Antwi-Birago, G. 27; Barker, R. 31(5); Boland, W. 32(2); Brown, J. 31(4); Budtz, J. 28; Bullock, L. (1); Clark, B. 14(5); Coles, D. 3; Collins, S. 10; Craddock, T. 1(3); Elliott, R. 14(1); Foley, D. 11(23); Gibb, A. 4(2); Humphreys, R. 43(2); Lee, G. 3; Lee-Barrett, A. 18; Liddle, G. 41; MacKay, M. 10(14); McCunnie, J. 23(6); Monkhouse, A. 21(4); Moore, I. 22(2); Nelson, M. 44(1); Nolan, E. 11; Porter, J. 24(15); Robson, M. 6(11); Sweeney, A. 27(9); Thompson, A. 7; Turnbull, S. (1).
Goals – League (63): Barker 13 (6 pens), Brown 10, Porter 9, Moore 6, MacKay 5, Sweeney 4, Humphreys 3, Collins 2, Liddle 2, Monkhouse 2, Nelson 2, Antwi-Birago 1, Clark 1, McCunnie 1, Robson 1, Thompson 1.
Carling Cup (3): Foley 2, Moore 1.
FA Cup (6): Barker 2, Brown 1, Liddle 1, Moore 1, Porter 1.
J Paint Trophy (9): Porter 3, Brown 2, Barker 1, Foley 1, Mackay 1, Moore 1.
Ground: Victoria Park, Clarence Road, Hartlepool TS24 8BZ. Telephone (01429) 272 584.
Record Attendance: 17,426 v Manchester U, FA Cup 3rd rd, 5 January 1957.
Capacity: 7,787.
Manager: Danny Wilson.
Secretary: Maureen Smith.
Most League Goals: 90, Division 3 (N), 1956–57.
Highest League Scorer in Season: William Robinson, 28, Division 3 (N), 1927–28; Joe Allon, 28, Division 4, 1990–91.
Most League Goals in Total Aggregate: Ken Johnson, 98, 1949–64.
Most Capped Player: Ambrose Fogarty, 1 (11), Republic of Ireland.
Most League Appearances: Wattie Moore, 447, 1948–64.
Honours – Nil.
Colours: White shirts with blue trim, blue shorts, white stockings.

HEREFORD UNITED FL CHAMPIONSHIP 1

Beckwith Dean (D)	6 3	13 01	Southwark	18 9 83	Gillingham
Broadhurst Karl (D)	6 1	11 07	Portsmouth	18 3 80	Bournemouth
Brown Wayne (G)	6 0	13 11	Southampton	14 1 77	Chester C
Easton Clint (M)	5 11	11 00	Barking	1 10 77	Gillingham
Esson Ryan (G)	6 1	12 06	Aberdeen	19 3 80	Shrewsbury T
Fitzpatrick Jordan (M)	6 0	12 00	Stourbridge	15 6 88	Wolverhampton W
Guinan Stephen (F)	6 1	13 02	Birmingham	24 12 75	Cheltenham T
Gwynne Sam (M)	5 9	11 11	Hereford	17 12 87	Scholar
Johnson Simon (F)	5 9	11 09	West Bromwich	9 3 83	Darlington
Jones Craig (M)	6 0	12 02	Hereford	12 12 89	Cardiff C
Macleod Jack (M)	5 8	10 00	Hereford	3 8 88	Carshalton Ath
McClenahan Trent (D)	5 11	12 00	Sydney	4 2 85	West Ham U
Palmer Marcus (F)	6 0	11 07	Gloucester	22 12 88	Cheltenham T
Rose Richard (D)	6 0	12 04	Pembury	8 9 82	Gillingham
Smith Ben (M)	5 9	11 09	Chelmsford	23 11 78	Weymouth
Taylor Kris (M)	5 9	11 05	Stafford	12 1 84	Walsall

League Appearances: Ainsworth, L. 13(2); Beckwith, D. 38; Benjamin, T. 15(19); Broadhurst, K. 22(1); Brown, W. 44; Collins, L. 14(2); Diagouraga, T. 41; Easton, C. 36(3); Esson, R. 1; Gleeson, S. 3(1); Guinan, S. 20(8); Gwynne, S. 9(6); Hooper, G. 19; Igoe, S. 4; Johnson, S. 22(11); MacDonald, S. 7; McClenahan, T. 38; McCombe, J. 23(4); Palmer, M. (1); Robinson, T. 32(11); Rose, R. 31; Smith, B. 42(2); Taylor, K. 22(9); Threlfall, R. 6(3); Weale, C. 1; Webb, L. 3(11).
Goals – League (72): Robinson 13 (1 pen), Hooper 11, Benjamin 10 (3 pens), MacDonald 6, Johnson 5 (1 pen), Smith 5, Ainsworth 4, Easton 3, Guinan 3, Webb 3, Beckwith 2, Diagouraga 2, McClenahan 1, Rose 1, Taylor 1, own goals 2.
Carling Cup (5): Ainsworth 3, Easton 1, Robinson 1.
FA Cup (7): Robinson 2, Ainsworth 1, Benjamin 1, Johnson 1, McCombe 1, Smith 1.
J Paint Trophy (0).
Ground: Edgar Street, Hereford, Herefordshire HR4 9JU. Telephone: (01432) 276 666.
Record Attendance: 18,114 v Sheffield Wed., FA Cup 3rd rd, 4 January 1958.
Capacity: 7,149.
Manager: Graham Turner.
Secretary: Joan Fennessey.
Most League Goals: 86, Division 3, 1975–76.
Highest League Scorer in Season: Dixie McNeil, 35, 1975–76.
Most League Goals in Total Aggregate: Stewart Phillips, 93, 1980–88, 1990–91.
Most Capped Player: Trevor Benjamin, 2, Jamaica.
Most League Appearances: Mel Pejic, 412, 1980–92.
Honours – Football League: Division 3 Champions – 1975–76. **Welsh Cup:** Winners – 1990.
Colours: White shirts, black shorts, white stockings.

HUDDERSFIELD TOWN FL CHAMPIONSHIP 1

Beckett Luke (F)	5 11	14 01	Sheffield	25 11 76	Sheffield U
Berrett James (M)	5 10	10 13	Halifax	13 1 89	Scholar
Booth Andy (F)	6 1	13 00	Huddersfield	6 12 73	Sheffield W
Broadbent Daniel (M)	5 10	12 00	Leeds	2 3 90	Scholar
Cadamarteri Danny (F)	5 7	13 05	Bradford	12 10 79	Leicester C
Clarke Nathan (D)	6 2	12 00	Halifax	30 11 83	Scholar
Clarke Tom (D)	5 11	12 02	Halifax	21 12 87	Scholar
Collins Michael (M)	6 0	10 12	Halifax	30 4 86	Scholar

Eastwood Simon (G)	6 2	12 09	Luton	26 6 89	Scholar
Glennon Matthew (G)	6 2	13 11	Stockport	8 10 78	St Johnstone
Holdsworth Andy (D)	5 9	11 02	Pontefract	29 1 84	Scholar
Jevons Phil (F)	5 11	12 00	Liverpool	1 8 79	Bristol C
Kamara Malvin (M)	5 11	13 00	Southwark	17 11 83	Port Vale
Killock Shane (D)	6 0	12 04	Huddersfield	12 3 89	Ossett Albion
Mirfin David (M)	6 2	14 05	Sheffield	18 4 85	Scholar
Skarz Joe (D)	5 11	13 00	Huddersfield	13 7 89	Scholar
Smithies Alex (G)	6 1	10 01	Huddersfield	25 3 90	Scholar
Williams Robbie (D)	5 10	11 13	Pontefract	2 10 84	Barnsley
Worthington Jon (M)	5 9	11 05	Dewsbury	16 4 83	Scholar

League Appearances: Akins, L. (3); Beckett, L. 25(11); Berrett, J. 10(5); Booth, A. 28(10); Brandon, C. 25(3); Broadbent, D. (5); Cadamarteri, D. 10(2); Clarke, N. 44; Clarke, T. 2(1); Collins, M. 35(6); Glennon, M. 45; Hardy, A. 5(1); Holdsworth, A. 43(1); Jevons, P. 17(4); Kamara, M. 33(10); Keogh, R. 9; Killock, S. 1; Mirfin, D. 23(6); Page, R. 18; Racchi, D. (3); Schofield, D. 19(6); Sinclair, F. 28(1); Skarz, J. 22(5); Smithies, A. 1(1); Wallwork, R. 16; Williams, R. 24(1); Worthington, J. 19(6); Young, M. 4(4).
Goals – League (50): Booth 9, Beckett 8 (3 pens), Jevons 7 (3 pens), Cadamarteri 3, Holdsworth 3, Kamara 3, Wallwork 3, Brandon 2, Clarke N 2, Collins 2, Schofield 2, Williams 2, Berrett 1, Keogh 1, Mirfin 1, Page 1.
Carling Cup (0).
FA Cup (10): Beckett 4, Jevons 2, Kamara 2, Brandon 1, Collins 1.
J Paint Trophy (1): Collins 1.
Ground: The Galpharm Stadium, Stadium Way, Leeds Road, Huddersfield HD1 6PX. Telephone 0870 4444 677.
Record Attendance: 67,037 v Arsenal, FA Cup 6th rd, 27 February 1932 (at Leeds Road); 23,678 v Liverpool, FA Cup 3rd rd, 12 December 1999 (at Alfred McAlpine Stadium).
Capacity: 24,500.
Manager: Stan Ternent.
Secretary: J. Ann Hough.
Most League Goals: 101, Division 4, 1979–80.
Highest League Scorer in Season: Sam Taylor, 35, Division 2, 1919–20; George Brown, 35, Division 1, 1925–26.
Most League Goals in Total Aggregate: George Brown, 142, 1921–29; Jimmy Glazzard, 142, 1946–56.
Most Capped Player: Jimmy Nicholson, 31 (41), Northern Ireland.
Most League Appearances: Billy Smith, 520, 1914–34.
Honours – Football League: Division 1 Champions – 1923–24, 1924–25, 1925–26. Division 2 Champions – 1969–70. Division 4 Champions – 1979–80. **FA Cup:** Winners – 1922.
Colours: Blue and white striped shirts, white shorts, white and blue hooped stockings.

HULL CITY   FA PREMIERSHIP

Ashbee Ian (M)	6 1	13 07	Birmingham	6 9 76	Cambridge U
Atkinson William (M)	5 10	10 07	Beverley	14 10 88	Scholar
Barmby Nick (M)	5 7	11 03	Hull	11 2 74	Leeds U
Bennett James (M)	5 10	12 03	Beverley	4 9 88	Scholar
Bridges Michael (F)	6 1	10 11	North Shields	5 8 78	Carlisle U
Brown Wayne (D)	6 0	12 06	Barking	20 8 77	Colchester U
Dawson Andy (D)	5 10	11 02	Northallerton	20 10 78	Scunthorpe U
Doyle Nathan (M)	5 11	12 06	Derby	12 1 87	Derby Co
Duke Matt (G)	6 5	13 04	Sheffield	16 7 77	Sheffield U
Featherstone Nicky (F)	5 7	11 03	Goole	22 9 89	Scholar

Folan Caleb (F)	6 2	14 07	Leeds	26 10 82	Wigan Ath
France Ryan (M)	5 11	11 11	Sheffield	13 12 80	Alfreton T
Garcia Richard (F)	5 11	12 01	Perth	4 9 81	Colchester U
Hughes Bryan (M)	5 10	11 08	Liverpool	19 6 76	Charlton Ath
Marney Dean (M)	6 0	11 05	Barking	31 1 84	Tottenham H
Myhill Boaz (G)	6 3	14 06	Modesto	9 11 82	Aston Villa
Pedersen Henrik (F)	6 1	13 03	Copenhagen	10 6 75	Bolton W
Plummer Matthew (D)	6 1	12 01	Hull	18 1 89	Scholar
Ricketts Sam (D)	6 1	12 01	Aylesbury	11 10 81	Swansea C
Turner Michael (D)	6 4	13 05	Lewisham	9 11 83	Brentford
Welsh John (M)	5 7	12 02	Liverpool	10 1 84	Liverpool
Windass Dean (F)	5 10	12 03	North Ferriby	1 4 69	Bradford C

League Appearances: Ashbee, I. 42; Barmby, N. 5(10); Bridges, M. 1(6); Brown, W. 41; Campbell, F. 32(2); Clement, N. 4(1); Coles, D. 1; Dawson, A. 24(5); Delaney, D. 20(2); Doyle, N. (1); Duke, M. 3; Elliott, S. 3(4); Fagan, C. 4(4); Featherstone, N. (6); Folan, C. 18(11); France, R. 3(10); Garcia, R. 35(3); Hughes, B. 26(9); Livermore, D. 9(11); Marney, D. 35(6); McPhee, S. 7(12); Myhill, B. 43; Okocha, J. 10(8); Pedersen, H. 18(3); Ricketts, S. 44; Turner, M. 44; Walton, S. 5(5); Windass, D. 29(8).
Goals – League (65): Campbell 15, Windass 11 (2 pens), Folan 8, Marney 6 (2 pens), Garcia 5, Turner 5, Pedersen 4, Ashbee 3, McPhee 2, Barmby 1, Brown 1, Dawson 1, Hughes 1, Livermore 1, own goal 1.
Carling Cup (4): Bridges 1, Elliott 1, Garcia 1, McPhee 1.
FA Cup (2): Windass 2.
Play-Offs (7): Barmby 2, Windass 2, Doyle 1, Folan 1, Garcia 1.
Ground: Kingston Communications Stadium, Walton St, Hull HU3 6HU. Telephone (0870) 837 0003.
Record Attendance: 55,019 v Manchester U, FA Cup 6th rd, 26 February 1949 (Boothferry Park); 25,512 v Sunderland, FL C, 28 October 2007 (KC Stadium).
Capacity: 25,417.
Manager: Phil Brown.
Secretary: Phil Hough.
Most League Goals: 109, Division 3, 1965–66.
Highest League Scorer in Season: Bill McNaughton, 39, Division 3 (N), 1932–33.
Most League Goals in Total Aggregate: Chris Chilton, 195, 1960–71.
Most Capped Player: Theo Whitmore, Jamaica.
Most League Appearances: Andy Davidson, 520, 1952–67.
Honours – Football League: Division 3 (N) Champions – 1932–33, 1948–49. Division 3 Champions – 1965–66.
Colours: Black and amber striped shirts, black shorts.

IPSWICH TOWN   FL CHAMPIONSHIP

Bowditch Dean (F)	5 11	10 08	Bishop's Stortford	15 6 86	Trainee
Bruce Alex (D)	6 0	11 06	Norwich	28 9 84	Birmingham C
Casement Chris (M)	6 0	12 02	Belfast	12 1 88	Scholar
Clarke Billy (F)	5 7	10 01	Cork	13 12 87	Scholar
Counago Pablo (F)	5 11	11 06	Pontevedra	9 8 79	Malaga
Garvan Owen (M)	6 0	10 07	Dublin	29 1 88	Scholar
Harding Dan (D)	6 0	11 11	Gloucester	23 12 83	Leeds U
Haynes Danny (F)	5 11	12 04	Peckham	19 1 88	Scholar
Lee Alan (F)	6 2	13 09	Galway	21 8 78	Cardiff C
Miller Tommy (M)	6 0	11 07	Easington	8 1 79	Sunderland
Naylor Richard (D)	6 1	13 07	Leeds	28 2 77	Trainee
Norris David (M)	5 7	11 06	Stamford	22 2 81	Plymouth Arg
Peters Jaime (M)	5 7	10 12	Toronto	4 5 87	Moor Green
Quinn Alan (M)	5 9	10 06	Dublin	13 6 79	Sheffield U

Rhodes Jordan (F)	6 1	11 03	Oldham	5 2 90	Barnsley
Richards Matt (D)	5 8	10 10	Harlow	26 12 84	Scholar
Roberts Gary (M)	5 10	11 09	Liverpool	18 3 84	Accrington S
Robinson Kurt (D)	5 8	11 05	Basildon	21 10 89	Southend U
Smith Tommy (D)	6 2	12 02	Macclesfield	31 3 90	Scholar
Sumulikoski Velice (M)	6 0	12 02	Macedonia	24 1 81	Zenit
Supple Shane (G)	5 11	11 07	Dublin	4 5 87	Scholar
Trotter Liam (M)	6 2	12 02	Ipswich	24 8 88	Scholar
Upson Edward (M)	5 10	11 07	Bury St Edmunds	21 11 89	Scholar
Walters Jon (F)	6 0	12 06	Birkenhead	20 9 83	Chester C
Williams Gavin (M)	5 10	11 05	Pontypridd	20 6 80	West Ham U
Wright David (D)	5 11	11 01	Warrington	1 5 80	Wigan Ath

League Appearances: Alexander, N. 29; Bruce, A. 35(1); Bywater, S. 17; Casement, C. 2(1); Clarke, B. 9(11); Counago, P. 35(8); De Vos, J. 46; Garvan, O. 39(4); Harding, D. 29(1); Haynes, D. 18(23); Kuqi, S. 2(2); Lee, A. 37(8); Legwinski, S. 9(6); Miller, T. 32(5); Naylor, R. 6(1); Norris, D. 9; O'Callaghan, G. 1; Peters, J. (5); Quinn, A. 14(2); Rhodes, A. (8); Roberts, G. 10(11); Simpson, D. 7(1); Sito, 11(2); Sumulikoski, V. 10(6); Trotter, L. 2(4); Walters, J. 39(1); Williams, G. 10(3); Wilnis, F. 9(4); Wright, D. 39(2).
Goals – League (65): Walters 13, Counago 12, Lee 11 (2 pens), Haynes 7, Miller T 5 (1 pen), De Vos 2, Garvan 2, Legwinski 2, Wright 2, Harding 1, Norris 1, Quinn 1, Rhodes 1, Roberts 1, Sito 1, Sumulikoski 1, Trotter 1, own goal 1.
Carling Cup (3): Garvan 1, Lee 1 (pen), own goal 1.
FA Cup (0).
Ground: Portman Road, Ipswich, Suffolk IP1 2DA. Telephone (01473) 400 500.
Record Attendance: 38,010 v Leeds U, FA Cup 6th rd, 8 March 1975.
Capacity: 30,311.
Manager: Jim Magilton.
Secretary: Sally Webb.
Most League Goals: 106, Division 3 (S), 1955–56.
Highest League Scorer in Season: Ted Phillips, 41, Division 3 (S), 1956–57.
Most League Goals in Total Aggregate: Ray Crawford, 204, 1958–63 and 1966–69.
Most Capped Player: Allan Hunter, 47 (53), Northern Ireland.
Most League Appearances: Mick Mills, 591, 1966–82.
Honours – Football League: Division 1 Champions – 1961–62. Division 2 Champions – 1960–61, 1967–68, 1991–92. Division 3 (S) Champions – 1953–54, 1956–57. **FA Cup:** Winners – 1977–78. **European Competitions: UEFA Cup:** Winners – 1980–81.
Colours: Blue shirts, white shorts, blue stockings.

LEEDS UNITED   FL CHAMPIONSHIP 1

Ameobi Tomi (F)	6 3	12 10	Newcastle	16 8 88	Scholar
Ankergren Casper (G)	6 3	14 07	Koge	9 11 79	Brondby
Bayly Robert (M)	5 8	11 00	Dublin	22 2 88	Scholar
Beckford Jermaine (F)	6 2	13 02	Ealing	9 12 83	Wealdstone
Carole Sebastien (M)	5 7	11 02	Pontoise	8 9 82	Brighton & HA
Constantine Leon (F)	6 2	12 00	Hackney	24 2 78	Port Vale
Delph Fabian (M)	5 8	10 00	Bradford	21 11 89	Scholar
Douglas Jonathan (M)	6 0	12 06	Monaghan	22 11 81	Blackburn R
Elding Anthony (F)	6 1	12 02	Boston	16 4 82	Stockport Co
Gardner Scott (M)	5 9	11 04	Luxembourg	1 4 88	Scholar
Heath Matt (D)	6 4	13 13	Leicester	1 11 81	Coventry C
Howson Jonathan (M)	5 11	12 01	Leeds	21 5 88	Scholar
Hughes Andy (M)	5 11	12 01	Stockport	2 1 78	Norwich C
Huntington Paul (D)	6 3	12 08	Carlisle	17 9 87	Newcastle U
Johnson Brad (M)	6 0	12 10	Hackney	28 4 87	Northampton T
Kandol Tresor (F)	6 1	11 05	Banga	20 8 81	Barnet

Kilkenny Neil (M)	5 8	10 08	Enfield	19 12 85	Birmingham C
Lucas David (G)	6 1	13 07	Preston	23 11 77	Barnsley
Lund Jonny (G)	5 10	11 10	Leeds	1 11 88	Scholar
Martin Alan (G)	6 0	11 11	Glasgow	1 1 89	Motherwell
Michalik Lubomir (D)	6 4	13 00	Cadca	13 8 83	Bolton W
Parker Ben (D)	5 11	11 06	Pontefract	8 11 87	Scholar
Prutton David (M)	5 10	13 00	Hull	12 9 81	Southampton
Richardson Frazer (D)	5 11	12 04	Rotherham	29 10 82	Trainee
Rui Marques Manuel (D)	5 11	11 13	Luanda	3 9 77	Maritimo
Sorsa Sebastian (M)	5 9	11 00	Finland	25 1 84	HJK Helsinki
Sweeney Peter (M)	6 0	12 11	Glasgow	25 9 84	Stoke C
Westlake Ian (M)	5 11	11 00	Clacton	10 11 83	Ipswich T
Weston Curtis (M)	5 11	11 09	Greenwich	24 1 87	Swindon T

League Appearances: Andrews, W. 1; Ankergren, C. 43; Beckford, J. 40; Carole, S. 17(11); Clapham, J. 12(1); Constantine, L. 1(3); Da Costa, F. (4); De Vries, M. 1(5); Delph, F. (1); Douglas, J. 22(2); Elding, A. 4(5); Flo, T. 4(18); Freedman, D. 9(2); Gardner, S. 1; Heath, M. 25(1); Howson, J. 21(5); Hughes, A. 32(8); Huntington, P. 12(5); Johnson, B. 18(3); Kandol, T. 32(9); Kenton, D. 16; Kilkenny, N. 16; Kishishev, R. 5(2); Lewis, E. 1; Lucas, D. 3; Michalik, L. 17; Parker, B. 6(3); Prutton, D. 38(5); Richardson, F. 39; Rui Marques, M. 34(2); Sheehan, A. 10; Sweeney, P. 6(3); Thompson, A. 9(4); Westlake, I. 10(10); Weston, C. 1(6).
Goals – League (72): Beckford 20 (2 pens), Kandol 11, Freedman 5, Prutton 4, Carole 3, Douglas 3, Flo 3, Howson 3, Johnson 3, Rui Marques 3, Thompson 3, Constantine 1, De Vries 1, Elding 1, Heath 1, Hughes 1, Huntington 1, Kilkenny 1, Richardson 1, Sheehan 1, Westlake 1, Weston 1.
Carling Cup (1): Westlake 1.
FA Cup (0).
J Paint Trophy (2): Constantine 1, Huntington 1.
Play-Offs (3): Howson 2, Freedman 1.
Ground: Elland Road Stadium, Elland Rd, Leeds LS11 0ES. Telephone (0113) 367 6000.
Record Attendance: 57,892 v Sunderland, FA Cup 5th rd (replay), 15 March 1967.
Capacity: 39,450.
Manager: Gary McAllister.
Most League Goals: 98, Division 2, 1927–28.
Highest League Scorer in Season: John Charles, 42, Division 2, 1953–54.
Most League Goals in Total Aggregate: Peter Lorimer, 168, 1965–79 and 1983–86.
Most Capped Player: Lucas Radebe, 58 (70), South Africa.
Most League Appearances: Jack Charlton, 629, 1953–73.
Honours – Football League: Division 1 Champions – 1968–69, 1973–74, 1991–92. Division 2 Champions – 1923–24, 1963–64, 1989–90. **FA Cup:** Winners – 1972. **Football League Cup:** Winners – 1967–68. **European Competitions: European Fairs Cup:** Winners – 1967–68, 1970–71.
Colours: White shirts, white shorts, white stockings.

LEICESTER CITY   FL CHAMPIONSHIP 1

Bori Gabor (M)	5 10	11 00	Hungary	16 1 84	MTK Budapest
Campbell Dudley (F)	5 10	11 00	London	12 11 81	Birmingham C
Chambers Ashley (F)	5 10	11 06	Leicester	1 3 90	Scholar
Chambers James (D)	5 10	11 11	West Bromwich	20 11 80	Watford
Cisak Aleksander (G)	6 3	14 11	Krakow	19 5 89	Scholar
Clemence Stephen (M)	6 0	12 09	Liverpool	31 3 78	Birmingham C
Dodds Louis (F)	5 10	12 04	Leicester	8 10 86	Scholar
Fryatt Matty (F)	5 10	11 00	Nuneaton	5 3 86	Walsall
Gradel Max (M)	5 8	12 03	Ivory Coast	30 9 87	Scholar
Hayes Jonathan (M)	5 7	11 00	Dublin	9 7 87	Reading

Hayles Barry (F)	5 10	12 11	Lambeth	17 5 72	Plymouth Arg
Hellings Sergio (M)	6 0	12 00	Amsterdam	11 10 84	AGOVV
					Apeldoorn
Henderson Paul (G)	6 1	12 06	Sydney	22 4 76	Bradford C
Howard Steve (F)	6 3	15 00	Durham	10 5 76	Derby Co
Hume Iain (F)	5 7	11 02	Brampton	31 10 83	Tranmere R
King Andy (M)	6 0	11 10	Luton	29 10 88	Scholar
Kisnorbo Patrick (D)	6 1	11 11	Melbourne	24 3 81	Hearts
Kisnorbo Patrick (D)	6 1	11 11	Melbourne	24 3 81	Hearts
Laczko Zsolt (F)	6 0	12 11	Szeged	18 12 86	Olympiakos
Logan Conrad (G)	6 0	14 09	Letterkenny	18 4 86	Scholar
Mattock Joe (D)	5 11	11 04	Leicester	15 5 90	Scholar
McAuley Gareth (D)	6 4	13 12	Larne	5 12 79	Lincoln C
N'Gottu Bruno (D)	6 1	13 07	Lyon	10 6 71	Birmingham C
Oakley Matthew (M)	5 10	12 06	Peterborough	17 8 77	Derby Co
Odhiambo Eric (F)	5 9	11 00	Oxford	12 5 89	Scholar
Porter Levi (F)	5 4	10 05	Leicester	6 4 87	Scholar
Sappleton Reneil (M)	5 10	11 13	Kingston	8 12 89	QPR
Sheehan Alan (D)	5 11	11 02	Athlone	14 9 86	Scholar
Stearman Richard (D)	6 2	10 08	Wolverhampton	19 8 87	Scholar
Wesolowski James (M)	5 8	11 11	Sydney	25 8 87	Scholar
Worley Harry (D)	6 3	13 00	Warrington	25 11 88	Chelsea

League Appearances: Alnwick, B. 8; Bell, D. 6; Bori, G. 4(2); Campbell, D. 17(11); Chambers, A. 1(4); Chambers, J. 15(9); Clapham, J. 11; Clarke, C. 2; Clemence, S. 30(1); Cort, C. 7(7); De Vries, M. 5(1); Etuhu, K. 2(2); Fryatt, M. 21(9); Fulop, M. 24; Hayes, J. 1(6); Hayles, B. 9(9); Henderson, P. 14; Hendrie, L. 9; Howard, S. 20(1); Hume, I. 34(6); John, C. 7(4); Kaebi, H. 2(1); Kenton, D. 6(4); King, A. 5(6); Kishishev, R. 2(5); Kisnorbo, P. 41; Laczko, Z. 5(4); Mattock, J. 26(5); Maybury, A. 1; McAuley, G. 43(1); N'Gotty, B. 30(8); Newton, S. 7(3); Oakley, M. 20; Porter, L. 1(3); Sappleton, R. (1); Sheehan, A. 17(3); Stearman, R. 37(2); Wesolowski, J. 15(7); Worley, H. 1(1).
Goals – League (42): Hume 11 (1 pen), Howard 6 (1 pen), Campbell 4, Kisnorbo 3, Clemence 2, Fryatt 2, Hayles 2, John 2, McAuley 2, Stearman 2, De Vries 1, Hendrie 1, King 1, Sheehan 1, own goals 2.
Carling Cup (8): Campbell 1, Clemence 1, Cort 1, Fryatt 1, McAuley 1, Sheehan 1, Stearman 1, Wesolowski 1.
FA Cup (0).
Ground: Walkers Stadium, Filbert Way, Leicester LE2 7FL. Telephone (0844) 815 6000.
Record Attendance: 47,298 v Tottenham H, FA Cup 5th rd, 18 February 1928.
Capacity: 32,312.
Manager: Nigel Pearson.
Secretary: Andrew Neville.
Most League Goals: 109, Division 2, 1956–57.
Highest League Scorer in Season: Arthur Rowley, 44, Division 2, 1956–57.
Most League Goals in Total Aggregate: Arthur Chandler, 259, 1923–35.
Most Capped Player: John O'Neill, 39, Northern Ireland.
Most League Appearances: Adam Black, 528, 1920–35.
Honours – Football League: Division 2 Champions – 1924–25, 1936–37, 1953–54, 1956–57, 1970–71, 1979–80. **Football League Cup:** Winners – 1964, 1997, 2000.
Colours: All blue.

LEYTON ORIENT   FL CHAMPIONSHIP 1

Boyd Adam (F)	5 9	10 12	Hartlepool	25 5 82	Luton T
Chambers Adam (M)	5 10	11 08	Sandwell	20 11 80	Kidderminster H
Demetriou Jason (M)	5 11	10 08	Newham	18 11 87	Scholar

Gray Wayne (F)	5 10	11 05	Dulwich	7 11 80	Yeovil T
Melligan John (M)	5 9	11 02	Dublin	11 2 82	Cheltenham T
Mkandawire Tamika (D)	6 1	12 03	Malawi	28 5 83	Hereford U
Morris Glenn (G)	5 11	11 00	Woolwich	20 12 83	Scholar
Palmer Aiden (M)	5 8	10 04	Enfield	2 1 87	Scholar
Purches Stephen (D)	5 11	11 13	Ilford	14 1 80	Bournemouth
Saah Brian (M)	6 1	11 05	Rush Green	16 12 86	Scholar
Terry Paul (M)	5 10	12 06	Barking	3 4 79	Yeovil T
Thelwell Alton (D)	6 0	12 05	London	5 9 80	Hull C
Thornton Sean (M)	5 10	11 00	Drogheda	18 5 83	Doncaster R

League Appearances: Barcham, A. 15(10); Boyd, A. 40(4); Chambers, A. 45; Corden, W. 17(9); Daniels, C. 24(7); Demetriou, J. 31(12); Echanomi, E. (14); Fortune, C. (1); Gray, W. 30(8); Ibehre, J. 18(13); Melligan, J. 25(7); Mkandawire, T. 35; Morris, G. 16; Nelson, S. 30; Oji, S. 9(4); Palmer, A. 23; Pires, L. (1); Purches, S. 35(2); Saah, B. 23(2); Terry, P. 41(2); Thelwell, A. 27(1); Thornton, S. 22(9).

Goals – League (49): Boyd 14 (5 pens), Gray 8 (1 pen), Ibehre 7, Chambers 3, Demetriou 3, Melligan 3, Mkandawire 3, Thornton 3, Daniels 2, Barcham 1, Purches 1, Saah 1.

Carling Cup (2): Boyd 1 (pen), Demetriou 1.

FA Cup (4): Boyd 2 (1 pen), Gray 2.

J Paint Trophy (1): Echanomi 1.

Ground: Matchroom Stadium, Brisbane Road, Leyton, London E10 5NE. Telephone 0871 310 1881.

Record Attendance: 34,345 v West Ham U, FA Cup 4th rd, 25 January 1964.

Capacity: 9,271.

Manager: Martin Ling.

Secretary: Lindsey Freeman.

Most League Goals: 106, Division 3 (S), 1955–56.

Highest League Scorer in Season: Tom Johnston, 35, Division 2, 1957–58.

Most League Goals in Total Aggregate: Tom Johnston, 121, 1956–58, 1959–61.

Most Capped Players: Tunji Banjo, 7 (7), Nigeria; John Chiedozie, 7 (9), Nigeria; Tony Grealish, 7 (45), Eire.

Most League Appearances: Peter Allen, 432, 1965–78.

Honours – Football League: Division 3 Champions – 1969–70. Division 3 (S) Champions – 1955–56.

Colours: Red and white.

LINCOLN CITY   FL CHAMPIONSHIP 2

Beevers Lee (D)	6 1	13 00	Doncaster	4 12 83	Boston U
Brown Nat (F)	6 2	12 05	Sheffield	15 6 81	Huddersfield T
Clarke Shane (D)	6 1	13 03	Lincoln	7 11 87	Scholar
Duffy Ayden (M)	5 8	10 12	Kettering	16 11 86	Scholar
Forrester Jamie (F)	5 7	11 00	Bradford	1 11 74	Bristol R
Frecklington Lee (M)	5 8	11 00	Lincoln	8 9 85	Scholar
Green Paul (D)	5 8	10 04	Birmigham	15 4 87	Aston Villa
Hone Daniel (D)	6 2	12 00	Croydon	15 9 89	Scholar
John-Lewis Leneli (M)	5 10	11 10	Hammersmith	17 5 89	Scholar
Kerr Scott (M)	5 9	10 07	Leeds	11 12 81	Scarborough
N'Guessan Dany (M)	6 0	12 13	Ivry-sur-Seine	11 8 87	Boston U
Warlow Owain (M)	6 0	12 00	Treforest	3 7 88	Scholar
Wright Ben (F)	6 1	13 07	Munster	1 7 80	Viking Stavanger

League Appearances: Amoo, R. 10(3); Beevers, L. 37; Bencherif, H. 11(1); Brown, N. 23(4); Clarke, S. 11(5); Croft, G. 20; Dodds, L. 38(3); Duffy, A. 3(1); Forrester, J. 37(3); Frecklington, L. 31(3); Green, P. 36; Hand, J. 19(6); Hone, D. 20(3); John-Lewis, L. 15(6); Kerr, S. 33(3); King, G. 3(3); Marriott, A. 34; Moses, A. 16(2);

64

N'Guessan, D. 23(14); Pembleton, M. 4(2); Ridley, L. 15; Ryan, O. 4(11); Smith, Adam (4); Smith, B. 9; Stallard, M. 14(11); Torpey, S. 7(6); Warlow, O. 6(11); Watt, P. 1; Wright, B. 26(8).
Goals – League (61): Wright 15, Forrester 12 (2 pens), Dodds 9, N'Guessan 7 (1 pen), Frecklington 4, John-Lewis 3, Stallard 2, Amoo 1, Beevers 1, Bencherif 1, Green 1, Hone 1, Kerr 1, King 1, own goals 2.
Carling Cup (1): Forrester 1.
FA Cup (2): Forrester 1, own goal 1.
J Paint Trophy (2): Stallard 2 (1 pen).
Ground: Sincil Bank Stadium, Sincil Bank, Lincoln LN5 8LD. Telephone (0870) 899 2005.
Record Attendance: 23,196 v Derby Co, League Cup 4th rd, 15 November 1967.
Capacity: 10,055.
Manager: Peter Jackson.
Secretary: Fran Martin.
Most League Goals: 121, Division 3 (N), 1951–52.
Highest League Scorer in Season: Allan Hall, 41, Division 3 (N), 1931–32.
Most League Goals in Total Aggregate: Andy Graver, 144, 1950–55 and 1958–61.
Most Capped Player: Gareth McAuley, 5(10), Northern Ireland.
Most League Appearances: Grant Brown, 407, 1989–2002.
Honours – Football League: Division 3 (N) Champions – 1931–32, 1947–48, 1951–52. Division 4 Champions – 1975–76. **GM Vauxhall Conference:** Champions – 1987–88.
Colours: Red and white.

LIVERPOOL   FA PREMIERSHIP

Player					
Agger Daniel (D)	6 2	12 06	Hvidovre	12 12 84	Brondby
Ajdarevic Astrit (M)			Kosovo	20 9 90	Falkenberg
Anderson Paul (M)	5 9	10 04	Leicester	23 7 88	Hull C
Antwi-Birago Godwin (D)	6 1	13 09	Tafu	7 6 88	San Gregorio
Arbeloa Alvaro (D)	6 0	12 06	Salamanca	17 1 83	La Coruna
Babel Ryan (F)	6 1	12 04	Amsterdam	19 12 86	Ajax
Benayoun Yossi (M)	5 10	11 00	Beer Sheva	6 6 80	West Ham U
Bouzanis Dean (G)	6 1	13 05	Sydney	2 10 90	Sydney
Brouwer Jordy (F)			Den Haag	26 2 88	Ajax
Carragher Jamie (D)	5 9	12 01	Liverpool	28 1 78	Trainee
Carson Scott (G)	6 3	13 12	Whitehaven	3 9 85	Leeds U
Crouch Peter (F)	6 7	13 03	Macclesfield	30 1 81	Southampton
Darby Stephen (D)			Liverpool	6 10 88	Scholar
Duran Vazquez Fransisco (M)			Malaga	28 4 88	Malaga
El Zhar Nabil (F)	5 9	11 05	Rabat	27 8 86	St Etienne
Fabio Aurelio (M)	5 10	11 11	Sao Carlos	24 9 79	Valencia
Finnan Steve (M)	6 0	12 03	Limerick	24 4 76	Fulham
Flynn Ryan (M)	5 8	10 00	Scotland	4 9 88	Falkirk
Gerrard Steven (M)	6 0	12 05	Whiston	30 5 80	Trainee
Guthrie Danny (M)	5 9	11 06	Shrewsbury	18 4 87	Scholar
Hammill Adam (M)			Liverpool	25 1 88	Scholar
Hansen Martin (G)	6 2	12 07	Denmark	15 6 90	Scholar
Hobbs Jack (D)	6 3	13 05	Portsmouth	18 8 88	Lincoln C
Huth Ronald (D)			Asuncion	30 10 89	Tacuary
Hyypia Sami (D)	6 3	13 09	Porvoo	7 10 73	Willem II
Itandje Charles (G)	6 3	13 01	Bobigny	2 11 82	Lens
Kelly Martin (D)	6 3	12 02	Bolton	27 4 90	Scholar
Kuyt Dirk (F)	6 0	12 02	Katwijk	22 7 80	Feyenoord
Le Tallec Anthony (M)	6 0	12 00	Hennebont	3 10 84	Le Havre
Leto Sebastian (M)	6 2	12 04	San Vicente	30 8 86	Lanus

Player			Birthplace			Previous Club
Lindfield Craig (F)	6 0	10 05	Wirral	7	9 88	Scholar
Lucas (M)	5 10	11 09	Dourados	9	1 87	Gremio
Martin David (G)	6 1	13 04	Romford	22	1 86	Milton Keynes D
Mascherano Javier (M)	5 10	12 02	San Lorenzo	8	6 84	West Ham U
Nemeth Krisztian (M)	5 10	11 07	Gyor	5	1 89	
Paletta Gabriel (D)	6 1	13 07	Longchamps	15	2 86	Banfield
Pennant Jermaine (M)	5 8	10 01	Nottingham	15	1 83	Birmingham C
Plessis Damien (M)	6 3	12 02	Neuvy-sous-Bois	5	3 88	Lyon
Putterill Ray (M)	5 8	12 03	Liverpool	2	3 89	Scholar
Reina Jose (G)	6 2	14 06	Madrid	31	8 82	Villarreal
Riise John Arne (M)	6 1	14 00	Molde	24	9 80	Monaco
Roque Miguel (M)	6 2	12 03	Tremp	8	7 88	UE Lleida
San Jose Mikel (M)	6 0	12 04	Pamplona	30	5 89	Athletic Bilbao
Simon Andras (F)	6 0	11 05	Salgotarjan	30	3 90	MTK Budapest
Skrtel Martin (D)	6 3	12 10	Hamdlova	15	12 84	Zenit
Spearing Jay (D)			Wirral	25	11 88	Scholar
Threlfall Robbie (D)	5 11	11 00	Liverpool	25	11 88	Scholar
Torres Fernando (F)	5 9	12 03	Madrid	20	3 84	Atletico Madrid
Voronin Andrei (F)	5 11	11 08	Odessa	21	7 79	Leverkusen
Xabi Alonso (M)	6 0	12 02	Tolosa	25	11 81	Real Sociedad

League Appearances: Agger, D. 4(1); Alonso, X. 16(3); Arbeloa, A. 26(2); Babel, R. 15(15); Benayoun, Y. 15(15); Carragher, J. 34(1); Crouch, P. 9(12); Fabio Aurelio, 13(3); Finnan, S. 21(3); Gerrard, S. 32(2); Hobbs, J. 1(1); Hyypia, S. 24(3); Insua, E. 2(1); Kewell, H. 8(2); Kuyt, D. 24(8); Lucas, 12(6); Mascherano, J. 25; Pennant, J. 14(4); Plessis, D. 2; Reina, J. 38; Riise, J. 22(7); Sissoko, M. 6(3); Skrtel, M. 13(1); Torres, F. 29(4); Voronin, A. 13(6).

Goals – League (67): Torres 24, Gerrard 11 (3 pens) Crouch 5, Voronin 5, Babel 4, Benayoun 4, Kuyt 3 (2 pens), Alonso 2, Pennant 2, Fabio Aurelio 1, Hyypia 1, Mascherano 1, Sissoko 1, own goals 3.

Carling Cup (6): Torres 3, Benayoun 1, El-Zhar 1, Gerrard 1.

FA Cup (12): Benayoun 3, Gerrard 3, Crouch 2, Babel 1, Hyypia 1, Kuyt 1, Lucas 1.

Champions League (34): Kuyt 7, Gerrard 6 (2 pens), Torres 6, Babel 5, Crouch 4, Benayoun 3, Hyypia 2, Voronin 1.

Ground: Anfield Stadium, Anfield Road, Liverpool L4 0TH. Telephone (0151) 263 2361.

Record Attendance: 61,905 v Wolverhampton W, FA Cup 4th rd, 2 February 1952.

Capacity: 45,362.

Manager: Rafael Benitez.

Secretary: William Bryce Morrison.

Most League Goals: 106, Division 2, 1895–96.

Highest League Scorer in Season: Roger Hunt, 41, Division 2, 1961–62.

Most League Goals in Total Aggregate: Roger Hunt, 245, 1959–69.

Most Capped Player: Ian Rush, 67 (73), Wales.

Most League Appearances: Ian Callaghan, 640, 1960–78.

Honours – Football League: Division 1 – Champions 1900–01, 1905–06, 1921–22, 1922–23, 1946–47, 1963–64, 1965–66, 1972–73, 1975–76, 1976–77, 1978–79, 1979–80, 1981–82, 1982–83, 1983–84, 1985–86, 1987–88, 1989–90 (Liverpool have a record number of 18 League Championship wins). Division 2 Champions – 1893–94, 1895–96, 1904–05, 1961–62. **FA Cup:** Winners – 1965, 1974, 1986, 1989, 1992, 2001, 2006. **League Cup:** Winners – 1981, 1982, 1983, 1984, 1995, 2001, 2003. **League Super Cup:** Winners 1985–86. **European Competitions: European Cup:** Winners – 1976–77, 1977–78, 1980–81, 1983–84. **Champions League:** Winners – 2004–05. **UEFA Cup:** Winners – 1972–73, 1975–76, 2001. **Super Cup:** Winners – 1977, 2005. **Colours:** Red shirts, red shorts, red stockings.

Andrew Calvin (F)	6 0	12 11	Luton	19 12 86	Scholar
Asafu-Adjaye Ed (D)	5 11	12 04	London	22 12 88	Scholar
Barrett Zac (G)	6 2	13 03	Stevenage	26 5 88	Scholar
Bell David (M)	5 10	11 05	Kettering	21 1 84	Rushden & D
Beresford Marlon (G)	6 1	13 05	Lincoln	2 9 69	Barnsley
Brill Dean (G)	6 2	14 05	Luton	2 12 85	Scholar
Currie Darren (M)	5 11	12 07	Hampstead	29 11 74	Ipswich T
Davis Sol (D)	5 8	11 13	Cheltenham	4 9 79	Swindon T
Emanuel Lewis (D)	5 8	12 01	Bradford	14 10 83	Bradford C
Goodall Alan (D)	5 7	11 08	Birkenhead	2 12 81	Rochdale
Jackson Richard (D)	5 8	12 10	Whitby	18 4 80	Derby Co
Keane Keith (M)	5 9	11 02	Luton	20 11 86	Scholar
McVeigh Paul (F)	5 7	11 00	Belfast	6 12 77	Norwich C
Morgan Dean (M)	5 11	13 00	Enfield	3 10 83	Reading
O'Leary Stephen (M)	6 0	11 09	Barnet	12 2 85	Scholar
Parkin Sam (F)	6 2	13 00	Roehampton	14 3 81	Ipswich T
Perry Chris (D)	5 8	11 03	Carshalton	26 4 73	WBA
Robinson Steve (M)	5 9	11 02	Lisburn	10 12 74	Preston NE
Spring Matthew (M)	5 11	12 05	Harlow	17 11 79	Watford
Talbot Drew (F)	5 11	11 00	Barnsley	19 7 86	Sheffield W
Underwood Paul (M)	5 11	12 11	Wimbledon	16 8 73	Rushden & D

League Appearances: Alnwick, B. 4; Andrew, C. 19(20); Asafu-Adjaye, E. 7; Beavan, G. 1(1); Bell, D. 37; Brill, D. 37; Brkovic, A. (1); Charles, R. 6(1); Coyne, C. 18; Currie, D. 25(6); Davis, S. 15; Edwards, D. 18(1); Emanuel, L. 15(2); Fojut, J. 15(1); Forde, D. 5; Furlong, P. 24(8); Goodall, A. 25(4); Grant, A. 1(3); Howells, J. (1); Hutchison, D. 15(6); Jackson, R. 27(2); Keane, K. 27(1); Langley, R. (1); McVeigh, P. 15(10); Morgan, D. 8(8); O'Leary, S. 10(6); Parkin, S. 12(7); Perry, C. 35; Peschisolido, P. 2(2); Robinson, S. 24(3); Spring, M. 44; Talbot, D. 16(11); Wilson, M. 4.

Goals – League (43): Spring 9 (7 pens), Furlong 8, Parkin 5, Bell 4, Edwards 4, Andrew 2, Currie 2, Emanuel 2, Fojut 2, Charles 1, Goodall 1, Keane 1, Morgan 1, Perry 1.

Carling Cup (8): Furlong 2, Spring 2 (1 pen), Talbot 2, Bell 1, Robinson 1.

FA Cup (5): Andrew 2, Coyne 1, Fojut 1, own goal 1.

J Paint Trophy (5): Furlong 2, Hutchison 1, Peschisolido 1, Spring 1 (pen).

Ground: Kenilworth Stadium, 1 Maple Road, Luton, Beds LU4 8AW. Telephone (01582) 411 622.

Record Attendance: 30,069 v Blackpool, FA Cup 6th rd replay, 4 March 1959.

Capacity: 10,260.

Manager: Mick Harford.

Secretary: Cherry Newbery.

Most League Goals: 103, Division 3 (S), 1936–37.

Highest League Scorer in Season: Joe Payne, 55, Division 3 (S), 1936–37.

Most League Goals in Total Aggregate: Gordon Turner, 243, 1949–64.

Most Capped Player: Mal Donaghy, 58 (91), Northern Ireland.

Most League Appearances: Bob Morton, 494, 1948–64.

Honours – Football League: Championship 1: Winners – 2004–05. Division 2 Champions – 1981–82. Division 4 Champions – 1967–68. Division 3 (S) Champions – 1936–37. **Football League Cup:** Winners – 1987–88.

Colours: White shirts, black shorts, white stockings.

MACCLESFIELD TOWN   FL CHAMPIONSHIP 2

Blackman Nick (M)	6 2	11 08	Whitefield	11 11 89	Scholar
Brain Jonny (G)	6 3	13 05	Carlisle	11 2 83	Port Vale
Dunfield Terry (M)	5 11	12 04	Vancouver	20 2 82	Bury
Evans Gary (F)	6 0	12 08	Macclesfield	26 4 88	
Flynn Matthew (D)	6 0	11 08	Warrington	10 5 89	Warrington T
Green Francis (F)	5 9	11 04	Nottingham	25 4 80	Boston U
Gritton Martin (F)	6 1	12 02	Glasgow	1 6 78	Lincoln C
Hadfield Jordan (M)	5 10	11 04	Swinton	12 8 87	Stockport Co
Reid Izak (M)	5 5	10 05	Sheffield	08 7 87	Scholar
Teague Andrew (D)	6 2	12 00	Preston	5 2 86	Scholar
Thomas Danny (M)	5 7	10 10	Leamington Spa	1 5 81	Hereford U

League Appearances: Ashmore, J. 7(1); Ashton, N. 19; Blackman, N. 1(10); Brain, J. 29; Brisley, S. 9(1); Cresswell, R. 19; Dennis, K. (1); Dimech, L. 23(3); Doughty, P. 5(1); Dunfield, T. 40(1); Edghill, R. 13(2); Evans, G. 20(22); Green, F. 35(6); Gritton, M. 27(4); Hadfield, J. (2); Hessey, S. 26; Husbands, M. 2; Jennings, J. 5(6); Lee, T. 17(1); McIntyre, K. 22(1); McNulty, J. 13(6); Millar, C. (2); Morley, D. 2(2); Murray, A. 22(1); Onibuje, F. (1); Regan, C. 18(2); Reid, I. 17(8); Reid, L. 29(2); Rooney, J. 1(1); Spencer, S. (3); Symes, M. 10(4); Teague, A. 1; Thomas, D. 43; Tolley, J. 20(4); Walker, R. 10; Wiles, S. 1(16).
Goals – League (47): Green 11, Gritton 8, Evans 7, Thomas 4, Brisley 2, McIntyre 2 (2 pens), Reid I 2, Reid L 2, Tolley 2, Ashton 1, Blackman 1, Cresswell 1, Dunfield 1, McNulty 1, Morley 1, Symes 1.
Carling Cup (0).
FA Cup (1): Gritton 1.
J Paint Trophy (0).
Ground: Moss Rose Ground, London Road, Macclesfield, Cheshire SK11 0DQ. Telephone (01625) 264 686.
Record Attendance: 9,008 v Winsford U, Cheshire Senior Cup 2nd rd, 4 February 1948. **Capacity:** 6,335.
Manager: Keith Alexander.
Most League Goals: 66, Division 3, 1999–2000.
Highest League Scorer in Season: Jon Parkin, 22, League 2, 2004–05.
Most League Goals in Total Aggregate: Matt Tipton, 45, 2002–05; 2006–07.
Most Capped Player: George Abbey, 10(16), Nigeria.
Most League Appearances: Darren Tinson, 263, 1997–2003.
Honours – None.
Colours: Blue shirts, white shorts, blue stockings.

MANCHESTER CITY   FA PREMIERSHIP

Ball Michael (D)	5 10	12 02	Liverpool	2 10 79	PSV Eindhoven
Bianchi Rolando (F)	5 10	10 11	Lovere	15 2 83	Reggina
Bojinov Valeri (F)	5 10	12 04	Oriahovizca	15 2 86	Juventus
Caicedo Felipe (F)	6 1	12 08	Guayaquil	5 9 88	Basle
Clayton Adam (M)	5 9	11 11	Manchester	14 1 89	Scholar
Corluka Vedran (D)	6 3	13 03	Zagreb	9 2 86	Dynamo Zagreb
Corradi Bernardo (F)	6 0	13 10	Siena	30 3 76	Valencia
Dunne Richard (D)	6 2	15 12	Dublin	21 9 79	Everton
Elano (M)	5 9	10 03	Iracemapolis	14 6 81	Shakhter Donetsk
Etuhu Calvin (F)	6 0	12 09	Nigeria	30 5 88	Scholar
Evans Ched (F)	6 0	12 00	Rhyl	28 12 88	Scholar
Garrido Javier (M)	5 10	11 11	Irun	15 3 85	Real Sociedad
Gelson (M)	6 0	11 03	Cape Verde Islands	2 9 86	Sion

Hamann Dietmar (M)	6 3	13 01	Waldasson	27 8 73	Liverpool	
Hart Joe (G)	6 5	14 05	Shrewsbury	19 4 87	Shrewsbury T	
Ireland Stephen (F)	5 8	10 07	Cobh	22 8 86	Scholar	
Isaksson Andreas (G)	6 6	13 07	Smygehamn	3 10 81	Rennes	
Johnson Michael (M)	6 0	12 07	Urmston	3 3 88	Scholar	
Logan Shaleum (D)	5 8	10 01	Manchester	29 1 88	Scholar	
Marshall Paul (M)	6 1	12 03	Manchester	9 7 89	Scholar	
McDonald Clayton (D)	6 6	16 05	Liverpool	26 12 88	Scholar	
Mills Danny (D)	5 11	12 06	Norwich	18 5 77	Leeds U	
Mills Matthew (D)	6 3	12 12	Swindon	14 7 86	Southampton	
Mwaruwari Benjamin (F)	6 2	12 03	Harare	13 8 78	Portsmouth	
Obeng Curtis (D)	5 8	10 08	Manchester	14 2 89	Scholar	
Onuoha Nedum (D)	6 2	12 04	Warri	12 11 86	Scholar	
Petrov Martin (F)	6 0	12 02	Vzatza	15 1 79	Atletico Madrid	
Richards Micah (D)	5 11	13 00	Birmingham	24 6 88	Scholar	
Samaras Georgios (F)	6 3	13 07	Heraklion	21 2 85	Heerenveen	
Schmeichel Kasper (G)	6 1	13 00	Copenhagen	5 11 86	Scholar	
Sturridge Danny (F)	5 11	12 02	Birmingham	1 9 89	Scholar	
Vassell Darius (F)	5 9	13 00	Birmingham	13 6 80	Aston Villa	
Vidal Javan (D)	5 10	10 10	Manchester	10 5 89	Scholar	
Williamson Sam (D)	5 8	11 09	Macclesfield	15 10 87	Scholar	

League Appearances: Ball, M. 19(9); Bianchi, R. 7(12); Bojinov, V. 1(2); Caicedo, F. (10); Castillo, N. 2(5); Corluka, V. 34(1); Dunne, R. 36; Elano, 29(5); Etuhu, K. 2(4); Garrido, J. 21(6); Gelson, 21(5); Geovanni, 2(17); Hamann, D. 26(3); Hart, J. 26; Ireland, S. 32(1); Isaksson, A. 5; Jihai, S. 7(7); Johnson, M. 23; Mpenza, E. 8(7); Mwaruwari, B. 13; Onuoha, N. 13(3); Petrov, M. 34; Richards, M. 25; Samaras, G. 2(3); Schmeichel, K. 7; Sturridge, D. 2(1); Vassell, D. 21(6); Williamson, S. (1).

Goals – League (45): Elano 8 (2 pens), Vassell 6, Petrov 5, Bianchi 4, Ireland 4, Geovanni 3, Mwaruwari 3, Gelson 2, Johnson 2, Mpenza 2, Etuhu 1, Onuoha 1, Sturridge 1, own goals 3.

Carling Cup (4): Bianchi 1, Elano 1 (pen), Mpenza 1, Sammaras 1.

FA Cup (2): Elano 1, Sturridge 1.

Ground: The City of Manchester Stadium, SportCity, Manchester M11 3FF. Telephone (0870) 062 1894.

Record Attendance: (at Maine Road) 85,569 v Stoke C, FA Cup 6th rd, 3 March 1934 (British record for any game outside London or Glasgow) (at City of Manchester Stadium) 47,304 v Chelsea, FA Premier League, 28 February 2004.

Capacity: 47,715.

Manager: Mark Hughes.

Secretary: J. B. Halford.

Most League Goals: 108, Division 2, 1926–27, 108, Division 1, 2001–02.

Highest League Scorer in Season: Tommy Johnson, 38, Division 1, 1928–29.

Most League Goals in Total Aggregate: Tommy Johnson, 158, 1919–30.

Most Capped Player: Colin Bell, 48, England.

Most League Appearances: Alan Oakes, 565, 1959–76.

Honours – Football League: Division 1 Champions – 1936–37, 1967–68, 2001–02. Division 2 Champions – 1898–99, 1902–03, 1909–10, 1927–28, 1946–47, 1965–66. **FA Cup:** Winners – 1904, 1934, 1956, 1969. **Football League Cup:** Winners – 1970, 1976. **European Competitions: European Cup-Winners' Cup:** Winners – 1969–70.

Colours: Sky blue shirts, white shorts, sky blue stockings.

MANCHESTER UNITED   FA PREMIERSHIP

Amos Ben (G)	6 2	13 00	Macclesfield	10 4 90	Scholar	
Anderson (M)	5 8	10 07	Porto Alegre	13 4 88	Porto	
Brandy Febian (F)	5 5	10 00	Manchester	4 2 89	Scholar	
Brown Wes (D)	6 1	13 11	Manchester	13 10 79	Scholar	

Player	Ht	Wt	Birthplace	Born	Previous Club
Campbell Frazier (F)	5 11	12 04	Huddersfield	13 9 87	Scholar
Carrick Michael (M)	6 2	13 03	Wallsend	28 7 81	Tottenham H
Cathcart Craig (D)	6 2	11 06	Belfast	6 2 89	Scholar
Chester James (D)	5 10	11 13	Warrington	23 1 89	Scholar
Cleverley Tom (M)	5 8	10 07	Basingstoke	12 8 89	Scholar
Dong Fangzhuo (F)	6 0	12 07	Liaoning	23 1 85	Dalian Shide
Eagles Chris (M)	6 0	10 08	Hemel Hempstead	19 11 85	Scholar
Eckersley Richard (D)	5 9	11 09	Salford	12 3 89	Scholar
Evans Corry (M)	5 8	10 12	Belfast	30 7 90	Scholar
Evans Jonny (D)	6 2	12 02	Belfast	3 1 88	Scholar
Evra Patrice (D)	5 8	11 10	Dakar	15 5 81	Monaco
Ferdinand Rio (D)	6 2	13 12	Peckham	7 11 78	Leeds U
Fletcher Darren (M)	6 0	13 01	Edinburgh	1 2 84	Scholar
Foster Ben (G)	6 2	12 08	Leamington Spa	3 4 83	Stoke C
Galbraith Daniel (F)	5 9	10 03	Manchester	5 3 90	Scholar
Gibson Darron (M)	6 0	12 04	Londonderry	25 10 87	Scholar
Giggs Ryan (F)	5 11	11 00	Cardiff	29 11 73	School
Gray David (F)	5 11	11 02	Edinburgh	4 5 88	Scholar
Hargreaves Owen (M)	5 11	11 07	Calgary	20 1 81	Bayern Munich
Heaton Tom (G)	6 1	13 12	Chester	15 4 86	Scholar
Hewson Sam (M)	5 8	11 02	Bolton	28 11 88	Scholar
Kuszczak Tomasz (G)	6 3	13 03	Krosno Odrzansia	20 3 82	WBA
Manucho (F)	6 2	13 00	Luanda	7 3 83	Petro Atletico
Martin Lee (M)	5 10	10 03	Taunton	9 2 87	Scholar
Nani (M)	5 9	10 04	Amadora	17 11 86	Sporting Lisbon
Neville Gary (D)	5 11	12 04	Bury	18 2 75	Scholar
O'Shea John (D)	6 3	12 10	Waterford	30 4 81	Waterford
Park Ji-Sung (M)	5 9	11 06	Seoul	25 2 81	PSV Eindhoven
Pique Gerard (D)	6 3	12 10	Barcelona	2 2 87	Scholar
Possebon Rodrigo (M)	6 0	11 13	Sapucaia do Sul	13 2 89	Internacional
Ronaldo Cristiano (M)	6 1	12 04	Funchal	5 2 85	Sporting Lisbon
Rooney Wayne (F)	5 10	12 04	Liverpool	24 10 85	Everton
Saha Louis (F)	6 1	12 06	Paris	8 8 78	Fulham
Scholes Paul (M)	5 7	11 00	Salford	16 11 74	Scholar
Silvestre Mikael (D)	6 0	13 01	Chambray les Tours	9 8 77	Internazionale
Simpson Danny (D)	5 9	11 05	Salford	4 1 87	Scholar
Tevez Carlos (F)	5 8	11 11	Cuidadela	5 2 84	West Ham U
Van der Sar Edwin (G)	6 5	14 11	Voorhout	29 10 70	Fulham
Vidic Nemanja (D)	6 1	13 02	Uzice	21 10 81	Spartak Moscow
Zieler Ron-Robert (G)	6 1	11 07	Cologne	12 2 89	Scholar

League Appearances: Anderson, 16(8); Brown, W. 34(2); Campbell, F. (1); Carrick, M. 24(7); Eagles, C. 1(3); Evra, P. 33; Ferdinand, R. 35; Fletcher, D. 5(11); Foster, B. 1; Giggs, R. 26(5); Hargreaves, O. 16(7); Kuszczak, T. 8(1); Nani, 16(10); O'Shea, J. 10(18); Park, J. 8(4); Pique, G. 5(4); Ronaldo, C. 31(3); Rooney, W. 25(2); Saha, L. 6(11); Scholes, P. 22(2); Silvestre, M. 3; Simpson, D. 1(2); Tevez, C. 31(3); Van der Sar, E. 29; Vidic, N. 32.

Goals – League (80): Ronaldo 31 (4 pens), Tevez 14, Rooney 12, Saha 5 (2 pens), Giggs 3, Nani 3, Carrick 2, Ferdinand 2, Hargreaves 2, Brown 1, Park 1, Scholes 1, Vidic 1, own goals 2.

Carling Cup (0).

FA Cup (9): Ronaldo 3 (1 pen), Fletcher 2, Rooney 2, Nani 1, Tevez 1.

Champions League (20): Ronaldo 8 (1 pen), Rooney 4, Tevez 4, Pique 2, Ferdinand 1, Scholes 1.

Community Shield (1): Giggs 1.

Ground: Old Trafford, Sir Matt Busby Way, Manchester M16 0RA. Telephone (0161) 868 8000.

Record Attendance: 76,962 Wolverhampton W v Grimsby T, FA Cup semi-final. 25 March 1939. **Club record:** 76,098 v Blackburn R, Premier League, 31 March 2007. **Capacity:** 76,212.
Manager: Sir Alex Ferguson CBE.
Secretary: Ken Ramsden.
Most League Goals: 103, Division 1, 1956–57 and 1958–59.
Highest League Scorer in Season: Dennis Viollet, 32, 1959–60.
Most League Goals in Total Aggregate: Bobby Charlton, 199, 1956–73.
Most Capped Player: Bobby Charlton, 106, England.
Most League Appearances: Bobby Charlton, 606, 1956–73.
Honours – FA Premier League: Champions – 1992–93, 1993–94, 1995–96, 1996–97, 1998–99, 1999–2000, 2000–01, 2002–03, 2006–07, 2007–08. **Football League:** Division 1 Champions – 1907–8, 1910–11, 1951–52, 1955–56, 1956–57, 1964–65, 1966–67. Division 2 Champions – 1935–36, 1974–75. **FA Cup:** Winners – 1909, 1948, 1963, 1977, 1983, 1985, 1990, 1994, 1996, 1999, 2004. **Football League Cup:** Winners – 1991–92, 2006. **European Competitions: European Cup:** Winners – 1967–68. **Champions League:** Winners – 1998–99, 2007–08. **European Cup-Winners' Cup:** Winners – 1990–91. **Super Cup:** Winners – 1991. **Inter-Continental Cup:** Winners – 1999.
Colours: Red shirts, white shorts, black stockings.

MANSFIELD TOWN BLUE SQUARE PREMIER

Arnold Nathan (F)	5 8	10 07	Mansfield	26 7 87	Scholar	
Boulding Mick (F)	5 10	11 05	Sheffield	8 2 76	Rotherham U	
Boulding Rory (F)	6 0	12 02	Sheffield	21 7 88	Ilkeston T	
Buxton Jake (D)	6 1	13 05	Sutton-in-Ashfield	4 3 85	Scholar	
Dawson Stephen (M)	5 6	11 01	Dublin	4 12 85	Leicester C	
Jelleyman Gareth (D)	5 10	11 05	Holywell	14 11 80	Peterborough U	
John-Baptiste Alex (D)	5 11	11 11	Sutton-in-Ashfield	31 1 86	Scholar	
Kitchen Ashley (D)	5 11	11 06	Edwinstowe	10 10 88	Scholar	
Mullins Johnny (D)	5 11	12 06	Hampstead	6 11 85	Scholar	
Trimmer Lewis (F)	5 7	10 00	Norwich	30 10 89		
White Jason (G)	6 2	12 13	Mansfield	28 1 83	Trainee	
Wood Chris (M)	6 0	10 11	Worksop	24 1 87	Scholar	

League Appearances: Arnold, N. 21(11); Atkinson, W. 10(2); Bell, L. 23; Boulding, M. 43; Boulding, R. 4(7); Briggs, K. 10(3); Brown, S. 15(14); Bullock, L. 5; Burrell, W. (1); Buxton, J. 40; D'Laryea, J. 23(6); Dawson, S. 43; Goward, R. (2); Hamshaw, M. 45; Holmes, I. 4(12); Horlock, K. (5); Jelleyman, G. 37(2); John-Baptiste, A. 25; Kitchen, A. 1; Louis, J. 14(4); Martin, D. 21(5); McAliskey, J. 9(7); McAllister, S. 5(2); McIntosh, M. 9(2); Muggleton, C. 36; Mullins, J. 42(1); Reet, D. (2); Sleath, D. 2(5); Trimmer, L. (2); Wainwright, N. 1(4); White, J. 10(3); Wood, C. 8(5).
Goals – League (48): Boulding M 21 (4 pens) Arnold 4, Brown 4, Louis 4 (1 pen), Buxton 2, Dawson 2, Hamshaw 2, McAliskey 2, Mullins 2, Bell 1, Holmes 1, McIntosh 1, own goals 2.
Carling Cup (1): Mullins 1.
FA Cup (8): Boulding M 3, Holmes 2, Boulding R 1, Hamshaw 1, Jelleyman 1.
J Paint Trophy (0).
Ground: Field Mill Ground, Quarry Lane, Mansfield, Nottinghamshire NG18 5DA. Telephone (0870) 756 3160.
Record Attendance: 24,467 v Nottingham F, FA Cup 3rd rd, 10 January 1953.
Capacity: 9,365.
Manager: Billy McEwan.
Secretary: Sharon Roberts.
Most League Goals: 108, Division 4, 1962–63.
Highest League Scorer in Season: Ted Harston, 55, Division 3 (N), 1936–37.

Most League Goals in Total Aggregate: Harry Johnson, 104, 1931–36.
Most Capped Player: John McClelland, 6 (53), Northern Ireland.
Most League Appearances: Rod Arnold, 440, 1970–83.
Honours – Football League: Division 3 Champions – 1976–77. Division 4
Champions – 1974–75. **Freight Rover Trophy:** Winners – 1986–87.
Colours: Amber shirts with royal blue trim, royal blue shorts with amber side
stripe, amber stockings.

MIDDLESBROUGH   FA PREMIERSHIP

Aliadiere Jeremie (F)	6 0	11 00	Rambouillet	30 3 83	Arsenal
Alves Afonso (F)	6 1	11 09	Belo Horizonte	30 1 81	Heerenveen
Arca Julio (M)	5 9	11 13	Quilmes	31 1 81	Sunderland
Bates Matthew (D)	5 10	12 03	Stockton	10 12 86	Scholar
Boateng George (M)	5 9	12 06	Nkawkaw	5 9 75	Aston Villa
Cattermole Lee (M)	5 10	11 13	Stockton	21 3 88	Scholar
Craddock Tom (F)	5 11	12 00	Darlington	14 10 86	Scholar
Downing Stewart (M)	5 11	10 04	Middlesbrough	22 7 84	Scholar
Franks Jonathan (M)	5 9	11 03	Stockton	8 4 90	Scholar
Goulon Herold (M)	6 4	14 07	Paris	12 6 88	Lyon
Grounds Jonathan (D)	6 1	13 10	Ingleby Barwick	2 2 88	Scholar
Hines Sebastian (M)	6 2	12 04	Wetherby	29 5 88	Scholar
Huth Robert (D)	6 3	14 07	Berlin	18 8 84	Chelsea
Johnson Adam (M)	5 9	9 11	Sunderland	14 7 87	Scholar
Johnson John (D)			Middlesbrough	16 9 88	Scholar
Jones Brad (G)	6 3	12 01	Armidale	19 3 82	Trainee
McMahon Anthony (D)	5 10	11 04	Bishop Auckland	24 3 86	Scholar
Mido (F)	6 2	14 09	Cairo	23 2 83	Tottenham H
O'Neil Gary (M)	5 10	11 00	Bromley	18 5 83	Portsmouth
Owens Graeme (M)	5 10	12 00	Ashington	1 6 88	Scholar
Pogatetz Emanuel (D)	6 2	13 05	Steinbock	16 1 83	Graz
Riggott Chris (D)	6 2	13 09	Derby	1 9 80	Derby Co
Schwarzer Mark (G)	6 4	14 07	Sydney	6 10 72	Bradford C
Shawky Mohamed (M)	5 11	11 11	Port Said	5 10 81	Al-Ahly
Steele Jason (G)	6 2	12 13	Bishop Auckland	18 8 90	Scholar
Taylor Andrew (D)	5 10	11 04	Hartlepool	1 8 86	Trainee
Tuncay Sanli (F)	5 10	11 00	Sakarya	16 1 82	Fenerbahce
Turnbull Ross (G)	6 4	15 00	Bishop Auckland	4 1 85	Trainee
Walker Josh (M)	5 11	11 13	Newcastle	21 2 89	Scholar
Wheater David (D)	6 4	12 12	Redcar	14 2 87	Scholar
Williams Rhys (D)			Perth	14 7 88	Scholar
Young Luke (D)	6 0	12 04	Harlow	19 7 79	Chalton Ath

League Appearances: Aliadiere, J. 26(3); Alves, A. 7(4); Arca, J. 23(1); Boateng,
G. 29(4); Cattermole, L. 10(14); Craddock, T. 1(2); Davies, A. 3(1); Downing, S.
38; Grounds, J. 5; Hines, S. (1); Hutchinson, B. (8); Huth, R. 9(4); Johnson, A.
3(16); Jones, B. 1; Lee, D. 5(9); McMahon, T. (1); Mido, 8(4); O'Neil, G. 25(1);
Pogatetz, E. 23(1); Riggott, C. 9(1); Rochemback, F. 21(5); Schwarzer, M. 34;
Shawki, M. 3(2); Taylor, A. 18(1); Tuncay, S. 27(7); Turnbull, R. 3; Wheater, D. 34;
Woodgate, J. 16; Yakubu, A. 2; Young, L. 35.
Goals – League (43): Downing 9 (2 pens), Tuncay 8, Alves 6, Aliadiere 5, Wheater
3, Arca 2, Mido 2, Boateng 1, Cattermole 1, Hutchinson 1, Huth 1, Johnson 1, Rig-
gott 1, Rochemback 1, Young 1.
Carling Cup (2): Lee 1, Rochemback 1.
FA Cup (5): Downing 1, Lee 1, Wheater 1, own goals 2.
Ground: Riverside Stadium, Middlesbrough TS3 6RS. Telephone (0844) 499 6789.

Record Attendance: Ayresome Park: 53,536 v Newcastle U, Division 1, 27 December 1949. Riverside Stadium: 34,814 v Newcastle U, FA Premier League, 5 March 2003. **Capacity:** 35,041.
Manager: Gareth Southgate.
Secretary: Karen Nelson.
Most League Goals: 122, Division 2, 1926–27.
Highest League Scorer in Season: George Camsell, 59, Division 2, 1926–27 (Second Division record).
Most League Goals in Total Aggregate: George Camsell, 325, 1925–39.
Most Capped Player: Wilf Mannion, 26, England.
Most League Appearances: Tim Williamson, 563, 1902–23.
Honours – Football League: Division 1 Champions 1994–95. Division 2 Champions 1926–27, 1928–29, 1973–74. **Football League Cup:** Winners – 2004. **Amateur Cup:** Winners – 1895, 1898. **Anglo-Scottish Cup:** Winners – 1975–76.
Colours: Red shirts with white chestband, red shorts, red stockings.

MILLWALL   FL CHAMPIONSHIP 1

Alexander Gary (F)	6 0	13 04	Lambeth	15 8 79	Leyton Orient
Barron Scott (D)	5 9	9 08	Preston	2 9 85	Ipswich T
Bignot Marcus (D)	5 7	11 04	Birmingham	22 8 74	QPR
Bowes Gary (F)	5 11	12 00	Bramborough		Scholar
Brammer David (M)	5 10	12 00	Bromborough	28 2 75	Stoke C
Brkovic Ahmet (M)	5 8	11 11	Dubrovnik	23 9 74	Luton T
Dunne Alan (D)	5 10	10 13	Dublin	23 8 82	Trainee
Ebsworth Darren (D)	5 10	10 02	London	23 8 90	Scholar
Edwards Preston (G)	6 0	12 07	Edmonton	5 9 89	Scholar
Forbes Adrian (F)	5 8	11 10	Greenford	23 1 79	Blackpool
Frampton Andrew (D)	5 11	10 10	Wimbledon	3 9 79	Brentford
Fuseini Ali (M)	5 6	9 10	Ghana	7 12 88	Scholar
Grabban Lewis (F)	6 0	11 03	Croydon	12 1 88	Crystal Palace
Hackett Chris (M)	6 0	11 06	Oxford	1 3 83	Hearts
Harris Neil (F)	5 11	12 09	Orsett	12 7 77	Nottingham F
Laird Marc (M)	6 1	10 07	Edinburgh	23 1 86	Manchester C
Martin David (M)	5 9	10 10	Erith	3 6 85	Crystal Palace
Pidgeley Lenny (G)	6 3	13 09	Isleworth	7 2 84	Chelsea
Robinson Paul (D)	6 1	11 09	Barnet	7 1 82	Scholar
Savage Bas (F)	6 3	13 08	London	7 1 82	Brighton & HA
Senda Danny (D)	5 10	10 02	Harrow	17 4 81	Wycombe W
Smith Ryan (M)	5 10	11 00	Islington	10 11 86	Derby Co
Spiller Danny (M)	5 8	11 00	Maidstone	10 10 81	Gillingham
Whitbread Zak (D)	6 2	11 04	Houston	10 1 84	Liverpool
Zebroski Chris (F)	6 1	11 08	Swindon	29 10 86	Plymouth Arg

League Appearances: Akinfenwa, A. 1(6); Alexander, G. 32(4); Ardley, N. (1); Bakayogo, Z. 5(5); Barron, S. 7(5); Bignot, M. 17(5); Bowes, G. (1); Brammer, D. 23; Brkovic, A. 15(10); Cochrane, J. (1); Craig, T. 5; Day, C. 5; Douglas, R. 7; Dunne, A. 17(2); Edwards, P. (1); Evans, R. 21; Forbes, A. 6(5); Frampton, A. 28(2); Fuseini, A. 31(6); Gaynor, R. 1(2); Grabban, L. 10(3); Hackett, C. 1(5); Harris, N. 19(8); Hodge, B. 10; Hoskins, W. 9(1); Karacan, J. 7; Laird, M. 16(1); Martin, D. 7(4); May, B. 4(4); O'Hara, J. 10(4); Pidgeley, L. 13; Robinson, P. 45; Savage, B. 9(2); Senda, D. 39(1); Shaw, R. 16(2); Simpson, J. 34(7); Smith, R. 9(7); Spiller, D. 6; Whitbread, Z. 21(2).
Goals – League (45): Alexander 7 (1 pen), Simpson 6, Dunne 3 (1 pen), Grabban 3, Harris 3 (2 pens), Robinson P 3, Whitbread 3, Brkovic 2, Fuseini 2, Hoskins 2, Martin 2, O'Hara 2, Savage 2, Craig 1, Frampton 1, Laird 1, Senda 1, Spiller 1.
Carling Cup (0).
FA Cup (7): Hoskins 2, Alexander 1, Brkovic 1, Dunne 1 (pen), May 1, Simpson 1.

73

J Paint Trophy (2): May 1, Simpson 1.
Ground: The Den, Zampa Road, London SE16 3LN. Telephone (020) 7232 1222.
Record Attendance: 20,093 v Arsenal, FA Cup 3rd rd, 10 January 1994. **Capacity:** 20,146.
Manager: Kenny Jackett.
Secretary: Yvonne Haines.
Most League Goals: 127, Division 3 (S), 1927–28.
Highest League Scorer in Season: Richard Parker, 37, Division 3 (S), 1926–27.
Most League Goals in Total Aggregate: Teddy Sheringham, 93, 1984–91 and Neil Harris, 101, 1995–2004; 2006–08.
Most Capped Player: Eamonn Dunphy, 22 (23), Republic of Ireland.
Most League Appearances: Barry Kitchener, 523, 1967–82.
Honours – Football League: Division 2 Champions – 1987–88, 2000–01. Division 3 (S) Champions – 1927–28, 1937–38. Division 4 Champions – 1961–62. **Football League Trophy:** Winners – 1982–83.
Colours: Royal blue shirts, white shorts, royal blue stockings.

MILTON KEYNES DONS   FL CHAMPIONSHIP 1

Abbey Nathan (G)	6 1	11 13	Islington	11	7 78	Brentford
Andrews Keith (M)	6 0	12 04	Dublin	13	9 80	Hull C
Baldock Sam (F)	5 7	10 07	Buckingham	15	3 89	Scholar
Cameron Colin (M)	5 8	11 00	Kirkcaldy	23	10 72	Coventry C
Carayol Mustapha (M)	5 10	11 11	Gambia	10	4 90	
Diallo Drissa (D)	6 1	11 13	Nouadhibou	4	1 73	Sheffield W
Dobson Craig (M)	5 6	10 06	Chingford	23	1 84	Stevenage B
Dyer Lloyd (M)	5 8	10 02	Birmingham	13	9 82	Millwall
Gallen Kevin (F)	5 11	13 03	Hammersmith	21	9 75	QPR
Gueret Willy (G)	6 1	13 02	Saint Claude	3	8 73	Swansea C
Howell Luke (D)	5 10	10 05	Cuckfield	5	1 87	Gillingham
Johnson Jemal (F)	5 8	11 09	New Jersey	3	5 84	Wolverhampton W
Lewington Dean (D)	5 11	11 07	Kingston	18	5 84	Scholar
Mitchell Paul (M)	5 9	12 01	Manchester	26	8 81	Scholar
Navarro Alan (M)	5 10	11 07	Liverpool	31	5 81	Macclesfield T
O'Hanlon Sean (D)	6 1	12 05	Southport	2	1 83	Swindon T
Regan Carl (D)	5 11	11 12	Liverpool	14	1 80	Macclesfield T
Stirling Jude (D)	6 2	11 12	Enfield	29	6 82	Peterborough U
Swailes Danny (D)	6 3	12 06	Bolton	1	4 79	Macclesfield T
Wilbraham Aaron (F)	6 3	12 04	Knutsford	21	10 79	Hull C
Wright Mark (M)	5 11	11 00	Wolverhampton	24	2 82	Walsall

League Appearances: Andrews, K. 40(1); Baldock, S. (5); Broughton, D. 2(11); Cameron, C. 21(8); Carbon, M. (3); Diallo, D. 30; Dobson, C. 1; Dyer, L. 43(2); Edds, G. 2(5); Gallen, K. 15(9); Gueret, W. 46; Hadfield, J. 6(7); Howell, L. 8; Johnson, J. 17(22); Knight, L. 15(2); Lewington, D. 45; Livermore, J. (5); McGovern, J. 2(1); Miles, J. 7(5); Murphy, K. 1(2); Navarro, A. 38(1); O'Hanlon, S. 41(2); Regan, C. 8(1); Smart, B. (8); Stirling, J. 21(13); Swailes, D. 40; Wilbraham, A. 28(7); Wright, M. 29(5).
Goals – League (82): Wright 13, Andrews 12, Dyer 11, Wilbraham 10, Gallen 8, Johnson 5, Knight 4, O'Hanlon 4, Swailes 4, Cameron 3, Navarro 3, Diallo 2, Stirling 2, Regan 1.
Carling Cup (5): Broughton 1, Gallen 1 (pen), Knight 1, McGovern 1, own goal 1.
FA Cup (1): Johnson 1 (pen).
J Paint Trophy (9): Andrews 2 (2 pens), Johnson 2, Wright 2, Cameron 1, O'Hanlon 1, Swailes 1.
Ground: *Stadium*mk, Stadium Way, Milton Keynes, Buckinghamshire MK9 1FA. Telephone (01908) 622 922.

Record Attendance: 30,115 v Manchester U, FA Premier League, 9 May 1993 (at Selhurst Park). **Capacity:** 8,836.
Manager: Roberto Di Matteo.
Head of Football Operations: Kirstine Nicholson.
Most League Goals: 97, Division 3, 1983–84.
Highest League Scorer in Season: Alan Cork, 29, 1983–84.
Most League Goals in Total Aggregate: Alan Cork, 145, 1977–92.
Most Capped Player: Kenny Cunningham, 40 (72), Republic of Ireland.
Most League Appearances: Alan Cork, 430, 1977–92.
Honours – Football League: Championship 2 Champions – 2007–08. Division 4 Champions – 1982–83. **FA Cup:** Winners – 1987–88. **Johnstone's Paint Trophy:** Winners – 2007–08.
Colours: White shirts, white shorts, white stockings.

MORECAMBE   FL CHAMPIONSHIP 2

Adams Danny (D)	6 1	14 00	Altrincham	3 1 76	Huddersfield T
Artell Dave (D)	6 3	14 01	Rotherham	22 11 80	Chester C
Baker Carl (M)	6 2	12 06	Whiston	26 12 82	Southport
Bentley Jim (M)	6 1	12 00	Liverpool	11 6 76	Telford U
Blinkhorn Matthew (F)	5 11	10 10	Blackpool	2 3 85	Blackpool
Curtis Wayne (F)	6 0	14 05	Barrow	6 3 80	Holker Old Boys
Davies Scott (G)			Blackpool	27 2 87	Scholar
Drummond Stuart (M)	6 2	13 08	Preston	11 12 75	Shrewsbury T
Howard Michael (D)	5 7	10 10	Birkenhead	2 12 78	Swansea C
Hunter Garry (M)	5 7	10 03	Morecambe	1 1 85	Scholar
Lloyd Paul (M)			Preston	25 3 87	Scholar
McLachlan Fraser (M)	5 11	12 11	Manchester	9 11 82	Mansfield T
McStay Henry (D)	6 0	11 11	Co Armagh	6 3 85	Antwerp
Stanley Craig (M)	6 0	12 06	Coventry	3 3 83	Hereford U
Thompson Gary (F)	6 0	14 02	Kendal	24 11 80	Scholar
Twiss Michael (F)	5 11	13 05	Salford	26 12 77	Chester C
Yates Adam (D)	5 11	13 10	Stoke	28 5 83	Leek T

League Appearances: Adams, D. 42; Allen, D. 16(4); Artell, D. 34(2); Baker, C. 40(2); Bentley, J. 43; Blinkhorn, M. 36(5); Burns, J. 4(3); Cresswell, R. 2; Curtis, W. 16(20); Davies, S. 10; Drench, S. 3(1); Drummond, S. 17(1); Grand, S. 4(2); Howard, M. 2(2); Hunter, G. 19(19); Jalal, S. 12; Lewis, J. 19; Lloyd, P. 1(6); Loach, S. 2; McLachlan, F. 1; McStay, H. 12(1); Newby, J. 11(21); Sorvel, N. 14(8); Stanley, C. 41; Thompson, G. 36(4); Twiss, M. 27(9); Yates, A. 42(2).
Goals – League (59): Baker 10 (3 pens), Blinkhorn 10, Thompson 7 (1 pen), Bentley 6, Newby 6, Twiss 6, Artell 3, Curtis 2, Drummond 2, Stanley 2, Grand 1, Hunter 1, own goals 3.
Carling Cup (5): Artell 1, Baker 1 (pen), Bentley 1, Newby 1, Thompson 1.
J Paint Trophy (6): Newby 3 (1 pen), Blinkhorn 1, Burns 1, Hunter 1.
Ground: Christie Park, Lancaster Road, Morecambe LA4 5TJ. Telephone (01524) 411 797.
Record Attendance: 9,383 v Weymouth FA Cup 3rd rd, 6 January 1962.
Capacity: 6,030.
Manager: Sammy McIlroy.
Secretary: Neil Marsdin.
Most League Goals: 86, Conference, 2002–03.
Highest League Scorer in Season: Justin Jackson, 29, 1999–2000.
Most League Goals in Total Aggregate: 100, John Norman, 1994–99; 2000–02.
Most League Appearances: 209, Dave McKeanney, 1995–2004.
Honours – Conference: Promoted to Football League (play-offs) 2006–07. **Presidents Cup:** Winners – 1991–92. **FA Trophy:** Winners 1973–74. **Lancs Senior Cup:** Winners 1967–68. **Lancs Combination:** Champions – 1924–25, 1961–62,

1962–63, 1967–68. **Lancs Combination Cup:** Winners – 1926–27, 1945–46, 1964–65, 1966–67, 1967–68. **Lancs Junior Cup:** Winners – 1927, 1928, 1962, 1963, 1969, 1986, 1987, 1994, 1996, 1999, 2004.
Colours: Red shirts, white shorts, white stockings.

NEWCASTLE UNITED   FA PREMIERSHIP

Ameobi Foluwashola (F)	6 3	11 13	Zaria	12 10 81	Scholar
Barton Joey (M)	5 11	12 05	Huyton	2 9 82	Manchester C
Beye Habib (D)	6 0	12 06	Suresnes	19 10 77	Marseille
Butt Nicky (M)	5 10	11 05	Manchester	21 1 75	Manchester U
Cacapa Claudio (D)	6 0	12 01	Lavras	29 5 76	Lyon
Carroll Andy (F)	6 3	13 08	Newcastle	6 1 89	Scholar
Diagne-Faye Aboulaye (M)	6 2	13 10	Dakar	26 2 78	Bolton W
Duff Damien (M)	5 9	12 06	Ballyboden	2 3 79	Chelsea
Edgar David (D)	6 2	12 13	Ontario	19 5 87	Scholar
Emre Belezoglu (M)	5 8	10 10	Istanbul	7 9 80	Internazionale
Forster Fraser (G)	6 4	14 00	Newcastle	17 3 88	Scholar
Geremi (M)	5 9	13 01	Bafoussam	20 12 78	Chelsea
Given Shay (G)	6 0	13 03	Lifford	20 4 76	Blackburn R
Harper Steve (G)	6 2	13 10	Easington	14 3 75	Seaham Red Star
Jose Enrique (D)	6 0	12 00	Valencia	23 1 86	Villarreal
Kadar Tamas (D)	6 0	12 10	Veszprem	14 3 90	Zalaegerszegi
Krul Tim (G)	6 2	11 08	Den Haag	3 4 88	Den Haag
LuaLua Kazenga (F)	5 11	12 00	Kinshasa	10 12 90	Scholar
Martins Obafemi (F)	5 10	11 06	Lagos	28 10 84	Internazionale
Milner James (M)	5 10	11 00	Leeds	4 1 86	Leeds U
N'Zogbia Charles (M)	5 9	11 00	Le Havre	28 5 86	Le Havre
Ngo Baheng Wesley (F)	5 11	11 06	Blanc Mesnil	23 9 89	Le Havre
Owen Michael (F)	5 8	10 12	Chester	14 12 79	Liverpool
Rozehnal David (D)	6 3	12 04	Stembeck	5 7 80	Paris St Germain
Smith Alan (F)	5 10	12 04	Rothwell	28 10 80	Manchester U
Soderberg Ole (D)			Norrkoping	20 7 90	BK Hacken
Taylor Steven (D)	6 1	13 01	Greenwich	23 1 86	Scholar
Tozer Ben (D)	6 1	13 05	Plymouth	1 3 90	Swindon T
Viduka Mark (F)	6 2	15 01	Melbourne	9 10 75	Middlesbrough

League Appearances: Ameobi, S. 2(4); Barton, J. 20(3); Beye, H. 27(2); Butt, N. 35; Cacapa, C. 16(3); Carr, S. 8(2); Carroll, A. 1(3); Diagne-Faye, A. 20(2); Diatta, L. (2); Duff, D. 12(4); Edgar, D. 2(3); Emre, B. 6(8); Geremi, 24(3); Given, S. 19; Harper, S. 19(2); Jose Enrique, 18(5); LuaLua, K. (2); Martins, O. 23(8); Milner, J. 25(4); N'Zogbia, C. 27(4); Owen, M. 24(5); Ramage, P. (3); Rozehnal, D. 16(5); Smith, A. 26(7); Solano, N. (1); Taylor, S. 29(2); Viduka, M. 19(7).
Goals – League (45): Owen 11 (2 pens), Martins 9 (1 pen), Viduka 7, Butt 3, N'Zogbia 3, Milner 2, Barton 1 (pen), Beye 1, Cacapa 1, Diagne-Faye 1, Emre 1, Geremi 1, Taylor 1, own goals 3.
Carling Cup (2): Martins 1, Owen 1.
FA Cup (4): Cacapa 1, Duff 1, Milner 1, Owen 1.
Ground: St James' Park, Newcastle upon Tyne NE1 4ST. Telephone (0191) 201 8400.
Record Attendance: 68,386 v Chelsea, Division 1, 3 Sept 1930. **Capacity:** 52,387.
Manager: Kevin Keegan.
Most League Goals: 98, Division 1, 1951–52.
Highest League Scorer in Season: Hughie Gallacher, 36, Division 1, 1926–27.
Most League Goals in Total Aggregate: Jackie Milburn, 177, 1946–57.
Most Capped Player: Shay Given, 77 (86), Republic of Ireland.
Most League Appearances: Jim Lawrence, 432, 1904–22.

Honours – Football League: Division 1 – Champions 1904–05, 1906–07, 1908–09, 1926–27, 1992–93. Division 2 Champions – 1964–65. **FA Cup:** Winners – 1910, 1924, 1932, 1951, 1952, 1955. **Texaco Cup:** Winners – 1973–74, 1974–75. **European Competitions: European Fairs Cup:** Winners – 1968–69. **Anglo-Italian Cup:** Winners – 1973. **Intertoto Cup:** Winners – 2006.
Colours: Black and white striped shirts, black shorts, black stockings.

NORTHAMPTON TOWN   FL CHAMPIONSHIP 1

Akinfenwa Adebayo (F)	5 11	13 07	Nigeria	10 5 82	Millwall
Bunn Mark (G)	6 0	12 02	Camden	16 11 84	Scholar
Coke Gilles (M)	6 0	11 11	London	3 6 86	Mansfield T
Crowe Jason (D)	5 9	10 09	Sidcup	30 9 78	Grimsby T
Doig Chris (D)	6 2	12 06	Dumfries	13 2 81	Nottingham F
Dolman Liam (D)	6 0	14 05	Brixworth	26 9 87	Scholar
Dunn Chris (G)	6 5	13 11	Essex	23 10 87	Scholar
Dyer Alex (M)	5 8	11 07	Sweden	1 6 90	Scholar
Gilligan Ryan (M)	5 10	11 07	Swindon	18 1 87	Watford
Gyepes Gabor (D)	6 3	13 01	Hungary	26 6 81	Wolverhampton W
Henderson Ian (F)	5 10	11 06	Thetford	24 1 85	Norwich C
Holt Andy (D)	6 1	12 07	Stockport	21 4 78	Wrexham
Hughes Mark (D)	6 1	13 10	Liverpool	9 12 86	Everton
Jackman Danny (D)	5 4	10 00	Worcester	3 1 83	Gillingham
Larkin Colin (F)	5 9	11 07	Dundalk	27 4 82	Chesterfield

League Appearances: Aiston, S. (1); Akinfenwa, A. 13(2); Bowditch, D. 7(3); Branston, G. 3; Bunn, M. 45; Burnell, J. 26(7); Coke, G. 11(9); Crowe, J. 44; Doig, C. 15; Dolman, L. 27(3); Dunn, C. 1; Dyer, A. 3(3); Gilligan, R. 28(10); Gyepes, G. 13; Hayes, J. 5(6); Henderson, I. 9(14); Holt, A. 29(7); Hubertz, P. 33(7); Hughes, M. 34(1); Jackman, D. 34(5); Johnson, Bradley 22(1); Johnson, Brett 10(6); Jones, D. 27(6); Kirk, A. 25; Larkin, C. 14(19); Little, M. 17; May, D. (2); Russell, A. 11(2).
Goals – League (60): Hubertz 13 (3 pens), Kirk 8, Akinfenwa 7, Coke 5, Crowe 4, Gilligan 4, Bradley Johnson 3, Jones 3, Bowditch 2, Holt 2, Larkin 2, Doig 1, Dolman 1, Dyer 1, Hughes 1, Jackman 1, Russell 1, own goal 1.
Carling Cup (2): Bradley Johnson 1, Kirk 1.
FA Cup (4): Kirk 2, Bradley Johnson 1, Larkin 1.
J Paint Trophy (0).
Ground: Sixfields Stadium, Upton Way, Northampton NN5 5QA. Telephone 01604 683 700
Record Attendance: (at County Ground): 24,523 v Fulham, Division 1, 23 April 1966; (at Sixfields Stadium): 7,557 v Manchester C, Division 2, 26 September 1998.
Capacity: 7,653.
Manager: Stuart Gray.
Secretary: Norman Howells.
Most League Goals: 109, Division 3, 1962–63 and Division 3 (S), 1952–53.
Highest League Scorer in Season: Cliff Holton, 36, Division 3, 1961–62.
Most League Goals in Total Aggregate: Jack English, 135, 1947–60.
Most Capped Player: Edwin Lloyd Davies, 12 (16), Wales.
Most League Appearances: Tommy Fowler, 521, 1946–61.
Honours – Football League: Division 3 Champions – 1962–63. Division 4 Champions – 1986–87.
Colours: Claret shirts, white shorts, claret stockings.

NORWICH CITY   FL CHAMPIONSHIP

Chadwick Luke (M)	5 11	11 08	Cambridge	18 11 80	Stoke C
Croft Lee (D)	5 11	12 12	Wigan	21 6 85	Manchester C
Cureton Jamie (F)	5 8	10 07	Bristol	28 8 75	Colchester U
Daley Luke (F)			Northampton	10 11 89	Scholar
Doherty Gary (D)	6 2	13 04	Carndonagh	31 1 80	Tottenham H
Drury Adam (D)	5 10	11 08	Cottenham	29 8 78	Peterborough U
Eagle Robert (M)	5 7	10 08	Ipswich	23 2 87	Scholar
Fotheringham Mark (M)	5 10	11 04	Dundee	22 10 83	Aarau
Gilks Matthew (G)	6 3	13 12	Rochdale	4 6 82	Rochdale
Lappin Simon (M)	5 9	10 10	Glasgow	25 1 83	St Mirren
Marshall David (G)	6 3	13 04	Glasgow	5 3 85	Celtic
Martin Chris (F)	6 2	12 06	Norwich	4 11 88	Scholar
Otsemobor John (D)	5 10	12 07	Liverpool	23 3 83	Crewe Alex
Pattison Matt (M)	5 9	11 00	Johannesburg	27 10 86	Newcastle U
Russell Darel (M)	5 10	11 09	Mile End	22 10 80	Stoke C
Shackell Jason (D)	6 3	12 09	Hitchin	27 9 83	Scholar
Spillane Michael (M)	5 9	11 10	Cambridge	23 3 89	Scholar
Velasco Juan (M)	5 10	11 11	Seville	17 5 77	Espanyol

League Appearances: Bates, M. 2(1); Bertrand, R. 18; Brellier, J. 8(2); Brown, C. 8(6); Camara, M. 20(1); Chadwick, L. 9(4); Croft, L. 19(22); Cureton, J. 29(12); Doherty, G. 32(2); Drury, A. 9; Dublin, D. 28(9); Evans, C. 20(8); Fotheringham, M. 26(2); Gibbs, K. 6(1); Hartson, J. 2(2); Henry, J. 1(2); Huckerby, D. 26(8); Jarvis, R. (1); Jarvis, R. 4; Lappin, S. 15; Marshall, D. 46; Martin, C. 3(4); Murray, I. 8(1); Otsemobor, J. 41(2); Pattison, M. 22(5); Pearce, A. 8(3); Rigters, M. (2); Russell, D. 37(2); Shackell, J. 36(3); Smith, J. 6(3); Spillane, M. 4(2); Strihavka, D. 3(7); Taylor, M. 8; Velasco, J. 2(3).
Goals – League (49): Cureton 12 (2 pens), Evans 10 (1 pen), Dublin 7, Huckerby 5 (1 pen), Russell 4, Fotheringham 2, Brown 1, Chadwick 1, Croft 1, Lappin 1, Otsemobor 1, Strihavka 1, Taylor 1, own goals 2.
Carling Cup (6): Cureton 2, Dublin 1, Fotheringham 1, Lappin 1, Russell 1.
FA Cup (2): Doherty 1, Dublin 1.
Ground: Carrow Road, Norwich NR1 1JE. Telephone (01603) 760 760.
Record Attendance: 43,984 v Leicester C, FA Cup 6th rd, 30 March 1963.
Capacity: 26,034.
Manager: Glenn Roeder.
Secretary: Kevan Platt.
Most League Goals: 99, Division 3 (S), 1952–53.
Highest League Scorer in Season: Ralph Hunt, 31, Division 3 (S), 1955–56.
Most League Goals in Total Aggregate: Johnny Gavin, 122, 1945–54, 1955–58.
Most Capped Player: Mark Bowen, 35 (41), Wales.
Most League Appearances: Ron Ashman, 592, 1947–64.
Honours – Football League: Division 1 Champions – 2003–04. Division 2 Champions – 1971–72, 1985–86. Division 3 (S) Champions – 1933–34. **Football League Cup:** Winners – 1962, 1985.
Colours: Yellow shirts, green shorts, yellow stockings.

NOTTINGHAM FOREST   FL CHAMPIONSHIP

Agogo Junior (F)	5 10	11 07	Accra	1 8 79	Bristol R
Bencherif Hamza (D)	5 9	12 03	France	9 2 88	Scholar
Bennett Julian (D)	6 1	13 00	Nottingham	17 12 84	Walsall
Breckin Ian (D)	6 2	13 05	Rotherham	24 2 75	Wigan Ath
Byrne Mark (M)			Dublin	9 11 88	Crumlin

Chambers Luke (D)	6 1	11 13	Kettering	28 9 85	Northampton T
Clingan Sammy (M)	5 11	11 06	Belfast	13 1 84	Wolverhampton W
Cohen Chris (M)	5 11	10 11	Norwich	5 3 87	Yeovil T
Davies Arron (M)	5 9	11 00	Cardiff	22 6 84	Yeovil T
Gamble Paddy (G)			Nottingham	1 9 88	Scholar
Heath Joseph (D)			Birkenhead	4 10 88	Scholar
Holt Grant (F)	6 1	14 02	Carlisle	12 4 81	Rochdale
Lockwood Matt (D)	5 11	11 10	Southend	17 10 76	Leyton Orient
McCleary Garath (F)	5 10	12 06	Oxford	15 5 87	Bromley
McGugan Lewis (M)	5 9	11 06	Long Eaton	25 10 88	Scholar
Moloney Brendan (M)	6 1	11 02	Enfield	18 1 89	Scholar
Morgan Wes (D)	6 2	14 00	Nottingham	21 1 84	Scholar
Newbold Adam (F)			Nottingham	16 11 89	Scholar
Perch James (D)	5 11	11 05	Mansfield	29 9 85	Scholar
Redmond Shane (G)			Dublin	23 3 89	Scholar
Roberts Dale (M)	6 3	11 06	Horden	22 10 86	Scholar
Sharpe Tom (D)			Nottingham	12 10 88	Scholar
Sinclair Emile (F)	6 0	11 04	Leeds	20 12 87	Scholar
Smith Paul (G)	6 3	14 00	Epsom	17 12 79	Southampton
Staples Reece (M)			Nottingham	10 9 89	Scholar
Tait Richard (D)			Galashiels	2 12 89	Curzon Ashton
Thornhill Matt (M)	6 1	13 10	Nottingham	11 10 88	Scholar
Tyson Nathan (F)	5 10	10 02	Reading	4 5 82	Wycombe W
Wilson Kelvin (D)	6 2	12 12	Nottingham	3 9 85	Preston NE

League Appearances: Agogo, J. 27(8); Bastians, F. (1); Bennett, J. 33(1); Breckin, I. 22(6); Byrne, M. (1); Chambers, L. 40(2); Clingan, S. 40(2); Cohen, C. 40(1); Commons, K. 29(10); Davies, A. 9(10); Dobie, S. 1(1); Holt, Grant 22(10); Hoskins, W. 2; Lennon, N. 15(3); Lockwood, M. 11; McCleary, G. 3(5); McGugan, L. 24(9); Moloney, B. 2; Morgan, W. 37(5); Ormerod, B. 13; Perch, J. 19(11); Sinclair, E. (12); Smith, P. 46; Thornhill, M. 5(9); Tyson, N. 26(8); Wilson, K. 40(2).

Goals – League (64): Agogo 13 (1 pen), Commons 9, Tyson 9 (1 pen), Chambers 6, McGugan 6, Bennett 4, Holt Grant 3 (1 pen), Cohen 2, Ormerod 2, Thornhill 2, Breckin 1, Clingan 1, Davies 1, McCleary 1, Morgan 1, Sinclair 1, own goals 2.

Carling Cup (2): Smith 1, Tyson 1.

FA Cup (4): Tyson 2, Commons 1, McGugan 1.

J Paint Trophy (2): Chambers 2.

Ground: The City Ground, Nottingham NG2 5FJ. Telephone (0115) 982 4444.

Record Attendance: 49,946 v Manchester U, Division 1, 28 October 1967.

Capacity: 30,576.

Manager: Colin Calderwood.

Football Administrator: Jane Carnelly.

Most League Goals: 110, Division 3 (S), 1950–51.

Highest League Scorer in Season: Wally Ardron, 36, Division 3 (S), 1950–51.

Most League Goals in Total Aggregate: Grenville Morris, 199, 1898–1913.

Most Capped Player: Stuart Pearce, 76 (78), England.

Most League Appearances: Bob McKinlay, 614, 1951–70.

Honours – Football League: Division 1 – Champions 1977–78, 1997–98. Division 2 Champions – 1906–07, 1921–22. Division 3 (S) Champions – 1950–51. **FA Cup:** Winners – 1898, 1959. **Football League Cup:** Winners – 1977–78, 1978–79, 1988–89, 1989–90. **Anglo-Scottish Cup:** Winners – 1976–77. **Simod Cup:** Winners – 1989. **Zenith Data Systems Cup:** Winners – 1991–92. **European Competitions: European Cup:** Winners – 1978–79, 1979–80. **Super Cup:** Winners – 1979–80.

Colours: Red shirts, white shorts, red stockings.

NOTTS COUNTY   FL CHAMPIONSHIP 2

Butcher Richard (M)	6 0	13 01	Peterborough	22 1 81	Peterborough U
Edwards Mike (D)	6 1	13 01	North Ferriby	25 4 80	Grimsby T
Hunt Steve (D)	6 1	13 05	Southampton	11 11 84	Colchester U
MacKenzie Neil (M)	6 2	12 05	Birmingham	15 4 76	Scunthorpe U
Mayo Paul (D)	5 11	11 09	Lincoln	13 10 81	Lincoln C
Pilkington Kevin (G)	6 1	13 00	Hitchin	8 3 74	Mansfield T
Sandercombe Tim (G)	6 4	13 12	Plymouth	15 6 89	Plymouth Arg
Smith Jay (M)	5 7	10 01	London	25 9 81	Southend U
Strachan Gavin (M)	5 10	11 07	Aberdeen	23 12 78	Peterborough U
Tann Adam (D)	6 0	11 05	Fakenham	12 5 82	Leyton Orient
Weir-Daley Spencer (F)	5 9	10 11	Leicester	5 9 85	Nottingham F
Weston Myles (F)	5 11	12 05	Lewisham	12 3 88	Charlton Ath

League Appearances: Bastians, F. 5; Branston, G. 1; Butcher, R. 46; Canoville, L. 32(3); Corden, W. 7(2); Crow, D. 13(1); Dudfield, L. 26(7); Edwards, M. 19; Frost, S. (2); Gibb, A. 9; Hoult, R. 14; Hunt, S. 36(1); Jarvis, R. 17; Johnson, M. 11(1); Lee, J. 22(9); Lindfield, C. 3; MacKenzie, N. 24(5); Mayo, P. 27(2); McCann, A. 13(9); Parkinson, A. 11(12); Pearce, K. 8; Pilkington, K. 32; Sam, H. 7(13); Silk, G. 22(11); Smith, J. 16(4); Somner, M. 12(4); Strachan, G. 7; Tann, A. 40(1); Weir-Daley, S. 12(18); Weston, M. 14(11).
Goals – League (37): Butcher 12, MacKenzie 6 (2 pens), Weir-Daley 3, Crow 2, Hunt 2, Jarvis 2, Silk 2, Dudfield 1, Edwards 1, Johnson 1, Lee 1, Lindfield 1, Pearce 1, Sam 1, Tann 1.
Carling Cup (0).
FA Cup (3): Dudfield 2, Sam 1.
J Paint Trophy (0).
Ground: Meadow Lane Stadium, Meadow Lane, Nottingham NG2 3HJ. Telephone (0115) 952 9000.
Record Attendance: 47,310 v York C, FA Cup 6th rd, 12 March 1955. **Capacity:** 20,300.
Manager: Ian McParland.
Secretary: Tony Cuthbert.
Most League Goals: 107, Division 4, 1959–60.
Highest League Scorer in Season: Tom Keetley, 39, Division 3 (S), 1930–31.
Most League Goals in Total Aggregate: Les Bradd, 125, 1967–78.
Most Capped Player: Kevin Wilson, 15 (42), Northern Ireland.
Most League Appearances: Albert Iremonger, 564, 1904–26.
Honours – Football League: Division 2 Champions – 1896–97, 1913–14, 1922–23. Division 3 Champions – 1997–98. Division 3 (S) Champions – 1930–31, 1949–50. Division 4 Champions – 1970–71. **FA Cup:** Winners – 1893–94. **Anglo-Italian Cup:** Winners – 1995.
Colours: Black and white striped shirts, black shorts, black stockings.

OLDHAM ATHLETIC   FL CHAMPIONSHIP 1

Alessandra Lewis (F)	5 9	11 07	Oldham	8 2 89	Scholar
Allott Mark (M)	5 11	11 07	Manchester	3 10 77	Chesterfield
Black Paul (D)	6 0	12 10	Middleton	18 1 90	Scholar
Crossley Mark (G)	6 3	15 09	Barnsley	16 6 69	Fulham
Davies Craig (F)	6 2	13 05	Burton-on-Trent	9 1 86	Wolverhampton W
Eardley Neal (D)	5 11	11 10	Llandudno	6 11 88	Scholar
Gregan Sean (D)	6 2	15 00	Billingham	29 3 74	Leeds U
Hazell Reuben (D)	5 11	12 05	Birmingham	24 4 79	Chesterfield
Hughes Lee (F)	5 10	12 00	Smethwick	22 5 76	WBA

Kamud'a Kalala Jean-Paul (M)	5 10	12 02	Lubumbashi	16 2 82	Yeovil T
Liddell Andy (F)	5 7	11 11	Leeds	28 6 73	Sheffield U
Lomax Kelvin (D)	5 10	12 03	Bury	12 11 86	Scholar
Smalley Deane (M)	6 0	11 10	Chadderton	5 9 88	Scholar
Stam Stefan (D)	6 2	13 02	Amersfoort	14 9 79	
Taylor Chris (M)	5 11	11 00	Oldham	20 12 86	Scholar
Thompson John (D)	6 0	12 01	Dublin	12 10 81	Nottingham F
Wolfenden Matthew (M)	5 9	11 01	Oldham	23 7 87	Scholar

League Appearances: Alessandra, L. 12(3); Allott, M. 34(8); Beresford, M. 5; Bertrand, R. 21; Black, P. (2); Chalmers, A. (2); Constantine, L. 7(1); Crossley, M. 38; Davies, C. 31(1); Eardley, N. 40(2); Giddings, S. 2; Gregan, S. 15; Hazell, R. 32(2); Hughes, L. 15(3); Jarrett, J. 12(3); Kamud'a Kalala, J. 14(6); Kelly, A. (1); Kilkenny, N. 19(1); Liddell, A. 16(2); Livermore, D. 10; Lomax, K. 17(4); McDonald, G. 31(4); O'Donnell, R. 3(1); Pearson, M. (1); Ricketts, M. 8(1); Robertson, J. 2(1); Smalley, D. 19(18); Stam, S. 34(2); Taylor, C. 40(2); Thompson, J. 6(1); Trotman, N. 16(1); Wolfenden, M. 7(18).
Goals – League (58): Davies 10 (1 pen), Hughes 7 (2 pens), Eardley 6 (3 pens), Taylor 5, Allott 4, McDonald 4, Jarrett 3, Alessandra 2, Constantine 2, Liddell 2 (1 pen), Ricketts 2 (1 pen), Smalley 2, Wolfenden 2, Hazell 1, Kilkenny 1, Livermore 1, Robertson 1, Trotman 1, own goals 2.
Carling Cup (4): Davies 1, Kamudimba Kalala 1, Kilkenny 1, Smalley 1.
FA Cup (6): McDonald 2, Davies 1, Hughes 1, Kilkenny 1, Trotman 1.
J Paint Trophy (3): Davies 1, Liddell 1, Wolfenden 1.
Ground: Boundary Park, Furtherwood Road, Oldham OL1 2PA. Telephone (0871) 226 2235.
Record Attendance: 46,471 v Sheffield W, FA Cup 4th rd, 25 January 1930.
Capacity: 10,850.
Manager: John Sheridan.
Secretary: Alan Hardy.
Most League Goals: 95, Division 4, 1962–63.
Highest League Scorer in Season: Tom Davis, 33, Division 3 (N), 1936–37.
Most League Goals in Total Aggregate: Roger Palmer, 141, 1980–94.
Most Capped Player: Gunnar Halle, 24 (64), Norway.
Most League Appearances: Ian Wood, 525, 1966–80.
Honours – Football League: Division 2 Champions – 1990–91, Division 3 (N) Champions – 1952–53. Division 3 Champions – 1973–74.
Colours: Blue shirts, blue shorts, white stockings.

PETERBOROUGH UNITED   FL CHAMPIONSHIP 1

Blackett Shane (D)	6 0	12 11	Luton	3 10 82	Dagenham & R
Blanchett Danny (M)	5 11	11 12	Derby	12 3 88	Cambridge C
Boyd George (M)	5 10	11 07	Stevenage	2 10 85	Stevenage B
Charnock Kieran (D)	6 1	13 07	Preston	3 8 84	Northwich Vic
Crow Danny (F)	5 10	11 00	Great Yarmouth	26 1 86	Norwich C
Day Jamie (M)	5 9	10 06	Wycombe	7 5 86	Scholar
Hatch Liam (F)	6 4	13 09	Hitchin	3 4 84	Barnet
Howe Rene (F)	6 0	14 03	Bedford	22 10 86	Kettering T
Hyde Micah (M)	5 10	11 02	Newham	10 11 74	Burnley
Jalal Shwan (G)	6 2	14 00	Baghdad	14 8 83	Woking
Keates Dean (M)	5 6	10 06	Walsall	30 6 78	Walsall
Lee Charlie (M)	5 11	11 07	Whitechapel	5 1 87	Tottenham H
Lewis Joe (G)	6 5	12 10	Bury St Edmunds	6 10 87	Norwich C
Low Josh (M)	6 0	14 00	Bristol	15 2 79	Leicester C
Mackail-Smith Craig (F)	6 3	12 04	Hertford	25 2 84	Dagenham & R
McKeown James (G)	6 1	13 07	Birmingham	24 7 89	Scholar

McLean Aaron (F)	5 8	10 03	Hammersmith	25 5 83	Grays Ath
Morgan Craig (D)	6 0	11 00	Asaph	16 6 85	Milton Keynes D
Newton Adam (M)	5 10	11 00	Ascot	4 12 80	West Ham U
Potter Alfie (M)	5 7	9 06	Peterborough	9 1 89	Millwall
Smith Adam (D)	5 7	10 05	Lingwood	11 9 85	Kings Lynn
Tyler Mark (G)	5 11	12 00	Norwich	2 4 77	Trainee
Westwood Chris (D)	5 11	12 10	Dudley	13 2 77	Walsall
Whelpdale Chris (M)	6 0	12 08	Harold Wood	27 1 87	Billericay T
Williams Tom (M)	5 11	12 06	Carshalton	8 7 80	Wycombe W

League Appearances: Blackett, S. 9(2); Blanchett, D. 1; Boyd, G. 41(5); Branston, G. 1(1); Charnock, K. 10; Crow, D. 2(2); Day, J. 42; Gnapka, C. 25(3); Hatch, L. 1(10); Howe, R. 2(13); Hughes, J. 2(5); Hyde, M. 33(4); Jalal, S. 7; Keates, D. 33(7); Lee, C. 32(10); Lewis, J. 22; Low, J. 9(6); Mackail-Smith, C. 34(2); McKeown, J. (1); McLean, A. 45; Mitchell, S. 1(4); Morgan, C. 41; Newton, A. 26(6); Potter, A. (2); Rendell, S. 3(7); Strachan, G. (3); Tyler, M. 17; Westwood, C. 35(2); Whelpdale, C. 29(6); Williams, T. 3(4).
Goals – League (84): McLean 29 (3 pens), Boyd 12, Mackail-Smith 12 (1 pen), Lee 6, Keates 5, Day 3, Rendell 3, Whelpdale 3, Crow 2, Hatch 2, Low 2, Morgan 2, Howe 1, Hughes 1, own goal 1.
Carling Cup (2): Boyd 1, own goal 1.
FA Cup (12): Mackail-Smith 7, McLean 3, Boyd 1, Lee 1.
J Paint Trophy (4): Boyd 1, Lee 1, McLean 1, own goal 1.
Ground: London Road Stadium, Peterborough PE2 8AL. Telephone (01733) 563 947.
Record Attendance: 30,096 v Swansea T, FA Cup 5th rd, 20 February 1965.
Capacity: 15,000.
Manager: Darren Ferguson.
Secretary: Karen Turner.
Most League Goals: 134, Division 4, 1960–61.
Highest League Scorer in Season: Terry Bly, 52, Division 4, 1960–61.
Most League Goals in Total Aggregate: Jim Hall, 122, 1967–75.
Most Capped Player: James Quinn, 9 (50), Northern Ireland.
Most League Appearances: Tommy Robson, 482, 1968–81.
Honours – Football League: Division 4 Champions – 1960–61, 1973–74.
Colours: Blue shirts, white shorts, blue stockings.

PLYMOUTH ARGYLE   FL CHAMPIONSHIP

Abdou Nadjim (M)	5 10	11 02	Martigues	13 7 84	Sedan
Barnes Ashley (F)	6 0	12 00	Bath	30 10 89	Paulton R
Clark Chris (F)	5 7	10 05	Aberdeen	15 9 80	
Doumbe Stephen (D)	6 1	12 05	Paris	28 0 79	Hibernian
Easter Jermaine (F)	5 9	12 02	Cardiff	15 1 82	Wycombe W
Fallon Rory (F)	6 2	11 09	Gisborne	20 3 82	Swansea C
Folly Yoann (M)	5 9	11 04	Togo	6 6 85	Sheffield W
Halmosi Peter (M)	5 10	10 12	Szombathely	25 9 79	Debrecen
Larrieu Romain (G)	6 2	13 00	Mont-de-Marsan	31 8 76	ASOA Valence
Mackie Jamie (F)	5 8	11 00	Dorking	22 9 85	Exeter C
MacLean Steve (F)	5 11	12 06	Edinburgh	23 8 82	Cardiff C
McCormick Luke (G)	6 0	13 12	Coventry	15 8 83	Scholar
Paterson Jim (M)	5 11	12 13	Bellshill	25 9 79	
Sawyer Gary (D)	6 0	11 08	Bideford	5 7 85	Scholar
Seip Marcel (D)	6 0	12 04	Wenschoten	5 4 82	Heerenveen
Smith Dan (M)	5 10	10 07	Saltash	5 10 86	Scholar
Summerfield Luke (M)	6 0	11 00	Ivybridge	6 12 87	Scholar
Timar Krisztian (D)	6 3	13 08	Budapest	4 10 79	Ferencvaros

League Appearances: Abdou, N. 22(9); Anderson, R. 14; Buzsaky, A. 8(3); Chadwick, N. 3(6); Clark, C. 8(4); Connolly, P. 42; Djordjic, B. 1; Douglas, R. 1; Doumbe, S. 10(2); Easter, J. 20(12); Ebanks-Blake, S. 19(6); Fallon, R. 13(16); Folly, Y. 1(3); Gosling, D. 5(5); Halmosi, P. 41(2); Hayles, B. 21(2); Hodges, L. 20(7); Jutkiewicz, L. 1(2); Larrieu, R. 15; MacLean, S. 14(3); Mackie, J. 4(9); Martin, L. 10(2); McCormick, D. 30; Nalis, L. 35(5); Norris, D. 27; Paterson, J. 7(1); Sawyer, G. 28(3); Seip, M. 32(2); Smith, D. (2); Summerfield, L. 5(2); Teale, G. 8(4); Timar, K. 36(2); Wotton, P. 5(3).
Goals – League (60): Ebanks-Blake 11 (4 pens), Halmosi 8, Fallon 7, Easter 6, Norris 5, MacLean 3, Mackie 3, Timar 3, Chadwick 2, Hayles 2, Martin 2, Abdou 1, Connolly 1, Nalis 1, Paterson 1, Sawyer 1, Seip 1, Wotton 1 (pen), own goal 1.
Carling Cup (4): Ebanks-Blake 1, Hodges 1, Summerfield 1, own goal 1.
FA Cup (4): Abdou 1, Clark 1, Ebanks-Blake 1, Halmosi 1.
Ground: Home Park, Plymouth, Devon PL2 3DQ. Telephone (01752) 562 561.
Record Attendance: 43,596 v Aston Villa, Division 2, 10 October 1936.
Capacity: 20,000.
Manager: Paul Sturrock.
Secretary: Carole Rowntree.
Most League Goals: 107, Division 3 (S), 1925–26 and 1951–52.
Highest League Scorer in Season: Jack Cock, 32, Division 3 (S), 1926–27.
Most League Goals in Total Aggregate: Sammy Black, 180, 1924–38.
Most Capped Player: Moses Russell, 20 (23), Wales.
Most League Appearances: Kevin Hodges, 530, 1978–92.
Honours – Football League: Division 2 Champions – 2003–04. Division 3 (S) Champions – 1929–30, 1951–52. Division 3 Champions – 1958–59, 2001–02.
Colours: Green shirts, white shorts, black stockings.

PORTSMOUTH   FA PREMIERSHIP

Ashdown Jamie (G)	6 1	13 05	Reading	30 11 80	Reading
Begovic Asmir (G)	6 6	13 01	Trebinje	20 6 87	La Louviere
Campbell Sol (D)	6 2	14 05	Newham	18 9 74	Arsenal
Christophe Jean-Francois (M)	6 1	13 01	Creil	13 6 82	Lens
Cranie Martin (D)	6 1	12 09	Yeovil	23 9 86	Southampton
Davis Sean (M)	5 10	12 00	Clapham	20 9 79	Tottenham H
Defoe Jermain (F)	5 7	10 04	Beckton	7 10 82	Tottenham H
Diarra Lassana (M)	5 8	11 02	Paris	10 3 85	Arsenal
Diop Papa Bouba (M)	6 4	14 12	Dakar	28 1 78	Fulham
Distin Sylvain (D)	6 3	14 06	Bagnolet	16 12 77	Manchester C
Duffy Richard (D)	5 10	9 05	Swansea	30 8 85	Swansea C
Hreidarsson Hermann (D)	6 3	12 12	Reykjavik	11 7 74	Charlton Ath
Hughes Richard (M)	6 0	13 03	Glasgow	25 6 79	Bournemouth
James David (G)	6 4	14 13	Welwyn	1 8 70	Manchester C
Johnson Glen (D)	6 0	13 04	Greenwich	23 8 84	Chelsea
Kanu Nwankwo (F)	6 5	13 00	Owerri	1 8 76	WBA
Kilbey Tom (M)	6 3	13 08	Waltham Forest	19 10 90	Millwall
Kranjcar Niko (M)	6 1	12 00	Zagreb	13 8 84	Hajduk Split
Lauren (D)	5 11	11 02	Londi Kribi	19 1 77	Arsenal
Muntari Sulley Ali (M)	5 10	12 00	Konongo	27 8 84	Udinese
Mvuemba Arnold (M)	5 8	10 07	Alencon	28 1 85	Rennes
Nugent Dave (F)	5 11	12 13	Liverpool	2 5 85	Preston NE
Pamarot Noe (D)	5 11	13 07	Fontenay-sous-Bois	14 4 79	Tottenham H
Pedro Mendes (M)	5 9	12 04	Guimaraes	26 2 79	Tottenham H
Primus Linvoy (D)	5 10	12 04	Forest Gate	14 9 73	Reading
Songo'o Frank (M)	6 2	12 06	Yaounde	14 5 87	Barcelona
Traore Djimi (D)	6 3	12 04	Laval	1 3 80	Charlton Ath

Utaka John (F)	5 9	11 02	Enugu	8	1 82	Rennes
Wilson Marc (M)	6 2	12 07	Belfast	17	8 87	Scholar

League Appearances: Ashdown, J. 3; Aubey, L. 1(2); Baros, M. 8(4); Campbell, S. 31; Cranie, M. 1(1); Davis, S. 18(4); Defoe, J. 12; Diarra, L. 11(1); Diop, P. 25; Distin, S. 36; Hreidarsson, H. 30(2); Hughes, R. 8(5); James, D. 35; Johnson, G. 29; Kanu, N. 13(12); Kranjcar, N. 31(3); Lauren, E. 11(4); Muntari, S. 27(2); Mvuemba, A. 3(5); Mwaruwari, B. 21(2); Nugent, D. 5(10); O'Neil, G. 2; Pamarot, N. 14(4); Pedro Mendes, 14(4); Songo'o, F. (1); Taylor, M. 3(10); Traore, D. 1(2); Utaka, J. 25(4).
Goals – League (48): Mwaruwari 12, Defoe 8 (2 pens), Utaka 5, Kanu 4, Kranjcar 4, Muntari 4 (1 pen), Hreidarsson 3, Campbell 1, Diarra 1, Johnson 1, Pamarot 1, Taylor 1 (pen), own goals 3.
Carling Cup (5): Nugent 2, Pamarot 2, Kanu 1.
FA Cup (7): Kanu 2, Diarra 1, Kranjcar 1, Muntari 1 (pen), Nugent 1, own goal 1.
Ground: Fratton Park, Frogmore Road, Portsmouth, Hampshire PO4 8RA. Telephone (02392) 731 204.
Record Attendance: 51,385 v Derby Co, FA Cup 6th rd, 26 February 1949.
Capacity: 20,338.
Manager: Harry Redknapp.
Secretary: Paul Weld.
Most League Goals: 97, Division 1, 2002–03.
Highest League Scorer in Season: Guy Whittingham, 42, Division 1, 1992–93.
Most League Goals in Total Aggregate: Peter Harris, 194, 1946–60.
Most Capped Player: Jimmy Dickinson, 48, England.
Most League Appearances: Jimmy Dickinson, 764, 1946–65.
Honours – Football League: Division 1 Champions – 1948–49, 1949–50, 2002–03. Division 3 (S) Champions – 1923–24. Division 3 Champions – 1961–62, 1982–83.
FA Cup: Winners – 1939, 2008.
Colours: Blue shirts, white shorts, red stockings.

PORT VALE   FL CHAMPIONSHIP 2

Anyon Joe (G)	6 1	12 11	Poulton-le-Fylde	29 12 86	Scholar
Davidson Ross (M)	6 2	11 05	Burton	6 9 89	Scholar
Edwards Paul (M)	5 11	10 12	Manchester	1 1 80	Oldham Ath
Glover Danny (M)	6 0	11 02	Crewe	24 10 89	Scholar
Griffith Anthony (M)	6 0	12 00	Huddersfield	28 10 86	Doncaster R
Harsley Paul (M)	5 8	11 09	Scunthorpe	29 5 78	Macclesfield T
Lawrie James (F)	6 0	12 05	Dindonald	18 12 90	Scholar
Martin Chris (G)	6 0	13 05	Mansfield	21 7 90	Scholar
Perry Kyle (F)	6 4	14 05	Birmingham	5 3 86	Chasetown
Prosser Luke (M)	6 3	10 05	Hertfordshire	28 5 88	Scholar
Richards Marc (F)	6 2	12 06	Wolverhampton	8 7 82	Barnsley
Richman Simon (M)	5 11	11 12	Ormskirk	2 6 90	Scholar
Rodgers Luke (F)	5 6	11 00	Birmingham	1 1 82	Crewe Alex
Slater Chris (D)	6 0	13 03	Dudley	14 1 84	Chasetown
Tudor Shane (M)	5 7	11 12	Wolverhampton	10 2 82	Leyton Orient
Whitaker Danny (M)	5 11	10 12	Manchester	14 11 80	Macclesfield T

League Appearances: Anyon, J. 44; Atkinson, W. 3(1); Cardle, J. 4(5); Chapman, L. (1); Davidson, R. (3); Eckersley, A. 18; Edwards, P. 17(8); Glover, D. 9(6); Harsley, P. 39(2); Herd, C. 11; Howland, D. 17; Hulbert, R. 15(7); Laird, M. 7; Lawrie, J. (6); Lowe, K. 24(4); Martin, C. 2; McGoldrick, D. 15(2); McGregor, M. 18(2); Mikaelsson, T. 5(1); Miles, C. 1(2); Miller, J. 12(2); Mulligan, D. 10(3); O'Loughlin, C. (3); Pearce, K. 11(1); Perry, K. 9(7); Pilkington, G. 45; Prosser, L. 3(2); Richards, M. 19(10); Richman, S. 6; Rocastle, C. 17(6); Rodgers, L. 29(7);

Salmon, M. 8(1); Slater, C. 1(4); Sodje, A. 3; Talbot, J. 21(4); Tudor, S. 8(6); Westwood, A. 11(1); Whitaker, D. 36(5); Willock, C. 8(7).
Goals – League (47): Rodgers 9 (3 pens), Whitaker 7, Harsley 5 (4 pens), Richards 5, Lowe 3, Willock 3, Edwards 2, Herd 2, McGoldrick 2, Pilkington 2, Eckersley 1, Glover 1, Howland 1, Laird 1, Mulligan 1, Rocastle 1, own goal 1.
Carling Cup (1): Rodgers 1 (pen).
FA Cup (3): Pilkington 1, Rodgers 1, Willock 1.
J Paint Trophy (2): Miller 1, Rodgers 1.
Ground: Vale Park, Hamil Road, Burslem, Stoke-on-Trent ST6 1AW. Telephone (01782) 655 800.
Record Attendance: 49,768 v Aston Villa, FA Cup 5th rd, 20 February 1960.
Capacity: 18,982.
Manager: Lee Sinnott.
Secretary: Bill Lodey.
Most League Goals: 110, Division 4, 1958–59.
Highest League Scorer in Season: Wilf Kirkham 38, Division 2, 1926–27.
Most League Goals in Total Aggregate: Wilf Kirkham 154, 1923–29, 1931–33.
Most Capped Player: Chris Birchall, 22 (26), Trinidad & Tobago.
Most League Appearances: Roy Sproson, 761, 1950–72.
Honours – Football League: Division 3 (N) Champions – 1929–30, 1953–54. Division 4 Champions – 1958–59. **Autoglass Trophy:** Winners – 1993. **LDV Vans Trophy:** Winners – 2001
Colours: White shirts white shorts, white stockings.

PRESTON NORTH END   FL CHAMPIONSHIP

Anyinsah Joe (M)	5 8	11 00	Bristol	8 10 84	Bristol C
Brown Chris (F)	6 3	13 01	Doncaster	11 12 84	Norwich C
Carter Darren (M)	6 2	12 11	Solihull	18 12 83	WBA
Chaplow Richard (M)	5 9	9 03	Accrington	2 2 85	WBA
Chilvers Liam (D)	6 2	12 08	Chelmsford	6 11 81	Colchester U
Davidson Callum (D)	5 10	11 00	Stirling	25 6 76	Leicester C
Hart Michael (M)	5 10	11 06	Bellshill	10 2 80	
Hawley Karl (F)	5 8	12 02	Walsall	6 12 81	Carlisle U
Henderson Wayne (G)	5 11	12 02	Dublin	16 9 83	Brighton & HA
Hill Matt (D)	5 8	11 13	Bristol	26 3 81	Bristol C
Jarrett Jason (M)	6 0	13 04	Bury	14 9 79	Leicester C
Jones Billy (M)	5 11	13 00	Shrewsbury	24 3 87	Crewe Alex
Lonergan Andrew (G)	6 2	13 00	Preston	19 10 83	Scholar
Mawene Youl (D)	6 1	13 00	Caen	16 7 79	Derby Co
McKenna Paul (M)	5 8	11 00	Eccleston	20 10 77	Trainee
Mellor Neil (F)	6 0	14 00	Sheffield	4 11 82	Liverpool
Murphy Andrew (G)	6 4	14 00		22 9 88	Scholar
Neal Chris (G)	6 2	12 04	St Albans	23 10 85	Scholar
Neal Lewis (M)	5 10	11 02	Leicester	14 7 81	Stoke C
Nicholls Kevin (M)	5 10	11 13	Newham	2 1 79	Leeds U
Ormerod Brett (F)	5 11	11 12	Blackburn	18 10 76	Southampton
Sedgwick Chris (M)	6 0	12 01	Sheffield	28 4 80	Rotherham U
St Ledger-Hall Sean (D)	6 0	11 09	Birmingham	28 12 84	Peterborough U
Trotman Neal (D)	6 3	13 08	Levenshulme	11 3 87	Oldham Ath
Whaley Simon (M)	5 10	11 11	Bolton	7 6 85	Bury

League Appearances: Agyemang, P. 11(11); Alexander, G. 3; Beattie, C. 1(1); Brown, C. 17; Carroll, A. 7(4); Carter, D. 30(9); Chaplow, R. 7(5); Chilvers, L. 27(1); Davidson, C. 39(1); Gallagher, P. 15(4); Halls, J. 4; Hart, M. 2; Hawley, K. 20(5); Henderson, W. 3; Hill, M. 21(5); Jones, B. 28(1); Lonergan, A. 43; Mawene, Y. 36(2); McKenna, P. 33; Mellor, N. 12(24); Neal, C. 8(9); Nicholls, K. 17(1);

Ormerod, B. 8(10); Priskin, T. 4(1); Pugh, D. 5(2); Sedgwick, C. 40(2); St Ledger-Hall, S. 34(3); Trotman, N. 2(1); Whaley, S. 29(14).
Goals – League (50): Mellor 9 (1 pen), Brown C 5, Agyemang 4, Carter 4, Davidson 4 (2 pens), Whaley 4, Chaplow 3, Hawley 3, Mawene 3, Neal L 2, Priskin 2, Sedgwick 2, Carroll 1, Gallagher 1, Ormerod 1, St Ledger-Hall 1, own goal 1.
Carling Cup (1): Pugh 1.
FA Cup (5): Hawley 2, Whaley 2, Mellor 1 (pen).
Ground: Deepdale, Sir Tom Finney Way, Preston PR1 6RU. Telephone (0870) 442 1964.
Record Attendance: 42,684 v Arsenal, Division 1, 23 April 1938. **Capacity:** 24,000 (with completion of new stand).
Manager: Alan Irvine.
Secretary: Janet Parr.
Most League Goals: 100, Division 2, 1927–28 and Division 1, 1957–58.
Highest League Scorer in Season: Ted Harper, 37, Division 2, 1932–33.
Most League Goals in Total Aggregate: Tom Finney, 187, 1946–60.
Most Capped Player: Tom Finney, 76, England.
Most League Appearances: Alan Kelly, 447, 1961–75.
Honours – Football League: Division 1 Champions – 1888–89 (first champions), 1889–90. Division 2 Champions – 1903–04, 1912–13, 1950–51, 1999–2000. Division 3 Champions – 1970–71, 1995–96. **FA Cup:** Winners – 1889, 1938.
Colours: White shirts, blue shorts, white and blue hooped stockings.

QUEENS PARK RANGERS FL CHAMPIONSHIP

Agyemang Patrick (F)	6 1	12 00	Walthamstow	29 9 80	Preston NE
Ainsworth Gareth (M)	5 10	12 05	Blackburn	10 5 73	Cardiff C
Balanta Angelo (F)	5 10	11 11	Colombia	1 7 90	Scholar
Barker Chris (D)	6 2	13 08	Sheffield	2 3 80	Cardiff C
Blackstock Dexter (F)	6 2	13 03	Oxford	20 5 86	Southampton
Bolder Adam (M)	5 9	10 08	Hull	25 10 80	Derby Co
Buzsaky Akos (M)	5 11	11 09	Hungary	7 5 82	Plymouth Arg
Camp Lee (G)	5 11	11 11	Derby	22 8 84	Derby Co
Cole Jake (G)	6 2	13 00	Hammersmith	11 9 85	Scholar
Connolly Matthew (D)	6 1	11 03	Barnet	24 9 87	Arsenal
Delaney Damien (D)	6 3	14 00	Cork	20 7 81	Hull C
Ephraim Hogan (F)	5 9	10 06	Islington	31 3 88	West Ham U
Hall Fitz (D)	6 3	13 00	Leytonstone	20 12 80	Wigan Ath
Leigertwood Mikele (D)	6 1	11 04	Enfield	12 11 82	Sheffield U
Mahon Gavin (M)	5 11	13 07	Birmingham	2 1 77	Watford
Nardiello Daniel (F)	5 11	11 04	Coventry	22 10 82	Barnsley
Rehman Zesh (D)	6 2	12 08	Birmingham	14 10 83	Fulham
Rowlands Martin (M)	5 9	10 10	Hammersmith	8 2 79	Brentford
Stewart Damion (D)	6 3	13 08	Kingston	8 8 80	Harbour View
Vine Rowan (F)	5 11	12 10	Basingstoke	21 9 82	Birmingham C
Walton Simon (D)	6 1	13 05	Sherburn-in-Elmet	13 9 87	Hull C

League Appearances: Agyemang, P. 17; Ainsworth, G. 16(8); Bailey, S. 1; Balanta, A. 6(5); Barker, C. 25; Bignot, M. (2); Blackstock, D. 26(9); Bolder, A. 20(4); Buzsaky, A. 24(3); Camp, L. 46; Connolly, M. 18(2); Cranie, M. 6; Cullip, D. 5(1); Curtis, J. 3(1); Delaney, D. 17; Ephraim, H. 20(9); Hall, F. 14; Jarrett, J. 1(1); Lee, K. 2(5); Leigertwood, M. 33(7); Mahon, G. 11(5); Malcolm, B. 10(1); Mancienne, M. 26(4); Moore, S. 5(6); Nardiello, D. 4(4); Nygaard, M. 6(13); Rehman, Z. 17(4); Rose, R. (1); Rowlands, M. 43(1); Sahar, B. 6(3); Sinclair, S. 8(1); Stewart, D. 35(4); Timoska, S. 3(4); Vine, R. 31(2); Walton, S. 1(4); Ward, N. (1).
Goals – League (60): Buzsaky 10, Agyemang 8, Blackstock 6 (1 pen), Rowlands 6 (3 pens), Vine 6, Leigertwood 5, Stewart 5, Ainsworth 3, Ephraim 3, Bolder 2, Balanta 1, Delaney 1, Mahon 1, Moore 1, Nygaard 1, Sinclair 1.

Carling Cup (1): Rowlands 1.
FA Cup (0).
Ground: Loftus Road Stadium, South Africa Road, Shepherds Bush, London W12 7PA. Telephone (020) 8743 0262.
Record Attendance: 35,353 v Leeds U, Division 1, 27 April 1974. **Capacity:** 18,682.
Manager: Iain Dowie.
Secretary: Sheila Marson.
Most League Goals: 111, Division 3, 1961–62.
Highest League Scorer in Season: George Goddard, 37, Division 3 (S), 1929–30.
Most League Goals in Total Aggregate: George Goddard, 172, 1926–34.
Most Capped Player: Alan McDonald, 52, Northern Ireland.
Most League Appearances: Tony Ingham, 519, 1950–63.
Honours – Football League: Division 2 Champions – 1982–83. Division 3 (S) Champions – 1947–48. Division 3 Champions – 1966–67. **Football League Cup:** Winners – 1966–67.
Colours: Blue and white hoops.

READING   FL CHAMPIONSHIP

Andersen Mikkel (G)	6 5	12 08	Herlev	17 12 88	AB Copenhagen
Bennett Alan (D)	6 2	12 08	Kilkenny	4 10 81	Cork C
Bikey Andre (D)	6 0	12 08	Douala	8 1 85	Lokomotiv Moscow
Bozanic Oliver (M)	6 0	12 00	Melbourne	8 1 89	Central Coast M
Church Simon (F)	6 0	13 04	Wycombe	10 12 88	Scholar
Cisse Kalifa (M)	6 2	12 11	Orleans	1 9 84	Boavista
Convey Bobby (M)	5 9	11 04	Philadelphia	27 5 83	DC United
Davies Scott (M)	5 11	12 00	Dublin	10 3 88	Wycombe W
Doyle Kevin (F)	5 11	12 06	Adamstown	18 9 83	Cork C
Duberry Michael (D)	6 1	13 10	Enfield	14 10 75	Leeds U
Fae Emerse (M)	5 8	11 00	Nantes	24 1 84	Nantes
Federici Adam (G)	6 2	14 02	Nowra	31 1 85	
Golbourne Scott (M)	5 8	11 08	Bristol	29 2 88	Bristol C
Gunnarsson Brynjar (M)	6 1	12 01	Reykjavik	16 10 75	Watford
Hahnemann Marcus (G)	6 3	16 04	Seattle	15 6 72	Fulham
Hamer Ben (G)	5 11	12 04	Reading	20 11 87	Crawley T
Harper James (M)	5 10	11 02	Chelmsford	9 11 80	Arsenal
Henry James (M)	6 1	11 11	Woodley	10 6 89	Scholar
Hunt Steve (M)	5 9	10 10	Port Laoise	1 8 80	Brentford
Illugason Viktor (F)	6 1	12 08	Reykjavik	25 1 90	
Ingimarsson Ivar (D)	6 0	12 07	Reykjavik	20 8 77	Wolverhampton W
Karacan Jem (M)	5 10	11 13	Lewisham	21 2 89	Scholar
Kebe Jimmy (M)	6 2	11 07	Vitry-sur-Seine	19 1 84	Boulogne
Kitson Dave (F)	6 3	13 00	Hitchin	21 1 80	Cambridge U
Lita Leroy (F)	5 7	11 12	Congo DR	28 12 84	Bristol C
Little Glen (M)	6 3	13 00	Wimbledon	15 10 75	Burnley
Long Shane (F)	5 10	11 02	Kilkenny	22 1 87	Cork C
Matejovsky Marek (M)	5 10	11 00	Brandys nad Labem	20 12 81	Mlada Boleslav
Murty Graeme (D)	5 10	11 10	Saltburn	13 11 74	York C
Pearce Alex (D)	6 0	11 10	Reading	9 11 88	Scholar
Robson-Kanu Hal (F)	5 7	11 08	Hammersmith	21 5 89	
Rosenior Liam (D)	5 10	11 05	Wandsworth	9 7 84	Fulham
Shorey Nicky (D)	5 9	10 10	Romford	19 2 81	Leyton Orient
Sodje Sam (D)	6 0	12 00	Greenwich	29 5 79	Brentford
Sonko Ibrahima (D)	6 3	13 07	Bignola	22 1 81	Brentford

League Appearances: Bikey, A. 14(8); Cisse, K. 11(11); Convey, B. 12(8); De la Cruz, U. 3(3); Doyle, K. 34(2); Duberry, M. 12(1); Fae, E. 3(5); Golbourne, S. 1; Gunnarsson, B. 18(2); Hahnemann, M. 38; Halls, J. (1); Harper, J. 38; Hunt, S. 37;

Ingimarsson, I. 33(1); Kebe, J. 1(4); Kitson, D. 28(6); Lita, L. 10(4); Little, G. (2); Long, S. 7(22); Matejovsky, M. 10(4); Murty, G. 28; Oster, J. 12(6); Rosenior, L. 15(2); Seol, K. 2(1); Shorey, N. 36; Sonko, I. 15(1).
Goals – League (41): Kitson 10, Doyle 6, Harper 6, Hunt 5 (2 pens), Bikey 3, Long 3, Ingimarsson 2, Shorey 2, Cisse 1, Lita 1, Matejovsky 1, own goal 1.
Carling Cup (3): Convey 1, Halls 1, Lita 1.
FA Cup (2): Hunt 2.
Ground: The Madejski Stadium, Junction 11, M4, Reading, Berkshire RG2 0FL. Telephone (0118) 968 1100.
Record Attendance: Elm Park: 33,042 v Brentford, FA Cup 5th rd, 19 February 1927; Madejski Stadium: 24,122 v Aston villa, Premiership, 10 February 2007.
Capacity: 24,161.
Manager: Steve Coppell.
Secretary: Sue Hewett.
Most League Goals: 112, Division 3 (S), 1951–52.
Highest League Scorer in Season: Ronnie Blackman, 39, Division 3 (S), 1951–52.
Most League Goals in Total Aggregate: Ronnie Blackman, 158, 1947–54.
Most Capped Player: Jimmy Quinn, 17 (46), Northern Ireland.
Most League Appearances: Martin Hicks, 500, 1978–91.
Honours – Football League: Championship Champions – 2005–06. Division 2 Champions – 1993–94. Division 3 Champions – 1985–86. Division 3 (S) Champions – 1925–26. Division 4 Champions – 1978–79. **Simod Cup:** Winners – 1987–88.
Colours: Blue and white.

ROCHDALE   FL CHAMPIONSHIP 2

Player		Born	Place	Date	Signed from
Buckley Will (F)	6 0	13 00	Burnley	12 8 88	Curzon Ashton
Dagnall Chris (F)	5 8	12 03	Liverpool	15 4 86	Tranmere R
D'Laryea Nathan (D)	5 10	12 02	Manchester	3 9 85	Manchester C
Higginbotham Kallum (F)	5 11	10 10	Manchester	15 6 89	Oldham Ath
Holness Marcus (D)	6 0	12 02	Oldham	8 12 88	Scholar
Jones Gary (M)	5 11	12 05	Birkenhead	3 6 77	Barnsley
Kennedy Tom (D)	5 10	11 01	Bury	24 6 85	Bury
Le Fondre Adam (F)	5 9	11 04	Stockport	2 12 86	Stockport Co
McArdle Rory (D)	6 1	11 05	Sheffield	1 5 87	Sheffield W
Muirhead Ben (M)	5 9	11 02	Doncaster	5 1 83	Bradford C
Perkins David (M)	5 6	11 06	St Asaph	21 6 82	Morecambe
Ramsden Simon (D)	6 0	12 06	Bishop Auckland	17 12 81	Grimsby T
Rundle Adam (M)	5 8	11 01	Durham	8 7 84	Mansfield T
Russell Sam (G)	6 0	10 13	Middlesbrough	4 10 82	Darlington
Spencer James (G)	6 3	15 04	Stockport	11 4 85	Stockport Co
Stanton Nathan (D)	5 9	12 06	Nottingham	6 5 81	Scunthorpe U
Thompson Joe (M)	6 0	9 07	Rochdale	5 3 89	Scholar

League Appearances: Atkinson, R. (2); Basham, C. 5(8); Bowyer, G. (1); Branston, G. 4; Buckley, W. 1(6); Crooks, L. 5(4); D'Laryea, N. 2(4); Dagnall, C. 7(7); Doolan, J. 19(6); Evans, R. 1; Higginbotham, K. 22(11); Holness, M. 13(6); Howe, R. 19(1); Jones, G. 43; Kennedy, T. 43; Le Fondre, A. 30(16); Lee, T. 11; Lomax, K. 10; McArdle, R. 42(1); McEvilly, L. 3(4); Muirhead, B. 18(13); Murray, G. 21(2); Perkins, D. 40; Prendergast, R. 2(12); Ramsden, S. 35; Rundle, A. 37(5); Russell, S. 15; Spencer, J. 20; Stanton, N. 27; Taylor, S. 2(2); Thompson, J. 4(7); Thorpe, L. 5(3); Wharton, B. (1).
Goals – League (77): Le Fondre 16 (4 pens), Howe 9, Murray 9, Dagnall 7 (1 pen), Jones 7, Rundle 5, Perkins 4, Higginbotham 3, McEvilly 3, Kennedy 2 (1 pen), McArdle 2, Ramsden 2, Prendergast 1, Thompson 1, Thorpe 1, own goals 5.
Carling Cup (3): Murray 1, Perkins 1, Prendergast 1.
FA Cup (1): Le Fondre 1.
J Paint Trophy (1): Prendergast 1.

Play-Offs (5): Dagnall 2, McArdle 1, Perkins 1, Rundle 1.
Ground: Spotland Stadium, Sandy Lane, Rochdale OL11 5DS. Telephone (01706) 644 648.
Record Attendance: 24,231 v Notts Co, FA Cup 2nd rd, 10 December 1949.
Capacity: 10,208.
Manager: Keith Hill.
Secretary: Colin Garlick.
Most League Goals: 105, Division 3 (N), 1926–27.
Highest League Scorer in Season: Albert Whitehurst, 44, Division 3 (N), 1926–27.
Most League Goals in Total Aggregate: Reg Jenkins, 119, 1964–73.
Most Capped Player: Leo Bertos, 6 (7), New Zealand.
Most League Appearances: Graham Smith, 317, 1966–74.
Honours – None.
Colours: Black and blue striped shirts, white shorts, blue stockings.

ROTHERHAM UNITED   FL CHAMPIONSHIP 2

Brogan Stephen (D)	5 7	10 04	Rotherham	12	4 88	Scholar
Cahill Tom (F)	5 10	12 08	Derby	21 11 86		Matlock T
Cann Steven (G)	6 2	12 06	South Africa	20	1 88	Derby Co
Coughlan Graham (D)	6 2	13 07	Dublin	18 11 74		Sheffield W
Green Jamie (F)	5 7	10 07	Doncaster	18	8 89	Scholar
Harrison Danny (M)	5 11	12 04	Liverpool	4 11 82		Tranmere R
Holmes Derek (F)	6 2	13 00	Lanark	18 10 78		Carlisle U
Holmes Peter (M)	5 11	11 13	Bishop Auckland	18 11 80		Luton T
Hudson Mark (M)	5 10	11 03	Bishop Auckland	24 10 80		Huddersfield T
Joseph Marc (D)	6 0	12 05	Leicester	10 11 76		Blackpool
Mills Pablo (D)	5 11	11 04	Birmingham	27	5 84	Derby Co
Newsham Mark (M)	5 10	9 11	Hatfield	24	3 87	Scholar
O'Grady Chris (F)	6 1	11 06	Nottingham	25	1 86	Leicester C
Sharps Ian (D)	6 3	13 05	Warrington	23 10 80		Tranmere R
Taylor Ryan (F)	6 2	10 10	Rotherham	4	5 88	Scholar
Todd Andrew (M)	6 0	11 03	Nottingham	22	2 79	Accrington S
Tonge Dale (D)	5 10	10 06	Doncaster	7	5 85	Barnsley
Warrington Andy (G)	6 3	12 13	Sheffield	10	6 76	Bury
Yates Jamie (F)	5 7	10 11	Sheffield	24 12 88		Scholar

League Appearances: Bean, M. 11(1); Brogan, S. 28(1); Cahill, T. 5(2); Coughlan, G. 45; Cresswell, R. 1(2); Duncum, S. (2); Dyer, B. 3; Green, J. 6(3); Haggarty, D. (1); Harrison, D. 44; Holmes, D. 33(4); Holmes, P. 19(5); Hudson, M. 30(1); Hurst, P. 8(3); Joseph, M. 34(2); King, L. (1); Mills, P. 32(1); Newsham, M. 11(14); O'Grady, C. 35(3); Pettigrew, A. 3(1); Ross, I. 9(8); Sharps, I. 33; Taylor, R. 22(13); Todd, A. 11(2); Tonge, D. 31(6); Warrington, A. 46; Widdowson, J. 3; Yates, J. 3(17).
Goals – League (62): Holmes D 11, Hudson 9 (1 pen), O'Grady 9, Taylor 6, Harrison D. 4, Joseph 4, Newsham 4, Brogan 3 (1 pen), Yates 3, Holmes P. 2, Sharps 2, Bean 1, Coughlan 1, Green 1, Mills 1, own goal 1.
Carling Cup (1): Harrison D 1.
FA Cup (2): Brogan 1 (pen), O'Grady 1.
J Paint Trophy (2): O'Grady 1, Sharps 1.
Ground: Don Valley Stadium, Worksop Road, Sheffield, South Yorkshire S9 3TL.
Record Attendance: 25,170 v Sheffield U, Division 2, 13 December 1952. **Capacity:** 25,000.
Manager: Mark Robins.
Secretary: J. Pilmner.
Most League Goals: 114, Division 3 (N), 1946–47.
Highest League Scorer in Season: Wally Ardron, 38, Division 3 (N), 1946–47.
Most League Goals in Total Aggregate: Gladstone Guest, 130, 1946–56.
Most Capped Player: Shaun Goater, 14 (19), Bermuda.

Most League Appearances: Danny Williams, 459, 1946–62.
Honours – Football League: Division 3 Champions – 1980–81. Division 3 (N)
Champions – 1950–51. Division 4 Champions – 1988–89. **Auto Windscreens Shield:**
Winners – 1996.
Colours: Red and white.

SCUNTHORPE UNITED   FL CHAMPIONSHIP 1

Baraclough Ian (M)	6 1	12 02	Leicester	4 12 70	Notts Co	
Butler Andy (D)	6 2	14 02	Doncaster	4 11 83	Scholar	
Byrne Cliff (D)	6 0	12 11	Dublin	27 4 82	Sunderland	
Crosby Andy (D)	6 2	13 07	Rotherham	3 3 73	Oxford U	
Forte Jonathan (M)	6 0	12 02	Sheffield	25 7 86	Sheffield U	
Hayes Paul (F)	6 0	12 12	Dagenham	20 9 83	Barnsley	
Hurst Kevan (M)	5 10	11 07	Chesterfield	27 8 85	Sheffield U	
Iriekpen Ezomo (D)	6 1	12 02	East London	14 5 82	Swansea C	
Lillis Joshua (G)	6 2	12 09	Scunthorpe	24 6 87	Scholar	
May Ben (F)	6 3	12 12	Gravesend	10 3 84	Millwall	
McCann Grant (M)	5 10	11 00	Belfast	14 4 80	Barnsley	
Morris Ian (M)	6 0	11 05	Dublin	27 2 87	Leeds U	
Murphy Joe (G)	6 2	13 06	Dublin	21 8 81	Sunderland	
Paterson Martin (F)	5 9	10 11	Tunstall	13 5 87	Stoke C	
Sparrow Matt (M)	5 11	11 06	Wembley	3 10 81	Scholar	
Wilcox Joe (D)	6 1	11 05	Northampton	18 4 89		
Williams Marcus (D)	5 10	10 07	Doncaster	8 4 86	Scholar	
Winn Peter (M)	6 0	11 09	Cleethorpes	19 12 88	Scholar	
Wright Andrew (M)	6 1	13 07	Southport	15 1 85	West Virginia Univ	

League Appearances: Ameobi, T. (9); Baraclough, I. 17; Butler, A. 34(2); Byrne,
C. 25; Cork, J. 32(2); Crosby, A. 38; Forte, J. 18(20); Goodwin, J. 39(1); Hayes, P.
32(8); Hobbs, J. 7(2); Horsfield, G. 11(1); Hurst, K. 31(2); Iriekpen, E. 12(5); Lillis,
J. 1(2); Logan, S. 4; Martis, S. 3; May, B. 6(15); McCann, G. 12(2); Morris, I. 20(5);
Murphy, J. 45; Paterson, M. 34(6); Seck, M. (1); Sparrow, M. 24(8); Taylor, C.
12(8); Weston, C. 2(5); Williams, M. 29(5); Winn, P. (4); Wright, A. (2); Youga, K.
18(1).
Goals – League (46): Paterson 13, Hayes 8 (1 pen), Crosby 4 (1 pen), Forte 4,
Goodwin 3, Morris 3, Butler 2, Cork 2, Hobbs 1, Hurst 1, Iriekpen 1, May 1,
McCann 1, Sparrow 1, Youga 1.
Carling Cup (1): Paterson 1.
FA Cup (0).
Ground: Glanford Park, Doncaster Road, Scunthorpe DN15 8TD. Telephone
(0871) 221 1899.
Record Attendance: Old Showground: 23,935 v Portsmouth, FA Cup 4th rd, 30
January 1954. Glanford Park: 8,906 v Nottingham F, FL 1, 10 March 2007.
Capacity: 9,203.
Manager: Nigel Adkins.
General Manager: Jamie Hammond.
Most League Goals: 88, Division 3 (N), 1957–58.
Highest League Scorer in Season: Barrie Thomas, 31, Division 2, 1961–62.
Most League Goals in Total Aggregate: Steve Cammack, 110, 1979–81, 1981–86.
Most Capped Player: Dave Mulligan, 1(12), New Zealand.
Most League Appearances: Jack Brownsword, 595, 1950–65.
Honours – Football League: FL 1 Champions – 2006–07; Division 3 (N)
Champions – 1957–58.
Colours: Claret and blue.

SHEFFIELD UNITED   FL CHAMPIONSHIP

Abdi Liban (F)			Somalia	5 10 88	Scholar
Annerson Jamie (G)	6 2	13 02	Sheffield	21 6 88	Scholar
Armstrong Chris (D)	5 9	11 00	Newcastle	5 8 82	Oldham Ath
Beattie James (F)	6 1	13 06	Lancaster	27 2 78	Everton
Carney David (M)	5 11	11 00	Sydney	30 11 83	Oldham Ath
Chanot Maxime (D)			Nancy	21 11 89	Scholar
Cresswell Ryan (D)	5 9	10 05	Rotherham	22 12 87	Scholar
Ehiogu Ugo (D)	6 2	14 10	Hackney	3 11 72	Rangers
Geary Derek (D)	5 6	10 08	Dublin	19 6 80	Sheffield W
Gillespie Keith (M)	5 10	11 03	Larne	18 2 75	Leicester C
Hendrie Lee (M)	5 10	11 00	Birmingham	18 5 77	Aston Villa
Hulse Rob (F)	6 1	12 04	Crewe	25 10 79	Leeds U
Kazim-Richards Colin (F)	6 1	10 10	Leyton	26 8 86	Brighton & HA
Kenny Paddy (G)	6 0	15 10	Halifax	17 5 78	Bury
Kilgallon Matt (D)	6 2	12 11	York	8 1 84	Leeds U
Law Nicky (M)	5 10	11 06	Nottingham	29 3 88	Scholar
Lucketti Chris (D)	6 0	13 06	Littleborough	28 9 71	Preston NE
Montgomery Nick (M)	5 8	12 08	Leeds	28 10 81	Scholar
Morgan Chris (D)	6 0	13 06	Barnsley	9 11 77	Barnsley
Naughton Kyle (M)			Sheffield	11 11 88	Scholar
Naysmith Gary (D)	5 9	12 01	Edinburgh	16 11 78	Everton
Quinn Keith (M)			Dublin	22 9 88	Scholar
Quinn Stephen (M)	5 6	9 08	Dublin	4 4 86	Scholar
Robertson Jordan (F)	6 0	12 06	Sheffield	12 2 88	Scholar
Seck Mamadou (D)	6 4	12 13	Rufisgue	23 8 79	Le Havre
Sharp Billy (F)	5 9	11 00	Sheffield	5 2 86	Scunthorpe U
Shelton Luton (F)	5 11	11 11	Kingston	11 11 85	Harbour View
S-Latef Zeyn (F)			Sweden	22 7 90	Scholar
Slavkovski Goran (F)			Skravlinge	8 4 89	Internazionale
Speed Gary (M)	5 10	12 10	Deeside	8 9 69	Bolton W
Starosta Ben (D)	6 0	12 00	Sheffield	7 1 87	Scholar
Stead Jon (F)	6 3	12 00	Huddersfield	7 4 83	Sunderland
Tonge Michael (M)	5 10	12 06	Manchester	7 4 83	Scholar
Travis Nicky (M)	6 0	12 01	Sheffield	12 3 87	Scholar
Webber Danny (F)	5 10	11 04	Manchester	28 12 81	Watford
Wedgbury Sam (D)			West Bromwich	26 2 89	Worcester C

League Appearances: Armstrong, C. 27(5); Bardsley, P. 16; Beattie, J. 36(3); Bennett, I. 6(1); Bromby, L. 11; Cahill, G. 16; Carney, D. 18(3); Cotterill, D. 15(1); Ehiogu, U. 5(5); Geary, D. 19(2); Gillespie, K. 23(12); Halls, J. 5(1); Hendrie, L. 7(5); Hulse, R. 10(11); Kenny, P. 40; Kilgallon, M. 39(1); Law, N. (1); Leigertwood, M. 1(1); Lucketti, C. 4(2); Martin, L. 5(1); Montgomery, N. 18(2); Morgan, C. 25; Naysmith, G. 38; Quinn, A. 4(4); Quinn, S. 15(4); Sharp, B. 21(8); Shelton, L. 5(10); Speed, G. 20; Stead, J. 12(12); Tonge, M. 37(8); Webber, D. 8(6).
Goals – League (56): Beattie 22 (6 pens), Sharp 4, Armstrong 3, Speed 3 (1 pen), Stead 3, Webber 3, Cahill 2, Carney 2, Gillespie 2, Kilgallon 2, Morgan 2, Quinn S 2, Hendrie 1, Shelton 1, Tonge 1, own goals 3.
Carling Cup (11): Sharp 2, Shelton 2, Stead 2, Hendrie 1, Horsfield 1, Law 1, Lucketti 1, Webber 1.
FA Cup (3): Carney 1, Shelton 1, Stead 1.
Ground: Bramall Lane, Cherry Street, Sheffield S2 4SU. Telephone (0871) 222 1899.
Record Attendance: 68,287 v Leeds U, FA Cup 5th rd, 15 February 1936.
Capacity: 32,500.
Manager: Kevin Blackwell.
Secretary: Donna Fletcher.
Most League Goals: 102, Division 1, 1925–26.
Highest League Scorer in Season: Jimmy Dunne, 41, Division 1, 1930–31.

Most League Goals in Total Aggregate: Harry Johnson, 205, 1919–30.
Most Capped Player: Billy Gillespie, 25, Northern Ireland.
Most League Appearances: Joe Shaw, 629, 1948–66.
Honours – Football League: Division 1 Champions – 1897–98. Division 2 Champions – 1952–53. Division 4 Champions – 1981–82. **FA Cup:** Winners – 1899, 1902, 1915, 1925.
Colours: Red and white striped shirts, black shorts, black stockings.

SHEFFIELD WEDNESDAY   FL CHAMPIONSHIP

Beevers Mark (D)	6 4	13 00	Barnsley	21 11 89	Scholar
Boden Luke (F)	6 1	12 00	Sheffield	26 11 88	Scholar
Burton Deon (F)	5 9	11 09	Ashford	25 10 76	Rotherham U
Clarke Leon (F)	6 2	14 02	Birmingham	10 2 85	Wolverhampton W
Esajas Etienne (F)	5 7	10 03	Amsterdam	4 11 84	Vitesse
Gilbert Peter (D)	5 11	12 00	Newcastle	31 7 83	Leicester C
Grant Lee (G)	6 3	13 01	Hemel Hempstead	27 1 83	Derby Co
Hinds Richard (D)	6 2	12 02	Sheffield	22 8 80	Scunthorpe U
Jeffers Francis (F)	5 10	11 02	Liverpool	25 1 81	Blackburn R
Johnson Jermaine (M)	6 0	12 08	Kingston	25 6 80	Bradford C
Lekaj Rocky (M)	5 10	10 05	Kosovo	12 10 89	Scholar
Lunt Kenny (M)	5 9	11 00	Runcorn	20 11 79	Crewe Alex
McAllister Sean (M)	5 8	10 07	Bolton	15 8 87	Scholar
McMenamin Liam (M)	5 11	10 11	Derry	10 4 89	Scholar
O'Donnell Richard (G)	6 2	13 05	Sheffield	12 9 89	Scholar
Simek Frankie (D)	6 0	11 06	St Louis	13 10 84	Arsenal
Small Wade (M)	5 7	11 00	Croydon	23 4 84	Milton Keynes D
Sodje Akpo (F)	6 2	12 08	Greenwich	31 1 81	Port Vale
Spurr Tommy (D)	6 1	11 05	Leeds	13 9 87	Scholar
Tudgay Marcus (F)	5 10	12 04	Worthing	3 2 83	Derby Co
Wallwork Ronnie (M)	5 10	12 09	Manchester	10 9 77	WBA
Watson Steve (D)	6 0	12 07	North Shields	1 4 74	WBA
Wood Richard (D)	6 3	12 03	Ossett	5 7 85	Scholar

League Appearances: Beevers, M. 26(2); Boden, L. (2); Bolder, A. 11(2); Brunt, C. 1; Bullen, L. 17(5); Burch, R. 2; Burton, D. 23(17); Clarke, L. 2(6); Esajas, E. 5(13); Folly, Y. 7(3); Gilbert, P. 9(1); Grant, L. 44; Hinds, R. 30(8); Jeffers, F. 7(3); Johnson, J. 30(5); Johnson, M. 13; Kavanagh, G. 21(2); Lunt, K. 3(1); McAllister, S. 5(3); O'Brien, B. 26(7); Sahar, B. 8(4); Showunmi, E. 6(4); Simek, F. 17; Slusarski, B. 3(4); Small, W. 18(11); Sodje, A. 16(3); Songo'o, F. 12; Spurr, T. 40(1); Tudgay, M. 29(6); Wallwork, R. 4(3); Watson, S. 20(3); Whelan, G. 25; Wood, R. 26(1).
Goals – League (54): Burton 7 (4 pens), Sodje 7, Tudgay 7, Small 4, Clarke 3, O'Brien 3, Sahar 3, Bolder 2, Hinds 2, Jeffers 2 (1 pen), Kavanagh 2, Spurr 2, Watson 2, Whelan 2 (1 pen), Wood 2, Bullen 1, Johnson J 1, Slusarski 1, Songo'o 1.
Carling Cup (5): Burton 2, Folly 1, Small 1, Whelan 1.
FA Cup (3): Beevers 1, Tudgay 1, Watson 1.
Ground: Hillsborough, Sheffield S6 1SW. Telephone 0870 999 1867.
Record Attendance: 72,841 v Manchester C, FA Cup 5th rd, 17 February 1934.
Capacity: 39,812.
Manager: Brian Laws.
Secretary: Kaven Walker (football secretary).
Most League Goals: 106, Division 2, 1958–59.
Highest League Scorer in Season: Derek Dooley, 46, Division 2, 1951–52.
Most League Goals in Total Aggregate: Andrew Wilson, 199, 1900–20.
Most Capped Player: Nigel Worthington, 50 (66), Northern Ireland.
Most League Appearances: Andrew Wilson, 501, 1900–20.
Honours – Football League: Division 1 Champions – 1902–03, 1903–04, 1928–29, 1929–30. Division 2 Champions – 1899–1900, 1925–26, 1951–52, 1955–56, 1958–59.
FA Cup: Winners – 1896, 1907, 1935. **Football League Cup:** Winners – 1990–91.
Colours: Blue and white striped shirts, black shorts, black stockings.

SHREWSBURY TOWN   FL CHAMPIONSHIP 2

Ashton Neil (M)	5 8	12 04	Liverpool	15 1 85	Tranmere R
Bevan Scott (G)	6 6	15 10	Southampton	16 9 79	Kidderminster H
Constable James (F)	6 2	12 12	Malmesbury	4 10 84	Kidderminster H
Davies Ben (M)	5 10	12 08	Birmingham	27 5 81	Chester C
Garner Glyn (G)	6 2	13 11	Pontypool	9 12 86	Leyton Orient
Herd Ben (D)	5 9	10 12	Welwyn	21 6 85	Watford
Hibbert Dave (F)	6 2	12 00	Eccleshall	28 1 86	Preston NE
Humphrey Chris (M)	5 10	10 08	Walsall	19 9 87	WBA
Hunt David (M)	5 11	11 09	Dulwich	10 9 82	Northampton T
Kempson Darran (D)	6 2	13 00	Blackpool	6 12 84	Crewe Alex
Langmead Kelvin (F)	6 1	12 00	Coventry	23 3 85	Preston NE
Leslie Steve (M)	5 11	12 10	Shrewsbury	5 11 87	Scholar
Madjo Guy (F)	6 0	13 05	Cameroon	1 6 84	Cheltenham T
McIntyre Kevin (M)	6 0	11 10	Liverpool	23 12 77	Macclesfield T
Meredith James (D)	6 0	11 09	Albury	4 4 88	Sligo R
Moss Darren (D)	5 10	11 00	Wrexham	24 5 81	Crewe Alex
Pugh Marc (M)	5 11	11 04	Burnley	2 4 87	Bury
Symes Michael (F)	6 3	12 04	Yarmouth	31 10 83	Bradford C
Tierney Marc (D)	5 11	12 04	Bury	23 8 85	Oldham Ath

League Appearances: Ashton, N. 6(9); Barnes, M. 2; Bevan, S. 5; Briggs, K. 1(1); Constable, J. 7(7); Cooke, A. 10(4); Davies, B. 26(1); Drummond, S. 22(1); Garner, G. 41; Hall, A. 13(2); Hall, D. 7(8); Herd, B. 42(3); Hibbert, D. 36(8); Humphrey, C. 7(18); Hunt, D. 22(5); Jones, L. 6(1); Kempson, D. 18(5); Langmead, K. 39; Lee, G. 4(1); Leslie, S. 10(7); Madjo, G. 10(5); McIntyre, K. 22; Meredith, J. 3; Moss, D. 28(3); Murdock, C. 29; Nicholson, S. 6(8); Pugh, M. 27(10); Ryan, J. 1(3); Symes, M. 12(9); Tierney, M. 42(1); Wainwright, N. 2(1).
Goals – League (56): Hibbert 12 (4 pens), Davies 6, Cooke 5, Constable 4, Pugh 4, Drummond 3, Hall A 3, Madjo 3, Symes 3, Hunt 2, McIntyre 2, Moss 2, Murdock 2, Briggs K 1, Langmead 1, Leslie 1, Nicholson 1, Tierney 1.
Carling Cup (1): Kempson 1.
FA Cup (0).
J Paint Trophy (0).
Ground: The New Stadium, Oteley Road, Shrewsbury, Shropshire SY2 6ST. Telephone (0871) 811 8800.
Record Attendance: 18,917 v Walsall, Division 3, 26 April 1961. **Capacity:** 9,875.
Manager: Paul Simpson.
Secretary/General Manager: Jonathan Harris.
Most League Goals: 101, Division 4, 1958–59.
Highest League Scorer in Season: Arthur Rowley, 38, Division 4, 1958–59.
Most League Goals in Total Aggregate: Arthur Rowley, 152, 1958–65 (completing his League record of 434 goals).
Most Capped Player: Jimmy McLaughlin, 5 (12), Northern Ireland; Bernard McNally, 5, Northern Ireland.
Most League Appearances: Mickey Brown, 418, 1986–91; 1992–94; 1996–2001.
Honours – Football League: Division 3 Champions – 1978–79, 1993–94. **Welsh Cup:** Winners – 1891, 1938, 1977, 1979, 1984, 1985.
Colours: Blue and amber.

SOUTHAMPTON   FL CHAMPIONSHIP

Baseya Cedric (F)	6 4	13 03	Bretigny	19 12 87	Scholar
Bialkowski Bartosz (G)	6 3	12 10	Braniewo	6 7 87	Gornik Zabrze
Davies Andrew (D)	6 3	14 08	Stockton	17 12 84	Middlesbrough
Davies Kyle (D)	6 1	12 06	Fremont	4 11 89	Scholar

Davis Kelvin (G)	6 1	14 09	Bedford	29 9 76	Sunderland
Dyer Nathan (M)	5 5	9 00	Trowbridge	29 11 87	Scholar
Euell Jason (F)	5 11	11 13	Lambeth	6 2 77	Middlesbrough
Gillett Simon (M)	5 6	11 07	Oxford	6 11 85	Scholar
Hatch Jamie (M)	5 9	11 03	Exeter	21 9 89	Scholar
James Lloyd (M)	5 11	11 01	Bristol	16 2 88	Scholar
John Stern (F)	6 1	12 13	Tunapuna	30 10 76	Sunderland
Lallana Adam (M)			Southampton	10 5 88	Scholar
Lancashire Oliver (D)	6 1	11 10	Basingstoke	13 12 88	Scholar
McGoldrick David (F)	6 1	11 10	Nottingham	29 11 87	Notts Co
Mills Joseph (F)	5 9	11 00	Swindon	30 10 89	Scholar
Poke Michael (G)	6 1	13 12	Staines	21 11 85	Trainee
Rasiak Grzegorz (F)	6 2	13 10	Szczecin	12 1 79	Tottenham H
Safri Youseff (M)	5 9	12 09	Casablanca	1 3 77	Norwich C
Saganowski Marek (F)	5 10	12 04	Lodz	31 10 78	Troyes
Skacel Rudi (M)	5 10	12 10	Trutnov	17 7 79	Hearts
Surman Andrew (M)	6 0	11 09	Johannesburg	20 8 86	Trainee
Thomas Wayne (D)	6 2	14 12	Gloucester	17 5 79	Burnley
Thomson Jake (M)	5 11	11 05	Southsea	12 5 89	Scholar
Viafara John (M)	6 1	12 12	Robles	27 10 78	Portsmouth
White Jamie (F)	5 8	10 07	Southampton	21 9 89	Scholar
Wright-Phillips Bradley (F)	5 10	11 00	Lewisham	12 3 85	Manchester C

League Appearances: Baseya, C. (1); Bennett, A. 10; Bialkowski, B. 1; Dailly, C. 11; Davies, A. 22(1); Davis, K. 35; Dyer, N. 15(2); Euell, J. 31(7); Gillett, S. (2); Hammill, A. 12(13); Idiakez, I. 14(7); Ifil, P. 11(1); John, S. 35(5); Jones, K. 1; Lallana, A. (5); Licka, M. 10(2); Lucketti, C. 4; Makin, C. 5; McGoldrick, D. 2(6); O'Halloran, S. (1); Ostlund, A. 8(4); Pearce, I. 1; Pericard, V. 1(4); Perry, C. 6; Poke, M. 3(1); Powell, D. 10; Rasiak, G. 13(10); Safri, Y. 37; Saganowski, M. 14(16); Skacel, R. 13(3); Surman, A. 35(5); Thomas, W. 29(1); Viafara, J. 30(10); Vignal, G. 20; Wright, J. 33(3); Wright, R. 7; Wright-Phillips, B. 27(12).
Goals – League (56): John 19, Wright-Phillips 8, Rasiak 6, Euell 3, Saganowski 3, Viafara 3, Vignal 3 (3 pens), Surman 2 (1 pen), Dyer 1, Idiakez 1, Jones 1, Lallana 1, Powell 1, Skacel 1, own goals 3.
Carling Cup (1): Rasiak 1.
FA Cup (4): Surman 2, Rasiak 1, Vignal 1.
Ground: St Mary's Stadium, Britannia Road, Southampton SO14 5FP. Telephone (0845) 688 9448.
Record Attendance: 32,104 v Liverpool, FA Premier League, 18 January 2003.
Capacity: 32,689.
Head Coach: Jan Poortvliet.
Secretary: Liz Coley.
Most League Goals: 112, Division 3 (S), 1957–58.
Highest League Scorer in Season: Derek Reeves, 39, Division 3, 1959–60.
Most League Goals in Total Aggregate: Mike Channon, 185, 1966–77, 1979–82.
Most Capped Player: Peter Shilton, 49 (125), England.
Most League Appearances: Terry Paine, 713, 1956–74.
Honours – Football League: Division 3 (S) Champions – 1921–22. Division 3 Champions – 1959–60. **FA Cup:** Winners – 1975–76.
Colours: Red and white striped shirts, black shorts, white and red hooped stockings.

SOUTHEND UNITED   FL CHAMPIONSHIP 1

Ademeno Charles (F)	5 10	11 13	Milton Keynes	12 12 88	Scholar
Bailey Nicky (M)	5 10	12 06	Hammersmith	10 6 84	Barnet
Barnard Lee (F)	5 10	10 10	Romford	18 7 84	Tottenham H
Barrett Adam (D)	6 1	12 09	Dagenham	29 11 79	Bristol R
Clarke Peter (D)	6 0	12 10	Southport	3 1 82	Blackpool

Flahavan Darryl (G)	5 11	12 06	Southampton	28 11 78	Woking
Foran Richie (F)	5 11	12 03	Dublin	16 6 80	Motherwell
Francis Simon (D)	6 3	14 00	Nottingham	16 2 85	Sheffield U
Gower Mark (M)	5 8	12 02	Edmonton	5 10 78	Barnet
Harrold Matt (F)	6 2	13 07	Walthamstow	25 7 84	Yeovil T
Hooper Gary (M)	5 10	12 07	Harlow	26 1 88	Grays Ath
Liptak Zoltan (D)	6 4	13 00	Hungary	10 12 84	Lombard-Papa
Lokando Mbive (M)	5 11	10 12	Congo	18 9 89	Scholar
MacDonald Charlie (F)	5 8	12 10	Southwark	13 2 81	Charlton Ath
Maher Kevin (M)	6 0	12 00	Ilford	17 10 76	Tottenham H
Masters Clark (G)	6 2	13 12	Hastings	31 5 87	Brentford
McCormack James (M)	5 9	11 09	Dublin	10 1 84	Preston NE
Moussa Franck (M)	5 8	10 08	Brussels	24 9 87	Scholar
Revell Alex (F)	6 3	13 00	Cambridge	7 7 83	Brighton & HA
Scannell Damian (M)	5 10	11 07	Croydon	28 4 85	Eastleigh

League Appearances: Bailey, N. 42(2); Barnard, L. 11(4); Barrett, A. 45; Black, T. 29(9); Bradbury, L. 1; Campbell-Ryce, J. 2; Clarke, L. 16; Clarke, P. 45; Collis, S. 20; Flahavan, D. 26; Foran, R. (6); Francis, S. 24(3); Gilbert, K. 5; Gower, M. 40(2); Grant, A. (10); Hammell, S. 16; Harrold, M. 12(4); Hooper, G. 9(4); Hunt, L. 23(1); MacDonald, C. 11(14); Maher, K. 18(1); McCormack, A. 42; Morgan, D. 6(2); Moussa, F. 6(10); Mulgrew, C. 18; Odhiambo, E. 2(3); Revell, A. 5(3); Richards, G. 8(2); Robson-Kanu, 6(2); Scannell, D. (9); Walker, J. 14(1); Wilson, C. 4(2).

Goals – League (70): Bailey 9, Barnard 9, Gower 9, Clarke L 8 (2 pens), McCormack 8, Barrett 6, Clarke P 4, Walker 4, Robson-Kanu 3, Black 2, Francis 2, Hammell 2 (1 pen), Hooper 2, MacDonald 1, Mulgrew 1.

Carling Cup (7): Bradbury 3 (1 pen), Harrold 2 (1 pen), Barrett 1, MacDonald 1.

FA Cup (10): MacDonald 3, Morgan 3 (1 pen), Bailey 2, Francis 1, Harrold 1 (pen).

J Paint Trophy (2): Foran 1, McCormack 1.

Play-Offs (1): Bailey 1.

Ground: Roots Hall Stadium, Victoria Avenue, Southend-on-Sea SS2 6NQ. Telephone (01702) 304 050.

Record Attendance: 31,090 v Liverpool FA Cup 3rd rd, 10 January 1979. **Capacity:** 12,168.

Manager: Steve Tilson.

Secretary: Helen Norbury.

Most League Goals: 92, Division 3 (S), 1950–51.

Highest League Scorer in Season: Jim Shankly, 31, 1928–29; Sammy McCrory, 1957–58, both in Division 3 (S).

Most League Goals in Total Aggregate: Roy Hollis, 122, 1953–60.

Most Capped Player: George Mackenzie, 9, Eire.

Most League Appearances: Sandy Anderson, 452, 1950–63.

Honours – Football League: Championship 1 Champions – 2005–06. Division 4 Champions – 1980–81.

Colours: Navy blue.

STOCKPORT COUNTY   FL CHAMPIONSHIP 1

Blizzard Dominic (M)	6 2	12 04	High Wycombe	2 9 83	Watford
Coward Chris (F)	6 1	11 07	Manchester	23 7 89	Scholar
Dicker Gary (M)	6 0	12 00	Dublin	31 7 86	Birmingham C
Dickinson Liam (F)	6 4	11 07	Salford	4 10 85	Woodley Sports
Havern Gianluca (F)	6 1	13 00	Manchester	24 9 88	Scholar
McNeil Matthew (F)	6 5	14 03	Macclesfield	14 7 76	Macclesfield T
McNulty Jim (D)	6 1	12 00	Liverpool	13 2 85	Macclesfield T
McSweeney Leon	5 10	10 11	Cork	19 2 83	Leicester C
Owen Gareth (D)	6 1	11 07	Stoke	21 9 82	Oldham Ath

Pilkington Anthony (M)	5 11	12 00	Manchester	3 11 87	Atherton CW
Raynes Michael (M)	6 4	12 00	Wythenshawe	15 10 87	Scholar
Rose Michael (D)	5 11	12 04	Salford	28 7 82	Yeovil T
Rowe Tommy (M)	5 11	12 11	Manchester	1 5 89	Scholar
Smith James (D)	5 10	11 08	Liverpool	17 10 85	Liverpool
Tansey Greg (M)	6 1	12 03	Huyton	21 11 88	Scholar
Taylor Jason (M)	6 1	11 03	Ashton-under-Lyne	28 1 87	Oldham Ath
Tunnicliffe James (D)	6 4	12 03	Denton	17 1 89	Scholar
Turnbull Paul (F)	5 10	11 07	Stockport	23 1 89	Scholar
Williams Ashley (D)	6 0	11 02	Wolverhampton	23 8 84	Hednesford T

League Appearances: Blizzard, D. 22(5); Bowler, M. 4(1); Briggs, K. 5(8); Dicker, G. 29(1); Dickinson, L. 34(6); Elding, A. 18(7); Gleeson, S. 4(2); Griffin, A. 19(9); Havern, G. 1; Logan, C. 34; Logan, S. 6(1); Lowe, R. 4; McNeil, M. 17; McNulty, J. 11; McSweeney, L. 5(6); Morgan-Smith, A. (1); Nowland, A. 4; Owen, G. 35(1); Pilkington, A. 23(6); Poole, D. 13(9); Proudlock, A. 18(15); Raynes, M. 20(7); Rose, M. 25(3); Rowe, T. 17(7); Ruddy, J. 12; Smith, James 24(2); Smith, Johann (2); Tansey, G. 5(8); Taylor, J. 40(2); Thompson, L. 3; Tierney, P. 15(1); Tunnicliffe, J. 1(4); Turnbull, P. 12(7); Vincent, J. (1); Williams, A. 26.
Goals – League (72): Dickinson 19 (2 pens), Elding 13 (4 pens), Proudlock 8, Pilkington 6, Rowe 6, Taylor 4, Rose 3, McNeil 2, Poole 2, Blizzard 1, Griffin 1, Havern 1, McSweeney 1, own goals 5.
Carling Cup (4): Blizzard 1, Elding 1, McNeil 1, Proudlock 1.
FA Cup (2): McNeil 2.
J Paint Trophy (5): Elding 1, McNeil 1, Pilkington 1, Proudlock 1, Tierney 1.
Play-Offs (5): Dickinson 2, Gleeson 1, Pilkington 1, own goal 1.
Ground: Edgeley Park, Hardcastle Road, Edgeley, Stockport, Cheshire SK3 9DD. Telephone (0161) 286 8888 (ext. 257).
Record Attendance: 27,833 v Liverpool, FA Cup 5th rd, 11 February 1950.
Capacity: 10,812.
Manager: Jim Gannon.
Secretary (acting): Rachael Moss.
Most League Goals: 115, Division 3 (N), 1933–34.
Highest League Scorer in Season: Alf Lythgoe, 46, Division 3 (N), 1933–34.
Most League Goals in Total Aggregate: Jack Connor, 132, 1951–56.
Most Capped Player: Jarkko Wiss, 9 (43), Finland.
Most League Appearances: Andy Thorpe, 489, 1978–86, 1988–92.
Honours – Football League: Division 3 (N) Champions – 1921–22, 1936–37. Division 4 Champions – 1966–67.
Colours: Reflex blue shirts, white shorts, white stockings.

STOKE CITY   FA PREMIERSHIP

Buxton Lewis (D)	6 1	13 10	Newport (IW)	10 12 83	Portsmouth
Cort Leon (D)	6 3	13 01	Bermondsey	11 9 79	Crystal Palace
Cresswell Richard (F)	6 0	11 08	Bridlington	20 9 77	Leeds U
De Laet Ritchie (D)	6 1	12 02	Belgium	28 11 88	Antwerp
Delap Rory (M)	6 0	11 10	Sutton Coldfield	6 7 76	Sunderland
Diao Salif (M)	6 1	13 03	Kedougou	10 2 77	Liverpool
Dickinson Carl (D)	6 0	12 00	Swadlincote	31 3 87	Scholar
Fuller Ricardo (F)	6 3	13 03	Kingston	31 10 79	Southampton
Griffin Andy (D)	5 9	10 10	Billinge	7 3 79	Derby Co
Lawrence Liam (M)	5 11	11 03	Retford	14 12 81	Sunderland
Parkin Jon (F)	6 4	13 07	Barnsley	30 12 81	Hull C
Pericard Vincent (F)	6 1	13 08	Efko	3 10 82	Portsmouth
Phillips Demar (F)	5 6	9 04	Kingston	23 9 83	Waterhouse
Pugh Danny (M)	6 0	12 10	Manchester	19 10 82	Preston NE
Pulis Anthony (M)	5 10	11 10	Bristol	21 7 84	Portsmouth
Rooney Adam (F)	5 10	12 03	Dublin	21 4 87	Scholar

Shawcross Ryan (D)　6 3　13 03　Chester　　　　　4 10 87　Manchester U
Shotton Ryan (D)　6 3　13 05　Stoke　　　　　30 9 88　Scholar
Sidibe Mamady (F)　6 4　12 02　Bamako　　　18 12 79　Gillingham
Simonsen Steve (G)　6 2　12 00　South Shields　　3 4 79　Everton
Whelan Glenn (M)　5 11　12 07　Dublin　　　13 1 84　Sheffield W
Wilkinson Andy (D)　5 11　11 00　Stone　　　　6 8 84　Scholar

League Appearances: Ameobi, S. 3(3); Bothroyd, J. 1(3); Buxton, L. (4); Cort, L. 33; Craddock, J. 4; Cresswell, R. 42(1); Delap, R. 44; Diao, S. 8(3); Dickinson, C. 19(8); Eustace, J. 20(6); Fuller, R. 39(3); Gallagher, P. 2(5); Griffin, A. 15; Higginbotham, D. 1; Hill, C. 4(1); Hoult, R. 1; Lawrence, L. 40(1); Matteo, D. 14; Nash, C. 10; Parkin, J. 4(25); Pearson, S. 3(1); Pericard, V. 2(3); Phillips, D. (2); Pugh, D. 27(3); Pulis, A. (1); Riggott, C. 9; Shawcross, R. 39(2); Sidibe, M. 33(2); Simonsen, S. 35(1); Sweeney, P. (5); Whelan, G. 13(1); Wilkinson, A. 16(7); Wright, S. 14(2); Zakuani, G. 11(8).
Goals – League (69): Fuller 15 (2 pens), Lawrence 14 (4 pens), Cresswell 11, Cort 8, Shawcross 7, Sidibe 4, Delap 2, Parkin 2, Whelan 1, own goals 5.
Carling Cup (2): Cresswell 1, Shawcross 1.
FA Cup (1): Lawrence 1.
Ground: Britannia Stadium, Stanley Matthews Way, Stoke-on-Trent ST4 4EG. Telephone (0871) 663 2008.
Record Attendance: 51,380 v Arsenal, Division 1, 29 March 1937 (at Victoria Ground). **Capacity:** 28,218.
Manager: Tony Pulis.
Football Administrator: Eddie Harrison.
Most League Goals: 92, Division 3 (N), 1926–27.
Highest League Scorer in Season: Freddie Steele, 33, Division 1, 1936–37.
Most League Goals in Total Aggregate: Freddie Steele, 142, 1934–49.
Most Capped Player: Gordon Banks, 36 (73), England.
Most League Appearances: Eric Skeels, 506, 1958–76.
Honours – Football League: Division 2 Champions – 1932–33, 1962–63, 1992–93. Division 3 (N) Champions – 1926–27. **Football League Cup:** Winners – 1971–72. **Autoglass Trophy:** Winners – 1992. **Auto Windscreens Shield:** Winners – 2000.
Colours: Red and white striped shirts, white shorts, white stockings.

SUNDERLAND　　　　　　FA PREMIERSHIP

Anderson Russell (D)　5 11　10 09　Aberdeen　　　25 10 78　Aberdeen
Arnau (M)　　　5 8　11 09　Manacor　　　1 10 81　Barcelona
Bardsley Phillip (D)　5 11　11 13　Salford　　　28 6 85　Manchester U
Carson Trevor (G)　6 0　14 11　Downpatrick　　5 3 88　Scholar
Chandler Jamie (M)　5 7　11 02　South Shields　24 3 89　Scholar
Chopra Michael (F)　5 9　10 10　Newcastle　　23 12 83　Cardiff C
Colback Jack (M)　5 9　11 05　Newcastle　　24 10 89　Scholar
Collins Danny (D)　6 2　12 00　Buckley　　　6 8 80　Chester C
Connolly David (F)　5 7　11 09　Willesden　　6 6 77　Wigan Ath
Dowson David (F)　5 10　12 00　Bishop Auckland　12 9 88　Scholar
Edwards Carlos (M)　5 8　11 02　Port of Spain　24 10 78　Luton T
Etuhu Dickson (M)　6 2　13 04　Kano　　　　8 6 82　Norwich C
Fulop Marton (G)　6 6　14 07　Budapest　　3 5 83　Tottenham H
Gordon Craig (G)　6 4　12 02　Edinburgh　31 12 82　Hearts
Halford Greg (D)　6 4　12 10　Chelmsford　8 12 84　Reading
Hartley Peter (D)　6 0　12 06　Hartlepool　　3 4 88　Scholar
Higginbotham Danny (D)　6 2　13 01　Manchester　29 12 78　Stoke C
Jones Kenwyne (F)　6 2　13 06　Trinidad & Tobago　5 10 84　Southampton
Kavanagh Graham (M)　5 10　13 03　Dublin　　2 12 73　Wigan Ath
Kay Michael (D)　6 0　11 05　Shotley Bridge　12 9 89　Scholar
Leadbitter Grant (M)　5 9　11 06　Sunderland　　7 1 86　Trainee
Liddle Michael (D)　5 6　11 00　London　　25 12 89　Scholar

McArdle Niall (D)	6 1	11 09	Dublin	22 3 90	Scholar
McShane Paul (D)	6 0	11 05	Wicklow	6 1 86	WBA
Miller Liam (M)	5 7	10 05	Cork	13 2 81	Manchester U
Murphy Daryl (F)	6 2	13 12	Waterford	15 3 83	Waterford
Nosworthy Nayron (D)	6 0	12 08	Brixton	11 10 80	Gillingham
O'Donovan Roy (F)	5 10	11 07	Cork	10 8 85	Cork C
Prica Rade (F)	6 1	12 08	Ljungby	30 6 80	Aalborg
Reid Andy (M)	5 9	12 08	Dublin	29 7 82	Charlton Ath
Richardson Kieran (M)	5 9	11 13	Greenwich	21 10 84	Manchester U
Stokes Anthony (F)	5 11	11 06	Dublin	25 7 88	Arsenal
Van der Gouw Raimond (G)	6 3	13 09	Oldenzaal	24 3 63	Apeldoorn
Waghorn Martyn (F)	5 9	13 01	South Shields	23 1 90	Scholar
Wallace Ross (M)	5 6	9 12	Dundee	23 5 85	Celtic
Ward Darren (G)	6 0	13 09	Worksop	11 5 74	Norwich C
Way Darren (M)	5 7	11 00	Plymouth	21 11 79	Yeovil T
Weir Robbie (M)	5 9	11 07	Belfast	12 12 88	Scholar
Whitehead Dean (M)	5 11	12 06	Oxford	12 1 82	Oxford U

League Appearances: Anderson, R. (1); Bardsley, P. 11; Chopra, M. 21(12); Cole, A. 3(4); Collins, D. 32(4); Connolly, D. 1(2); Edwards, C. 11(2); Etuhu, D. 18(2); Evans, J. 15; Fulop, M. 1; Gordon, C. 34; Halford, G. 8; Harte, I. 3(5); Higginbotham, D. 21; John, S. (1); Jones, K. 33; Leadbitter, G. 17(14); McShane, P. 20(1); Miller, L. 16(8); Murphy, D. 20(8); Nosworthy, N. 29; O'Donovan, R. 4(13); Prica, R. (6); Reid, A. 11(2); Richardson, K. 15(2); Stokes, A. 8(12); Waghorn, M. 1(2); Wallace, R. 18(3); Ward, D. 3; Whitehead, D. 27; Yorke, D. 17(3).
Goals – League (36): Jones 7, Chopra 6 (1 pen), Higginbotham 3, Murphy 3, Richardson K 3, Leadbitter 2, Wallace 2, Collins 1, Etuhu 1, John 1, Miller 1, Prica 1, Reid 1, Stokes 1, Whitehead 1, Yorke 1, own goal 1.
Carling Cup (0).
FA Cup (0).
Ground: Stadium of Light, Sunderland, Tyne and Wear SR5 1SU. Telephone (0191) 551 5000.
Record Attendance: 75,118 v Derby Co, FA Cup 6th rd replay, 8 March 1933 (Roker Park). 48,353 v Liverpool, FA Premier League, 13 April 2002 (Stadium of Light). **Capacity:** 49,000.
Manager: Roy Keane.
Club Secretary: Margaret Byrne.
Most League Goals: 109, Division 1, 1935–36.
Highest League Scorer in Season: Dave Halliday, 43, Division 1, 1928–29.
Most League Goals in Total Aggregate: Charlie Buchan, 209, 1911–25.
Most Capped Player: Charlie Hurley, 38 (40), Republic of Ireland.
Most League Appearances: Jim Montgomery, 537, 1962–77.
Honours – Football League: Championship – Winners – 2004–05, 2006–07. Division 1 Champions – 1891–92, 1892–93, 1894–95, 1901-02, 1912–13, 1935–36, 1995–96, 1998–99. Division 2 Champions – 1975–76. Division 3 Champions – 1987–88. **FA Cup:** Winners – 1937, 1973.
Colours: Red and white striped shirts, black shorts, red stockings.

SWANSEA CITY   FL CHAMPIONSHIP

Allen Joe (M)	5 6	9 10	Carmarthen	14 3 90	Scholar
Amankwaah Kevin (D)	6 1	12 12	Harrow	19 5 82	Yeovil T
Austin Kevin (D)	6 2	15 00	Hackney	12 2 73	Bristol R
Bauza Guillem (F)	5 11	12 01	Palma de Mallorca	25 10 84	Espanyol
Bodde Ferrie (M)	5 10	12 06	Delft	4 5 82	Den Haag
Britton Leon (M)	5 6	10 00	Merton	16 9 82	West Ham U
Butler Thomas (M)	5 7	12 00	Dublin	25 4 81	Hartlepool U
Collins Matthew (M)	5 9	11 07	Merthyr	31 3 86	Fulham

De Vries Dorus (G)	6 1	12 08	Beverwijk	29 12 80	Dunfermline Ath
Duffy Darryl (F)	5 11	12 01	Glasgow	16 4 84	Hull C
Evans Scott (M)	6 0	11 07	Swansea	6 1 89	Manchester C
Jones Chris (F)	5 9	11 00	Swansea	12 9 89	Scholar
Lawrence Dennis (D)	6 7	11 13	Trinidad	1 8 74	Wrexham
MacDonald Shaun (M)	6 1	11 04	Swansea	17 6 88	Scholar
Monk Garry (D)	6 1	13 00	Bedford	6 3 79	Barnsley
O'Leary Kristian (M)	6 0	12 09	Port Talbot	30 8 77	Trainee
Orlandi Andrea (M)	6 0	12 01	Barcelona	3 8 84	Alaves
Painter Marcos (D)	5 11	12 04	Solihull	17 8 86	Birmingham C
Pratley Darren (M)	6 1	11 00	Barking	22 4 85	Fulham
Rangel Angel (D)	5 11	11 09	Tortosa	28 10 82	Terrassa
Robinson Andy (M)	5 8	11 04	Birkenhead	3 11 79	Cammell Laird
Scotland Jason (F)	5 8	11 10	Morvant	18 2 79	St Johnstone
Tate Alan (D)	6 1	13 05	Easington	2 9 82	Manchester U
Tudur-Jones Owain (M)	6 2	12 00	Bangor	15 10 84	Bangor C
Way Darren (M)	5 7	11 00	Plymouth	21 11 79	Yeovil T

League Appearances: Allen, J. 2(4); Anderson, P. 22(9); Austin, K. 17(2); Bauza, G. 12(16); Bodde, F. 33; Brandy, F. 2(17); Britton, L. 35(5); Butler, T. 29(13); Craney, I. (1); De Vries, D. 46; Duffy, D. 12(8); Feeney, W. 7(3); Lawrence, D. 40; Macdonald, S. (1); Monk, G. 32; O'Leary, K. 5(6); Orlandi, A. 1(7); Painter, M. 29(1); Pratley, D. 39(3); Rangel, A. 43; Robinson, A. 34(6); Scotland, J. 43(2); Tate, A. 18(3); Tudur Jones, O. 2(6); Way, D. (2); Williams, A. 3.
Goals – League (82): Scotland 24 (8 pens), Robinson 8 (1 pen), Anderson 7, Bauza 7, Bodde 6, Butler 6, Feeney 5 (1 pen), Pratley 5, Brandy 3, Lawrence 2, Rangel 2, Duffy 1, Monk 1, Tate 1, own goals 4.
Carling Cup (2): Anderson 1, Scotland 1.
FA Cup (12): Bauza 4, Robinson 2, Scotland 2, Bodde 1, Britton 1, Feeney 1, Pratley 1.
J Paint Trophy (8): Anderson 2, Bauza 2, Scotland 2 (1 pen), Duffy 1, own goal 1.
Ground: Liberty Stadium, Landore, Swansea SA1 2FA. Telephone (01792) 616 600.
Record Attendance: 32,796 v Arsenal, FA Cup 4th rd, 17 February 1968 (at Vetch Field). **Capacity:** 20,520.
Manager: Roberto Martinez.
Secretary: Jackie Rockey.
Most League Goals: 90, Division 2, 1956–57.
Highest League Scorer in Season: Cyril Pearce, 35, Division 2, 1931–32.
Most League Goals in Total Aggregate: Ivor Allchurch, 166, 1949–58, 1965–68.
Most Capped Player: Ivor Allchurch, 42 (68), Wales.
Most League Appearances: Wilfred Milne, 585, 1919–37.
Honours – Football League: Championship 1 – Winners – 2007–08, Division 3 Champions – 1999–2000. Division 3 (S) Champions – 1924–25, 1948–49. **Autoglass Trophy:** Winners – 1994, 2006. **Football League Trophy:** Winners – 2006. **Welsh Cup:** Winners – 11 times.
Colours: All white.

SWINDON TOWN   FL CHAMPIONSHIP 1

Aljofree Hasney (D)	6 0	12 00	Manchester	11 7 78	Plymouth Arg
Allen Chris (M)	5 11	11 10	Bristol	3 1 89	Scholar
Brezovan Peter (G)	6 6	15 04	Bratislava	9 12 79	Brno
Comminges Miguel (D)	5 9	11 03	Les Abymes	16 3 82	Reims
Corr Barry (F)	6 3	12 07	County Wicklow	2 4 85	Sheffield W
Cox Simon (M)	5 10	10 12	Reading	28 4 87	Reading
Easton Craig (M)	5 11	11 03	Bellshill	26 2 79	Leyton Orient
Ifil Jerel (D)	6 1	12 11	Wembley	27 6 82	Watford
Joyce Ben (F)	5 8	11 04	Plymouth	9 9 90	

Kanyuka Patrick (D)	6 0	12 06	Kinshasa	19 7 87	QPR
Kennedy Callum (M)	6 1	12 10	Cheltenham	6 1 89	Scholar
McGovern John-Paul (M)	5 10	12 02	Glasgow	3 10 80	Milton Keynes D
McNamee Anthony (M)	5 6	10 03	Kensington	13 7 84	Watford
Morrison Sean (M)	6 4	14 00	Plymouth	8 1 91	Plymouth Arg
Paynter Billy (F)	6 1	14 01	Liverpool	13 7 84	Southend U
Peacock Lee (F)	6 0	12 08	Paisley	9 10 76	Sheffield W
Pook Michael (M)	5 11	11 10	Swindon	22 10 85	Scholar
Roberts Chris (F)	5 9	13 02	Cardiff	22 10 79	Bristol C
Scott Mark (M)	5 9	12 04	Cheltenham	14 3 86	
Smith Jack (D)	5 11	11 05	Hemel Hempstead	14 10 83	Watford
Smith Phil (G)	6 0	15 02	Harrow	14 12 79	Crawley T
Sturrock Blair (F)	5 10	12 09	Dundee	25 8 81	Rochdale
Vincent Jamie (D)	5 11	11 13	Wimbledon	18 6 75	Yeovil T

League Appearances: Adams, S. 2; Aljofree, H. 38(1); Allen, C. 7(1); Arrieta, I. (4); Ashikodi, M. 4(6); Blackburn, C. 4(3); Brezovan, P. 31; Collins, S. 3(1); Comminges, M. 32(8); Corr, B. 7(10); Cox, S. 35(1); Easton, C. 40; Ifil, J. 39(1); Joyce, B. (3); Kanyuka, P. 3(1); McGovern, J. 34(7); McNamee, A. 18(1); Mohammed, K. 3(8); Morrison, S. 1(1); Nicholas, A. 8(3); Paynter, B. 23(13); Peacock, L. 36(1); Pook, M. 13(9); Roberts, C. 16(11); Scott, M. 1(1); Smith, P. 15; Sturrock, B. 13(8); Timlin, M. 9(1); Tozer, B. 1(1); Vincent, J. 32; Williams, A. (1); Zaaboub, S. 18(11).
Goals – League (63): Cox 15 (2 pens), Paynter 8, Easton 6, Peacock 6, Corr 5 (1 pen), Roberts 5 (2 pens), Sturrock 3, Aljofree 2, McGovern 2, McNamee 2, Ifil 1, Joyce 1, Nicholas 1, Pook 1, Smith J 1, Timlin 1, own goals 3.
Carling Cup (0).
FA Cup (7): Paynter 2, Sturrock 2, Aljofree 1, McGovern 1, Roberts 1.
J Paint Trophy (5): Blackburn 2, Arrieta 1, Cox 1, Sturrock 1.
Ground: The County Ground, County Road, Swindon, Wiltshire SN1 2ED. Telephone (0871) 423 6433.
Record Attendance: 32,000 v Arsenal, FA Cup 3rd rd, 15 January 1972. **Capacity:** 14,800.
Manager: Maurice Malpas.
Secretary: Louise Fletcher.
Most League Goals: 100, Division 3 (S), 1926–27.
Highest League Scorer in Season: Harry Morris, 47, Division 3 (S), 1926–27.
Most League Goals in Total Aggregate: Harry Morris, 216, 1926–33.
Most Capped Player: Rod Thomas, 30 (50), Wales.
Most League Appearances: John Trollope, 770, 1960–80.
Honours – Football League: Division 2 Champions – 1995–96. Division 4 Champions – 1985–86. **Football League Cup:** Winners – 1968–69, 2007–08. **Anglo-Italian Cup:** Winners – 1970.
Colours: All red.

TOTTENHAM HOTSPUR   FA PREMIERSHIP

Alnwick Ben (G)	6 0	12 09	Prudhoe	1 1 87	Sunderland
Archibald-Henville Troy (D)	6 2	13 03	Newham	4 11 88	Scholar
Assou-Ekotto Benoit (D)	5 10	11 00	Douala	24 3 84	Lens
Bale Gareth (D)	6 0	11 10	Cardiff	16 7 89	Southampton
Barcham Andy (F)	5 8	11 10	Basildon	16 12 86	Scholar
Bent Darren (F)	5 11	12 07	Wandsworth	6 2 84	Charlton Ath
Berbatov Dimitar (F)	6 2	12 06	Sofia	30 1 81	Leverkusen
Berchiche Yuri (D)			Resideus	10 2 90	Athletic Bilbao
Boateng Kevin-Prince (M)	6 0	11 09	Berlin	6 3 87	Hertha Berlin
Button David (G)	6 3	13 00	Stevenage	27 2 89	Scholar
Chimbonda Pascal (D)	5 11	11 11	Les Abymes	21 2 79	Wigan Ath

Daniels Charlie (M)	6 1	12 12	Harlow	7 9 86	Scholar
Dawkins Simon (F)	5 10	11 01	Edgware	1 12 87	Scholar
Dawson Michael (D)	6 2	12 02	Northallerton	18 11 83	Nottingham F
Dervite Dorian (D)			Lille	25 7 88	
Forecast Tommy (G)	6 6	11 10	Newham	15 10 86	Scholar
Gardner Anthony (D)	6 3	14 00	Stafford	19 9 80	Port Vale
Ghali Hossam (M)	5 11	12 04	Cairo	15 12 81	Feyenoord
Gilberto (D)	5 11	12 04	Rio de Janeiro	28 2 77	Hertha Berlin
Gunter Chris (D)	5 11	11 02	Newport	21 7 89	Cardiff C
Huddlestone Tom (M)	6 2	11 02	Nottingham	28 12 86	Derby Co
Hughton Cian (D)			Enfield	25 1 89	Scholar
Hutchins Daniel (M)			London	23 9 89	Scholar
Hutton Alan (D)	6 1	11 05	Glasgow	30 11 84	Rangers
Jenas Jermaine (M)	5 11	11 00	Nottingham	18 2 83	Newcastle U
Kaboul Younes (D)	6 2	13 07	St-Julien-en-Genevois	4 1 86	Auxerre
Keane Robbie (F)	5 9	12 06	Dublin	8 7 80	Leeds U
King Ledley (D)	6 2	14 05	Bow	12 10 80	Trainee
Lee Young-Pyo (D)	5 8	10 10	Hong Chung	23 4 77	PSV Eindhoven
Lennon Aaron (M)	5 6	10 03	Leeds	16 4 87	Leeds U
Livermore Jake (M)			Enfield	14 11 89	Scholar
Maghoma Jacques (M)	5 9	11 06	Lubumbashi	23 10 87	Scholar
Malbranque Steed (M)	5 8	11 12	Mouscron	6 1 80	Fulham
Martin Joe (M)	6 0	12 13	Dagenham	29 11 88	Scholar
McKenna Kieran (M)	5 10	10 07	London	14 5 86	Academy
Mills Leigh (D)	6 2	13 00	Winchester	8 2 88	Scholar
O'Hara Jamie (M)	5 11	12 04	Dartford	25 9 86	Scholar
Olsen Alex (F)			Gjovik	9 9 89	Gjovik
Pekhart Tomas (F)			Susice	26 5 89	
Robinson Paul (G)	6 4	15 07	Beverley	15 10 79	Leeds U
Rocha Ricardo (D)	6 0	12 08	Braga	3 10 78	Benfica
Rose Danny (M)	5 8	11 11	Doncaster	2 7 90	Scholar
Stalteri Paul (D)	5 11	11 13	Toronto	18 10 77	Werder Bremen
Taarabt Adel (M)	5 9	10 12	Berre-l'Etang	24 5 89	
Tainio Teemu (M)	5 9	11 09	Tornio	27 11 79	Auxerre
Woodgate Jonathan (D)	6 2	12 06	Middlesbrough	22 1 80	Middlesbrough
Zokora Didier (M)	5 11	12 04	Abidjan	14 12 80	St Etienne

League Appearances: Assou-Ekotto, B. 1; Bale, G. 8; Bent, D. 11(16); Berbatov, D. 33(3); Boateng, K. 7(6); Cerny, R. 13; Chimbonda, P. 31(1); Dawson, M. 26(1); Defoe, J. 3(16); Gardner, A. 4; Gilberto, 3(3); Gunter, C. 1(1); Huddlestone, T. 18(10); Hutton, A. 14; Jenas, J. 28(1); Kaboul, Y. 19(2); Keane, R. 32(4); King, L. 4; Lee, Y. 17(1); Lennon, A. 25(4); Malbranque, S. 35(2); O'Hara, J. 9(8); Ricardo Rocha, 4(1); Robinson, P. 25; Routledge, W. 1(1); Stalteri, P. 3; Taarabt, A. (6); Tainio, T. 6(10); Woodgate, J. 12; Zokora, D. 25(3).
Goals – League (66): Berbatov 15 (1 pen), Keane 15 (3 pens), Bent 6, Defoe 4, Jenas 4, Malbranque 4, Huddlestone 3, Kaboul 3, Bale 2, Chimbonda 2, Lennon 2, Dawson 1, Gardner 1, Gilberto 1, O'Hara 1, Woodgate 1, own goal 1.
Carling Cup (14): Jenas 2, Keane 2, Malbranque 2, Bale 1, Berbatov 1 (pen), Chimbonda 1, Defoe 1, Huddlestone 1, Lennon 1, Woodgate 1, own goal 1.
FA Cup (4): Berbatov 2 (1 pen), Keane 2.
UEFA Cup (18): Berbatov 5 (1 pen), Keane 4, Defoe 3, Bent 2, Dawson 1, Kaboul 1, Malbranque 1, O'Hara 1.
Ground: White Hart Lane, Bill Nicholson Way, 748 High Road, Tottenham, London N17 0AP. Telephone (0870) 420 5000.
Record Attendance: 75,038 v Sunderland, FA Cup 6th rd, 5 March 1938.
Capacity: 36,310.
Manager: Juande Ramos.
Secretary: John Alexander.
Most League Goals: 115, Division 1, 1960–61.
Highest League Scorer in Season: Jimmy Greaves, 37, Division 1, 1962–63.

Most League Goals in Total Aggregate: Jimmy Greaves, 220, 1961–70.
Most Capped Player: Pat Jennings, 74 (119), Northern Ireland.
Most League Appearances: Steve Perryman, 655, 1969–86.
Honours – Football League: Division 1 Champions – 1950–51, 1960–61. Division 2 Champions – 1919–20, 1949–50. **FA Cup:** Winners – 1901 (as non-League club), 1921, 1961, 1962, 1967, 1981, 1982, 1991. **Football League Cup:** Winners – 1970–71, 1972–73, 1998–99, 2007–08. **European Competitions: European Cup-Winners' Cup:** Winners – 1962–63. **UEFA Cup:** Winners – 1971–72, 1983–84.
Colours: White shirts, blue shorts, white and blue hooped stockings.

TRANMERE ROVERS   FL CHAMPIONSHIP 1

Achterberg John (G)	6 1	13 00	Utrecht	8 7 71	Eindhoven
Ahmed Adnan (M)	5 10	11 02	Burnley	7 6 84	Huddersfield T
Cansdell-Sheriff Shane (D)	6 0	12 00	Sydney	10 11 82	Aarhus
Chorley Ben (M)	6 3	13 02	Sidcup	30 9 82	Milton Keynes D
Coyne Danny (G)	6 0	13 00	Prestatyn	27 8 73	Burnley
Curran Craig (F)	5 11	11 11	Liverpool	23 8 89	Scholar
Davies Steve (F)	6 0	12 00	Liverpool	29 12 87	Scholar
Goodison Ian (D)	6 1	12 06	St James, Jam	21 11 72	Seba U
Greenacre Chris (F)	5 9	12 09	Halifax	23 12 77	Stoke C
Henry Paul (M)	5 8	11 06	Liverpool	28 1 88	Scholar
Holmes Daniel (D)	5 10	12 00	Wirral	6 1 89	Scholar
Jennings Steven (M)	5 7	11 07	Liverpool	28 10 84	Scholar
Kay Antony (D)	5 11	11 08	Barnsley	21 10 82	Barnsley
McLaren Paul (M)	6 1	13 04	High Wycombe	17 11 76	Rotherham U
Moore Ian (F)	5 11	12 00	Birkenhead	26 8 76	Hartlepool U
Shuker Chris (M)	5 5	9 03	Liverpool	9 5 82	Barnsley
Taylor Andy (D)	5 11	11 07	Blackburn	14 3 86	Blackburn R
Zola Makongo Calvin (F)	6 3	13 07	Kinshasa	31 12 84	Newcastle U

League Appearances: Achterberg, J. 5; Ahmed, A. 3(3); Cansdell-Sherriff, S. 43(1); Chorley, B. 30(1); Cooper, K. 3(1); Coyne, D. 41; Curran, C. 1(34); Davies, S. 8(2); Goodison, I. 42; Greenacre, C. 36(4); Henry, P. 1(1); Jennings, S. 39(2); Jones, M. 4(5); Kay, A. 30(8); McLaren, P. 43; Moore, I. 17; Mullin, J. 4(6); Myrie-Williams, J. 21(4); Shuker, C. 22(1); Stockdale, R. 43(1); Taylor, A. 29(1); Taylor, G. 19(4); Tremarco, C. 4(4); Zola, C. 18(12).
Goals – League (52): Greenacre 11 (2 pens), Kay 6, Zola 5, McLaren 4, Cansdell-Sherriff 3, Moore 3, Myrie-Williams 3 (1 pen), Shuker 3, Taylor G 3, Curran 2, Davies 2, Jennings 2, Taylor A 2, Chorley 1, Jones 1, own goal 1.
Carling Cup (0).
FA Cup (7): Greenacre 3 (1 pen), Jennings 2, Kay 1, Taylor G 1.
J Paint Trophy (0).
Ground: Prenton Park, Prenton Road West, Birkenhead, Merseyside CH42 9PY. Telephone (0870) 460 3333.
Record Attendance: 24,424 v Stoke C, FA Cup 4th rd, 5 February 1972.
Capacity: 16,567.
Manager: Ronnie Moore.
Secretary: Mick Horton.
Most League Goals: 111, Division 3 (N), 1930–31.
Highest League Scorer in Season: Bunny Bell, 35, Division 3 (N), 1933–34.
Most League Goals in Total Aggregate: Ian Muir, 142, 1985–95.
Most Capped Player: John Aldridge, 30 (69), Republic of Ireland.
Most League Appearances: Harold Bell, 595, 1946–64 (incl. League record 401 consecutive appearances).
Honours – Football League: Division 3 (N) Champions – 1937–38. **Welsh Cup:** Winners – 1935. **Leyland Daf Cup:** Winners – 1990.
Colours: White.

Bradley Mark (D)	6 0	11 05	Dudley	14 1 88	Scholar
Craddock Josh (M)	5 11	10 08	Wolverhampton	5 3 91	Scholar
Deeney Troy (F)	5 11	12 00	Birmingham	29 6 88	Chelmsley T
Demontagnac Ishmel (F)	5 10	11 05	Newham	15 6 88	Charlton Ath
Gerrard Anthony (D)	6 2	13 07	Liverpool	6 2 86	Everton
Gilmartin Rene (G)	6 5	13 06	Islington	31 5 87	St Patrick's BC
Ince Clayton (G)	6 3	13 02	Trinidad	13 7 72	Coventry C
Nicholls Alex (F)	5 10	11 00	Stourbridge	19 12 87	Scholar
Sansara Netan (D)	6 0	12 00	Walsall	3 8 89	Scholar
Smith Emmanuel (D)	6 2	12 03	Birmingham	8 11 88	Scholar
Taundry Richard (D)	5 9	12 10	Walsall	15 2 89	Scholar
Weston Rhys (D)	6 1	12 12	Kingston	27 10 80	Port Vale

League Appearances: Betsy, K. 16; Boertien, P. 20; Bradley, M. 29(6); Brittain, M. (1); Butler, M. 5; Carneiro, C. 2(1); Craddock, J. (1); Dann, S. 28; Deeney, T. 16(19); Demontagnac, I. 10(20); Dobson, M. 21(3); Fox, D. 21(1); Gerrard, A. 44; Hall, P. 7(12); Holmes, L. 19; Ince, C. 46; Mattis, D. 4; McDermott, D. 1(12); Mooney, T. 36; Moore, S. 3(2); N'Dour, A. 3(6); Nicholls, A. 7(12); Ricketts, M. 12; Roper, I. 19; Smith, E. 4; Sonko, E. 30(7); Sonner, D. 6; Sweeney, P. 7; Taundry, R. 12(9); Weston, R. 43(1); Wrack, D. 35(2).
Goals – League (52): Mooney 11 (3 pens), Sonko 5, Holmes 4, Bradley 3, Dann 3, Demontagnac 3, Fox 3, Gerrard 3, Ricketts 3, Betsy 2, Nicholls 2, Butler 1, Deeney 1, Dobson 1, Hall 1, Moore 1, N'Dour 1, Roper 1, Wrack 1, own goals 2.
Carling Cup (0).
FA Cup (5): Ricketts 2 (1 pen), Demontagnac 1, Mooney 1, Nicholls 1.
J Paint Trophy (0).
Ground: Banks's Stadium, Bescot Crescent, Walsall WS1 4SA. Telephone (0871) 221 0442.
Record Attendance: 11,037 v Wolverhampton W, Division 1, 11 January 2003.
Capacity: 11,230.
Manager: Jimmy Mullen.
Secretary: Roy Whalley.
Most League Goals: 102, Division 4, 1959–60.
Highest League Scorer in Season: Gilbert Alsop, 40, Division 3 (N), 1933–34 and 1934–35.
Most League Goals in Total Aggregate: Tony Richards, 184, 1954–63; Colin Taylor, 184, 1958–63, 1964–68, 1969–73.
Most Capped Player: Mick Kearns, 15 (18), Republic of Ireland.
Most League Appearances: Colin Harrison, 467, 1964–82.
Honours – Football League: FL 2 Champions – 2006–07. Division 4 Champions – 1959–60.
Colours: White shirts with red trim, red shorts with white stripe, black stockings with white stripe.

WATFORD   FL CHAMPIONSHIP

Ainsworth Lionel (F)	5 9	9 10	Nottingham	1 10 87	Hereford U
Ashikodi Moses (F)	5 10	10 07	Lagos	27 6 87	Rangers
Avinel Cedric (D)	6 2	13 03	Paris	11 9 86	Creteil
Bangura Al Hassan (M)	5 8	10 07	Sierra Leone	24 1 88	Scholar
Bromby Leigh (D)	5 11	11 06	Dewsbury	2 6 80	Sheffield U
DeMerit Jay (D)	6 1	13 05	Wisconsin	4 12 79	Northwood
Diagouraga Toumani (M)	6 2	11 05	Paris	10 6 87	Scholar
Doyley Lloyd (D)	5 10	12 05	Whitechapel	1 12 82	Scholar
Ellington Nathan (F)	5 10	13 01	Bradford	2 7 81	WBA

Eustace John (M)	5 11	11 12	Solihull	3 11 79	Stoke C
Francis Fran (M)	6 2	14 03	Jamaica	18 1 87	Stoke C
Henderson Darius (F)	6 3	14 03	Sutton	7 9 81	Gillingham
Hoskins Will (F)	5 9	11 11	Nottingham	6 5 86	Rotherham U
Jackson Matt (D)	6 1	14 00	Leeds	19 10 71	Wigan Ath
Kabba Steve (F)	5 10	11 03	Lambeth	7 3 81	Sheffield U
Lee Richard (G)	6 0	13 03	Oxford	5 10 82	Scholar
Loach Scott (G)	6 1	13 01	Nottingham	27 5 88	Lincoln C
Mariappa Adrian (D)	5 10	11 12	Harrow	3 10 86	Scholar
McAnuff Jobi (M)	5 11	11 05	Edmonton	9 11 81	Crystal Palace
Osborne Junior (M)	5 10	12 03	Watford	12 2 88	Scholar
O'Toole John (M)	6 2	13 07	Harrow	30 9 88	
Parkes Jordan (D)	6 0	12 00	Watford	26 7 89	Scholar
Poom Mart (G)	6 4	14 02	Tallinn	3 2 72	Arsenal
Prisken Tamas (F)	6 1	11 07	Komarno	27 6 86	Gyor
Rinaldi Douglas (D)	6 0	12 03	Erval Seco	10 2 84	Veranopolis
Robinson Theo (M)	5 11	11 00	Birmingham	22 1 89	Scholar
Sadler Matthew (D)	5 11	11 08	Birmingham	26 2 85	Birmingham C
Shittu Dan (D)	6 3	15 00	Lagos	2 9 80	QPR
Smith Tommy (M)	5 8	11 04	Hemel Hempstead	22 5 80	Derby Co
Williams Gareth (M)	5 11	12 08	Glasgow	16 12 81	Leicester C
Williamson Lee (M)	5 10	10 04	Derby	7 6 82	Rotherham U

League Appearances: Ainsworth, L. 3(5); Bangura, A. 3(4); Bromby, L. 16; Davenport, C. 1; DeMerit, J. 30(5); Doyley, L. 36; Ellington, N. 18(16); Eustace, J. 13; Francis, D. 6(5); Henderson, D. 34(6); Hoskins, W. (1); Jackson, M. 6; John, C. 3(2); Johnson, A. 11(1); Kabba, S. 7(7); King, M. 25(2); Lee, R. 34(1); Mahon, G. 19; Mariappa, A. 13(12); McAnuff, J. 31(8); O'Toole, J. 23(12); Poom, M. 12; Prisken, T. 7(7); Sadler, M. 14(1); Shittu, D. 37(2); Smith, T. 44; Stewart, J. 33(6); Williamson, L. 27(5).
Goals – League (62): Henderson 12, King 11 (3 pens), Shittu 7, Smith 7, Johnson 5, Ellington 4, O'Toole 3, Francis 2, McAnuff 2, Stewart 2, Williamson 2, Bromby 1, DeMerit 1, Kabba 1, Priskin 1, own goal 1.
Carling Cup (3): Campana 1, Priskin 1, Rinaldi 1.
FA Cup (3): Shittu 2, O'Toole 1.
Play-Offs (1): Henderson 1.
Ground: Vicarage Road Stadium, Vicarage Road, Watford, Hertfordshire WD18 0ER. Telephone (0845) 442 1881.
Record Attendance: 34,099 v Manchester U, FA Cup 4th rd (replay), 3 February 1969. **Capacity:** 18,400.
Manager: Aidy Boothroyd.
Secretary: Michelle Ives.
Most League Goals: 92, Division 4, 1959–60.
Highest League Scorer in Season: Cliff Holton, 42, Division 4, 1959–60.
Most League Goals in Total Aggregate: Luther Blissett, 148, 1976–83, 1984–88, 1991–92.
Most Capped Player: John Barnes, 31 (79), England and Kenny Jackett, 31, Wales.
Most League Appearances: Luther Blissett, 415, 1976–83, 1984–88, 1991–92.
Honours – Football League: Division 2 Champions – 1997–98. Division 3 Champions – 1968–69. Division 4 Champions – 1977–78.
Colours: Yellow shirts, black shorts, yellow stockings.

WEST BROMWICH ALBION   FA PREMIERSHIP

Albrechtsen Martin (D)	6 1	12 13	Copenhagen	30 3 80	FC Copenhagen
Barnett Leon (D)	6 0	12 04	Stevenage	30 11 85	Luton T
Beattie Craig (F)	6 0	11 07	Glasgow	16 1 84	Celtic
Bednar Roman (F)	6 3	13 03	Prague	26 3 83	Hearts
Brunt Chris (M)	6 1	13 04	Belfast	14 12 84	Sheffield W

Clement Neil (D)	6 0	12 03	Reading	3 10 78	Chelsea
Danek Michal (G)	6 5	15 00	Czech Republic	6 7 83	Viktoria Plzen
Daniels Luke (G)	6 1	12 10	Bolton	5 1 88	Manchester U
Davies Curtis (D)	6 2	11 13	Waltham Forest	15 3 85	Luton T
Gera Zoltan (M)	6 0	11 11	Pecs	22 4 79	Ferencvaros
Greening Jonathan (M)	5 11	11 00	Scarborough	2 1 79	Middlesbrough
Hodgkiss Jared (M)	5 6	11 02	Stafford	15 11 86	Scholar
Hoefkens Carl (D)	6 1	12 13	Lier	6 10 78	Stoke C
Kiely Dean (G)	6 1	12 05	Salford	10 10 70	Portsmouth
Koren Robert (M)	5 9	11 03	Ljubljana	20 9 80	Lillestrom
MacDonald Sherjill (F)	6 0	12 06	Amsterdam	20 11 84	Hereford U
Martis Shelton (D)	6 0	11 11	Willemstad	29 11 82	Darlington
Miller Ishmael (F)	6 3	14 00	Manchester	5 3 87	Manchester C
Morrison James (M)	5 10	10 06	Darlington	25 5 86	Middlesbrough
Pele (D)	6 1	13 08	Albufeira	2 5 78	Southampton
Phillips Kevin (F)	5 7	11 00	Hitchin	25 7 73	Aston Villa
Robinson Paul (D)	5 9	11 12	Watford	14 12 78	Watford
Slusarski Bartosz (F)	6 1	12 11	Szamocin	11 12 81	Groclin
Steele Luke (G)	6 2	12 00	Peterborough	24 9 84	Manchester U
Teixeira Felipe (F)	5 9	10 10	Paris	2 10 80	Academica
Tininho (D)	5 9	12 00	Mozambique	13 10 80	Beira Mar
Worrall David (M)	6 0	11 03	Manchester	12 6 90	Bury

League Appearances: Albrechtsen, M. 28(4); Barnett, L. 30(2); Beattie, C. 6(15); Bednar, R. 18(11); Brunt, C. 22(12); Cesar, B. 19(1); Chaplow, R. 2(3); Clement, N. 8(1); Ellington, N. (3); Gera, Z. 33(10); Greening, J. 46; Hodgkiss, J. 3(1); Hoefkens, C. 42; Kiely, D. 44; Kim, D. 1(3); Koren, R. 38(2); MacDonald, S. (10); Martis, S. 2; Miller, I. 24(10); Moore, L. 3(7); Morrison, J. 25(10); Pele, 13(8); Phillips, K. 29(6); Robinson, P. 43; Slusarski, B. (1); Steele, L. 2; Teixeira, F. 24(6); Tininho, 1.
Goals – League (88): Phillips 22 (1 pen), Bednar 13, Koren 9, Miller 9, Gera 8, Teixeira 5, Brunt 4, Morrison 4, Barnett 3, Beattie 3, Albrechtsen 2, Cesar 1, Greening 1, Kim 1, Robinson 1, own goals 2.
Carling Cup (5): Miller 2 (1 pen), Beattie 1, Ellington 1, Gera 1.
FA Cup (16): Miller 5, Bednar 4 (1 pen), Morrison 2, Phillips 2 (1 pen), Brunt 1, Gera 1, Koren 1.
Ground: The Hawthorns, West Bromwich, West Midlands B71 4LF. Telephone (0871) 271 1100
Record Attendance: 64,815 v Arsenal, FA Cup 6th rd, 6 March 1937. **Capacity:** 27,877.
Manager: Tony Mowbray.
Secretary: Darren Eales.
Most League Goals: 105, Division 2, 1929–30.
Highest League Scorer in Season: William 'Ginger' Richardson, 39, Division 1, 1935–36.
Most League Goals in Total Aggregate: Tony Brown, 218, 1963–79.
Most Capped Player: Stuart Williams, 33 (43), Wales.
Most League Appearances: Tony Brown, 574, 1963–80.
Honours – Football League: Division 1 Champions – 1919–20. Championship winners – 2007–08. Division 2 Champions – 1901–02, 1910–11. **FA Cup:** Winners – 1888, 1892, 1931, 1954, 1968. **Football League Cup:** Winners – 1965–66.
Colours: Navy blue and white striped shirts, white shorts, navy blue stockings.

WEST HAM UNITED   FA PREMIERSHIP

Ashton Dean (F)	6 2	14 07	Crewe	24 11 83	Norwich C
Bellamy Craig (F)	5 9	10 12	Cardiff	13 7 79	Liverpool
Blackmore David (G)	6 1	13 00	Chelmsford	23 3 89	Scholar
Boa Morte Luis (F)	5 9	12 06	Lisbon	4 8 77	Fulham
Bowyer Lee (M)	5 9	10 12	Canning Town	3 1 77	Newcastle U

Name	Ht	Wt	Birthplace	Date of Birth	Club
Cole Carlton (F)	6 3	14 02	Croydon	12 11 83	Chelsea
Collins James (D)	6 2	14 05	Newport	23 8 83	Cardiff C
Collison Jack (M)	6 0	13 10	Watford	2 10 88	Scholar
Davenport Calum (D)	6 4	14 00	Bedford	1 1 83	Tottenham H
Dyer Kieron (M)	5 8	10 01	Ipswich	29 12 78	Newcastle U
Etherington Matthew (M)	5 10	10 12	Truro	14 8 81	Tottenham H
Faubert Julien (M)	5 10	11 08	Le Havre	1 8 83	Bordeaux
Ferdinand Anton (D)	6 2	11 00	Peckham	2 85	Trainee
Gabbidon Daniel (D)	6 0	13 05	Cwmbran	8 8 79	Cardiff C
Green Robert (G)	6 3	14 09	Chertsey	18 1 80	Norwich C
Hines Zavon (F)	5 10	10 07	Jamaica	27 12 88	Scholar
Katan Yaniv (F)	6 1	12 13	Haifa	27 1 81	Maccabi Haifa
Ljungberg Frederik (M)	5 9	11 00	Vittsjo	16 4 77	Arsenal
McCartney George (D)	5 11	11 02	Belfast	29 4 81	Sunderland
Miller Ashley (D)			Barking	5 9 89	Scholar
Mullins Hayden (D)	5 11	11 12	Reading	27 3 79	Crystal Palace
Neill Lucas (D)	6 0	12 03	Sydney	9 3 78	Blackburn R
N'Gala Bondz (D)			Newham	13 9 89	Scholar
Noble Mark (M)	5 11	12 00	West Ham	8 5 87	Scholar
Pantsil John (D)	6 0	11 10	Berekum	15 6 81	Hapoel Tel Aviv
Parker Scott (M)	5 9	11 10	Lambeth	13 10 80	Newcastle U
Quashie Nigel (M)	6 0	13 10	Peckham	20 7 78	WBA
Reid Kyel (M)	5 10	12 05	Deptford	26 11 87	Scholar
Sears Freddie (F)	5 8	10 01	Hornchurch	27 11 89	Scholar
Spector Jonathan (D)	6 0	12 08	Arlington	1 3 86	Manchester U
Spence Jordan (M)			Woodford	24 5 90	Scholar
Stokes Tony (M)	5 10	11 10	Bethnal Green	7 1 87	Scholar
Tomkins James (D)	6 3	11 10	Basildon	29 3 89	Scholar
Upson Matthew (D)	6 1	11 04	Stowmarket	18 4 79	Birmingham C
Walker Jim (G)	5 11	13 04	Sutton-in-Ashfield	9 7 73	Walsall
Wright Richard (G)	6 2	14 04	Ipswich	5 11 77	Everton
Zamora Bobby (F)	6 1	11 11	Barking	16 1 81	Tottenham H

League Appearances: Ashton, D. 20(11); Bellamy, C. 7(1); Boa Morte, L. 18(9); Bowyer, L. 12(3); Camara, H. 3(7); Cole, C. 21(10); Collins, J. 2(1); Collison, J. 1(1); Dyer, K. 2; Etherington, M. 15(3); Faubert, J. 4(3); Ferdinand, A. 22(3); Gabbidon, D. 8(2); Green, R. 38; Ljungberg, F. 22(3); McCartney, G. 38; Mullins, H. 32(2); Neill, L. 34; Noble, M. 25(6); Pantsil, J. 4(10); Parker, S. 17(1); Reid, K. (1); Sears, F. 1(6); Solano, N. 14(9); Spector, J. 13(13); Tomkins, J. 5(1); Upson, M. 29; Zamora, B. 11(2).

Goals – League (42): Ashton 10, Bowyer 4, Cole 4, Solano 4, Etherington 3, Noble 3 (2 pens), Bellamy 2, Ferdinand 2, Ljungberg 2, McCartney 1, Parker 1, Sears 1, Upson 1, Zamora 1, own goals 3.

Carling Cup (6): Bellamy 2, Cole 2, Ashton 1, own goal 1.

FA Cup (0).

Ground: The Boleyn Ground, Upton Park, Green Street, London E13 9AZ. Telephone (020) 8548 2748.

Record Attendance: 42,322 v Tottenham H, Division 1, 17 October 1970. **Capacity:** 35,303.

Manager: Alan Curbishley.

Secretary: Peter Barnes.

Most League Goals: 101, Division 2, 1957–58.

Highest League Scorer in Season: Vic Watson, 42, Division 1, 1929–30.

Most League Goals in Total Aggregate: Vic Watson, 298, 1920–35.

Most Capped Player: Bobby Moore, 108, England.

Most League Appearances: Billy Bonds, 663, 1967–88.

Honours – Football League: Division 2 Champions – 1957–58, 1980–81. **FA Cup:** Winners – 1964, 1975, 1980. **European Competitions: European Cup-Winners' Cup:** Winners – 1964–65. **Intertoto Cup:** Winners – 1999.

Colours: Claret and sky blue shirts, white shorts, white stockings.

Aghahowa Julius (F)	5 10	11 07	Benin City	12	2 82	Shakhtar Donetsk
Bouaouzan Rachid (M)	5 6	11 02	Rotterdam	20	2 84	Sparta Rotterdam
Boyce Emmerson (D)	6 0	12 06	Aylesbury	24	9 79	Crystal Palace
Bramble Titus (D)	6 2	13 10	Ipswich	31	7 81	Newcastle U
Brown Michael (M)	5 9	12 04	Hartlepool	25	1 77	Fulham
Camara Henri (F)	5 9	10 08	Dakar	10	5 77	Wolverhampton W
Cotterill David (M)	5 10	11 04	Cardiff	4	12 87	Bristol C
Cywka Tomasz (M)	5 10	11 09	Gliwice	27	6 88	Gwarek Zabrze
Edman Erik (D)	5 10	12 04	Huskvarna	11	11 78	Rennes
Granqvist Andreas (D)	6 3	13 03	Helsingborg	16	4 85	Helsingborg
Heskey Emile (F)	6 2	13 08	Leicester	11	1 78	Birmingham C
Kilbane Kevin (M)	6 1	12 08	Preston	1	2 77	Everton
King Marlon (F)	5 10	12 10	Dulwich	26	4 80	Watford
Kirkland Chris (G)	6 5	14 05	Leicester	2	5 81	Liverpool
Koumas Jason (M)	5 10	11 02	Wrexham	25	9 79	WBA
Kupisz Tomasz (M)			Radom	2	1 90	Piaseczno
Melchiot Mario (D)	6 2	11 09	Amsterdam	4	11 76	Rennes
Montrose Lewis (M)	6 0	12 00	Manchester	17	11 88	Scholar
Nash Carlo (G)	6 5	14 01	Bolton	13	9 73	Preston NE
Palacios Wilson (M)	5 10	11 11	La Ceiba	29	7 84	Birmingham C
Pollitt Mike (G)	6 4	15 03	Farnworth	29	2 72	Rotherham U
Scharner Paul (D)	6 3	13 03	Prugstall	11	3 80	Brann
Sibierski Antoine (M)	6 2	12 04	Lille	5	8 74	Newcastle U
Taylor Ryan (M)	5 8	10 04	Liverpool	19	8 84	Tranmere R
Valencia Luis Antonio (M)	5 11	12 09	Lago Agrio	4	8 85	Villarreal
Webster Andrew (D)	6 2	13 07	Dundee	23	4 82	Hearts

League Appearances: Aghahowa, J. 2(12); Bent, M. 25(6); Boyce, E. 24(1); Bramble, T. 26; Brown, M. 27(4); Cotterill, D. 2; Edman, E. 5; Figueroa, M. 1(1); Folan, C. 1(1); Granqvist, A. 13(1); Hagen, E. 1; Hall, F. (1); Heskey, E. 27(1); Kilbane, K. 33(2); King, M. 8(7); Kirkland, C. 37; Koumas, J. 21(9); Landzaat, D. 19; Melchiot, M. 31; Olembe, S. 2(6); Palacios, W. 16; Pollitt, M. 1; Scharner, P. 37; Sibierski, A. 10(20); Skoko, J. 7(5); Taylor, R. 12(5); Valencia, L. 30(1).
Goals – League (34): Bent 7, Heskey 4, Scharner 4, Sibierski 4 (1 pen), Landzaat 3 (1 pen), Taylor 3, Valencia 3, Bramble 2, Kilbane 1, King 1 (pen), Koumas 1 (pen), own goal 1.
Carling Cup (0).
FA Cup (4): Cotterill 1, Scharner 1, Sibierski 1, own goal 1.
Ground: JJB Stadium, Robin Park, Newtown, Wigan WN5 OUZ. Telephone (01942) 774 000.
Record Attendance: 27,526 v Hereford U, FA Cup 2nd rd, 12 December 1953 (at Springfield Park). **Capacity:** 25,138.
Manager: Steve Bruce.
Secretary: Stuart Hayton.
Most League Goals: 84, Division 3, 1996–97.
Highest League Scorer in Season: Graeme Jones, 31, Division 3, 1996–97.
Most League Goals in Total Aggregate: Andy Liddell, 70, 1998–2004.
Most Capped Player: Lee McCulloch, 11(15), Scotland.
Most League Appearances: Kevin Langley, 317, 1981–86, 1990–94.
Honours – Football League: Division 2 Champions – 2002–03. Division 3 Champions – 1996–97. **Freight Rover Trophy:** Winners – 1984–85. **Auto Windscreens Shield:** Winners – 1998–99.
Colours: Blue and white striped shirts, blue shorts, white stockings.

Bailey Matthew (M)	5 10	9 11	Birmingham	24 9 88	Scholar
Bennett Elliott (M)	5 9	10 13	Telford	18 12 88	Scholar
Bothroyd Jay (F)	6 3	13 00	Islington	7 5 82	Charlton Ath
Collins Lee (D)	6 1	11 10	Telford	23 9 83	Scholar
Collins Neill (D)	6 3	12 06	Irvine	2 9 83	Sunderland
Craddock Jody (D)	6 2	12 00	Bromsgrove	25 7 75	Sunderland
Davies Mark (M)	5 11	11 08	Willenhall	18 2 88	Scholar
Eastwood Freddy (F)	5 11	12 04	Epsom	29 10 83	Southend U
Ebanks-Blake Sylvan (F)	5 10	13 04	Cambridge	29 3 86	Plymouth Arg
Edwards Dave (M)	5 11	11 04	Shrewsbury	3 2 86	Luton T
Edwards Rob (D)	6 1	11 10	Telford	25 12 82	Aston Villa
Elliott Stephen (F)	5 8	11 07	Dublin	6 1 84	Sunderland
Elokobi George (D)	5 10	13 02	Cameroon	31 1 86	Colchester U
Foley Kevin (D)	5 9	11 11	Luton	1 11 84	Luton T
Gleeson Stephen (M)	6 2	11 00	Dublin	3 8 88	Scholar
Gobern Lewis (M)	5 10	11 07	Birmingham	28 1 85	Scholar
Hennessey Wayne (G)	6 0	11 06	Anglesey	24 1 87	Scholar
Henry Karl (M)	6 0	11 02	Wolverhampton	26 11 82	Stoke C
Hughes Liam (F)	6 2	11 09	Gornal	11 9 88	Scholar
Ikeme Carl (G)	6 2	13 09	Sutton Coldfield	8 6 86	Scholar
Jarvis Matthew (M)	5 8	11 10	Middlesbrough	22 5 86	Gillingham
Jones Daniel (D)	6 2	13 00	Rowley Regis	14 7 86	Scholar
Keogh Andy (F)	6 0	11 00	Dublin	16 5 86	Scunthorpe U
Kightly Michael (F)	5 9	11 09	Basildon	24 1 86	Grays Ath
Little Mark (D)	6 1	12 11	Worcester	20 8 88	Scholar
Mulgrew Charlie (D)	6 2	13 02	Glasgow	6 3 86	Celtic
Murray Matt (G)	6 4	13 10	Solihull	2 5 81	Trainee
Olofinjana Seyi (M)	6 2	13 05	Nigeria	30 6 80	Brann
Potter Darren (M)	6 1	11 07	Liverpool	21 12 84	Liverpool
Rosa Denes (M)	5 8	10 05	Hungary	7 4 77	Ferencvaros
Salmon Mark (M)	5 10	10 07	Dublin	31 10 88	Scholar
Ward Darren (D)	6 3	11 04	Kenton	13 9 78	Crystal Palace
Ward Stephen (F)	5 11	12 01	Dublin	20 8 85	Bohemians

League Appearances: Bothroyd, J. 13(9); Breen, G. 18(1); Collins N. 34(5); Craddock, J. 22(1); Eastwood, F. 10(21); Ebanks-Blake, S. 20; Edwards, D. 10; Edwards, R. 4(4); Elliott, S. 18(11); Elokobi, G. 15; Foley, K. 42(2); Gibson, D. 15(6); Gray, M. 29(4); Hennessey, W. 46; Henry, K. 38(2); Jarvis, M. 17(9); Jones, D. (1); Keogh, A. 33(10); Kightly, M. 20(17); Kyle, K. 3(9); Little, M. (1); Olofinjana, S. 35(1); Potter, D. 11(7); Stack, G. (2); Ward, D. 30; Ward, S. 23(6).

Goals – League (53): Ebanks-Blake 12 (2 pens), Keogh 8, Elliott 4 (1 pen), Kightly 4, Bothroyd 3, Collins N 3, Eastwood 3, Gray 3, Henry 3, Olofinjana 3, Craddock 1, Edwards D 1, Edwards R 1, Foley 1, Gibson 1, Jarvis 1, Kyle 1.

Carling Cup (3): Craddock 1, Eastwood 1, Keogh 1 (pen).

FA Cup (6): Keogh 2, Bothroyd 1, Collins, N. 1, Elliott 1, Kightly 1.

Ground: Molineux, Waterloo Road, Wolverhampton WV1 4QR. Telephone (0870) 442 0123.

Record Attendance: 61,315 v Liverpool, FA Cup 5th rd, 11 February 1939.

Capacity: 29,277.

Manager: Mick McCarthy.

Secretary: Richard Skirrow.

Most League Goals: 115, Division 2, 1931–32.

Highest League Scorer in Season: Dennis Westcott, 38, Division 1, 1946–47.

Most League Goals in Total Aggregate: Steve Bull, 250, 1986–99.

Most Capped Player: Billy Wright, 105, England (70 consecutive).

Most League Appearances: Derek Parkin, 501, 1967–82.

Honours – Football League: Division 1 Champions – 1953–54, 1957–58, 1958–59. Division 2 Champions – 1931–32, 1976–77. Division 3 (N) Champions – 1923–24. Division 3 Champions – 1988–89. Division 4 Champions – 1987–88. **FA Cup:** Winners – 1893, 1908, 1949, 1960. **Football League Cup:** Winners – 1973–74, 1979–80. **Texaco Cup:** Winners – 1971. **Sherpa Van Trophy:** Winners – 1988. **Colours:** Old gold and black.

WREXHAM   BLUE SQUARE PREMIER

Name						
Aiston Sam (M)	6 1	14 00	Newcastle	21 11 76	Northampton T
Baynes Wes (M)	5 11	10 10	Chester	12 10 88	Scholar
Done Matt (M)	5 10	10 04	Oswestry	22 6 88	Scholar
Evans Gareth (D)	6 1	12 12	Wrexham	10 1 87	Scholar
Evans Steve (D)	6 4	13 05	Wrexham	26 2 79	TNS
Fleming Andy (M)	6 1	12 00	Liverpool	1 4 87	Scholar
Hope Richard (D)	6 2	12 06	Stockton	22 6 78	Shrewsbury T
Mackin Levi (M)	6 1	12 00	Chester	4 4 86	Scholar
Murtagh Conall (M)	6 0	11 11	Belfast	29 6 85	Rhyl
Pejic Shaun (D)	6 0	11 07	Hereford	16 11 82	Trainee
Proctor Michael (F)	5 11	11 11	Sunderland	3 10 80	Hartlepool U
Spann Silvio (M)	5 9	11 11	Couva	21 8 81	W Connection
Spender Simon (D)	5 11	11 00	Mold	15 11 85	Scholar
Taylor Neil (D)	5 9	10 02	St Asaph	7 2 89	Scholar
Tremarco Carl (D)	5 8	11 11	Liverpool	11 10 85	Tranmere R
Ward Gavin (G)	6 3	14 12	Sutton Coldfield	30 6 70	Chester C
Williams Marc (F)	5 10	11 12	Colwyn Bay	27 7 88	Scholar
Williams Mike (D)	5 11	12 00	Colwyn Bay	27 10 86	Scholar
Williams Tony (G)	6 2	13 09	Maesteg	20 9 77	Carlisle U

League Appearances: Aiston, S. 13(6); Baynes, W. 10(2); Bolland, P. 18; Broughton, D. 16; Carvill, M. 5(3); Collins, M. 2; Crowell, M. 3(3); Done, M. 13(13); Duffy, R. 6(3); Evans, G. 10(3); Evans, S. 30(1); Fleming, A. 2(2); Garrett, R. 9(3); Hall, P. 7(4); Hope, R. 33; Johnson, J. (7); Jones, M. 14(2); Jones, M. 2; Llewellyn, C. 38(2); Mackin, L. 8(1); Murtagh, C. 3(1); Nicholson, S. 9(4); Pejic, S. 17(2); Proctor, M. 23(17); Roberts, N. 35(1); Sonner, D. 9; Spann, S. 7(2); Spender, S. 32(2); Taylor, N. 21(5); Tremarco, C. 10; Ugarte, J. (1); Valentine, R. 14; Ward, G. 22; Whitley, Jeff 5(6); Williams, D. 11(4); Williams, E. 7(6); Williams, Marc 11(8); Williams, Mike 15(3); Williams, T. 22.
Goals – League (38): Proctor 11 (2 pens), Roberts 8 (2 pens), Evans S 3, Llewellyn 3, Marc Williams 3, Baynes 2, Broughton 2, Hall 1, Mackin 1, Sonner 1 (pen), Spann 1, Spender 1, Williams E 1.
Carling Cup (1): Proctor 1.
FA Cup (1): Roberts 1.
Ground: Racecourse Ground, Mold Road, Wrexham LL11 2AH. Telephone (01978) 262 129.
Record Attendance: 34,445 v Manchester U, FA Cup 4th rd, 26 January 1957.
Capacity: 15,500.
Manager: Brian Little.
Secretary: Geraint Parry.
Most League Goals: 106, Division 3 (N), 1932–33.
Highest League Scorer in Season: Tom Bamford, 44, Division 3 (N), 1933–34.
Most League Goals in Total Aggregate: Tom Bamford, 175, 1928–34.
Most Capped Player: Joey Jones, 29 (72), Wales.
Most League Appearances: Arfon Griffiths, 592, 1959–61, 1962–79.
Honours – Football League: Division 3 Champions – 1977–78. **LDV Vans Trophy:** Winners – 2004–05. **Welsh Cup:** Winners – 22 times. **FAW Premier Cup:** Winners – 1998, 2000, 2001, 2003.
Colours: Red shirts, white shorts, red stockings.

WYCOMBE WANDERERS   FL CHAMPIONSHIP 2

Antwi Will (D)	6 2	12 08	Epsom	19 10 82	Aldershot T
Bloomfield Matt (M)	5 9	11 00	Ipswich	8 2 84	Ipswich T
Christon Lewis (M)	6 0	12 02	Milton Keynes	21 1 89	Scholar
Crooks Leon (M)	6 0	11 12	Greenwich	21 11 85	Milton Keynes D
Doherty Tom (M)	5 8	10 06	Bristol	17 3 79	QPR
Duncan Derek (M)	5 10	10 11	Newham	23 4 87	Leyton Orient
Holt Gary (M)	6 0	12 00	Irvine	9 3 73	Nottingham F
Johnson Leon (D)	6 1	13 05	Shoreditch	10 5 81	Gillingham
Knight Leon (F)	5 5	9 06	Hackney	16 9 82	Milton Keynes D
Martin Russell (M)	6 0	11 08	Brighton	4 1 86	Lewes
McCracken David (D)	6 2	11 06	Glasgow	16 10 81	Dundee U
McGleish Scott (F)	5 9	11 09	Barnet	10 2 74	Northampton T
Oakes Stefan (M)	6 1	13 07	Leicester	6 9 78	Notts Co
Rice Robert (D)	5 8	11 11	Hendon	23 2 89	Scholar
Shearer Scott (G)	6 3	12 00	Glasgow	15 2 81	Bristol R
Sutton John (F)	6 2	13 11	Norwich	26 12 83	St Mirren
Torres Sergio (M)	6 2	12 04	Mar del Plata	8 11 83	Basingstoke T
Williamson Mike (D)	6 4	13 03	Stoke	8 11 83	Southampton
Woodman Craig (D)	5 9	10 11	Tiverton	22 12 82	Bristol C
Young Jamie (G)	5 11	13 00	Brisbane	25 8 85	Reading

League Appearances: Antwi, W. 6; Bloomfield, M. 26(9); Boucaud, A. 2(8); Bullock, M. 17(8); Christon, L. 2; Daly, G. (2); Doherty, T. 21(3); Douglas, R. 3; Easter, J. 6; Facey, D. 4(2); Fielding, F. 36; Herd, C. 3(1); Holt, G. 42(1); Johnson, L. 44(1); Knight, L. 12(8); Lennon, N. 8(1); Martin, R. 44; McCracken, D. 35(2); McGleish, S. 45(1); Oakes, S. 23(11); Palmer, C. 1; Phillips, M. 1(1); Reid, R. 1(10); Rice, R. (1); Shearer, S. 4(1); Stockley, S. 18(4); Sutton, J. 23(20); Torres, S. 36(6); Williams, T. 6(4); Williamson, M. 7(5); Woodman, C. 27(2); Young, J. 3(1).
Goals – League (56): McGleish 25 (4 pens), Sutton 6 (1 pen), Knight 5, Torres 5, Bloomfield 4, Oakes 3, Easter 2 (2 pens), Holt 2, Facey 1, McCracken 1, Reid 1, own goal 1.
Carling Cup (1): Oakes 1.
FA Cup (1): Bloomfield 1.
J Paint Trophy (0).
Play-Offs (1): Facey 1.
Ground: Adams Park, Hillbottom Road, Sands, High Wycombe HP12 4HJ. Telephone (01494) 472 100.
Record Attendance: 9,921 v Fulham, FA Cup 3rd rd, 9 January 2002.
Capacity: 10,000.
Manager: Peter Taylor.
Secretary: Keith Allen.
Most League Goals: 72, Championship 2, 2005–06.
Highest League Goalscorer in Season: Sean Devine, 23, 1999–2000.
Most League Goals in Total Aggregate: Nathan Tyson, 42, 2005–06.
Most Capped Player: Mark Rogers, 7, Canada.
Most League Appearances: Steve Brown, 371, 1994–2004.
Honours – GM Vauxhall Conference: Winners – 1993. **FA Trophy:** Winners – 1991, 1993.
Colours: Light and dark blue.

YEOVIL TOWN   FL CHAMPIONSHIP 1

Alcock Craig (D)	5 8	11 00	Truro	8 12 87	Scholar
Bircham Marc (M)	5 11	11 06	Wembley	11 5 78	QPR
Forbes Terrell (D)	5 11	12 07	Southwark	17 8 81	Oldham Ath

Guyett Scott (D)	6 2	13 06	Ascot	20 1 76	Chester C
Jones Nathan (M)	5 6	10 06	Rhondda	28 5 73	Brighton & HA
Kirk Andy (F)	5 11	11 01	Belfast	29 5 79	Northampton T
Mildenhall Stephen (G)	6 5	15 00	Swindon	13 5 78	Grimsby T
Owusu Lloyd (F)	6 2	14 00	Slough	12 12 76	Brentford
Peltier Lee (F)	5 10	12 00	Liverpool	11 12 86	Liverpool
Rose Matthew (D)	5 11	11 04	Dartford	24 9 75	QPR
Skiverton Terry (D)	6 1	13 06	Mile End	26 6 75	Wycombe W
Smith Nathan (D)	5 11	12 00	Enfield	11 1 87	Potters Bar T
Stewart Marcus (F)	5 9	11 00	Bristol	8 11 72	Bristol C
Warne Paul (M)	5 10	11 07	Norwich	8 5 73	Oldham Ath
Williams Marvin (M)	5 11	11 06	London	12 8 87	Millwall

League Appearances: Alcock, C. 5(3); Barry, A. 25(11); Begovic, A. 2; Betsy, K. 5; Bircham, M. 9(4); Bridcutt, L. 6(3); Christophe, J. 4(1); Church, S. 2(4); Cochrane, J. 6(6); Dempsey, G. 10(6); Domoraud, W. (5); Downes, A. 3(2); Flinders, S. 9; Forbes, T. 41; Gillett, S. 3(1); Guyett, S. 34; Hughes, J. (1); Jones, N. 29(2); Jones, R. 6(3); Kirk, A. 15(4); Knights, D. (3); Larrieu, R. 6; Lynch, M. 12(2); Maher, S. 4(2); Mildenhall, S. 29; Morris, L. (1); Owusu, L. 31(12); Peltier, L. 34; Peters, J. 12(2); Rose, M. 27(3); Skiverton, T. 27(4); Smith, N. 6(1); Stewart, M. 35(1); Stieber, Z. 14(1); Walker, J. 11(2); Warne, P. 26(7); Way, D. 7; Welsh, I. (3); Williams, M. 8(15); Woods, M. 3.
Goals – League (38): Owusu 9, Skiverton 5, Kirk 4, Stewart 4, Walker 3, Cochrane 2, Dempsey 2, Betsy 1, Downes 1, Jones N 1, Peters 1, Rose 1, Stieber 1, Warne 1, Way 1, own goal 1.
Carling Cup (1): Owusu 1.
FA Cup (1): Stewart 1.
J Paint Trophy (1): Owusu 1.
Ground: Huish Park, Lufton Way, Yeovil, Somerset BA22 8YF. Telephone (01935) 423 662.
Record Attendance: 9,527 v Leeds U, FL 1, 25 April 2008 (16,318 v Sunderland at Huish). **Capacity:** 9,665.
Manager: Russell Slade.
Secretary: Jean Cotton.
Most League Goals: 90, FL 2, 2004–05.
Highest League Goalscorer in Season: Phil Jevons, 27, 2004–05.
Most League Goals in Total Aggregate: Phil Jevons, 42, 2004–06.
Most Capped Player: Andrejs Stolcers, 1 (81), Latvia and Arron Davies, 1, Wales.
Most League Appearances: Terry Skiverton, 139, 2003–.
Honours – Football League: Championship 2 – Winners 2004–05. **Football Conference:** Champions – 2002–03. **FA Trophy:** Winners 2001–02.
Colours: Green and white shirts, green shorts, white stockings.

LEAGUE POSITIONS: FA PREMIER from 1992–93 and DIVISION 1 1982–83 to 1991–92

	2006-07	2005-06	2004-05	2003-04	2002-03	2001-02	2000-01	1999-2000	1998-99	1997-98	1996-97	1995-96	1994-95
Arsenal	4	4	2	1	2	1	2	2	2	1	3	5	12
Aston Villa	11	16	10	6	16	8	8	6	6	7	5	4	18
Barnsley	–	–	–	–	–	–	–	–	–	19	–	–	–
Birmingham C	–	18	12	10	13	–	–	–	–	–	–	–	–
Blackburn R	10	6	15	15	6	10	–	–	19	6	13	7	1
Bolton W	7	8	6	8	17	16	–	–	–	18	–	20	–
Bradford C	–	–	–	–	–	20	17	–	–	–	–	–	–
Brighton & HA	–	–	–	–	–	–	–	–	–	–	–	–	–
Charlton Ath	19	13	11	7	12	14	9	–	18	–	–	–	–
Chelsea	2	1	1	2	4	6	6	5	3	4	6	11	11
Coventry C	–	–	–	–	–	–	19	14	15	11	17	16	16
Crystal Palace	–	–	18	–	–	–	–	–	–	20	–	–	19
Derby Co	–	–	–	–	–	19	17	16	8	9	12	–	–
Everton	6	11	4	17	7	15	16	13	14	17	15	6	15
Fulham	16	12	13	9	14	13	–	–	–	–	–	–	–
Ipswich T	–	–	–	–	–	18	5	–	–	–	–	–	22
Leeds U	–	–	–	19	15	5	4	3	4	5	11	13	5
Leicester C	–	–	–	18	–	20	13	8	10	10	9	–	21
Liverpool	3	3	5	4	5	2	3	4	7	3	4	3	4
Luton T	–	–	–	–	–	–	–	–	–	–	–	–	–
Manchester C	14	15	8	16	9	–	18	–	–	–	–	18	17
Manchester U	1	2	3	3	1	3	1	1	1	2	1	1	2
Middlesbrough	12	14	7	11	11	12	14	12	9	–	19	12	–
Millwall	–	–	–	–	–	–	–	–	–	–	–	–	–
Newcastle U	13	7	14	5	3	4	11	11	13	13	2	2	6
Norwich C	–	–	19	–	–	–	–	–	–	–	–	–	20
Nottingham F	–	–	–	–	–	–	–	–	20	–	20	9	3
Notts Co	–	–	–	–	–	–	–	–	–	–	–	–	–
Oldham Ath	–	–	–	–	–	–	–	–	–	–	–	–	–
Oxford U	–	–	–	–	–	–	–	–	–	–	–	–	–
Portsmouth	9	17	16	13	–	–	–	–	–	–	–	–	–
QPR	–	–	–	–	–	–	–	–	–	–	–	19	8
Readng	8	–	–	–	–	–	–	–	–	–	–	–	–
Sheffield U	18	–	–	–	–	–	–	–	–	–	–	–	–
Sheffield W	–	–	–	–	–	–	–	19	12	16	7	15	13
Southampton	–	–	20	12	8	11	10	15	17	12	16	17	10
Stoke C	–	–	–	–	–	–	–	–	–	–	–	–	–
Sunderland	–	20	–	–	20	17	7	7	–	–	18	–	–
Swansea C	–	–	–	–	–	–	–	–	–	–	–	–	–
Swindon T	–	–	–	–	–	–	–	–	–	–	–	–	–
Tottenham H	5	5	9	14	10	9	12	10	11	14	10	8	7
Watford	20	–	–	–	–	–	–	20	–	–	–	–	–
WBA	–	19	17	–	19	–	–	–	–	–	–	–	–
West Ham U	15	9	–	–	18	7	15	9	5	8	14	10	14
Wigan Ath	17	10	–	–	–	–	–	–	–	–	–	–	–
Wimbledon	–	–	–	–	–	–	–	18	16	15	8	14	9
Wolverhampton W	–	–	–	20	–	–	–	–	–	–	–	–	–

	1993-94	1992-93	1991-92	1990-91	1989-90	1988-89	1987-88	1986-87	1985-86	1984-85	1983-84	1982-83
Arsenal	4	10	4	1	4	1	6	4	7	7	6	10
Aston Villa	10	2	7	17	2	17	–	22	16	10	10	6
Barnsley	–	–	–	–	–	–	–	–	–	–	–	–
Birmingham C	–	–	–	–	–	–	–	–	21	–	20	17
Blackburn R	2	4	–	–	–	–	–	–	–	–	–	–
Bolton W	–	–	–	–	–	–	–	–	–	–	–	–
Bradford C	–	–	–	–	–	–	–	–	–	–	–	–
Brighton & HA	–	–	–	–	–	–	–	–	–	–	–	22
Charlton Ath	–	–	–	–	19	14	17	19	–	–	–	–
Chelsea	14	11	14	11	5	–	18	14	6	6	–	–
Coventry C	11	15	19	16	12	7	10	10	17	18	19	19
Crystal Palace	–	20	10	3	15	–	–	–	–	–	–	–
Derby Co	–	–	–	20	16	5	15	–	–	–	–	–
Everton	17	13	12	9	6	8	4	1	2	1	7	7
Fulham	–	–	–	–	–	–	–	–	–	–	–	–
Ipswich T	19	16	–	–	–	–	–	–	20	17	12	9
Leeds U	5	17	1	4	–	–	–	–	–	–	–	–
Leicester C	–	–	–	–	–	–	20	19	15	15	–	1
Liverpool	8	6	6	2	1	2	1	2	1	2	1	1
Luton T	–	–	20	18	17	16	9	7	9	13	16	18
Manchester C	16	9	5	5	14	–	21	15	–	–	–	20
Manchester U	1	1	2	6	13	11	2	11	4	4	4	3
Middlesbrough	–	21	–	–	–	18	–	–	–	–	–	–
Millwall	–	–	–	20	10	–	–	–	–	–	–	–
Newcastle U	3	–	–	–	–	20	8	17	11	14	–	–
Norwich C	12	3	18	15	10	4	14	5	–	20	14	14
Nottingham F	–	22	8	8	9	3	3	8	8	9	3	5
Notts Co	–	–	21	–	–	–	–	–	–	–	21	15
Oldham Ath	21	19	17	–	–	–	–	–	–	–	–	–
Oxford U	–	–	–	–	–	–	21	18	18	–	–	–
Portsmouth	–	–	–	–	–	–	–	19	–	–	–	–
QPR	9	5	11	12	11	9	5	16	13	19	5	–
Reading	–	–	–	–	–	–	–	–	–	–	–	–
Sheffield U	20	14	9	13	–	–	–	–	–	–	–	–
Sheffield W	7	7	3	–	18	15	11	13	5	8	–	–
Southampton	18	18	16	14	7	13	12	12	14	5	2	12
Stoke C	–	–	–	–	–	–	–	–	–	22	18	13
Sunderland	–	–	–	19	–	–	–	–	–	21	13	16
Swansea C	–	–	–	–	–	–	–	–	–	–	–	21
Swindon T	22	–	–	–	–	–	–	–	–	–	–	–
Tottenham H	15	8	15	10	3	6	13	3	10	3	8	4
Watford	–	–	–	–	–	–	20	9	12	11	11	2
WBA	–	–	–	–	–	–	–	–	22	12	17	11
West Ham U	13	–	22	–	–	19	16	15	3	16	9	8
Wigan Ath	–	–	–	–	–	–	–	–	–	–	–	–
Wimbledon	6	12	13	7	8	12	7	6	–	–	–	–
Wolverhampton W	–	–	–	–	–	–	–	–	–	–	22	–

LEAGUE POSITIONS: DIVISION 1 from 1992–93, CHAMPIONSHIP from 2004–05 and DIVISION 2 1982–83 to 1991–92

	2006-07	2005-06	2004-05	2003-04	2002-03	2001-02	2000-01	1999-2000	1998-99	1997-98	1996-97	1995-96	1994-95
Aston Villa	–	–	–	–	–	–	–	–	–	–	–	–	–
Barnsley	20	–	–	–	–	23	16	4	13	–	2	10	6
Birmingham C	2	–	–	–	–	5	5	5	4	7	10	15	–
Blackburn R	–	–	–	–	–	–	2	11	–	–	–	–	–
Bolton W	–	–	–	–	–	3	6	6	–	1	–	–	3
Bournemouth	–	–	–	–	–	–	–	–	–	–	–	–	–
Bradford C	–	–	–	23	19	15	–	–	2	13	21	–	–
Brentford	–	–	–	–	–	–	–	–	–	–	–	–	–
Brighton & HA	–	22	20	–	23	–	–	–	–	–	–	–	–
Bristol C	–	–	–	–	–	–	–	24	–	–	–	–	23
Bristol R	–	–	–	–	–	–	–	–	–	–	–	–	–
Burnley	15	17	13	19	16	7	7	–	–	–	–	–	22
Bury	–	–	–	–	–	–	–	–	22	17	–	–	–
Cambridge U	–	–	–	–	–	–	–	–	–	–	–	–	–
Cardiff C	13	11	16	13	–	–	–	–	–	–	–	–	–
Carlisle U	–	–	–	–	–	–	–	–	–	–	–	–	–
Charlton Ath	–	–	–	–	–	–	–	1	–	4	15	6	15
Chelsea	–	–	–	–	–	–	–	–	–	–	–	–	–
Colchester U	10	–	–	–	–	–	–	–	–	–	–	–	–
Coventry C	17	8	19	12	20	11	–	–	–	–	–	–	–
Crewe Alex	–	22	21	18	–	22	14	19	18	11	–	–	–
Crystal Palace	12	6	–	6	14	10	21	15	14	–	6	3	–
Derby Co	3	20	4	20	18	–	–	–	–	–	–	2	9
Fulham	–	–	–	–	–	–	1	9	–	–	–	–	–
Gillingham	–	–	22	21	11	12	13	–	–	–	–	–	–
Grimsby T	–	–	–	–	24	19	18	20	11	–	22	17	10
Huddersfield T	–	–	–	–	–	–	22	8	10	16	20	8	–
Hull C	21	18	–	–	–	–	–	–	–	–	–	–	–
Ipswich T	14	15	3	5	7	–	–	3	3	5	4	7	–
Leeds U	24	5	14	–	–	–	–	–	–	–	–	–	–
Leicester C	19	16	15	–	2	–	–	–	–	–	–	5	–
Leyton Orient	–	–	–	–	–	–	–	–	–	–	–	–	–
Luton T	23	10	–	–	–	–	–	–	–	–	–	24	16
Manchester C	–	–	–	–	–	1	–	2	–	22	14	–	–
Mansfield T	–	–	–	–	–	–	–	–	–	–	–	–	–
Middlesbrough	–	–	–	–	–	–	–	–	–	2	–	–	1
Millwall	–	23	10	10	9	4	–	–	–	–	–	22	12
Newcastle U	–	–	–	–	–	–	–	–	–	–	–	–	–
Norwich C	16	9	–	1	8	6	15	12	9	15	13	16	–
Nottingham F	–	–	23	14	6	16	11	14	–	1	–	–	–
Notts Co	–	–	–	–	–	–	–	–	–	–	–	–	24
Oldham Ath	–	–	–	–	–	–	–	–	–	–	23	18	14
Oxford U	–	–	–	–	–	–	–	–	23	12	17	–	–
Peterborough U	–	–	–	–	–	–	–	–	–	–	–	–	–
Plymouth Arg	11	14	17	–	–	–	–	–	–	–	–	–	–
Port Vale	–	–	–	–	–	–	–	23	21	19	8	12	17
Portsmouth	–	–	–	–	1	17	20	18	19	20	7	21	18
Preston NE	7	4	5	15	12	8	4	–	–	–	–	–	–
QPR	18	21	11	–	–	–	23	10	20	21	9	–	–

1993-94	1992-93	1991-92	1990-91	1989-90	1988-89	1987-88	1986-87	1985-86	1984-85	1983-84	1982-83	
–	–	–	–	–	–	2	–	–	–	–	–	Aston Villa
18	13	16	8	19	7	14	11	12	11	14	10	Barnsley
22	19	–	–	23	19	19	–	2	–	–	–	Birmingham C
–	–	6	19	5	5	5	12	19	5	6	11	Blackburn R
14	–	–	–	–	–	–	–	–	–	–	22	Bolton W
–	–	–	–	22	12	17	–	–	–	–	–	Bournemouth
–	–	–	–	23	14	4	10	13	–	–	–	Bradford C
–	22	–	–	–	–	–	–	–	–	–	–	Brentford
–	–	23	6	18	19	–	22	11	6	9	–	Brighton & HA
13	15	17	9	–	–	–	–	–	–	–	–	Bristol C
–	24	13	13	–	–	–	–	–	–	–	–	Bristol R
–	–	–	–	–	–	–	–	–	–	–	21	Burnley
–	–	–	–	–	–	–	–	–	–	–	–	Bury
–	23	5	–	–	–	–	–	–	–	22	12	Cambridge U
–	–	–	–	–	–	–	–	–	21	15	–	Cardiff C
–	–	–	–	–	–	–	–	20	16	7	14	Carlisle U
11	12	7	16	–	–	–	–	2	17	13	17	Charlton Ath
–	–	–	–	–	1	–	–	–	–	1	18	Chelsea
–	–	–	–	–	–	–	–	–	–	–	–	Colchester U
–	–	–	–	–	–	–	–	–	–	–	–	Coventry C
–	–	–	–	–	–	–	–	–	–	–	–	Crewe Alex
1	–	–	–	–	3	6	6	5	15	18	15	Crystal Palace
6	8	3	–	–	–	–	1	–	–	20	13	Derby Co
–	–	–	–	–	–	–	–	22	9	11	4	Fulham
–	–	–	–	–	–	–	–	–	–	–	–	Gillingham
16	9	19	–	–	–	21	15	10	5	19	–	Grimsby T
–	–	–	–	–	–	23	17	16	13	12	–	Huddersfield T
–	–	24	14	21	15	14	6	–	–	–	–	Hull C
–	–	1	14	9	8	8	5	–	–	–	–	Ipswich T
–	–	–	–	1	10	7	4	14	7	10	8	Leeds U
4	6	4	22	13	15	13	–	–	–	–	3	Leicester C
–	–	–	–	–	–	–	–	–	–	–	–	Leyton Orient
20	20	–	–	–	–	–	–	–	–	–	–	Luton T
–	–	–	–	–	2	9	–	–	3	4	–	Manchester C
–	–	–	–	–	–	–	–	–	–	–	–	Mansfield T
9	–	2	7	21	–	3	–	21	19	17	16	Middlesbrough
3	7	15	5	–	–	1	16	9	–	–	–	Millwall
–	1	20	11	3	–	–	–	–	–	3	5	Newcastle U
–	–	–	–	–	–	–	–	1	–	–	–	Norwich C
2	–	–	–	–	–	–	–	–	–	–	–	Nottingham F
7	17	–	4	–	–	–	–	–	20	–	–	Notts Co
–	–	–	1	8	16	10	3	8	14	19	7	Oldham Ath
23	14	21	10	17	17	–	–	–	1	–	–	Oxford U
24	10	–	–	–	–	–	–	–	–	–	–	Peterborough U
–	–	22	18	16	18	16	7	–	–	–	–	Plymouth Arg
–	–	24	15	11	–	–	–	–	–	–	–	Port Vale
17	3	9	17	12	20	–	2	4	4	16	–	Portsmouth
–	–	–	–	–	–	–	–	–	–	–	–	Preston NE
–	–	–	–	–	–	–	–	–	–	–	1	QPR

LEAGUE POSITIONS: DIVISION 1 from 1992–93, CHAMPIONSHIP from 2004–05 and DIVISION 2 1982–83 to 1991–92 (cont.)

	2006-07	2005-06	2004-05	2003-04	2002-03	2001-02	2000-01	1999-2000	1998-99	1997-98	1996-97	1995-96	1994-95
Reading	–	1	7	9	4	–	–	–	–	24	18	19	2
Sheffield U	–	2	8	8	3	13	10	16	8	6	5	9	8
Sheffield W	9	19	–	–	22	20	17	–	–	–	–	–	–
Shrewsbury T	–	–	–	–	–	–	–	–	–	–	–	–	–
Southampton	6	12	–	–	–	–	–	–	–	–	–	–	–
Southend U	22	–	–	–	–	–	–	–	–	–	24	14	13
Stockport Co	–	–	–	–	–	24	19	17	16	8	–	–	–
Stoke C	8	13	12	11	21	–	–	–	–	23	12	4	11
Sunderland	1	–	1	3	–	–	–	–	1	3	–	1	20
Swansea C	–	–	–	–	–	–	–	–	–	–	–	–	–
Swindon T	–	–	–	–	–	–	–	24	17	18	19	–	21
Tranmere R	–	–	–	–	–	–	24	13	15	14	11	13	5
Walsall	–	–	–	22	17	18	–	22	–	–	–	–	–
Watford	–	3	18	16	13	14	9	–	5	–	–	23	7
WBA	4	–	–	2	–	2	6	21	12	10	16	11	19
West Ham U	–	–	6	4	–	–	–	–	–	–	–	–	–
Wigan Ath	–	–	2	7	–	–	–	–	–	–	–	–	–
Wimbledon	–	–	–	24	10	9	8	–	–	–	–	–	–
Wolverhampton W	5	7	9	–	5	3	12	7	7	9	3	20	4

LEAGUE POSITIONS: DIVISION 2 from 1992–93, LEAGUE 1 from 2004–05 and DIVISION 3 1982–83 to 1991–92

	2006-07	2005-06	2004-05	2003-04	2002-03	2001-02	2000-01	1999-2000	1998-99	1997-98	1996-97	1995-96	1994-95
Aldershot	–	–	–	–	–	–	–	–	–	–	–	–	–
Barnet	–	–	–	–	–	–	–	–	–	–	–	–	–
Barnsley	–	5	13	12	19	–	–	–	–	–	–	–	–
Birmingham C	–	–	–	–	–	–	–	–	–	–	–	–	1
Blackpool	3	19	16	14	13	16	–	22	14	12	7	3	12
Bolton W	–	–	–	–	–	–	–	–	–	–	–	–	–
Bournemouth	19	17	8	9	–	21	7	16	7	9	16	14	19
Bradford C	22	11	11	–	–	–	–	–	–	–	–	6	14
Brentford	24	3	4	17	16	3	14	17	–	21	4	15	2
Brighton & HA	18	–	–	4	–	1	–	–	–	–	–	23	16
Bristol C	2	9	7	3	3	7	9	9	–	2	5	13	–
Bristol R	–	–	–	–	–	–	21	7	13	5	17	10	4
Burnley	–	–	–	–	–	–	–	2	15	20	9	17	–
Bury	–	–	–	–	–	22	16	15	–	–	1	–	–
Cambridge U	–	–	–	–	–	24	19	19	–	–	–	–	20
Cardiff C	–	–	–	6	4	–	21	–	–	–	–	–	22
Carlisle U	8	–	–	–	–	–	–	–	–	23	–	21	–

	1993–94	1992–93	1991–92	1990–91	1989–90	1988–89	1987–88	1986–87	1985–86	1984–85	1983–84	1982–83
Reading	–	–	–	–	–	–	22	13	–	–	–	–
Sheffield U	–	–	–	–	2	–	21	9	7	18	–	–
Sheffield W	–	–	–	3	–	–	–	–	–	–	2	6
Shrewsbury T	–	–	–	–	–	22	18	18	17	8	8	9
Southampton	–	–	–	–	–	–	–	–	–	–	–	–
Southend U	15	18	12	–	–	–	–	–	–	–	–	–
Stockport Co	–	–	–	–	–	–	–	–	–	–	–	–
Stoke C	10	–	–	–	24	13	11	8	10	–	–	–
Sunderland	12	21	18	–	6	11	–	20	18	–	–	–
Swansea C	–	–	–	–	–	–	–	–	–	21	–	–
Swindon T	–	5	8	21	4	6	12	–	–	–	–	–
Tranmere R	5	4	14	–	–	–	–	–	–	–	–	–
Walsall	–	–	–	–	–	24	–	–	–	–	–	–
Watford	19	16	10	20	15	4	–	–	–	–	–	–
WBA	21	–	–	23	20	9	20	15	–	–	–	–
West Ham U	–	2	–	2	7	–	–	–	–	–	–	–
Wigan Ath	–	–	–	–	–	–	–	–	–	–	–	–
Wimbledon	–	–	–	–	–	–	–	–	3	12	–	–
Wolverhampton W	8	11	11	12	10	–	–	–	–	22	–	2

	1993–94	1992–93	1991–92	1990–91	1989–90	1988–89	1987–88	1986–87	1985–86	1984–85	1983–84	1982–83
Aldershot	–	–	–	–	–	24	20	–	–	–	–	–
Barnet	24	–	–	–	–	–	–	–	–	–	–	–
Barnsley	–	–	–	–	–	–	–	–	–	–	–	–
Birmingham C	–	–	2	12	7	–	–	–	–	–	–	–
Blackpool	20	18	–	–	23	19	10	9	12	–	–	–
Bolton W	–	2	13	4	6	10	–	21	18	17	10	–
Bournemouth	17	17	8	9	–	–	1	15	10	17	14	–
Bradford C	7	10	16	8	–	–	–	–	1	7	12	–
Brentford	16	–	1	6	13	7	12	11	10	13	20	9
Brighton & HA	14	9	–	–	–	2	–	–	–	–	–	–
Bristol C	–	–	–	2	11	5	6	9	5	–	–	–
Bristol R	8	–	–	1	5	8	19	16	6	5	7	–
Burnley	6	13	–	–	–	–	–	–	21	12	–	–
Bury	–	–	21	7	5	13	14	16	20	–	–	–
Cambridge U	10	–	–	1	–	–	–	–	24	–	–	–
Cardiff C	19	–	–	–	21	16	–	22	–	–	–	2
Carlisle U	–	–	–	–	–	–	22	–	–	–	–	–

117

LEAGUE POSITIONS: DIVISION 2 from 1992–93, LEAGUE 1 from 2004–05 and DIVISION 3 1982–83 to 1991–92 (cont.)

	2006-07	2005-06	2004-05	2003-04	2002-03	2001-02	2000-01	1999-2000	1998-99	1997-98	1996-97	1995-96	1994-95
Cheltenham T	17	–	–	–	21	–	–	–	–	–	–	–	–
Chester C	–	–	–	–	–	–	–	–	–	–	–	–	23
Chesterfield	21	16	17	20	20	18	–	24	9	10	10	7	–
Colchester U	–	2	15	11	12	15	17	18	18	–	–	–	–
Crewe Alex	13	–	–	–	2	–	–	–	–	–	6	5	3
Darlington	–	–	–	–	–	–	–	–	–	–	–	–	–
Derby Co	–	–	–	–	–	–	–	–	–	–	–	–	–
Doncaster R	11	8	10	–	–	–	–	–	–	–	–	–	–
Exeter C	–	–	–	–	–	–	–	–	–	–	–	–	–
Fulham	–	–	–	–	–	–	–	1	6	–	–	–	–
Gillingham	16	14	–	–	–	–	–	3	4	8	11	–	–
Grimsby T	–	–	–	21	–	–	–	–	–	3	–	–	–
Hartlepool U	–	21	6	6	–	–	–	–	–	–	–	–	–
Huddersfield T	15	4	9	–	22	6	–	–	–	–	–	–	5
Hull C	–	–	2	–	–	–	–	–	–	–	–	24	8
Leyton Orient	20	–	–	–	–	–	–	–	–	–	–	–	24
Lincoln C	–	–	–	–	–	–	–	23	–	–	–	–	–
Luton T	–	–	1	10	9	–	22	13	12	17	3	–	–
Macclesfield T	–	–	–	–	–	–	–	–	24	–	–	–	–
Manchester C	–	–	–	–	–	–	–	–	3	–	–	–	–
Mansfield T	–	–	–	–	23	–	–	–	–	–	–	–	–
Middlesbrough	–	–	–	–	–	–	–	–	–	–	–	–	–
Millwall	10	–	–	–	–	–	1	5	10	18	14	–	–
Newport Co	–	–	–	–	–	–	–	–	–	–	–	–	–
Northampton T	14	–	–	–	24	20	18	–	22	4	–	–	–
Nottingham F	4	7	–	–	–	–	–	–	–	–	–	–	–
Notts Co	–	–	–	23	15	19	8	8	16	–	24	4	–
Oldham Ath	6	10	19	15	5	9	15	14	20	13	–	–	–
Oxford U	–	–	–	–	–	–	24	20	–	–	–	2	7
Peterborough U	–	–	23	18	11	17	12	–	–	–	21	19	15
Plymouth Arg	–	–	–	1	8	–	–	–	–	22	19	–	21
Portsmouth	–	–	–	–	–	–	–	–	–	–	–	–	–
Port Vale	12	13	18	7	17	14	11	–	–	–	–	–	–
Preston NE	–	–	–	–	–	–	–	1	5	15	15	–	–
QPR	–	–	–	2	4	8	–	–	–	–	–	–	–
Reading	–	–	–	–	–	2	3	10	11	–	–	–	–
Rotherham U	23	20	–	–	–	–	2	–	–	–	23	16	17
Rushden & D	–	–	–	22	–	–	–	–	–	–	–	–	–
Scunthorpe U	1	12	–	–	–	–	–	23	–	–	–	–	–
Sheffield U	–	–	–	–	–	–	–	–	–	–	–	–	–
Sheffield W	–	–	5	16	–	–	–	–	–	–	–	–	–
Shrewsbury T	–	–	–	–	–	–	–	–	–	–	22	18	18
Southend U	–	1	–	–	–	–	–	–	–	24	–	–	–
Stockport Co	–	–	24	19	14	–	–	–	–	–	2	9	11
Stoke C	–	–	–	–	–	5	5	6	8	–	–	–	–
Sunderland	–	–	–	–	–	–	–	–	–	–	–	–	–
Swansea C	7	6	–	–	–	–	23	–	–	–	–	22	10
Swindon T	–	23	12	5	10	13	20	–	–	–	–	1	–
Torquay U	–	–	21	–	–	–	–	–	–	–	–	–	–

1993–94	1992–93	1991–92	1990–91	1989–90	1988–89	1987–88	1986–87	1985–86	1984–85	1983–84	1982–83	
–	–	–	–	–	–	–	–	–	–	–	–	Cheltenham T
–	24	18	19	16	8	15	15	–	–	–	–	Chester C
–	–	–	–	–	22	18	17	17	–	–	24	Chesterfield
–	–	–	22	12	–	–	–	–	–	–	–	Colchester U
–	–	24	–	–	–	–	23	13	–	–	–	Crewe Alex
–	–	–	–	–	–	–	–	3	7	–	–	Darlington
–	–	–	–	–	–	24	13	11	14	–	23	Derby Co
22	19	20	16	–	–	–	–	–	–	24	19	Doncaster R
21	12	9	21	20	4	9	18	–	–	–	–	Exeter C
–	–	–	–	–	23	13	5	5	4	8	13	Fulham
–	–	–	3	–	22	–	–	–	–	–	–	Gillingham
23	16	11	–	–	–	–	–	–	–	–	–	Grimsby T
11	15	3	11	8	14	–	–	–	–	–	3	Hartlepool U
9	20	14	–	–	–	–	–	–	3	4	–	Huddersfield T
18	7	10	13	14	–	–	–	–	22	11	20	Hull C
–	–	–	–	–	–	–	–	–	–	–	–	Leyton Orient
–	–	–	–	–	–	–	21	19	14	6	–	Lincoln C
–	–	–	–	–	–	–	–	–	–	–	–	Luton T
–	–	–	–	–	–	–	–	–	–	–	–	Macclesfield T
–	–	–	–	–	–	–	–	–	–	–	–	Manchester C
–	22	–	24	15	15	19	10	–	–	–	–	Mansfield T
–	–	–	–	–	–	–	2	–	–	–	–	Middlesbrough
–	–	–	–	–	–	–	–	–	2	9	17	Millwall
–	–	–	–	–	–	23	19	18	13	4	–	Newport Co
–	–	–	–	22	20	6	–	–	–	–	–	Northampton T
–	–	–	–	3	9	4	7	8	–	–	–	Nottingham F
–	–	–	–	–	–	–	–	–	–	–	–	Notts Co
–	–	–	–	–	–	–	–	–	–	1	5	Oldham Ath
–	–	–	–	–	–	–	–	–	–	–	–	Oxford U
–	–	6	–	–	–	–	–	–	–	–	–	Peterborough U
3	14	–	–	–	–	–	2	15	19	8	–	Plymouth Arg
–	–	–	–	–	–	–	–	–	–	–	1	Portsmouth
2	3	–	–	3	11	12	–	–	23	–	–	Port Vale
–	21	17	17	19	6	16	–	–	23	16	16	Preston NE
–	–	–	–	–	–	–	–	–	–	–	–	QPR
1	8	12	15	10	18	–	–	1	9	–	21	Reading
15	11	–	23	9	–	21	14	14	12	18	–	Rotherham U
–	–	–	–	–	–	–	–	–	–	–	–	Rushden & D
–	–	–	–	–	–	–	–	–	–	21	–	Scunthorpe U
–	–	–	–	–	2	–	–	–	3	11	–	Sheffield U
–	–	–	–	–	–	–	–	–	–	–	–	Sheffield W
–	–	22	18	11	–	–	–	–	–	–	–	Shrewsbury T
–	–	–	2	–	21	17	–	–	–	22	15	Southend U
4	6	5	–	–	–	–	–	–	–	–	–	Stockport Co
–	1	4	14	–	–	–	–	–	–	–	–	Stoke C
–	–	–	–	–	–	1	–	–	–	–	–	Sunderland
13	5	19	20	17	12	–	–	24	20	–	–	Swansea C
–	–	–	–	–	–	–	3	–	–	–	–	Swindon T
–	–	23	–	–	–	–	–	–	–	–	–	Torquay U

	2006-07	2005-06	2004-05	2003-04	2002-03	2001-02	2000-01	1999-2000	1998-99	1997-98	1996-97	1995-96	1994-95
Tranmere R	9	18	3	8	7	12	–	–	–	–	–	–	–
Walsall	–	24	14	–	–	–	4	–	2	19	12	11	–
Watford	–	–	–	–	–	–	–	–	1	13	–	–	–
WBA	–	–	–	–	–	–	–	–	–	–	–	–	–
Wigan Ath	–	–	–	1	10	6	4	6	11	–	–	–	–
Wimbledon	–	22†	20†	–	–	–	–	–	–	–	–	–	–
Wolverhampton W	–	–	–	–	–	–	–	–	–	–	–	–	–
Wrexham	–	–	22	13	–	23	10	11	17	7	8	8	13
Wycombe W	–	–	–	24	18	11	13	12	19	14	18	12	6
Yeovil T	5	15	–	–	–	–	–	–	–	–	–	–	–
York C	–	–	–	–	–	–	–	21	16	20	20	9	–

†As Milton Keynes D

LEAGUE POSITIONS: DIVISION 3 from 1992–93, LEAGUE 2 from 2004–05 and DIVISION 4 1982–83 to 1991–92

	2006-07	2005-06	2004-05	2003-04	2002-03	2001-02	2000-01	1999-2000	1998-99	1997-98	1996-97	1995-96	1994-95
Accrington S	20	–	–	–	–	–	–	–	–	–	–	–	–
Aldershot	–	–	–	–	–	–	–	–	–	–	–	–	–
Barnet	14	18	–	–	–	–	24	6	16	7	15	9	11
Blackpool	–	–	–	–	–	7	–	–	–	–	–	–	–
Bolton W	–	–	–	–	–	–	–	–	–	–	–	–	–
Boston U	23	11	16	11	15	–	–	–	–	–	–	–	–
Bournemouth	–	–	–	–	4	–	–	–	–	–	–	–	–
Brentford	–	–	–	–	–	–	–	–	1	–	–	–	–
Brighton & HA	–	–	–	–	–	1	11	17	23	23	–	–	–
Bristol C	–	–	–	–	–	–	–	–	–	–	–	–	–
Bristol R	6	12	12	15	20	23	–	–	–	–	–	–	–
Burnley	–	–	–	–	–	–	–	–	–	–	–	–	–
Bury	21	19	17	12	7	–	–	–	–	–	–	3	4
Cambridge U	–	–	24	13	12	–	–	2	16	10	16	–	–
Cardiff C	–	–	–	–	–	–	2	–	3	21	7	22	–
Carlisle U	–	1	–	23	22	17	22	23	23	–	3	–	1
Cheltenham T	–	5	14	14	–	4	9	8	–	–	–	–	–
Chester C	18	15	20	–	–	–	–	24	14	14	6	8	–
Chesterfield	–	–	–	–	–	3	–	–	–	–	–	–	3
Colchester U	–	–	–	–	–	–	–	–	–	4	8	7	10
Crewe Alex	–	–	–	–	–	–	–	–	–	–	–	–	–

*Record expunged

1993-94	1992-93	1991-92	1990-91	1989-90	1988-89	1987-88	1986-87	1985-86	1984-85	1983-84	1982-83	
–	–	–	5	4	–	–	–	–	–	–	–	Tranmere R
–	–	–	–	24	–	3	8	6	11	6	10	Walsall
–	–	–	–	–	–	–	–	–	–	–	–	Watford
–	4	7	–	–	–	–	–	–	–	–	–	WBA
–	23	15	10	18	17	7	4	4	16	15	18	Wigan Ath
–	–	–	–	–	–	–	–	–	–	2	–	Wimbledon
–	–	–	–	–	1	–	–	23	–	–	–	Wolverhampton W
12	–	–	–	–	–	–	–	–	–	–	22	Wrexham
–	–	–	–	–	–	–	–	–	–	–	–	Wycombe W
–	–	–	–	–	–	–	–	–	–	–	–	Yeovil T
5	–	–	–	–	–	23	20	7	8	–	–	York C

1993-94	1992-93	1991-92	1990-91	1989-90	1988-89	1987-88	1986-87	1985-86	1984-85	1983-84	1982-83	
–	–	–	–	–	–	–	–	–	–	–	–	Accrington S
–	–	*	23	22	–	–	6	16	13	5	18	Aldershot
–	3	7	–	–	–	–	–	–	–	–	–	Barnet
–	–	4	5	–	–	–	–	–	2	6	21	Blackpool
–	–	–	–	–	3	–	–	–	–	–	–	Bolton W
–	–	–	–	–	–	–	–	–	–	–	–	Boston U
–	–	–	–	–	–	–	–	–	–	–	–	Bournemouth
–	–	–	–	–	–	–	–	–	–	–	–	Brentford
–	–	–	–	–	–	–	–	–	–	4	14	Brighton & HA
–	–	–	–	–	–	–	–	–	–	–	–	Bristol C
–	–	1	6	16	16	10	22	14	–	–	–	Bristol R
13	7	–	–	–	–	–	–	–	4	15	5	Burnley
–	–	–	6	8	15	11	22	–	–	–	–	Bury
–	1	9	13	–	–	2	13	–	–	–	–	Cambridge U
7	18	22	20	8	12	23	–	–	–	–	–	Cardiff C
–	–	–	–	–	–	–	–	–	–	–	–	Carlisle U
–	–	–	–	–	–	–	–	–	–	–	–	Cheltenham T
2	–	–	–	–	–	–	–	2	16	24	13	Chester C
8	12	13	18	7	–	–	–	–	1	13	–	Chesterfield
17	10	–	–	24	22	9	5	6	7	8	6	Colchester U
3	6	6	–	–	3	17	17	12	10	16	23	Crewe Alex

LEAGUE POSITIONS: DIVISION 3 from 1992–93, LEAGUE 2 from 2004–05 and DIVISION 4 1982–83 to 1991–92 (cont.)

	2006–07	2005–06	2004–05	2003–04	2002–03	2001–02	2000–01	1999–2000	1998–99	1997–98	1996–97	1995–96	1994–95
Darlington	11	8	8	18	14	15	20	4	11	19	18	5	20
Doncaster R	–	–	–	1	–	–	–	–	–	24	19	13	9
Exeter C	–	–	–	–	23	16	19	21	12	15	22	14	22
Fulham	–	–	–	–	–	–	–	–	–	–	2	17	8
Gillingham	–	–	–	–	–	–	–	–	–	–	–	2	19
Grimsby T	15	4	18	–	–	–	–	–	–	–	–	–	–
Halifax T	–	–	–	–	–	24	23	18	10	–	–	–	–
Hartlepool U	2	–	–	–	2	7	4	7	22	17	20	20	18
Hereford U	16	–	–	–	–	–	–	–	–	–	24	6	16
Huddersfield T	–	–	–	4	–	–	–	–	–	–	–	–	–
Hull C	–	–	–	2	13	11	6	14	21	22	17	–	–
Kidderminster H	–	23	16	11	10	16	–	–	–	–	–	–	–
Leyton Orient	–	3	11	19	18	18	5	19	6	11	16	21	–
Lincoln C	5	7	6	7	6	22	18	15	–	3	9	18	12
Luton T	–	–	–	–	–	2	–	–	–	–	–	–	–
Macclesfield T	22	17	5	20	16	13	14	13	–	2	–	–	–
Maidstone U	–	–	–	–	–	–	–	–	–	–	–	–	–
Mansfield T	17	16	13	5	–	3	13	17	8	12	11	19	6
Newport Co	–	–	–	–	–	–	–	–	–	–	–	–	–
Northampton T	–	2	7	6	–	–	–	3	–	–	4	11	17
Notts Co	13	21	19	–	–	–	–	–	–	1	–	–	–
Oxford U	–	23	15	9	8	21	–	–	–	–	–	–	–
Peterborough U	10	9	–	–	–	–	–	5	9	10	–	–	–
Plymouth Arg	–	–	–	–	1	12	12	13	–	–	4	–	–
Port Vale	–	–	–	–	–	–	–	–	–	–	–	–	–
Preston NE	–	–	–	–	–	–	–	–	–	–	–	1	5
Reading	–	–	–	–	–	–	–	–	–	–	–	–	–
Rochdale	9	14	9	21	19	5	8	10	19	18	14	15	15
Rotherham U	–	–	–	–	–	–	–	2	5	9	–	–	–
Rushden & D	–	24	22	–	1	6	–	–	–	–	–	–	–
Scarborough	–	–	–	–	–	–	–	24	6	12	23	21	
Scunthorpe U	–	–	2	22	5	8	10	–	4	8	13	12	7
Shrewsbury T	7	10	21	–	24	9	15	22	15	13	–	–	–
Southend U	–	–	4	17	17	12	11	16	18	–	–	–	–
Stockport Co	8	22	–	–	–	–	–	–	–	–	–	–	–
Swansea C	–	–	3	10	21	20	–	1	7	20	5	–	–
Swindon T	3	–	–	–	–	–	–	–	–	–	–	–	–
Torquay U	24	20	–	3	9	19	21	9	20	5	21	24	13
Tranmere R	–	–	–	–	–	–	–	–	–	–	–	–	–
Walsall	1	–	–	–	–	–	–	–	–	–	–	–	2
Wigan Ath	–	–	–	–	–	–	–	–	–	–	1	10	14
Wimbledon	4†	–	–	–	–	–	–	–	–	–	–	–	–
Wolverhampton W	–	–	–	–	–	–	–	–	–	–	–	–	–
Wrexham	19	13	–	–	3	–	–	–	–	–	–	–	–
Wycombe W	12	6	10	–	–	–	–	–	–	–	–	–	–
Yeovil T	–	–	1	8	–	–	–	–	–	–	–	–	–
York C	–	–	–	24	10	14	17	20	–	–	–	–	–

†As Milton Keynes D

1993–94	1992–93	1991–92	1990–91	1989–90	1988–89	1987–88	1986–87	1985–86	1984–85	1983–84	1982–83	
21	15	–	1	–	24	13	–	–	3	14	17	Darlington
15	16	21	11	20	23	–	–	–	–	2	–	Doncaster R
–	–	–	1	13	22	14	21	18	–	–	–	Exeter C
												Fulham
16	21	11	15	14	–	–	–	–	–	–	–	Gillingham
–	–	–	–	2	9	–	–	–	–	–	–	Grimsby T
–	22	20	22	23	21	18	15	20	21	21	11	Halifax T
–	–	–	3	19	19	16	18	7	19	23	22	Hartlepool U
20	17	17	17	17	15	19	16	10	5	11	24	Hereford U
												Huddersfield T
–	–	–	–	–	–	–	–	–	–	–	2	Hull C
												Kidderminster H
–	–	–	–	6	8	7	5	–	–	–	–	Leyton Orient
18	8	10	14	10	10	–	24	–	–	–	–	Lincoln C
												Luton T
												Macclesfield T
–	–	18	19	5	–	–	–	–	–	–	–	Maidstone U
12	–	3	–	–	–	–	–	3	14	19	10	Mansfield T
–	–	–	–	–	–	24	–	–	–	–	–	Newport Co
22	20	16	10	–	–	–	1	8	23	18	15	Northampton T
												Notts Co
												Oxford U
–	–	4	9	17	7	10	17	11	7	9	–	Peterborough U
												Plymouth Arg
–	–	–	–	–	–	–	4	12	–	–	3	Port Vale
5	–	–	–	–	–	2	23	–	–	–	–	Preston NE
–	–	–	–	–	–	–	–	–	–	3	–	Reading
9	11	8	12	12	18	21	21	18	17	22	20	Rochdale
–	–	2	–	–	–	1	–	–	–	–	–	Rotherham U
												Rushden & D
14	13	12	9	18	5	12	–	–	–	–	–	Scarborough
11	14	5	8	11	4	4	8	15	9	–	4	Scunthorpe U
1	9	–	–	–	–	–	–	–	–	–	–	Shrewsbury T
–	–	–	–	3	–	–	3	9	20	–	–	Southend U
–	–	2	4	20	20	19	11	22	12	16	–	Stockport Co
–	–	–	–	–	–	6	12	–	–	–	–	Swansea C
–	–	–	–	–	–	–	1	8	17	8	–	Swindon T
6	19	–	7	15	14	5	23	24	24	9	12	Torquay U
–	–	–	–	–	2	14	20	19	6	10	19	Tranmere R
10	5	15	16	–	–	–	–	–	–	–	–	Walsall
19	–	–	–	–	–	–	–	–	–	–	–	Wigan Ath
–	–	–	–	–	–	–	–	–	–	–	1	Wimbledon
–	–	–	–	–	–	1	4	–	–	–	–	Wolverhampton W
–	2	14	24	21	7	11	9	13	15	20	–	Wrexham
4	–	–	–	–	–	–	–	–	–	–	–	Wycombe W
												Yeovil T
–	4	19	21	13	11	–	–	–	–	1	7	York C

LEAGUE CHAMPIONSHIP HONOURS
FA PREMIER LEAGUE
Maximum points: 126

	First	*Pts*	*Second*	*Pts*	*Third*	*Pts*
1992–93	Manchester U	84	Aston Villa	74	Norwich C	72
1993–94	Manchester U	92	Blackburn R	84	Newcastle U	77
1994–95	Blackburn R	89	Manchester U	88	Nottingham F	77

Maximum points: 114

1995–96	Manchester U	82	Newcastle U	78	Liverpool	71
1996–97	Manchester U	75	Newcastle U*	68	Arsenal*	68
1997–98	Arsenal	78	Manchester U	77	Liverpool	65
1998–99	Manchester U	79	Arsenal	78	Chelsea	75
1999–00	Manchester U	91	Arsenal	73	Leeds U	69
2000–01	Manchester U	80	Arsenal	70	Liverpool	69
2001–02	Arsenal	87	Liverpool	80	Manchester U	77
2002–03	Manchester U	83	Arsenal	78	Newcastle U	69
2003–04	Arsenal	90	Chelsea	79	Manchester U	75
2004–05	Chelsea	95	Arsenal	83	Manchester U	77
2005–06	Chelsea	91	Manchester U	83	Liverpool	82
2006–07	Manchester U	89	Chelsea	83	Liverpool*	68
2007–08	Manchester U	87	Chelsea	85	Arsenal	83

FOOTBALL LEAGUE CHAMPIONSHIP
Maximum points: 138

2004–05	Sunderland	94	Wigan Ath	87	Ipswich T††	85
2005–06	Reading	106	Sheffield U	90	Watford	81
2006–07	Sunderland	88	Birmingham C	86	Derby Co	84
2007–08	WBA	81	Stoke C	79	Hull C	75

DIVISION 1
Maximum points: 138

1992–93	Newcastle U	96	West Ham U*	88	Portsmouth††	88
1993–94	Crystal Palace	90	Nottingham F	83	Millwall††	74
1994–95	Middlesbrough	82	Reading††	79	Bolton W	77
1995–96	Sunderland	83	Derby Co	79	Crystal Palace††	75
1996–97	Bolton W	98	Barnsley	80	Wolverhampton W††	76
1997–98	Nottingham F	94	Middlesbrough	91	Sunderland††	90
1998–99	Sunderland	105	Bradford C	87	Ipswich T††	86
1999–00	Charlton Ath	91	Manchester C	89	Ipswich T	87
2000–01	Fulham	101	Blackburn R	91	Bolton W	87
2001–02	Manchester C	99	WBA	89	Wolverhampton W††	86
2002–03	Portsmouth	98	Leicester C	92	Sheffield U††	80
2003–04	Norwich C	94	WBA	86	Sunderland††	79

FOOTBALL LEAGUE CHAMPIONSHIP 1
Maximum points: 138

2004–05	Luton T	98	Hull C	86	Tranmere R††	79
2005–06	Southend U	82	Colchester U	79	Brentford††	76
2006–07	Scunthorpe U	91	Bristol C	85	Blackpool	83
2007–08	Swansea C	92	Nottingham F	82	Doncaster R	80

DIVISION 2

Maximum points: 138

1992–93	Stoke C	93	Bolton W	90	Port Vale††	89
1993–94	Reading	89	Port Vale	88	Plymouth Arg††	85
1994–95	Birmingham C	89	Brentford††	85	Crewe Alex††	83
1995–96	Swindon T	92	Oxford U	83	Blackpool††	82
1996–97	Bury	84	Stockport Co	82	Luton T††	78
1997–98	Watford	88	Bristol C	85	Grimsby T	72
1998–99	Fulham	101	Walsall	87	Manchester C	82
1999–00	Preston NE	95	Burnley	88	Gillingham	85
2000–01	Millwall	93	Rotherham U	91	Reading††	86
2001–02	Brighton & HA	90	Reading	84	Brentford*††	83
2002–03	Wigan Ath	100	Crewe Alex	86	Bristol C††	83
2003–04	Plymouth Arg	90	QRP	83	Bristol C††	82

FOOTBALL LEAGUE CHAMPIONSHIP 2

Maximum points: 138

2004–05	Yeovil T	83	Scunthorpe U*	80	Swansea C	80
2005–06	Carlisle U	86	Northampton T	83	Leyton Orient	81
2006–07	Walsall	89	Hartlepool U	88	Swindon T	85
2007–08	Milton Keynes D	97	Peterborough U	92	Hereford U	88

DIVISION 3

Maximum points: 126

1992–93	Cardiff C	83	Wrexham	80	Barnet	79
1993–94	Shrewsbury T	79	Chester C	74	Crewe Alex	73
1994–95	Carlisle U	91	Walsall	83	Chesterfield	81

Maximum points: 138

1995–96	Preston NE	86	Gillingham	83	Bury	79
1996–97	Wigan Ath*	87	Fulham	87	Carlisle U	84
1997–98	Notts Co	99	Macclesfield T	82	Lincoln C	75
1998–99	Brentford	85	Cambridge U	81	Cardiff C	80
1999–00	Swansea C	85	Rotherham U	84	Northampton T	82
2000–01	Brighton & HA	92	Cardiff C	82	Chesterfield¶	80
2001–02	Plymouth Arg	102	Luton T	97	Mansfield T	79
2002–03	Rushden & D	87	Hartlepool U	85	Wrexham	84
2003–04	Doncaster R	92	Hull C	88	Torquay U*	81

* Won or placed on goal average (ratio)/goal difference.
†† Not promoted after play-offs. ¶ 9 pts deducted for irregularities.

FOOTBALL LEAGUE

Maximum points: a 44; b 60

1888–89a	Preston NE	40	Aston Villa	29	Wolverhampton W	28
1889–90a	Preston NE	33	Everton	31	Blackburn R	27
1890–91a	Everton	29	Preston NE	27	Notts Co	26
1891–92b	Sunderland	42	Preston NE	37	Bolton W	36

DIVISION 1 to 1991–92

Maximum points: a 44; b 52; c 60; d 68; e 76; f 84; g 126; h 120; k 114.

1892–93c	Sunderland	48	Preston NE	37	Everton	36
1893–94c	Aston Villa	44	Sunderland	38	Derby Co	36
1894–95c	Sunderland	47	Everton	42	Aston Villa	39
1895–96c	Aston Villa	45	Derby Co	41	Everton	39
1896–97c	Aston Villa	47	Sheffield U*	36	Derby Co	36

	First	Pts	Second	Pts	Third	Pts
1897–98c	Sheffield U	42	Sunderland	37	Wolverhampton W*	35
1898–99d	Aston Villa	45	Liverpool	43	Burnley	39
1899–1900d	Aston Villa	50	Sheffield U	48	Sunderland	41
1900–01d	Liverpool	45	Sunderland	43	Notts Co	40
1901–02d	Sunderland	44	Everton	41	Newcastle U	37
1902–03d	The Wednesday	42	Aston Villa*	41	Sunderland	41
1903–04d	The Wednesday	47	Manchester C	44	Everton	43
1904–05d	Newcastle U	48	Everton	47	Manchester C	46
1905–06e	Liverpool	51	Preston NE	47	The Wednesday	44
1906–07e	Newcastle U	51	Bristol C	48	Everton*	45
1907–08e	Manchester U	52	Aston Villa*	43	Manchester C	43
1908–09e	Newcastle U	53	Everton	46	Sunderland	44
1909–10e	Aston Villa	53	Liverpool	48	Blackburn R*	45
1910–11e	Manchester U	52	Aston Villa	51	Sunderland*	45
1911–12e	Blackburn R	49	Everton	46	Newcastle U	44
1912–13e	Sunderland	54	Aston Villa	50	Sheffield W	49
1913–14e	Blackburn R	51	Aston Villa	44	Middlesbrough*	43
1914–15e	Everton	46	Oldham Ath	45	Blackburn R*	43
1919–20f	WBA	60	Burnley	51	Chelsea	49
1920–21f	Burnley	59	Manchester C	54	Bolton W	52
1921–22f	Liverpool	57	Tottenham H	51	Burnley	49
1922–23f	Liverpool	60	Sunderland	54	Huddersfield T	53
1923–24f	Huddersfield T*	57	Cardiff C	57	Sunderland	53
1924–25f	Huddersfield T	58	WBA	56	Bolton W	55
1925–26f	Huddersfield T	57	Arsenal	52	Sunderland	48
1926–27f	Newcastle U	56	Huddersfield T	51	Sunderland	49
1927–28f	Everton	53	Huddersfield T	51	Leicester C	48
1928–29f	Sheffield W	52	Leicester C	51	Aston Villa	50
1929–30f	Sheffield W	60	Derby Co	50	Manchester C*	47
1930–31f	Arsenal	66	Aston Villa	59	Sheffield W	52
1931–32f	Everton	56	Arsenal	54	Sheffield W	50
1932–33f	Arsenal	58	Aston Villa	54	Sheffield W	51
1933–34f	Arsenal	59	Huddersfield T	56	Tottenham H	49
1934–35f	Arsenal	58	Sunderland	54	Sheffield W	49
1935–36f	Sunderland	56	Derby Co*	48	Huddersfield T	48
1936–37f	Manchester C	57	Charlton Ath	54	Arsenal	52
1937–38f	Arsenal	52	Wolverhampton W	51	Preston NE	49
1938–39f	Everton	59	Wolverhampton W	55	Charlton Ath	50
1946–47f	Liverpool	57	Manchester U*	56	Wolverhampton W	56
1947–48f	Arsenal	59	Manchester U*	52	Burnley	52
1948–49f	Portsmouth	58	Manchester U*	53	Derby Co	53
1949–50f	Portsmouth*	53	Wolverhampton W	53	Sunderland	52
1950–51f	Tottenham H	60	Manchester U	56	Blackpool	50
1951–52f	Manchester U	57	Tottenham H*	53	Arsenal	53
1952–53f	Arsenal*	54	Preston NE	54	Wolverhampton W	51
1953–54f	Wolverhampton W	57	WBA	53	Huddersfield T	51
1954–55f	Chelsea	52	Wolverhampton W*	48	Portsmouth*	48
1955–56f	Manchester U	60	Blackpool*	49	Wolverhampton W	49
1956–57f	Manchester U	64	Tottenham H*	56	Preston NE	56
1957–58f	Wolverhampton W	64	Preston NE	59	Tottenham H	51
1958–59f	Wolverhampton W	61	Manchester U	55	Arsenal*	50
1959–60f	Burnley	55	Wolverhampton W	54	Tottenham H	53
1960–61f	Tottenham H	66	Sheffield W	58	Wolverhampton W	57
1961–62f	Ipswich T	56	Burnley	53	Tottenham H	52

126

	First	Pts	Second	Pts	Third	Pts
1962–63f	Everton	61	Tottenham H	55	Burnley	54
1963–64f	Liverpool	57	Manchester U	53	Everton	52
1964–65f	Manchester U*	61	Leeds U	61	Chelsea	56
1965–66f	Liverpool	61	Leeds U*	55	Burnley	55
1966–67f	Manchester U	60	Nottingham F*	56	Tottenham H	56
1967–68f	Manchester C	58	Manchester U	56	Liverpool	55
1968–69f	Leeds U	67	Liverpool	61	Everton	57
1969–70f	Everton	66	Leeds U	57	Chelsea	55
1970–71f	Arsenal	65	Leeds U	64	Tottenham H*	52
1971–72f	Derby Co	58	Leeds U*	57	Liverpool*	57
1972–73f	Liverpool	60	Arsenal	57	Leeds U	53
1973–74f	Leeds U	62	Liverpool	57	Derby Co	48
1974–75f	Derby Co	53	Liverpool*	51	Ipswich T	51
1975–76f	Liverpool	60	QPR	59	Manchester U	56
1976–77f	Liverpool	57	Manchester C	56	Ipswich T	52
1977–78f	Nottingham F	64	Liverpool	57	Everton	55
1978–79f	Liverpool	68	Nottingham F	60	WBA	59
1979–80f	Liverpool	60	Manchester U	58	Ipswich T	53
1980–81f	Aston Villa	60	Ipswich T	56	Arsenal	53
1981–82g	Liverpool	87	Ipswich T	83	Manchester U	78
1982–83g	Liverpool	82	Watford	71	Manchester U	70
1983–84g	Liverpool	80	Southampton	77	Nottingham F*	74
1984–85g	Everton	90	Liverpool*	77	Tottenham H	77
1985–86g	Liverpool	88	Everton	86	West Ham U	84
1986–87g	Everton	86	Liverpool	77	Tottenham H	71
1987–88h	Liverpool	90	Manchester U	81	Nottingham F	73
1988–89k	Arsenal*	76	Liverpool	76	Nottingham F	64
1989–90k	Liverpool	79	Aston Villa	70	Tottenham H	63
1990–91k	Arsenal†	83	Liverpool	76	Crystal Palace	69
1991–92g	Leeds U	82	Manchester U	78	Sheffield W	75

No official competition during 1915–19 and 1939–46; Regional Leagues operating.
* Won or placed on goal average (ratio)/goal difference.
† 2 pts deducted

DIVISION 2 to 1991–92

Maximum points: a 44; b 56; c 60; d 68; e 76; f 84; g 126; h 132; k 138.

	First	Pts	Second	Pts	Third	Pts
1892–93a	Small Heath	36	Sheffield U	35	Darwen	30
1893–94b	Liverpool	50	Small Heath	42	Notts Co	39
1894–95c	Bury	48	Notts Co	39	Newton Heath*	38
1895–96c	Liverpool*	46	Manchester C	46	Grimsby T*	42
1896–97c	Notts Co	42	Newton Heath	39	Grimsby T	38
1897–98c	Burnley	48	Newcastle U	45	Manchester C	39
1898–99d	Manchester C	52	Glossop NE	46	Leicester Fosse	45
1899–1900d	The Wednesday	54	Bolton W	52	Small Heath	46
1900–01d	Grimsby T	49	Small Heath	48	Burnley	44
1901–02d	WBA	55	Middlesbrough	51	Preston NE*	42
1902–03d	Manchester C	54	Small Heath	51	Woolwich A	48
1903–04d	Preston NE	50	Woolwich A	49	Manchester U	48
1904–05d	Liverpool	58	Bolton W	56	Manchester U	53
1905–06e	Bristol C	66	Manchester U	62	Chelsea	53
1906–07e	Nottingham F	60	Chelsea	57	Leicester Fosse	48
1907–08e	Bradford C	54	Leicester Fosse	52	Oldham Ath	50
1908–09e	Bolton W	52	Tottenham H*	51	WBA	51
1909–10e	Manchester C	54	Oldham Ath*	53	Hull C*	53

	First	Pts	Second	Pts	Third	Pts
1910–11e	WBA	53	Bolton W	51	Chelsea	49
1911–12e	Derby Co*	54	Chelsea	54	Burnley	52
1912–13e	Preston NE	53	Burnley	50	Birmingham	46
1913–14e	Notts Co	53	Bradford PA*	49	Woolwich A	49
1914–15e	Derby Co	53	Preston NE	50	Barnsley	47
1919–20f	Tottenham H	70	Huddersfield T	64	Birmingham	56
1920–21f	Birmingham*	58	Cardiff C	58	Bristol C	51
1921–22f	Nottingham F	56	Stoke C*	52	Barnsley	52
1922–23f	Notts Co	53	West Ham U*	51	Leicester C	51
1923–24f	Leeds U	54	Bury*	51	Derby Co	51
1924–25f	Leicester C	59	Manchester U	57	Derby Co	55
1925–26f	Sheffield W	60	Derby Co	57	Chelsea	52
1926–27f	Middlesbrough	62	Portsmouth*	54	Manchester C	54
1927–28f	Manchester C	59	Leeds U	57	Chelsea	54
1928–29f	Middlesbrough	55	Grimsby T	53	Bradford PA*	48
1929–30f	Blackpool	58	Chelsea	55	Oldham Ath	53
1930–31f	Everton	61	WBA	54	Tottenham H	51
1931–32f	Wolverhampton W	56	Leeds U	54	Stoke C	52
1932–33f	Stoke C	56	Tottenham H	55	Fulham	50
1933–34f	Grimsby T	59	Preston NE	52	Bolton W*	51
1934–35f	Brentford	61	Bolton W*	56	West Ham U	56
1935–36f	Manchester U	56	Charlton Ath	55	Sheffield U*	52
1936–37f	Leicester C	56	Blackpool	55	Bury	52
1937–38f	Aston Villa	57	Manchester U*	53	Sheffield U	53
1938–39f	Blackburn R	55	Sheffield U	54	Sheffield W	53
1946–47f	Manchester C	62	Burnley	58	Birmingham C	55
1947–48f	Birmingham C	59	Newcastle U	56	Southampton	52
1948–49f	Fulham	57	WBA	56	Southampton	52
1949–50f	Tottenham H	61	Sheffield W*	52	Sheffield U*	52
1950–51f	Preston NE	57	Manchester C	52	Cardiff C	50
1951–52f	Sheffield W	53	Cardiff C*	51	Birmingham C	51
1952–53f	Sheffield U	60	Huddersfield T	58	Luton T	52
1953–54f	Leicester C*	56	Everton	56	Blackburn R	55
1954–55f	Birmingham C*	54	Luton T*	54	Rotherham U	54
1955–56f	Sheffield W	55	Leeds U	52	Liverpool*	48
1956–57f	Leicester C	61	Nottingham F	54	Liverpool	53
1957–58f	West Ham U	57	Blackburn R	56	Charlton Ath	55
1958–59f	Sheffield W	62	Fulham	60	Sheffield U*	53
1959–60f	Aston Villa	59	Cardiff C	58	Liverpool*	50
1960–61f	Ipswich T	59	Sheffield U	58	Liverpool	52
1961–62f	Liverpool	62	Leyton Orient	54	Sunderland	53
1962–63f	Stoke C	53	Chelsea*	52	Sunderland	52
1963–64f	Leeds U	63	Sunderland	61	Preston NE	56
1964–65f	Newcastle U	57	Northampton T	56	Bolton W	50
1965–66f	Manchester C	59	Southampton	54	Coventry C	53
1966–67f	Coventry C	59	Wolverhampton W	58	Carlisle U	52
1967–68f	Ipswich T	59	QPR*	58	Blackpool	58
1968–69f	Derby Co	63	Crystal Palace	56	Charlton Ath	50
1969–70f	Huddersfield T	60	Blackpool	53	Leicester C	51
1970–71f	Leicester C	59	Sheffield U	56	Cardiff C*	53
1971–72f	Norwich C	57	Birmingham C	56	Millwall	55
1972–73f	Burnley	62	QPR	61	Aston Villa	50
1973–74f	Middlesbrough	65	Luton T	50	Carlisle U	49
1974–75f	Manchester U	61	Aston Villa	58	Norwich C	53

128

	First	*Pts*	*Second*	*Pts*	*Third*	*Pts*
1975–76f	Sunderland	56	Bristol C*	53	WBA	53
1976–77f	Wolverhampton W	57	Chelsea	55	Nottingham F	52
1977–78f	Bolton W	58	Southampton	57	Tottenham H*	56
1978–79f	Crystal Palace	57	Brighton & HA*	56	Stoke C	56
1979–80f	Leicester C	55	Sunderland	54	Birmingham C*	53
1980–81f	West Ham U	66	Notts Co	53	Swansea C*	50
1981–82g	Luton T	88	Watford	80	Norwich C	71
1982–83g	QPR	85	Wolverhampton W	75	Leicester C	70
1983–84g	Chelsea*	88	Sheffield W	88	Newcastle U	80
1984–85g	Oxford U	84	Birmingham C	82	Manchester C	74
1985–86g	Norwich C	84	Charlton Ath	77	Wimbledon	76
1986–87g	Derby Co	84	Portsmouth	78	Oldham Ath††	75
1987–88h	Millwall	82	Aston Villa*	78	Middlesbrough	78
1988–89k	Chelsea	99	Manchester C	82	Crystal Palace	81
1989–90k	Leeds U*	85	Sheffield U	85	Newcastle U††	80
1990–91k	Oldham Ath	88	West Ham U	87	Sheffield W	82
1991–92k	Ipswich T	84	Middlesbrough	80	Derby Co	78

No official competition during 1915–19 and 1939–46; Regional Leagues operating.
* Won or placed on goal average (ratio)/goal difference.
†† Not promoted after play-offs.

DIVISION 3 to 1991–92
Maximum points: 92; 138 from 1981–82.

1958–59	Plymouth Arg	62	Hull C	61	Brentford*	57
1959–60	Southampton	61	Norwich C	59	Shrewsbury T*	52
1960–61	Bury	68	Walsall	62	QPR	60
1961–62	Portsmouth	65	Grimsby T	62	Bournemouth*	59
1962–63	Northampton T	62	Swindon T	58	Port Vale	54
1963–64	Coventry C*	60	Crystal Palace	60	Watford	58
1964–65	Carlisle U	60	Bristol C*	59	Mansfield T	59
1965–66	Hull C	69	Millwall	65	QPR	57
1966–67	QPR	67	Middlesbrough	55	Watford	54
1967–68	Oxford U	57	Bury	56	Shrewsbury T	55
1968–69	Watford*	64	Swindon T	64	Luton T	61
1969–70	Orient	62	Luton T	60	Bristol R	56
1970–71	Preston NE	61	Fulham	60	Halifax T	56
1971–72	Aston Villa	70	Brighton & HA	65	Bournemouth*	62
1972–73	Bolton W	61	Notts Co	57	Blackburn R	55
1973–74	Oldham Ath	62	Bristol R*	61	York C	61
1974–75	Blackburn R	60	Plymouth Arg	59	Charlton Ath	55
1975–76	Hereford U	63	Cardiff C	57	Millwall	56
1976–77	Mansfield T	64	Brighton & HA	61	Crystal Palace*	59
1977–78	Wrexham	61	Cambridge U	58	Preston NE*	56
1978–79	Shrewsbury T	61	Watford*	60	Swansea C	60
1979–80	Grimsby T	62	Blackburn R	59	Sheffield W	58
1980–81	Rotherham U	61	Barnsley*	59	Charlton Ath	59
1981–82	Burnley*	80	Carlisle U	80	Fulham	78
1982–83	Portsmouth	91	Cardiff C	86	Huddersfield T	82
1983–84	Oxford U	95	Wimbledon	87	Sheffield U*	83
1984–85	Bradford C	94	Millwall	90	Hull C	87
1985–86	Reading	94	Plymouth Arg	87	Derby Co	84
1986–87	Bournemouth	97	Middlesbrough	94	Swindon T	87
1987–88	Sunderland	93	Brighton & HA	84	Walsall	82
1988–89	Wolverhampton W	92	Sheffield U*	84	Port Vale	84

	First	Pts	Second	Pts	Third	Pts
1989–90	Bristol R	93	Bristol C	91	Notts Co	87
1990–91	Cambridge U	86	Southend U	85	Grimsby T*	83
1991–92	Brentford	82	Birmingham C	81	Huddersfield T	78

* Won or placed on goal average (ratio)/goal difference.

DIVISION 4 (1958–1992)
Maximum points: 92; 138 from 1981–82.

	First	Pts	Second	Pts	Third	Pts
1958–59	Port Vale	64	Coventry C*	60	York C	60
1959–60	Walsall	65	Notts Co*	60	Torquay U	60
1960–61	Peterborough U	66	Crystal Palace	64	Northampton T*	60
1961–62†	Millwall	56	Colchester U	55	Wrexham	53
1962–63	Brentford	62	Oldham Ath*	59	Crewe Alex	59
1963–64	Gillingham*	60	Carlisle U	60	Workington	59
1964–65	Brighton & HA	63	Millwall*	62	York C	62
1965–66	Doncaster R*	59	Darlington	59	Torquay U	58
1966–67	Stockport Co	64	Southport*	59	Barrow	59
1967–68	Luton T	66	Barnsley	61	Hartlepools U	60
1968–69	Doncaster R	59	Halifax T	57	Rochdale*	56
1969–70	Chesterfield	64	Wrexham	61	Swansea C	60
1970–71	Notts Co	69	Bournemouth	60	Oldham Ath	59
1971–72	Grimsby T	63	Southend U	60	Brentford	59
1972–73	Southport	62	Hereford U	58	Cambridge U	57
1973–74	Peterborough U	65	Gillingham	62	Colchester U	60
1974–75	Mansfield T	68	Shrewsbury T	62	Rotherham U	59
1975–76	Lincoln C	74	Northampton T	68	Reading	60
1976–77	Cambridge U	65	Exeter C	62	Colchester U*	59
1977–78	Watford	71	Southend U	60	Swansea C*	56
1978–79	Reading	65	Grimsby T*	61	Wimbledon*	61
1979–80	Huddersfield T	66	Walsall	64	Newport Co	61
1980–81	Southend U	67	Lincoln C	65	Doncaster R	56
1981–82	Sheffield U	96	Bradford C*	91	Wigan Ath	91
1982–83	Wimbledon	98	Hull C	90	Port Vale	88
1983–84	York C	101	Doncaster R	85	Reading*	82
1984–85	Chesterfield	91	Blackpool	86	Darlington	85
1985–86	Swindon T	102	Chester C	84	Mansfield T	81
1986–87	Northampton T	99	Preston NE	90	Southend U	80
1987–88	Wolverhampton W	90	Cardiff C	85	Bolton W	78
1988–89	Rotherham U	82	Tranmere R	80	Crewe Alex	78
1989–90	Exeter C	89	Grimsby T	79	Southend U	75
1990–91	Darlington	83	Stockport Co*	82	Hartlepool U	82
1991–92§	Burnley	83	Rotherham U*	77	Mansfield T	77

* Won or placed on goal average (ratio)/goal difference.
†Maximum points: 88 owing to Accrington Stanley's resignation. ††Not promoted after play-offs.
§Maximum points: 126 owing to Aldershot being expelled.

DIVISION 3—SOUTH (1920–1958)
1920–21 Season as Division 3.
Maximum points: a 84; b 92.

	First	Pts	Second	Pts	Third	Pts
1920–21a	Crystal Palace	59	Southampton	54	QPR	53
1921–22a	Southampton*	61	Plymouth Arg	61	Portsmouth	53
1922–23a	Bristol C	59	Plymouth Arg*	53	Swansea T	53
1923–24a	Portsmouth	59	Plymouth Arg	55	Millwall	54
1924–25a	Swansea T	57	Plymouth Arg	56	Bristol C	53

	First	Pts	Second	Pts	Third	Pts
1925–26a	Reading	57	Plymouth Arg	56	Millwall	53
1926–27a	Bristol C	62	Plymouth Arg	60	Millwall	56
1927–28a	Millwall	65	Northampton T	55	Plymouth Arg	53
1928–29a	Charlton Ath*	54	Crystal Palace	54	Northampton T*	52
1929–30a	Plymouth Arg	68	Brentford	61	QPR	51
1930–31a	Notts Co	59	Crystal Palace	51	Brentford	50
1931–32a	Fulham	57	Reading	55	Southend U	53
1932–33a	Brentford	62	Exeter C	58	Norwich C	57
1933–34a	Norwich C	61	Coventry C*	54	Reading*	54
1934–35a	Charlton Ath	61	Reading	53	Coventry C	51
1935–36a	Coventry C	57	Luton T	56	Reading	54
1936–37a	Luton T	58	Notts Co	56	Brighton & HA	53
1937–38a	Millwall	56	Bristol C	55	QPR*	53
1938–39a	Newport Co	55	Crystal Palace	52	Brighton & HA	49
1939–46	Competition cancelled owing to war.					
1946–47a	Cardiff C	66	QPR	57	Bristol C	51
1947–48a	QPR	61	Bournemouth	57	Walsall	51
1948–49a	Swansea T	62	Reading	55	Bournemouth	52
1949–50a	Notts Co	58	Northampton T*	51	Southend U	51
1950–51b	Nottingham F	70	Norwich C	64	Reading*	57
1951–52b	Plymouth Arg	66	Reading*	61	Norwich C	61
1952–53b	Bristol R	64	Millwall*	62	Northampton T	62
1953–54b	Ipswich T	64	Brighton & HA	61	Bristol C	56
1954–55b	Bristol C	70	Leyton Orient	61	Southampton	59
1955–56b	Leyton Orient	66	Brighton & HA	65	Ipswich T	64
1956–57b	Ipswich T*	59	Torquay U	59	Colchester U	58
1957–58b	Brighton & HA	60	Brentford*	58	Plymouth Arg	58

Won or placed on goal average (ratio).

DIVISION 3—NORTH (1921–1958)
Maximum points: a 76; b 84; c 80; d 92.

	First	Pts	Second	Pts	Third	Pts
1921–22a	Stockport Co	56	Darlington*	50	Grimsby T	50
1922–23a	Nelson	51	Bradford PA	47	Walsall	46
1923–24b	Wolverhampton W	63	Rochdale	62	Chesterfield	54
1924–25b	Darlington	58	Nelson*	53	New Brighton	53
1925–26b	Grimsby T	61	Bradford PA	60	Rochdale	59
1926–27b	Stoke C	63	Rochdale	58	Bradford PA	55
1927–28b	Bradford PA	63	Lincoln C	55	Stockport Co	54
1928–29g	Bradford C	63	Stockport Co	62	Wrexham	52
1929–30b	Port Vale	67	Stockport Co	63	Darlington*	50
1930–31b	Chesterfield	58	Lincoln C	57	Wrexham*	54
1931–32c	Lincoln C*	57	Gateshead	57	Chester	50
1932–33b	Hull C	59	Wrexham	57	Stockport Co	54
1933–34b	Barnsley	62	Chesterfield	61	Stockport Co	59
1934–35b	Doncaster R	57	Halifax T	55	Chester	54
1935–36b	Chesterfield	60	Chester*	55	Tranmere R	55
1936–37b	Stockport Co	60	Lincoln C	57	Chester	53
1937–38b	Tranmere R	56	Doncaster R	54	Hull C	53
1938–39b	Barnsley	67	Doncaster R	56	Bradford C	52
1939–46	Competition cancelled owing to war.					
1946–47b	Doncaster R	72	Rotherham U	60	Chester	56
1947–48b	Lincoln C	60	Rotherham U	59	Wrexham	50
1948–49b	Hull C	65	Rotherham U	62	Doncaster R	50
1949–50b	Doncaster R	55	Gateshead	53	Rochdale*	51

	First	Pts	Second	Pts	Third	Pts
1950–51d	Rotherham U	71	Mansfield T	64	Carlisle U	62
1951–52d	Lincoln C	69	Grimsby T	66	Stockport Co	59
1952–53d	Oldham Ath	59	Port Vale	58	Wrexham	56
1953–54d	Port Vale	69	Barnsley	58	Scunthorpe U	57
1954–55d	Barnsley	65	Accrington S	61	Scunthorpe U*	58
1955–56d	Grimsby T	68	Derby Co	63	Accrington S	59
1956–57d	Derby Co	63	Hartlepools U	59	Accrington S*	58
1957–58d	Scunthorpe U	66	Accrington S	59	Bradford C	57

* Won or placed on goal average (ratio).

PROMOTED AFTER PLAY-OFFS

(Not accounted for in previous section)

1986–87 Aldershot to Division 3.

1987–88 Swansea C to Division 3.

1988–89 Leyton Orient to Division 3.

1989–90 Cambridge U to Division 3; Notts Co to Division 2; Sunderland to Division 1.

1990–91 Notts Co to Division 1; Tranmere R to Division 2; Torquay U to Division 3.

1991–92 Blackburn R to Premier League; Peterborough U to Division 1.

1992–93 Swindon T to Premier League; WBA to Division 1; York C to Division 2.

1993–94 Leicester C to Premier League; Burnley to Division 1; Wycombe W to Division 2.

1994–95 Huddersfield T to Division 1.

1995–96 Leicester C to Premier League; Bradford C to Division 1; Plymouth Arg to Division 2.

1996–97 Crystal Palace to Premier League; Crewe Alex to Division 1; Northampton T to Division 2.

1997–98 Charlton Ath to Premier League; Colchester U to Division 2.

1998–99 Watford to Premier League; Scunthorpe to Division 2.

1999–00 Peterborough U to Division 2.

2000–01 Walsall to Division 1; Blackpool to Division 2.

2001–02 Birmingham C to Premier League; Stoke C to Division 1; Cheltenham T to Division 2.

2002–03 Wolverhampton W to Premier League; Cardiff C to Division 1; Bournemouth to Division 2.

2003–04 Crystal Palace to Premier League; Brighton & HA to Division 1; Huddersfield T to Division 2.

2004–05 West Ham U to Premier League; Sheffield W to Football League Championship, Southend U to Football League Championship 1.

2005–06 Watford to Premier League; Barnsley to Football League Championship; Cheltenham T to Football League Championship 1.

2006–07 Derby Co to Premier League; Blackpool to Football League Championship; Bristol R to Football League Championship 1.

2007–08 Hull C to Premier League; Doncaster R to Football League Championship; Stockport Co to Football League Championship 1.

RELEGATED CLUBS
FA PREMIER LEAGUE TO DIVISION 1
1992–93 Crystal Palace, Middlesbrough, Nottingham F.
1993–94 Sheffield U, Oldham Ath, Swindon T.
1994–95 Crystal Palace, Norwich C, Leicester C, Ipswich T.
1995–96 Manchester C, QPR, Bolton W.
1996–97 Sunderland, Middlesbrough, Nottingham F.
1997–98 Bolton W, Barnsley, Crystal Palace.
1998–99 Charlton Ath, Blackburn R, Nottingham F.
1999–90 Wimbledon, Sheffield W, Watford.
2000–01 Manchester C, Coventry C, Bradford C.
2001–02 Ipswich T, Derby Co, Leicester C.
2002–03 West Ham U, WBA, Sunderland.
2003–04 Leicester C, Leeds U, Wolverhampton W.

FA PREMIER LEAGUE TO FOOTBALL LEAGUE CHAMPIONSHIP
2004–05 Crystal Palace, Norwich C, Southampton.
2005–06 Birmingham C, WBA, Sunderland.
2006–07 Sheffield U, Charlton Ath, Watford
2007–08 Reading, Birmingham C, Derby Co

DIVISION 1 TO DIVISION 2
1898–99 Bolton W and Sheffield W
1899–1900 Burnley and Glossop
1900–01 Preston NE and WBA
1901–02 Small Heath and Manchester C
1902–03 Grimsby T and Bolton W
1903–04 Liverpool and WBA
1904–05 League extended. Bury and
         Notts Co, two bottom clubs in
         First Division, re-elected.
1905–06 Nottingham F and
         Wolverhampton W
1906–07 Derby Co and Stoke C
1907–08 Bolton W and Birmingham C
1908–09 Manchester C and Leicester Fosse
1909–10 Bolton W and Chelsea
1910–11 Bristol C and Nottingham F
1911–12 Preston NE and Bury
1912–13 Notts Co and Woolwich Arsenal
1913–14 Preston NE and Derby Co
1914–15 Tottenham H and Chelsea*
1919–20 Notts Co and Sheffield W
1920–21 Derby Co and Bradford PA
1921–22 Bradford C and Manchester U
1922–23 Stoke C and Oldham Ath
1923–24 Chelsea and Middlesbrough
1924–25 Preston NE and Nottingham F
1925–26 Manchester C and Notts Co
1926–27 Leeds U and WBA
1927–28 Tottenham H and Middlesbrough
1928–29 Bury and Cardiff C
1929–30 Burnley and Everton
1930–31 Leeds U and Manchester U
1931–32 Grimsby T and West Ham U

1932–33 Bolton W and Blackpool
1933–34 Newcastle U and Sheffield U
1934–35 Leicester C and Tottenham H
1935–36 Aston Villa and Blackburn R
1936–37 Manchester U and Sheffield W
1937–38 Manchester C and WBA
1938–39 Birmingham C and Leicester C
1946–47 Brentford and Leeds U
1947–48 Blackburn R and Grimsby T
1948–49 Preston NE and Sheffield U
1949–50 Manchester C and Birmingham C
1950–51 Sheffield W and Everton
1951–52 Huddersfield T and Fulham
1952–53 Stoke C and Derby Co
1953–54 Middlesbrough and Liverpool
1954–55 Leicester C and Sheffield W
1955–56 Huddersfield T and Sheffield U
1956–57 Charlton Ath and Cardiff C
1957–58 Sheffield W and Sunderland
1958–59 Portsmouth and Aston Villa
1959–60 Luton T and Leeds U
1960–61 Preston NE and Newcastle U
1961–62 Chelsea and Cardiff C
1962–63 Manchester C and Leyton Orient
1963–64 Bolton W and Ipswich T
1964–65 Wolverhampton W and
         Birmingham C
1965–66 Northampton T and Blackburn R
1966–67 Aston Villa and Blackpool
1967–68 Fulham and Sheffield U
1968–69 Leicester C and QPR
1969–70 Sunderland and Sheffield W
1970–71 Burnley and Blackpool

1971–72	Huddersfield T and Nottingham F	1988–89	Middlesbrough, West Ham U, Newcastle U
1972–73	Crystal Palace and WBA		
1973–74	Southampton, Manchester U, Norwich C	1989–90	Sheffield W, Charlton Ath, Millwall
1974–75	Luton T, Chelsea, Carlisle U	1990–91	Sunderland and Derby Co
1975–76	Wolverhampton W, Burnley, Sheffield U	1991–92	Luton T, Notts Co, West Ham U
		1992–93	Brentford, Cambridge U, Bristol R
1976–77	Sunderland, Stoke C, Tottenham H	1993–94	Birmingham C, Oxford U, Peterborough U
1977–78	West Ham U, Newcastle U, Leicester C	1994–95	Swindon T, Burnley, Bristol C, Notts Co
1978–79	QPR, Birmingham C, Chelsea	1995–96	Millwall, Watford, Luton T
1979–80	Bristol C, Derby Co, Bolton W	1996–97	Grimsby T, Oldham Ath, Southend U
1980–81	Norwich C, Leicester C, Crystal Palace	1997–98	Manchester C, Stoke C, Reading
1981–82	Leeds U, Wolverhampton W, Middlesbrough	1998–99	Bury, Oxford U, Bristol C
		1999–00	Walsall, Port Vale, Swindon T
1982–83	Manchester C, Swansea C, Brighton & HA	2000–01	Huddersfield T, QPR, Tranmere R
1983–84	Birmingham C, Notts Co, Wolverhampton W	2001–02	Crewe Alex, Barnsley, Stockport Co
1984–85	Norwich C, Sunderland, Stoke C	2002–03	Sheffield W, Brighton & HA, Grimsby T
1985–86	Ipswich T, Birmingham C, WBA		
1986–87	Leicester C, Manchester C, Aston Villa	2003–04	Walsall, Bradford C, Wimbledon
1987–88	Chelsea**, Portsmouth, Watford, Oxford U		

**Relegated after play-offs.
*Subsequently re-elected to Division 1 when League was extended after the War.

FOOTBALL LEAGUE CHAMPIONSHIP
TO FOOTBALL LEAGUE CHAMPIONSHIP 1

2004–05	Gillingham, Nottingham F, Rotherham U.
2005–06	Crewe Alex, Millwall, Brighton & HA.
2006–07	Southend U, Luton T, Leeds U
2007–08	Leicester C, Scunthorpe U, Colchester U

DIVISION 2 TO DIVISION 3

1920–21	Stockport Co	1937–38	Barnsley and Stockport Co
1921–22	Bradford PA and Bristol C	1938–39	Norwich C and Tranmere R
1922–23	Rotherham Co and Wolverhampton W	1946–47	Swansea T and Newport Co
		1947–48	Doncaster R and Millwall
1923–24	Nelson and Bristol C	1948–49	Nottingham F and Lincoln C
1924–25	Crystal Palace and Coventry C	1949–50	Plymouth Arg and Bradford PA
1925–26	Stoke C and Stockport Co	1950–51	Grimsby T and Chesterfield
1926–27	Darlington and Bradford C	1951–52	Coventry C and QPR
1927–28	Fulham and South Shields	1952–53	Southampton and Barnsley
1928–29	Port Vale and Clapton Orient	1953–54	Brentford and Oldham Ath
1929–30	Hull C and Notts Co	1954–55	Ipswich T and Derby Co
1930–31	Reading and Cardiff C	1955–56	Plymouth Arg and Hull C
1931–32	Barnsley and Bristol C	1956–57	Port Vale and Bury
1932–33	Chesterfield and Charlton Ath	1957–58	Doncaster R and Notts Co
1933–34	Millwall and Lincoln C	1958–59	Barnsley and Grimsby T
1934–35	Oldham Ath and Notts Co	1959–60	Bristol C and Hull C
1935–36	Port Vale and Hull C	1960–61	Lincoln C and Portsmouth
1936–37	Doncaster R and Bradford C	1961–62	Brighton & HA and Bristol R

1962–63 Walsall and Luton T
1963–64 Grimsby T and Scunthorpe U
1964–65 Swindon T and Swansea T
1965–66 Middlesbrough and Leyton Orient
1966–67 Northampton T and Bury
1967–68 Plymouth Arg and Rotherham U
1968–69 Fulham and Bury
1969–70 Preston NE and Aston Villa
1970–71 Blackburn R and Bolton W
1971–72 Charlton Ath and Watford
1972–73 Huddersfield T and Brighton & HA
1973–74 Crystal Palace, Preston NE, Swindon T
1974–75 Millwall, Cardiff C, Sheffield W
1975–76 Oxford U, York C, Portsmouth
1976–77 Carlisle U, Plymouth Arg, Hereford U
1977–78 Blackpool, Mansfield T, Hull C
1978–79 Sheffield U, Millwall, Blackburn R
1979–80 Fulham, Burnley, Charlton Ath
1980–81 Preston NE, Bristol C, Bristol R
1981–82 Cardiff C, Wrexham, Orient
1982–83 Rotherham U, Burnley, Bolton W
1983–84 Derby Co, Swansea C, Cambridge U
1984–85 Notts Co, Cardiff C, Wolverhampton W
1985–86 Carlisle U, Middlesbrough, Fulham
1986–87 Sunderland**, Grimsby T, Brighton & HA
1987–88 Huddersfield T, Reading, Sheffield U**

1988–89 Shrewsbury T, Birmingham C, Walsall
1989–90 Bournemouth, Bradford C, Stoke C
1990–91 WBA and Hull C
1991–92 Plymouth Arg, Brighton & HA, Port Vale
1992–93 Preston NE, Mansfield T, Wigan Ath, Chester C
1993–94 Fulham, Exeter C, Hartlepool U, Barnet
1994–95 Cambridge U, Plymouth Arg, Cardiff C, Chester C, Leyton Orient
1995–96 Carlisle U, Swansea C, Brighton & HA, Hull C
1996–97 Peterborough U, Shrewsbury T, Rotherham U, Notts Co
1997–98 Brentford, Plymouth Arg, Carlisle U, Southend U
1998–99 York C, Northampton T, Lincoln C, Macclesfield T
1999–00 Cardiff C, Blackpool, Scunthorpe U, Chesterfield
2000–01 Bristol R, Luton T, Swansea C, Oxford U
2001–02 Bournemouth, Bury, Wrexham, Cambridge U
2002–03 Cheltenham T, Huddersfield T, Mansfield T, Northampton T
2003–04 Grimsby T, Rushden & D, Notts Co, Wycombe W

FOOTBALL LEAGUE CHAMPIONSHIP 1 TO FOOTBALL LEAGUE CHAMPIONSHIP 2

2004–05 Torquay U, Wrexham, Peterborough U, Stockport Co.
2005–06 Hartlepool U, Milton Keynes D, Swindon T, Walsall.
2006–07 Chesterfield, Bradford C, Rotherham U, Brentford
2007–08 Bournemouth, Gillingham, Port Vale, Luton T

DIVISION 3 TO DIVISION 4

1958–59 Rochdale, Notts Co, Doncaster R, Stockport Co
1959–60 Accrington S, Wrexham, Mansfield T, York C
1960–61 Chesterfield, Colchester U, Bradford C, Tranmere R
1961–62 Newport Co, Brentford, Lincoln C, Torquay U
1962–63 Bradford PA, Brighton & HA, Carlisle U, Halifax T
1963–64 Millwall, Crewe Alex, Wrexham, Notts Co

1964–65 Luton T, Port Vale, Colchester U, Barnsley
1965–66 Southend U, Exeter C, Brentford, York C
1966–67 Doncaster R, Workington, Darlington, Swansea T
1967–68 Scunthorpe U, Colchester U, Grimsby T, Peterborough U (demoted)
1968–69 Oldham Ath, Crewe Alex, Hartlepool, Northampton T

135

1969–70	Bournemouth, Southport, Barrow, Stockport Co	1981–82	Wimbledon, Swindon T, Bristol C, Chester
1970–71	Reading, Bury, Doncaster R, Gillingham	1982–83	Reading, Wrexham, Doncaster R, Chesterfield
1971–72	Mansfield T, Barnsley, Torquay U, Bradford C	1983–84	Scunthorpe U, Southend U, Port Vale, Exeter C
1972–73	Rotherham U, Brentford, Swansea C, Scunthorpe U	1984–85	Burnley, Orient, Preston NE, Cambridge U
1973–74	Cambridge U, Shrewsbury T, Southport, Rochdale	1985–86	Lincoln C, Cardiff C, Wolverhampton W, Swansea C
1974–75	Bournemouth, Tranmere R, Watford, Huddersfield T	1986–87	Bolton W**, Carlisle U, Darlington, Newport Co
1975–76	Aldershot, Colchester U, Southend U, Halifax T	1987–88	Doncaster R, York C, Grimsby T, Rotherham U**
1976–77	Reading, Northampton T, Grimsby T, York C	1988–89	Southend U, Chesterfield, Gillingham, Aldershot
1977–78	Port Vale, Bradford C, Hereford U, Portsmouth	1989–90	Cardiff C, Northampton T, Blackpool, Walsall
1978–79	Peterborough U, Walsall, Tranmere R, Lincoln C	1990–91	Crewe Alex, Rotherham U, Mansfield T
1979–80	Bury, Southend U, Mansfield T, Wimbledon	1991–92	Bury, Shrewsbury T, Torquay U, Darlington
1980–81	Sheffield U, Colchester U, Blackpool, Hull C		

**Relegated after play-offs.

LEAGUE STATUS FROM 1986–1987

	RELEGATED FROM LEAGUE	PROMOTED TO LEAGUE
1986–87	Lincoln C	Scarborough
1987–88	Newport Co	Lincoln C
1988–89	Darlington	Maidstone U
1989–90	Colchester U	Darlington
1990–91	—	Barnet
1991–92	—	Colchester U
1992–93	Halifax T	Wycombe W
1993–94	—	—
1994–95	—	—
1995–96	—	—
1996–97	Hereford U	Macclesfield T
1997–98	Doncaster R	Halifax T
1998–99	Scarborough	Cheltenham T
1999–2000	Chester C	Kidderminster H
2000–01	Barnet	Rushden & D
2001–02	Halifax T	Boston U
2002–03	Shrewsbury T, Exeter C	Yeovil T, Doncaster R
2003–04	Carlisle U, York C	Chester C, Shrewsbury T
2004–05	Kidderminster H, Cambridge U	Barnet, Carlisle U
2005–06	Oxford U, Rushden & D	Accrington S, Hereford U
2006–07	Boston U, Torquay U	Dagenham & R, Morecambe
2007–08	Mansfield T, Wrexham	Aldershot T, Exeter C

LEAGUE TITLE WINS

FA PREMIER LEAGUE – Manchester U 10, Arsenal 3, Chelsea 2, Blackburn R 1.

FOOTBALL LEAGUE CHAMPIONSHIP – Sunderland 2, Reading 1, WBA 1.

LEAGUE DIVISION 1 – Liverpool 18, Arsenal 10, Everton 9, Sunderland 8, Aston Villa 7, Manchester U 7, Newcastle U 5, Sheffield W 4, Huddersfield T 3, Leeds U 3, Manchester C 3, Portsmouth 3, Wolverhampton W 3, Blackburn R 2, Burnley 2, Derby Co 2, Nottingham F 2, Preston NE 2, Tottenham H 2; Bolton W, Charlton Ath, Chelsea, Crystal Palace, Fulham, Ipswich T, Middlesbrough, Norwich C, Sheffield U, WBA 1 each.

FOOTBALL LEAGUE CHAMPIONSHIP 1 – Luton T 1, Scunthorpe U, Southend U 1, Swansea C 1.

LEAGUE DIVISION 2 – Leicester C 6, Manchester C 6, Birmingham C (one as Small Heath) 5, Sheffield W 5, Derby Co 4, Liverpool 4, Preston NE 4, Ipswich T 3, Leeds U 3, Middlesbrough 3, Notts Co 3, Stoke C 3, Aston Villa 2, Bolton W 2, Burnley 2, Bury 2, Chelsea 2, Fulham 2, Grimsby T 2, Manchester U 2, Millwall 2, Norwich C 2, Nottingham F 2, Tottenham H 2, WBA 2, West Ham U 2, Wolverhampton W 2; Blackburn R, Blackpool, Bradford C, Brentford, Brighton & HA, Bristol C, Coventry C, Crystal Palace, Everton, Huddersfield T, Luton T, Newcastle U, Plymouth Arg, QPR, Oldham Ath, Oxford U, Reading, Sheffield U, Sunderland, Swindon T, Watford, Wigan Ath 1 each.

FOOTBALL LEAGUE CHAMPIONSHIP 2 – Carlisle U 1, Milton Keynes D 1, Walsall 1, Yeovil T 1.

LEAGUE DIVISION 3 – Brentford 2, Carlisle U 2, Oxford U 2, Plymouth Arg 2, Portsmouth 2, Preston NE 2, Shrewsbury T 2; Aston Villa, Blackburn R, Bolton W, Bournemouth, Bradford C, Brighton & HA, Bristol R, Burnley, Bury, Cambridge U, Cardiff C, Coventry C, Doncaster R, Grimsby T, Hereford U, Hull C, Leyton Orient, Mansfield T, Northampton T, Notts Co, Oldham Ath, QPR, Reading, Rotherham U, Rushden & D, Southampton, Sunderland, Swansea C, Watford, Wigan Ath, Wolverhampton W, Wrexham 1 each.

LEAGUE DIVISION 4 – Chesterfield 2, Doncaster R 2, Peterborough U 2; Brentford, Brighton & HA, Burnley, Cambridge U, Darlington, Exeter C, Gillingham, Grimsby T, Huddersfield T, Lincoln C, Luton T, Mansfield T, Millwall, Northampton T, Notts Co, Port Vale, Reading, Rotherham U, Sheffield U, Southend U, Southport, Stockport Co, Swindon T, Walsall, Watford, Wimbledon, Wolverhampton W, York C 1 each.

DIVISION 3 (South) – Bristol C 3, Charlton Ath 2, Ipswich T 2, Millwall 2, Notts Co 2, Plymouth Arg 2, Swansea T 2; Brentford, Brighton & HA, Bristol R, Cardiff C, Coventry C, Crystal Palace, Fulham, Leyton Orient, Luton T, Newport Co, Norwich C, Nottingham F, Portsmouth, QPR, Reading, Southampton 1 each.

DIVISION 3 (North) – Barnsley 3, Doncaster R 3, Lincoln C 3, Chesterfield 2, Grimsby T 2, Hull C 2, Port Vale 2, Stockport Co 2; Bradford C, Bradford PA, Darlington, Derby Co, Nelson, Oldham Ath, Rotherham U, Scunthorpe U, Stoke C, Tranmere R, Wolverhampton W 1 each.

FOOTBALL LEAGUE PLAY-OFFS 2007–2008

CHAMPIONSHIP FIRST LEG

Crystal Palace	(0) 1	Bristol C	(0) 2
Watford	(0) 0	Hull C	(2) 2

CHAMPIONSHIP SECOND LEG

Bristol C	(0) 2	Crystal Palace	(1) 1
(aet.)			
Hull C	(1) 4	Watford	(1) 1

CHAMPIONSHIP FINAL Saturday, 24 May 2008 *(at Wembley)*   86,703

Bristol C (0) 0

Hull C (1) 1 *(Windass 38)*

Bristol C: Basso; Orr (Johnson), McAllister, Carle (Byfield), Carey, Fontaine, Noble (Sproule), Elliott, Trundle, Adebola, McIndoe.
Hull C: Myhill; Ricketts, Dawson, Ashbee, Turner, Brown, Garcia, Barmby (Fagan), Campbell (Marney), Windass (Folan), Hughes.
Referee: A. Wiley (Staffordshire).

LEAGUE 1 FIRST LEG

Southend U	(0) 0	Doncaster R	(0) 0
Leeds U	(0) 1	Carlisle U	(1) 2

LEAGUE 1 SECOND LEG

Carlisle U	(0) 0	Leeds U	(1) 2
Doncaster R	(3) 5	Southend U	(0) 1

LEAGUE 1 FINAL Sunday, 25 May 2008 *(at Wembley)*   75,132

Doncaster R (0) 1 *(Hayter 48)*

Leeds U (0) 0

Doncaster R: Sullivan; O'Connor, Roberts G, Hird, Mills, Stock, Green, Wellens (McCammon), Hayter, Price (Lockwood), Coppinger (Guy).
Leeds U: Ankergren; Richardson, Johnson, Kilkenny, Michalik, Huntington, Prutton (Kandol), Howson, Beckford, Freedman (Hughes), Douglas.
Referee: A. D'Urso (Essex).

LEAGUE 2 FIRST LEG

Darlington	(1) 2	Rochdale	(0) 1
Wycombe W	(1) 1	Stockport Co	(0) 1

LEAGUE 2 SECOND LEG

Rochdale	(1) 2	Darlington	(1) 1
(aet; Rochdale won 5-4 on penalties.)			
Stockport Co	(1) 1	Wycombe W	(0) 0

LEAGUE 2 FINAL Monday, 26 May 2008 *(at Wembley)*   35,715

Stockport Co (1) 3 *(Stanton 34 (og), Pilkington 49, Dickinson 67)*

Rochdale (1) 2 *(McArdle 23, Rundle 77)*

Stockport Co: Logan C; Rose, Turnbull, McNulty, Owen, Pilkington, Dicker, Rowe, Dickinson (McNeil), Gleeson (McSweeney).
Rochdale: Lee; Ramsden, Kennedy, D'Laryea (Buckley), Stanton, McArdle, Higginbotham (Muirhead), Jones, Le Fondre (Howe), Dagnall, Rundle.
Referee: S. Attwell (Warwickshire).

LEAGUE ATTENDANCES 2007–2008

FA BARCLAYCARD PREMIERSHIP ATTENDANCES

	Average Gate			Season 2007–08	
	2006–07	2007–08	+/–%	Highest	Lowest
Arsenal	60,045	60,070	+0.04	60,161	59,442
Aston Villa	36,214	40,029	+10.53	42,640	32,288
Birmingham City	22,274	26,181	+17.54	29,252	22,089
Blackburn Rovers	21,275	23,944	+12.55	30,316	19,316
Bolton Wanderers	23,606	20,901	–11.46	25,414	17,014
Chelsea	41,542	41,397	–0.35	41,837	39,447
Derby County	25,945	32,432	+25.00	33,087	30,048
Everton	36,739	36,955	+0.59	40,049	31,885
Fulham	22,279	23,774	+6.71	25,357	20,774
Liverpool	43,563	43,532	–0.07	44,459	42,308
Manchester City	39,997	42,126	+5.32	47,321	38,261
Manchester United	75,826	75,691	–0.18	76,013	75,055
Middlesbrough	27,730	26,708	–3.69	33,952	22,920
Newcastle United	50,686	51,321	+1.25	52,307	49,948
Portsmouth	19,862	19,914	+0.26	20,556	17,108
Reading	23,829	23,585	–1.02	24,374	21,379
Sunderland	31,887	43,344	+35.93	47,802	37,369
Tottenham Hotspur	35,739	35,967	+0.64	36,178	35,504
West Ham United	34,719	34,601	–0.34	34,980	33,629
Wigan Athletic	18,159	19,046	+4.88	25,133	14,007

FOOTBALL LEAGUE CHAMPIONSHIP ATTENDANCES

	Average Gate			Season 2007–08	
	2006–07	2007–08	+/–%	Highest	Lowest
Barnsley	12,733	11,425	–10.3	18,257	8,531
Blackpool	6,877	8,861	+28.8	9,640	7,214
Bristol City	12,818	16,276	+27.0	19,332	12,474
Burnley	11,956	12,365	+3.4	16,843	9,779
Cardiff City	15,219	13,939	–8.4	18,840	11,006
Charlton Athletic	26,195	23,191	–11.5	26,337	20,737
Colchester United	5,466	5,509	+0.8	6,300	4,450
Coventry City	20,342	19,123	–6.0	27,992	14,036
Crystal Palace	17,541	16,031	–8.6	23,950	13,048
Hull City	18,758	18,025	–3.9	24,350	14,822
Ipswich Town	22,445	21,935	–2.3	29,656	17,938
Leicester City	23,206	23,509	+1.3	31,892	19,264
Norwich City	24,545	24,527	–0.1	25,497	23,176
Plymouth Argyle	13,012	13,000	–0.1	17,511	10,451
Preston North End	14,430	12,647	–12.4	17,807	10,279
Queens Park Rangers	12,936	13,959	+7.9	18,309	10,514
Scunthorpe United	5,669	6,434	+13.5	8,801	4,407
Sheffield United	30,512	25,631	–16.0	31,760	23,161
Sheffield Wednesday	23,638	21,418	–9.4	36,208	17,211
Southampton	23,556	21,254	–9.8	31,957	17,741
Stoke City	15,749	16,823	+6.8	26,609	11,147
Watford	18,750	16,876	–10.0	18,698	15,021
West Bromwich Albion	20,472	22,311	+9.0	27,493	18,310
Wolverhampton Wanderers	20,968	23,499	+12.1	27,883	20,763

Premiership and Football League attendance averages and highest crowd figures for 2007–08 are unofficial.

FOOTBALL LEAGUE CHAMPIONSHIP 1 ATTENDANCES

	Average Gate			Season 2007–08	
	2006–07	2007–08	+/–%	Highest	Lowest
AFC Bournemouth	6,028	5,504	–8.7	9,632	3,489
Brighton & Hove Albion	6,048	5,937	–1.8	8,691	4,395
Bristol Rovers	5,480	6,850	+25.0	11,883	3,933
Carlisle United	7,907	7,835	–0.9	16,668	5,477
Cheltenham Town	4,359	4,310	–1.1	7,043	3,169
Crewe Alexandra	5,462	4,932	–9.7	6,786	3,929
Doncaster Rovers	7,746	7,978	+3.0	15,001	5,967
Gillingham	6,282	6,077	–3.3	8,719	4,402
Hartlepool United	5,096	4,507	–11.6	7,784	3,217
Huddersfield Town	10,573	9,391	–11.2	16,413	6,004
Leeds United	21,613	26,543	+22.8	38,256	19,095
Leyton Orient	4,857	5,210	+7.3	7,602	3,082
Luton Town	8,580	6,492	–24.3	9,297	5,417
Millwall	9,234	8,691	–5.9	13,895	6,520
Northampton Town	5,573	5,409	–2.9	7,260	4,555
Nottingham Forest	20,612	19,964	–3.1	28,520	15,860
Oldham Athletic	6,334	5,326	–15.9	10,054	3,633
Port Vale	4,725	4,417	–6.5	7,908	2,869
Southend United	10,024	8,173	–18.5	9,828	6,844
Swansea City	12,720	13,520	+6.3	19,010	10,135
Swindon Town	7,419	7,170	–3.4	13,270	4,840
Tranmere Rovers	6,930	6,504	–6.1	11,008	5,006
Walsall	5,643	5,620	–0.4	10,102	4,309
Yeovil Town	5,765	5,468	–5.2	9,527	4,319

FOOTBALL LEAGUE CHAMPIONSHIP 2 ATTENDANCES

	Average Gate			Season 2007–08	
	2006–07	2007–08	+/–%	Highest	Lowest
Accrington Stanley	2,260	1,634	–27.7	2,898	1,149
Barnet	2,279	2,147	–5.8	3,074	1,303
Bradford City	8,694	13,659	+57.1	15,510	13,019
Brentford	5,600	4,469	–20.2	6,246	3,155
Bury	2,588	2,601	+0.5	6,271	1,690
Chester City	2,473	2,479	+0.2	3,849	1,566
Chesterfield	4,235	4,103	–3.1	6,300	3,274
Dagenham & Redbridge	1,756	2,007	+14.3	3,451	1,328
Darlington	3,814	3,818	+0.1	6,965	2,628
Grimsby Town	4,379	4,115	–6.0	5,829	2,537
Hereford United	3,328	3,421	+2.8	6,020	2,271
Lincoln City	5,176	4,078	–21.2	5,286	3,189
Macclesfield Town	2,863	2,298	–19.7	3,585	1,378
Mansfield Town	3,176	2,821	–11.2	5,271	1,606
Milton Keynes Dons	6,034	9,456	+56.7	17,250	6,483
Morecambe	1,598	2,812	+76.0	4,761	1,634
Notts County	4,974	4,732	–4.9	10,027	3,421
Peterborough United	4,662	5,995	+28.6	10,400	4,200
Rochdale	2,898	3,057	+5.5	4,692	2,278
Rotherham United	4,763	4,201	–11.8	6,709	2,979
Shrewsbury Town	4,730	5,659	+19.6	7,707	4,499
Stockport County	5,514	5,643	+2.3	8,838	4,477
Wrexham	5,030	4,234	–15.8	7,687	2,805
Wycombe Wanderers	4,983	4,747	–4.7	6,202	3,821

TRANSFERS 2007–2008

JUNE 2007	*From*	*To*
29 Bent, Darren	Charlton Athletic	Tottenham Hotspur
4 Bramble, Titus M.	Newcastle United	Wigan Athletic
20 Corr, Barry	Sheffield Wednesday	Swindon Town
27 Craig, Tony A.	Millwall	Crystal Palace
29 Earnshaw, Robert	Norwich City	Derby County
25 Forster, Nicholas	Hull City	Brighton & Hove Albion
27 Frampton, Andrew J.K.	Brentford	Millwall
11 Halford, Gregory	Reading	Sunderland
7 Hayter, James E.	AFC Bournemouth	Doncaster Rovers
18 Hibbert, David J.	Preston North End	Shrewsbury Town
1 Hreidarsson, Hermann	Charlton Athletic	Portsmouth
5 Hurst, Kevan	Sheffield United	Scunthorpe United
5 McAnuff, Joel J.	Crystal Palace	Watford
13 McCann, Gavin P.	Aston Villa	Bolton Wanderers
13 McCarthy, Patrick	Leicester City	Charlton Athletic
28 Nash, Carlo J.	Preston North End	Wigan Athletic
2 Odejayi, Olukayode	Cheltenham Town	Barnsley
13 O'Donnell, Daniel	Liverpool	Crewe Alexandra
7 Parker, Scott M.	Newcastle United	West Ham United
5 Sibierski, Antoine	Newcastle United	Wigan Athletic
1 Spencer, James M.	Stockport County	Rochdale
26 Weir-Daley, Spencer J.A.	Nottingham Forest	Notts County
21 Windass, Dean	Bradford City	Hull City

JULY 2007		
10 Aliadiere, Jeremie	Arsenal	Middlesbrough
3 Aljofree, Hasney	Plymouth Argyle	Swindon Town
5 Allott, Mark S.	Chesterfield	Oldham Athletic
17 Baird, Christopher P.	Southampton	Fulham
30 Barnett, Leon P.	Luton Town	West Bromwich Albion
3 Barton, Joseph A.	Manchester City	Newcastle United
11 Bellamy, Craig D.	Liverpool	West Ham United
20 Benayoun, Yossi S.	West Ham United	Liverpool
12 Best, Leon J.B.	Southampton	Coventry City
13 Blake, Robert J.	Leeds United	Burnley
24 Blinkhorn, Matthew D.	Blackpool	Morecambe
5 Borrowdale, Gary I.	Crystal Palace	Coventry City
31 Brown, Michael R.	Fulham	Wigan Athletic
16 Brown, Wayne L.	Colchester United	Hull City
23 Butcher, Richard T.	Peterborough United	Notts County
5 Cahill, Thomas	Matlock Town	Rotherham United
23 Campbell, Dudley J.	Birmingham City	Leicester City
20 Carlton, Daniel	Morecambe	Carlisle United
12 Charnock, Kieran J.	Northwich Victoria	Peterborough United
13 Chopra, Rocky M.	Cardiff City	Sunderland
16 Clemence, Stephen N.	Birmingham City	Leicester City
1 Cohen, Christopher D.	Yeovil Town	Nottingham Forest
2 Coke, Giles C.	Mansfield Town	Northampton Town
20 Cook, Lee	Queens Park Rangers	Fulham
19 Crowther, Ryan J.	Stockport County	Liverpool
2 Cureton, Jamie	Colchester United	Norwich City
20 Davies, Aaron R.	Yeovil Town	Nottingham Forest
25 Davis, Claude	Sheffield United	Derby County
17 Davis, Steven	Aston Villa	Fulham
25 Duffy, Darryl A.	Hull City	Swansea City
1 Eastwood, Freddy	Southend United	Wolverhampton Wanderers
31 Elliott, Marvin C.	Millwall	Bristol City
20 Elliott, Stephen W.	Sunderland	Wolverhampton Wanderers
26 Ellison, Kevin	Tranmere Rovers	Chester City
17 Etuhu, Dixon P.	Norwich City	Sunderland

18 Facey, Delroy M.	Rotherham United	Gillingham
9 Forte, Jonathan	Sheffield United	Scunthorpe United
14 Geremi	Chelsea	Newcastle United
18 Gray, Wayne W.	Yeovil Town	Leyton Orient
19 Harewood, Marlon A.	West Ham United	Aston Villa
16 Healy, David J.	Leeds United	Fulham
20 Helguson, Heidar	Fulham	Bolton Wanderers
9 Howarth, Christopher	Bolton Wanderers	Carlisle United
5 Howe, Jermaine R.	Kettering Town	Peterborough United
5 Hughes, Aaron W.	Aston Villa	Fulham
4 Hughes, Jeffrey	Lincoln City	Crystal Palace
5 Jagielka, Philip N.	Sheffield United	Everton
3 Jarvis, Matthew	Gillingham	Wolverhampton Wanderers
12 Jones, Billy	Crewe Alexandra	Preston North End
16 Kamara, Diomansky M.	West Bromwich Albion	Fulham
30 King, Simon D.R.	Barnet	Gillingham
16 Konchesky, Paul M.	West Ham United	Fulham
10 Koumas, Jason	West Bromwich Albion	Wigan Athletic
2 Kuszczak, Tomasz	West Bromwich Albion	Manchester United
1 Le Fondre, Adam J.	Stockport County	Rochdale
25 Ljungberg, Fredrik	Arsenal	West Ham United
20 Lockwood, Matthew D.	Leyton Orient	Nottingham Forest
30 McIndoe, Michael	Wolverhampton Wanderers	Bristol City
27 McShane, Paul D.	West Bromwich Albion	Sunderland
5 Mears, Tyrone	West Ham United	Derby County
5 Naysmith, Gary	Everton	Sheffield United
5 Nicholls, Kevin J.	Leeds United	Preston North End
11 Nugent, David J.	Preston North End	Portsmouth
18 Parkin, Jonathan	Hull City	Stoke City
3 Partridge, Richard J.	Rotherham United	Chester City
14 Pipe, David R.	Notts County	Bristol Rovers
14 Platt, Clive L.	Milton Keynes Dons	Colchester United
27 Price, Lewis P.	Ipswich Town	Derby County
6 Pugh, Marc	Bury	Shrewsbury Town
16 Reo-Coker, Nigel	West Ham United	Aston Villa
16 Richardson, Kieran E.	Manchester United	Sunderland
11 Ridley, Lee	Scunthorpe United	Cheltenham Town
4 Rocastle, Craig A.	Oldham Athletic	Port Vale
30 Russell, Darel F.R.G.	Stoke City	Norwich City
5 Sharp, William	Scunthorpe United	Sheffield United
31 Sinclair, Dean M.	Barnet	Charlton Athletic
6 Smith, Ryan C.M.	Derby County	Millwall
9 Taylor-Fletcher, Gary	Huddersfield Town	Blackpool
9 Todd, Andrew J.J.	Blackburn Rovers	Derby County
31 Trundle, Lee C.	Swansea City	Bristol City
3 Ward, Darren P.	Crystal Palace	Wolverhampton Wanderers
19 Williams, Andrew	Hereford United	Bristol Rovers
16 Wilson, Kelvin J.	Preston North End	Nottingham Forest
20 Yeates, Mark	Tottenham Hotspur	Colchester United
27 Young, Luke P.	Charlton Athletic	Middlesbrough

TEMPORARY TRANSFERS
12 Antwi-Birago, Godwin – Liverpool – Hartlepool United; 17 Basey, Grant W. – Charlton Athletic – Brentford; 10 Connolly, Matthew T. – Arsenal – Colchester United; 25 Davies, Scott – Reading – Aldershot Town; 31 Dodds, Louis B. – Leicester City – Lincoln City; 18 Gilmartin, Rene – Walsall – Hednesford Town; 5 Guthrie, Danny S. – Liverpool – Bolton Wanderers; 12 Hammill, Adam J. – Liverpool – Southampton; 25 Harban, Thomas J. – Barnsley – Bradford City; 17 Heckingbottom, Paul – Barnsley – Bradford City; 27 Joynes, Nathan – Barnsley – Bradford City; 9 Lowe, Keith S. – Wolverhampton Wanderers – Port Vale; 31 Miller, Ian J. – Ipswich Town – Darlington; 25 Moore, Sammy – Ipswich Town – Brentford; 27 Nyatanga, Lewin J. – Derby County – Barnsley; 11 Richards, Justin D. – Peterborough United – Boston United; 19 Smith, James D. – Chelsea – Norwich City; 31 Turnbull, Ross – Middlesbrough – Cardiff City; 18 Wiles, Simon P. – Blackpool – Macclesfield Town; 10 Youga, Kelly A. – Charlton Athletic – Scunthorpe United

AUGUST 2007

2 Abbott, Pawel T.H.	Swansea City	Darlington
31 Alexander, Graham	Preston North End	Burnley
10 Aljofree, Hasney	Plymouth Argyle	Swindon Town
4 Bailey, Nicholas F.	Barnsley	Southend United
7 Baines, Leighton	Wigan Athletic	Everton
8 Batt, Shaun	Dagenham & Redbridge	Fisher Athletic
7 Beattie, James S.	Everton	Sheffield United
8 Bouazza, Hameur	Watford	Fulham
31 Bradbury, Lee	Southend United	AFC Bournemouth
15 Brunt, Christopher	Sheffield Wednesday	West Bromwich Albion
8 Butcher, Richard T.	Peterborough United	Notts County
30 Byfield, Darren	Millwall	Bristol City
3 Camp, Lee M.J.	Derby County	Queens Park Rangers
7 Campbell, Dudley J.	Birmingham City	Leicester City
31 Campbell-Ryce, Jamal	Southend United	Barnsley
17 Carlisle, Clarke J.	Watford	Burnley
10 Carter, Darren A.	West Bromwich Albion	Preston North End
7 Clemence, Stephen N.	Birmingham City	Leicester City
8 Cook, Lee	Queens Park Rangers	Fulham
10 Cranie, Martin J.	Southampton	Portsmouth
3 Cresswell, Richard P.W.	Leeds United	Stoke City
10 Dean, James	Northwich Victoria	Bury
31 Diarra, Lassana	Chelsea	Arsenal
31 Diop, Papa B.	Fulham	Portsmouth
16 Dyer, Kieron C.	Newcastle United	West Ham United
7 Edwards, David A.	Shrewsbury Town	Luton Town
30 Ellington, Nathan L.F.	West Bromwich Albion	Watford
3 Ellison, Kevin	Tranmere Rovers	Chester City
31 Faye, Abdoulaye D.	Bolton Wanderers	Newcastle United
31 Folan, Caleb C.	Wigan Athletic	Hull City
14 Foley, Kevin P.	Luton Town	Wolverhampton Wanderers
24 Foster, Stephen J.	Burnley	Barnsley
15 Garner, Joseph A.	Blackburn Rovers	Carlisle United
1 Griffin, Andrew	Portsmouth	Derby County
10 Gueret, Willy J.	Swansea City	Milton Keynes Dons
17 Hand, Jamie	Chester City	Lincoln City
31 Harte, Ian P.	Leeds United	Sunderland
6 Healy, David J.	Leeds United	Fulham
30 Higginbotham, Daniel J.	Stoke City	Sunderland
7 Hoefkens, Carl	Stoke City	West Bromwich Albion
31 Holmes, Ian D.	Matlock Town	Mansfield Town
31 Hughes, Andrew J.	Norwich City	Leeds United
31 Huntington, Paul	Newcastle United	Leeds United
8 Jacobson, Joseph M.	Cardiff City	Bristol Rovers
9 Jeffers, Francis	Blackburn Rovers	Sheffield Wednesday
30 John, Stern	Sunderland	Southampton
31 Johnson, Glen M.C.	Chelsea	Portsmouth
31 Johnson, Jemal J.	Wolverhampton Wanderers	Milton Keynes Dons
30 Jones, Kenwyne J.	Southampton	Sunderland
29 Knight, Zatyiah	Fulham	Aston Villa
31 Leigertwood, Mikele B.	Sheffield United	Queens Park Rangers
20 Lewis, Edward J.	Leeds United	Derby County
22 Martin, Richard W.	Brighton & Hove Albion	Manchester City
10 McCarthy, Patrick	Leicester City	Charlton Athletic
31 McGovern, Jon P.	Milton Keynes Dons	Swindon Town
10 McLeod, Izale M.	Milton Keynes Dons	Charlton Athletic
17 Mido	Tottenham Hotspur	Middlesbrough
7 Morrison, James C.	Middlesbrough	West Bromwich Albion
31 Murphy, Daniel B.	Tottenham Hotspur	Fulham
14 O'Brien, Andrew J.	Portsmouth	Bolton Wanderers
10 O'Donovan, Roy S.	Cork City	Sunderland

31	O'Neil, Gary	Portsmouth	Middlesbrough
10	Owen, Gareth J.	Oldham Athletic	Stockport County
9	Paterson, Martin A.	Stoke City	Scunthorpe United
31	Paynter, William P.	Southend United	Swindon Town
9	Pearce, Jason D.	Portsmouth	AFC Bournemouth
9	Pele	Southampton	West Bromwich Albion
3	Queudrue, Franck	Fulham	Birmingham City
8	Richards, Gary	Colchester United	Southend United
3	Ridgewell, Liam M.	Aston Villa	Birmingham City
31	Rosenior, Liam J.	Fulham	Reading
7	Safri, Youssef	Norwich City	Southampton
31	Seol, Ki-Hyeon	Reading	Fulham
7	Sharp, Billy L.	Scunthorpe United	Sheffield United
3	Smith, Alan	Manchester United	Newcastle United
30	Sodje, Akpo	Port Vale	Sheffield Wednesday
31	Solano, Nolberto	Newcastle United	West Ham United
31	Stefanovic, Dejan	Portsmouth	Fulham
20	Swailes, Daniel	Macclesfield Town	Milton Keynes Dons
16	Thomas, Wayne	Burnley	Southampton
3	Walton, Simon W.	Charlton Athletic	Queens Park Rangers
7	Williams, Marvin T.	Millwall	Yeovil Town
24	Williams, Robert I.	Barnsley	Huddersfield Town
30	Yakubu, Ayegbeni	Middlesbrough	Everton
10	Young, Luke P.	Charlton Athletic	Middlesbrough

TEMPORARY TRANSFERS

31 Aiston, Sam J. – Northampton Town – Burton Albion; 23, Anderson – Everton – Barnsley; 7 Anderson, Paul – Liverpool – Swansea City; 10 Artus, Frankie – Bristol City – Exeter City; 10 Aspden, Curtis – Hull City – Harrogate Town; 30 Barnard, Lee J. – Tottenham Hotspur – Crewe Alexandra; 10 Bean, Marcus T. – Blackpool – Rotherham United; 10 Begovic, Asmir – Portsmouth – AFC Bournemouth; 17 Behcet, Darren – Yeovil Town – Dorchester Town; 1 Bennett, Alan J. – Reading – Southampton; 30 Bennett, Dean A. – Chester City – Kidderminster Harriers; 31 Bent, Marcus N. – Charlton Athletic – Wigan Athletic; 21 Bertrand, Ryan D. – Chelsea – Oldham Athletic; 24 Bradbury, Lee – Southend United – AFC Bournemouth; 24 Branston, Guy – Peterborough United – Rochdale; 30 Bullock, Lee – Hartlepool United – Mansfield Town; 10 Cadmore, Tom – Wycombe Wanderers – Hayes & Yeading United; 31 Camara, Henri – Wigan Athletic – West Ham United; 16 Carroll, Andrew T. – Newcastle United – Preston North End; 10 Carson, Scott P. – Liverpool – Aston Villa; 24 Caton, Andrew J. – Swindon Town – Swindon Supermarine; 9 Chamberlain, Scott D. – Brighton & Hove Albion – Eastbourne Borough; 10 Charles, Wesley D.D. – Brentford – Sutton United; 10 Christophe, Jean F. – Portsmouth – AFC Bournemouth; 20 Clapham, James R. – Wolverhampton Wanderers – Leeds United; 16 Clarke, Clive – Sunderland – Leicester City; 31 Clarke, Leon M. – Sheffield Wednesday – Southend United; 17 Cobbs, Sonny H. – Brighton & Hove Albion – Worthing; 17 Cork, Jack F.P. – Chelsea – Scunthorpe United; 31 Coulson, Michael – Barnsley – Northwich Victoria; 31 Cox, Simon – Reading – Swindon Town; 17 Craddock, Jody – Wolverhampton Wanderers – Stoke City; 4 Daniels, Charlie – Tottenham Hotspur – Leyton Orient; 31 Davies, Curtis E. – West Bromwich Albion – Aston Villa; 9 Diagouraga, Toumani – Watford – Hereford United; 31 Dickov, Paul – Manchester City – Crystal Palace; 16 Dickson, Christopher M. – Charlton Athletic – Crewe Alexandra; 10 Djourou, Johan – Arsenal – Birmingham City; 24 Doran, Peter J. – Walsall – Worcester City; 10 Ephraim, Hogan – West Ham United – Queens Park Rangers; 31 Feeney, Warren J. – Cardiff City – Swansea City; 31 Fojut, Jaroslaw – Bolton Wanderers – Luton Town; 24, Forde, David – Cardiff City – Luton Town; 15 Fulop, Marton – Sunderland – Leicester City; 31 Gallagher, Paul – Blackburn Rovers – Preston North End; 1 Gamble, Patrick J. – Nottingham Forest – Stalybridge Celtic; 10 Gargan, Sam J. – Brighton & Hove Albion – Worthing; 10 Garner, Joseph A. – Blackburn Rovers – Carlisle United; 3 Gaynor, Ross – Millwall – Fisher Athletic; 10 Giddings, Stuart J. – Coventry City – Oldham Athletic; 8 Gilbert, Kerrea K. – Arsenal – Southend United; 31 Gooding, Andrew M. – Coventry City – Burton Albion; 9 Gradel, Max – Leicester City – AFC Bournemouth; 24 Grant, Gavin – Millwall – Grays Athletic; 10 Green, Dominic A. – Dagenham & Redbridge – Thurrock; 10 Gregory, Steven M. – Wycombe Wanderers – Hayes & Yeading United; 13 Griffiths, Anthony J. – Doncaster Rovers – Halifax Town;

10 Hamer, Ben – Reading – Brentford; 17 Hardman, Lewis T. – Darlington – Whitby Town; 14 Hazley, Matthew – Stoke City – Stafford Rangers; 31 Henderson, Stephen – Bristol City – York City; 24 Holness, Marcus L. – Oldham Athletic – Ossett Town; 31 Idrizaj, Besian – Liverpool – Crystal Palace; 23 Jefferies, Michael J. – Macclesfield Town – Leek Town; 7 Jones, Daniel J. – Wolverhampton Wanderers – Northampton Town; 14 Jones, Richard G. – Manchester United – Yeovil Town; 31 Keogh, Richard J. – Bristol City – Huddersfield Town; 24 Kilkenny, Neil M. – Birmingham City – Oldham Athletic; 31 Kuqi, Shefki – Crystal Palace – Fulham; 1 Lewis, Joseph P. – Norwich City – Morecambe; 10 Logan, Conrad – Leicester City – Stockport County; 31 Maher, Stephen J. – Yeovil Town – Dorchester Town; 10 Maidens, Michael D. – Hartlepool United – Blyth Spartans; 9 Mancienne, Michael I. – Chelsea – Queens Park Rangers; 17 Marsh-Evans, Robert W. – Chester City – Droylsden; 12 Massey, Alan – Wycombe Wanderers – Wealdstone; 31 Masters, Clark J. – Brentford – Welling United; 31 McGoldrick, David J. – Southampton – Port Vale; 20 McGrail, Christopher – Preston North End – Accrington Stanley; 10 McKeown, James K. – Peterborough United – Kettering Town; 31 Miller, Ian – Ipswich Town – Darlington; 15 Miller, Ishmael – Manchester City – West Bromwich Albion; 31 Mills, Daniel J. – Manchester City – Charlton Athletic; 14 Mills, Matthew C.C. – Manchester City – Doncaster Rovers; 24 Mills, Pablo S.I. – Rotherham United – Crawley Town; 10 Montague, Ross P. – Brentford – Sutton United; 30 Mulligan, David – Scunthorpe United – Grimsby Town; 10 Murphy, Andrew – Preston North End – Northwich Victoria; 10 Myrie-Williams, Jennison – Bristol City – Cheltenham Town; 9 N'Dumbu-N'Sungu, Guy – Gillingham – Bradford City; 10 Newton, Sean – Chester City – Southport; 16 Nicholson, Stuart I. – West Bromwich Albion – Shrewsbury Town; 31 O'Callaghan, George – Ipswich Town – Brighton & Hove Albion; 10 O'Connor, Gareth – Burnley – AFC Bournemouth; 31 Odhiambo, Eric – Leicester City – Southend United; 24 O'Hara, Jamie – Tottenham Hotspur – Millwall; 28 Oji, Samuel U.U. – Birmingham City – Leyton Orient; 8 Palmer, Christopher L. – Wycombe Wanderers – Darlington; 16 Palmer, James – Bristol Rovers – Tiverton Town; 2 Peltier, Lee A. – Liverpool – Yeovil Town; 10 Pentney, Carl – Leicester City – York City; 10 Pettigrew, Adrian R.J. – Chelsea – Brentford; 17 Reed, Jamie – Wrexham – Aberystwyth Town; 31 Reid, Reuben – Plymouth Argyle – Wycombe Wanderers; 17 Rigley, Alex – Swindon Town – Cirencester Town; 9 Robinson, Theo – Watford – Hereford United; 31 Rooney, Adam – Stoke City – Chesterfield; 31 Russell, Alexander J. – Bristol City – Northampton Town; 14 Ryan, James – Liverpool – Shrewsbury Town; 9 Sahar, Ben – Chelsea – Queens Park Rangers; 17 Sandell, Andrew C. – Bristol Rovers – Salisbury City; 10 Semple, Ryan D. – Lincoln City – Rushden & Diamonds; 9 Shawcross, Ryan J. – Manchester United – Stoke City; 31 Simpson, Jay-Alistaire F. – Arsenal – Millwall; 10 Skinner, Lloyd E. – Brighton & Hove Albion – Burgess Hill Town; 23 Smith, Adam – Peterborough United – Kings Lynn; 10 Smith, James – Liverpool – Stockport County; 31 Sodje, Samuel – Reading – Charlton Athletic; 9 Stack, Graham – Reading – Wolverhampton Wanderers; 1 Starosta, Ben M. – Sheffield United – Brentford; 24 Thomas, Sean I.S. – Queens Park Rangers – Wealdstone; 10 Tearney, Paul T. – Blackpool – Stockport County; 16 Travis, Nicholas – Sheffield United – Chesterfield; 10 Ujah, Curtis – Yeovil Town – Crawley Town; 31 Warburton, Callum S. – Rochdale – Kendal Town; 8 Weale, Christopher – Bristol City – Hereford United; 14 Welsh, Ishmael – Yeovil Town – Torquay United; 30 Westwood, Ashley M. – Chester City – Port Vale; 17 Winterton, Christopher C. – Brighton & Hove Albion – Burgess Hill Town; 31 Worley, Harry J. – Chelsea – Carlisle United; 31 Wright, Joshua W. – Charlton Athletic – Barnet; 3 Wright, Stephen J. – Sunderland – Stoke City; 31 Zakuani, Gabriel A. – Fulham – Stoke City; 2 Zebroski, Christopher – Millwall – Torquay United

SEPTEMBER 2007 TEMPORARY TRANSFERS

28 Alnwick, Ben – Tottenham Hotspur – Luton Town; 14 Annerson, Jamie – Sheffield United – Rotherham United; 20 Anyinsah, Joseph G. – Preston North End – Carlisle United; 14 Avinel, Cedric M. – Watford – Stafford Rangers; 8 Bennett, Dean A. – Chester City – Kidderminster Harriers; 14 Blackmore, David – West Ham United – Thurrock; 14 Boulding, Rory J.J. – Mansfield Town – Hucknall Town; 20 Cahill, Gary J. – Aston Villa – Sheffield United; 25 Carder-Andrews, Karle S. – Brentford – Margate; 21 Cattell, Stuart – Wycombe Wanderers – Oxford United; 17 Chamberlain, Scott D. – Brighton & Hove Albion – Bognor Regis Town; 24 Cisak, Alex – Leicester City – Oxford United; 14 Clarke, Tom – Yeovil Town – Bridgwater Town; 21 Clarke, Wayne J. – Darlington – Shildon; 29 Cole, James W. – Barnet – Wingate & Finchley; 28 Collins, Sam – Hull City – Swindon Town; 27 Collins, Sam C. – Milton Keynes Dons – Kettering Town; 28 Craney, Ian T.W. –

145

Swansea City – Accrington Stanley; 21 Cresswell, Ryan – Sheffield United – Rotherham United; 21 Dailly, Christian – West Ham United – Southampton; 21 Davies, Gareth – Chesterfield – Stalybridge Celtic; 24 Davis, Sol S. – Luton Town – Peterborough United; 21 Dickson, Christopher M. – Charlton Athletic – Gillingham; 14 Douglas, Robert J. – Leicester City – Millwall; 14 Dyer, Bruce A. – Doncaster Rovers – Rotherham United; 21 Ellis, Mark I.I. – Bolton Wanderers – Torquay United; 14 Evans, Gareth D. – Wrexham – Northwich Victoria; 28 Fielding, Frank D. – Blackburn Rovers – Wycombe Wanderers; 28 Frizzell, Brewster – Hull City – North Ferriby United; 28 Garrett, Robert – Stoke City – Wrexham; 12 Gatting, Joe S. – Brighton & Hove Albion – Woking; 21 Gillett, Simon J. – Southampton – Yeovil Town; 6 Goode, Aaron M.O. – Queens Park Rangers – Kingstonian; 7 Grazioli, Giuliano – Barnet – AFC Wimbledon; 21 Hardman, Lewis – Darlington – Shildon; 17 Hastings, John J.D. – Milton Keynes Dons – Ebbsfleet United; 13 Hegarty, Nicholas – Grimsby Town – York City; 7 Hernandez, Stephen – Sheffield United – Worksop Town; 26 Heslop, Simon – Barnsley – Northwich Victoria; 18 Hoskins, William – Watford – Millwall; 28 Ifil, Phillip – Tottenham Hotspur – Southampton; 14 Johnson, Adam – Middlesbrough – Watford; 21 Johnson, Michael O. – Derby County – Sheffield Wednesday; 14 Jones, Zachariah S. – Blackburn Rovers – Stockport County; 21 Kavanagh, Graham A. – Sunderland – Sheffield Wednesday; 28 Kazimierczak, Przemyslaw – Bolton Wanderers – Wycombe Wanderers; 8 Kelly, Shaun – Chester City – Vauxhall Motors; 20 Laird, Scott – Plymouth Argyle – Torquay United; 21 Larrieu, Romain – Plymouth Argyle – Yeovil Town; 20 Leonard, Benjamin P. – Bury – Tamworth; 17 Loach, Scott J.J. – Watford – Stafford Rangers; 12 Lomax, Kelvin – Oldham Athletic – Rochdale; 21 MacKenzie, Christopher – Shrewsbury Town – Kidderminster Harriers; 28 Marsh-Evans, Robert W. – Chester City – Vauxhall Motors; 28 Mattis, Dwayne A.A. – Barnsley – Walsall; 28 May, Ben S. – Millwall – Scunthorpe United; 8 McAllister, Sean B. – Sheffield Wednesday – Mansfield Town; 21 Montague, Ross P. – Brentford – Welling United; 21 Nowland, Adam C. – Preston North End – Gillingham; 14 Page, Sam T. – Milton Keynes Dons – Walton & Hersham; 21 Potter, Alfie – Peterborough United – Grays Athletic; 14 Reet, Daniel – Mansfield Town – Alfreton Town; 21 Richards, Matthew – Ipswich Town – Brighton & Hove Albion; 21 Saunders, Russell – Wigan Athletic – Altrincham; 14 Shotton, Ryan – Stoke City – Altrincham; 12 Smart, Bally – Norwich City – Milton Keynes Dons; 27 Smith, Adam – Peterborough United – Boston United; 21 Stephens, Dale – Bury – Drolysden; 21 Taylor, Ryan – Rotherham United – Burton Albion; 28 Wallwork, Ronald – West Bromwich Albion – Huddersfield Town; 21 Wilson, Marc D. – Portsmouth – AFC Bournemouth

OCTOBER 2007 TEMPORARY TRANSFERS

11 Allison, Scott – Hartlepool United – Gateshead; 1 Andrews, Wayne M.H. – Coventry City – Leeds United; 21 Anyinsah, Joseph G. – Preston North End – Carlisle United; 4 Aspden, Curtis – Hull City – Harrogate Town; 19 Atkinson, Robert – Barnsley – Rochdale; 12 Atkinson, William H. – Hull City – Port Vale; 11 Bailey, Stefan K.L.K. – Queens Park Rangers – Oxford United; 19 Bardsley, Phillip A. – Manchester United – Sheffield United; 29 Bastians, Felix – Nottingham Forest – Chesterfield; 29 Bencherif, Hamza – Nottingham Forest – Lincoln City; 25 Bennett, Elliott – Wolverhampton Wanderers – Crewe Alexandra; 18 Beresford, Marlon – Luton Town – Oldham Athletic; 5 Betsy, Kevin – Bristol City – Yeovil Town; 5 Bradley, Jason – Sheffield Wednesday – Buxton; 25 Brkovic, Ahmet – Luton Town – Millwall; 1 Brooks-Meade, Corrin – Fulham – Darlington; 5 Bullock, Lee – Hartlepool United – Bury; 16 Butler, Martin N. – Walsall – Grimsby Town; 30 Buzsaky, Akos – Plymouth Argyle – Queens Park Rangers; 18 Campbell, Fraizer L. – Manchester United – Hull City; 26 Carayol, Mustapha – Milton Keynes Dons – Crawley Town; 8 Caton, Andrew J. – Swindon Town – North Leigh; 19 Church, Simon R. – Reading – Crewe Alexandra; 1 Clapham, James R. – Wolverhampton Wanderers – Leeds United; 14 Clarke, Tom – Yeovil Town – Bridgwater Town; 24 Colbeck, Philip J. – Bradford City – Darlington; 8 Cole, James W. – Barnet – Wingate & Finchley; 1 Coles, Daniel R. – Hull City – Hartlepool United; 25 Cooper, Kevin L. – Cardiff City – Tranmere Rovers; 5 Cotton, Jack M. – Lincoln City – Ilkeston Town; 5 Coward, Christopher D. – Stockport County – Northwich Victoria; 8 Cranie, Martin J. – Portsmouth – Queens Park Rangers; 9 Crow, Daniel – Peterborough United – Notts County; 26 Dark, Lewis K. – Brentford – Farnborough; 9 Davies, Andrew – Middlesbrough – Southampton; 1 De Vries, Mark – Leicester City – Leeds United; 11 Dean, James – Bury – Altrincham; 23 Doherty, Thomas – Queens Park Rangers – Wycombe Wanderers; 23 Douglas, Robert J. – Leicester City – Wycombe Wanderers; 26 Easter, Jermaine – Wycombe Wanderers – Plymouth Argyle; 12 Eckersley, Adam – Manchester United – Port Vale; 25 Emanuel, Lewis J. – Luton Town –

146

Brentford; 4 Evans, Rhys K. – Blackpool – Bradford City; 5 Fogden, Wesley K. – Brighton & Hove Albion – Dorchester Town; 19 Gibson, Darron – Manchester United – Wolverhampton Wanderers; 8 Green, Matthew J. – Cardiff City – Darlington; 12 Hart, Daniel – Barnet – Northwood; 15 Hartson, John – West Bromwich Albion – Norwich City; 16 Heslop, Simon – Barnsley – Halifax Town; 2 Holness, Marcus L. – Oldham Athletic – Rochdale; 5 Jackson, Matthew A. – Watford – Blackpool; 2 Jarrett, Jason L. – Preston North End – Queens Park Rangers; 5 Jefferies, Michael J. – Macclesfield Town – Leek Town; 23 John, Collins – Fulham – Leicester City; 18 Karacan, Jem P. – Reading – AFC Bournemouth; 29 Kay, James – Sheffield Wednesday – Guiseley; 19 Kelly, Ashley C. – Oldham Athletic – Leigh RMI; 1 Keogh, Richard J. – Bristol City – Huddersfield Town; 23 Kishishev, Radostin – Leicester City – Leeds United; 19 Knights, Darryl J. – Yeovil Town – Cambridge United; 9 Lallana, Adam D. – Southampton – AFC Bournemouth; 5 Law, Joshua – Chesterfield – Alfreton Town; 5 Law, Nicholas – Sheffield United – Bradford City; 1 Legzdins, Adam R. – Birmingham City – Halifax Town; 11 Logan, Shaleum – Manchester City – Grimsby Town; 5 Martin, Lee R. – Manchester United – Plymouth Argyle; 4 Masters, Clark J. – Brentford – Welling United; 5 McBreen, Daniel J. – Scunthorpe United – York City; 17 McClements, David – Sheffield Wednesday – Hinckley United; 22 McKeown, James K. – Peterborough United – Worcester City; 30 Minto-St Aimie, Kieron L. – Queens Park Rangers – Oxford United; 19 Murphy, Andrew – Preston North End – Vauxhall Motors; 26 Obersteller, Jack – Wycombe Wanderers – Grays Athletic; 4 Odhiambo, Eric – Leicester City – Southend United; 1 Oji, Samuel U. – Birmingham City – Leyton Orient; 8 Oliver, Dean – Sheffield United – Halifax Town; 15 Page, Sam T. – Milton Keynes Dons – Hendon; 8 Pearson, Michael T. – Oldham Athletic – Farsley Celtic; 11 Peatfield, Lee – Bury – Fleetwood Town; 1 Peters, Ryan V. – Brentford – Margate; 25 Potter, Luke A. – Barnsley – Stafford Rangers; 19 Puddy, Willem J.S. – Cheltenham Town – Stafford Rangers; 22 Pugh, Andrew J. – Gillingham – Welling United; 10 Rhodes, Jordan L. – Ipswich Town – Oxford United; 26 Rigby, Lloyd J. – Rochdale – Rossendale United; 4 Russell, Alexander J. – Bristol City – Northampton Town; 26 Schmeichel, Kasper P. – Manchester City – Cardiff City; 5 Sinclair, Dean M. – Charlton Athletic – Cheltenham Town; 12 Smith, Johann A.R. – Bolton Wanderers – Darlington; 29 Songo'o Franck S. – Portsmouth – Crystal Palace; 19 Taylor, Scott J. – Milton Keynes Dons – Rochdale; 26 Thomas, Anthony C. – Barnet – Cambridge City; 4 Thompson, Leslie – Bolton Wanderers – Stockport County; 5 Tunnicliffe, James – Stockport County – Northwich Victoria; 2 Vine, Rowan – Birmingham City – Queens Park Rangers; 25 Wainwright, Neil – Darlington – Shrewsbury Town; 19 Walker, James L.N. – Charlton Athletic – Yeovil Town; 5 Warburton, Callum S. – Rochdale – Kendal Town; 2 Wright, Joshua M. – Charlton Athletic – Barnet

NOVEMBER 2007 TEMPORARY TRANSFERS
9 Ademeno, Charles – Southend United – Welling United; 22 Ainsworth, Lionel – Hereford United – Watford; 22, Aiston, Sam J. – Northampton Town – Wrexham; 15 Ameobi, Tommy – Leeds United – Scunthorpe United; 22 Atkinson, Robert – Barnsley – Grimsby Town; 22 Baidoo, Shabazz K.K. – Queens Park Rangers – Gillingham; 30 Ball, Gary – Morecambe – Kendal Town; 22 Barcham, Andrew – Tottenham Hotspur – Leyton Orient; 22 Barnes, Ashley L. – Plymouth Argyle – Oxford United; 15 Baseya, Cedric – Southampton – Crewe Alexandra; 29 Belford, Cameron D. – Bury – Worcester City; 9 Bignot, Marcus J. – Queens Park Rangers – Millwall; 15 Branston, Guy – Peterborough United – Northampton Town; 13 Brooks-Meade, Corrin – Fulham – AFC Wimbledon; 1 Byron, Michael J. – Notts County – Hinckley United; 20 Camara, Mohamed – Derby County – Norwich City; 22 Carden, Paul A. – Accrington Stanley – Cambridge United; 30 Cobbs, Sonny H. – Brighton & Hove Albion – Dorchester Town; 2 Coles, Daniel R. – Hull City – Bristol Rovers; 2 Collins, Matthew J. – Swansea City – Wrexham; 9 Collins, Patrick – Darlington – Oxford United; 2 Cort, Leon T. – Crystal Palace – Stoke City; 9 Coward, Christopher D. – Stockport County – Ashton United; 1 Cresswell, Ryan – Sheffield United – Morecambe; 22 D'Agostino, Michael J. – Blackpool – Cheltenham Town; 9 Davies, Jamie – Morecambe – Leigh RMI; 22 Dennehy, Billy – Sunderland – Accrington Stanley; 19 Derry, Shaun – Leeds United – Crystal Palace; 23 Duncan, Derek – Wycombe Wanderers – Lewes; 22 Evans, Chedwyn M. – Manchester City – Norwich City; 22 Farquharson, Nicholas A. – Crewe Alexandra – Northwich Victoria; 22 Flynn, Matthew E. – Macclesfield Town – Warrington Town; 22 Flynn, Ryan – Liverpool – Hereford United; 8 Foulkes, Luke – Grimsby Town – Boston United; 16 Grant, Anthony P.S. – Chelsea – Luton Town; 22 Gray, David P. – Manchester United – Crewe Alexandra; 22 Green, Matthew J. – Cardiff City – Oxford United; 12 Hales, Lee A. – West Ham United – Rushden & Diamonds; 1 Halls, John – Reading – Preston North End; 20 Hastings, John – Milton Keynes Dons –

Maidenhead United; 9 Havern, Gianluca – Stockport County – Ashton United; 9 Hessey,
Sean P. – Chester City – Macclesfield Town; 6 Hill, Clinton – Stoke City – Crystal Palace; 22
Hinshelwood, Paul – Torquay United – Tiverton Town; 2 Hodge, Bryan – Blackburn
Rovers – Millwall; 22 Hughes, Jeffrey – Crystal Palace – Peterborough United; 22 Hughes,
Liam J. – Wolverhampton Wanderers – Bury; 2 Humphrey, Chris – Shrewsbury Town –
Stafford Rangers; 30 Jeffery, Jack C. – West Ham United – Hampton & Richmond
Borough; 22 Jones, Carl M. – York City – Gateshead; 22 Keogh, Richard J. – Bristol City –
Carlisle United; 14 Langford, Andrew – Morecambe – Leek Town; 29 Ledgister, Aaron T. –
Cheltenham Town – Weston-Super-Mare; 2 Lindfield, Craig A. – Liverpool – Notts County;
22 Liptak, Zoltan – Sheffield United – Stevenage Borough; 2 Loach, Scott J. – Watford –
Stafford Rangers; 9 Logan, Shaleum – Manchester City – Scunthorpe United; 1 Macken,
Jonathan P. – Derby County – Barnsley; 22 Madjo, Guy B. – Crawley Town – Cheltenham
Town; 16 Malcolm, Robert – Derby County – Queens Park Rangers; 21 McEvilly, Lee –
Accrington Stanley – Rochdale; 9 McMahon, Anthony – Middlesbrough – Blackpool; 22
Miller, Adam E. – Stevenage Borough – Gillingham; 16 Morgan, Dean – Luton Town –
Southend United; 5 Noble, Matthew J. – Doncaster Rovers – Spennymoor Town; 9
Nowland, Adam C. – Preston North End – Stockport County; 22 Nutter, John R.W. –
Stevenage Borough – Gillingham; 12 Oli, Dennis C. – Grays Athletic – Gillingham; 23
O'Loughlin, Charlie M. – Port Vale – Nantwich Town; 15 Palethorpe, Phillip J. – Chester
City – Tamworth; 15 Pattison, Matthew J. – Newcastle United – Norwich City; 1 Potter,
Alfie – Peterborough United – Havant & Waterlooville; 22 Power, Alan T.D. – Nottingham
Forest – Grays Athletic; 2 Pugh, Daniel – Preston North End – Stoke City; 2 Ricketts,
Michael B. – Oldham Athletic – Walsall; 22 Ridley, Lee – Cheltenham Town – Darlington;
7 Ross, Ian – Sheffield United – Rotherham United; 22 Salmon, Mark M. – Wolverhampton
Wanderers – Port Vale; 21 Saynor, Ben K.G. – Bradford City – Leigh RMI; 9 Seanla,
Stephane – Barnet – St Albans City; 22 Sharpe, Thomas R. – Nottingham Forest – Bury; 22
Shimmin, Dominic E. – Queens Park Rangers – AFC Bournemouth; 6 Sinclair, Scott A. –
Chelsea – Queens Park Rangers; 22 Sleath, Daniel J. – Mansfield Town – Boston United; 21
Slusarski, Bartosz – West Bromwich Albion – Blackpool; 30 Stephens, Dale – Bury – Hyde
United; 22 Stieber, Zoltan – Aston Villa – Yeovil Town; 22 Stokes, Anthony – West Ham
United – Stevenage Borough; 22 Sweeney, Peter – Stoke City – Walsall; 2 Taylor, Martin –
Birmingham City – Norwich City; 2 Threlfall, Robert R. – Liverpool – Hereford United; 22
Thurgood, Stuart A. – Grays Athletic – Gillingham; 20 Torpey, Stephen D.J. – Lincoln City
– Farsley Celtic; 19 Tudor, Shane A. – Port Vale – Shrewsbury Town; 22 White, John –
Colchester United – Stevenage Borough; 16 Wilson, Marc D. – Portsmouth – Luton Town

DECEMBER 2007

31 Scannell, Damian   Eastleigh   Southend United

TEMPORARY TRANSFERS
8 Aspden, Curtis – Hull City – Boston United; 9 Bignot, Marcus J. – Queens Park Rangers
– Millwall; 20 Blackmore, David – West Ham United – Thurrock; 22 Bowditch, Dean –
Ipswich Town – Northampton Town; 5 Brkovic, Ahmet – Luton Town – Millwall; 11
Brown, David P. – Nottingham Forest – Eastwood Town; 9 Brown, Junior – Crewe
Alexandra – Kidsgrove Athletic; 3 Buckley, Kyle – Rochdale – Woodley Sports; 28
Campana, Alessandro – Watford – Wealdstone; 9 Carroll, Neil – Chester City – Leigh RMI;
21 Caton, Andrew J. – Swindon Town – Brackley Town; 7 Davies, Charlton – Walsall –
Solihull Moors; 18 Dickson, Ryan A. – Plymouth Argyle – Brentford; 18 Donnelly-Jackson,
Jamie – Chesterfield – Matlock Town; 13 Doughty, Philip M. – Blackpool – Macclesfield
Town; 14 Erskine, Jacob – Dagenham & Redbridge – Tooting & Mitcham United; 6
Fogden, Wesley K. – Brighton & Hove Albion – Dorchester Town; 21 Gargan, Sam J. –
Brighton & Hove Albion – Bognor Regis Town; 12 Golbourne, Julio S. – Reading – AFC
Bournemouth; 14 Hanna, Christopher J. – Walsall – Hednesford Town; 21 Harris, Harry –
Walsall – Hinckley United; 6 Hart, Gary J. – Brighton & Hove Albion – Havant &
Waterlooville; 12 Henry, James – Reading – AFC Bournemouth; 3 Holness, Marcus L. –
Oldham Athletic – Rochdale; 3 Hopkins, Damian L. – Bradford City – Ossett Albion; 10
Howard, Charlie S. – Gillingham – Bromley; 18 Husbands, Michael P. – Macclesfield Town
– AFC Telford United; 24 Jevons, Phillip – Bristol City – Huddersfield Town; 27 Kelly,
Ashley C. – Oldham Athletic – Barrow; 17 Klein-Davies, Joshua – Bristol Rovers – Yate
Town; 9 Laird, Marc – Manchester City – Port Vale; 11 Liversedge, Nicholas – Darlington –
Bishop Auckland; 14 Mason, Anthony – Plymouth Argyle – Bridgwater Town; 27
McAllister, Sean B. – Sheffield Wednesday – Bury; 3 Morgan, Luke W.M. – Bradford City –
Ossett Albion; 24 Nolan, Edward W. – Blackburn Rovers – Hartlepool United; 10

O'Donnell, Richard M. – Sheffield Wednesday – Buxton; 17 Page, Sam T. – Milton Keynes Dons – Hendon; 12 Pearce, Alex – Reading – AFC Bournemouth; 9 Pearce, Krystian M.V. – Birmingham City – Notts County; 16 Reet, Daniel – Mansfield Town – Alfreton Town; 7 Sansara, Netan – Walsall – Solihull Moors; 13 Sinclair, Dean M. – Charlton Athletic – Cheltenham Town; 21 Sinclair, Emile A. – Nottingham Forest – Brentford; 17 Smith, Benjamin J. – Doncaster Rovers – Lincoln City; 3 Songo'o, Franck S. – Portsmouth – Crystal Palace; 17 Taylor, Andrew – Blackburn Rovers – Tranmere Rovers; 10 Wilkinson, David M. – Crystal Palace – Dover Athletic; 20 Yao, Sosthene A. – Cheltenham Town – Weston-Super-Mare; 3 Young, Neil A. – AFC Bournemouth – Weymouth

JANUARY 2008

31 Adebola, Bamberdele O.	Coventry City	Bristol City
3 Agyemang, Patrick	Preston North End	Queens Park Rangers
7 Ainsworth, Lionel	Hereford United	Watford
3 Akurang, Cliff D.	Histon	Barnet
21 Anelka, Nicolas	Bolton Wanderers	Chelsea
31 Aspden, Curtis	Hull City	Farsley Celtic
24 Bardsley, Philip A.	Manchester United	Sunderland
25 Barnard, Lee J.	Tottenham Hotspur	Southend United
31 Bevan, Scott A.	Kidderminster Harriers	Shrewsbury Town
8 Bolland, Philip C.	Chester City	Wrexham
10 Brkovic, Ahmet	Luton Town	Millwall
31 Bromby, Leigh	Sheffield United	Watford
10 Brown, Christopher	Norwich City	Preston North End
31 Brown, David P.	Nottingham Forest	Bradford City
31 Bullock, Lee	Hartlepool United	Bradford City
7 Butler, Martin N.	Walsall	Grimsby Town
2 Buzsaky, Akos	Plymouth Argyle	Queens Park Rangers
30 Cahill, Gary J.	Aston Villa	Bolton Wanderers
10 Chaplow, Richard D.	West Bromwich Albion	Preston North End
7 Coles, Daniel R.	Hull City	Bristol Rovers
31 Collins, Sam	Hull City	Hartlepool United
4 Connolly, Matthew T.	Arsenal	Queens Park Rangers
31 Constable, James A.	Kidderminster Harriers	Shrewsbury Town
14 Cort, Leon T.	Crystal Palace	Stoke City
31 Cox, Simon	Reading	Swindon Town
11 Coyne, Christopher	Luton Town	Colchester United
4 Craney, Ian T.W.	Swansea City	Accrington Stanley
31 Dann, Scott	Walsall	Coventry City
22 Danns, Neil A.	Birmingham City	Crystal Palace
10 Davies, Andrew	Middlesbrough	Southampton
17 Delaney, Damien	Hull City	Queens Park Rangers
24 Derry, Shaun	Leeds United	Crystal Palace
17 Diarra, Lassana	Arsenal	Portsmouth
11 Dickson, Ryan A.	Plymouth Argyle	Brentford
30 Dixon, Jonathan J.	Aldershot Town	Brighton & Hove Albion
23 Dobie, Scott	Nottingham Forest	Carlisle United
31 Dobson, Craig G.	Stevenage Borough	Milton Keynes Dons
4 Drummond, Stewart	Shrewsbury Town	Morecambe
28 D'Sane, Roscoe	Accrington Stanley	Torquay United
3 Easter, Jermaine	Wycombe Wanderers	Plymouth Argyle
10 Ebanks-Blake, Sylvan	Plymouth Argyle	Wolverhampton Wanderers
1 Eckersley, Adam	Manchester United	Port Vale
14 Edwards, David	Luton Town	Wolverhampton Wanderers
31 Elder, Nathan	Brighton & Hove Albion	Brentford
31 Elding, Anthony L.	Stockport County	Leeds United
31 Elokobi, George N.	Colchester United	Wolverhampton Wanderers
2 Ephraim, Hogan	West Ham United	Queens Park Rangers
31 Eustace, John M.	Stoke City	Watford
22 Evans, Rhys K.	Blackpool	Millwall
11 Folly, Yoann	Sheffield Wednesday	Plymouth Argyle
4 Forbes, Adrian E.	Blackpool	Millwall
28 Fox, Daniel J.	Walsall	Coventry City

149

28 Fuller, Barry M.	Stevenage Borough	Gillingham
14 Gosling, Daniel	Plymouth Argyle	Everton
21 Grabban, Lewis	Crystal Palace	Millwall
25 Gray, Andrew D.	Burnley	Charlton Athletic
11 Griffin, Andrew	Derby County	Stoke City
4 Hall, Fitz	Wigan Athletic	Queens Park Rangers
31 Hammond, Dean	Brighton & Hove Albion	Colchester United
3 Hatch, Liam M.	Barnet	Peterborough United
3 Hayles, Barrington	Plymouth Argyle	Leicester City
16 Hill, Clinton	Stoke City	Crystal Palace
4 Holness, Marcus L.	Oldham Athletic	Rochdale
15 Horwood, Evan D.	Sheffield United	Carlisle United
3 Howard, Steven J.	Derby County	Leicester City
10 Ifil, Phillip	Tottenham Hotspur	Colchester United
31 Jackson, Simeon A.	Rushden & Diamonds	Gillingham
9 Jevons, Phillip	Bristol City	Huddersfield Town
9 Johnson, Bradley	Northampton Town	Leeds United
31 Kazimierczak, Przemyslaw	Bolton Wanderers	Darlington
7 Kilkenny, Neil M.	Birmingham City	Leeds United
11 King, Mark	Blackburn Rovers	Accrington Stanley
25 King, Marlon F.	Watford	Wigan Athletic
7 Knight, Leon L.	Milton Keynes Dons	Wycombe Wanderers
9 Laird, Marc	Manchester City	Millwall
31 Laird, Scott	Plymouth Argyle	Stevenage Borough
31 Lennon, Neil F.	Nottingham Forest	Wycombe Wanderers
7 Lewis, Joseph	Norwich City	Peterborough United
28 Lewis, Stuart A.	Stevenage Borough	Gillingham
28 Macken, Jonathan P.	Derby County	Barnsley
25 Mackie, James	Exeter City	Plymouth Argyle
18 MacLean, Steven	Cardiff City	Plymouth Argyle
11 Madjo, Guy B.	Crawley Town	Shrewsbury Town
2 Mahon, Gavin A.	Watford	Queens Park Rangers
31 Marsh-Evans, Robert W.	Chester City	Leigh RMI
31 Martin, David	Crystal Palace	Millwall
11 Masters, Clark J.	Brentford	Southend United
18 May, Ben S.	Millwall	Scunthorpe United
16 McCann, Grant S.	Barnsley	Scunthorpe United
31 McCleary, Garath J.	Bromley	Nottingham Forest
18 McFadden, James	Everton	Birmingham City
4 McIntyre, Kevin	Macclesfield Town	Shrewsbury Town
18 McNamee, Anthony	Watford	Swindon Town
8 McPhee, Stephen	Hull City	Blackpool
31 Michalik, Lubomir	Bolton Wanderers	Leeds United
10 Miller, Adam E.	Stevenage Borough	Gillingham
11 Miller, Ian	Ipswich Town	Darlington
31 Miller, Ishmael	Manchester City	West Bromwich Albion
31 Moore, Ian R.	Hartlepool United	Tranmere Rovers
10 Mulligan, David	Scunthorpe United	Port Vale
4 Murray, Adam D.	Macclesfield Town	Oxford United
25 Murray, Glenn	Rochdale	Brighton & Hove Albion
30 Ndumbu-Nsungu, Guylain	Gillingham	Darlington
31 Norris, David M.	Plymouth Argyle	Ipswich Town
7 Nutter, John R.W.	Stevenage Borough	Gillingham
11 Oakley, Matthew	Derby County	Leicester City
14 Oli, Dennis C.	Grays Athletic	Gillingham
4 Pattison, Matthew J.	Newcastle United	Norwich City
31 Peltier, Lee A.	Liverpool	Yeovil Town
13 Pugh, Daniel	Preston North End	Stoke City
24 Quinn, Alan	Sheffield United	Ipswich Town
31 Regan, Carl A.	Macclesfield Town	Milton Keynes Dons
31 Reid, Andrew M.	Charlton Athletic	Sunderland
30 Revell, Alexander D.	Brighton & Hove Albion	Southend United

25 Richards, Gary	Southend United	Gillingham
8 Ross, Ian	Sheffield United	Rotherham United
30 Routledge, Wayne N.	Tottenham Hotspur	Aston Villa
25 Sadler, Matthew	Birmingham City	Watford
9 Savage, Robert W.	Blackburn Rovers	Derby County
17 Shawcross, Ryan J.	Manchester United	Stoke City
31 Silva De Franca, Anderson	Everton	Barnsley
11 Slater, Christopher J.	Chasetown	Port Vale
8 Speed, Gary A.	Bolton Wanderers	Sheffield United
31 Stubbs, Alan	Everton	Derby County
10 Sweeney, Peter	Stoke City	Leeds United
18 Taylor, Andrew	Blackburn Rovers	Tranmere Rovers
31 Taylor, Cleveland	Scunthorpe United	Carlisle United
17 Taylor, Matthew S.	Portsmouth	Bolton Wanderers
9 Thurgood, Stuart A.	Grays Athletic	Gillingham
31 Trotman, Neal	Oldham Athletic	Preston North End
31 Vernon, Scott M.	Blackpool	Colchester United
11 Vine, Rowan	Birmingham City	Queens Park Rangers
8 Ward, Gavin J.	Chester City	Wrexham
31 Whelan, Glenn D.	Sheffield Wednesday	Stoke City
3 Williams, Thomas A.	Wycombe Wanderers	Peterborough United
29 Woodgate, Jonathan S.	Middlesbrough	Tottenham Hotspur

TEMPORARY TRANSFERS

31 Ainge, Simon C. – Bradford City – Halifax Town; 20 Akins, Lucas – Huddersfield Town – Northwich Victoria; 1 Akurang, Cliff D. – Histon – Barnet; 7 Alnwick, Ben – Tottenham Hotspur – Leicester City; 10 Ameobi, Tomi – Leeds United – Scunthorpe United; 11 Anelka, Nicolas – Bolton Wanderers – Chelsea; 18 Ashikodi, Moses – Watford – Swindon Town; 30 Ashmore, James – Sheffield United – Macclesfield Town; 10 Ashton, Neil J. – Shrewsbury Town – Macclesfield Town; 18 Aspden, Curtis – Hull City – Farsley Celtic; 31 Atkinson, Robert – Barnsley – Grimsby Town; 27 Austin, Robert D. – Notts County – Eastwood Town; 31 Bailey, Matthew – Wolverhampton Wanderers – Kidderminster Harriers; 3 Ball, Gary – Morecambe – Kendal Town; 7 Barcham, Andrew – Tottenham Hotspur – Leyton Orient; 2 Barnes, Michael T. – Manchester United – Chesterfield; 4 Bastians, Felix – Nottingham Forest – Notts County; 3 Bates, Matthew D. – Middlesbrough – Norwich City; 1 Belford, Cameron D. – Bury – Worcester City; 3 Belt, Frank J. – Hull City – Bridlington Town; 4 Bennett, Dean A. – Chester City – Kidderminster Harriers; 31 Bennett, Elliott – Wolverhampton Wanderers – Bury; 4 Bertrand, Ryan D. – Chelsea – Norwich City; 31 Betsy, Kevin – Bristol City – Walsall; 7 Bradley, Jason – Sheffield Wednesday – Buxton; 18 Brooks-Meade, Corrin – Fulham – Carshalton Athletic; 31 Brown, David A. – Accrington Stanley – Rushden & Diamonds; 10 Bryant, Thomas J. – Gillingham – Folkestone Invicta; 1 Bullock, Lee – Hartlepool United – Bradford City; 3 Butcher, Lee A. – Tottenham Hotspur – AFC Wimbledon; 10 Button, David R. – Tottenham Hotspur – Grays Athletic; 21 Bygrave, Adam M. – Reading – Gillingham; 31 Bywater, Stephen – Derby County – Ipswich Town; 4 Camara, Mohamed – Derby County – Norwich City; 4 Campbell, Fraizer L. – Manchester United – Hull City; 27 Carayol, Mustapha – Milton Keynes Dons – Crawley Town; 3 Carden, Paul A. – Accrington Stanley – Cambridge United; 1 Chamberlain, Scott D. – Brighton & Hove Albion – Bognor Regis Town; 11 Christon, Lewis – Wycombe Wanderers – Woking; 30 Church, Simon R. – Reading – Yeovil Town; 10 Cisak, Alex – Leicester City – Tamworth; 30 Cole, Steven A. – Sunderland – Burnley; 24 Collins, Lee H. – Wolverhampton Wanderers – Hereford United; 24 Collins, Sam C. – Milton Keynes Dons – Hendon; 31 Cook, Lee – Fulham – Charlton Athletic; 4 Cork, Jack F.P. – Chelsea – Scunthorpe United; 25 Coward, Christopher D. – Stockport County – Woodley Sports; 10 Cresswell, Ryan – Sheffield United – Macclesfield Town; 2 D'Agostino, Michael J. – Blackpool – Cheltenham Town; 7 Daniel, Colin – Crewe Alexandra – Grays Athletic; 18 Davenport, Callum R.P. – West Ham United – Watford; 11 Dean, James – Bury – Stalybridge Celtic; 31 Defoe, Jermaine C. – Tottenham Hotspur – Portsmouth; 3 Dennehy, Billy – Sunderland – Accrington Stanley; 1 Diagouraga, Toumani – Watford – Hereford United; 31 Dickov, Paul – Manchester City – Blackpool; 2 Domoraud, Wilfried – Yeovil Town – Weymouth; 21 Donnelly, Martin – Sheffield United – Rochdale; 18 Doughty, Philip M. – Blackpool – Accrington Stanley; 31 Drench, Steven M. – Morecambe – Southport; 25 Duffy, Robert J. – Oxford United – Wrexham; 31 Edge, Lewis J.S. – Blackpool – Northwich Victoria; 31 Elliott, Stuart – Hull City – Doncaster Rovers; 25

151

Ellis, Daniel J. – Stockport County – Droylsden; 1 Ellis, Mark I. – Bolton Wanderers – Torquay United; 10 Evans, Chedwyn M. – Manchester City – Norwich City; 4 Evans, Jonathan – Manchester United – Sunderland; 14 Fazenda, Miguel A.K. – West Bromwich Albion – Barnsley; 11 Fielding, Francis D. – Blackburn Rovers – Wycombe Wanderers; 17 Foran, Richard – Southend United – Darlington; 28 Frost, Stef – Notts County – Gainsborough Trinity; 31 Gallagher, Paul – Blackburn Rovers – Stoke City; 31 Gardner, Anthony – Tottenham Hotspur – Everton; 22 Gardner, Scott A. – Leeds United – Farsley Celtic; 28 Garrett, Robert – Stoke City – Wrexham; 24 Gerrard, Paul W. – Sheffield United – Blackpool; 11 Ghaly, Hossam E.S. – Tottenham Hotspur – Derby County; 31 Gibb, Alistair S. – Hartlepool United – Notts County; 31 Gibbs, Kieran J.R. – Arsenal – Norwich City; 3 Gibson, Darron – Manchester United – Wolverhampton Wanderers; 11 Gradel, Max-Alain – Leicester City – AFC Bournemouth; 31 Grant, Anthony P.S. – Chelsea – Southend United; 19 Gray, Andrew D. – Burnley – Charlton Athletic; 17 Gregory, Steven M. – Wycombe Wanderers – Havant & Waterlooville; 17 Hadfield, Jordan – Macclesfield Town – Milton Keynes Dons; 8 Hales, Lee A. – West Ham United – Rushden & Diamonds; 31 Halford, Gregory – Sunderland – Charlton Athletic; 16 Hall, Asa – Birmingham City – Shrewsbury Town; 11 Hall, Paul A. – Walsall – Wrexham; 10 Halls, John – Reading – Crystal Palace; 28 Hamer, Ben – Reading – Brentford; 18 Hamilton-Omole, Marvin D. – Gillingham – Folkestone Invicta; 11 Harkin, Ruari B. – Charlton Athletic – Heybridge Swifts; 1 Hatch, Liam M.A. – Barnet – Peterborough United; 8 Hayes, Jonathan – Leicester City – Northampton Town; 1 Hayles, Barrington – Plymouth Argyle – Leicester City; 31 Henry, James – Reading – Norwich City; 31 Hernandez, Stephen – Sheffield United – Worksop Town; 16 Heslop, Simon – Barnsley – Halifax Town; 11 Hessey, Sean P. – Chester City – Macclesfield Town; 21 Hird, Adrian S. – Doncaster Rovers – Grimsby Town; 25 Hobbs, Jack – Liverpool – Scunthorpe United; 11 Holmes, Lee D. – Derby County – Walsall; 28 Hooper, Gary – Southend United – Hereford United; 31 Horsfield, Geoffrey M. – Sheffield United – Scunthorpe United; 1 Howard, Steven J. – Derby County – Leicester City; 8 Howe, Jermaine R. – Peterborough United – Rochdale; 23 Howland, David – Birmingham City – Port Vale; 10 Jalal, Shwan S. – Peterborough United – Morecambe; 31 Jarrett, Jason L. – Preston North End – Oldham Athletic; 31 Jarvis, Ryan – Norwich City – Notts County; 1 Jennings, James R. – Macclesfield Town – Altrincham; 31 Jones, Luke J. – Shrewsbury Town – Kidderminster Harriers; 1 Jutkiewicz, Lukas I.P. – Everton – Plymouth Argyle; 31 Kavanagh, Graham A. – Sunderland – Sheffield Wednesday; 10 Kenton, Darren E. – Leicester City – Leeds United; 23 Kerr, Nathaniel J. – Rotherham United – Northwich Victoria; 4 Kilkenny, Neil M. – Birmingham City – Leeds United; 16 Kitchen, Ashley – Mansfield Town – Gainsborough Trinity; 31 Knights, Darryl J. – Yeovil Town – Kidderminster Harriers; 30 Kyle, Kevin – Coventry City – Wolverhampton Wanderers; 1 Laird, Scott – Plymouth Argyle – Stevenage Borough; 6 Law, Joshua – Chesterfield – Alfreton Town; 5 Lawlor, Matthew – Blackpool – Farsley Celtic; 2 Lee, Kieran C. – Manchester United – Queens Park Rangers; 3 Legzdins, Adam R. – Birmingham City – Halifax Town; 18 Lindfield, Craig A. – Liverpool – Chester City; 1 Loach, Scott J. – Watford – Morecambe; 29 Loach, Scott J. – Watford – Bradford City; 4 Lynch, Ryan P. – Crewe Alexandra – Stafford Rangers; 25 Mackin, Levi A. – Wrexham – Droylsden; 1 Mahon, Gavin A. – Watford – Queens Park Rangers; 11 Martin, Lee R. – Manchester United – Sheffield United; 8 Martis, Shelton – West Bromwich Albion – Scunthorpe United; 18 Massey, Alan – Wycombe Wanderers – Hendon; 15 Masters, Clark J. – Southend United – Stevenage Borough; 8 Mayo, Paul – Notts County – Darlington; 18 McEvilly, Lee – Accrington Stanley – Cambridge United; 31 McKay, William – Leicester City – Hinckley United; 11 Medley, Luke – Bradford City – Cambridge City; 17 Mikaelsson, Tobias – Aston Villa – Port Vale; 24 Miles, John F. – Accrington Stanley – Milton Keynes Dons; 4 Mills, Daniel J. – Manchester City – Derby County; 14 Mills, Matthew C. – Manchester City – Doncaster Rovers; 11 Moloney, Brendon A. – Nottingham Forest – Chesterfield; 29 Moncur, Thomas J. – Fulham – Bradford City; 8 Morgan, Luke W.M. – Bradford City – Droylsden; 31 Mulgrew, Charles P. – Wolverhampton Wanderers – Southend United; 18 Murphy, Kieran – Milton Keynes Dons – Crawley Town; 25 Murtagh, Conal F. – Wrexham – Droylsden; 28 Myrie-Williams, Jennison – Bristol City – Tranmere Rovers; 24 Nardiello, Daniel A. – Queens Park Rangers – Barnsley; 29 Ndumbu-Nsungu, Guylain – Gillingham – Darlington; 31 Nyatanga, Lewin J. – Derby County – Barnsley; 11 Oakley, Matthew – Derby County – Leicester City; 25 Obersteller, Jack – Wycombe Wanderers – Grays Athletic; 8 O'Donnell, Richard M. – Sheffield Wednesday – Rotherham United; 16 O'Halloran, Stephen – Aston Villa – Southampton; 31 O'Loughlin, Charlie M. – Port Vale – Hinckley United; 17 Parkes, Jordan – Watford – Brentford; 31 Pearce, Alex –

Reading – Norwich City; 31 Pearce, Krystian M.V. – Birmingham City – Port Vale; 29
Pentney, Carl – Leicester City – Ilkeston Town; 30 Peters, Jaime B. – Ipswich Town –
Yeovil Town; 30 Pettigrew, Adrian R.J. – Chelsea – Rotherham United; 4 Power, Alan T.D.
– Nottingham Forest – Grays Athletic; 24 Prosser, Luke B. – Port Vale – Leigh RMI; 18
Quinn, Alan – Sheffield United – Ipswich Town; 31 Randall, Mark L. – Arsenal – Burnley;
31 Rasiak, Grzegorz – Southampton – Bolton Wanderers; 17 Rayner, Simon – Torquay
United – Boston United; 11 Reed, Jamie L. – Wrexham – Tamworth; 31 Reid, Reuben –
Plymouth Argyle – Brentford; 17 Rice, Robert – Wycombe Wanderers – Wealdstone; 17
Richards, Matthew – Ipswich Town – Brighton & Hove Albion; 4 Ridley, Lee –
Cheltenham Town – Lincoln City; 4 Rigby, Lloyd J. – Rochdale – Vauxhall Motors; 1
Robinson, Theo – Watford – Hereford United; 31 Robson-Kanu, Thomas H. – Reading –
Southend United; 10 Rocastle, Craig A. – Port Vale – Gillingham; 3 Rooney, Adam – Stoke
City – Chesterfield; 1 Ross, Ian – Sheffield United – Rotherham United; 11 Russell,
Alexander J. – Bristol City – Cheltenham Town; 21 Sankofa, Osey O.K. – Charlton Athletic
– Brentford; 29 Seck, Mamadou – Sheffield United – Scunthorpe United; 11 Sharpe,
Thomas R. – Nottingham Forest – Halifax Town; 4 Shawcross, Ryan J. – Manchester
United – Stoke City; 31 Sheehan, Alan – Leicester City – Leeds United; 1 Shotton, Ryan –
Stoke City – Altrincham; 31 Showunmi, Enoch – Bristol City – Sheffield Wednesday; 2
Simpson, Jay-Alistaire F. – Arsenal – Millwall; 31 Sinclair, Robert J. – Luton Town –
Salisbury City; 3 Slusarski, Bartosz – West Bromwich Albion – Blackpool; 4 Smith, Nathan
A. – Chesterfield – Lincoln City; 25 Sorvel, Neil – Morecambe – Southport; 1 Speed, Gary
A. – Bolton Wanderers – Sheffield United; 7 Spencer, Scott K. – Everton – Yeovil Town; 4
Stack, Graham – Reading – Wolverhampton Wanderers; 31 Stalteri, Paul – Tottenham
Hotspur – Fulham; 21 Starosta, Ben M. – Sheffield United – Bradford City; 4 Stepien,
Jordan – Bury – Nuneaton Borough; 2 Stieber, Zoltan – Aston Villa – Yeovil Town; 10
Symes, Michael – Shrewsbury Town – Macclesfield Town; 11 Taylforth, Sean J. – Bradford
City – Droylsden; 31 Taylor, Gareth K. – Tranmere Rovers – Doncaster Rovers; 4 Teague,
Andrew H. – Macclesfield Town – Tamworth; 22 Thompson, Alan – Leeds United –
Hartlepool United; 3 Thompson, Leslie A. – Bolton Wanderers – Torquay United; 29
Threlfall, Robert R. – Liverpool – Hereford United; 1 Todd, Andrew J. – Rotherham
United – Accrington Stanley; 31 Tyler, Mark R. – Peterborough United – Hull City; 18
Valentine, Ryan D. – Wrexham – Darlington; 29 Varga, Stanislav – Sunderland – Burnley; 4
Walker, James L. N. – Charlton Athletic – Yeovil Town; 30 Walton, Simon W. – Queens
Park Rangers – Hull City; 31 Warner, Anthony R. – Fulham – Barnsley; 25 Watt, Philip A.
– Lincoln City – Corby Town; 1 Welsh, John J. – Hull City – Chester City; 24 Wilkinson,
David M. – Crystal Palace – Eastleigh; 1 Williams, Thomas A. – Wycombe Wanderers –
Peterborough United; 25 Winterton, Christopher C. – Brighton & Hove Albion – Horsham
YMCA; 11 Wright, Joshua W. – Charlton Athletic – Barnet; 3 Yeo, Simon J. – Chester City
– Bury

FEBRUARY 2008

21 Defoe, Jermain C.	Tottenham Hotspur	Portsmouth
5 Mwaruwari, Benjani	Portsmouth	Manchester City
5 Taylor, Gareth K.	Tranmere Rovers	Doncaster Rovers

TEMPORARY TRANSFERS

21 Ademeno, Charles – Southend United – Rushden & Diamonds; 26 Andersen, Mikkel –
Reading – Torquay United; 19 Anderson, Russell – Sunderland – Plymouth Argyle; 5
Arestidou, Andreas J. – Blackburn Rovers – Lancaster City; 12 Asafu-Adjaye, Edward
Y.O. – Luton Town – Salisbury City; 29 Atkinson, William H. – Hull City – Mansfield
Town; 25 Austin, Matthew S. – Notts County – Gainsborough Trinity; 8 Basham,
Christopher P. – Bolton Wanderers – Rochdale; 15 Bastians, Felix – Nottingham Forest –
Milton Keynes Dons; 28 Bedeau, Anthony C. – Torquay United – Weymouth; 4 Bentham,
Craig M. – Bradford City – Farsley Celtic; 8 Bolder, Adam P. – Queens Park Rangers –
Sheffield Wednesday; 11 Bowditch, Dean – Ipswich Town – Brighton & Hove Albion; 18
Boyle, Patrick – Everton – Crewe Alexandra; 8 Bridcutt, Liam R. – Chelsea – Yeovil Town;
15 Briggs, Keith – Shrewsbury Town – Mansfield Town; 14 Brooker, Stephen M.L. – Bristol
City – Cheltenham Town; 29 Brooks-Meade, Corrin – Fulham – Cheshunt; 26 Broughton,
Drewe O. – Milton Keynes Dons – Wrexham; 25 Brown, Wayne – Fulham – Brentford; 1
Cahill, Thomas – Rotherham United – Altrincham; 22 Clarke, Tom – Huddersfield Town –
Halifax Town; 29 Clement, Neil – West Bromwich Albion – Hull City; 25 Cobbs, Sonny H.
– Brighton & Hove Albion – Welling United; 11 Compton, Jack L.P. – West Bromwich
Albion – Weymouth; 8 Cotterill, David – Wigan Athletic – Sheffield United; 14 Craddock,

Thomas – Middlesbrough – Hartlepool United; 15 Crow, Daniel – Peterborough United – Notts County; 11 Dark, Lewis K. – Brentford – Ramsgate; 14 Domoraud, Wilfried – Yeovil Town – Weston-Super-Mare; 21 Dowson, David – Sunderland – Chesterfield; 19 Duncum, Samuel – Rotherham United – York City; 15 Dutton-Black, Joshua R. – Southampton – Crawley Town; 1 Erskine, Jacob – Dagenham & Redbridge – Maidstone Unied; 27 Farquharson, Nicholas A. – Crewe Alexandra – Nantwich Town; 11 Flinders, Scott L. – Crystal Palace – Yeovil Town; 22 Flynn, Matthew E. – Macclesfield Town – Ashton United; 28 Fraser, James – Bristol Rovers – Tiverton Town; 22 Fulop, Marton – Sunderland – Stoke City; 28 Gall, Kevin A. – Carlisle United – Darlington; 25 Gargan, Sam J. – Brighton & Hove Albion – Welling United; 21 Gleeson, Stephen M. – Wolverhampton Wanderers – Hereford United; 15 Grant, Gavin – Millwall – Stevenage Borough; 15 Grundy, Aaron – Bury – FC United of Manchester; 14 Hall, Ryan – Crystal Palace – Dagenham & Redbridge; 26 Hand, Jamie – Lincoln City – Oxford United; 8 Hart, Daniel – Barnet – Wivenhoe Town; 21 Hartley, Peter – Sunderland – Chesterfield; 28 Henderson, Stephen – Bristol City – Weymouth; 28 Hendrie, Lee A. – Sheffield United – Leicester City; 10 Herd, Christopher – Aston Villa – Port Vale; 8 Hodge, Bryan – Blackburn Rovers – Darlington; 8 Holmes, Daniel – Tranmere Rovers – Southport; 8 Hoskins, William – Watford – Nottingham Forest; 22 Hoult, Russell – Stoke City – Notts County; 24 Howard, Michael A. – Morecambe – Oxford United; 22 Howell, Andrew – Queens Park Rangers – Wealdstone; 5 Hughes, Jerahl – Yeovil Town – Worthing; 29 Hughes, Liam J. – Wolverhampton Wanderers – Stafford Rangers; 15 Hurst, Paul – Rotherham United – Burton Albion; 25 Hyde, Jake M. – Swindon Town – Weymouth; 6 Jackson, Jamie D. – Chesterfield – Gainsborough Trinity; 22 Jeffery, Jack C. – West Ham United – Cambridge United; 22 John, Collins – Fulham – Watford; 29 Johnson, Michael O. – Derby County – Notts County; 15 Jones, Zachariah S. – Blackburn Rovers – Ashton United; 29 Kempson, Darran – Shrewsbury Town – Accrington Stanley; 29 Kennedy, Jason – Middlesbrough – Darlington; 15 Kerry, Lloyd – Sheffield United – Chesterfield; 14 Killock, Shane – Huddersfield Town – Hyde United; 1 King, Liam – Rotherham United – Altrincham; 28 Kirkup, Daniel – Carlisle United – Workington; 22 Lawlor, Matthew – Blackpool – Leigh RMI; 14 Lee, Graeme B. – Doncaster Rovers – Hartlepool United; 11 Little, Mark D. – Wolverhampton Wanderers – Northampton Town; 29 Livermore, David – Hull City – Oldham Athletic; 29 Livermore, Jake – Tottenham Hotspur – Milton Keynes Dons; 22 Logan, Shaleum – Manchester City – Stockport County; 19 Lunt, Kenny V. – Sheffield Wednesday – Crewe Alexandra; 8 MacDonald, Sherjill – West Bromwich Albion – Hereford United; 22 Mangan, Andrew F. – Bury – Accrington Stanley; 21 McGrail, Christopher – Preston North End – Vauxhall Motors; 29 McLeod, Izale M. – Charlton Athletic – Colchester United; 14 McLuckie, Philip – Morecambe – Workington; 11 Milsom, Robert S. – Fulham – Brentford; 26 Mohamed, Kaid – Swindon Town – Torquay United; 22 Moore, Luke – Aston Villa – West Bromwich Albion; 26 Morfaw, Alexandre – Scunthorpe United – Lincoln City; 11 Nelthorpe, Craig R. – Doncaster Rovers – Halifax Town; 29 Newton, Sean – Chester City – Droylsden; 15 Noble, Matthew J. – Doncaster Rovers – Guiseley; 29 O'Halloran, Stephen – Aston Villa – Leeds United; 21 Okuonghae, Magnus E. – Dagenham & Redbridge – Weymouth; 25 Palmer, Marcus J. – Hereford United – Gloucester City; 27 Parker, Ben B.C. – Leeds United – Darlington; 25 Patterson, Marlon – Dagenham & Redbridge – Grays Athletic; 22 Pearce, Ian A. – Fulham – Southampton; 8 Poke, Michael H. – Southampton – Torquay United; 29 Potter, Alfie – Peterborough United – AFC Wimbledon; 15 Pugh, Andrew J. – Gillingham – Maidstone United; 8 Pulis, Anthony J. – Stoke City – Bristol Rovers; 8 Randolph, Darren E. – Charlton Athletic – Bury; 21 Rendell, Scott – Cambridge United – Peterborough United; 29 Riggott, Christopher M. – Middlesbrough – Stoke City; 27 Roberts, Dale – Nottingham Forest – Rushden & Diamonds; 12 Roberts, Gary M. – Ipswich Town – Crewe Alexandra; 26 Robertson, Jordan – Sheffield United – Oldham Athletic; 8 Rooney, Adam – Stoke City – Bury; 22 Ruddy, John T.G. – Everton – Stockport County; 21 Sahar, Ben – Chelsea – Sheffield Wednesday; 28 Sinclair, Scott A. – Chelsea – Charlton Athletic; 19 Skinner, Lloyd E. – Brighton & Hove Albion – Worthing; 28 Smith, Dorian – Charlton Athletic – Tooting & Mitcham United; 21 Smith, Thomas J. – Ipswich Town – Stevenage Borough; 15 Sodje, Efetobore – Gillingham – Bury; 14 Steele, Luke D. – West Bromwich Albion – Stoke City; 16 Stone, Craig B.R. – Gillingham – Brentford; 27 Swaibu, Moses – Crystal Palace – Weymouth; 22 Taylor, Jamie – Dagenham & Redbridge – Grays Athletic; 18 Teague, Andrew H. – Macclesfield Town – Hyde United; 19 Teale, Gary – Derby County – Plymouth Argyle; 29 Thomas, Aswad – Charlton Athletic – Accrington Stanley; 21 Tomlinson, Stuart C. – Crewe Alexandra – Burton Albion; 29 Vaughan, Stephen J. – Chester City – Droylsden; 15 Walker, James L.N. – Charlton Athletic –

Southend United; 28 Webb, Thomas J.J. – Colchester United – Folkestone Invicta; 16 Welsh, Ishmael – Yeovil Town – Forest Green Rovers; 12 Widdowson, Joseph – West Ham United – Rotherham United; 14 Woods, Martin P. – Doncaster Rovers – Yeovil Town

MARCH 2008 TEMPORARY TRANSFERS

27 Ameobi, Foluwashola – Newcastle United – Stoke City; 18 Anderson, Russell – Sunderland – Plymouth Argyle; 27 Andrews, Wayne M.H. – Coventry City – Bristol Rovers; 7 Annerson, James – Sheffield United – Chesterfield; 7 Anyinsah, Joseph G. – Preston North End – Crewe Alexandra; 27 Ashton, Nathan – Fulham – Millwall; 19 Bailey, Matthew – Crewe Alexandra – Weymouth; 7 Barnes, Ashley L. – Plymouth Argyle – Salisbury City; 27 Barnes, Michael T. – Manchester United – Shrewsbury Town; 4 Beattie, Craig – West Bromwich Albion – Preston North End; 27 Bell, David A. – Luton Town – Leicester City; 7 Bennett, Alan J. – Reading – Brentford; 2 Bennett, Elliott – Wolverhampton Wanderers – Bury; 4 Bentham, Craig M. – Bradford City – Farsley Celtic; 27 Begovic, Asmir – Portsmouth – Yeovil Town; 3 Blackburn, Christopher R. – Swindon Town – Weymouth; 7 Bolder, Adam P. – Queens Park Rangers – Sheffield Wednesday; 14 Bothroyd, Jay – Wolverhampton Wanderers – Stoke City; 19 Boyle, Patrick – Everton – Crewe Alexandra; 12 Brooker, Stephen M.L. – Bristol City – Cheltenham Town; 27 Brown, Aaron – Reading – Walsall; 27 Brown, David A. – Accrington Stanley – Northwich Victoria; 27 Brown, Junior – Crewe Alexandra – Witton Albion; 21 Burgess, Kevin M. – Darlington – Whitby Town; 27 Button, David R. – Tottenham Hotspur – Rochdale; 2 Cahill, Thomas – Rotherham United – Altrincham; 20 Charles, Wesley D.D. – Brentford – Ebbsfleet United; 27 Christon, Lewis – Wycombe Wanderers – AFC Wimbledon; 10 Christophe, Jean F. – Portsmouth – Yeovil Town; 25 Cobbs, Sonny H. – Brighton & Hove Albion – Welling United; 14 Cogan, Barry C. – Gillingham – Grays Athletic; 4 Constantine, Leon – Leeds United – Oldham Athletic; 14 Corden, Wayne – Leyton Orient – Notts County; 27 Craig, Tony A. – Crystal Palace – Millwall; 27 Daniel, Colin – Crewe Alexandra – Leek Town; 27 Devaux, Thomas – Colchester United – Heybridge Swifts; 18 Domoraud, Wilfried – Yeovil Town – Weston-Super-Mare; 14 Douglas, Robert J. – Leicester City – Plymouth Argyle; 27 Downes, Aiden – Everton – Yeovil Town; 26 Dowson, David – Sunderland – Chesterfield; 21 Duffy, Richard – Portsmouth – Coventry City; 20 Duncum, Samuel – Rotherham United – York City; 29 Ehui, Ismael – Fulham – Carshalton Athletic; 28 Erskine, Emmanuel J. – Dagenham & Redbridge – Maidstone United; 5 Etuhu, Kelvin – Manchester City – Leicester City; 27 Facey, Delroy M. – Gillingham – Wycombe Wanderers; 8 Fagan, Craig – Derby County – Hull City; 27 Farquharson, Nicholas A. – Crewe Alexandra – Nuneaton Borough; 7 Fitzgerald, Lorcan – West Ham United – Cheshunt; 28 Fitzpatrick, Jordan P. – Hereford United – Bromsgrove Rovers; 12 Flinders, Scott L. – Crystal Palace – Yeovil Town; 27 Flinders, Scott L. – Crystal Palace – Blackpool; 31 Fogden, Wesley K. – Brighton & Hove Albion – Bognor Regis Town; 28 Foley, Sam – Cheltenham Town – Bath City; 7 Freedman, Douglas A. – Crystal Palace – Leeds United; 7 Frost, Stef – Notts County – Matlock Town; 25 Gargan, Sam J. – Brighton & Hove Albion – Welling United; 27 Gleeson, Stephen M. – Wolverhampton Wanderers – Stockport County; 4 Goode, Aaron M.O. – Queens Park Rangers – Wealdstone; 15 Grant, Gavin – Millwall – Stevenage Borough; 7 Groves, Matt – Bristol Rovers – Chippenham Town; 27 Hall, Ryan – Crystal Palace – Crawley Town; 14 Halls, John – Reading – Sheffield United; 27 Hanson, Mitchell G.B. – Derby County – Port Vale; 9 Hart, Daniel – Barnet – Wivenhoe Town; 26 Hartley, Peter – Sunderland – Chesterfield; 27 Hawkins, Colin J. – Coventry City – Chesterfield; 14 Heath, Matthew P. – Leeds United – Colchester United; 30 Henderson, Stephen – Bristol City – Weymouth; 14 Hird, Christopher – Aston Villa – Wycombe Wanderers; 27 Hines, Zavon – West Ham United – Coventry City; 9 Hodge, Bryan – Blackburn Rovers – Darlington; 27 Holmes, Ian D. – Mansfield Town – AFC Telford United; 20 Holt, Grant – Nottingham Forest – Blackpool; 3 Hooper, Gary – Southend United – Hereford United; 21 Horlock, Kevin – Scunthorpe United – Mansfield Town; 6 Hoult, Russell – Stoke City – Notts County; 27 Hughes, Jeffrey – Crystal Palace – Bristol Rovers; 14 Hughes, Jerahl – Yeovil Town – Worthing; 16 Hurst, Paul – Rotherham United – Burton Albion; 7 Ide, Charles J. – Brentford – Lewes; 27 Igoe, Samuel – Bristol Rovers – Hereford United; 27 Jackson, Jamie D. – Chesterfield – Matlock Town; 23 Jeffery, Jack C. – West Ham United – Cambridge United; 25 John, Collins – Fulham – Watford; 28 Jones, Craig N. – Hereford United – Bromsgrove Rovers; 7 Jones, Daniel J. – Wolverhampton Wanderers – Northampton Town; 3 Jones, Luke J. – Shrewsbury Town – Kidderminster Harriers; 27 Jones, Stephen G. – Burnley – Crewe Alexandra; 20 Karacan, Jem P. – Reading – Millwall; 29 Kempson, Darran – Shrewsbury Town – Accrington Stanley; 10 Keogh, Richard J. – Bristol City – Cheltenham Town; 17 Kerry, Lloyd – Sheffield United –

Chesterfield; 17 Killock, Shane – Huddersfield Town – Hyde United; 2 King, Liam –
Rotherham United – Altrincham; 25 Konstantopoulos, Dimitrios – Coventry City –
Nottingham Forest; 14 Kuqi, Shefki – Crystal Palace – Ipswich Town; 27 Lawlor, Matthew –
Blackpool – Leigh RMI; 29 Ledgister, Aaron T. – Cheltenham Town – Bath City; 19 Lee,
Graeme B. – Doncaster Rovers – Shrewsbury Town; 27 Lee, Thomas E. – Macclesfield
Town – Rochdale; 5 Lita, Leroy – Reading – Charlton Athletic; 13 Little, Mark D. –
Wolverhampton Wanderers – Northampton Town; 27 Logan, Shaleum – Manchester City –
Stockport County; 27 Lowe, Ryan – Crewe Alexandra – Stockport County; 27 Lucketti,
Christopher J. – Sheffield United – Southampton; 4 Lunt, Kenny V. – Sheffield Wednesday
– Crewe Alexandra; 10 Lynch, Ryan P. – Crewe Alexandra – Altrincham; 7 Maher, Kevin
A. – Southend United – Gillingham; 27 Martin, Joseph J. – Tottenham Hotspur –
Blackpool; 3 McClements, David – Sheffield Wednesday – Buxton; 26 Mitchell, Scott –
Peterborough United – Stevenage Borough; 1 Moncur, Thomas J. – Fulham – Bradford
City; 27 Montrose, Lewis – Wigan Athletic – Rochdale; 7 Morgan, Dean – Luton Town –
Crewe Alexandra; 27 Moult, Jake O. – Plymouth Argyle – Kidderminster Harriers; 4 Nash,
Carlo J. – Wigan Athletic – Stoke City; 27 Nelthorpe, Craig R. – Doncaster Rovers –
Darlington; 30 Newton, Sean – Chester City – Droylsden; 17 Noble, Matthew J. – Doncaster
Rovers – Guiseley; 28 O'Donnell, Richard M. – Sheffield Wednesday – Oldham Athletic; 7
Ormerod, Brett R. – Preston North End – Nottingham Forest; 27 Owens, Graeme A. –
Middlesbrough – Chesterfield; 30 Parker, Ben B.C. – Leeds United – Darlington; 14 Parkes,
Jordan – Watford – Barnet; 27 Patterson, Marlon – Dagenham & Redbridge – Grays
Athletic; 3 Pearce, Krystian M.V. – Birmingham City – Port Vale; 27 Pearson, Stephen –
Derby County – Stoke City; 14 Pericard, Vincent D.P. – Stoke City – Southampton; 27
Perry, Christopher J. – Luton Town – Southampton; 7 Priskin, Tamas – Watford – Preston
North End; 6 Prosser, Luke B. – Port Vale – Leigh RMI; 20 Racon, Therry – Charlton
Athletic – Brighton & Hove Albion; 7 Rae, Michael E. – Hartlepool United – Southport; 10
Randolph, Darren E. – Charlton Athletic – Bury; 27 Reid, Kyel – West Ham United –
Crystal Palace; 27 Reid, Paul M. – Barnsley – Carlisle United; 19 Rigters, Maceo –
Blackburn Rovers – Norwich City; 27 Roberts, Mark A. – Accrington Stanley – Northwich
Victoria; 27 Rochester, Kraig – Dagenham & Redbridge – Dulwich Hamlet; 10 Rooney,
Adam – Stoke City – Bury; 27 Ruddy, John T.G. – Everton – Stockport County; 25 Sahar,
Ben – Chelsea – Sheffield Wednesday; 28 Saunders, Russell – Wigan Athletic –
Gainsborough Trinity; 14 Schmeichel, Kasper P. – Manchester City – Coventry City; 7
Seanla, Stephane – Barnet – Wivenhoe Town; 3 Showunmi, Enoch – Bristol City – Sheffield
Wednesday; 27 Simmonds, Donovan – Coventry City – Gillingham; 7 Simmonds, James R.
– Chelsea – Dover Athletic; 21 Simpson, Daniel P. – Manchester United – Ipswich Town; 27
Sinclair, Scott A. – Chelsea – Crystal Palace; 28 Sleath, Daniel J. – Mansfield Town –
Gainsborough Trinity; 27 Slusarski, Bartosz – West Bromwich Albion – Sheffield
Wednesday; 20 Smith, Johann – Bolton Wanderers – Stockport County; 29 Smith, Thomas
J. – Ipswich Town – Stevenage Borough; 17 Sodje, Efetobore – Gillingham – Bury; 7
Songo'o, Franck S. – Portsmouth – Sheffield Wednesday; 7 Spencer, Scott K. – Everton –
Macclesfield Town; 20 Steele, Luke D. – West Bromwich Albion – Barnsley; 27 Tansey,
Gregory J. – Stockport County – Altrincham; 14 Taylforth, Sean J. – Bradford City –
Guiseley; 27 Taylor, Jamie – Dagenham & Redbridge – Grays Athletic; 18 Teague, Andrew
H. – Macclesfield Town – Hyde United; 11 Tejan-Sie, Thomas M. – Dagenham &
Redbridge – Billericay Town; 29 Thomas, Aswad – Charlton Athletic – Accrington Stanley;
13 Thurgood, Stuart A. – Gillingham – Grays Athletic; 13 Timlin, Michael – Fulham –
Swindon Town; 27 Turnbull, Paul – Stockport County – Altrincham; 21 Wainwright, Neil –
Darlington – Mansfield Town; 4 Waite, Jamie – Bradford City – Droylsden; 17 Welsh,
Ishmael – Yeovil Town – Forest Green Rovers; 4 Westlake, Ian J. – Leeds United –
Brighton & Hove Albion; 4 Weston, Curtis J. – Leeds United – Scunthorpe United; 7
Worley, Harry J. – Chelsea – Leicester City; 20 Wright, Richard I. – West Ham United –
Southampton; 27 Wylde, Michael J. – Cheltenham Town – Kidderminster Harriers

APRIL 2008 TEMPORARY TRANSFERS
1 Adamson, Chris – Stockport County – Northwich Victoria; 16 Andersen, Mikkel –
Reading – Rushden & Diamonds; 10 Annerson, James – Sheffield United – Chesterfield; 15
Bailey, Matthew – Crewe Alexandra – Weymouth; 4 Bennett, Alan J. – Reading –
Brentford; 7 Bennett, Elliott – Wolverhampton Wanderers – Bury; 7 Bolder, Adam P. –
Queens Park Rangers – Sheffield Wednesday; 14 Bothroyd, Jay – Wolverhampton
Wanderers – Stoke City; 22 Burgess, Kevin M. – Darlington – Whitby Town; 30 Carayol,
Mustapha – Milton Keynes Dons – Crawley Town; 14 Cogan, Barry C. – Gillingham –
Grays Athletic; 27 Craig, Tony A. – Crystal Palace – Millwall; 20 Crow, Daniel –

156

Peterborough United – Notts County; 26 Ellis, Mark I. – Bolton Wanderers – Torquay United; 2 Goode, Aaron M.O. – Queens Park Rangers – Wealdstone; 30 Hall, Ryan – Crystal Palace – Crawley Town; 14 Halls, John – Reading – Sheffield United; 13 Hart, Daniel – Barnet – Wivenhoe Town; 13 Heath, Matthew P. – Leeds United – Colchester United; 14 Hurst, Paul – Rotherham United – Burton Albion; 20 Karacan, Jem P. – Reading – Millwall; 13 Keogh, Richard J. – Bristol City – Cheltenham Town; 19 Lee, Thomas E. – Macclesfield Town – Rochdale; 1 Lita, Leroy – Reading – Charlton Athletic; 10 Lynch, Ryan P. – Crewe Alexandra – Altrincham; 18 Martin, Alan – Leeds United – Hinckley United; 4 Morgan, Dean – Luton Town – Crewe Alexandra; 30 Murphy, Kieran – Milton Keynes Dons – Crawley Town; 28 Nelthorpe, Craig R. – Doncaster Rovers – Darlington; 14 Parkes, Jordan – Watford – Barnet; 9 Pearce, Krystian M.V. – Birmingham City – Port Vale; 6 Rae, Michael E. – Hartlepool United – Southport; 29 Reid, Kyel – West Ham United – Crystal Palace; 14 Rooney, Adam – Stoke City – Bury; 7 Sahar, Ben – Chelsea – Sheffield Wednesday; 4 Simmonds, James R. – Chelsea – Dover Athletic; 28 Sinclair, Robert J. – Luton Town – Salisbury City; 5 Smith, Thomas J. – Ipswich Town – Stevenage Borough; 21 Sodje, Efetobore – Gillingham – Bury; 7 Songo'o, Franck S. – Portsmouth – Sheffield Wednesday; 15 Taylforth, Sean J. – Bradford City – Guiseley; 25 Teague, Andrew H. – Macclesfield Town – Hyde United; 14 Thurgood, Stuart A. – Gillingham – Grays Athletic; 24 Turnbull, Paul – Stockport County – Altrincham; 6 Westlake, Ian J. – Leeds United – Brighton & Hove Albion; 20 Wright, Richard I. – West Ham United – Southampton

MAY 2008

30 Earnshaw, Robert	Derby County	Nottingham Forest
8 Griffith, Anthony	Doncaster Rovers	Port Vale
14 Heath, Matthew P.	Leeds United	Colchester United
28 O'Grady, Christopher	Rotherham United	Oldham Athletic
22 Rendell, Scott	Cambridge United	Peterborough United
23 Steele, Luke D.	WBA	Barnsley
20 Walker, James L.N.	Charlton Athletic	Southend United
6 Worley, Harry J.	Chelsea	Leicester City

TEMPORARY TRANSFERS

3 Basham, Christopher P. – Bolton Wanderers – Rochdale; 30 Ellington, Nathan L.F. – Watford – Derby County; 4 Facey, Delroy M. – Gillingham – Wycombe Wanderers; 4 Holmes, Ian D. – Mansfield Town – AFC Telford United; 2 Howe, Jermaine R. – Peterborough United – Rochdale; 2 Parker, Ben B.C. – Leeds United – Darlington; 1 Pentney, Carl – Leicester City – Fisher Athletic; 7 Robson-Kanu, Thomas H. – Reading – Southend United; 2 Sheehan, Alan – Leicester City – Leeds United; 4 Zebroski, Christopher – Millwall – Torquay United

FOREIGN TRANSFERS 2007–2008

MAY 2007	From	To
18 Cisse, Kalifa	Boavista	Reading
25 Fabianski, Lukosz	Legia Warsaw	Arsenal
12 Lucas	Gremio	Liverpool
30 Muntari, Sulley	Udinese	Portsmouth
JUNE 2007		
19 Granqvist, Andreas	Helsingborg	Wigan Athletic
29 Kapo, Olivier	Juventus	Birmingham City
29 Rozehnal, David	Paris St Germain	Newcastle United
9 Taarabt, Adel	Lens	Tottenham Hotspur
JULY 2007		
16 Alonso, Mikel	Real Sociedad	Bolton Wanderers
2 Anderson	Porto	Manchester United
13 Babel, Ryan	Ajax	Liverpool
13 Bianchi, Rolando	Reggina	Manchester City
1 Cid, Gerald	Bordeaux	Bolton Wanderers
3 De Ridder, Daniel	Celta Vigo	Birmingham City
1 Dzemaili, Blerim	Zurich	Bolton Wanderers
2 Eduardo	Dinamo Zagreb	Arsenal
1 Faubert, Julien	Bordeaux	West Ham United

14 Gelson	Sion	Manchester City
17 Geovanni	Cruzeiro	Manchester City
1 Hargreaves, Owen	Bayern Munich	Manchester United
5 Kaboul, Younes	Auxerre	Tottenham Hotspur
4 Kingson, Richard	Hammarby	Birmingham City
10 Malouda, Florent	Lyon	Chelsea
5 Mvuemba, Arnold	Rennes	Portsmouth
2 Nani	Sporting Lisbon	Manchester United
26 Petrov, Martin	Atletico Madrid	Manchester City
20 Pienaar, Steven	Borussia Dortmund	Everton
1 Pizarro, Claudio	Bayern Munich	Chelsea
30 Prince-Boateng, Kevin	Hertha Berlin	Tottenham Hotspur
2 Rigters, Maceo	NAC Breda	Blackburn Rovers
12 Sagna, Bacary	Auxerre	Arsenal
28 Santa Cruz, Roque	Bayern Munich	Blackburn Rovers
6 Schmitz, Rafael	Lille	Birmingham City
4 Torres, Fernando	Atletico Madrid	Liverpool
4 Tuncay	Fenerbahce	Middlesbrough
11 Utaka, John	Rennes	Portsmouth
6 Voronin, Andriy	Leverkusen	Liverpool
27 Wilhelmsson, Christian	Nantes	Bolton Wanderers

AUGUST 2007

10 Alex	PSV Eindhoven	Chelsea
23 Belletti, Juliano	Barcelona	Chelsea
31 Beye, Habib	Marseille	Newcastle United
3 Bojinov, Valeri	Fiorentina	Manchester City
3 Braaten, Daniel	Rosenborg	Bolton Wanderers
4 Cacapa, Claudio	Lyon	Newcastle United
2 Corluka, Vedran	Dinamo Zagreb	Manchester City
2 Elano	Shakhtar Donetsk	Manchester City
2 Fae, Emerse	Nantes	Reading
17 Feilhaber, Benny	Hamburg	Derby County
2 Garrido, Javier	Real Sociedad	Manchester City
6 Jose Enrique	Villarreal	Newcastle United
31 Palacios, Wilson	Olimpia	Birmingham City
31 Plessis, Damian	Lyon	Liverpool
31 Salifou, Moustapha	Wil	Aston Villa
31 Shawky, Mohamed	Al-Ahly	Middlesbrough
21 Wessels, Stefan	Cologne	Everton

JANUARY 2008

29 Andreasen, Leon	Werder Bremen	Fulham
31 Alves, Afonso	Heerenveen	Middlesbrough
18 Aubey, Lucien	Lens	Portsmouth
31 Caicedo, Felipe	Basle	Manchester City
4 Castillo, Nery	Shakhtar Donetsk	Manchester City
4 Cohen, Tamir	Maccabi Netanya	Bolton Wanderers
10 Fernandes, Manuel	Valencia	Everton
22 Figueroa, Maynor	Dep Olimpia	Wigan Athletic
31 Gilberto	Hertha Berlin	Tottenham Hotspur
31 Hagen, Erik	Zenit	Wigan Athletic
22 Hangeland, Brede	FC Copenhagen	Fulham
31 Johnson, Eddie	Kansas City Wizards	Fulham
31 Kebe, Jimmy	Lens	Reading
11 Matejovsky, Marek	Mlada Boleslav	Reading
25 Prica, Rade	Aalborg	Sunderland
14 Skrtel, Martin	Zenit	Liverpool
31 Sterjovski, Mile	Genclerbirligi	Derby County
17 Steinsson, Gretar	AZ	Bolton Wanderers
8 Villa, Emanuel	UAG Tecos	Derby County
21 Zarate, Mauro	Al-Saad	Birmingham City

MARCH 2008

7 Lamine, Diatta	Besiktas	Newcastle United
18 Vogel, Johann	Real Betis	Blackburn Rovers

Three players signed in earlier seasons made their debut: Armand Traore (Arsenal), Martin Olsson (Blackburn Rovers) and Ali Al-Habsi (Bolton Wanderers).

FA CUP REVIEW 2007–2008

You might have had an idea the 2007–08 FA Cup competition would yield two unfashionable finalists despite the domination of all tournaments these days by the leading Premier League clubs for two good reasons. Firstly because of their involvement in European games, the top teams have a rather cavalier attitude to the world's oldest trophy, and secondly some of the romance was returning with more than a share of giant-killing by the minnows who still regard the FA Cup as something special.

Thus it finished up at the new look Wembley Stadium with Portsmouth who last won the cup in 1939 playing Cardiff City who were the only club to take the pot out of the country way back in 1927.

There was an irony, too, over the outcome harking back to that 1920s final when a slip by the Welsh born Arsenal goalkeeper, arguably the softest goal ever seen at Wembley in an FA Cup final, virtually sent the cup to Wales. In 2008 it was Cardiff who suffered when a fumble by goalkeeper Peter Enckelman allowed Nwankwo Kanu the comparatively easy task of wrapping it up for Portsmouth.

But that was May and the trek to West London starts way back and once the first round proper was reached, only the most determined of gallant upstarts had held on. Former Football League clubs were among their number as well as those from more modest surroundings. Perhaps not too many eyebrows were raised when Havant & Waterlooville won at York City, or Chasetown were successful at Team Bath, but Staines Town drawing at Stockport County was a slightly different result as was the Sunday best effort by Torquay United over those perennial giant-killers of old Yeovil Town.

A waterlogged pitch held up the Staines replay but when it happened, Stockport were held again and lost in the subsequent shoot-out. Come round two and Horsham who had seen off Maidenhead United in comfortable fashion were drawn at home to promotion chasing Swansea City. They earned a replay in Wales. Havant, meanwhile, were seeing off Notts County at Meadow Lane and again on Sunday Chasetown were holding Port Vale on their own ground. Sadly Staines were hit for five by Peterborough United.

Swansea recovered from Horsham twice taking the lead before winning 6-2, but Chasetown beat Port Vale to reach the third round. Then came the Premier casualties. Blackburn Rovers – 4-1 to Coventry City – Bolton Wanderers and Everton lost at home. Bristol Rovers drew at Fulham, Luton Town at home to Liverpool. Havant kept going with a Swansea draw, too. But Chasetown after taking the lead over Cardiff were beaten and Pompey started with a win at Ipswich.

Then came the shock of Havant taking out Swansea 4-2 and Rovers winning on penalties against Fulham. The fourth round and plucky Havant twice led at Anfield before losing 5-2. Preston won easily at Derby County and Sheffield United beat another Premier team Manchester City. Cardiff were successful at Hereford, Portsmouth at home to Plymouth.

The fifth round and Bristol Rovers were still going strong beating Southampton, West Bromwich Albion won 5-0 at Coventry and both Cardiff against Wolves and Portsmouth at Preston were through safely. Manchester United hit Arsenal for four, but the surprise was Barnsley winning at Liverpool. Middlesbrough beat Sheffield United on penalties in a replay.

When the last eight gathered for the quarter-finals, Bristol Rovers from the third tier were drawn against Albion, Cardiff at Middlesbrough, Portsmouth away to Manchester United, while Barnsley entertained Chelsea. Pompey won for the first time at Old Trafford in 51 years, West Bromwich won 5-1, Cardiff 2-0 but Barnsley stunned Chelsea 1-0.

This left just Pompey to fly the Premier flag in the semi-finals. Portsmouth again needed just one goal to beat West Bromwich as did Cardiff against Barnsley. In fact Pompey's winning final goal was only their seventh in the entire campaign!

THE FA CUP 2007–2008

FIRST ROUND

Hereford U	(0) 0	Leeds U	(0) 0
Accrington S	(2) 2	Huddersfield T	(1) 3
Altrincham	(1) 1	Millwall	(0) 2
Barnet	(0) 2	Gillingham	(1) 1
Barrow	(1) 1	Bournemouth	(1) 1
Billericay T	(1) 1	Swansea C	(0) 2
Bradford C	(1) 1	Chester C	(0) 0
Bury	(1) 4	Workington	(0) 1
Cambridge U	(0) 2	Aldershot T	(1) 1
Carlisle U	(0) 1	Grimsby T	(1) 1
Cheltenham T	(0) 1	Brighton & HA	(0) 1
Chesterfield	(1) 1	Tranmere R	(1) 2
Crewe Alex	(1) 2	Milton Keynes D	(0) 1
Darlington	(1) 1	Northampton T	(1) 1
Eastbourne B	(0) 0	Weymouth	(0) 4
Exeter C	(2) 4	Stevenage B	(0) 0
Halifax T	(0) 0	Burton Alb	(1) 4
Hampton & R	(0) 0	Dagenham & R	(0) 3
Harrogate RA	(0) 2	Droylsden	(0) 0
Horsham	(1) 4	Maidenhead U	(0) 1
Leyton Orient	(1) 1	Bristol R	(0) 1
Lincoln C	(1) 1	Nottingham F	(1) 1
Luton T	(0) 1	Brentford	(1) 1
Mansfield T	(2) 3	Lewes	(0) 0
Morecambe	(0) 0	Port Vale	(2) 2
Notts Co	(0) 3	Histon	(0) 0
Oldham Ath	(1) 2	Doncaster R	(0) 2
Oxford U	(2) 3	Northwich Vic	(1) 1
Peterborough U	(2) 4	Wrexham	(0) 1
Rushden & D	(2) 3	Macclesfield T	(0) 1
Southend U	(2) 2	Rochdale	(1) 1
Stockport Co	(0) 1	Staines T	(0) 1
Team Bath	(0) 0	Chasetown	(2) 2
Walsall	(1) 2	Shrewsbury T	(0) 0
Ware	(0) 0	Kidderminster H	(0) 2
Wycombe W	(0) 1	Swindon T	(0) 2
York C	(0) 0	Havant & W	(1) 1
Forest Green R	(2) 2	Rotherham U	(0) 2
Gainsborough T	(0) 0	Hartlepool U	(2) 6
Torquay U	(2) 4	Yeovil T	(1) 1

FIRST ROUND REPLAYS

Bournemouth	(1) 3	Barrow	(0) 2
(aet.)			
Brighton & HA	(1) 2	Cheltenham T	(0) 1
Grimsby T	(0) 1	Carlisle U	(0) 0
Leeds U	(0) 0	Hereford U	(1) 1
Northampton T	(2) 2	Darlington	(0) 1
Rotherham U	(0) 0	Forest Green R	(1) 3
Staines T	(1) 1	Stockport Co	(0) 1
(aet; Staines T won 4-3 on penalties.)			
Brentford	(0) 0	Luton T	(1) 2
Bristol R	(1) 3	Leyton Orient	(1) 3
(aet; Bristol R won 6-5 on penalties.)			

| Doncaster R | (1) 1 | Oldham Ath | (1) 2 |
| Nottingham F | (1) 3 | Lincoln C | (0) 1 |

SECOND ROUND

Horsham	(0) 1	Swansea C	(1) 1
Bradford C	(0) 0	Tranmere R	(2) 3
Bristol R	(2) 5	Rushden & D	(1) 1
Burton Alb	(0) 1	Barnet	(1) 1
Bury	(0) 1	Exeter C	(0) 0
Cambridge U	(1) 1	Weymouth	(0) 0
Dagenham & R	(1) 3	Kidderminster H	(1) 1
Hereford U	(1) 2	Hartlepool U	(0) 0
Huddersfield T	(0) 3	Grimsby T	(0) 0
Millwall	(0) 2	Bournemouth	(0) 1
Northampton T	(1) 1	Walsall	(1) 1
Notts Co	(0) 0	Havant & W	(0) 1
Oldham Ath	(1) 1	Crewe Alex	(0) 0
Oxford U	(0) 0	Southend U	(0) 0
Staines T	(0) 0	Peterborough U	(3) 5
Swindon T	(1) 3	Forest Green R	(0) 2
Torquay U	(0) 0	Brighton & HA	(0) 2
Harrogate RA	(0) 2	Mansfield T	(1) 3
Port Vale	(1) 1	Chasetown	(1) 1
Luton T	(0) 1	Nottingham F	(0) 0

SECOND ROUND REPLAYS

Swansea C	(4) 6	Horsham	(2) 2
Barnet	(0) 1	Burton Alb	(0) 0
Chasetown	(0) 1	Port Vale	(0) 0
Southend U	(2) 3	Oxford U	(0) 0
Walsall	(0) 1	Northampton T	(0) 0

THIRD ROUND

Aston Villa	(0) 0	Manchester U	(0) 2
Barnsley	(0) 2	Blackpool	(1) 1
Blackburn R	(0) 1	Coventry C	(1) 4
Bolton W	(0) 0	Sheffield U	(1) 1
Brighton & HA	(1) 1	Mansfield T	(2) 2
Bristol C	(1) 1	Middlesbrough	(1) 2
Charlton Ath	(1) 1	WBA	(1) 1
Chasetown	(1) 1	Cardiff C	(1) 3
Chelsea	(1) 1	QPR	(0) 0
Colchester U	(1) 1	Peterborough U	(1) 3
Everton	(0) 0	Oldham Ath	(1) 1
Huddersfield T	(1) 2	Birmingham C	(1) 1
Ipswich T	(0) 0	Portsmouth	(0) 1
Norwich C	(0) 1	Bury	(0) 1
Plymouth Arg	(2) 3	Hull C	(0) 2
Preston NE	(0) 1	Scunthorpe U	(0) 0
Southampton	(2) 2	Leicester C	(0) 0
Southend U	(1) 5	Dagenham & R	(1) 2
Sunderland	(0) 0	Wigan Ath	(1) 3
Swansea C	(0) 1	Havant & W	(0) 1
Swindon T	(0) 1	Barnet	(0) 1
Tottenham H	(1) 2	Reading	(1) 2
Tranmere R	(0) 2	Hereford U	(0) 2
Walsall	(0) 0	Millwall	(0) 0
Watford	(1) 2	Crystal Palace	(0) 0

West Ham U	(0) 0	Manchester C	(0) 0
Wolverhampton W	(0) 2	Cambridge U	(1) 1
Burnley	(0) 0	Arsenal	(1) 2
Derby Co	(2) 2	Sheffield W	(2) 2
Fulham	(1) 2	Bristol R	(1) 2
Luton T	(0) 1	Liverpool	(0) 1
Stoke C	(0) 0	Newcastle U	(0) 0

THIRD ROUND REPLAYS

Bury	(1) 2	Norwich C	(0) 1
Liverpool	(1) 5	Luton T	(0) 0
Millwall	(1) 2	Walsall	(0) 1
Reading	(0) 0	Tottenham H	(1) 1
WBA	(1) 2	Charlton Ath	(0) 2

(aet; WBA won 4-3 on penalties.)

Havant & W	(3) 4	Swansea C	(1) 2
Hereford U	(0) 1	Tranmere R	(0) 0
Manchester C	(0) 1	West Ham U	(0) 0
Newcastle U	(2) 4	Stoke C	(0) 1
Barnet	(0) 1	Swindon T	(1) 1

(aet; Barnet won 2-0 on penalties.)

| Bristol R | (0) 0 | Fulham | (0) 0 |

(aet; Bristol R won 5-3 on penalties.)

| Sheffield W | (1) 1 | Derby Co | (0) 1 |

(aet; Derby Co won 4-2 on penalties.)

FOURTH ROUND

Southend U	(0) 0	Barnsley	(1) 1
Arsenal	(0) 3	Newcastle U	(0) 0
Barnet	(0) 0	Bristol R	(0) 1
Coventry C	(1) 2	Millwall	(1) 1
Derby Co	(0) 1	Preston NE	(3) 4
Liverpool	(2) 5	Havant & W	(2) 2
Mansfield T	(0) 0	Middlesbrough	(1) 2
Oldham Ath	(0) 0	Huddersfield T	(1) 1
Peterborough U	(0) 0	WBA	(2) 3
Portsmouth	(2) 2	Plymouth Arg	(1) 1
Southampton	(0) 2	Bury	(0) 0
Watford	(0) 1	Wolverhampton W	(1) 4
Wigan Ath	(0) 1	Chelsea	(0) 2
Hereford U	(0) 1	Cardiff C	(1) 2
Manchester U	(1) 3	Tottenham H	(1) 1
Sheffield U	(2) 2	Manchester C	(0) 1

FIFTH ROUND

Bristol R	(0) 1	Southampton	(0) 0
Cardiff C	(2) 2	Wolverhampton W	(0) 0
Chelsea	(1) 3	Huddersfield T	(1) 1
Coventry C	(0) 0	WBA	(1) 5
Liverpool	(1) 1	Barnsley	(0) 2
Manchester U	(3) 4	Arsenal	(0) 0
Preston NE	(0) 0	Portsmouth	(0) 1
Sheffield U	(0) 0	Middlesbrough	(0) 0

FIFTH ROUND REPLAY

| Middlesbrough | (0) 1 | Sheffield U | (0) 0 |

(aet.)

SIXTH ROUND

Barnsley	(0) 1	Chelsea	(0) 0
Manchester U	(0) 0	Portsmouth	(0) 1
Bristol R	(1) 1	WBA	(2) 5
Middlesbrough	(0) 0	Cardiff C	(2) 2

SEMI-FINALS

WBA	(0) 0	Portsmouth	(0) 1
Barnsley	(0) 0	Cardiff C	(1) 1

THE FA CUP FINAL

Saturday, 17 May 2008

(at Wembley Stadium, attendance 89,874)

Portsmouth (1) 1   Cardiff C (0) 0

Portsmouth: James; Johnson, Hreidarsson, Diarra, Campbell, Distin, Utaka (Nugent), Pedro Mendes (Diop), Kranjcar, Kanu (Baros), Muntari.

Scorer: Kanu 37.

Cardiff C: Enckelman; McNaughton, Capaldi, Rae (Sinclair), Johnson, Loovens, Ledley, McPhail, Hasselbaink (Thompson), Whittingham (Ramsey), Parry.

Referee: M. Dean (Wirral).

PAST FA CUP FINALS

Details of one goalscorer is not available in 1878.

1872	The Wanderers 1		Royal Engineers 0	
	Betts			
1873	The Wanderers 2		Oxford University 0	
	Kinnaird, Wollaston			
1874	Oxford University.............2		Royal Engineers 0	
	Mackarness, Patton			
1875	Royal Engineers 1		Old Etonians 1*	
	Renny-Tailyour		*Bonsor*	
Replay	Royal Engineers 2		Old Etonians 0	
	Renny-Tailyour, Stafford			
1876	The Wanderers 1		Old Etonians 1*	
	Edwards		*Bonsor*	
Replay	The Wanderers 3		Old Etonians 0	
	Wollaston, Hughes 2			
1877	The Wanderers 2		Oxford University 1*	
	Lindsay, Kenrick		*Kinnaird (og)*	
1878	The Wanderers 3		Royal Engineers 1	
	Kenrick 2, Kinnaird		*Unknown*	
1879	Old Etonians 1		Clapham Rovers 0	
	Clerke			
1880	Clapham Rovers 1		Oxford University 0	
	Lloyd-Jones			
1881	Old Carthusians 3		Old Etonians 0	
	Wyngard, Parry, Todd			
1882	Old Etonians 1		Blackburn Rovers 0	
	Anderson			
1883	Blackburn Olympic 2		Old Etonians 1*	
	Costley, Matthews		*Goodhart*	
1884	Blackburn Rovers...............2		Queen's Park, Glasgow 1	
	Sowerbutts, Forrest		*Christie*	
1885	Blackburn Rovers...............2		Queen's Park, Glasgow 0	
	Forrest, Brown			
1886	Blackburn Rovers...............0		West Bromwich Albion 0	
Replay	Blackburn Rovers...............2		West Bromwich Albion 0	
	Brown, Sowerbutts			
1887	Aston Villa 2		West Bromwich Albion 0	
	Hunter, Hodgetts			
1888	West Bromwich Albion 2		Preston NE 1	
	Woodhall, Bayliss		*Dewhurst*	
1889	Preston NE 3		Wolverhampton W.............................0	
	Dewhurst, J. Ross, Thompson			
1890	Blackburn Rovers...............6		Sheffield W 1	
	Walton, John Southworth,		*Bennett*	
	Lofthouse, Townley 3			
1891	Blackburn Rovers...............3		Notts Co...1	
	Dewar, John Southworth,		*Oswald*	
	Townley			
1892	West Bromwich Albion 3		Aston Villa 0	
	Geddes, Nicholls, Reynolds			
1893	Wolverhampton W 1		Everton 0	
	Allen			

1894	Notts Co 4	Bolton W 1
	Watson, Logan 3	*Cassidy*
1895	Aston Villa 1	West Bromwich Albion 0
	J. Devey	
1896	Sheffield W 2	Wolverhampton W 1
	Spiksley 2	*Black*
1897	Aston Villa 3	Everton 2
	Campbell, Wheldon, Crabtree	*Boyle, Bell*
1898	Nottingham F 3	Derby Co 1
	Cape 2, McPherson	*Bloomer*
1899	Sheffield U 4	Derby Co 1
	Bennett, Beers, Almond, Priest	*Boag*
1900	Bury 4	Southampton 0
	McLuckie 2, Wood, Plant	
1901	Tottenham H 2	Sheffield U 2
	Brown 2	*Bennett, Priest*
Replay	Tottenham H 3	Sheffield U 1
	Cameron, Smith, Brown	*Priest*
1902	Sheffield U 1	Southampton 1
	Common	*Wood*
Replay	Sheffield U 2	Southampton 1
	Hedley, Barnes	*Brown*
1903	Bury 6	Derby Co 0
	Ross, Sagar, Leeming 2, Wood, Plant	
1904	Manchester C 1	Bolton W 0
	Meredith	
1905	Aston Villa 2	Newcastle U 0
	Hampton 2	
1906	Everton 1	Newcastle U 0
	Young	
1907	Sheffield W 2	Everton 1
	Stewart, Simpson	*Sharp*
1908	Wolverhampton W 3	Newcastle U 1
	Hunt, Hedley, Harrison	*Howey*
1909	Manchester U 1	Bristol C 0
	A. Turnbull	
1910	Newcastle U 1	Barnsley 1
	Rutherford	*Tufnell*
Replay	Newcastle U 2	Barnsley 0
	Shepherd 2 (1 pen)	
1911	Bradford C 0	Newcastle U 0
Replay	Bradford C 1	Newcastle U 0
	Speirs	
1912	Barnsley 0	West Bromwich Albion 0
Replay	Barnsley 1	West Bromwich Albion 0*
	Tufnell	
1913	Aston Villa 1	Sunderland 0
	Barber	
1914	Burnley 1	Liverpool 0
	Freeman	
1915	Sheffield U 3	Chelsea 0
	Simmons, Masterman, Kitchen	

Year	Winner	Score	Runner-up	Score
1920	Aston Villa *Kirton*	1	Huddersfield T	0*
1921	Tottenham H *Dimmock*	1	Wolverhampton W	0
1922	Huddersfield T *Smith (pen)*	1	Preston NE	0
1923	Bolton W *Jack, J.R. Smith*	2	West Ham U	0
1924	Newcastle U *Harris, Seymour*	2	Aston Villa	0
1925	Sheffield U *Tunstall*	1	Cardiff C	0
1926	Bolton W *Jack*	1	Manchester C	0
1927	Cardiff C *Ferguson*	1	Arsenal	0
1928	Blackburn Rovers *Roscamp 2, McLean*	3	Huddersfield T *A. Jackson*	1
1929	Bolton W *Butler, Blackmore*	2	Portsmouth	0
1930	Arsenal *James, Lambert*	2	Huddersfield T	0
1931	West Bromwich Albion *W.G. Richardson 2*	2	Birmingham *Bradford*	1
1932	Newcastle U *Allen 2*	2	Arsenal *John*	1
1933	Everton *Stein, Dean, Dunn*	3	Manchester C	0
1934	Manchester C *Tilson 2*	2	Portsmouth *Rutherford*	1
1935	Sheffield W *Rimmer 2, Palethorpe, Hooper*	4	West Bromwich Albion *Boyes, Sandford*	2
1936	Arsenal *Drake*	1	Sheffield U	0
1937	Sunderland *Gurney, Carter, Burbanks*	3	Preston NE *F. O'Donnell*	1
1938	Preston NE *Mutch (pen)*	1	Huddersfield T	0*
1939	Portsmouth *Parker 2, Barlow, Anderson*	4	Wolverhampton W *Dorsett*	1
1946	Derby Co *H. Turner (og), Doherty, Stamps 2*	4	Charlton Ath *H. Turner*	1*
1947	Charlton Ath *Duffy*	1	Burnley	0*
1948	Manchester U *Rowley 2, Pearson, Anderson*	4	Blackpool *Shimwell (pen), Mortensen*	2
1949	Wolverhampton W *Pye 2, Smyth,*	3	Leicester C *Griffiths*	1
1950	Arsenal *Lewis 2*	2	Liverpool	0

166

1951	Newcastle U	2	Blackpool	0
	Milburn 2			
1952	Newcastle U	1	Arsenal	0
	G. Robledo			
1953	Blackpool	4	Bolton W	3
	Mortensen 3, Perry		*Lofthouse, Moir, Bell*	
1954	West Bromwich Albion	3	Preston NE	2
	Allen 2 (1 pen), Griffin		*Morrison, Wayman*	
1955	Newcastle U	3	Manchester C	1
	Milburn, Mitchell,		*Johnstone*	
	Hannah			
1956	Manchester C	3	Birmingham C	1
	Hayes, Dyson, Johnstone		*Kinsey*	
1957	Aston Villa	2	Manchester U	1
	McParland 2		*T. Taylor*	
1958	Bolton W	2	Manchester U	0
	Lofthouse 2			
1959	Nottingham F	2	Luton T	1
	Dwight, Wilson		*Pacey*	
1960	Wolverhampton W	3	Blackburn Rovers	0
	McGrath (og), Deeley 2			
1961	Tottenham H	2	Leicester C	0
	Smith, Dyson			
1962	Tottenham H	3	Burnley	1
	Greaves, Smith,		*Robson*	
	Blanchflower (pen)			
1963	Manchester U	3	Leicester C	1
	Herd 2, Law		*Keyworth*	
1964	West Ham U	3	Preston NE	2
	Sissons, Hurst, Boyce		*Holden, Dawson*	
1965	Liverpool	2	Leeds U	1*
	Hunt, St John		*Bremner*	
1966	Everton	3	Sheffield W	2
	Trebilcock 2, Temple		*McCalliog, Ford*	
1967	Tottenham H	2	Chelsea	1
	Robertson, Saul		*Tambling*	
1968	West Browmich Albion	1	Everton	0*
	Astle			
1969	Manchester C	1	Leicester C	0
	Young			
1970	Chelsea	2	Leeds U	2*
	Houseman, Hutchinson		*Charlton, Jones*	
Replay	Chelsea	2	Leeds U	1*
	Osgood, Webb		*Jones*	
1971	Arsenal	2	Liverpool	1*
	Kelly, George		*Heighway*	
1972	Leeds U	1	Arsenal	0
	Clarke			
1973	Sunderland	1	Leeds U	0
	Porterfield			
1974	Liverpool	3	Newcastle	0
	Keegan 2, Heighway			
1975	West Ham U	2	Fulham	0
	A. Taylor 2			

Year	Winner	Score	Scorers	Runner-up	Score	Scorers
1976	Southampton	1	Stokes	Manchester U	0	
1977	Manchester U	2	Pearson, J. Greenhoff	Liverpool	1	Case
1978	Ipswich T	1	Osborne	Arsenal	0	
1979	Arsenal	3	Talbot, Stapleton, Sunderland	Manchester U	2	McQueen, McIlroy
1980	West Ham U	1	Brooking	Arsenal	0	
1981	Tottenham H	1	Hutchison (og)	Manchester C	1*	Hutchison
Replay	Totteham H	3	Villa 2, Crooks	Manchester C	2	MacKenzie, Reeves (pen)
1982	Tottenham H	1	Hoddle	QPR	1*	Fenwick
Replay	Tottenham H	1	Hoddle (pen)	QPR	0	
1983	Manchester U	2	Stapleton, Wilkins	Brighton & HA	2*	Smith, Stevens
Replay	Manchester U	4	Robson 2, Whiteside, Muhren (pen)	Brighton & HA	0	
1984	Everton	2	Sharp, Gray	Watford	0	
1985	Manchester U	1	Whiteside	Everton	0*	
1986	Liverpool	3	Rush 2, Johnston	Everton	1	Lineker
1987	Coventry C	3	Bennett, Houchen, Mabbutt (og)	Tottenham H	2*	C. Allen, Kilcline (og)
1988	Wimbledon	1	Sanchez	Liverpool	0	
1989	Liverpool	3	Aldridge, Rush 2	Everton	2*	McCall 2
1990	Manchester U	3	Robson, Hughes 2	Crystal Palace	3*	O'Reilly, Wright 2
Replay	Manchester U	1	Martin	Crystal Palace	0	
1991	Tottenham H	2	Stewart, Walker (og)	Nottingham F	1*	Pearce
1992	Liverpool	2	Thomas, Rush	Sunderland	0	
1993	Arsenal	1	Wright	Sheffield W	1*	Hirst
Replay	Arsenal	2	Wright, Linighan	Sheffield W	1*	Waddle
1994	Manchester U	4	Cantona 2 (2 pens), Hughes, McClair	Chelsea	0	
1995	Everton	1	Rideout	Manchester U	0	
1996	Manchester U	1	Cantona	Liverpool	0	

1997	Chelsea..................................2	Middlesbrough.................................0
	Di Matteo, Newton	
1998	Arsenal....................................2	Newcastle U 0
	Overmars, Anelka	
1999	Manchester U..........................2	Newcastle U 0
	Sheringham, Scholes	
2000	Chelsea..................................1	Aston Villa 0
	Di Matteo	
2001	Liverpool 2	Arsenal 1
	Owen 2	*Ljungberg*
2002	Arsenal....................................2	Chelsea 0
	Parlour, Ljungberg	
2003	Arsenal....................................1	Southampton....................................0
	Pires	
2004	Manchester U..........................3	Millwall 0
	Ronaldo, Van Nistelrooy 2 (1 pen)	
2005	Arsenal....................................0	Manchester U 0*
	Arsenal won 5-4 on penalties	
2006	Liverpool 3	West Ham U 3*
	Cisse, Gerrard 2	*Carragher (og), Ashton, Konchesky*
	Liverpool won 3-1 on penalties	
2007	Chelsea..................................1	Manchester U 0*
	Drogba	
2008	Portsmouth 1	Cardiff C..0
	Kanu	

*After extra time

SUMMARY OF FA CUP WINNERS SINCE 1872

Manchester United	11
Arsenal	10
Tottenham Hotspur	8
Aston Villa	7
Liverpool	7
Blackburn Rovers	6
Newcastle United	6
Everton	5
The Wanderers	5
West Bromwich Albion	5
Bolton Wanderers	4
Chelsea	4
Manchester City	4
Sheffield United	4
Wolverhampton Wanderers	4
Sheffield Wednesday	3
West Ham United	3
Bury	2
Nottingham Forest	2
Old Etonians	2
Portsmouth	2
Preston North End	2
Sunderland	2
Barnsley	1
Blackburn Olympic	1
Blackpool	1
Bradford City	1
Burnley	1
Cardiff City	1
Charlton Athletic	1
Clapham Rovers	1
Coventry City	1
Derby County	1
Huddersfield Town	1
Ipswich Town	1
Leeds United	1
Notts County	1
Old Carthusians	1
Oxford University	1
Royal Engineers	1
Southampton	1
Wimbledon	1

APPEARANCES IN FA CUP FINAL

Manchester United	18
Arsenal	17
Liverpool	13
Newcastle United	13
Everton	12
Aston Villa	10
West Bromwich Albion	10
Tottenham Hotspur	9
Blackburn Rovers	8
Chelsea	8
Manchester City	8
Wolverhampton Wanderers	8
Bolton Wanderers	7
Preston North End	7
Old Etonians	6
Sheffield United	6
Sheffield Wednesday	6
Huddersfield Town	5
The Wanderers	5
West Ham United	5
Derby County	4
Leeds United	4
Leicester City	4
Oxford University	4
Portsmouth	4
Royal Engineers	4
Southampton	4
Sunderland	4
Blackpool	3
Burnley	3
Cardiff City	3
Nottingham Forest	3
Barnsley	2
Birmingham City	2
Bury	2
Charlton Athletic	2
Clapham Rovers	2
Notts County	2
Queen's Park (Glasgow)	2
Blackburn Olympic	1
Bradford City	1
Brighton & Hove Albion	1
Bristol City	1
Coventry City	1
Crystal Palace	1
Fulham	1
Ipswich Town	1
Luton Town	1
Middlesbrough	1
Millwall	1
Old Carthusians	1
Queen's Park Rangers	1
Watford	1
Wimbledon	1

CARLING CUP REVIEW 2007-2008

Tottenham Hotspur have had a pretty miserable record against Chelsea and the fact that both teams managed to reach the final of the Carling Cup in February could not have been the best of opponents for the occupants of White Hart Lane. But though Chelsea took the lead through Didier Drogba, Dimitar Bertatov from the penalty spot ensured extra time and Jonathan Woodgate in overtime sent the cup to Spurs for the first time in nine years.

Middle August is now the time for the opening encounters and the first round produced Norwich City as the highest scorers with a 5-2 win over Barnet. There were several fours, too, for Doncaster Rovers, Hereford United, Oldham Athletic and Southend United. Enter the Premier League teams with no European interest and exit Sunderland at Luton Town, Wigan Athletic at home to Hull City plus Derby County on penalties against Blackpool. But Aston Villa saw off Wrexham with five goals.

For the third round those with commitments on the continent survived without too much trauma. Arsenal beat Newcastle United 2-0 as did Spurs against Middlesbrough. Liverpool were 4-2 winners at Reading with Fernando Torres scoring a hat-trick. Blackburn Rovers beat Birmingham City 3-0, Bolton Wanderers won 2-1 at Fulham and Everton 3-0 away to Sheffield Wednesday. Chelsea for their part were the top scorers on travel hitting Hull for four, while Sheffield United with a 5-0 victory over Morecambe were the highest overall marksmen.

However, Aston Villa were beaten 1-0 at home by Leicester City and the big shock was the exit of Manchester United at Old Trafford as Coventry City won 2-0 there, given the use of domestic cup competitions for younger players, but it in no way detracts from the performances of clubs in lower divisions.

The fourth round draw made it obvious that two more Premier League teams were due to be eliminated as Portsmouth were at home to Blackburn Rovers and Bolton Wanderers entertained Manchester City. Both produced success for the visitors. Of the other six ties, Liverpool edged Cardiff City 2-1 at Anfield, Everton won 1-0 at Luton, Arsenal 3-0 at Sheffield United and West Ham 2-1 at Coventry. This left the eventual finalists Chelsea and Tottenham. Chelsea were a goal down to Leicester but with a Frank Lampard hat-trick ran out 4-2 winners while Spurs beat Blackpool 2-0.

Naturally with those clubs still having to fulfil European fixtures, the decision concerning the calibre of teams put into the field is a difficult one. Thus for the quarter-finals Arsenal travelled to Blackburn, Spurs to Manchester City and Chelsea hosted Liverpool at Stamford Bridge. The remaining tie involving Everton at West Ham had been played a week earlier because the Merseyside club had a UEFA Cup tie in Holland the week of the scheduled Carling Cup game.

Everton duly won 2-1 at Upton Park, Arsenal needed the extra period to overcome Rovers, but Spurs were 2-0 winners at the City of Manchester Stadium while Chelsea overcame Liverpool.

Thus the semi-finals arrived in early January with Chelsea playing Everton and Arsenal in a north London derby against rivals Tottenham. Unluckily for Everton it was an own goal in the dying seconds which ended in their defeat at Stamford Bridge while the Gunners found themselves needing to go to Spurs seeking victory after being held 1-1. So to the return legs and for Spurs one of their most convincing wins against Arsenal. Spurs rattled up five goals to just one in reply, while on the following day Chelsea won 1-0 at Goodison Park to wrap up their tie successfully.

For the Associate Members of the Football League they also have the Johnstone's Paint Trophy competition to offer another route towards Wembley. Appropriately perhaps the winners proved to be Milton Keynes Dons, the onetime Wimbledon club who defeated Grimsby Town 2-0 in the final exactly 20 years after their predecessors had won the FA Cup beating Liverpool. In the Northern Section final, Grimsby had beaten League newcomers Morecambe on aggregate, the losers reminding everyone of the continual progress made by teams from the Conference area of the pyramid.

CARLING CUP 2007–2008

FIRST ROUND

Peterborough U	(2) 2	Southampton	(1) 1
Accrington S	(0) 0	Leicester C	(1) 1
Barnsley	(0) 2	Darlington	(0) 1
Blackpool	(0) 1	Huddersfield T	(0) 0
Brentford	(0) 0	Bristol C	(2) 3
Bristol R	(0) 1	Crystal Palace	(1) 1

(aet; Bristol R won 4-1 on penalties.)

Bury	(0) 0	Carlisle U	(1) 1
Cardiff C	(0) 1	Brighton & HA	(0) 0

(aet.)

Chester C	(0) 0	Nottingham F	(0) 0

(aet; Nottingham F won 4-2 on penalties.)

Coventry C	(0) 3	Notts Co	(0) 0
Dagenham & R	(0) 1	Luton T	(1) 2
Doncaster R	(1) 4	Lincoln C	(0) 1
Grimsby T	(0) 1	Burnley	(0) 1

(aet; Burnley won 4-2 on penalties.)

Hereford U	(4) 4	Yeovil T	(0) 1
Macclesfield T	(0) 0	Leeds U	(0) 1
Milton Keynes D	(2) 3	Ipswich T	(1) 3

(aet; Milton Keynes D won 5-3 on penalties.)

Northampton T	(1) 2	Millwall	(0) 0
Norwich C	(5) 5	Barnet	(0) 2
Oldham Ath	(2) 4	Mansfield T	(0) 1
Plymouth Arg	(2) 2	Wycombe W	(0) 1
Port Vale	(1) 1	Wrexham	(1) 1

(aet; Wrexham won 5-3 on penalties.)

Preston NE	(0) 1	Morecambe	(1) 2
QPR	(0) 1	Leyton Orient	(0) 2
Rochdale	(0) 2	Stoke C	(1) 2

(aet; Rochdale won 4-2 on penalties.)

Scunthorpe U	(0) 1	Hartlepool U	(0) 2
Sheffield U	(2) 3	Chesterfield	(1) 1
Shrewsbury T	(0) 1	Colchester U	(0) 0

(aet.)

Southend U	(1) 4	Cheltenham T	(0) 1

(aet.)

Stockport Co	(0) 1	Tranmere R	(0) 0
Swansea C	(1) 2	Walsall	(0) 0
Swindon T	(0) 0	Charlton Ath	(0) 2
Watford	(2) 3	Gillingham	(0) 0
WBA	(1) 1	Bournemouth	(0) 0
Crewe Alex	(0) 0	Hull C	(1) 3
Wolverhampton W	(0) 2	Bradford C	(0) 1
Rotherham U	(1) 1	Sheffield W	(1) 3

SECOND ROUND

Birmingham C	(2) 2	Hereford U	(0) 1
Bristol R	(0) 1	West Ham U	(2) 2
Burnley	(0) 3	Oldham Ath	(0) 0
Cardiff C	(0) 1	Leyton Orient	(0) 0
Carlisle U	(0) 0	Coventry C	(1) 2
Charlton Ath	(2) 4	Stockport Co	(0) 3
Derby Co	(0) 2	Blackpool	(0) 2

(aet; Blackpool won 7-6 on penalties.)

Luton T	(2) 3	Sunderland	(0) 0
Milton Keynes D	(1) 2	Sheffield U	(1) 3
(aet.)			
Nottingham F	(0) 0	Leicester C	(0) 0
(abandoned due to injury to Clarke (Leicester C).)			
Peterborough U	(0) 0	WBA	(2) 2
Plymouth Arg	(1) 2	Doncaster R	(0) 0
Portsmouth	(1) 3	Leeds U	(0) 0
Rochdale	(1) 1	Norwich C	(0) 1
(aet; Norwich C won 4-3 on penalties.)			
Sheffield W	(0) 2	Hartlepool U	(0) 1
(aet.)			
Shrewsbury T	(0) 0	Fulham	(0) 1
Southend U	(1) 2	Watford	(0) 0
Swansea C	(0) 0	Reading	(0) 1
(aet.)			
Wigan Ath	(0) 0	Hull C	(1) 1
Wolverhampton W	(0) 1	Morecambe	(0) 3
(aet.)			
Wrexham	(0) 0	Aston Villa	(1) 5
Bristol C	(0) 1	Manchester C	(1) 2
Middlesbrough	(0) 2	Northampton T	(0) 0
Newcastle U	(0) 2	Barnsley	(0) 0
Nottingham F	(1) 2	Leicester C	(1) 3

THIRD ROUND

Arsenal	(0) 2	Newcastle U	(0) 0
Blackpool	(0) 2	Southend U	(1) 1
(aet.)			
Burnley	(0) 0	Portsmouth	(0) 1
Luton T	(1) 3	Charlton Ath	(1) 1
(aet.)			
Manchester C	(0) 1	Norwich C	(0) 0
Reading	(1) 2	Liverpool	(1) 4
Sheffield U	(2) 5	Morecambe	(0) 0
WBA	(1) 2	Cardiff C	(4) 4
Aston Villa	(0) 0	Leicester C	(0) 1
Blackburn R	(0) 3	Birmingham C	(0) 0
Fulham	(0) 1	Bolton W	(0) 2
(aet.)			
Hull C	(0) 0	Chelsea	(1) 4
Manchester U	(0) 0	Coventry C	(1) 2
Sheffield W	(0) 0	Everton	(0) 3
Tottenham H	(0) 2	Middlesbrough	(0) 0
West Ham U	(0) 1	Plymouth Arg	(0) 0

FOURTH ROUND

Coventry C	(0) 1	West Ham U	(0) 2
Bolton W	(0) 0	Manchester C	(0) 1
Chelsea	(2) 4	Leicester C	(1) 3
Liverpool	(0) 2	Cardiff C	(0) 1
Luton T	(0) 0	Everton	(0) 1
(aet.)			
Portsmouth	(0) 1	Blackburn R	(1) 2
Sheffield U	(0) 0	Arsenal	(1) 3
Tottenham H	(1) 2	Blackpool	(0) 0

QUARTER-FINALS

West Ham U	(1) 1	Everton	(1) 2

173

Blackburn R	(1) 2	Arsenal	(2) 3
(aet.)			
Manchester C	(0) 0	Tottenham H	(1) 2
Chelsea	(0) 2	Liverpool	(0) 0

SEMI-FINALS FIRST LEG

| Chelsea | (1) 2 | Everton | (0) 1 |
| Arsenal | (0) 1 | Tottenham H | (1) 1 |

SEMI-FINALS SECOND LEG

| Tottenham H | (2) 5 | Arsenal | (0) 1 |
| Everton | (0) 0 | Chelsea | (0) 1 |

CARLING CUP FINAL

Sunday, 24 February 2008
(at Wembley Stadium, attendance 87,660)

Tottenham H (0) 2   Chelsea (1) 1

(aet.)

Tottenham H: Robinson; Hutton, Chimbonda (Huddlestone), Zokora, Woodgate, King, Lennon, Jenas, Berbatov, Keane (Kaboul), Malbranque (Tainio).

Scorers: Berbatov 70 (pen), Woodgate 94.

Chelsea: Cech; Belletti, Bridge, Mikel (Cole J), Terry, Ricardo Carvalho, Essien (Ballack), Lampard, Drogba, Anelka, Wright-Phillips (Kalou).

Scorer: Drogba 39.

Referee: M. Halsey (Lancashire).

PAST LEAGUE CUP FINALS

Played as two legs up to 1966

1961	Rotherham U 2	Aston Villa 0	
	Webster, Kirkman		
	Aston Villa 3	Rotherham U 0*	
	O'Neill, Burrows, McParland		
1962	Rochdale 0	Norwich C 3	
	Lythgoe 2, Punton		
	Norwich C 1	Rochdale 0	
	Hill		
1963	Birmingham C 3	Aston Villa 1	
	Leek 2, Bloomfield	*Thomson*	
	Aston Villa 0	Birmingham C 0	
1964	Stoke C 1	Leicester C 1	
	Bebbington	*Gibson*	
	Leicester C 3	Stoke C 2	
	Stringfellow, Gibson, Riley	*Viollet, Kinnell*	
1965	Chelsea 3	Leicester C 2	
	Tambling, Venables (pen),	*Appleton, Goodfellow*	
	McCreadie		
	Leicester C 0	Chelsea 0	
1966	West Ham U 2	WBA 1	
	Moore, Byrne	*Astle*	
	WBA 4	West Ham U 1	
	Kaye, Brown, Clark, Williams	*Peters*	
1967	QPR 3	WBA 2	
	Morgan R, Marsh, Lazarus	*Clark C 2*	
1968	Leeds U 1	Arsenal 0	
	Cooper		
1969	Swindon T 3	Arsenal 1*	
	Smart, Rogers 2	*Gould*	
1970	Manchester C 2	WBA 1*	
	Doyle, Pardoe	*Astle*	
1971	Tottenham H 2	Aston Villa 0	
	Chivers 2		
1972	Chelsea 1	Stoke C 2	
	Osgood	*Conroy, Eastham*	
1973	Tottenham H 1	Norwich C 0	
	Coates		
1974	Wolverhampton W 2	Manchester C 1	
	Hibbitt, Richards	*Bell*	
1975	Aston Villa 1	Norwich C 0	
	Graydon		
1976	Manchester C 2	Newcastle U 1	
	Barnes, Tueart	*Gowling*	
1977	Aston Villa 0	Everton 0	
Replay	Aston Villa 1	Everton 1*	
	Kenyon (og)	*Latchford*	

Year	Team	Score	Team	Score
Replay	Aston Villa	3	Everton	2*
	Little 2, Nicholl		*Latchford, Lyons*	
1978	Nottingham F	0	Liverpool	0*
Replay	Nottingham F	1	Liverpool	0
	Robertson (pen)			
1979	Nottingham F	3	Southampton	2
	Birtles 2, Woodcock		*Peach, Holmes*	
1980	Wolverhampton W	1	Nottingham F	0
	Gray			
1981	Liverpool	1	West Ham U	1*
	Kennedy A		*Stewart (pen)*	
Replay	Liverpool	2	West Ham U	1
	Dalglish, Hansen		*Goddard*	
1982	Liverpool	3	Tottenham H	1*
	Whelan 2, Rush		*Archibald*	
1983	Liverpool	2	Manchester U	1*
	Kennedy A, Whelan		*Whiteside*	
1984	Liverpool	0	Everton	0*
Replay	Liverpool	1	Everton	0
	Souness			
1985	Norwich C	1	Sunderland	0
	Chisholm (og)			
1986	Oxford U	3	QPR	0
	Hebberd, Houghton, Charles			
1987	Arsenal	2	Liverpool	1
	Nicholas 2		*Rush*	
1988	Luton T	3	Arsenal	2
	Stein B 2, Wilson		*Hayes, Smith*	
1989	Nottingham F	3	Luton T	1
	Clough 2, Webb		*Harford*	
1990	Nottingham F	1	Oldham Ath	0
	Jemson			
1991	Sheffield W	1	Manchester U	0
	Sheridan			
1992	Manchester U	1	Nottingham F	0
	McClair			
1993	Arsenal	2	Sheffield W	1
	Merson, Morrow		*Harkes*	
1994	Aston Villa	3	Manchester U	1
	Atkinson, Saunders 2 (1 pen)		*Hughes*	
1995	Liverpool	2	Bolton W	1
	McManaman 2		*Thompson*	
1996	Aston Villa	3	Leeds U	0
	Milosevic, Taylor, Yorke			
1997	Leicester C	1	Middlesbrough	1*
	Heskey		*Ravanelli*	
Replay	Leicester C	1	Middlesbrough	0*
	Claridge			
1998	Chelsea	2	Middlesbrough	0*
	Sinclair, Di Matteo			

1999	Tottenham H	1	Leicester C	0
	Nielsen			
2000	Leicester C	2	Tranmere R	1
	Elliott 2		Kelly	
2001	Liverpool	1	Birmingham C	1
	Fowler		Purse (pen)	

Liverpool won 5-4 on penalties.

2002	Blackburn	2	Tottenham H	1
	Jansen, Cole		Ziege	
2003	Liverpool	2	Manchester U	0
	Gerrard, Owen			
2004	Middlesbrough	2	Bolton W	1
	Job, Zenden (pen)		Davies	
2005	Chelsea	3	Liverpool	2*
	Gerrard (og), Drogba, Kezman		Riise, Nunez	
2006	Manchester U	4	Wigan Ath	0
	Rooney 2, Saha, Ronaldo			
2007	Chelsea	2	Arsenal	1
	Drogba 2		Walcott	
2008	Tottenham H	2	Chelsea	1*
	Berbatov, Woodgate		Drogba	

*After extra time

JOHNSTONE'S PAINT TROPHY 2007–2008

NORTHERN SECTION FIRST

Accrington S	(2) 2	Oldham Ath	(0) 3
Chester C	(0) 1	Crewe Alex	(1) 1

(Chester C won 4-3 on penalties.)

Chesterfield	(0) 1	Hartlepool U	(1) 3
Doncaster R	(3) 5	Bradford C	(0) 1
Grimsby T	(1) 4	Huddersfield T	(1) 1
Mansfield T	(0) 0	Rotherham U	(0) 1
Tranmere R	(0) 0	Morecambe	(0) 1
Wrexham	(0) 0	Macclesfield T	(0) 1

SOUTHERN SECTION FIRST

Notts Co	(0) 0	Leyton Orient	(1) 1
Bournemouth	(2) 2	Walsall	(0) 0
Luton T	(1) 2	Northampton T	(0) 1
Nottingham F	(1) 2	Peterborough U	(0) 3
Southend U	(1) 2	Dagenham & R	(0) 2

(Dagenham & R won 7-6 on penalties.)

Swansea C	(1) 3	Millwall	(1) 2
Swindon T	(2) 4	Brentford	(1) 1
Yeovil T	(0) 1	Shrewsbury T	(0) 0

NORTHERN SECTION SECOND

Carlisle U	(2) 4	Chester C	(1) 2
Darlington	(0) 0	Leeds U	(0) 1
Lincoln C	(1) 2	Hartlepool U	(1) 5
Macclesfield T	(0) 0	Stockport Co	(0) 1
Morecambe	(0) 2	Port Vale	(2) 2

(Morecambe won 4-2 on penalties.)

Rochdale	(1) 1	Bury	(0) 3
Rotherham U	(1) 1	Grimsby T	(0) 1

(Grimsby T won 4-2 on penalties.)

Doncaster R	(0) 3	Oldham Ath	(0) 0

SOUTHERN SECTION SECOND

Brighton & HA	(1) 2	Barnet	(0) 1
Bristol R	(0) 0	Bournemouth	(0) 1
Gillingham	(1) 4	Luton T	(3) 3
Hereford U	(0) 0	Yeovil T	(0) 0

(Yeovil T won 4-2 on penalties.)

Leyton Orient	(0) 0	Dagenham & R	(0) 1
Milton Keynes D	(1) 3	Peterborough U	(1) 1
Swansea C	(2) 2	Wycombe W	(0) 0
Swindon T	(0) 1	Cheltenham T	(2) 3

NORTHERN QUARTER-FINALS

Carlisle U	(0) 0	Stockport Co	(0) 3
Grimsby T	(2) 2	Doncaster R	(1) 2

(Grimsby T won 5-4 on penalties.)

Hartlepool U	(1) 1	Morecambe	(0) 1

(Morecambe won 4-2 on penalties.)

Leeds U	(1) 1	Bury	(2) 2

SOUTHERN QUARTER-FINALS

Bournemouth	(0) 0	Milton Keynes D		(2) 2
Gillingham	(2) 4	Dagenham & R		(0) 0
Swansea C	(1) 1	Yeovil T		(0) 0
Brighton & HA	(2) 4	Cheltenham T		(1) 1

NORTHERN SEMI-FINALS

Morecambe	(1) 2	Bury		(0) 0
Stockport Co	(0) 1	Grimsby T		(0) 2

SOUTHERN SEMI-FINALS

Gillingham	(0) 1	Milton Keynes D	(0) 1

(Milton Keynes D won 5-4 on penalties.)

Swansea C	(1) 1	Brighton & HA	(0) 0

SOUTHERN FINAL FIRST LEG

Swansea C	(0) 0	Milton Keynes D	(0) 1

SOUTHERN FINAL SECOND LEG

Milton Keynes D	(0) 0	Swansea C	(1) 1

(Milton Keynes D won 5-4 on penalties.)

NORTHERN FINAL FIRST LEG

Morecambe	(0) 0	Grimsby T	(0) 1

NORTHERN FINAL SECOND LEG

Grimsby T	(0) 0	Morecambe	(0) 0

JOHNSTONE'S PAINT TROPHY FINAL

Sunday, 30 March 2008

(at Wembley Stadium, attendance 56,618)

Grimsby T (0) 0   Milton Keynes D (0) 2

Grimsby T: Barnes; Clarke, Newey, Hunt (Toner), Fenton, Atkinson, Hegarty, Bolland, North (Bore), Till (Jones), Boshell.

Milton Keynes D: Gueret; Stirling, Lewington, Andrews, O'Hanlon, Swailes, Cameron (Baldock), Navarro, Gallen (Wilbraham), Johnson (Wright), Dyer.

Scorers: Andrews 74 (pen), O'Hanlon 81.

Referee: P. Joslin (Nottinghamshire).

FA CHARITY SHIELD WINNERS 1908–2007

1908	Manchester U v QPR		1964	Liverpool v West Ham U	2-2*
		4-0 after 1-1 draw	1965	Manchester U v Liverpool	2-2*
1909	Newcastle U v Northampton T	2-0	1966	Liverpool v Everton	1-0
1910	Brighton v Aston Villa	1-0	1967	Manchester U v Tottenham H	3-3*
1911	Manchester U v Swindon T	8-4	1968	Manchester C v WBA	6-1
1912	Blackburn R v QPR	2-1	1969	Leeds U v Manchester C	2-1
1913	Professionals v Amateurs	7-2	1970	Everton v Chelsea	2-1
1920	Tottenham H v Burnley	2-0	1971	Leicester C v Liverpool	1-0
1921	Huddersfield T v Liverpool	1-0	1972	Manchester C v Aston Villa	1-0
1922	Not played		1973	Burnley v Manchester C	1-0
1923	Professionals v Amateurs	2-0	1974	Liverpool† v Leeds U	1-1
1924	Professionals v Amateurs	3-1	1975	Derby Co v West Ham U	2-0
1925	Amateurs v Professionals	6-1	1976	Liverpool v Southampton	1-0
1926	Amateurs v Professionals	6-3	1977	Liverpool v Manchester U	0-0*
1927	Cardiff C v Corinthians	2-1	1978	Nottingham F v Ipswich T	5-0
1928	Everton v Blackburn R	2-1	1979	Liverpool v Arsenal	3-1
1929	Professionals v Amateurs	3-0	1980	Liverpool v West Ham U	1-0
1930	Arsenal v Sheffield W	2-1	1981	Aston Villa v Tottenham H	2-2*
1931	Arsenal v WBA	1-0	1982	Liverpool v Tottenham H	1-0
1932	Everton v Newcastle U	5-3	1983	Manchester U v Liverpool	2-0
1933	Arsenal v Everton	3-0	1984	Everton v Liverpool	1-0
1934	Arsenal v Manchester C	4-0	1985	Everton v Manchester U	2-0
1935	Sheffield W v Arsenal	1-0	1986	Everton v Liverpool	1-1*
1936	Sunderland v Arsenal	2-1	1987	Everton v Coventry C	1-0
1937	Manchester C v Sunderland	2-0	1988	Liverpool v Wimbledon	2-1
1938	Arsenal v Preston NE	2-1	1989	Liverpool v Arsenal	1-0
1948	Arsenal v Manchester U	4-3	1990	Liverpool v Manchester U	1-1*
1949	Portsmouth v Wolverhampton W	1-1*	1991	Arsenal v Tottenham H	0-0*
1950	World Cup Team v	4-2	1992	Leeds U v Liverpool	4-3
	Canadian Touring Team		1993	Manchester U† v Arsenal	1-1
1951	Tottenham H v Newcastle U	2-1	1994	Manchester U v Blackburn R	2-0
1952	Manchester U v Newcastle U	4-2	1995	Everton v Blackburn R	1-0
1953	Arsenal v Blackpool	3-1	1996	Manchester U v Newcastle U	4-0
1954	Wolverhampton W v WBA	4-4*	1997	Manchester U† v Chelsea	1-1
1955	Chelsea v Newcastle U	3-0	1998	Arsenal v Manchester U	3-0
1956	Manchester U v Manchester C	1-0	1999	Arsenal v Manchester U	2-1
1957	Manchester U v Aston Villa	4-0	2000	Chelsea v Manchester U	2-0
1958	Bolton W v Wolverhampton W	4-1	2001	Liverpool v Manchester U	2-1
1959	Wolverhampton W v	3-1	2002	Arsenal v Liverpool	1-0
	Nottingham F		2003	Manchester U† v Arsenal	1-1
1960	Burnley v Wolverhampton W	2-2*	2004	Arsenal v Manchester U	3-1
1961	Tottenham H v FA XI	3-2	2005	Chelsea v Arsenal	2-1
1962	Tottenham H v Ipswich T	5-1	2006	Liverpool v Chelsea	2-1
1963	Everton v Manchester U	4-0	2007	Manchester U† v Chelsea	1-1

*Each club retained shield for six months. †Won on penalties.

THE FA COMMUNITY SHIELD 2007

Chelsea (1) 1, Manchester United (1) 1

aet; Manchester U won 3-0 on penalties.

At Wembley Stadium, 5 August 2007, attendance 80,731

Chelsea: Cech; Johnson (Sidwell), Cole A (Diarra), Mikel, Ben Haim, Ricardo Carvalho, Wright-Phillips, Lampard, Cole J (Sinclair), Essien, Malouda (Pizarro).
Scorer: Malouda 45.

Manchester United: Van der Sar; Brown, Evra, Silvestre (Nani), Ferdinand, Vidic, Ronaldo, O'Shea, Rooney, Giggs (Fletcher), Carrick.
Scorer: Giggs 35.

Referee: M. Halsey (Lancashire).

SCOTTISH LEAGUE REVIEW 2007–2008

If not exactly the tortoise and the hare, the Scottish Premier League title was as close enough to a photo finish as happens in the game. Rangers will claim with much justification that their involvement in European affairs and the reluctance of the SPL to allow them an easing of their ensuing fixture congestion was a contributory cause of ultimate failure. Celtic, for their part, will point to the significance of two crucial victories over their rivals in the closing weeks to justify their own success, the third in a row. Level on points on D-Day, Celtic had a better goal difference anyway, but it was academic with Rangers losing at Aberdeen.

Nine games in 23 days including the UEFA Cup final and the Scottish Cup, too, was a daunting end to the season for the Ibrox club. They were able to take the pot and couple it with the CIS Insurance Cup achieved in March, though neither matches were comfortable. Dundee United provided stiff opposition and Rangers only won the CIS on penalties, while Queen of the South battling bravely against albeit a tired Rangers outfit to claw back two goals before losing 3-2 in the Scottish Cup. Rangers had previously beaten League Cup winners St Johnstone on penalties.

However, it was Hibernian who were the last team to lose its unbeaten record, going nine matches before defeat. Their victories included a home win over Celtic and away to Rangers, too. Alas they were unable to sustain that kind of form in the following months. For Edinburgh rivals Hearts, it was worse. They even failed to make the cut when the two halves of the League split.

Motherwell and Dundee United fought for third place for much of the season, before the Fir Park outfit prevailed. Indeed Aberdeen sneaked above United after the satisfaction of inflicting the crucial defeat of Rangers.

Seventh place for Falkirk was as they had been the previous season, but Inverness Caley recovered from a slow start to finish ninth, just below Hearts. St Mirren edged Kilmarnock out of tenth place, but the heartbreak story of the season was the demise of Gretna and a sorry end to the fairy story surrounding them.

Put into administration with the deduction of ten points, bankrupt and likely to fold completely, relegation was inevitable long before these decisions and then the Scottish League decided to demote them to Division Three. The administrators subsequently pulled the plug to leave a vacancy subsequently filled by Annan Athletic.

Hamilton Academical deserved their Scottish League success, a more convincing team overall than Dundee, who still had chances to catch the leaders but invariably failed to take advantage at crucial stages. Clyde survived the challengers from Division Two after Stirling Albion's early departure. Ross County won promotion and with Gretna's situation, a lift up, too, for Airdrie United. East Fife, runaway winners of the Third Division, were originally joined by fourth place Arbroath from the play-offs who saw off Cowdenbeath and then Stranraer, the latter also given an unexpected elevation. Berwick Rangers in the toils for most of the season were another destined for the drop.

Internationally Scotland gave a more than decent account of themselves in arguably the most difficult European Championship group of any of the home countries. Having to face France and Italy was an arduous task for any opposition. Even so, Alex McLeish decided to move on and joined the Premier League in charge of Birmingham City, though this proved a short-lived acquaintance in terms of status as they were relegated. George Burley from Southampton took over.

As mentioned previously, Rangers did well to reach the UEFA Cup final having filtered down from the Champions League but their opponents Zenit St Petersburg had the luxury of having all League matches postponed to enable them to concentrate on the game in hand. Ironically, of course, Rangers' games in hand in another sense proved their undoing in the timescale available.

Celtic, despite Parkhead successes over AC Milan and Benfica, did not reach the Champions League knockout stage, Dunfermline exited early from the UEFA Cup, but Aberdeen made it to the third round before losing to Bayern Munich.

SCOTTISH LEAGUE TABLES 2007–2008

Premier League	P	W	D	L	F	A	W	D	L	F	A	W	D	L	F	A	GD	Pts
			Home					Away					Total					
1 Celtic	38	14	4	1	42	7	14	1	4	42	19	28	5	5	84	26	58	89
2 Rangers	38	18	0	1	50	10	9	5	5	34	23	27	5	6	84	33	51	86
3 Motherwell	38	9	4	6	30	26	9	2	8	20	20	18	6	14	50	46	4	60
4 Aberdeen	38	11	5	3	31	21	4	3	11	17	37	15	8	15	50	58	–8	53
5 Dundee U	38	9	6	4	26	14	5	4	10	27	33	14	10	14	53	47	6	52
6 Hibernian	38	10	5	4	34	22	4	5	10	15	23	14	10	14	49	45	4	52
7 Falkirk	38	8	6	5	21	16	5	4	10	24	33	13	10	15	45	49	–4	49
8 Hearts	38	8	4	7	27	26	5	5	9	20	29	13	9	16	47	55	–8	48
9 Inverness CT	38	9	2	8	32	28	4	2	13	19	34	13	4	21	51	62	–11	43
10 St Mirren	38	7	4	8	17	27	3	7	9	9	27	10	11	17	26	54	–28	41
11 Kilmarnock	38	7	5	7	26	23	3	5	11	13	29	10	10	18	39	52	–13	40
12 Gretna*	38	4	3	11	18	34	1	5	14	14	49	5	8	25	32	83	–51	13

Gretna deducted 10 points.

First Division	P	W	D	L	F	A	W	D	L	F	A	W	D	L	F	A	GD	Pts
			Home					Away					Total					
1 Hamilton A	36	14	4	0	29	9	9	3	6	33	24	23	7	6	62	27	35	76
2 Dundee	36	13	3	2	34	13	7	6	5	24	17	20	9	7	58	30	28	69
3 St Johnstone	36	10	7	1	38	21	5	6	7	22	24	15	13	8	60	45	15	58
4 Queen of the S	36	9	6	3	29	20	5	4	9	18	23	14	10	12	47	43	4	52
5 Dunfermline Ath	36	7	5	6	19	20	6	7	5	17	21	13	12	11	36	41	–5	51
6 Partick Th	36	7	8	3	23	15	4	4	10	17	24	11	12	13	40	39	1	45
7 Livingston	36	8	4	6	29	26	2	5	11	26	40	10	9	17	55	66	–11	39
8 Morton	36	4	5	9	22	29	5	5	8	18	29	9	10	17	40	58	–18	37
9 Clyde	36	5	3	10	22	32	4	7	7	18	27	9	10	17	40	59	–19	37
10 Stirling A	36	3	7	8	22	33	1	5	12	19	38	4	12	20	41	71	–30	24

Second Division	P	W	D	L	F	A	W	D	L	F	A	W	D	L	F	A	GD	Pts
			Home					Away					Total					
1 Ross Co	36	11	4	3	45	23	11	3	4	33	21	22	7	7	78	44	34	73
2 Airdrie U	36	11	3	4	32	12	9	3	6	32	22	20	6	10	64	34	30	66
3 Raith R	36	8	3	7	28	27	11	0	7	32	23	19	3	14	60	50	10	60
4 Alloa Ath	36	12	1	5	32	27	4	7	7	25	29	16	8	12	57	56	1	56
5 Peterhead	36	10	2	6	37	25	6	5	7	28	29	16	7	13	65	54	11	55
6 Brechin C	36	7	7	4	35	23	6	6	6	28	25	13	13	10	63	48	15	52
7 Ayr U	36	6	2	10	26	32	7	5	6	25	30	13	7	16	51	62	–11	46
8 Queen's Park	36	6	3	9	23	26	7	2	9	25	25	13	5	18	48	51	–3	44
9 Cowdenbeath	36	5	4	9	20	33	5	3	10	27	40	10	7	19	47	73	–26	37
10 Berwick R	36	2	6	10	25	42	1	1	16	15	59	3	7	26	40	101	–61	16

Third Division	P	W	D	L	F	A	W	D	L	F	A	W	D	L	F	A	GD	Pts
			Home					Away					Total					
1 East Fife	36	14	2	2	40	8	14	2	2	37	16	28	4	4	77	24	53	88
2 Stranraer	36	10	3	5	29	21	9	5	4	36	22	19	8	9	65	43	22	65
3 Montrose	36	9	3	6	31	22	8	5	5	28	14	17	8	11	59	36	23	59
4 Arbroath	36	6	7	5	24	20	8	3	7	30	27	14	10	12	54	47	7	52
5 Stenhousemuir	36	6	5	7	23	27	7	4	7	27	32	13	9	14	50	59	–9	48
6 Elgin C	36	9	2	7	35	33	4	6	8	21	35	13	8	15	56	68	–12	47
7 Albion R	36	4	7	7	29	35	5	3	10	22	33	9	10	17	51	68	–17	37
8 Dumbarton	36	7	5	6	17	19	2	5	11	14	29	9	10	17	31	48	–17	37
9 East Stirling	36	6	3	9	32	35	4	1	13	16	36	10	4	22	48	71	–23	34
10 Forfar Ath	36	6	3	9	20	26	2	6	10	15	36	8	9	19	35	62	–27	33

CLYDESDALE BANK SCOTTISH PREMIER LEAGUE RESULTS 2007–2008

Home \ Away	Aberdeen	Celtic	Dundee U	Falkirk	Gretna	Hearts	Hibernian	Inverness CT	Kilmarnock	Motherwell	Rangers	St Mirren
Aberdeen	—	1-3, 1-5	2-0	1-1, 2-1	2-0, 3-0	1-1, 0-1	3-1	1-0	2-1	1-2, 1-1	1-1	4-0, 1-1
Celtic	3-0, 1-0	—	3-0, 0-0	2-0	3-0	5-0, 3-0	1-1	5-0, 2-1	0-0, 1-0	1-1, 3-0	2-1, 3-3	2-0, 4-0
Dundee U	1-0, 3-0, 0-0	0-2	—	2-0, 0-0	1-2	3-2, 0-3	1-1, 0-3	1-0, 2-1	1-1, 2-0	5-3, 2-2	2-0, 3-1	2-1, 1-1
Falkirk	1-0	1-4, 0-1	3-0	—	2-0, 0-0	0-4, 2-0	1-1, 0-3	1-1, 0-3	1-1, 0-2	0-1	2-1, 3-3, 1-3	2-0, 1-5
Gretna	1-1	1-2, 0-3, 1-1	3-2, 0-3	1-2	—	2-1, 1-1	1-0, 0-1	0-4, 1-2, 2-3	1-0, 1-2, 4-2	1-0, 1-3, 1-2	4-2, 0-4	0-1, 3-2
Hearts	4-1	3-2, 0-2, 3-2	2-1	1-1	1-0	—	1-1	1-0, 0-1	0-2, 0-1, 2-1	0-2, 0-1, 2-1	1-3, 1-1	1-1
Hibernian	3-1, 3-3	1-2	1-1, 1-3, 1-0	4-2, 0-1	2-0, 4-2, 4-0	2-1, 0-3	—	1-0, 2-0	4-1, 2-0, 3-1	1-0, 1-2	0-3, 0-1	0-1, 2-0
Inverness CT	1-2, 3-4	1-2	2-1, 1-0	4-2, 0-1, 0-1	3-3, 1-1	0-2, 0-1, 2-1	2-1	—	2-2, 4-1, 3-1	0-1	2-2, 4-1, 3-1, 2-0	0-1
Kilmarnock	0-1, 3-1, 3-0	1-2	1-1, 2-1, 5-3	0-1	3-0	0-2, 0-1	2-1	2-2	—	0-1	0-2, 1-2, 1-1, 1-1	0-0, 1-0, 1-1
Motherwell	2-1, 3-0	1-2, 5-3	2-0	7-2, 2-0, 1-5	4-0, 4-2, 1-0	0-2, 0-1, 2-1	2-1, 1-0, 0-1	2-1, 4-1, 3-1, 2-0	0-0, 1-2, 1-0, 2-0	—	3-1, 1-0	2-0, 4-0
Rangers	3-0, 3-1	1-5	2-0, 3-1	7-2, 2-0, 1-5	1-0, 2-0	1-3, 2-0, 1-1	0-1, 2-1, 2-1	2-1, 0-1, 1-0	0-0, 3-1, 0-1	0-1, 3-1	—	2-0, 4-0
St Mirren	0-1	0-1	0-3	0-3	2-0, 1-0, 1-1	1-3, 1-1	2-1, 2-1, 2-1	2-1, 1-1	0-0	0-1, 3-1	0-3	—

IRN BRU SCOTTISH LEAGUE—DIVISION ONE RESULTS 2007–2008

Home \ Away	Clyde	Dundee	Dunfermline Ath	Hamilton A	Livingston	Morton	Partick Th	Queen of the S	St Johnstone	Stirling Albion
Clyde	—	1-2	2-1	0-2	2-1	0-1	1-2	0-0	1-0	1-3
Dundee	0-1	—	1-2	2-3	3-2	1-1	1-4	1-4	1-3	3-0
Dunfermline Ath	2-0	1-1	—	1-0	4-1	2-1	3-0	2-1	2-1	3-1
Hamilton A	1-1	1-0	0-0	—	2-0	2-0	1-0	2-3	3-2	3-0
Livingston	2-1	0-1	0-5	1-1	—	2-0	1-1	4-0	0-1	2-1
Morton	0-0	2-0	1-1	0-2	1-1	—	2-0	1-0	1-0	4-0
Partick Th	4-2	1-0	0-1	1-3	3-1	6-1	—	1-0	1-0	0-0
Queen of the S	3-2	0-2	0-2	0-2	3-1	4-0	4-2	—	2-2	4-3
St Johnstone	1-2	1-0	0-1	3-0	2-1	1-3	1-0	0-3	—	2-1
Stirling Albion	1-1	1-6	2-3	0-1	1-4	1-2	1-0	0-0	3-1	—

IRN BRU SCOTTISH LEAGUE—DIVISION TWO RESULTS 2007–2008

	Airdrie U	Alloa Ath	Ayr U	Berwick R	Brechin C	Cowdenbeath	Peterhead	Queen's Park	Raith R	Ross Co
Airdrie U	—	2-0 1-1	0-0 0-2	3-0 4-0	2-1 1-2	3-1 4-0	1-1 2-0	1-0 3-2	0-1 3-0	0-1 2-0
Alloa Ath	0-6	—	2-1 1-2	4-0 2-1	1-2 2-2	4-0 3-2	2-0 2-0	1-2 3-1	2-0 2-1	3-1 2-0
Ayr U	1-2 1-1	0-3 3-1	—	2-2 5-0	3-3 2-2	3-2 1-4	2-0 1-2	2-3 3-1	0-3 0-1	1-4 0-2
Berwick R	1-2	1-2 0-1	2-2 5-0	—	0-4 0-3	1-1 1-1	0-3 1-2	1-1 1-4	2-1 2-5	0-1 1-2
Brechin C	2-0 2-4	2-2 3-3	3-3 2-2	1-1 2-2	—	4-5 1-1	2-2 3-1	2-1 2-1	0-1 3-2	3-3 2-2
Cowdenbeath	4-2 2-1	0-2 2-2	4-5 1-1	4-3 1-2	1-0 0-2	—	0-4 0-2	2-4 1-0	1-0 1-4	2-4 1-2
Peterhead	1-1 0-1	3-1 0-2	3-0 4-1	9-2 1-0	4-2 1-0	4-2 1-0	—	1-0 1-0	0-1 1-0	1-1 3-2
Queen's Park	1-4 0-2	1-1 1-4	5-1 1-1	1-0 3-1	2-0 3-0	0-1 2-3	1-1 2-0	—	2-5 0-1	0-1 0-2
Raith R	2-1 3-2	2-1 2-5	2-1 3-0	3-1 3-0	2-3 1-1	2-0 3-2	2-2 2-5	0-2 0-1	—	0-1 2-3
Ross Co	1-1 3-2	0-2 6-1	2-0 2-4	2-1 4-0	2-1 0-0	4-1 3-0	1-0 5-1	3-2 1-1	2-3 2-3	—

IRN BRU SCOTTISH LEAGUE—DIVISION THREE RESULTS 2007–2008

	Albion R	Arbroath	Dumbarton	East Fife	East Stirling	Elgin	Forfar Ath	Montrose	Stenhousemuir	Stranraer
Albion R	—	5-2	2-0	1-4	2-3	3-4	2-1	1-3	1-1	3-2
Arbroath	1-0	—	0-1	1-1	2-2	1-1	0-0	0-3	1-1	1-1
Dumbarton	1-4	1-1	—	1-1	2-0	4-0	3-4	0-0	2-2	2-2
East Fife	2-0	2-1	2-0	—	1-0	1-0	0-0	0-0	0-1	0-0
East Stirling	4-0	0-2	2-0	0-3	—	1-4	3-0	3-1	7-0	0-1
Elgin	0-0	2-1	2-1	0-3	4-0	—	3-0	0-2	0-1	3-1
Forfar Ath	1-0	2-3	2-1	2-3	1-0	4-0	—	1-4	1-1	2-1
Montrose	2-1	3-3	3-1	0-3	3-2	3-2	2-4	—	3-4	2-3
Stenhousemuir	3-1	1-0	1-1	0-1	2-0	2-3	2-0	0-0	—	1-3
Stranraer	3-0	0-3	2-0	0-2	2-1	0-0	2-1	0-2	3-1	—

ABERDEEN   PREMIER LEAGUE

Ground: Pittodrie Stadium, Aberdeen AB24 5QH (01224) 650400
Ground capacity: 21,421 (all seated). **Colours:** All red.
Manager: Jimmy Calderwood.
League Appearances: Aluko S 10(10); Brewster C 2(1); Bus D 3(3); Byrne R 11(2); Clark C 17(1); Considine A 21(1); De Visscher J 13(9); Diamond Z 26; Duff S 6(4); Foster R 27(6); Hart M 18; Langfield J 25; Lovell S 7(15); Mackie D 13(6); Maguire C 14(14); Mair L 15(3); Maybury A 13; McNamara J 12(5); Miller L 32(4); Nicholson B 38; Severin S 33(2); Smith D 1(2); Smith Jamie 16(1); Smith Jonathan (1); Soutar D 13; Touzani K 8(6); Walker J 3(5); Young D 21(3).
Goals – League (50): Miller 12 (2 pens), Nicholson 5 (2 pens), Maguire 4, Aluko 3, Brewster 3, Diamond 3, Lovell 3, Mackie 3, Severin 3 (3 pens), Jamie Smith 3, Young 2, Clark 1, De Visscher 1, Foster 1, Mair 1, Touzani 1, own goal 1.
Scottish Cup (12): Considine 3, Jamie Smith 3, De Visscher 2, Diamond 1, Lovell 1, Mackie 1, Nicholson 1.
CIS Cup (6): Nicholson 3 (2 pens), Considine 1, Miller 1, Young 1.
Honours – Division 1: Champions – 1954-55, **Premier Division:** Champions – 1979-80, 1983-84, 1984-85. **Scottish Cup winners** 1947, 1970, 1982, 1983, 1984, 1986, 1990. **League Cup winners** 1956, 1977, 1986, 1990, 1996. **European Cup-Winners' Cup winners** 1983.

AIRDRIE UNITED   DIV. 1

Ground: Shyberry Excelsior Stadium, Airdrie ML6 8QZ (01236) 622000
Postal address: 60 St Enoch Square, Glasgow G1 4AG.
Ground capacity: 10,000 (all seated). **Colours:** White shirts with red diamond, white shorts.
Manager: Kenny Black.
League Appearances: Andreoni M 16(1); Brady C 1(3); Byrne P (1); Campbell S 7(1); Craig F 1; Donnelly R 24(1); Gillies D 1(15); Hollis L 2(1); Holmes G 17(2); Lovering P 30; McCarry M 1; McDonald K 33; McDougall S 8(9); McKenna S 29(1); McKeown S 15; McMennamin C 1(1); Noble S 29(5); Prunty B 17(15); Robertson S 34; Russell A 32; Sharp J 8; Smith D 30(2); Smyth M 28; Soutar W 1(1); Waddell R 29(3); Watt K 2(1).
Goals – League (64): Russell 19, Noble 14, McDonald 6, McKeown 6 (3 pens), Prunty 5, Watt 4, Andreoni 2 (1 pen), Holmes 2, McDougall 2, Waddell 2, Gillies 1, Smith 1.
Play-Offs (4): Russell 2, Donnelly 1, Prunty 1.
Scottish Cup (5): McDonald 1, McKeown 1, Noble 1, Russell 1, Watt 1.
CIS Cup McKenna 1.
Challenge Cup (7): Russell 4 (1 pen), Noble 1, own goals 2.
Honours – Second Division: Champions – 2003–04; **Division II:** Champions – 1902-03, 1954-55, 1973-74. **Scottish Cup winners** 1924. **B&Q Cup winners** 1995. **Bell's League Challenge winners** 2000-01, 2001-02.

ALBION ROVERS   DIV. 3

Ground: Cliffhill Stadium, Main Street, Coatbridge ML5 3RB (01236) 606334
Ground capacity: 1249 (seated: 489). **Colours:** Primrose yellow shirts, red shorts, red stockings.
Manager: Paul Martin.
League Appearances: Adam C 14; Barr R 9(1); Benton A 32; Buckley R 20; Chisholm I 15(9); Connell P (1); Dimilta D 1(6); Donald B 23; Donnelly C 23(2); Ferry D 9; Friel S 2(2); Gemmell J 20(1); Hughes C 10; Hunter R 14(3); Martin A 4(8); Martin W 6(2); McDougal J (4); McGeough J 2(3); McGowan M 18; McKenzie J 23(2); McStay J 1(2); Mitchell T 3; Reid A 26(5); Scott D 32; Smith B 7(5); Thompson L 1; Walker P 25(6); Walker R 22(5); Watson G 15(9); Wright K 19.

Goals – League (51): Gemmell 11 (2 pens), Wright 10 (2 pens), Hunter 8, Walker P 5, McKenzie 4, Barr 3, Martin W 3, Donnelly 2 (1 pen), Adam 1, Benton 1, Chisholm 1, Ferry 1, Watson 1.
Scottish Cup (9): Hunter 4, Gemmell 2, Adams 1, Martin 1, Walker P 1.
CIS Cup (2): Chisholm 1, Hunter 1.
Challenge Cup (1): McKenzie 1.
Honours – Division II: Champions – 1933-34. Second Division: Champions 1988-89.

ALLOA ATHLETIC   DIV. 2

Ground: Recreation Park, Alloa FK10 1RY (01259) 722695
Ground capacity: 3100. **Colours:** Gold shirts with black trim, black shorts with gold stripe.
Manager: Allan Maitland.
League Appearances: Agnew S 27(3); Andrew J 16(12); Barker S (1); Brown G 18(5); Buist S 22(2); Clark R 14(1); Coakley A 13(3); Coleman P (1); Creer A 2(1); Fairbairn B 2(10); Ferguson A 5(7); Ferguson B 31(2); Fleming D 22; Forrest F 26(1); Foster A (1); Grant J 26(3); Hay J 1(2); Hodge S 14(3); Jellema R 34; Kelly F 1(6); Kerr H (3); Mackie C (5); McAulay K 11(1); McClune D 20(6); McKeown S 25(4); McLeod P 1; O'Neill M (1); Scott A 9(8); Townsley C 31; Ure M ; Wilson D 25.
Goals – League (57): Brown 11 (1 pen), Ferguson B 8 (2 pens), Ferguson A 6, Grant 4, McAulay 4, Wilson 4, Agnew 3, Andrew 3, Coakley 3, Townsley 3, Buist 2, McKeown 2 (2 pens), Scott 2, Forrest 1, own goal 1.
Play-Offs (5): Coakley 1, Ferguson B 1, Forrest 1, Scott 1, own goal 1.
Scottish Cup (1): Coakley 1.
CIS Cup (1): Mackie 1.
Challenge Cup (0).
Honours – Division II: Champions – 1921-22. Third Division: Champions – 1997-98. Bell's League Challenge winners 1999-2000.

ARBROATH   DIV. 2

Ground: Gayfield Park, Arbroath DD11 1QB (01241) 872157
Ground capacity: 8488. **Colours:** Maroon shirts with white trim, white shorts.
Manager: John McGlashan.
League Appearances: Bishop J 24(1); Black R 18; Brazil A 27(4); Campbell A 13(3); Clark B 1(5); Deasley B 4(4); Fellows G 5; Ferguson S 16(1); Hegarty C 12; Hill D 17; Lunan P 8; MacKay S 1(2); Marvin P 1(1); Masson T (3); McBride S 9(3); McMullan K 29(3); Morrison S 4; Pepper J (1); Raeside R 30; Rattray A 13; Reilly A 13(13); Rennie S 10(3); Scott B 19(9); Scott D (4); Sellars B 24; Smith N 10(4); Tosh P 19(12); Tully C 23; Watson P 22(8); Webster K 9(8); Wight C 15.
Goals – League (54): Scott B 11, Sellars 8 (2 pens), Watson 7, Tosh 6, Brazil 5 (2 pens), Raeside 3, McBride 2, Webster 2, Bishop 1, Campbell 1, Deasley 1, Ferguson 1, Hegarty 1 (pen), Lunan 1, Reilly 1, Rennie 1, Smith 1, own goal 1.
Play-Offs (5): Raeside 2, Black 1, Sellars 1, Watson 1.
Scottish Cup (5): Scott B 2, Sellars 1, Watson 1, Webster 1.
CIS Cup (5): Brazil 2, Scott B 2, Sellars 1.
Challenge Cup (3): McKay 1, Reilly 1, Tosh 1.
Honours – Nil.

AYR UNITED   DIV. 2

Ground: Somerset Park, Ayr KA8 9NB (01292) 263435
Ground capacity: 10,185 (1549 seated). **Colours:** White shirts with black trim, black shorts.
Manager: Brian Reid.
League Appearances: Anderson I 5(1); Baldacchino R 4; Campbell M 12; Casey M 7(5); Corr B 5; Dunn D 14(4); Easton W 8(3); Forrest E 34; Hamilton D 7(3);

Henderson M 30(1); Higgins C 1; Keenan D 15; Kinneard L (1); Lowing D 16(1); Marshall C 4(3); McGeown M 31(1); McGowan N 16; McLaren A 3(5); McLeod P 6(7); Moore M 13(1); Pettigrew C 13(3); Robertson C 21(5); Staunton M 2; Stevenson R 33; Stewart F (1); Swift S 13; Vareille J 16(7); Wardlaw G 16(12); Weaver P 17(5); Williams A 32(2); Woodburn A 2(4).
Goals – League (51): Williams 16 (1 pen), Stevenson 15, Moore 4, Forrest 3, Wardlaw 3, Lowing 2, Swift 2, Anderson 1, Easton 1, Henderson 1, McLaren 1, McLeod 1, Robertson 1.
Scottish Cup (1): Williams 1.
CIS Cup (0).
Challenge Cup (6): Williams 3 (1 pen), Stevenson 2, Moore 1.
Honours – Division II: Champions – 1911-12, 1912-13, 1927-28, 1936-37, 1958-59, 1965-66. **Second Division:** Champions – 1987-88, 1996-97.

BERWICK RANGERS   DIV. 3

Ground: Shielfield Park, Berwick-on-Tweed TD15 2EF (01289) 307424
Ground capacity: 4131. **Colours:** Black shirt with broad gold vertical stripes, black shorts with white trim, black stockings with gold tops.
Manager: Alan McGonigal.
League Appearances: Anderson C (1); Ayre K 9; Bolochoweckjy M 12(4); Callaghan S 10; Coult L 1(6); Davison K 5; Diack I 22; Fairbairn B 13; Flockhart C 9(1); Fraser S 14(2); Gemmill S 21(6); Greenhill D 22(10); Greenhill G 2(1); Henderson R 1; Horn R 19(3); Howat A 8(3); Lennox T 11(4); Little I 25(1); Logan P 8; Manson R 9(2); McGlynn G 1; McGroarty C 12; McLaren F 4(1); McLean A 2(2); McLeish K 21(4); McMullan P 20(3); McNicoll G 6(1); Murdoch S 4; Noble S 5(2); O'Connor G 18; Smith J 15; Staunton M 3; Stevenson M (12); Swanson D 11(3); Thomson I 30(3); Tolmie B 12; Wood G 11(4).
Goals – League (40): Diack 9, Gemmill 7 (1 pen), Little 7, Greenhill D 3, Swanson 3 (1 pen), McLaren 2 (1 pen), McLeish 2, Anderson 1, Ayre 1, Davison 1, Fairbairn 1, Greenhill G 1, Thomson 1, Tolmie 1.
Scottish Cup (0).
CIS Cup (5): Bolochoweckyj 1, Diack 1, Gemmill 1 (pen), Wood 1, own goal 1.
Challenge Cup (2): Swanson 1, Thomson 1.
Honours – Second Division: Champions – 1978-79. **Third Division:** Champions – 2006-07.

BRECHIN CITY   DIV. 2

Ground: Glebe Park, Brechin DD9 6BJ (01356) 622856
Ground capacity: 3960. **Colours:** Red with white trim.
Manager: Michael O'Neill.
League Appearances: Byers K 29(2); Callaghan B 1(1); Callaghan S 17(1); Diack I 10(3); Dyer W 23(2); Fusco G 14(4); Geddes C 4(7); Gribben D 6(2); Hughes C 3; Janczyk N 18(4); Johnston M 12(3); King C 32(4); McCluskey C 1(1); McNicholl G 1; Murie D 22; Nelson A 20(3); Nelson C 35; Paton M 15(1); Rusin L (1); Russell I 4; Smith C 9(12); Smith D 35; Walker N 2(11); Walker R 16(10); Walker S 26(2); Ward J 13(1); White D 28(1).
Goals – League (63): King 10, Smith D 8, Smith C 6, Byers 4, Callaghan S 4 (3 pens), Diack 4, Paton 4, Russell 4, Gribben 2, Johnston 2, Nelson A 2, Walker N 2, Walker S 2, Dyer 1, Fusco 1, Geddes 1, Janczyk 1, Murie 1 (pen), Ward 1, White 1, own goals 2.
Scottish Cup (5): Byers 2, King 2, Callaghan 1 (pen).
CIS Cup (0).
Challenge Cup (7): Johnson 2, Russell 2 (1 pen), Janczyk 1, Nelson A 1, Smith 1.
Honours – Second Division: Champions – 1982-83, 1989-90, 2004-05. **Third Division:** Champions – 2001-02. **C Division:** Champions – 1953-54.

189

CELTIC   PREMIER LEAGUE

Ground: Celtic Park, Glasgow G40 3RE (0871) 226 1888
Ground capacity: 60,355 (all seated). **Colours:** Green and white hooped shirts, white shorts.
Manager: Gordon Strachan.
League Appearances: Balde B 4; Boruc A 30; Brown M 8; Brown S 31(4); Caddis P (2); Caldwell G 35; Conroy R 2; Donati M 22(3); Hartley P 23(4); Hinkel A 16; Hutchinson B (2); Jarosik J 6(2); Kennedy J 5(2); Killen C 2(18); McDonald S 35(1); McGeady A 35(1); McGowan P (1); McManus S 37; Miller K 1(1); Nakamura S 24(2); Naylor L 33; O'Brien J (1); O'Dea D 3(3); Perrier Doumbe 2; Pressley S 5; Riordan D 2(6); Robson B 9(6); Samaras G 5(10); Sheridan C (1); Sno E 3(9); Vennegoor J 31(1); Wilson M 8(3); Zurawski M 1(4).
Goals – League (84): McDonald 25 (3 pens), Vennegoor 15 (1 pen), Nakamura 7, McGeady 6, Samaras 5, McManus 4, Brown S 3, Donati 3, Miller 3, Robson 2 (1 pen), Caldwell 1, Hinkel 1, Jarosik 1, Killen 1, Naylor 1, Riordan 1, own goals 5.
Scottish Cup (9): McDonald 3, Vennegoor 3, Caldwell 1, Nakamura 1, Samaras 1.
CIS Cup (2): McDonald 1, Vennegoor 1.
Honours – Division I: Champions – 1892-93, 1893-94, 1895-96, 1897-98, 1904-05, 1905-06, 1906-07, 1907-08, 1908-09, 1909-10, 1913-14, 1914-15, 1915-16, 1916-17, 1918-19, 1921-22, 1925-26, 1935-36, 1937-38, 1953-54, 1965-66, 1966-67, 1967-68, 1968-69, 1969-70, 1970-71, 1971-72, 1972-73, 1973-74. **Premier Division:** Champions – 1976-77, 1978-79, 1980-81, 1981-82, 1985-86, 1987-88, 1997-98. **Premier League:** 2000-01, 2001-02, 2003-04, 2005–06, 2006–07, 2007-08. **Scottish Cup winners** 1892, 1899, 1900, 1904, 1907, 1908, 1911, 1912, 1914, 1923, 1925, 1927, 1931, 1933, 1937, 1951, 1954, 1965, 1967, 1969, 1971, 1972, 1974, 1975, 1977, 1980, 1985, 1988, 1989, 1995, 2001, 2004, 2005, 2007. **League Cup winners** 1957, 1958, 1966, 1967, 1968, 1969, 1970, 1975, 1983, 1998, 2000, 2001, 2004, 2006. **European Cup winners** 1967.

CLYDE   DIV. 1

Ground: Broadwood Stadium, Cumbernauld G68 9NE (01236) 451511
Ground capacity: 8200. **Colours:** White shirts with red and black trim, black shorts.
Manager: John Brown.
League Appearances: Albertz J 7; Arbuckle G 16(11); Bestvina D 22(1); Bradley K 17(10); Campbell I 4; Cardell J 8; Clarke P 11; Connolly S (1); Doherty M (1); Fagan S 2(1); Gibson B 12(1); Gibson J 4(3); Higgins C 32; Hutton D 36; Imrie D 19; Kirkup D 6(1); Roddy MacLennan 3(5); Ruari MacLennan 27(4); Masterton S 20(6); McCusker M (3); McGowan D 20(8); McGowan M 28(4); McGregor N 33; McKay D 7(5); McKenna S 1(7); McKeown C 16(5); McKeown T (4); McSwegan G 5(1); Potter C 4; Smith C 20(7); Thomson D (1); Traub A 1; Wilson M 15(4).
Goals – League (40): Clarke 6 (2 pens), Arbuckle 4, Imrie 4 (2 pens), Ruari MacLennan 4, Masterton 3 (1 pen), McGowan D 3, McGregor 3, McKeown 3, Albertz 2, Bradley 2, Higgins 2, Fagan 1 (pen), McGowan M 1 (pen), McSwegan 1, own goal 1.
Play-Offs (9): Clarke 3, McSwegan 2, Arbuckle 1, Gibson J 1, Gibson W 1, Masterton 1.
Scottish Cup (2): Arbuckle 1, Imrie 1.
CIS Cup (0).
Challenge Cup (2): Ruari MacLennan 1, Masterton 1.
Honours – Division II: Champions – 1904-05, 1951-52, 1956-57, 1961-62, 1972-73. **Second Division:** Champions – 1977-78, 1981-82, 1992-93, 1999-2000. **Scottish Cup winners** 1939, 1955, 1958. **League Challenge Cup winners** 2006-07.

COWDENBEATH   DIV. 3

Ground: Central Park, Cowdenbeath KY4 9EY (01383) 610166
Ground capacity: 5268. **Colours:** Royal blue with white cuffs and collar, white shorts.

Manager: Brian Welsh.
League Appearances: Adamson K 27(2); Anton C 4(2); Armstrong D 13; Armstrong J 19; Baxter M 8; Bingham D 6(2); Boyle M (1); Bryan T (1); Clarke P 10(2); Dalziel S 6(10); Deasley B 5(1); Dempster J 11(2); Docherty M 4(1); Drough D 4(2); Ferguson J (1); Galloway M 12; Gates S 12(1); Gilfillan B 22(1); Hannah D 3; Hay D 36; Hill D 26(1); Howatt A 2(8); Lennon D 2(1); Linton S 4(2); Lynch M 2; Mackle S 2(1); Manson S 3(4); Matusik O 1(2); McBride M 17(13); McCay D (1); McConalogue S 12(3); McLaughlin D 8(4); McQuade P 14(3); O'Neil J 20(10); Ramsay M 20(1); Ried J 1; Robertson J 6(4); Scullion P 26(4); Shanks C 7(4); Shields J 12; Tennerazzo G 3; Tomana M 6; Young C (1).
Goals – League (47): Clarke 6 (1 pen), McLaughlin 6, Dempster 5 (2 pens), McQuade 4, McBride 3 (1 pen), Scullion 3, Dalziel 2, Gates 2, Gilfillan 2, Manson 2, McConalogue 2, Ramsay 2, Armstrong J 1, Deasley 1, Docherty 1, Drough 1, Hill 1, Howatt 1, own goals 2.
Play-Offs (2): McQuade 1, Scullion 1 (pen).
Scottish Cup (1): Clarke 1 (pen).
CIS Cup (3): Clarke 1, Dalziel 1, O'Neil 1.
Challenge Cup (0).
Honours – Division II: Champions – 1913-14, 1914-15, 1938-39. **Third Division:** Champions – 2005-06.

DUMBARTON DIV. 3

Ground: Strathclyde Homes Stadium, Dumbarton G82 1JJ (01389) 762569/767864
Ground capacity: 2050. **Colours:** Gold shirts with black sleeves and black side panels, black shorts with three black side panels, black stockings.
Manager: Jim Chapman.
League Appearances: Brannon K 2(5); Brittain C 20(1); Campbell R 15(1); Canning M 29; Canning M 2; Coyne T 16(12); Craig D 7; Crawford D 26; Cusack L 5; Evans G 8(1); Ferry D (1); Geggan A 28; Gentile C 10(9); Hamilton C 19(9); Hasswell K 6(2); Henderson N 13; Kerr S 2(3); Lennon G 16; Mackie C 2(2); McFarlane D 10(1); McKillen R 1(1); McLaughlin J 3(1); McNaught D 6(12); McPhee B 17(6); McQuilken P 4(7); Moore M 7; Nugent A 8(1); O'Byrne M 30; Orrstarm A 6(1); Pierman F 1; Potter C 23; Russell R 21(7); Shaw P 2; Stokes M 6; Tiernan F 22(4); Wright K 1; Yule J 2.
Goals – League (31): Tiernan 6, McPhee 4, Campbell 3, Canning 3, Coyne 3 (2 pens), Hamilton 3, Geggan 2, McNaught 2, Moore 2, Brittain 1, Gentile 1, O'Byrne 1.
Scottish Cup (3): McPhee 2, MacFarlane 1.
CIS Cup (0).
Challenge Cup (2): Campbell 2.
Honours – Division I: Champions – 1890-91 (Shared), 1891-92. **Division II:** Champions – 1910-11, 1971-72. **Second Division:** Champions – 1991-92. **Scottish Cup winners** 1883.

DUNDEE DIV. 1

Ground: Dens Park, Dundee DD3 7JY (01382) 889966
Ground capacity: 11,760 (all seated). **Colours:** Navy shirts with white and red shoulder and sleeve flashes, white shorts with navy and red piping, navy stockings with two white hoops.
Manager: Alex Rae.
League Appearances: Antoine-Curier M 11; Clark B (2); Corrigan M 4; Cowan D 12; Daquin F 22(9); Davidson B 18(9); Deasley B 1; Dixon P 26(4); Griffin D 4(3); Lyle D 13(13); MacKenzie G 33; Malone E 25; McDonald K 34; McHale P 15(10); McMenamin C 12; Noubissie P 7(2); O'Brien D 9(9); Palenik M 22; Rae A (1); Robertson S 29(1); Roy L 5; Samson D 30(1); Sturm J 9(10); Swankie G 26(4); White M 1; Worrell D 21(1); Žemlik J 7(10).

Goals – League (58): McDonald 9, Antoine-Curier 8 (1 pen), Davidson 8 (1 pen), Lyle 6 (1 pen), McMenamin 6, Robertson 5, Palenik 4, Swankie 3, Daquin 2, O'Brien 2, MacKenzie 1, McHale 1, Sturm 1, Zemlik 1, own goal 1.
Scottish Cup (5): Daquin 1, McDonald 1, McHale 1, Malone 1, Robertson 1.
CIS Cup (5): Lyle 1 (pen), McDonald 1, Swankie 1, Robertson 1, Zemlik 1.
Challenge Cup (1): Sturm 1.
Honours – Division I: Champions – 1961-62. **First Division:** Champions – 1978-79, 1991-92, 1997-98. **Division II:** Champions – 1946-47. **Scottish Cup winners** 1910. **League Cup winners** 1952, 1953, 1974. **B&Q (Centenary) Cup winners** 1991.

DUNDEE UNITED   PREMIER LEAGUE

Ground: Tannadice Park, Dundee DD3 7JW (01382) 833166
Ground capacity: 14,223. **Colours:** Tangerine shirts, tangerine shorts.
Manager: Craig Levein.
League Appearances: Buaben P 20(4); Cameron G 1(2); Conway C 7(8); Daly J 3(6); De Vries M 11(3); Dillon S 33; Dods D 33; Duff S 4(5); Flood W 33(3); Gomis M 36; Goodwillie D (2); Grainger D 12(2); Hunt N 34(2); Kalvenes C 18(1); Kenneth G 14(5); Kerr M 24(6); Kovacevic M 4; McLean E 5(1); Milligan F (1); O'Brien J 5(5); Odhiambo E 1(3); Robb S 3(9); Robertson J 12(2); Robson J 22(5); Russell J 2(2); Swanson D 4(8); Szamotulski Z 18; Wilkie L 31; Zaluska L 15.
Goals – League (53): Hunt 13 (2 pens), Robson 11 (6 pens), Robertson D 6, Buaben 3, Robertson J 3, Wilkie 3, De Vries 2, Dillon 2, Swanson 2, Conway 1, Dods 1, Flood 1, Gomis 1, Kalvenes 1, Kenneth 1, own goals 2.
Scottish Cup (5): Conway 1, Dods 1, Gomis 1, Kalvenes 1, Robson 1.
CIS Cup (8): Hunt 5 (1 pen), De Vries 1, Robertson J 1, Wilkie 1.
Honours – Premier Division: Champions – 1982-83. **Division II:** Champions – 1924-25, 1928-29. **Scottish Cup winners** 1994. **League Cup winners** 1980, 1981.

DUNFERMLINE ATHLETIC   DIV. 1

Ground: East End Park, Dunfermline KY12 7RB (01383) 724295
Ground capacity: 11,780. **Colours:** Black and white striped shirt, white shorts, black stockings.
Manager: Jim McIntyre.
League Appearances: Bamba S 13(2); Burchill M 28(5); Burke A 11(2); Crawford S 28(6); Dearden S (1); Gallacher P 30; Glass S 31; Hamilton J 17(4); Harper K 1(3); Harris J 7(2); Labonte A 2; McBride S 1(2); McGlinchey M 6(2); McGuire P 1(1); McIntyre J 6(11); McKenzie R 2; McManus T 9(9); Morrison O 5(6); Morrison S 16(3); Muirhead S 12; Murdoch S 4(1); Murphy D 12; Phinn N 12(7); Ross G 1; Ryan B 7(1); Shields S 8(1); Simmons S 25(6); Thomson R ; Thomson S 22(2); Williamson I 1(9); Willis P (3); Wilson S 27(2); Woods C 25; Young D 15(1).
Goals – League (36): Burchill 11, Glass 4 (3 pens), Harper 4, Crawford 3, Hamilton 3, Simmons 3, Burke 1, McIntyre 1, McManus 1, Morrison O 1, Morrison S 1, Phinn 1, Thomson S 1, Williamson 1.
Scottish Cup (1): Wilson 1.
CIS Cup (1): Simmons 1.
Challenge Cup (9): Burchill 4, Glass 2 (1 pen), Morrison O 2, Wilson 1.
Honours – First Division: Champions – 1988-89, 1995-96. **Division II:** Champions – 1925-26. **Second Division:** Champions – 1985-86. **Scottish Cup winners** 1961, 1968.

EAST FIFE   DIV. 2

Ground: Bayview Park, Methil, Fife KY8 3RW (01333) 426323
Ground capacity: 2000 (all seated). **Colours:** Gold and black shirts, white shorts.
Manager: David Baikie.
League Appearances: Blackadder R 22(3); Cameron D 36; Davison K 3(4); Fotheringham K 34; Fox S 11; Gordon K 8(24); Greenhill G 10(3); Guy G 7(4); Linn B

24(4); Linton S 1; Martin J (4); McCulloch W 14; McDonald G 33(1); McGowan J 2; McManus P 24(3); Muir D (1); Nicholas S 5(11); O'Reilly C 12(17); Smart J 33; Stewart P 33(1); Templeman C 12(1); Tweed S 31; Walker P 6(2); Wight C 11; Young L 24(3).
Goals – League (77): McManus 17 (1 pen), Cameron 8 (4 pens), Fotheringham 7, McDonald 7, Smart 7, Linn 6, Stewart 4, O'Reilly 3, Templeman 3, Walker 3, Blackadder 2, Gordon 2, Nicholas 2, Tweed 2, Davison 1, McGowan 1, own goals 2.
Scottish Cup (4): Cameron 2 (1 pen), Smart 1, Tweed 1.
CIS Cup (2): McDonald 1, O'Reilly 1.
Challenge Cup (2): O'Reilly 1, Walker 1.
Honours – Division II: Champions – 1947-48. **Third Division:** Champions – 2007-08.
Scottish Cup winners 1938. **League Cup winners** 1948, 1950, 1954.

EAST STIRLINGSHIRE   DIV. 3

Ground: Firs Park, Falkirk FK2 7AY (01324) 623583
Ground capacity: 1880. **Colours:** Black shirts with white hoops, black shorts with white and red stripes.
Manager: Jim McInally.
League Appearances: Black C 2(2); Bolochoweckyj M 9; Brand A 30; Brown M 7; Brownlie P 16(7); Carr R 2(2); Colquhoun D 1; Donaldson C 25(4); Doyle P 14(2); Gibb S 24(1); Hill D 14; Kelly G 15(5); King D 25(2); McBride K 28(2); McBride P 5(7); McIntyre N 1; McKenzie M 12(14); McLaren G 2(1); McShane J (1); Mitchell T 1; Moffat G 12(2); Nicholls S 21(5); O'Connor G 13; Oates S 21(5); Richardson D 2; Rodgers A 13; Savage J 25(3); Simpson S 11(12); Smith A 3; Struthers K 1(5); Thywissen C 26(3); Upton S (1); Ure D 30(4).
Goals – League (48): Brand 11, Savage 10, Simpson 5, Donaldson 4, Bolochoweckyj 3, McBride K 3, Kelly 2 (2 pens), Brownlie 1, Colquhoun 1, Doyle 1, McKenzie 1, Moffat 1, Nicholls 1, Oates 1, Rodgers 1, Ure 1, own goal 1.
Scottish Cup (7): Savage 2, Brand 1, Donaldson 1, Kelly 1 (pen), Simpson 1, Ure 1.
CIS Cup (1): McBride K 1 (pen).
Challenge Cup (5): Simpson 3, Struthers 2.
Honours – Division II: Champions – 1931-32. **C Division:** Champions – 1947-48.

ELGIN CITY   DIV. 3

Ground: Borough Briggs, Elgin IV30 1AP (01343) 551114
Ground capacity: 3927 (478 seated). **Colours:** Black and white vertical striped shirts, black shorts.
Manager: Robbie Williamson.
League Appearances: Bowden M 1; Cameron B (1); Campbell C 27(3); Charlesworth M 6(6); Crooks J 7(4); Dempsie A 27(2); Dickson H 15; Dunn S 2; Frizzel C 30(6); Gibert K 25(1); Hind D 25(5); Kaczan P 29(3); Lewis A (1); Mackay S 10(2); Malin J 2; Martin W 10(1); Nicolson M 30; Niven D 14; O'Donoghue R 27(5); Ridgers A 31; Ross D 8(12); Shallicker D 18(5); Smith M 21(5); Sutherland Z 31(1); Tansley A (2).
Goals – League (56): Shallicker 12 (1 pen), Frizzel 7, Martin 5, Smith 5, Campbell 4, Charlesworth 4 (1 pen), Kaczan 4, Mackay 3 (1 pen), Sutherland 3, Crooks 2, Dickson 2, O'Donoghue 2, Nicolson 1, Tansley 1, own goal 1.
Scottish Cup (0).
CIS Cup (1): Charlesworth 1.
Challenge Cup (1): Nicolson 1.
Honours – Nil.

FALKIRK   PREMIER LEAGUE

Ground: Brockville Park, Falkirk FK1 5AX (01324) 624121
Ground capacity: 6123. **Colours:** Navy blue shirts with white seams, navy shorts.
Head Coach: John Hughes.

League Appearances: Aafjes J 23(3); Allison B 1(2); Arfield S 31(4); Arnau 13(6); Barr D 33; Barrett G 26(7); Bradley S 1(2); Clarke B 1(7); Craig L (6); Cregg P 36; Finnigan C 19(12); Higdon M 24(4); Holden D 20; Krul T 22; Latapy R 12(20); McBride K 15; Milne K 24(4); Mitchell C 3(2); Moffat K (3); Moutinho P 29(8); Olejnik R 12(1); Robertson D (1); Ross J 23; Scobbie T 29(3); Stewart M (3); Supple S 4; Thomson S 17(1); Wallner R (2).
Goals – League (45): Higdon 8, Moutinho 8, Finnigan 7, Barrett 6, Cregg 4, Arfield 3, Latapy 2, Aafjes 1, Arnau 1, Barr 1, Clarke 1, Milne 1, Scobbie 1, Thomson 1.
Scottish Cup (3): Arnau 1, Barr 1, Barrett 1.
CIS Cup (2): Higdon 1, Thomson 1.
Honours – Division II: Champions – 1935-36, 1969-70, 1974-75. **First Division:** Champions – 1990-91, 1993-94, 2002-03, 2004-05. **Second Division:** Champions – 1979-80. **Scottish Cup winners** 1913, 1957. **League Challenge Cup winners** 1998, 2005.

FORFAR ATHLETIC   DIV. 3

Ground: Station Park, Forfar, Angus (01307) 463576
Ground capacity: 4602. **Colours:** Sky blue shirts with navy side panels and shoulder/sleeve bands, navy shorts with sky blue trims, sky blue stockings with navy band on top.
Manager: Dick Campbell.
League Appearances: Allison M 3(1); Anderson C (2); Anton C 9(2); Beith G 4(3); Cruickshank A 2(3); Donachie B 15; Duell B 23(5); Dunn D 10; Fotheringham M 17(5); Fraser G 3; Fraser J 21(2); Geddes C 6(6); Grady S 6(5); Graham M 10; Kerrigan S 21(6); Kilgannon S 15(2); Lombardi M 14(5); Lumsden C 9(1); Lunan P 14; Mackie C 4(1); McCallum N 6(6); McNally S 32; Ovenstone J 32(2); Rattray A 7; Reid A 3(1); Smith E 30(3); Stephen N 13; Stuart M 16(7); Tulloch S 18(2); Watson S (2); Wood S 33.
Goals – League (35): Ovenstone 4, Stuart 4, Duell 3, Kilgannon 3, Lunan 3, Fotheringham 2, Fraser J 2, Graham 2, Kerrigan 2, Rattray 2, Anton 1, Geddes 1, Grady 1, Lombardi 1, McCallum 1, McNally 1, Smith 1, Tulloch 1.
Scottish Cup (1): Mackay 1.
CIS Cup (0).
Challenge Cup (3): Lombardi 1, Lunan 1, Tulloch 1.
Honours – Second Division: Champions – 1983-84. **Third Division:** Champions – 1994-95.

GRETNA

Ground: Raydale Park, Gretna DG16 5AP (01461) 337602. Currently playing home games at Motherwell.
Ground capacity: 2200. **Colours:** Black shirt with white hoops, black shorts with white trim.
League Appearances: Baldacchino R 4(4); Barr C 22(4); Buscher M 8(9); Caig T 7; Canning M (1); Collin A 18(1); Cowan D 10(1); Deuchar K 11(4); Deverdics N 20(5); Fisher N (1); Fleming G 28; Grady J 6(2); Graham D 2(8); Grainger D 9(1); Griffiths R 9(3); Hall D 14(1); Hogg S 4(7); Horwood E 15; Innes C 21; Jenkins A 16(4); Kissock J 10(1); Krysiak A 3(1); Makinwa H 7(6); McGill B 15(5); McGuffie R 5(4); McLaren F (3); McMenamin C 7(5); Meynell R 14(2); Murray P 31(1); Naughton K 18; Osman A 16(2); Paartalu E 3(6); Schultz-Eklund E (1); Skelton G 37(1); Taylor N (6); Wilkinson B 7(6); Yantorno F 21.
Goals – League (32): Deuchar 6, Skelton 4, Barr 3, Yantorno 3, Cowan 2, Deverdics 2, Jenkins 2, Buscher 1, Grainger 1 (pen), Hogg 1, Horwood 1, McGill 1, McMenamin 1, Meynell 1, Murray 1, Osman 1, own goal 1.
Scottish Cup (2): Horwood 1, Yantorno 1.
CIS Cup (3): Barr 1, Jenkins 1, Yantorno 1.
Honours – First Division: Champions – 2006–07. **Second Division: Champions** – 2005–06. **Third Division: Champions** – 2004–05.

HAMILTON ACADEMICAL   PREMIER LEAGUE

Ground: New Douglas Park, Cadzow Avenue, Hamilton ML3 0FT (01698) 368652
Ground capacity: 6078. **Colours:** Red and white hooped shirts, white shorts.
Manager: Billy Reid.
League Appearances: Barrau X 2(2); Cerny T 13(2); Davison K (1); Easton B 36; Elebert D 29; Evans G 1; Gibson J 4(11); Gilhaney M 24(11); Gillespie G 1; Gow G 1; Grady J 1(4); Graham D 17(3); Halliwell B 23; Kirkpatrick J (1); McArthur J 33(1); McCarthy J 27(8); McLaughlin M 33; McLeod P 1(6); Mensing S 17; Neil A 30; Offiong R 34; Parratt T 17(1); Potter B (1); Potter T (1); Stevenson T 12(4); Swailes C 14(5); Taylor S 8(5); Teggart N 1; Twigg G 2(1); Wake B 19); Wallner R 4; Waterworth A 1(9); Winters D 10(4).
Goals – League (62): Offiong 19 (4 pens), McCarthy 6, McArthur 5, Mensing 5, Stevenson 4 (2 pens), Taylor 4, Elebert 2, Gilhaney 2, Graham 2, McLaughlin 2, Winters 2, Gibson 1, Grady 1, McLeod 1, Neil 1, Swailes 1, Wake 1, Wallner 1, Waterworth 1, own goal 1.
Scottish Cup (1): McLaughlin 1.
CIS Cup (8): Offiong 2 (1 pen), Wake 2, McArthur 1, McCarthy 1, McLeod 1, Winters 1.
Challenge Cup (1): Taylor 1.
Honours – First Division: Champions – 1985-86, 1987-88, 2007-08. **Division II:** Champions – 1903-04. **Division III:** Champions – 2000-01. **B&Q Cup winners** 1992, 1993.

HEART OF MIDLOTHIAN   PREMIER LEAGUE

Ground: Tynecastle Park, Gorgie Road, Edinburgh EH11 2NL (0871) 663 1874
Ground capacity: 17,402. **Colours:** Maroon shirts, white shorts.
Manager: Laszlo Csaba.
League Appearances: Banks S 28; Basso A 7; Beniusis R 1(7); Berra C 35; Cesnauskis D 10(3); Driver A 23(2); Elliot C 14(10); Glen G 5(1); Goncalves J 23; Ivaskevicius K 8(9); Jonsson E 25(3); Kancelskis T 1; Karipidis C 15(1); Kingston L 16(2); Ksanavicius A 17(5); Kurskis E 3; Makela J 1(4); McCann N (3); McGowan R (1); Mikoliunas S 14(11); Mole J 2(4); Nade C 17(7); Neilson R 33; Palazuelos R 24(5); Pinilla M (2); Pospisil M (8); Robinson S (1); Screpis F 3(2); Stewart M 23(4); Tall I 12; Thomson J 5; Velicka A 16(4); Wallace L 16(5); Zaliukas M 21(5).
Goals – League (47): Velicka 11 (3 pens), Driver 5, Kingston 5, Nade 4, Stewart 3 (2 pens), Tall 3, Berra 2, Elliot 2, Glen 2, Cesnauskis 1, Ivaskevicius 1, Jonsson 1, Karipidis 1, Ksanavicius 1, Mikoliunas 1, Palazuelos 1, Zaliukas 1, own goals 2.
Scottish Cup (2): Cesnauskis 1, Velicka 1.
CIS Cup (8): Elliot 2, Velicka 2, Berra 1, Kingston 1, Nade 1 (pen), own goal 1.
Honours – Division I: Champions – 1894-95, 1896-97, 1957-58, 1959-60. **First Division:** Champions – 1979-80. **Scottish Cup winners** 1891, 1896, 1901, 1906, 1956, 1998, 2006. **League Cup winners** 1955, 1959, 1960, 1963.

HIBERNIAN   PREMIER LEAGUE

Ground: Easter Road Stadium, Edinburgh EH7 5QG (0131) 661 2159
Ground capacity: 17,400. **Colours:** Green shirts with white sleeves and collar, white shorts with green stripe.
Manager: Mixu Paatelainen.
League Appearances: Antoine-Curier M 8(5); Benjelloun A 5(10); Beuzelin G 25(2); Campbell R 2(3); Canning M 11; Chisholm R 13(5); Donaldson C 11(6); Fletcher S 29(3); Gathuessi T 18(5); Gray D (2); Hanlon P 5(2); Hogg C 34; Joneleit T (2); Jones R 30; Kerr B 23(3); Ma-Kalambay Y 29; McCann K 19; McCormack D 2(2); McNeil A 9(1); Morais F 19(9); Murphy D 17; Murray I 14(1); Nish C 13(2); Noubissie P 4; O'Brien A 6(17); Rankin J 15(2); Shiels D 14(8); Stevenson L 18(3); Zarabi A 7; Zemmama M 18(10).

195

Goals – League (49): Fletcher 13 (3 pens), Shiels 7 (1 pen), Zemmama 6, Donaldson 5 (4 pens), Nish 4, Antoine-Curier 3 (1 pen), Murphy 2, Rankin 2, Benjelloun 1, Gathuessi 1, Kerr 1, McCann 1, Morais 1, own goals 2.
Scottish Cup (3): Shiels 3.
CIS Cup (4): Antoine-Curier 1, Donaldson 1, Fletcher 1, Morais 1.
Honours – Division I: Champions – 1902-03, 1947-48, 1950-51, 1951-52. **First Division:** Champions – 1980-81, 1998-99. **Division II:** Champions – 1893-94, 1894-95, 1932-33. **Scottish Cup winners** 1887, 1902. **League Cup winners** 1973, 1992, 2007.

INVERNESS CALEDONIAN THISTLE
PREMIER LEAGUE

Ground: Tulloch Caledonian Stadium, East Longman, Inverness IV1 1FF (01463) 715816
Ground capacity: 7780. **Colours:** Royal blue and red shirts, royal blue and red shorts, royal blue stockings.
Manager: Craig Brewster.
League Appearances: Bayne G 9(17); Black I 31(2); Brewster C 1(1); Cowie D 35(2); Duncan R 33(1); Fraser M 36; Hart R (7); Hastings R 31(2); Imrie D 12(3); Kerr G (1); Malkowski Z 2; McAllister R 3(7); McBain R 31(2); McCaffrey S 7; McDonald D (5); McGuire P 23(1); Morgan A (3); Munro G 33; Niculae M 33(2); Paatelainen M 4(7); Proctor D 16(5); Rankin J 11(4); Tokely R 34(1); Vigurs I 1(3); Wilson B 13(12); Wyness D 19(5).
Goals – League (51): Cowie 9, Niculae 8, Wyness 5 (1 pen), Black 3 (1 pen), Duncan 3, McBain 3, Rankin 3 (3 pens), Wilson 3 (1 pen), Imrie 2, Tokely 2, Bayne 1, Brewster 1, McAllister 1, Munro 1, Paatelainen 1, Proctor 1, Vigurs 1, own goals 3.
Scottish Cup (7): Bayne 2, Niculae 2, Wyness 2, Wilson 1.
CIS Cup (0).
Honours – First Division: Champions – 2003-04. **Third Division:** Champions – 1996-97. **Bell's League Challenge winners** 2004.

KILMARNOCK
PREMIER LEAGUE

Ground: Rugby Park, Kilmarnock KA1 2DP (01563) 525184
Ground capacity: 18,128. **Colours:** Blue and white striped shirts, blue shorts.
Manager: Jim Jefferies.
League Appearances: Bryson C 16(3); Clancy T 10(1); Combe A 37; Corrigan M 7; Cox D (2); Dalglish P 3(3); Di Giacomo P 4(6); Dodds R 6(3); Fernandez D 16(13); Flannigan I 7(1); Ford S 28; Fowler J 34; Gibson W 9(14); Hamill J 29(3); Harpur C 1; Hay G 26; Invincibile D 27; Jarvis R 4(5); Johnston A 14(8); Koudou A 2(4); Lilley D 23(1); Locke G 7(10); Morgan A (3); Murray G 8(3); Naismith S 4; Nish C 20(2); O'Leary R 16(3); Skora E (1); Taouil M 19(3); Wales G 16(8); Wright F 25.
Goals – League (39): Nish 7 (2 pens), Bryson 4, Gibson 4, Wright 4, Di Giacomo 3, Fernandez 3, Invincibile 3, Taouil 2, Dodds 1, Flannigan 1, Ford 1, Hay 1, Jarvis 1, Koudou 1, Lilley 1, Murray 1, Wales 1.
Scottish Cup (3): Hamill 2, Nish 1 (pen).
CIS Cup (3): Naismith 1, Nish 1, Wright 1.
Honours – Division I: Champions – 1964-65. **Division II:** Champions – 1897-98, 1898-99. **Scottish Cup winners** 1920, 1929, 1997.

LIVINGSTON
DIV. 1

Ground: Almondvale Stadium, Alderton Road, Livingston EH54 7DN (01506) 417 000
Ground capacity: 10,005. **Colours:** Gold shirts, black shorts, white stockings.
Team Manager: Roberto Landi.
League Appearances: Craig S 20(8); Davidson M 3(3); Dorrans G 34; Fox L 28(4);

Griffiths L 13(5); Halliday A (1); Hamill J 2(2); Hottek J (1); Jacobs K 2(4); James C 26(3); Kennedy J 18; Liberda M 14; Lunn M 1; MacDonald C 7(3); MacKay D 33(1); Makel L 18; Malone C 4(2); Matthews L 4(2); McCaffrey D 28; McMenamin C 8(2); McPake J 19; Mitchell S 9; Noubissie P 5(3); Pesir T 14(6); Quitongo J (2); Raliukonis J 9; Sinclair D 2; Smith G (1); Snodgrass R 27(4); Stewart C 21; Tinkler M 18(1); Trialist ; Walker A 6(2); Weir S 3(12).
Goals – League (55): Dorrans 11, Snodgrass 9, Pesir 7, MacKay 6 (5 pens), Craig 5, Griffiths 5, Fox 3, Kennedy 2, McMenamin 2, Tinkler 2, Davidson 1, Walker 1, Weir 1.
Scottish Cup (7): MacKay 2 (1 pen), Craig 1, Dorrans 1, Jacobs 1, McMenamin 1, Raliukonis 1.
CIS Cup (7): Craig 2, MacKay 2 (1 pen), Mitchell 1, Snodgrass 1, own goal 1.
Challenge Cup (0).
Honours – First Division: Champions – 2000-01. **Second Division:** Champions – 1986-87, 1998-99. **Third Division:** Champions – 1995-96. **League Cup winners** 2004.

MONTROSE   DIV. 3

Ground: Links Park, Montrose DD10 8QD (01674) 673200
Ground capacity: 3292. **Colours:** Royal blue shirts and shorts.
Manager: Jim Weir.
League Appearances: Andreoni M 11(1); Baird J 28(6); Black S 20(4); Buchan J 13; Cumming S 19(2); Davidson H 22(3); Dobbins I 19(1); Donachie B 2(4); Doris R 21(4); Forsythe C 9; Gardiner R 31(1); Gates S 7(8); Gibson K 33; Heggerty C 8; Hunter R 5(5); Maitland J 2(8); McGowne K 3; McKenzie S 3(2); McLaren F (4); McLeod C 33; Mitchell C 5; Nicol D (1); Peat M 33; Rodgers A 8(14); Stein J 22(10); Stephen N 1; Stewart P 2(15); Thomson S 13(1); Wood G 23(1).
Goals – League (59): Baird 18 (6 pens), Wood 7, Stein 6, Doris 4, Gibson 4, Hunter 4, Rodgers 4, Andreoni 2, Black 2, Gates 2, Dobbins 1, Gardiner 1, McLeod 1, Stewart 1, own goals 2.
Play-Offs (1): Wood 1.
Scottish Cup (2): Baird 1, Rogers 1.
CIS Cup (3): Gibson 1, Stein 1, Wood 1.
Challenge Cup (6): Baird 3 (1 pen), Wood 2, Stein 1.
Honours – Second Division: Champions – 1984-85.

MORTON   DIV. 1

Ground: Cappielow Park, Greenock (01475) 723571
Ground capacity: 11,612. **Colours:** Royal blue and white hooped shirts, white shorts with royal blue panel down side.
Manager: Davie Irons.
League Appearances: Adams J ; Coakley A (2); Finlayson K 29(3); Gardyne M 3(7); Graham B 3(10); Greacen S 34; Harding R 34; Jenkins A 8(1); Keenan D 6(2); Linn B 1(2); MacGregor D 15(2); McAlister J 36; McAnespie K 10(4); McGuffie R 16(1); McGurn D 16; McLaughlin S 23(1); Millar C 23(2); Paartalu E 5; Robinson L 20; Russell I 24(6); Shields J 17(2); Smith B 5; Stevenson J 12(11); Templeman C 7(10); Wake B 4(7); Walker A 12(1); Weatherson P 33(2).
Goals – League (40): Weatherson 9, Russell 8 (3 pens), McAlister 4, Wake 4, Millar 3, Finlayson 2, Harding 2, Stevenson 2 (1 pen), Graham 1, Jenkins 1, McAnespie 1, McGuffie 1, own goals 2.
Scottish Cup (7): Finlayson 1, McAlistair 1, McLaughlin 1, Miller 1, Russell 1, Templeman 1, Weatherston 1.
CIS Cup (0).
Challenge Cup (7): Graham 2, Templeman 2, Linn 1, McAlistair 1, own goal 1.
Honours – First Division: Champions – 1977-78, 1983-84, 1986-87. **Division II:** Champions – 1949-50, 1963-64, 1966-67. **Second Division:** Champions – 1994-95, 2006-07. **Third Division:** Champions 2002-03. **Scottish Cup winners** 1922.

MOTHERWELL   PREMIER LEAGUE

Ground: Fir Park, Motherwell ML1 2QN (01698) 333333
Ground capacity: 13,742. **Colours:** Amber shirts with claret hoop and trim, amber shorts, amber stockings with claret trim.
First Team Coach: Mark McGhee.
League Appearances: Clarkson D 34(1); Craigan S 38; Daniels L 2; Fitzpatrick M 19(10); Grabban L (6); Grehan M (1); Hammell S 15; Hughes S 29(2); Kinniburgh W (2); Lappin S 7(7); Lasley K 25(7); Malcolm R 8; McCormack R 30(6); McGarry S 27(4); McHugh R (1); McLean B 6(3); Mensing S (1); Murphy D (3); Murphy J (16); O'Donnell P 15(3); Paterson J 20; Porter C 34(3); Quinn P 31; Reynolds M 38; Smith D 4(18); Smith G 36.
Goals – League (50): Porter 14, Clarkson 12, McCormack 9 (2 pens), Smith D 3, Lappin 2, McGarry 2, O'Donnell 2, Quinn 2, Hughes 1, Lasley 1, Murphy J 1 (pen), own goal 1.
Scottish Cup (4): Porter 2, McCormack 1 (pen), Smith D 1.
CIS Cup (8): McCormack 2, Porter 2, Clarkson 1, Lasley 1, McLean 1, Quinn 1.
Honours – Division I: Champions – 1931-32. **First Division:** Champions – 1981-82, 1984-85. **Division II:** Champions – 1953-54, 1968-69. **Scottish Cup winners** 1952, 1991. **League Cup winners** 1951.

PARTICK THISTLE   DIV. 1

Ground: Firhill Stadium, Glasgow G20 7AL (0141) 579 1971
Ground capacity: 13,141. **Colours:** Red and yellow striped shirts, red shorts.
Manager: Ian McCall.
League Appearances: Archibald A 27; Ardalany P (1); Buchanan L 19(3); Cameron G 3; Chaplain S 25(5); Connor S (1); Di Giacomo P 4(2); Donnelly S 8(10); Eaglesham G (2); Gibson J 4(4); Grey D 10(1); Harkins G 24(5); Hinchcliffe C 11; Keegan P 4(17); Kinniburgh W 18(1); Little R 2(1); McKeown S 13(1); McKinlay K 18(8); McStay R 12(8); Mooc V 3; Murray S 13(16); Roberts M 23(6); Robertson J 30; Rowson D 34; Storey S 31(4); Strachan A 3(1); Tuffey J 25(1); Twaddle M 32(1).
Goals – League (40): Buchanan 11 (1 pen), Chaplain 5, Roberts 5, Grey 3, McKinlay 3, Keegan 2, McKeown 2, Strachan 2, Twaddle 2, Di Giacomo 1, Donnelly 1, Harkins 1, Storey 1, own goal 1.
Scottish Cup (6): Buchanan 3, Grey 1, Roberts 1, Twaddle 1.
CIS Cup (2): Harkins 1, Murray 1.
Challenge Cup (4): Di Giacomo 1, Harkins 1, Keegan 1, own goal 1.
Honours – First Division: Champions – 1975-76, 2001-02. **Division II:** Champions – 1896-97, 1899-1900, 1970-71. **Second Division:** Champions 2000-01. **Scottish Cup winners** 1921. **League Cup winners** 1972.

PETERHEAD   DIV. 2

Ground: Balmoor Stadium, Peterhead AB42 1EU (01779) 478256
Ground capacity: 3250 (1000 seated). **Colours:** Royal blue with white shirts, royal blue shorts.
Manager: Neil Cooper.
League Appearances: Anderson S 26(3); Bagshaw A 10(18); Ballard D (1); Bavidge M 30(2); Bruce S (1); Buchan J 22(1); Cowie D 8(5); Donald D 23(3); Gilfillan B (1); Good I 11(1); Istead S 12(12); Keith M 1(1); Kelly D 3(3); Kozmanski K 11(12); Kula M 33; Leask P 1; MacDonald C 33(1); Mackay S 16(2); Mann B 32; McAllister R 4; McKay S 30(2); McVitie N 13; Monroe D 12(2); Munro H 2(3); Ross D 7(1); Sharp G 33(1); Smith S 13; Soane S 8(1); Will J 2.
Goals – League (65): Bavidge 15, Mann 12 (6 pens), McKay 8, Sharp 5, Ross 4, Anderson 3, Bagshaw 3, Kozmanski 3, MacDonald 3, Mackay 2, Buchan 1, Cowie 1, Good 1, Istead 1, McAllister 1, own goals 2.
Scottish Cup (0).

CIS Cup (1): Istead 1.
Challenge Cup (1): Cowie 1.
Honours – None.

QUEEN OF THE SOUTH   DIV. 1

Ground: Palmerston Park, Dumfries DG2 9BA (01387) 254853
Ground capacity: 7412 (seated: 3509). **Colours:** Royal blue shirts with white sleeves, white shorts with blue piping.
Manager: Gordon Chisholm.
League Appearances: Adams J (1); Aitken A 26; Atkin L 2; Bingham D 4(11); Burns P 26(2); Campbell R 1(3); Dobbie S 28(8); Gilmour B 14(10); Grindlay S 2; Harris R 26; Lauchlan J 6; MacDonald J 34; MacFarlane N 27(1); McCann R 14; McGowan N 2(1); McQuilken J 30(2); Mole J 2(6); Nixon D 2; O'Connor S 32; O'Neill J 5(18); Paton E 16(4); Reid C 8; Robertson S 9(5); Scally N 17; Stewart J 6(10); Thomson J 29(1); Tosh S 28.
Goals – League: (47): Dobbie 16 (1 pen), O'Connor 8, Burns 5, Tosh 5 (2 pens), Harris 2, O'Neill 2 (1 pen), Gilmour 1, MacFarlane 1, McQuilken 1, Scally 1, Stewart 1, Thomson 1, own goals 3.
Scottish Cup (19): O'Connor 5, Dobbie 4, Burns 2, Stewart 2, Thomson 2, Tosh 2, McCann 1, own goal 1.
CIS Cup (0).
Challenge Cup (0).
Honours – Division II: Champions – 1950-51. **Second Division:** Champions – 2001-02.
Challenge Cup winners 2003

QUEEN'S PARK   DIV. 2

Ground: Hampden Park, Glasgow G42 9BA (0141) 632 1275
Ground capacity: 52,000. **Colours:** Black and white hooped shirts, white shorts.
Coach: Billy Stark.
League Appearances: Agostini D 30; Boslen A 1(1); Bowers R 2(7); Brough J 4(1); Cairney P 35; Cairns M 18; Canning S 27(3); Cowie A 12; Dunlop M 25; Dunn R 9(9); Ferry M 34; Kettlewell S 27(1); McGrady S 17(15); Molloy S 6(5); Murray S 5(1); Neill J 11; Paton R 34; Quinn T 18(10); Reilly S 11(3); Ronald P 10(10); Sinclair R 17; Terry Z 1; Torrence D (3); Trouten A 33; Ure M 9(2).
Goals – League: (48): Trouten 12 (7 pens), Ferry 9, Cairney 7, Canning 5, Kettlewell 4, Quinn 4, Dunn 2, McGrady 2, Sinclair 1, own goals 2.
Scottish Cup (3): Ferry 2, Trouten 1.
CIS Cup (3): Canning 1, Dunlop 1, Trouten 1.
Challenge Cup (1): Canning 1.
Second Division: Champions – 1980-81. **Third Division:** Champions – 1999-2000.
Scottish Cup winners 1874, 1875, 1876, 1880, 1881, 1882, 1884, 1886, 1890, 1893.

RAITH ROVERS   DIV. 2

Ground: Stark's Park, Pratt Street, Kirkcaldy KY1 1SA (01592) 263514
Ground capacity: 10,104 (all seated). **Colours:** Navy blue shirts with white sleeves, white shorts with navy blue and red edges.
Manager: John McGlynn.
League Appearances: Andrews M 19; Borris R 19(8); Brown M 1; Bryce L (4); Campbell M 25(1); Carcary D 7(21); Darling J (2); Davidson I 30; Dingwall J 17(2); Fahey C 19(1); Goodwillie D 20(1); Helley J (4); Henderson N 11(3); Hislop S 28(6); Lumsden T 7(2); Main D 1; Pelosi M 19; Renton K 16(1); Silvestro C 17(1); Sloan R 30(4); Templeton G 15; Tod A 17(7); Walker A 6(1); Watley M (1); Weir G 20(11); Wilson C 36; Winter C 16(10).
Goals – League: (60): Weir 10 (2 pens), Goodwillie 9 (1 pen), Hislop 9 (2 pens), Sloan 7, Andrews 4, Carcary 4, Templeton 4, Davidson 3, Bryce 2, Campbell 2, Tod 2, Borris 1, Silvestro 1, own goals 2.

Play-Offs (2): Weir 2 (1 pen).
Scottish Cup (6): Carcary 2, Hislop 2, Davidson 1, Weir 1.
CIS Cup (4): Carcary 2, Tod 1, Weir 1.
Challenge Cup (1): Tod 1.
Honours – First Division: Champions – 1992-93, 1994-95. **Second Division:** Champions – 2002-03. **Division II:** Champions – 1907-08, 1909-10 (Shared), 1937-38, 1948-49.
League Cup winners 1995.

RANGERS   PREMIER LEAGUE

Ground: Ibrox Stadium, Glasgow G51 2XD 0871 7021972
Ground capacity: 51,082. **Colours:** Royal blue shirts with red and white trim, white shorts with blue and red trim.
Manager: Walter Smith
League Appearances: Adam C 12(4); Alexander N 7(1); Beasley D 8(3); Boyd K 17(11); Broadfoot K 14(1); Buffel T (1); Burke C 10(1); Cousin D 20(6); Cuellar C 36; Dailly C 12(1); Darcheville J 14(16); Davis S 11(1); Faye A 2(2); Ferguson B 37(1); Fleck J (1); Furman D (1); Hemdani B 12; Hutton A 20; McCulloch L 19(3); McGregor A 31; Naismith S 12(9); Novo N 10(18); Papac S 22; Thomson K 25(1); Webster A 1; Weir D 37; Whittaker S 29(1).
Goals – League (84): Boyd 14 (2 pens), Darcheville 12, Cousin 10 (2 pens), Novo 10 (1 pen), Ferguson 7, Naismith 5, Cuellar 4, Whittaker 4, Adam 2, Beasley 2, Burke 2, Dailly 2, McCulloch 2, Weir 2, Broadfoot 1, Thomson 1, Webster 1, own goals 3.
Scottish Cup (14): Boyd 6 (1 pen), Burke 2, McCulloch 2, Novo 2 (1 pen), Beasley 1, Hutton 1.
CIS Cup (10): Boyd 5 (1 pen), Novo 2, Cuellar 1, Darcheville 1, Ferguson 1.
Honours – Division I: Champions – 1890-91 (Shared), 1898-99, 1899-1900, 1900-01, 1901-02, 1910-11, 1911-12, 1912-13, 1917-18, 1919-20, 1920-21, 1922-23, 1923-24, 1924-25, 1926-27, 1927-28, 1928-29, 1929-30, 1930-31, 1932-33, 1933-34, 1934-35, 1936-37, 1938-39, 1946-47, 1948-49, 1949-50, 1952-53, 1955-56, 1956-57, 1958-59, 1960-61, 1962-63, 1963-64, 1974-75. **Premier Division:** Champions – 1975-76, 1977-78, 1986-87, 1988-89, 1989-90, 1990-91, 1991-92, 1992-93, 1993-94, 1994-95, 1995-96, 1996-97. **Premier League:** Champions – 1998-99, 1999-2000, 2002-03, 2004-05. **Scottish Cup winners** 1894, 1897, 1898, 1903, 1928, 1930, 1932, 1934, 1935, 1936, 1948, 1949, 1950, 1953, 1960, 1962, 1963, 1964, 1966, 1973, 1976, 1978, 1979, 1981, 1992, 1993, 1996, 1999, 2000, 2002, 2003, 2008. **League Cup winners** 1947, 1949, 1961, 1962, 1964, 1965, 1971, 1976, 1978, 1979, 1982, 1984, 1985, 1987, 1988, 1989, 1991, 1993, 1994, 1997, 1999, 2002, 2003, 2005, 2008. **European Cup-Winners' Cup winners** 1972.

ROSS COUNTY   DIV. 1

Ground: Victoria Park, Dingwall IV15 9QW (01349) 860860
Ground capacity: 6700. **Colours:** Navy blue with white and red pin stripe on collar and sleeves, white shorts with navy and red side stripe, navy stockings.
Manager: Derek Adam
League Appearances: Adams D 11; Anderson I 3(4); Barrowman A 32(1); Boyd S 21(2); Brady D 14(3); Bullock T 24; Campbell I 10; Creer A 4; Dowie A 33(1); Gardyne M 9(7); Girvan G 2; Golabek S 26; Grant R (1); Gunn C 2(13); Higgins S 23(11); Keddie A 27(1); Lawson P 24; Malin J 8; McCulloch M 30; Miller G 19(1); Moore D 7(12); Niven D (1); Petrie S 15(9); Robertson H (4); Sancho B 2; Scott M 21(10); Shields D 17(8); Strachan A 10(8); Winters D 2(4).
Goals – League (78): Barrowman 24 (2 pens), Higgins 10, Petrie 8, Shields 6, Gardyne 4, Keddie 3, Scott 3, Adams 2, Dowie 2, Golabek 2, Lawson 2, Moore 2, Winters 2, Anderson 1, Boyd 1, Brady 1, McCulloch 1, Strachan 1, own goals 3.
Scottish Cup (14): Shields 4, Barrowman 2 (1 pen), Dowie 2, Higgins 2, Boyd 1, Golabek 1, Keddie 1, Scott 1.
CIS Cup (4): Barrowman 3, Dowie 1.
Challenge Cup (2): Barrowman 1 (pen), Keddie 1.

Honours – **Second Division:** Champions – 2007-08. **Third Division:** Champions – 1998-99. **League Challenge Cup:** Winners – 2007.

ST JOHNSTONE   DIV. 1

Ground: McDiarmid Park, Crieff Road, Perth PH1 2SJ (01738) 459090
Ground capacity: 10,673. **Colours:** Royal blue shirts with white trim, white shorts.
Manager: Derek McInnes.
League Appearances: Anderson S 27(1); Cameron G 4(1); Craig L 19; Cuthbert K 2; Daal D 3(5); Deuchar K 10; Dyer W 1; Fairbairn J 1; Hardie M 6(2); Irvine G 33; Jackson A 26(8); James K 4(1); Kerr S 1(1); Lawrie A 4(3); Lynch S 1; MacDonald P 22(11); Main A 34; McBreen D 3(3); McCaffrey S 1; McCluskey J 1(3); McInnes D 14; McLaren W 6(1); McManus A 29(2); Milne S 17(5); Monaghan A 1; Moon K 8(12); Morris J 4(1); Quinn R 20(1); Rutkiewicz K 20; Sheerin P 33(3); Stanic G 29; Stewart J 4(4); Weatherston D 9(18); Wilson B 2(4).
Goals – League (60): Jackson 14, Sheerin 9 (8 pens), Milne 7, Deuchar 6, MacDonald 5 (1 pen), Quinn 4, Moon 3, Craig 2, Hardie 2, James 2, McCaffrey 1, McManus 1, Morris 1, Rutkiewicz 1, Stewart 1, Wilson 1.
Scottish Cup (9): Craig 2 (1 pen), Jackson 2, McBreen 1, MacDonald 1, Milne 1, Quinn 1, Sheerin 1 (pen).
CIS Cup (0).
Challenge Cup (13): Deuchar 4, Jackson 3, MacDonald 2, Sheerin 2 (2 pens), Quinn 1, Weatherson 1.
Honours – First Division: Champions – 1982-83, 1989-90, 1996-97. **Division II:** Champions – 1923-24, 1959-60, 1962-63. **League Challenge Cup:** Winners – 2008.

ST MIRREN   PREMIER LEAGUE

Ground: St Mirren Park, Paisley PA3 2EJ (0141) 889 2558
Ground capacity: 10,476 (all seated). **Colours:** Black and white striped shirts, white shorts with black trim.
Manager: Gus MacPherson.
League Appearances: Barron D 18; Birchall C 5(4); Brady G 16(2); Brittain R 2(4); Burke A 7(3); Corcoran M 18(8); Dargo C 15(1); Docherty M (1); Dorman A 18; Haining W 29; Hamilton J 7(8); Howard M 10; Kean S 15(17); Mason G 31; Maxwell I 17; McAusland M (1); McCay R 10(2); McGinn S 10(15); Mehmet B 32(5); Millen A 8(1); Miranda F 20(4); Molloy C (5); Murray H 27(2); O'Donnell S 5(5); Potter J 31; Reid A 10(2); Smith C 28; Van Zanten D 29.
Goals – League (26): Mehmet 6, Corcoran 3, Dorman 3, Maxwell 3, Mason 2, McGinn 2, Miranda 2, Dargo 1, Haining 1, Hamilton 1, Kean 1, McCay 1.
Scottish Cup (6): Dorman 2, Mehmet 2 (1 pen), Barron 1, Corcoran 1.
CIS Cup (0).
Honours – First Division: Champions – 1976-77, 1999-2000, 2005-06. **Division II:** Champions – 1967-68. **Scottish Cup winners** 1926, 1959, 1987.
League Challenge Cup: Winners – 2005-06.

STENHOUSEMUIR   DIV. 3

Ground: Ochilview Park, Stenhousemuir FK5 4QL (01324) 562992
Ground capacity: 3746. **Colours:** Maroon shirts with dark blue trim, white shorts.
Manager: John Coughlin.
League Appearances: Brown A 24; Dalziel S 15; Dempster J 17; Desmond S 1(3); Dillon J 18(4); Felvus B (1); Ferguson S 17(2); Flynn M 2; Galloway R 6(1); Gibson G 13(5); Gilbride A 30(1); Hamilton R 15(10); Hampshire S 19(4); Harty I 8(1); Hillcoat J 11; Johnstone S 1; Lennon G 10; Lindsay A 6(3); Lister J 1; Love R 2(2); Lyle W 30(2); Mailey P 12; McCulloch S 9(1); McEwan C 31(3); McKeown J 1; McLaughlin B 14(9); McManus S 2(4); Menzies C 8(13); Murdoch T 6(4); Quitongo J 3(7); Sideserf M 1; Smith J 17; Stewart M (1); Thom G 5(2); Thomson A 6(2); Tyrrell P 35.

Goals – League (50): Dalziel 9 (2 pens), Dempster 7 (5 pens), Ferguson 5, Harty 4 (1 pen), Dillon 3, Hampshire 3, Love 3, Lyle 3, Tyrrell 3, Gilbride 2, Thomson 2, Desmond 1, Gibson 1, Hamilton 1, Mailey 1, McEwan 1, McLaughlin 1.
Scottish Cup (0).
CIS Cup (1): Lyle 1.
Challenge Cup (1): Dempster 1.
Honours – League Challenge Cup: Winners – 1996.

STIRLING ALBION   DIV. 2

Ground: Forthbank Stadium, Springkerse Industrial Estate, Stirling FK7 7UJ (01786) 450399
Ground capacity: 3808. **Colours:** All red.
Manager: Allan Moore.
League Appearances: Aitken C 32(2); Allison B 3; Bell S 26(1); Christie S 12; Churchill G (1); Corr L (2); Cramb C 10(13); Devine S 13(4); Easton W 6(1); Ellis L 33; Forsyth R 18; Graham A 26; Gribben D 1(2); Harris R 11(6); Hay C 9(5); Hogarth M 24; Lilley D 12(12); Lithgow A 2(1); Malloy C 5; McBride J 14(5); McKay R 4; McKenna D 30(5); Moffat K (3); Muir G 1(5); Murphy P 8(2); Nugent P 31; Paartalu E 10; Reid C 13; Rodriguez J 10(1); Taggart N 24(6); Tomana M 2(11); Walker N 6(3).
Goals – League (41): Aitken 13 (8 pens), McKenna 7, Bell 6, Cramb 4, Rodriguez 3, McBride 2, Allison 1, Easton 1, Ellis 1, Paartalu 1, Taggart 1, own goal 1.
Scottish Cup (6): Aitken 2 (1 pen), Walker 2, Cramb 1, McKenna 1.
CIS Cup (1): McKenna 1.
Challenge Cup (1): Harris 1.
Honours – Division II: Champions – 1952-53, 1957-58, 1960-61, 1964-65. **Second Division:** Champions – 1976-77, 1990-91, 1995-96.

STRANRAER   DIV. 2

Ground: Stair Park, Stranraer DG9 8BS (01776) 703271
Ground capacity: 5600. **Colours:** Blue shirts with white side panels, blue shorts with white side panels.
Manager: Derek Ferguson.
League Appearances: Beggs S (1); Black S 32; Bonar S 22; Caddis R (5); Cashmore I 8(21); Coakley A 1(3); Cochrane J (9); Creaney J 9(3); Dobbins I 13; Ferguson A 4(1); Gibson A 33(1); Gillies R 5(1); Gribben D 3(6); Kane J 28(3); Keogh P 3(2); McColm S 5(5); McConalogue S 12(3); McCusker M 3(4); McGowan N 8; McKinstry J 29(2); McLaughlin G 26(3); McLoughlin J (1); Mitchell D 31; Mullen M 28(4); Nicoll K 2(3); Noble S 14(2); Paddy G 2; Paisley R (1); Payne S 1; Stewart M 8; Tade G 31(1); Thomson M 5(1); White A 30(5).
Goals – League (65): Mullen 13, Tade 12, Gibson 6 (2 pens), Stewart 6, Mitchell 5, Cashmore 3, McConalogue 3, White 3, Gillies 2 (1 pen), McColm 2, Nicoll 2, Bonar 1, Cochrane 1, Dobbins 1, Kane 1, Keogh 1, McKinstry 1, own goals 2.
Play-Offs (5): Tade 2, Gibson 1 (pen), McConalogue 1, Mullen 1.
Scottish Cup (2): Keogh 1 (pen), Tade 1.
CIS Cup (1): Keogh 1.
Challenge Cup (0).
Honours – Second Division: Champions – 1993-94, 1997-98. **Third Division:** Champions – 2003–04. **League Challenge Cup winners** 1997.

ANNAN ATHLETIC   DIV. 3

Ground: Galabank, North Street, Annan (01461) 204108
Ground capacity: 3500 (500 seated). **Colours:** Black and gold striped shirts, black shorts.
Manager: Harry Cairney.

SCOTTISH LEAGUE HONOURS

*On goal average (ratio)/difference. †Held jointly after indecisive play-off.
‡Won on deciding match. ††Held jointly. ¶Two points deducted for fielding ineligible
player. Competition suspended 1940–45 during war; Regional Leagues operating.
‡‡Two points deducted for registration irregularities. §Not promoted after play-offs.

PREMIER LEAGUE

Maximum points: 108

	First	Pts	Second	Pts	Third	Pts
1998–99	Rangers	77	Celtic	71	St Johnstone	57
1999–00	Rangers	90	Celtic	69	Hearts	54

Maximum points: 114

2000–01	Celtic	97	Rangers	82	Hibernian	66
2001–02	Celtic	103	Rangers	85	Livingston	58
2002–03	Rangers*	97	Celtic	97	Hearts	63
2003–04	Celtic	98	Rangers	81	Hearts	68
2004–05	Rangers	93	Celtic	92	Hibernian*	61
2005–06	Celtic	91	Hearts	74	Rangers	73
2006–07	Celtic	84	Rangers	72	Aberdeen	65
2007–08	Celtic	89	Rangers	86	Motherwell	60

PREMIER DIVISION

Maximum points: 72

1975–76	Rangers	54	Celtic	48	Hibernian	43
1976–77	Celtic	55	Rangers	46	Aberdeen	43
1977–78	Rangers	55	Aberdeen	53	Dundee U	40
1978–79	Celtic	48	Rangers	45	Dundee U	44
1979–80	Aberdeen	48	Celtic	47	St Mirren	42
1980–81	Celtic	56	Aberdeen	49	Rangers*	44
1981–82	Celtic	55	Aberdeen	53	Rangers	43
1982–83	Dundee U	56	Celtic*	55	Aberdeen	55
1983–84	Aberdeen	57	Celtic	50	Dundee U	47
1984–85	Aberdeen	59	Celtic	52	Dundee U	47
1985–86	Celtic*	50	Hearts	50	Dundee U	47

Maximum points: 88

1986–87	Rangers	69	Celtic	63	Dundee U	60
1987–88	Celtic	72	Hearts	62	Rangers	60

Maximum points: 72

1988–89	Rangers	56	Aberdeen	50	Celtic	46
1989–90	Rangers	51	Aberdeen*	44	Hearts	44
1990–91	Rangers	55	Aberdeen	53	Celtic*	41

Maximum points: 88

1991–92	Rangers	72	Hearts	63	Celtic	62
1992–93	Rangers	73	Aberdeen	64	Celtic	60
1993–94	Rangers	58	Aberdeen	55	Motherwell	54

Maximum points: 108

1994–95	Rangers	69	Motherwell	54	Hibernian	53
1995–96	Rangers	87	Celtic	83	Aberdeen*	55
1996–97	Rangers	80	Celtic	75	Dundee U	60
1997–98	Celtic	74	Rangers	72	Hearts	67

DIVISION 1

Maximum points: 52

1975–76	Partick Th	41	Kilmarnock	35	Montrose	30

1976–77	St Mirren	62	Clydebank	58	Dundee	51
1977–78	Morton*	58	Hearts	58	Dundee	57
1978–79	Dundee	55	Kilmarnock*	54	Clydebank	54
1979–80	Hearts	53	Airdrieonians	51	Ayr U*	44
1980–81	Hibernian	57	Dundee	52	St Johnstone	51
1981–82	Motherwell	61	Kilmarnock	51	Hearts	50
1982–83	St Johnstone	55	Hearts	54	Clydebank	50
1983–84	Morton	54	Dumbarton	51	Partick Th	46
1984–85	Motherwell	50	Clydebank	48	Falkirk	45
1985–86	Hamilton A	56	Falkirk	45	Kilmarnock	44

1986–87	Morton	57	Dunfermline Ath	56	Dumbarton	53
1987–88	Hamilton A	56	Meadowbank Th	52	Clydebank	49

1988–89	Dunfermline Ath	54	Falkirk	52	Clydebank	48
1989–90	St Johnstone	58	Airdrieonians	54	Clydebank	44
1990–91	Falkirk	54	Airdrieonians	53	Dundee	52

1991–92	Dundee	58	Partick Th*	57	Hamilton A	57
1992–93	Raith R	65	Kilmarnock	54	Dunfermline Ath	52
1993–94	Falkirk	66	Dunfermline Ath	65	Airdrieonians	54

1994–95	Raith R	69	Dunfermline Ath*	68	Dundee	68
1995–96	Dunfermline Ath	71	Dundee U*	67	Morton	67
1996–97	St Johnstone	80	Airdrieonians	60	Dundee*	58
1997–98	Dundee	70	Falkirk	65	Raith R*	60
1998–99	Hibernian	89	Falkirk	66	Ayr U	62
1999–00	St Mirren	76	Dunfermline Ath	71	Falkirk	68
2000–01	Livingston	76	Ayr U	69	Falkirk	56
2001–02	Partick Th	66	Airdrieonians	56	Ayr U	52
2002–03	Falkirk	81	Clyde	72	St Johnstone	67
2003–04	Inverness CT	70	Clyde	69	St Johnstone	57
2004–05	Falkirk	75	St Mirren*	60	Clyde	60
2005–06	St Mirren	76	St Johnstone	66	Hamilton A	59
2006–07	Gretna	66	St Johnstone	65	Dundee*	53
2007–08	Hamilton A	76	Dundee	69	St Johnstone	58

DIVISION 2

1975–76	Clydebank*	40	Raith R	40	Alloa Ath	35

1976–77	Stirling A	55	Alloa Ath	51	Dunfermline Ath	50
1977–78	Clyde*	53	Raith R	53	Dunfermline Ath	48
1978–79	Berwick R	54	Dunfermline Ath	52	Falkirk	50
1979–80	Falkirk	50	East Stirling	49	Forfar Ath	46
1980–81	Queen's Park	50	Queen of the S	46	Cowdenbeath	45
1981–82	Clyde	59	Alloa Ath*	50	Arbroath	50
1982–83	Brechin C	55	Meadowbank Th	54	Arbroath	49
1983–84	Forfar Ath	63	East Fife	47	Berwick R	43
1984–85	Montrose	53	Alloa Ath	50	Dunfermline Ath	49
1985–86	Dunfermline Ath	57	Queen of the S	55	Meadowbank Th	49
1986–87	Meadowbank Th	55	Raith R*	52	Stirling A*	52
1987–88	Ayr U	61	St Johnstone	59	Queen's Park	51
1988–89	Albion R	50	Alloa Ath	45	Brechin C	43

1989–90	Brechin C	49	Kilmarnock	48	Stirling A	47
1990–91	Stirling A	54	Montrose	46	Cowdenbeath	45
1991–92	Dumbarton	52	Cowdenbeath	51	Alloa Ath	50
1992–93	Clyde	54	Brechin C*	53	Stranraer	53
1993–94	Stranraer	56	Berwick R	48	Stenhousemuir*	47

Maximum points: 108

1994–95	Morton	64	Dumbarton	60	Stirling A	58
1995–96	Stirling A	81	East Fife	67	Berwick R	60
1996–97	Ayr U	77	Hamilton A	74	Livingston	64
1997–98	Stranraer	61	Clydebank	60	Livingston	59
1998–99	Livingston	77	Inverness CT	72	Clyde	53
1999–00	Clyde	65	Alloa Ath	64	Ross County	62
2000–01	Partick Th	75	Arbroath	58	Berwick R*	54
2001–02	Queen of the S	67	Alloa Ath	59	Forfar Ath	53
2002–03	Raith R	59	Brechin C	55	Airdrie U	54
2003–04	Airdrie U	70	Hamilton A	62	Dumbarton	60
2004–05	Brechin C	72	Stranraer	63	Morton	62
2005–06	Gretna	88	Morton§	70	Peterhead*§	57
2006–07	Morton	77	Stirling A	69	Raith R§	62
2007–08	Ross Co	73	Airdrie U	66	Raith R§	60

DIVISION 3
Maximum points: 108

1994–95	Forfar Ath	80	Montrose	67	Ross Co	60
1995–96	Livingston	72	Brechin C	63	Caledonian T	57
1996–97	Inverness CT	76	Forfar Ath*	67	Ross Co	67
1997–98	Alloa Ath	76	Arbroath	68	Ross Co*	67
1998–99	Ross Co	77	Stenhousemuir	64	Brechin C	59
1999–00	Queen's Park	69	Berwick R	66	Forfar Ath	61
2000–01	Hamilton A*	76	Cowdenbeath	76	Brechin C	72
2001–02	Brechin C	73	Dumbarton	61	Albion R	59
2002–03	Morton	72	East Fife	71	Albion R	70
2003–04	Stranraer	79	Stirling A	77	Gretna	68
2004–05	Gretna	98	Peterhead	78	Cowdenbeath	51
2005–06	Cowdenbeath*	76	Berwick R§	76	Stenhousemuir§	73
2006–07	Berwick R	75	Arbroath§	70	Queen's Park	68
2007–08	East Fife	88	Stranraer	65	Montrose§	59

DIVISION 1 to 1974–75
Maximum points: a 36; b 44; c 40; d 52; e 60; f 68; g 76; h 84.

	First	Pts	Second	Pts	Third	Pts
1890–91a	Dumbarton††	29	Rangers††	29	Celtic	21
1891–92b	Dumbarton	37	Celtic	35	Hearts	34
1892–93a	Celtic	29	Rangers	29	St Mirren	20
1893–94a	Celtic	29	Hearts	26	St Bernard's	23
1894–95a	Hearts	31	Celtic	26	Rangers	22
1895–96a	Celtic	30	Rangers	26	Hibernian	24
1896–97a	Hearts	28	Hibernian	26	Rangers	25
1897–98a	Celtic	33	Rangers	29	Hibernian	22
1898–99a	Rangers	36	Hearts	26	Celtic	24
1899–1900a	Rangers	32	Celtic	25	Hibernian	24
1900–01c	Rangers	35	Celtic	29	Hibernian	25
1901–02a	Rangers	28	Celtic	26	Hearts	22
1902–03b	Hibernian	37	Dundee	31	Rangers	29
1903–04d	Third Lanark	43	Hearts	39	Celtic*	38
1904–05d	Celtic‡	41	Rangers	41	Third Lanark	35
1905–06e	Celtic	49	Hearts	43	Airdrieonians	38

1906–07*f*	Celtic	55	Dundee	48	Rangers	45
1907–08*f*	Celtic	55	Falkirk	51	Rangers	50
1908–09*f*	Celtic	51	Dundee	50	Clyde	48
1909–10*f*	Celtic	54	Falkirk	52	Rangers	46
1910–11*f*	Rangers	52	Aberdeen	48	Falkirk	44
1911–12*f*	Rangers	51	Celtic	45	Clyde	42
1912–13*f*	Rangers	53	Celtic	49	Hearts*	41
1913–14*g*	Celtic	65	Rangers	59	Hearts*	54
1914–15*g*	Celtic	65	Hearts	61	Rangers	50
1915–16*g*	Celtic	67	Rangers	56	Morton	51
1916–17*g*	Celtic	64	Morton	54	Rangers	53
1917–18*f*	Rangers	56	Celtic	55	Kilmarnock*	43
1918–19*f*	Celtic	58	Rangers	57	Morton	47
1919–20*h*	Rangers	71	Celtic	68	Motherwell	57
1920–21*h*	Rangers	76	Celtic	66	Hearts	50
1921–22*h*	Celtic	67	Rangers	66	Raith R	51
1922–23*g*	Rangers	55	Airdrieonians	50	Celtic	46
1923–24*g*	Rangers	59	Airdrieonians	50	Celtic	46
1924–25*g*	Rangers	60	Airdrieonians	57	Hibernian	52
1925–26*g*	Celtic	58	Airdrieonians*	50	Hearts	50
1926–27*g*	Rangers	56	Motherwell	51	Celtic	49
1927–28*g*	Rangers	60	Celtic*	55	Motherwell	55
1928–29*g*	Rangers	67	Celtic	51	Motherwell	50
1929–30*g*	Rangers	60	Motherwell	55	Aberdeen	53
1930–31*g*	Rangers	60	Celtic	58	Motherwell	56
1931–32*g*	Motherwell	66	Rangers	61	Celtic	48
1932–33*g*	Rangers	62	Motherwell	59	Hearts	50
1933–34*g*	Rangers	66	Motherwell	62	Celtic	47
1934–35*g*	Rangers	55	Celtic	52	Hearts	50
1935–36*g*	Celtic	66	Rangers*	61	Aberdeen	61
1936–37*g*	Rangers	61	Aberdeen	54	Celtic	52
1937–38*g*	Celtic	61	Hearts	58	Rangers	49
1938–39*g*	Rangers	59	Celtic	48	Aberdeen	46
1946–47*e*	Rangers	46	Hibernian	44	Aberdeen	39
1947–48*e*	Hibernian	48	Rangers	46	Partick Th	36
1948–49*e*	Rangers	46	Dundee	45	Hibernian	39
1949–50*e*	Rangers	50	Hibernian	49	Hearts	43
1950–51*e*	Hibernian	48	Rangers*	38	Dundee	38
1951–52*e*	Hibernian	45	Rangers	41	East Fife	37
1952–53*e*	Rangers*	43	Hibernian	43	East Fife	39
1953–54*e*	Celtic	43	Hearts	38	Partick Th	35
1954–55*e*	Aberdeen	49	Celtic	46	Rangers	41
1955–56*f*	Rangers	52	Aberdeen	46	Hearts*	45
1956–57*f*	Rangers	55	Hearts	53	Kilmarnock	42
1957–58*f*	Hearts	62	Rangers	49	Celtic	46
1958–59*f*	Rangers	50	Hearts	48	Motherwell	44
1959–60*f*	Hearts	54	Kilmarnock	50	Rangers*	42
1960–61*f*	Rangers	51	Kilmarnock	50	Third Lanark	42
1961–62*f*	Dundee	54	Rangers	51	Celtic	46
1962–63*f*	Rangers	57	Kilmarnock	48	Partick Th	46
1963–64*f*	Rangers	55	Kilmarnock	49	Celtic*	47
1964–65*f*	Kilmarnock*	50	Hearts	50	Dunfermline Ath	49
1965–66*f*	Celtic	57	Rangers	55	Kilmarnock	45
1966–67*f*	Celtic	58	Rangers	55	Clyde	46
1967–68*f*	Celtic	63	Rangers	61	Hibernian	45
1968–69*f*	Celtic	54	Rangers	49	Dunfermline Ath	45
1969–70*f*	Celtic	57	Rangers	45	Hibernian	44

1970–71f	Celtic	56	Aberdeen	54	St Johnstone	44
1971–72f	Celtic	60	Aberdeen	50	Rangers	44
1972–73f	Celtic	57	Rangers	56	Hibernian	45
1973–74f	Celtic	53	Hibernian	49	Rangers	48
1974–75f	Rangers	56	Hibernian	49	Celtic	45

DIVISION 2 to 1974–75

Maximum points: a 76; b 72; c 68; d 52; e 60; f 36; g 44.

1893–94f	Hibernian	29	Cowlairs	27	Clyde	24
1894–95f	Hibernian	30	Motherwell	22	Port Glasgow	20
1895–96f	Abercorn	27	Leith Ath	23	Renton	21
1896–97f	Partick Th	31	Leith Ath	27	Kilmarnock*	21
1897–98f	Kilmarnock	29	Port Glasgow	25	Morton	22
1898–99f	Kilmarnock	32	Leith Ath	27	Port Glasgow	25
1899–1900f	Partick Th	29	Morton	28	Port Glasgow	20
1900–01f	St Bernard's	25	Airdrieonians	23	Abercorn	21
1901–02g	Port Glasgow	32	Partick Th	31	Motherwell	26
1902–03g	Airdrieonians	35	Motherwell	28	Ayr U*	27
1903–04g	Hamilton A	37	Clyde	29	Ayr U	28
1904–05g	Clyde	32	Falkirk	28	Hamilton A	27
1905–06g	Leith Ath	34	Clyde	31	Albion R	27
1906–07g	St Bernard's	32	Vale of Leven*	27	Arthurlie	27
1907–08g	Raith R	30	Dumbarton‡‡	27	Ayr U	27
1908–09g	Abercorn	31	Raith R*	28	Vale of Leven	28
1909–10g	Leith Ath‡	33	Raith R	33	St Bernard's	27
1910–11g	Dumbarton	31	Ayr U	27	Albion R	25
1911–12g	Ayr U	35	Abercorn	30	Dumbarton	27
1912–13d	Ayr U	34	Dunfermline Ath	33	East Stirling	32
1913–14g	Cowdenbeath	31	Albion R	27	Dunfermline Ath*	26
1914–15d	Cowdenbeath*	37	St Bernard's*	37	Leith Ath	37
1921–22a	Alloa Ath	60	Cowdenbeath	47	Armadale	45
1922–23a	Queen's Park	57	Clydebank ¶	50	St Johnstone ¶	45
1923–24a	St Johnstone	56	Cowdenbeath	55	Bathgate	44
1924–25a	Dundee U	50	Clydebank	48	Clyde	47
1925–26a	Dunfermline Ath	59	Clyde	53	Ayr U	52
1926–27a	Bo'ness	56	Raith R	49	Clydebank	45
1927–28a	Ayr U	54	Third Lanark	45	King's Park	44
1928–29b	Dundee U	51	Morton	50	Arbroath	47
1929–30a	Leith Ath*	57	East Fife	57	Albion R	54
1930–31a	Third Lanark	61	Dundee U	50	Dunfermline Ath	47
1931–32a	East Stirling*	55	St Johnstone	55	Raith R*	46
1932–33c	Hibernian	54	Queen of the S	49	Dunfermline Ath	47
1933–34c	Albion R	45	Dunfermline Ath*	44	Arbroath	44
1934–35c	Third Lanark	52	Arbroath	50	St Bernard's	47
1935–36c	Falkirk	59	St Mirren	52	Morton	48
1936–37c	Ayr U	54	Morton	51	St Bernard's	48
1937–38c	Raith R	59	Albion R	48	Airdrieonians	47
1938–39c	Cowdenbeath	60	Alloa Ath*	48	East Fife	48
1946–47d	Dundee	45	Airdrieonians	42	East Fife	31
1947–48e	East Fife	53	Albion R	42	Hamilton A	40
1948–49e	Raith R*	42	Stirling A	42	Airdrieonians*	41
1949–50e	Morton	47	Airdrieonians	44	Dunfermline Ath*	36
1950–51e	Queen of the S*	45	Stirling A	45	Ayr U*	36
1951–52e	Clyde	44	Falkirk	43	Ayr U	39
1952–53e	Stirling A	44	Hamilton A	43	Queen's Park	37
1953–54e	Motherwell	45	Kilmarnock	42	Third Lanark*	36

1954–55e	Airdrieonians	46	Dunfermline Ath	42	Hamilton A	39
1955–56b	Queen's Park	54	Ayr U	51	St Johnstone	49
1956–57b	Clyde	64	Third Lanark	51	Cowdenbeath	45
1957–58b	Stirling A	55	Dunfermline Ath	53	Arbroath	47
1958–59b	Ayr U	60	Arbroath	51	Stenhousemuir	46
1959–60b	St Johnstone	53	Dundee U	50	Queen of the S	49
1960–61b	Stirling A	55	Falkirk	54	Stenhousemuir	50
1961–62b	Clyde	54	Queen of the S	53	Morton	44
1962–63b	St Johnstone	55	East Stirling	49	Morton	48
1963–64b	Morton	67	Clyde	53	Arbroath	46
1964–65b	Stirling A	59	Hamilton A	50	Queen of the S	45
1965–66b	Ayr U	53	Airdrieonians	50	Queen of the S	47
1966–67a	Morton	69	Raith R	58	Arbroath	57
1967–68b	St Mirren	62	Arbroath	53	East Fife	49
1968–69b	Motherwell	64	Ayr U	53	East Fife*	48
1969–70b	Falkirk	56	Cowdenbeath	55	Queen of the S	50
1970–71b	Partick Th	56	East Fife	51	Arbroath	46
1971–72b	Dumbarton*	52	Arbroath	52	Stirling A	50
1972–73b	Clyde	56	Dumfermline Ath	52	Raith R*	47
1973–74b	Airdrieonians	60	Kilmarnock	58	Hamilton A	55
1974–75a	Falkirk	54	Queen of the S*	53	Montrose	53

Elected to Division 1: 1894 Clyde; 1895 Hibernian; 1896 Abercorn; 1897 Partick Th; 1899 Kilmarnock; 1900 Morton and Partick Th; 1902 Port Glasgow and Partick Th; 1903 Airdrieonians and Motherwell; 1905 Falkirk and Aberdeen; 1906 Clyde and Hamilton A; 1910 Raith R; 1913 Ayr U and Dumbarton.

SCOTTISH LEAGUE PLAY-OFFS 2007–2008

SCOTTISH DIVISION 1 SEMI-FINALS FIRST LEG

Alloa Ath	(1) 2	Clyde	(0) 1
Raith R	(0) 0	Airdrie U	(2) 2

SCOTTISH DIVISION 1 SEMI-FINALS SECOND LEG

Airdrie U	(1) 2	Raith R	(1) 2
Clyde	(1) 5	Alloa Ath	(2) 3
(aet.)			

SCOTTISH DIVISION 1 FINAL FIRST LEG

Airdrie U	(0) 0	Clyde	(0) 1

SCOTTISH DIVISION 1 FINAL SECOND LEG

Clyde	(0) 2	Airdrie U	(0) 0

SCOTTISH DIVISION 2 SEMI-FINALS FIRST LEG

Arbroath	(0) 1	Cowdenbeath	(0) 1
Montrose	(1) 1	Stranraer	(0) 1

SCOTTISH DIVISION 2 SEMI-FINALS SECOND LEG

Cowdenbeath	(0) 1	Arbroath	(0) 2
(aet.)			
Stranraer	(0) 3	Montrose	(0) 0

SCOTTISH DIVISION 2 FINAL FIRST LEG

Arbroath	(1) 2	Stranraer	(0) 0

SCOTTISH DIVISION 2 FINAL SECOND LEG

Stranraer	(0) 1	Arbroath	(0) 0

RELEGATED CLUBS

From Premier League

1998–99 Dunfermline Ath
1999–00 *No relegated team*
2000–01 St Mirren
2001–02 St Johnstone
2002–03 *No relegated team*

2003–04 Partick Th
2004–05 Dundee
2005–06 Livingston
2006–07 Dunfermline Ath
2007–08 Gretna

From Premier Division

1974–75 *No relegation due to League reorganisation*
1975–76 Dundee, St Johnstone
1976–77 Hearts, Kilmarnock
1977–78 Ayr U, Clydebank
1978–79 Hearts, Motherwell
1979–80 Dundee, Hibernian
1980–81 Kilmarnock, Hearts
1981–82 Partick Th, Airdrieonians
1982–83 Morton, Kilmarnock
1983–84 St Johnstone, Motherwell
1984–85 Dumbarton, Morton
1985–86 *No relegation due to League reorganisation*

1986–87 Clydebank, Hamilton A
1987–88 Falkirk, Dunfermline Ath, Morton
1988–89 Hamilton A
1989–90 Dundee
1990–91 None
1991–92 St Mirren, Dunfermline Ath
1992–93 Falkirk, Airdrieonians
1993–94 *See footnote, page 210*
1994–95 Dundee U
1995–96 Partick Th, Falkirk
1996–97 Raith R
1997–98 Hibernian

From Division 1

1974–75 *No relegation due to League reorganisation*
1975–76 Dunfermline Ath, Clyde
1976–77 Raith R, Falkirk
1977–78 Alloa Ath, East Fife
1978–79 Montrose, Queen of the S
1979–80 Arbroath, Clyde
1980–81 Stirling A, Berwick R
1981–82 East Stirling, Queen of the S
1982–83 Dunfermline Ath, Queen's Park
1983–84 Raith R, Alloa Ath
1984–85 Meadowbank Th, St Johnstone
1985–86 Ayr U, Alloa Ath
1986–87 Brechin C, Montrose
1987–88 East Fife, Dumbarton
1988–89 Kilmarnock, Queen of the S
1989–90 Albion R, Alloa Ath
1990–91 Clyde, Brechin C

1991–92 Montrose, Forfar Ath
1992–93 Meadowbank Th, Cowdenbeath
1993–94 *See footnote*
1994–95 Ayr U, Stranraer
1995–96 Hamilton A, Dumbarton
1996–97 Clydebank, East Fife
1997–98 Partick Th, Stirling A
1998–99 Hamilton A, Stranraer
1999–00 Clydebank
2000–01 Morton, Alloa Ath
2001–02 Raith R
2002–03 Alloa Ath, Arbroath
2003–04 Ayr U, Brechin C
2004–05 Partick Th, Raith R
2005–06 Stranraer, Brechin C
2006–07 Airdrie U, Ross Co
2007–08 Stirling A

From Division 2

1994–95 Meadowbank Th, Brechin C
1995–96 Forfar Ath, Montrose
1996–97 Dumbarton, Berwick R
1997–98 Stenhousemuir, Brechin C
1998–99 East Fife, Forfar Ath
1999–00 Hamilton A**
2000–01 Queen's Park, Stirling A

2001–02 Morton
2002–03 Stranraer, Cowdenbeath
2003–04 East Fife, Stenhousemuir
2004–05 Arbroath, Berwick R
2005–06 Dumbarton
2006–07 Stranraer, Forfar Ath
2007–08 Cowdenbeath, Berwick R

From Division 1 1973–74

1921–22 *Queen's Park, Dumbarton, Clydebank
1922–23 Albion R, Alloa Ath
1923–24 Clyde, Clydebank
1924–25 Third Lanark, Ayr U
1925–26 Raith R, Clydebank
1926–27 Morton, Dundee U
1927–28 Dunfermline Ath, Bo'ness
1928–29 Third Lanark, Raith R
1929–30 St Johnstone, Dundee U
1930–31 Hibernian, East Fife
1931–32 Dundee U, Leith Ath
1932–33 Morton, East Stirling
1933–34 Third Lanark, Cowdenbeath
1934–35 St Mirren, Falkirk
1935–36 Airdrieonians, Ayr U
1936–37 Dunfermline Ath, Albion R
1937–38 Dundee, Morton
1938–39 Queen's Park, Raith R
1946–47 Kilmarnock, Hamilton A
1947–48 Airdrieonians, Queen's Park
1948–49 Morton, Albion R
1949–50 Queen of the S, Stirling A

1950–51 Clyde, Falkirk
1951–52 Morton, Stirling A
1952–53 Motherwell, Third Lanark
1953–54 Airdrieonians, Hamilton A
1954–55 No clubs relegated
1955–56 Stirling A, Clyde
1956–57 Dunfermline Ath, Ayr U
1957–58 East Fife, Queen's Park
1958–59 Queen of the S, Falkirk
1959–60 Arbroath, Stirling A
1960–61 Ayr U, Clyde
1961–62 St Johnstone, Stirling A
1962–63 Clyde, Raith R
1963–64 Queen of the S, East Stirling
1964–65 Airdrieonians, Third Lanark
1965–66 Morton, Hamilton A
1966–67 St Mirren, Ayr U
1967–68 Motherwell, Stirling A
1968–69 Falkirk, Arbroath
1969–70 Raith R, Partick Th
1970–71 St Mirren, Cowdenbeath
1971–72 Clyde, Dunfermline Ath
1972–73 Kilmarnock, Airdrieonians
1973–74 East Fife, Falkirk

*Season 1921–22 – only 1 club promoted, 3 clubs relegated.
**15 pts deducted for failing to field a team.*

Scottish League championship wins: Rangers 51, Celtic 41, Aberdeen 4, Hearts 4, Hibernian 4, Dumbarton 2, Dundee 1, Dundee U 1, Kilmarnock 1, Motherwell 1, Third Lanark 1.

The Scottish Football League was reconstructed into three divisions at the end of the 1974–75 season, so the usual relegation statistics do not apply. Further reorganization took place at the end of the 1985–86 season. From 1986–87, the Premier and First Division had 12 teams each. The Second Division remained at 14. From 1988–89, the Premier Division reverted to 10 teams, and the First Division to 14 teams but in 1991–92 the Premier and First Division reverted to 12. At the end of the 1997–98 season, the top nine clubs in Premier Division broke away from the Scottish League to form a new competition, the Scottish Premier League, with the club promoted from Division One. At the end of the 1999–2000 season two teams were added to the Scottish League. There was no relegation from the Premier League but two promoted from the First Division and three from each of the Second and Third Divisions. One team was relegated from the First Division and one from the Second Division, leaving 12 teams in each division. In season 2002–03, Falkirk were not promoted to the Premier League due to the failure of their ground to meet League standards. Inverness CT were promoted after a previous refusal in 2003–04 because of ground sharing. At the end of 2005–06 the Scottish League introduced play-offs for the team finishing second from the bottom of Division 1 against the winners of the second, third and fourth finishing teams in Division 2 and with a similar procedure for Division 2 and Division 3.

PAST SCOTTISH LEAGUE CUP FINALS

Season	Winner		Runner-up	
1946–47	Rangers	4	Aberdeen	0
1947–48	East Fife	0 4	Falkirk	0* 1
1948–49	Rangers	2	Raith Rovers	0
1949–50	East Fife	3	Dunfermline	0
1950–51	Motherwell	3	Hibernian	0
1951–52	Dundee	3	Rangers	2
1952–53	Dundee	2	Kilmarnock	0
1953–54	East Fife	3	Partick Th	2
1954–55	Hearts	4	Motherwell	2
1955–56	Aberdeen	2	St Mirren	1
1956–57	Celtic	0 3	Partick Th	0 0
1957–58	Celtic	7	Rangers	1
1958–59	Hearts	5	Partick Th	1
1959–60	Hearts	2	Third Lanark	1
1960–61	Rangers	2	Kilmarnock	0
1961–62	Rangers	1 3	Hearts	1 1
1962–63	Hearts	1	Kilmarnock	0
1963–64	Rangers	5	Morton	0
1964–65	Rangers	2	Celtic	1
1965–66	Celtic	2	Rangers	1
1966–67	Celtic	1	Rangers	0
1967–68	Celtic	5	Dundee	3
1968–69	Celtic	6	Hibernian	2
1969–70	Celtic	1	St Johnstone	0
1970–71	Rangers	1	Celtic	0
1971–72	Partick Th	4	Celtic	1
1972–73	Hibernian	2	Celtic	1
1973–74	Dundee	1	Celtic	0
1974–75	Celtic	6	Hibernian	3
1975–76	Rangers	1	Celtic	0
1976–77	Aberdeen	2	Celtic	1
1977–78	Rangers	2	Celtic	1*
1978–79	Rangers	2	Aberdeen	1
1979–80	Aberdeen	0 0	Dundee U	0* 3
1980–81	Dundee	0	Dundee U	3
1981–82	Rangers	2	Dundee U	1
1982–83	Celtic	2	Rangers	1
1983–84	Rangers	3	Celtic	2
1984–85	Rangers	1	Dundee U	0
1985–86	Aberdeen	3	Hibernian	0
1986–87	Rangers	2	Celtic	1
1987–88	Rangers†	3	Aberdeen	3*
1988–89	Aberdeen	2	Rangers	3*
1989–90	Aberdeen	2	Rangers	1
1990–91	Rangers	2	Celtic	1
1991–92	Hibernian	2	Dunfermline Ath	0
1992–93	Rangers	2	Aberdeen	1*
1993–94	Rangers	2	Hibernian	1
1994–95	Raith R†	2	Celtic	2*

1995–96	Aberdeen	2	Dundee	0
1996–97	Rangers	4	Hearts	3
1997–98	Celtic	3	Dundee U	0
1998–99	Rangers	2	St Johnstone	1
1999–2000	Celtic	2	Aberdeen	0
2000–01	Celtic	3	Kilmarnock	0
2001–02	Rangers	4	Ayr U	0
2002–03	Rangers	2	Celtic	1
2003–04	Livingston	2	Hibernian	0
2004–05	Rangers	5	Motherwell	1
2005–06	Celtic	3	Dunfermline Ath	0
2006–07	Hibernian	5	Kilmarnock	1
2007–08	Rangers†	2	Dundee U	2*

†*Won on penalties* *After extra time*

PAST LEAGUE CHALLENGE FINALS

1990–91	Dundee	3	Ayr U	2
1991–92	Hamilton A	1	Ayr U	0
1992–93	Hamilton A	3	Morton	2
1993–94	St Mirren	9	Falkirk	3
1994–95	Airdrieonians	3	Dundee	2
1995–96	Stenhousemuir	0	Dundee U	0
	(aet; Stenhousemuir won 5-4 on penalties.)			
1996–97	Stranraer	1	St Johnstone	0
1997–98	Falkirk	1	Qeeen of the South	0
1998–99	no competition			
1999–2000	Alloa Ath	4	Inverness CT	4
	(aet; Alloa Ath won 5-4 on penalties.)			
2000–01	Airdrieonians	2	Livingston	2
	(aet; Airdrieonians won 3-2 on penalties.)			
2001–02	Airdrieonians	2	Alloa Ath	1
2002–03	Queen of the S	2	Brechin C	0
2003–04	Inverness CT	2	Airdrie U	0
2004–05	Falkirk	2	Ross Co	1
2005–06	St Mirren	2	Hamilton A	1
2006–07	Ross Co	1	Clyde	1
	(aet; Ross Co won 5-4 on penalties.)			
2007–08	St Johnstone	3	Dunfermline Ath	2

CIS SCOTTISH LEAGUE CUP 2007–2008

FIRST ROUND

Berwick R	(1) 3	Stenhousemuir	(0) 1

(aet.)

Brechin C	(0) 0	Stirling Albion	(1) 1
Clyde	(0) 0	Raith R	(1) 3
Cowdenbeath	(0) 2	Dumbarton	(0) 0
Dundee	(0) 2	Morton	(0) 0
Forfar Ath	(0) 0	Peterhead	(1) 1
Hamilton A	(1) 2	East Stirling	(0) 1
Livingston	(3) 5	Ayr U	(0) 0
Queen's Park	(2) 2	Alloa Ath	(0) 1
Ross Co	(1) 3	Elgin C	(1) 1
Arbroath	(4) 4	Albion R	(0) 2
East Fife	(0) 1	Queen of the S	(0) 0
Partick Th	(1) 2	Airdrie U	(0) 1
Stranraer	(0) 1	Montrose	(2) 2

SECOND ROUND

Berwick R	(1) 2	Hamilton A	(1) 3
Dundee	(1) 2	Livingston	(1) 2

(aet; Dundee won 6-5 on penalties.)

Gretna	(0) 3	Cowdenbeath	(1) 1
Inverness CT	(1) 3	Arbroath	(0) 1
Montrose	(0) 1	Falkirk	(1) 2
Partick Th	(0) 0	St Johnstone	(0) 0

(aet; Partick T won 5-4 on penalties.)

Peterhead	(0) 0	Kilmarnock	(1) 3
Queen's Park	(0) 1	Hibernian	(0) 2
St Mirren	(0) 0	East Fife	(0) 1
Stirling Albion	(0) 0	Hearts	(1) 2
Dundee U	(0) 2	Ross Co	(0) 1
Motherwell	(1) 3	Raith R	(0) 1

THIRD ROUND

Falkirk	(0) 0	Dundee U	(0) 1
Hamilton A	(2) 2	Kilmarnock	(0) 0
Hearts	(1) 4	Dunfermline Ath	(0) 1

(aet.)

Inverness CT	(1) 3	Gretna	(0) 0
Dundee	(0) 1	Celtic	(1) 2
East Fife	(0) 0	Rangers	(2) 4
Hibernian	(1) 2	Motherwell	(3) 4
Partick Th	(0) 0	Aberdeen	(1) 2

QUARTER-FINALS

Aberdeen	(3) 4	Inverness CT	(0) 1
Celtic	(0) 0	Hearts	(0) 2
Dundee U	(1) 3	Hamilton A	(0) 1
Motherwell	(0) 1	Rangers	(1) 2

SEMI-FINALS

Rangers	(0) 2	Hearts	(0) 0
Aberdeen	(1) 1	Dundee U	(1) 4

FINAL (at Hampden Park)

Dundee U	(1) 2	Rangers	(0) 2

(aet; Rangers won 3-2 on penalties.)

LEAGUE CHALLENGE CUP 2007–2008

FIRST ROUND NORTH EAST

Dundee	(0) 1	Ross Co	(2) 2
Elgin C	(0) 1	Brechin C	(1) 4
Forfar Ath	(1) 3	East Fife	(0) 2
(aet.)			
Montrose	(2) 5	Stirling Alb	(0) 1
Peterhead	(0) 1	Cowdenbeath	(0) 0
Raith R	(0) 1	St Johnstone	(1) 1
(aet; St Johnstone won 5-4 on penalties.)			

FIRST ROUND SOUTH WEST

Albion R	(0) 1	Berwick R	(0) 1
(aet; Berwick R won 4-3 on penalties.)			
Clyde	(1) 1	Queen of the S	(0) 0
East Stirling	(1) 4	Dumbarton	(1) 2
Hamilton A	(1) 1	Ayr U	(0) 2
Morton	(1) 1	Livingston	(0) 0
Queen's Park	(0) 1	Stranraer	(0) 0
Stenhousemuir	(0) 1	Airdrie U	(1) 3

FIRST ROUND NORTH EAST

Arbroath	(1) 2	Alloa Ath	(0) 0

SECOND ROUND

Airdrie U	(2) 5	Arbroath	(1) 1
East Stirling	(1) 1	Queen's Park	(0) 0
Forfar Ath	(0) 0	Ayr U	(1) 2
Montrose	(0) 1	Brechin C	(0) 2
(aet.)			
Partick Th	(1) 3	Berwick R	(0) 1
Peterhead	(0) 0	Morton	(1) 1
Clyde	(0) 1	Dunfermline Ath	(1) 4
Ross Co	(0) 0	St Johnstone	(1) 2

QUARTER-FINALS

Airdrie U	(0) 0	Dunfermline Ath	(0) 2
Ayr U	(0) 2	Partick Th	(0) 1
(aet.)			
East Stirling	(0) 0	Morton	(0) 4
St Johnstone	(4) 4	Brechin C	(0) 1

SEMI-FINALS

Dunfermline Ath	(0) 1	Ayr U	(0) 0
Morton	(1) 1	St Johnstone	(1) 3

FINAL (at East End Park)

Dunfermline Ath	(1) 2	St Johnstone	(3) 3

TENNENT'S SCOTTISH CUP 2007–2008

FIRST ROUND

Brora Rangers v Cove Rangers	0-5
Civil Service Strollers v Selkirk	1-2
Clachnacuddon v Edinburgh City	2-2, 0-1
Coldstream v Dalbeattie Star	0-4
Culter v Hawick Royal Albert	7-0
Fort William v Spartans	0-6
Fraserburgh v Huntly	1-1, 0-2
Girvan v Forres Mechanics	2-0
Glasgow University v Buckie Thistle	1-2
Golspie Sutherland v Preston Athletic	3-1
Lossiemouth v Whitehill Welfare	1-3
Newton Stewart v Linlithgow Rose	0-6
Rothes v Nairn County	1-4
St Cuthbert's Wanderers v Pollok	2-6
Vale of Leithen v Gala Fairydean	3-1
Wick Academy v Deveronvale	0-5
Wigtown & Bladnoch v Burntisland Shipyard	3-5

SECOND ROUND

Albion Rovers v Burntisland Shipyard	8-0
Annan Athletic v Huntly	2-5
Arbroath v Elgin City	5-0
Buckie Thistle v Nairn County	4-1
Cove Rangers v Keith	3-0
Culter v Vale of Leithen	2-1
Edinburgh City v East Stirling	1-2
Edinburgh University v Deveronvale	3-1
Forfar Athletic v Dumbarton	1-1, 0-3
Girvan v Stranraer	1-2
Inverurie Loco Works v East Fife	0-2
Linlithgow Rose v Spartans	4-1
Montrose v Pollok	2-2, 1-0
Selkirk v Dalbeattie Star	0-2
Threave Rovers v Stenhousemuir	1-0
Whitehill Welfare v Golspie Sutherland	6-1

THIRD ROUND

Airdrie U	(0) 1	Queen's Park	(0) 1
Albion R	(0) 1	East Stirling	(3) 5
Arbroath	(0) 0	Cowdenbeath	(1) 1
Brechin C	(0) 1	East Fife	(1) 1
Clyde	(1) 2	Montrose	(0) 0
Cove R	(0) 1	Edinburgh Univ	(0) 0
Culter	(1) 1	Huntly	(2) 3
Dumbarton	(2) 2	Berwick R	(0) 0
Linlithgow Rose	(1) 1	Dalbeattie Star	(0) 0
Livingston	(1) 4	Alloa Ath	(0) 0
Morton	(2) 3	Buckie Th	(1) 2
Partick Th	(1) 2	Ayr U	(1) 1
Peterhead	(0) 0	Queen of the S	(2) 5
Ross Co	(2) 4	Whitehill Welfare	(0) 0
Stranraer	(0) 0	Stirling Albion	(3) 6
Threave R	(0) 0	Raith R	(1) 5

THIRD ROUND REPLAYS

Queen's Park	(0) 2	Airdrie U	(2) 4
(aet.)			
East Fife	(1) 1	Brechin C	(1) 2

215

FOURTH ROUND

Celtic	(1) 3	Stirling Albion	(0) 0
Falkirk	(1) 2	Aberdeen	(2) 2
Hamilton A	(0) 0	Brechin C	(0) 0
Hearts	(1) 2	Motherwell	(0) 2
Hibernian	(1) 3	Inverness CT	(0) 0
Morton	(0) 2	Gretna	(1) 2
Queen of the S	(3) 4	Linlithgow Rose	(0) 0
St Mirren	(2) 3	Dumbarton	(0) 0
Huntly	(0) 1	Dundee	(1) 3
Livingston	(2) 2	Cowdenbeath	(0) 0
St Johnstone	(1) 3	Raith R	(0) 1
Clyde	(0) 0	Dundee U	(0) 1
Partick Th	(0) 2	Dunfermline Ath	(0) 1
Cove R	(0) 2	Ross Co	(4) 4
Rangers	(4) 6	East Stirling	(0) 0
Airdrie U	(0) 0	Kilmarnock	(2) 2

FOURTH ROUND REPLAYS

Aberdeen	(2) 3	Falkirk	(0) 1
Motherwell	(0) 1	Hearts	(0) 0
Brechin C	(0) 2	Hamilton A	(1) 1

(aet; Brechin C subsequently removed for fielding two ineligible players.)

Gretna	(0) 0	Morton	(0) 3

FIFTH ROUND

Aberdeen	(0) 1	Hamilton A	(0) 0
Kilmarnock	(0) 1	Celtic	(1) 5
Livingston	(0) 0	Partick Th	(0) 0
Morton	(0) 0	Queen of the S	(0) 2
St Mirren	(0) 0	Dundee U	(0) 0
Hibernian	(0) 0	Rangers	(0) 0
Motherwell	(0) 1	Dundee	(0) 2
Ross Co	(0) 0	St Johnstone	(1) 1

FIFTH ROUND REPLAYS

Partick Th	(0) 1	Livingston	(1) 1

(aet; Partick Th won 5-4 on penalties.)

Dundee U	(0) 0	St Mirren	(0) 1
Rangers	(1) 1	Hibernian	(0) 0

QUARTER-FINALS

Queen of the S	(0) 2	Dundee	(0) 0
St Johnstone	(1) 1	St Mirren	(0) 1
Aberdeen	(0) 1	Celtic	(0) 1
Rangers	(0) 1	Partick Th	(0) 1

QUARTER-FINAL REPLAYS

Celtic	(0) 0	Aberdeen	(0) 1
St Mirren	(0) 1	St Johnstone	(3) 3
Partick Th	(0) 0	Rangers	(2) 2

SEMI-FINALS

Queen of the S	(1) 4	Aberdeen	(1) 3
St Johnstone	(0) 1	Rangers	(0) 1

(aet; Rangers won 4-3 on penalties.)

FINAL (at Hampden Park)

Queen of the S	(0) 2	Rangers	(2) 3

PAST SCOTTISH CUP FINALS

1874	Queen's Park	2	Clydesdale	0
1875	Queen's Park	3	Renton	0
1876	Queen's Park	1 2	Third Lanark	1 0
1877	Vale of Leven	0 1 3	Rangers	0 1 2
1878	Vale of Leven	1	Third Lanark	0
1879	Vale of Leven	1	Rangers	1
	Vale of Leven awarded cup, Rangers did not appear for replay			
1880	Queen's Park	3	Thornlibank	0
1881	Queen's Park	2 3	Dumbarton	1 1
	Replayed because of protest			
1882	Queen's Park	2 4	Dumbarton	2 1
1883	Dumbarton	2 2	Vale of Leven	2 1
1884	*Queen's Park awarded cup when Vale of Leven did not appear for the final*			
1885	Renton	0 3	Vale of Leven	0 1
1886	Queen's Park	3	Renton	1
1887	Hibernian	2	Dumbarton	1
1888	Renton	6	Cambuslang	1
1889	Third Lanark	3 2	Celtic	0 1
	Replayed because of protest			
1890	Queen's Park	1 2	Vale of Leven	1 1
1891	Hearts	1	Dumbarton	0
1892	Celtic	1 5	Queen's Park	0 1
	Replayed because of protest			
1893	Queen's Park	2	Celtic	1
1894	Rangers	3	Celtic	1
1895	St Bernards	3	Renton	1
1896	Hearts	3	Hibernian	1
1897	Rangers	5	Dumbarton	1
1898	Rangers	2	Kilmarnock	0
1899	Celtic	2	Rangers	0
1900	Celtic	4	Queen's Park	3
1901	Hearts	4	Celtic	3
1902	Hibernian	1	Celtic	0
1903	Rangers	1 0 2	Hearts	1 0 0
1904	Celtic	3	Rangers	2
1905	Third Lanark	0 3	Rangers	0 1
1906	Hearts	1	Third Lanark	0
1907	Celtic	3	Hearts	0
1908	Celtic	5	St Mirren	1
1909	*After two drawn games between Celtic and Rangers, 2.2, 1.1, there was a riot and the cup was withheld*			
1910	Dundee	2 0 2	Clyde	2 0 1
1911	Celtic	0 2	Hamilton Acad	0 0
1912	Celtic	2	Clyde	0
1913	Falkirk	2	Raith R	0
1914	Celtic	0 4	Hibernian	0 1
1920	Kilmarnock	3	Albion R	2
1921	Partick Th	1	Rangers	0
1922	Morton	1	Rangers	0
1923	Celtic	1	Hibernian	0
1924	Airdrieonians	2	Hibernian	0
1925	Celtic	2	Dundee	1
1926	St Mirren	2	Celtic	0

1927	Celtic	3	East Fife	1
1928	Rangers	4	Celtic	0
1929	Kilmarnock	2	Rangers	0
1930	Rangers	0 2	Partick Th	0 1
1931	Celtic	2 4	Motherwell	2 2
1932	Rangers	1 3	Kilmarnock	1 0
1933	Celtic	1	Motherwell	0
1934	Rangers	5	St Mirren	0
1935	Rangers	2	Hamilton A	1
1936	Rangers	1	Third Lanark	0
1937	Celtic	2	Aberdeen	1
1938	East Fife	1 4	Kilmarnock	1 2
1939	Clyde	4	Motherwell	0
1947	Aberdeen	2	Hibernian	1
1948	Rangers	1 1	Morton	1 0
1949	Rangers	4	Clyde	1
1950	Rangers	3	East Fife	0
1951	Celtic	1	Motherwell	0
1952	Motherwell	4	Dundee	0
1953	Rangers	1 1	Aberdeen	1 0
1954	Celtic	2	Aberdeen	1
1955	Clyde	1 1	Celtic	1 0
1956	Hearts	3	Celtic	1
1957	Falkirk	1 2	Kilmarnock	1 1
1958	Clyde	1	Hibernian	0
1959	St Mirren	3	Aberdeen	1
1960	Rangers	2	Kilmarnock	0
1961	Dunfermline Ath	0 2	Celtic	0 0
1962	Rangers	2	St Mirren	0
1963	Rangers	1 3	Celtic	1 0
1964	Rangers	3	Dundee	1
1965	Celtic	3	Dunfermline Ath	2
1966	Rangers	0 1	Celtic	0 0
1967	Celtic	2	Aberdeen	0
1968	Dunfermline Ath	3	Hearts	1
1969	Celtic	4	Rangers	0
1970	Aberdeen	3	Celtic	1
1971	Celtic	1 2	Rangers	1 1
1972	Celtic	6	Hibernian	1
1973	Rangers	3	Celtic	2
1974	Celtic	3	Dundee U	0
1975	Celtic	3	Airdrieonians	1
1976	Rangers	3	Hearts	1
1977	Celtic	1	Rangers	0
1978	Rangers	2	Aberdeen	1
1979	Rangers	0 0 3	Hibernian	0 0 2
1980	Celtic	1	Rangers	0
1981	Rangers	0 4	Dundee U	0 1
1982	Aberdeen	4	Rangers	1 (aet)
1983	Aberdeen	1	Rangers	0 (aet)
1984	Aberdeen	2	Celtic	1 (aet)
1985	Celtic	2	Dundee U	1
1986	Aberdeen	3	Hearts	0
1987	St Mirren	1	Dundee U	0 (aet)
1988	Celtic	2	Dundee U	1

1989	Celtic	1	Rangers	0
1990	Aberdeen	0	Celtic	0
	(aet; Aberdeen won 9-8 on penalties)			
1991	Motherwell	4	Dundee U	3 (aet)
1992	Rangers	2	Airdrieonians	1
1993	Rangers	2	Aberdeen	1
1994	Dundee U	1	Rangers	0
1995	Celtic	1	Airdrieonians	0
1996	Rangers	5	Hearts	1
1997	Kilmarnock	1	Falkirk	0
1998	Hearts	2	Rangers	1
1999	Rangers	1	Celtic	0
2000	Rangers	4	Aberdeen	0
2001	Celtic	3	Hibernian	0
2002	Rangers	3	Celtic	2
2003	Rangers	1	Dundee	0
2004	Celtic	3	Dunfermline Ath	1
2005	Celtic	1	Dundee U	0
2006	Hearts	1	Gretna	1
	(aet; Hearts won 4-2 on penalties)			
2007	Celtic	1	Dunfermline Ath	0
2008	Rangers	3	Queen of the S	2

SCOTS-ADS HIGHLAND LEAGUE 2007–2008

	P	W	D	L	F	A	GD	Pts
Cove Rangers	28	19	7	2	85	33	52	64
Keith	28	18	7	3	80	27	53	61
Deveronvale	28	17	7	4	85	33	52	58
Buckie Thistle	28	17	6	5	54	24	30	57
Fraserburgh	28	16	3	9	65	43	22	51
Inverurie Loco Works	28	15	4	9	67	39	28	49
Huntly	28	13	6	9	60	44	16	45
Forres Mechanics	28	13	5	10	67	46	21	44
Nairn County	28	12	4	12	44	49	−5	40
Clachnacuddin	28	10	7	11	49	50	−1	37
Wick Academy	28	9	5	14	49	60	−11	32
Rothes	28	5	4	19	49	75	−26	19
Lossiemouth	28	4	5	19	22	66	−44	17
Brora Rangers	28	4	4	20	29	74	−45	16
Fort William	28	1	0	27	16	158	−142	3

TYREMAN EAST OF SCOTLAND LEAGUE PREMIER DIVISION 2007–2008

	P	W	D	L	F	A	GD	Pts
Whitehill Welfare	22	16	2	4	56	21	35	50
Edinburgh University	22	15	4	3	41	14	27	49
Spartans	22	14	5	3	57	23	34	47
Edinburgh City	22	12	4	6	50	34	16	40
Preston Athletic	22	11	7	4	41	28	13	40
Dalbeattie Star	22	11	2	9	45	37	8	35
Annan Athletic	22	7	7	8	40	33	7	28
Lothian Thistle	22	7	5	10	30	44	−14	26
Easthouses Lily	22	6	2	14	31	50	−19	20
Coldstream	22	5	4	13	26	62	−36	19
Selkirk	22	3	3	16	22	44	−22	12
Craigroyston	22	2	1	19	21	70	−49	7

WELSH LEAGUE 2007–2008

VAUXHALL MASTERFIT RETAILERS WELSH PREMIER LEAGUE

			Home					Away					Total					
		P	W	D	L	F	A	W	D	L	F	A	W	D	L	F	A	GD	Pts
1	Llanelli	34	13	2	2	52	13	14	2	1	47	22	27	4	3	99	35	64	85
2	The New Saints	34	15	1	1	53	16	10	2	5	32	19	25	3	6	85	30	55	78
3	Rhyl	34	12	2	3	29	12	9	4	4	31	12	21	6	7	60	24	36	69
4	Port Talbot T	34	10	5	2	36	18	7	3	7	21	30	17	8	9	57	48	9	59
5	Bangor City	34	8	7	2	34	16	7	3	7	28	15	15	10	9	62	31	31	55
6	Carmarthen T	34	7	6	4	31	22	8	3	6	28	25	15	9	10	59	47	12	54
7	Neath Athletic	34	9	4	4	31	23	6	5	6	26	29	15	9	10	57	52	5	54
8	Haverfordwest Co	34	9	3	5	36	25	5	2	10	25	34	14	5	15	61	59	2	47
9	Aberystwyth T	34	8	3	6	35	23	5	4	8	22	22	13	7	14	57	45	12	46
10	Welshpool T	34	6	4	7	23	27	6	6	5	26	25	12	10	12	49	52	–3	46
11	Airbus UK	34	7	4	6	19	18	4	5	8	17	26	11	9	14	36	44	–8	42
12	NEWI Cefn Druids	34	9	1	7	33	29	3	1	13	12	37	12	2	20	45	66	–21	38
13	Newtown	34	6	5	6	28	26	3	5	9	19	40	9	10	15	47	66	–19	37
14	Caernarfon T	34	5	4	8	20	32	5	2	10	22	42	10	6	18	42	74	–32	36
15	Connah's Quay N	34	7	3	7	21	30	2	4	11	21	55	9	7	18	42	85	–43	34
16	Porthmadog	34	1	4	12	19	38	6	2	9	29	32	7	6	21	48	70	–22	27
17	Caersws	34	2	3	12	20	43	4	5	8	17	29	6	8	20	37	72	–35	26
18	Llangefni Town	34	5	0	12	21	35	2	3	12	18	47	7	3	24	39	82	–43	24

NORTHERN IRELAND LEAGUE 2007–2008

CARNEGIE IRISH PREMIER LEAGUE

		Home						Away					Total					
	P	W	D	L	F	A	W	D	L	F	A	W	D	L	F	A	GD	Pts
Linfield	30	13	2	0	34	5	10	3	2	37	13	23	5	2	71	18	53	74
Glentoran	30	12	2	1	35	12	10	3	2	34	12	22	5	3	69	24	45	71
Cliftonville	30	9	4	2	35	20	9	2	4	20	12	18	6	6	55	32	23	60
Lisburn Distillery	30	7	4	4	16	8	10	3	2	34	20	17	7	6	50	28	22	58
Portadown	30	8	0	7	23	24	7	2	6	21	15	15	2	13	44	39	5	47
Ballymena United	30	7	5	3	20	17	5	3	7	22	24	12	8	10	42	41	1	44
Crusaders	30	8	2	5	25	20	4	5	6	20	27	12	7	11	45	47	–2	43
Newry City	30	7	4	4	23	21	6	0	9	22	31	13	4	13	45	52	–7	43
Coleraine	30	5	4	6	22	28	6	3	6	19	22	11	7	12	41	50	–9	40
Dungannon Swifts	30	6	3	6	23	23	3	6	6	15	21	9	9	12	38	44	–6	36
Donegal Celtic	30	6	3	6	26	21	3	5	7	13	26	9	8	13	39	47	–8	35
Glenavon	30	4	0	11	17	27	5	3	7	20	24	9	3	18	37	51	–14	30
Larne	30	3	2	10	13	35	4	2	9	21	36	7	4	19	44	71	–27	25
Institute	30	2	5	8	12	19	3	3	9	11	22	5	8	17	23	41	–18	23
Limavady United	30	4	3	8	16	25	2	2	11	10	32	6	5	19	26	57	–31	23
Armagh City	30	3	4	8	17	26	2	2	11	12	33	5	6	19	29	56	–27	23

No promotion or relegation. New invitational 12 club Premier League for 2008–09. Competing clubs as above, minus Donegal Celtic, Larne, Limavady United, Armagh City and Portadown, plus Bangor. Portadown's application submitted too late. They lost a subsequent appeal as did Donegal Celtic.

EUROPEAN REVIEW 2007–2008

An historic situation in the Champions League with the finalists both English clubs. Manchester United edged Chelsea in a penalty shoot-out after a dramatic match. United started as the more confident team and might have added to their one opening goal from Cristiano Ronaldo before Chelsea equalised near half-time through Frank Lampard.

The goal gave Chelsea a tremendous boost and twice they struck the woodwork before the game went into extra time. But Didier Drogba became only the second player to be sent off in a Champions League final which removed him from the list of penalty takers.

Surprisingly Ronaldo fired weakly at Petr Cech to miss and John Terry could have won it for Chelsea, but slipped as he took the kick, the ball glancing off the foot of the post. Then Nicolas Anelka had his shot saved by Erwin Van der Sar in the United goal. Thus it was European Cup trophy No.3 for Manchester United.

In the UEFA Cup final Rangers were beaten by Zenit St Petersburg. A backlog of fixtures as the season neared its end cost Rangers dearly while their Russian opponents had been given the luxury of postponed domestic fixtures.

So a much better season for British clubs all round which began back in July with the Intertoto and Blackburn Rovers emerging as qualifiers for the UEFA Cup itself. In its first qualifying round Carmarthen Town shipped eight goals at home to Brann, Glentoran five against visiting AIK Stockholm but Rhyl took a 3-1 lead against Haka and Dungannon Swifts in their first such outing edged Sudova 1-0. Drogheda United drew away to Libertas, St Patrick's Athletic at home to Odense.

Unlucky Rhyl were out on away goals along with Carmarthen, Dungannon, St Patrick's and Glentoran but Drogheda progressed. The Champions League under way, too, saw Linfield just edged out, as were Derry City 2-0 and The New Saints unfortunately on away goals. Rangers' marathon started well enough in the second qualifying round.

Arsenal, Liverpool and Celtic were successfully introduced at the next round and Rangers continued on. The UEFA Cup second qualifier ended Dunfermline Athletic and Drogheda's interest while Blackburn reached the first round before surprisingly losing to Larissa. But with Bolton Wanderers, Tottenham Hotspur, Everton and Aberdeen on away goals moving forward there was plenty of home interest.

Everton even topped their group, Aberdeen and Bolton were each third, Spurs runners-up in their section. Meanwhile the Champions League groups had an impressive list of winners – Porto, Chelsea, Real Madrid, AC Milan, Barcelona, Manchester United, Internazionale and Sevilla. But Liverpool after a poor start also qualified as did Arsenal. Rangers went into the UEFA Cup.

In that competition's third round the Dons lost out to Bayern Munich, Rangers, Spurs and Everton all won along with Bolton impressively over Atletico Madrid.

The Champions League knock-out stage saw Arsenal win outstandingly away to AC Milan and Manchester United beating Lyon, Chelsea eased through as did Liverpool away to Inter, but Celtic lost out to Barcelona. The last sixteen of the UEFA Cup exited Everton on penalties against Fiorentina as well as Spurs in similar fashion against PSV Eindhoven. Bolton were also beaten but Rangers stayed.

The quarter-finals saw Liverpool beating Arsenal, Chelsea defeating Fenerbahce and Manchester United overcoming Roma. Barcelona were the lone foreigners to survive. The last eight of the UEFA Cup had Rangers flying the UK flag. In the Champions League Chelsea for once had the better of Liverpool and Manchester United finished off Barcelona. Rangers held their nerve in the UEFA semi-final when it came to penalties. Meanwhile the task confronting the Scottish club was underlined when Zenit trounced Bayern Munich 4-0 in the second leg after holding the Germans to a 1-1 draw in the first match.

UEFA CHAMPIONS LEAGUE 2007–2008

■ *Denotes player sent off.*
* *Winner after extra time.*

FIRST QUALIFYING ROUND FIRST LEG

Apoel	(1) 2	BATE Borisov	(0) 0
Lenkoran	(0) 1	Dinamo Zagreb	(0) 1
Linfield	(0) 0	Elfsborg	(0) 0
Murata	(1) 1	Tampere	(0) 2
Olimpi	(0) 0	Astana	(0) 0
The New Saints	(1) 3	Ventspils	(1) 2
Zeta	(2) 3	Kaunas	(0) 1
Derry City	(0) 0	Pyunik	(0) 0
Domzale	(1) 1	SK Tirana	(0) 0
F91 Dudelange	(1) 1	Zilina	(0) 2
Hafnarfjordur	(2) 4	HB Torshavn	(1) 1
Marsaxlokk	(0) 0	Sarajevo	(4) 6
Pobeda	(0) 0	Levadia	(0) 1
Sheriff	(1) 2	Ranger's	(0) 0

Tuesday, 17 July 2007

Linfield (0) 0   Elfsborg (0) 0   2009

Linfield: Mannus; Douglas, O'Kane, Gault, Murphy, McAreavey (Mouncey 77), Curran, Dickson (Ferguson 87), Mulgrew, Thompson (Stewart 80), Bailie.
Elfsborg: Wiland; Augustsson, Bjorck, Karlsson, Andersson, Ishizaki (Alexandersson 89), Berglund (Keene 68), Svensson A, Svensson M (Avdic 52), Holmen, Mobaeck.

The New Saints (1) 3 *(Wilde 14, Baker 54, Hogan 90)*

Ventspils (1) 2 *(Rimkus 26, 89)*   649

The New Saints: Harrison; Courtney, King, Baker, Holmes, Toner (Morgan 46), Ruscoe (Leah 81), Hogan, Wilde, Beck, Wood (Taylor 85).
Ventspils: Davidovs; Soleicuks, Sernetskiy, Dubenskiy, Ndeki, Zizilevs, Tigirlas (Zangareyev 69), Kacanovs, Rimkus, Menteshashvili, Kolesnicenko (Kosmacovs 65).

Wednesday, 18 July 2007

Derry City (0) 0   Pyunik (0) 0   2285

Derry City: Jennings; McCallion, Hargan, Hutton, McCourt, Farren (Hynes 85), Molloy, Morrow (McHugh 67), Oman, Martyn, McGlynn (Deery 57).
Pyunik: Kasparov; Mkrtchian (Sahakian 78), Tadevosian, Hovsepian, Yedigarian, Nazarian, Cre (Hzeina 46), Pachajian, Arzumanian, Dokhoian, Ghazarian (Henrik Mkhitarian 62).

FIRST QUALIFYING ROUND SECOND LEG

Astana	(1) 3	Olimpi	(0) 0
BATE Borisov*	(1) 3	Apoel	(0) 0
Dinamo Zagreb*	(0) 3	Lenkoran	(1) 1
Kaunas	(3) 3	Zeta	(1) 2
Ranger's	(0) 0	Sheriff	(0) 3
Sarajevo	(1) 3	Marsaxlokk	(0) 1
Elfsborg	(1) 1	Linfield	(0) 0
HB Torshavn	(0) 0	Hafnarfjordur	(0) 0
Levadia	(0) 0	Pobeda	(0) 0
Pyunik	(1) 2	Derry City	(0) 0
SK Tirana	(0) 1	Domzale	(1) 2
Tampere	(2) 2	Murata	(0) 0
Ventspils	(1) 2	The New Saints	(0) 1
Zilina	(3) 5	F91 Dudelange	(1) 4

Wednesday, 25 July 2007

Elfsborg (1) 1 *(Svensson M 32)*   **Linfield (0) 0**   1023

Elfsborg: Wiland; Bjorck, Augustsson, Karlsson, Andersson, Ishizaki, Berglund (Alexandersson 83), Svensson A (Avdic 60), Svensson M (Keene 49), Holmen, Mobaeck.
Linfield: Mannus; Douglas (Mouncey 76), Dickson, Gault, McAreavey, O'Kane, Curran (Ferguson 74), Thompson, Lindsam, Mulgrew (Stewart 64), Bailie.

Pyunik (1) 2 *(Avetisian 28, Ghazarian 67)*   **Derry City (0) 0**   5300

Pyunik: Kasparov; Mkrtchian, Tadevosian, Hovsepian, Nazarian (Yedigarian 59), Hamlet Mkhitarian, Pachajian, Arzumanian, Avetisian (Henrik Mkhitarian 70), Ghazarian (Sahakian 81), Dokhoyan.
Derry City: Jennings; McCallion, Deery (Higgins 82), McCourt (Farren 65), Kelly, Molloy (O'Halloran 40), Martyn, Morrow, Oman, McHugh, Brennan.

Ventspils (1) 2 *(Ndeki 17, Kacanovs 53)*   **The New Saints (0) 1** *(Naylor 90)* 1500

Ventspils: Davidovs; Ndeki, Sernetskiy (Slesarcuks 90), Dubenskiy, Tigirlas, Zizilevs, Cilinsek, Kacanovs, Rimkus, Menteshashvili (Mysikov 90), Kolesnicenko (Kosmacovs 70).
The New Saints: Harrison; Courtney, King, Baker, Holmes, Lamb (Carter 57), Ruscoe, Hogan (Naylor 72), Wilde (Morgan 64), Beck, Wood.

SECOND QUALIFYING ROUND FIRST LEG

Debrecen	(0) 0	Elfsborg	(0) 1
FC Copenhagen	(1) 1	Beitar Jerusalem	(0) 0
Genk	(1) 1	Sarajevo	(1) 2
Pyunik	(0) 0	Shakhtar Donetsk	(1) 2
Rangers	(0) 2	Zeta	(0) 0
Tampere	(1) 1	Levski	(0) 0
Zaglebie	(0) 0	Steaua	(0) 1
Astana	(1) 1	Rosenborg	(1) 3
Besiktas	(0) 1	Sheriff	(0) 0
Domzale	(0) 1	Dinamo Zagreb	(1) 2
Hafnarfjordur	(1) 1	BATE Borisov	(1) 3
Red Star Belgrade	(1) 1	Levadia	(0) 0
Ventspils	(0) 0	Salzburg	(2) 3
Zilina	(0) 0	Slavia Prague	(0) 0

Tuesday, 31 July 2007

Rangers (0) 2 *(Weir 55, Novo 72)*   **Zeta (0) 0**   36,145

Rangers: McGregor; Hutton■, Papac, Cuellar, Weir, Ferguson, Hemdani, Darcheville (Sebo 83), Boyd (Broadfoot 83), McCulloch, Adam (Novo 46).
Zeta: Ivanovic S; Korac, Vuckovic, Radulovic (Durovic 77), Kaluderovic M, Tumbasevic, Ivanovic B, Markovic, Igumanovic, Cetkovic (Boljevic 83), Stjepanovic.

SECOND QUALIFYING ROUND SECOND LEG

Beitar Jerusalem	(0) 1	FC Copenhagen*	(1) 1
Dinamo Zagreb	(2) 3	Domzale	(1) 1
Levski	(0) 0	Tampere	(1) 1
Zeta	(0) 0	Rangers	(0) 1
BATE Borisov	(0) 1	Hafnarfjordur	(1) 1
Elfsborg	(0) 0	Debrecen	(0) 0
Levadia	(1) 2	Red Star Belgrade	(1) 1
Rosenborg	(4) 7	Astana	(1) 1
Salzburg	(1) 4	Ventspils	(0) 0
Sarajevo	(0) 0	Genk	(0) 1
Sheriff	(0) 0	Besiktas	(0) 3
Shakhtar Donetsk	(1) 2	Pyunik	(1) 1
Slavia Prague	(0) 0	Zilina	(0) 0
(aet; Slavia Prague won 4-3 on penalties.)			
Steaua	(1) 2	Zaglebie	(1) 1

Tuesday, 7 August 2007

Zeta (0) 0

Rangers (0) 1 *(Beasley 81)*   11,000

Zeta: Ivanovic S; Tumbasevic (Vuckovic 84), Igumanovic, Kaluderovic M, Radulovic, Cetkovic, Ivanovic B (Boljevic 71), Markovic, Durovic (Knezevic 56), Stjepanovic, Korac.

Rangers: McGregor; Broadfoot, Papac, Cuellar, Weir, Ferguson, Hemdani, Thomson (Adam 87), Darcheville (Novo 61), Beasley, McCulloch.

THIRD QUALIFYING ROUND FIRST LEG

Benfica	(1) 2	FC Copenhagen	(1) 1
Lazio	(0) 1	Dinamo Bucharest	(1) 1
Rangers	(0) 1	Red Star Belgrade	(0) 0
Valencia	(1) 3	Elfsborg	(0) 0
Ajax	(0) 0	Slavia Prague	(0) 1
BATE Borisov	(1) 2	Steaua	(0) 2
Fenerbahce	(1) 1	Anderlecht	(0) 0
Salzburg	(1) 1	Shakhtar Donetsk	(0) 0
Sarajevo	(0) 0	Dynamo Kiev	(1) 1
Sevilla	(0) 2	AEK Athens	(0) 0
Sparta Prague	(0) 0	Arsenal	(0) 2
Spartak Moscow	(1) 1	Celtic	(1) 1
Tampere	(0) 0	Rosenborg	(2) 3
Toulouse	(0) 0	Liverpool	(1) 1
Werder Bremen	(0) 2	Dinamo Zagreb	(1) 1
Zurich	(0) 1	Besiktas	(1) 1

Tuesday, 14 August 2007

Rangers (0) 1 *(Novo 90)*

Red Star Belgrade (0) 0   35,364

Rangers: McGregor; Hutton, Buffel, Cuellar, Weir, Ferguson, Hemdani, Thomson, Darcheville (Cousin 65), Beasley (Novo 65), McCulloch.

Red Star Belgrade: Randelovic; Andelkovic, Tutoric, Bronowicki, Gueye, Milijas, Koroman, Lucas, Castillo, Raskovic (Molina 70), Dordevic (Milovanovic 83).

Wednesday, 15 August 2007

Sparta Prague (0) 0

Arsenal (0) 2 *(Fabregas 72, Hleb 90)*   19,586

Sparta Prague: Postulka; Repka (Brezinsky 36), Kladrubsky, Pospech, Kadlec, Horvath (Limbersky 86), Abraham, Husek, Dosek, Rezek (Matusovic 59), Kulic.

Arsenal: Lehmann; Sagna, Clichy, Flamini, Toure, Gallas, Eboue, Fabregas, Hleb, Van Persie, Rosicky (Song Billong 80).

Spartak Moscow (1) 1 *(Pavlyuchenko 42)*

Celtic (1) 1 *(Hartley 21)*   67,000

Spartak Moscow: Pletikosa; Stranzl, Soava, Shishkin, Mozart, Titov, Torbinskiy, Kovac, Bystrov (Kalynychenko 76), Pavlyuchenko, Welliton.

Celtic: Brown M; Wilson, Naylor, Donati (Sno 74), Kennedy, McManus, Hartley, Brown S, McDonald (Caldwell 79), Vennegoor (McGeady 82), Nakamura.

Toulouse (0) 0

Liverpool (1) 1 *(Voronin 43)*   30,380

Toulouse: Douchez; Fofana, Mathieu, Ebondo (Sissoko 83), Paulo Cesar (Gignac 69), Cetto, Sirieix, Emana Edzimbi, Dieuze, Elmander, Bergougnoux (Mansare 46).

Liverpool: Reina; Finnan, Arbeloa, Mascherano, Carragher, Hyypia, Benayoun (Riise 59), Gerrard (Sissoko 65), Crouch, Voronin (Torres 78), Babel.

THIRD QUALIFYING ROUND SECOND LEG

Dinamo Bucharest	(1) 1	Lazio	(0) 3
Liverpool	(1) 4	Toulouse	(0) 0
Red Star Belgrade	(0) 0	Rangers	(0) 0
Anderlecht	(0) 0	Fenerbahce	(1) 2
Arsenal	(1) 3	Sparta Prague	(0) 0
Besiktas	(0) 2	Zurich	(0) 0
Celtic	(1) 1	Spartak Moscow	(1) 1

(aet; Celtic won 4-3 on penalties.)

Dynamo Kiev	(1) 3	Sarajevo	(0) 0
Dinamo Zagreb	(2) 2	Werder Bremen	(2) 3
Elfsborg	(1) 1	Valencia	(1) 2
FC Copenhagen	(0) 0	Benfica	(1) 1
Rosenborg	(1) 2	Tampere	(0) 0
Shakhtar Donetsk	(1) 3	Salzburg	(1) 1
Slavia Prague	(1) 2	Ajax	(1) 1
Steaua	(1) 2	BATE Borisov	(0) 0
AEK Athens	(0) 1	Sevilla	(3) 4

Tuesday, 28 August 2007

Liverpool (1) 4 *(Crouch 19, Hyypia 49, Kuyt 87, 90)*

Toulouse (0) 0   43,118

Liverpool: Reina; Arbeloa, Riise, Mascherano, Agger (Finnan 80), Hyypia, Benayoun, Sissoko (Lucas 68), Crouch, Kuyt, Leto (Babel 75).
Toulouse: Douchez; Fofana, Mathieu (Sissoko 82), Paulo Cesar, Ilunga, Cetto, Sirieix, Emana Edzimbi (Fabinho 77), Dieuze, Elmander, Gignac (Bergougnoux 54).

Red Star Belgrade (0) 0

Rangers (0) 0   40,104

Red Star Belgrade: Randelovic; Andelkovic, Tutoric, Gueye, Basta, Milijas (Raskovic 74), Koroman, Burzanovic (Barcos 71), Lucas, Castillo, Dordevic.
Rangers: McGregor; Hutton, Papac, Cuellar, Weir, Ferguson, Hemdani, Thomson, Darcheville (Cousin 70), McCulloch, Whittaker (Beasley 79).

Wednesday, 29 August 2007

Arsenal (1) 3 *(Rosicky 8, Fabregas 82, Eduardo 90)*

Sparta Prague (0) 0   58,462

Arsenal: Almunia; Hoyte J, Clichy, Silva, Toure, Senderos, Diaby (Fabregas 68), Walcott, Eduardo, Van Persie (Adebayor 68), Rosicky (Denilson 73).
Sparta Prague: Postulka; Repka, Kladrubsky (Limbersky 77), Pospech, Kadlec, Horvath, Abraham, Husek, Dosek, Rezek (Kolar 73), Kulic (Zofcak 46).

Celtic (1) 1 *(McDonald 27)*

Spartak Moscow (1) 1 *(Pavlyuchenko 45)*   57,644

Celtic: Boruc; Wilson, Naylor (O'Dea 110), Donati, Caldwell, McManus, Nakamura, Brown S, McDonald (Zurawski 97), Vennegoor, McGeady (Riordan 104).
Spartak Moscow: Pletikosa; Stranzl■, Soava, Shishkin, Mozart, Titov, Torbinskiy (Boyarintsev 100), Kovac, Bystrov (Kalynychenko 105), Pavlyuchenko, Welliton (Dedura 88).
aet; Celtic won 4-3 on penalties.

GROUP STAGE

GROUP A

Marseille	(0) 2	Besiktas	(0) 0
Porto	(1) 1	Liverpool	(1) 1
Besiktas	(0) 0	Porto	(0) 1
Liverpool	(0) 0	Marseille	(0) 1
Besiktas	(1) 2	Liverpool	(0) 1
Marseille	(0) 1	Porto	(0) 1

Liverpool	(2) 8	Besiktas	(0) 0
Porto	(1) 2	Marseille	(0) 1
Besiktas	(1) 2	Marseille	(0) 1
Liverpool	(1) 4	Porto	(1) 1
Marseille	(0) 0	Liverpool	(2) 4
Porto	(1) 2	Besiktas	(0) 0

Tuesday, 18 September 2007

Porto (1) 1 *(Lucho Gonzalez 8 (pen))*

Liverpool (1) 1 *(Kuyt 18)*   41,208

Porto: Nuno; Bruno Alves, Fucile, Joao Paulo, Paulo Assuncao, Quaresma, Lucho Gonzalez, Bosingwa, Raul Meireles (Mariano Gonzalez 64), Sektioui (Farias 64), Lisandro Lopez.
Liverpool: Reina; Finnan, Arbeloa, Mascherano, Carragher, Hyypia, Pennant■, Gerrard, Torres (Voronin 76), Kuyt, Babel (Fabio Aurelio 85).

Wednesday, 3 October 2007

Liverpool (0) 0

Marseille (0) 1 *(Valbuena 77)*   41,355

Liverpool: Reina; Finnan, Fabio Aurelio (Voronin 70), Leto (Riise 52), Carragher, Hyypia, Gerrard, Sissoko, Torres, Crouch (Kuyt 75), Benayoun.
Marseille: Mandanda; Taiwo, Rodriguez, Bonnart, Givet, Ziani, Cheyrou, Zenden (Arrache 88), Cana, Valbuena (Oruma 84), Niang (Cisse 70).

Wednesday, 24 October 2007

Besiktas (1) 2 *(Hyypia 13 (og), Bobo 82)*

Liverpool (0) 1 *(Gerrard 85)*   25,837

Besiktas: Hakan; Serdar K (Koray 42), Gokhan, Ibrahim U, Ibrahim T, Delgado (Higuain 62), Tello, Cisse, Serdar O, Ali, Bobo (Diatta 86).
Liverpool: Reina; Finnan, Riise, Mascherano (Lucas 76), Carragher, Hyypia (Crouch 83), Pennant (Benayoun 59), Gerrard, Voronin, Kuyt, Babel.

Tuesday, 6 November 2007

Liverpool (2) 8 *(Crouch 19, 89, Benayoun 32, 53, 56, Gerrard 69, Babel 78, 81)*

Besiktas (0) 0   41,143

Liverpool: Reina; Arbeloa, Fabio Aurelio (Babel 63), Mascherano, Carragher, Hyypia, Benayoun, Gerrard (Lucas 73), Crouch, Voronin (Kewell 72), Riise.
Besiktas: Hakan; Serdar K (Higuain 62), Diatta, Ibrahim U, Ibrahim T, Mehmet (Ricardinho 78), Delgado, Cisse, Serdar O (Ali 46), Koray, Bobo.

Wednesday, 28 November 2007

Liverpool (1) 4 *(Torres 19, 78, Gerrard 84 (pen), Crouch 87)*

Porto (1) 1 *(Lisandro Lopez 33)*   41,095

Liverpool: Reina; Finnan, Arbeloa, Mascherano, Carragher, Hyypia, Benayoun (Crouch 71), Gerrard, Torres, Voronin (Kewell 63), Babel (Kuyt 85).
Porto: Helton; Bruno Alves, Stepanov, Cech, Paulo Assuncao (Helder Postiga 81), Quaresma, Lucho Gonzalez, Mariano Gonzalez (Sektioui 77), Bosingwa, Kazmierczak (Raul Meireles 65), Lisandro Lopez.

Tuesday, 11 December 2007

Marseille (0) 0

Liverpool (2) 4 *(Gerrard 4, Torres 10, Kuyt 47, Babel 90)*   53,097

Marseille: Mandanda; Taiwo, Rodriguez, Bonnart, Givet (Faty 46), Ziani, Cheyrou (Nasri 34), Zenden (Cisse 46), Cana, Valbuena, Niang.
Liverpool: Reina; Arbeloa, Riise, Mascherano, Carragher, Hyypia, Benayoun, Gerrard, Torres (Babel 77), Kuyt (Lucas 86), Kewell (Fabio Aurelio 67).

Group A Final Table	P	W	D	L	F	A	Pts
Porto	6	3	2	1	8	7	11
Liverpool	6	3	1	2	18	5	10
Marseille	6	2	1	3	6	9	7
Besiktas	6	2	0	4	4	15	6

GROUP B

Chelsea	(0) 1	Rosenborg	(1) 1
Schalke	(0) 0	Valencia	(0) 1
Rosenborg	(0) 0	Schalke	(0) 2
Valencia	(1) 1	Chelsea	(1) 2
Chelsea	(1) 2	Schalke	(0) 0
Rosenborg	(0) 2	Valencia	(0) 0
Schalke	(0) 0	Chelsea	(0) 0
Valencia	(0) 0	Rosenborg	(1) 2
Rosenborg	(0) 0	Chelsea	(3) 4
Valencia	(0) 0	Schalke	(0) 0
Chelsea	(0) 0	Valencia	(0) 0
Schalke	(3) 3	Rosenborg	(1) 1

Tuesday, 18 September 2007

Chelsea (0) 1 *(Shevchenko 53)*

Rosenborg (1) 1 *(Koppinen 24)*   24,973

Chelsea: Cech; Belletti, Cole A (Ben Haim 74), Makelele, Terry, Alex, Cole J (Wright-Phillips 74), Essien, Kalou, Shevchenko, Malouda.
Rosenborg: Hirschfeld; Koppinen, Basma (Kvarme 46), Dorsin, Strand, Riseth, Skjelbred (Iversen 85), Tettey, Traore, Sapara (Ya Konan 69), Kone.

Wednesday, 3 October 2007

Valencia (1) 1 *(Villa 9)*

Chelsea (1) 2 *(Cole J 21, Drogba 70)*   52,000

Valencia: Hildebrand; Albiol, Marchena, Helguera, Miguel, Moretti, Albelda (Baraja 75), Joaquin (Arizmendi 88), Silva, Villa, Morientes (Zigic 69).
Chelsea: Cech; Paulo Ferreira, Cole A, Makelele, Terry, Ricardo Carvalho, Essien (Sidwell 83), Mikel (Alex 88), Drogba, Cole J, Malouda (Kalou 85).

Wednesday, 24 October 2007

Chelsea (1) 2 *(Malouda 4, Drogba 47)*

Schalke (0) 0   40,910

Chelsea: Cech; Paulo Ferreira, Bridge, Makelele, Alex, Ricardo Carvalho, Essien (Mikel 70), Lampard, Drogba, Cole J (Shevchenko 89), Malouda (Kalou 84).
Schalke: Neuer; Westermann, Bordon, Rodriguez (Bajramovic 81), Rafinha, Ernst, Jones, Grossmuller (Azaouagh 77), Larsen, Lovenkrands, Asamoah (Rakitic 61). Moretti, Albelda, Gavilan (Zigic 67), Joaquin, Silva, Morientes.

Tuesday, 6 November 2007

Schalke (0) 0

Chelsea (0) 0   53,951

Schalke: Neuer; Westermann, Bordon, Rafinha, Krstajic, Rakitic, Jones, Ozil (Lovenkrands 60), Bajramovic, Larsen, Asamoah.
Chelsea: Cech (Cudicini 46); Belletti (Mikel 64), Bridge, Makelele, Alex, Ricardo Carvalho, Essien, Lampard, Drogba, Cole J, Malouda (Wright-Phillips 78).

Wednesday, 28 November 2007

Rosenborg (0) 0

Chelsea (3) 4 *(Drogba 8, 20, Alex 40, Cole J 73)*   21,582

Rosenborg: Hirschfeld; Stoor, Kvarme, Dorsin (Basma 86), Riseth, Skjelbred, Tettey, Traore (Strand 57), Sapara, Kone (Ya Konan 63), Iversen.
Chelsea: Cudicini; Belletti, Cole A, Makelele, Terry, Alex, Essien, Lampard (Pizarro 76), Drogba (Shevchenko 68), Cole J, Wright-Phillips (Kalou 69).

Tuesday, 11 December 2007

Chelsea (0) 0

Valencia (0) 0   41,139

Chelsea: Cech; Paulo Ferreira (Belletti 72), Bridge, Essien, Terry, Ben Haim, Wright-Phillips, Lampard (Cole J 62), Shevchenko (Makelele 46), Kalou, Pizarro.
Valencia: Canizares; Albiol, Marchena, Helguera, Miguel (Manuel Fernandes 65), Moretti, Obayan, Vicente (Mata 75), Silva, Villa (Arizmendi 50), Morientes.

Group B Final Table	P	W	D	L	F	A	Pts
Chelsea	6	3	3	0	9	2	12
Schalke	6	2	2	2	5	4	8
Rosenborg	6	2	1	3	6	10	7
Valencia	6	1	2	3	2	6	5

GROUP C

Olympiakos	(0) 1	Lazio	(0) 1
(Behind closed doors.)		
Real Madrid	(1) 2	Werder Bremen	(1) 1
Lazio	(1) 2	Real Madrid	(1) 2
Werder Bremen	(1) 1	Olympiaks	(0) 3
Real Madrid	(1) 4	Olympiakos	(1) 2
Werder Bremen	(1) 2	Lazio	(0) 1
Lazio	(0) 2	Werder Bremen	(0) 1
Olympiakos	(0) 0	Real Madrid	(0) 0
Lazio	(1) 1	Olympiakos	(1) 2
Werder Bremen	(2) 3	Real Madrid	(1) 2
Olympiakos	(1) 3	Werder Bremen	(0) 0
Real Madrid	(3) 3	Lazio	(0) 1

Group C Final Table	P	W	D	L	F	A	Pts
Real Madrid	6	3	2	1	13	9	11
Olympiakos	6	3	2	1	11	7	11
Werder Bremen	6	2	0	4	8	13	6
Lazio	6	1	2	3	8	11	5

GROUP D

AC Milan	(2) 2	Benfica	(0) 1
Shakhtar Donetsk	(2) 2	Celtic	(0) 0
Benfica	(0) 0	Shakhtar Donetsk	(1) 1
Celtic	(0) 2	AC Milan	(0) 1
AC Milan	(2) 4	Shakhtar Donetsk	(0) 1
Benfica	(0) 1	Celtic	(0) 0
Celtic	(1) 1	Benfica	(0) 0
Shakhtar Donetsk	(0) 0	AC Milan	(0) 3
Benfica	(1) 1	AC Milan	(1) 1
Celtic	(1) 2	Shakhtar Donetsk	(1) 1
AC Milan	(0) 1	Celtic	(0) 0
Shakhtar Donetsk	(1) 1	Benfica	(2) 2

Tuesday, 18 September 2007

Shakhtar Donetsk (2) 2 *(Brandao 5, Lucarelli 8)*

Celtic (0) 0   26,100

Shakhtar Donetsk: Pyatov; Hubschmann, Kucher, Ilsinho, Rat, Fernandinho (Duljaj 86), Jadson (Nery Castillo 65), Lewandowski, Srna, Brandao, Lucarelli (Gladkiy 70).
Celtic: Boruc, Wilson, Naylor, Donati, Caldwell, McManus, Hartley, Brown S, McDonald (Killen 68), Vennegoor (Zurawski 85), Nakamura (McGeady 65).

Wednesday, 3 October 2007

Celtic (0) 2 *(McManus 63, McDonald 90)*

AC Milan (0) 1 *(Kaka 68 (pen))*   58,643

Celtic: Boruc; Perrier Doumbe (Kennedy 79), Naylor, Donati, Caldwell, McManus, Hartley, Brown S, McDonald, Jarosik (Nakamura 84), McGeady (Killen 84).
AC Milan: Dida (Kalac 90); Nesta, Jankulovski, Bonera, Oddo, Gattuso, Seedorf (Gourcuff 55), Pirlo, Kaka, Ambrosini, Inzaghi (Gilardino 77).

Wednesday, 24 October 2007

Benfica (0) 1 *(Cardozo 87)*

Celtic (0) 0   38,512

Benfica: Quim; Luisao, Leo, Katsouranis, Rui Costa, Pereira, Binya, Nuno Assis (Di Maria 82), Rodriguez (Luis Filipe 84), Cardozo, Bergessio (Adu 62).
Celtic: Boruc; Kennedy, Naylor, Donati (Sno 63), Caldwell, McManus, Hartley, Brown S, Killen (McDonald 74), Jarosik, McGeady.

Tuesday, 6 November 2007

Celtic (1) 1 *(McGeady 45)*

Benfica (0) 0   58,691

Celtic: Boruc; Caldwell, Naylor, Hartley, Kennedy, McManus, Jarosik (Donati 66), Brown S (Sno 89), McDonald, Vennegoor (Killen 66), McGeady.
Benfica: Quim; Luis Filipe, Edcarlos, Luisao, Leo, Katsouranis, Rui Costa (Bergessio 77), Pereira (Di Maria 61), Binya[a], Rodriguez, Cardozo (Nuno Gomes 77).

Wednesday, 28 November 2007

Celtic (1) 2 *(Jarosik 45, Donati 90)*

Shakhtar Donetsk (1) 1 *(Brandao 4)*   59,396

Celtic: Boruc; Caldwell, Naylor (Donati 16), Hartley, Kennedy (Pressley 41), McManus, Jarosik, Brown S, McDonald, Vennegoor (Killen 79), McGeady.
Shakhtar Donetsk: Pyatov; Hubschmann, Kucher, Ilsinho (Yezerskiy 84), Rat, Chygrynskiy, Jadson, Lewandowski, Srna, Brandao, Lucarelli (Gladkiy 88).

Tuesday, 4 December 2007

AC Milan (0) 1 *(Inzaghi 70)*

Celtic (0) 0   38,409

AC Milan: Kalac; Cafu, Simic (Kaladze 30), Favalli, Bonera, Gattuso, Seedorf (Gourcuff 69), Pirlo (Brocchi 74), Kaka, Ambrosini, Inzaghi.
Celtic: Boruc; Caldwell, O'Dea, Donati (Sno 71), Pressley, McManus, Hartley, Brown S, McDonald (Vennegoor 65), Jarosik (Zurawski 78), McGeady.

Group D Final Table	P	W	D	L	F	A	Pts
AC Milan	6	4	1	1	12	5	13
Celtic	6	3	0	3	5	6	9
Benfica	6	2	1	3	5	6	7
Shakhtar Donetsk	6	2	0	4	6	11	6

GROUP E

Barcelona	(1) 3	Lyon	(0) 0
Rangers	(0) 2	Stuttgart	(0) 1
Lyon	(0) 0	Rangers	(1) 3
Stuttgart	(0) 0	Barcelona	(0) 2
Rangers	(0) 0	Barcelona	(0) 0
Stuttgart	(0) 0	Lyon	(0) 2
Barcelona	(2) 2	Rangers	(0) 0
Lyon	(3) 4	Stuttgart	(1) 2
Lyon	(1) 2	Barcelona	(1) 2
Stuttgart	(1) 3	Rangers	(1) 2
Barcelona	(1) 3	Stuttgart	(1) 1
Rangers	(0) 0	Lyon	(1) 3

Wednesday, 19 September 2007

Rangers (0) 2 *(Adam 62, Darcheville 75 (pen))*

Stuttgart (0) 1 *(Gomez 56)*   49,795

Rangers: McGregor; Hutton, Papac, Cuellar, Weir, Ferguson, Hemdani, Thomson, Darcheville (Novo 83), Adam (Beasley 67), Whittaker (Faye 86).
Stuttgart: Schafer; Osorio, Tasci, Fernando Meira, Boka, Pardo, Hilbert, Da Silva (Ewerthon 70), Khedira (Basturk 78), Cacau, Gomez.

Tuesday, 2 October 2007

Lyon (0) 0

Rangers (1) 3 *(McCulloch 23, Cousin 48, Beasley 53)*   38,076

Lyon: Vercoutre; Grosso, Reveillere (Clerc 81), Anderson, Squillaci, Bodmer (Ben Arfa 60), Kallstrom, Juninho Pernambucano, Baros (Keita 60), Benzema, Govou.
Rangers: McGregor; Hutton, Papac, Cuellar, Weir, Ferguson, Hemdani, Thomson, Cousin (Whittaker 66), McCulloch (Novo 81), Beasley (Adam 90).

Tuesday, 23 October 2007

Rangers (0) 0

Barcelona (0) 0   49,957

Rangers: McGregor; Hutton, Papac, Cuellar, Weir, Ferguson, Adam, Thomson, Novo (Beasley 72), Cousin, McCulloch.
Barcelona: Victor Valdes; Milito, Puyol, Thuram, Abidal, Xavi, Iniesta, Ronaldinho, Gudjohnsen, Henry (Giovanni Dos Santos 82), Messi.

Wednesday, 7 November 2007

Barcelona (2) 2 *(Henry 6, Messi 43)*

Rangers (0) 0   82,887

Barcelona: Victor Valdes; Gabi Milito, Puyol (Oleguer 85), Thuram, Abidal, Xavi, Iniesta (Gudjohnsen 71), Ronaldinho (Bojan Krkic 77), Toure Yaya, Henry, Messi.
Rangers: McGregor; Hutton, Papac, Cuellar, Weir, Ferguson, Hemdani, Beasley (Novo 69), Cousin (Naismith 78), McCulloch, Adam (Darcheville 62).

Tuesday, 27 November 2007

Stuttgart (1) 3 *(Cacau 45, Pardo 62, Marica 85)*

Rangers (1) 2 *(Adam 27, Ferguson 70)*   51,300

Stuttgart: Schafer; Beck, Fernando Meira, Delpierre, Magnin, Hitzlsperger, Pardo, Hilbert (Ewerthon 83), Khedira (Da Silva 46), Cacau (Tasci 88), Marica.
Rangers: McGregor; Hutton, Papac, Cuellar, Weir, Ferguson, Hemdani, Thomson, Darcheville (Cousin 82), Beasley (Naismith 49), McCulloch (Adam 26).

Wednesday, 12 December 2007

Rangers (0) 0

Lyon (1) 3 *(Govou 16, Benzema 85, 88)*   50,260

Rangers: McGregor; Hutton, Papac (Darcheville■ 71), Cuellar, Weir, Ferguson, Hemdani (Boyd 84), Thomson, Cousin (Naismith 46), McCulloch, Whittaker.
Lyon: Vercoutre; Clerc, Grosso, Anderson, Squillaci, Kallstrom, Juninho Pernambucano (Baros 85), Ben Arfa (Bodmer 68), Toulalan, Benzema, Govou (Reveillere 77).

Group E Final Table	P	W	D	L	F	A	Pts
Barcelona	6	4	2	0	12	3	14
Lyon	6	3	1	2	11	10	10
Rangers	6	2	1	3	7	9	7
Stuttgart	6	1	0	5	7	15	3

GROUP F

Roma	(1) 2	Dynamo Kiev	(0) 0
Sporting Lisbon	(0) 0	Manchester United	(0) 1
Dynamo Kiev	(1) 1	Sporting Lisbon	(2) 2
Manchester United	(0) 1	Roma	(0) 0
Dynamo Kiev	(1) 2	Manchester United	(3) 4
Roma	(1) 2	Sporting Lisbon	(1) 1
Manchester United	(2) 4	Dynamo Kiev	(0) 0
Sporting Lisbon	(1) 2	Roma	(1) 2
Dynamo Kiev	(0) 1	Roma	(3) 4
Manchester United	(0) 2	Sporting Lisbon	(1) 1
Roma	(0) 1	Manchester United	(1) 1
Sporting Lisbon	(1) 3	Dynamo Kiev	(0) 0

Wednesday, 19 September 2007

Sporting Lisbon (0) 0

Manchester United (0) 1 *(Ronaldo 62)*   39,514

Sporting Lisbon: Stojkovic; Anderson Polga, Ronny (Pereirinha 74), Tonel, Miguel Veloso, Abel, Izmailov (Vukcevic 56), Joao Moutinho, Romagnoli (Purovic 68), Yannick, Liedson.
Manchester United: Van der Sar; Brown, Evra, Carrick, Ferdinand, Vidic, Nani, Scholes, Ronaldo (Tevez 87), Rooney (Saha 72), Giggs (Anderson 76).

Tuesday, 2 October 2007

Manchester United (0) 1 *(Rooney 70)*

Roma (0) 0   73,652

Manchester United: Kuszczak; O'Shea, Evra, Carrick, Ferdinand, Vidic, Ronaldo, Scholes, Saha (Tevez 66), Rooney (Anderson 85), Nani (Giggs 80).
Roma: Curci; Juan, Mexes, Cicinho, Aquilani (Pizarro 62), De Rossi, Perrotta, Tonetto, Mancini (Vucinic 74), Totti, Giuly (Esposito 80).

Tuesday, 23 October 2007

Dynamo Kiev (1) 2 *(Diogo Rincon 34, Bangoura 78)*

Manchester United (3) 4 *(Ferdinand 10, Rooney 18, Ronaldo 41, 68 (pen))*   42,000

Dynamo Kiev: Shovkovskiy; Diakhate, Nesmachni, Gavrancic, Ghioane (Belkevich 46), Correa (Rotan 83), Diogo Rincon, Gusev, Ayila, Bangoura, Shatskikh (Milevski 46).
Manchester United: Van der Sar (Kuszczak 80); Brown, O'Shea, Anderson, Ferdinand, Vidic, Ronaldo, Fletcher, Rooney, Tevez (Nani 73), Giggs (Simpson 80).

Wednesday, 7 November 2007

Manchester United (2) 4 *(Pique 31, Tevez 37, Rooney 76, Ronaldo 88)*

Dynamo Kiev (0) 0   75,017

Manchester United: Van der Sar (Kuszczak 46); Pique (Evans 73), Evra, Carrick, Simpson, Vidic, Ronaldo, Fletcher, Rooney, Tevez (Saha 68), Nani.
Dynamo Kiev: Shovkovskiy; Fedorov, Diakhate, Vashchuk, Markovic, Ghioane, Correa, Rotan (Diogo Rincon 46), Gusev (Rebrov 46), El-Kaddouri, Milevski (Bangoura 76).

Tuesday, 27 November 2007

Manchester United (0) 2 *(Tevez 61, Ronaldo 90)*

Sporting Lisbon (1) 1 *(Abel 21)*   75,162

Manchester United: Kuszczak; O'Shea, Evra, Carrick, Ferdinand, Vidic, Ronaldo, Anderson, Saha (Hargreaves 79), Fletcher (Tevez 46), Nani (Giggs 46).
Sporting Lisbon: Rui Patricio; Had, Anderson Polga, Tonel, Miguel Veloso, Abel, Izmailov (Farnerud 82), Joao Moutinho, Romagnoli (Vukcevic 68), Purovic (Pereirinha 82), Liedson.

Wednesday, 12 December 2007

Roma (0) 1 *(Mancini 71)*

Manchester United (1) 1 *(Pique 34)*   29,490

Roma: Doni; Cicinho, Mexes, Antunes, Ferrari, Pizarro, Taddei (De Rossi 46), Barusso (Vucinic 62), Mancini, Totti, Esposito (Giuly 62).
Manchester United: Kuszczak; Pique, O'Shea (Brown 54), Carrick, Evans, Simpson, Eagles, Fletcher, Saha, Rooney (Dong 72), Nani.

Group F Final Table	P	W	D	L	F	A	Pts
Manchester United	6	5	1	0	13	4	16
Roma	6	3	2	1	11	6	11
Sporting Lisbon	6	2	1	3	9	8	7
Dynamo Kiev	6	0	0	6	4	19	0

GROUP G

Fenerbahce	(1) 1	Internazionale	(0) 0
PSV Eindhoven	(0) 2	CSKA Moscow	(0) 1
CSKA Moscow	(0) 2	Fenerbahce	(1) 2
Internazionale	(2) 2	PSV Eindhoven	(0) 0
CSKA Moscow	(1) 1	Internazionale	(0) 2
PSV Eindhoven	(0) 0	Fenerbahce	(0) 0
Fenerbahce	(2) 2	PSV Eindhoven	(0) 0
Internazionale	(2) 4	CSKA Moscow	(2) 2
CSKA Moscow	(0) 0	PSV Eindhoven	(1) 1
Internazionale	(0) 3	Fenerbahce	(0) 0
Fenerbahce	(2) 3	CSKA Moscow	(1) 1
PSV Eindhoven	(0) 0	Internazionale	(0) 1

Group F Final Table	P	W	D	L	F	A	Pts
Internazionale	6	5	0	1	12	4	15
Fenerbahce	6	3	2	1	8	6	11
PSV Eindhoven	6	2	1	3	3	6	7
CSKA Moscow	6	0	1	5	7	14	1

GROUP H

Arsenal	(1) 3	Sevilla	(0) 0
Slavia Prague	(1) 2	Steaua	(1) 1
Sevilla	(2) 4	Slavia Prague	(1) 2
Steaua	(0) 0	Arsenal	(0) 1
Arsenal	(3) 7	Slavia Prague	(0) 0
Sevilla	(2) 2	Steaua	(0) 1
Slavia Prague	(0) 0	Arsenal	(0) 0
Steaua	(0) 0	Sevilla	(1) 2

Sevilla	(2) 3	Arsenal	(1) 1
Steaua	(1) 1	Slavia Prague	(0) 1
Arsenal	(2) 2	Steaua	(0) 1
Slavia Prague	(0) 0	Sevilla	(0) 3

Wednesday, 19 September 2007

Arsenal (1) 3 *(Fabregas 27, Van Persie 59, Eduardo 90)*

Sevilla (0) 0   59,992

Arsenal: Almunia; Sagna, Clichy, Flamini, Toure, Senderos, Hleb, Fabregas, Adebayor (Eduardo 83), Van Persie (Diarra 88), Rosicky (Diaby 50).
Sevilla: Palop; Dragutinovic, Daniel Alves, Escude, Fazio, Jesus Navas, Poulsen, Diego Capel (Renato 67), Marti (Keita 66), Luis Fabiano (Kerzhakov 46), Kanoute.

Tuesday, 2 October 2007

Steaua (0) 0

Arsenal (0) 1 *(Van Persie 76)*   15,000

Steaua: Zapata; Rada, Emeghara, Baciu, Marin, Petre O, Nicolita, Badea (Iacob 60), Dica, Neaga (Zaharia 77), Surdu (Badoi 84).
Arsenal: Almunia; Sagna, Clichy, Flamini, Toure, Senderos, Eboue (Silva 73), Fabregas, Adebayor, Van Persie, Hleb.

Tuesday, 23 October 2007

Arsenal (3) 7 *(Fabregas 5, 58, Hubacek 24 (og), Walcott 41, 55, Hleb 51, Bendtner 89)*

Slavia Prague (0) 0   59,621

Arsenal: Almunia; Sagna, Clichy, Flamini (Silva 63), Toure, Gallas, Eboue, Fabregas, Adebayor (Rosicky 64), Walcott, Hleb (Bendtner 63).
Slavia Prague: Vaniak; Hubacek, Svec, Tavares (Belaid 63), Pudil, Suchy, Krajcik, Kalivoda (Jablonsky 46), Vlcek, Senkerik, Ivana (Volesak 56).

Wednesday, 7 November 2007

Slavia Prague (0) 0

Arsenal (0) 0   18,000

Slavia Prague: Vorel; Brabec, Hubacek, Svec, Drizdal, Tavares, Smicer (Kalivoda 64), Pudil (Jablonsky 90), Suchy, Krajcik, Senkerik (Ivana 77).
Arsenal: Almunia; Diarra, Clichy, Silva, Song Billong, Gallas, Denilson, Walcott, Eduardo (Eboue 81), Bendtner (Adebayor 78), Diaby.

Tuesday, 27 November 2007

Sevilla (2) 3 *(Keita 24, Luis Fabiano 34, Kanoute 89 (pen))*

Arsenal (1) 1 *(Eduardo 11)*   35,529

Sevilla: Palop; Dragutinovic, Daniel Alves, Jesus Navas, Poulsen, Fazio, Keita, Adriano (Marti 90), Luis Fabiano (Kerzhakov 75), Crespo (Mosquera 64), Kanoute.
Arsenal: Almunia; Hoyte J (Sagna 66), Traore, Silva, Toure, Senderos, Eboue (Walcott 78), Fabregas (Rosicky 56), Eduardo, Bendtner, Denilson.

Wednesday, 12 December 2007

Arsenal (2) 2 *(Diaby 8, Bendtner 42)*

Steaua (0) 1 *(Zaharia 68)*   59,786

Arsenal: Lehmann; Sagna (Eboue 71), Traore, Song-Billong, Senderos, Gallas, Walcott, Denilson, Van Persie (Eduardo 65), Bendtner, Diaby (Diarra 71).
Steaua: Zapata; Goian, Rada, Emeghara, Nesu, Petre O, Cristocea (Surdu 57), Lovin, Badea (Golanski 81), Dica, Neaga (Zaharia 64).

233

Group H Final Table	P	W	D	L	F	A	Pts
Sevilla	6	5	0	1	14	7	15
Arsenal	6	4	1	1	14	4	13
Slavia Prague	6	1	2	3	5	16	5
Steaua	6	0	1	5	4	10	1

KNOCK-OUT STAGE

KNOCK-OUT ROUND FIRST LEG

Liverpool	(0) 2	Internazionale	(0) 0
Olympiakos	(0) 0	Chelsea	(0) 0
Roma	(1) 2	Real Madrid	(1) 1
Schalke	(1) 1	Porto	(0) 0
Arsenal	(0) 0	AC Milan	(0) 0
Celtic	(2) 2	Barcelona	(1) 3
Fenerbahce	(1) 3	Sevilla	(1) 2
Lyon	(0) 1	Manchester United	(0) 1

Tuesday, 19 February 2008

Liverpool (0) 2 *(Kuyt 85, Gerrard 90)*

Internazionale (0) 0   41,999

Liverpool: Reyna; Finnan, Fabio Aurelio, Mascherano, Carragher, Hyypia, Lucas (Crouch 64), Gerrard, Torres, Kuyt, Babel (Pennant 72).
Internazionale: Julio Cesar; Cordoba (Burdisso 76), Zanetti, Maxwell, Maicon, Materazzi■, Chivu, Stankovic, Cambiasso, Ibrahimovic, Cruz (Vieira 55).

Olympiakos (0) 0

Chelsea (0) 0   31,302

Olympiakos: Nikopolidis; Julio Cesar, Zewlakow, Antzas, Torosidis, Stoltidis, Galletti (Leonardo 83), Djordjevic (Belluschi 76), Ledesma, Pantos, Kovacevic (Nunez 87).
Chelsea: Cech; Belletti, Cole A, Makelele, Alex, Ricardo Carvalho, Essien, Ballack (Lampard 86), Drogba, Cole J (Kalou 75), Malouda (Anelka 75).

Wednesday, 20 February 2008

Arsenal (0) 0

AC Milan (0) 0   60,082

Arsenal: Lehmann; Sagna, Clichy, Flamini, Toure (Senderos 7), Gallas, Eboue (Walcott 90), Fabregas, Adebayor, Eduardo (Bendtner 74), Hleb.
AC Milan: Kalac; Maldini, Kaladze, Nesta (Jankulovski 50), Oddo, Gattuso, Seedorf (Emerson 86), Pirlo, Kaka, Ambrosini, Pato (Gilardino 77).

Celtic (2) 2 *(Vennegoor 16, Robson 38)*

Barcelona (1) 3 *(Messi 18, 79, Henry 52)*   56,395

Celtic: Boruc; Caddis (Wilson 61), Naylor, Hartley (Donati 65), Caldwell, McManus, Nakamura, Robson, McDonald, Vennegoor (Samaras 55), McGeady.
Barcelona: Victor Valdes; Gabi Milito, Marquez, Puyol, Abidal, Iniesta, Ronaldinho (Eto'o 73), Deco (Xavi 66), Toure Yaya, Henry (Gudjohnsen 88), Messi.

Lyon (0) 1 *(Benzema 54)*

Manchester United (0) 1 *(Tevez 87)*   39,219

Lyon: Coupet; Clerc (Ben Arfa 78), Grosso, Reveillere, Squillaci, Boumsong, Kallstrom, Juninho Pernambucano (Bodmer 74), Toulalan, Benzema (Fred 83), Govou.
Manchester United: Van der Sar; Brown, Evra, Hargreaves (Carrick 78), Ferdinand, Vidic, Anderson, Scholes (Nani 65), Rooney, Ronaldo, Giggs (Tevez 65).

KNOCK-OUT ROUND SECOND LEG

AC Milan	(0) 0	Arsenal	(0) 2
Barcelona	(1) 1	Celtic	(0) 0
Manchester United	(1) 1	Lyon	(0) 0
Sevilla	(3) 3	Fenerbahce	(1) 2
(aet; Fenerbahce won 3-2 on penalties.)			
Chelsea	(2) 3	Olympiakos	(0) 0
Porto	(0) 1	Schalke	(0) 0
(aet; Schalke won 4-1 on penalties.)			
Real Madrid	(0) 1	Roma	(0) 2
Internazionale	(0) 0	Liverpool	(0) 1

Tuesday, 4 March 2008

AC Milan (0) 0

Arsenal (0) 2 *(Fabregas 84, Adebayor 90)*   81,879

AC Milan: Kalac; Maldini, Kaladze, Nesta, Oddo, Gattuso, Pirlo, Kaka, Ambrosini, Pato, Inzaghi (Gilardino 69).
Arsenal: Almunia; Sagna, Clichy, Flamini, Senderos, Gallas, Eboue (Walcott 72), Fabregas, Adebayor, Hleb (Silva 90), Diaby.

Barcelona (1) 1 *(Xavi 3)*

Celtic (0) 0   75,326

Barcelona: Victor Valdes; Puyol, Sylvinho, Thuram, Xavi (Gudjohnsen 82), Ronaldinho, Zambrotta, Deco, Toure Yaya (Edmilson 68), Eto'o, Messi (Henry 38).
Celtic: Boruc; Wilson, Naylor, Donati (Sno 46), Caldwell, McManus, Nakamura, Hartley (McDonald 78), Brown S, Vennegoor (Samaras 55), McGeady.

Manchester United (1) 1 *(Ronaldo 41)*

Lyon (0) 0   75,521

Manchester United: Van der Sar; Brown, Evra, Carrick, Ferdinand, Vidic, Ronaldo (Hargreaves 90), Anderson (Tevez 70), Rooney, Fletcher, Nani.
Lyon: Coupet; Clerc, Cris, Grosso, Squillaci, Kallstrom (Fred 79), Juninho Pernambucano, Ben Arfa, Toulalan, Benzema, Govou (Keita 68).

Wednesday, 5 March 2008

Chelsea (2) 3 *(Ballack 5, Lampard 25, Kalou 48)*

Olympiakos (0) 0   37,721

Chelsea: Cudicini; Paul Ferreira, Cole A, Makelele, Terry, Ricardo Carvalho, Ballack, Lampard (Essien 76), Drogba, Kalou (Malouda 71), Cole J (Wright-Phillips 79).
Olympiakos: Nikopolidis; Patsatzoglou, Julio Cesar, Zewlakow, Antzas, Torosidis (Sisic 75), Stoltidis, Djordjevic (Leonardo 57), Ledesma (Belluschi 54), Pantos, Kovacevic.

Tuesday, 11 March 2008

Internazionale (0) 0

Liverpool (0) 1 *(Torres 63)*   71,501

Internazionale: Julio Cesar; Zanetti, Maicon, Burdisso■, Rivas, Chivu, Stankovic (Jimenez 84), Vieira (Pele 77), Cambiasso, Ibrahimovic (Suazo 80), Cruz.
Liverpool: Reina; Carragher, Fabio Aurelio, Mascherano (Pennant 87), Skrtel, Hyypia, Lucas, Gerrard, Torres, Kuyt (Riise 81), Babel (Benayoun 61).

QUARTER-FINALS FIRST LEG

Roma	(0) 0	Manchester United	(1) 2
Schalke	(0) 0	Barcelona	(1) 1
Arsenal	(1) 1	Liverpool	(1) 1
Fenerbahce	(0) 2	Chelsea	(1) 1

Tuesday, 1 April 2008

Roma (0) 0

Manchester United (1) 2 *(Ronaldo 39, Rooney 66)*   60,931

Roma: Doni; Panucci, Mexes, Cassetti, Pizarro, Aquilani (Esposito 77), Taddei (Giuly 59), De Rossi, Tonetto (Cicinho 68), Mancini, Vucinic.
Manchester United: Van der Sar; Brown, Evra, Carrick, Ferdinand, Vidic (O'Shea 33), Ronaldo, Anderson (Hargreaves 55), Rooney (Tevez 84), Scholes, Park.

Wednesday, 2 April 2008

Arsenal (1) 1 *(Adebayor 23)*

Liverpool (1) 1 *(Kuyt 25)*   60,041

Arsenal: Almunia; Toure, Clichy, Flamini, Senderos, Gallas, Eboue (Bendtner 67), Fabregas, Adebayor, Van Persie (Walcott 46), Hleb.
Liverpool: Reina; Carragher, Fabio Aurelio, Xabi Alonso (Lucas 77), Skrtel, Hyypia, Gerrard, Mascherano, Torres (Voronin 86), Kuyt, Babel (Benayoun 58).

Fenerbahce (0) 2 *(Kazim-Richards 64, Deivid 80)*

Chelsea (1) 1 *(Deivid 12 (og))*   49,055

Fenerbahce: Volkan; Lugano, Onder, Edu Dracena, Wederson, Mehmet, Alex, Ugur (Kazim-Richards 54), Maldonado, Kezman (Semih 72), Deivid.
Chelsea: Cudicini; Essien, Cole A, Makelele, Terry, Ricardo Carvalho, Ballack, Lampard (Mikel 76), Drogba, Cole J (Anelka 86), Malouda.

QUARTER-FINALS SECOND LEG

Chelsea	(1) 2	Fenerbahce	(0) 0
Liverpool	(1) 4	Arsenal	(1) 2
Barcelona	(1) 1	Schalke	(0) 0
Manchester United	(0) 1	Roma	(0) 0

Tuesday, 8 April 2008

Chelsea (1) 2 *(Ballack 3, Lampard 88)*

Fenerbahce (0) 0   38,369

Chelsea: Cudicini (Hilario 26); Essien, Cole A, Makelele, Terry, Ricardo Carvalho, Ballack, Lampard, Drogba, Kalou (Belletti 58), Cole J (Malouda 85).
Fenerbahce: Volkan; Lugano, Edu Dracena, Gokhan, Wederson (Ali 89), Mehmet, Alex, Maldonado (Kezman 60), Semih (Ugur 75), Kazim-Richards, Deivid.

Liverpool (1) 4 *(Hyypia 30, Torres 69, Gerrard 86 (pen), Babel 90)*

Arsenal (1) 2 *(Diaby 13, Adebayor 84)*   41,985

Liverpool: Reina; Carragher, Fabio Aurelio, Xabi Alonso, Skrtel, Hyypia, Gerrard, Mascherano, Torres (Riise 87), Kuyt (Arbeloa 90), Crouch (Babel 78).
Arsenal: Almunia; Toure, Clichy, Flamini (Silva 42), Senderos, Gallas, Eboue (Van Persie 72), Fabregas, Adebayor, Hleb, Diaby (Walcott 72).

Wednesday, 9 April 2008

Manchester United (0) 1 *(Tevez 70)*

Roma (0) 0   74,423

Manchester United: Van der Sar; Brown, Silvestre, Carrick (O'Shea 74), Ferdinand, Pique, Park, Hargreaves, Anderson (Neville 81), Tevez, Giggs (Rooney 74).
Roma: Doni; Panucci, Juan, Mexes, Cassetti (Tonetto 57), Pizarro (Giuly 69), Taddei (Esposito 81), De Rossi, Perrotta, Mancini, Vucinic.

SEMI-FINALS FIRST LEG

Liverpool	(1) 1	Chelsea	(0) 1
Barcelona	(0) 0	Manchester United	(0) 0

Tuesday, 22 April 2008
Liverpool (1) 1 *(Kuyt 43)*
Chelsea (0) 1 *(Riise 90 (og))*   42,180
Liverpool: Reina; Arbeloa, Fabio Aurelio (Riise 62), Xabi Alonso, Carragher, Skrtel, Gerrard, Mascherano, Torres, Kuyt, Babel (Benayoun 76).
Chelsea: Cech; Paulo Ferreira, Cole A, Makelele, Terry, Ricardo Carvalho, Ballack (Anelka 86), Lampard, Drogba, Cole J (Kalou 63), Malouda.

Wednesday, 23 April 2008
Barcelona (0) 0
Manchester United (0) 0   95,949
Barcelona: Victor Valdes; Gabi Milito, Marquez, Abidal, Xavi, Iniesta, Zambrotta, Deco (Henry 77), Toure Yaya, Eto'o, Messi (Bojan Krkic 62).
Manchester United: Van der Sar; Brown, Evra, Carrick, Ferdinand, Hargreaves, Ronaldo, Scholes, Rooney (Nani 76), Tevez (Giggs 85), Park.

SEMI-FINALS SECOND LEG

| Manchester United | (1) 1 | Barcelona | (0) 0 |
| Chelsea* | (1) 3 | Liverpool | (0) 2 |

Tuesday, 29 April 2008
Manchester United (1) 1 *(Scholes 14)*
Barcelona (0) 0   75,061
Manchester United: Van der Sar; Brown, Evra (Silvestre 90), Carrick, Ferdinand, Hargreaves, Ronaldo, Scholes (Fletcher 77), Nani (Giggs 77), Tevez, Park.
Barcelona: Victor Valdes; Gabi Milito, Puyol, Abidal, Xavi, Iniesta (Henry 61), Zambrotta, Deco, Toure Yaya (Gudjohnsen 88), Eto'o (Bojan Krkic 72), Messi.

Wednesday, 30 April 2008
Chelsea (1) 3 *(Drogba 33, 105, Lampard 98 (pen))*
Liverpool (0) 2 *(Torres 64, Babel 117)*   38,900
Chelsea: Cech; Essien, Cole A, Makelele, Terry, Ricardo Carvalho, Ballack, Lampard (Shevchenko 119), Drogba, Kalou (Malouda 70), Cole J (Anelka 91).
Liverpool: Reina; Arbeloa, Riise, Xabi Alonso, Carragher, Skrtel (Hyypia 22), Gerrard, Mascherano, Torres (Babel 98), Kuyt, Benayoun (Pennant 78).
aet.

UEFA CHAMPIONS LEAGUE FINAL 2008

Wednesday, 21 May 2008

Manchester United (1) 1 *(Ronaldo 26)*   **Chelsea (1) 1** *(Lampard 45)*

(in Moscow, 69,552)

Manchester United: Van der Sar; Brown (Anderson 120), Evra, Carrick, Ferdinand, Vidic, Hargreaves, Scholes (Giggs 87), Rooney (Nani 101), Tevez, Ronaldo.

Chelsea: Cech; Essien, Cole A, Makelele (Belletti 120), Terry, Ricardo Carvalho, Ballack, Lampard, Drogba**, Cole J (Anelka 99), Malouda (Kalou 92).

aet; Manchester United won 6-5 on penalties: Tevez scored; Ballack scored; Carrick scored; Belletti scored; Ronaldo saved; Lampard scored; Hargreaves scored; Cole A scored; Nani scored; Terry hit post; Anderson scored; Kalou scored; Giggs scored; Anelka saved.

Referee: L. Michel (Slovakia).

INTERTOTO CUP 2007

* *Denotes player sent off.*

FIRST ROUND, FIRST LEG
Sant Julia 2, Slavija 3
Tobol 3, Zestaponi 0
Valur 0, Cork City 2
Zagreb 2, Vllaznia 1
Achnas 1, Makedonija 0
Baku 1, Dacia 1
Differdange 0, Slovan 2
Hammarby 1, KI 0
Cliftonville 1, Dinaburg 1
Shakhtyor 4, Ararat 1
Gloria 2, Grbalj 1
Birkirkara 0, Maribor 3
Vetra 3, Llanelli 1
Honka 0, VMK 0

FIRST ROUND, SECOND LEG
Slavija 3, Sant Julia 2
Zestaponi 2, Tobol 0
Cork City 0, Valur 1
Vllaznia 1, Zagreb 0
Makedonija 2, Achnas 0
Dacia 4, Baku 2
Slovan 3, Differdange 0
KI 1, Hammarby 2
Dinaburg 0, Cliftonville 1
Ararat 2, Shakhtyor 0
Grbalj 1, Gloria 1
Maribor 2, Birkirkara 1
Llanelli 5, Vetra 3
VMK 2, Honka 4

SECOND ROUND, FIRST LEG
Maccabi Haifa 0, Gloria 2
Dacia 0, St Gallen 1
Gent 2, Cliftonville 0
Cork City 1, Hammarby 1
ZTE 0, Rubin 3
Rapid Vienna 3, Slovan 1
Slavija 0, Otelul 0
Makedonija 0, Chernomore 4
Maribor 2, Kula 0
Chernomorets 4, Shakhtyor 2
Tobol 1, Liberec 1
Honka 2, Aalborg 2
Vetra v Legia match cancelled.
Trabzonspor 6, Vllaznia 0

SECOND ROUND, SECOND LEG
Gloria 3, Maccabi Haifa 4
St Gallen 0, Dacia 5
Cliftonville 0, Gent 4
Hammarby 1, Cork City 0
Rubin 2, ZTE 0
Slovan 1, Rapid Vienna 0

Otelul 3, Slavija 0
Chernomore 3, Makedonija 0
Kula 5, Maribor 0
Shakhtyor 0, Chernomorets 2
Liberec 0, Tobol 2
Aalborg 1, Honka 1
Legia v Vetra match cancelled.
Vllaznia 0, Trabzonspor 4

THIRD ROUND, FIRST LEG
Chernomore 0, Sampdoria 1
Gloria 2, Atletico Madrid 1
Otelul 2, Trabzonspor 1
Chernomorets 0, Lens 0
Rapid Vienna 3, Rubin 1
Dacia 1, Hamburg 1
Gent 1, Aalborg 1
Vetra 1, Blackburn Rovers 2
Hammarby 0, Utrecht 0
Tobol 1, OFI Crete 0
Kula 1, Leiria 0

THIRD ROUND, SECOND LEG
Sampdoria 1, Chernomore 0
Atletico Madrid 1, Gloria 0
Trabzonspor 1, Otelul 2
Lens 1, Chernomorets 1
Rubin 0, Rapid Vienna 0
Hamburg 4, Dacia 0
Aalborg 2, Gent 1
Blackburn Rovers 4, Vetra 0
Utrecht 1, Hammarby 1
OFI Crete 0, Tobol 1
Leiria 4, Kula 1
Legia expelled because of crowd trouble.
Eleven winners qualify for UEFA Cup
Second Qualifying Round.

Vetra (0) 0

Blackburn Rovers (1) 2 *(McCarthy 30,*
Derbyshire 81)   5200

Blackburn Rovers: Friedel; Ooijer,
Warnock, Tugay (Mokoena 46), Nelsen,
Samba, Bentley (Derbyshire 65), Sav-
age, Roberts, McCarthy (Rigters 65),
Pedersen.

Blackburn Rovers (1) 4 *(Pedersen 25,*
Roberts 48, McCarthy 54, Samba 55)
Vetra (0) 0 *Milosevski*■   11,854

Blackburn Rovers: Friedel; Ooijer,
Warnock, Mokoena (Dunn 53), Nelsen,
Samba, Bentley, Savage, Roberts
(Rigters 57), McCarthy (Derbyshire 57),
Pedersen.

UEFA CUP 2007–2008

▪ *Denotes player sent off.*
* *Winner after extra time.* †*Winner after extra time and penalties*

FIRST QUALIFYING ROUND FIRST LEG

Aktobe	(0) 1	Mattersburg	(0) 0
Artmedia	(1) 1	Zimbru	(0) 1
B36	(1) 1	Ekranas	(2) 3
Banants	(0) 1	Young Boys	(1) 1
Belchatow	(0) 2	Ameri	(0) 0
Bezanija	(1) 2	Besa	(0) 0
Buducnost	(0) 1	Hajduk Split	(1) 1
Carmarthen Town	(0) 0	Brann	(5) 8
Dungannon Swifts	(1) 1	Suduva	(0) 0
Dynamo Tbilisi	(0) 2	Vaduz	(0) 0
Flora	(0) 0	Valerenga	(1) 1
Glentoran	(0) 0	AIK Stockholm	(1) 5
Gorica	(0) 1	Rabotnicki	(0) 2
HJK Helsinki	(1) 2	Etzella	(0) 0
Hacken	(1) 1	KR Reykjavik	(0) 1
Helsingborg	(2) 6	Trans	(0) 0
Keflavik	(2) 3	Midtjylland	(2) 2
Libertas	(0) 1	Drogheda United	(1) 1
Lillestrom	(2) 2	Kaerjeng	(1) 1
MKT Araz	(0) 0	Groclin	(0) 0
MTK Budapest	(1) 2	Mika	(1) 1
Metalurgs Liepaja	(1) 1	Dynamo Brest	(0) 1
Moravce	(0) 3	Alma-Ata	(0) 1
MyPa	(0) 1	EB/Streymur	(0) 0
Omonia	(1) 2	Rudar	(0) 0
Otaci	(1) 1	Honved	(0) 1
Rhyl	(2) 3	Haka	(1) 1
Ried	(1) 3	Neftchi	(1) 1
Santa Coloma	(0) 1	Maccabi Tel Aviv	(0) 0
Siroki	(3) 3	Koper	(1) 1
Skonto Riga	(1) 1	Dynamo Minsk	(1) 1
Slaven	(2) 6	Teuta	(1) 2
Sliema Wanderers	(0) 0	Litex	(1) 3
St Patrick's Ath	(0) 0	Odense	(0) 0
Vardar	(0) 0	Anorthosis	(0) 1
Vojvodina	(2) 5	Hibernians	(0) 1
Zrinjski	(0) 1	Partizan Belgrade	(2) 6

(Partizan Belgrade allowed to play in the second leg while disqualification hearing was being conducted; club also fined for conduct of their supporters.)

Thursday, 19 July 2007

Carmarthen Town (0) 0

Brann (5) 8 *(Winters 8, 30, 45, Helstad 17, 28, Sigurdsson K 70, Solli 83, Bjornsson 90)*
769

Carmarthen Town: Thomas N; Hancock, Smothers▪, Palmer, Warton, Thomas C, Walters, Ramasut, Fowler, Hicks, Cotterrall.
Brann: Thorbjornsen; Bjarnason, Dahl, Hanstveit, Helstad (Bjornsson 58), Huseklepp (Gashi 74), Sigurdsson K, Andresen (Jaiteh 46), Solli, Winters, Vaagan Moen.

Dungannon Swifts (1) 1 *(McAllister 17)*

Suduva (0) 0
500

Dungannon Swifts: Wells; McConkey, Gallagher, Montgomery, Hegarty, Curran, McCabe, McMinn, Campbell (McGinn 74), McCluskey, McAllister (Baron 89).
Suduva: Klevinskas S; Sobol, Skinderis, Klevinskas G, Mikuckis, Feldmann (Urbsys 46), Miklinevicius, Maciulevicius, Potapov, Viller, Braga (Juska 69).

Glentoran (0) 0

AIK Stockholm (1) 5 *(Figueiredo 21, 62, Valdemarin 68, Stephenson 73, Johnson 84)*
2033

Glentoran: Dougherty; Nixon, Fitzgerald, Hill (Morgan 69), Leeman, Smyth, Ward S, Hamill (Carson 69), Halliday, Hamilton, Berry (Ward M 80).
AIK Stockholm: Orlund; Karlsson, Tamandi, Johansson, Ivan (Mendes 76), Arnefjord, Johnson, Tjernstrom (Bengtsson 82), Pavey, Figueiredo (Valdemarin 66), Stephenson.

Libertas (0) 1 *(Pari 77)*

Drogheda United (1) 1 *(Zayed 44)*
250

Libertas: Ceccoli; Macerata, Gazzi, Sottili, Simoncini (Pari 53), Cevoli, Santini, Semprini, Fambri, Tarini, Cavalli (Nanni 71).
Drogheda United: Connor; Tambouras, Shelley, Gray (Webb 67), Ristila, Gartland, Robinson, Whelan, Zayed (Grant 71), Byrne, O'Keeffe (Baker 79).

Rhyl (2) 3 *(Moran 26, Hunt 36, Garside 47)*

Haka (1) 1 *(Lehtinen 15)*
1787

Rhyl: Gann; Powell M, Brewerton (Desormeaux 90), Connolly, Horan, Ruffer, Garside, Kelly, Hunt (Cameron 80), Moran, Graves (Roberts C 76).
Haka: Dovbnya; Kangaskorpi, Fowler, Okkonen, Holopainen, Strandvall, Innanen, Kauppila, Manninen (Mattila■ 72), Parviainen, Lehtinen.

St Patrick's Ath (0) 0

Odense (0) 0
2800

St Patrick's Ath: Ryan; Brennan, Rogers, Murphy, Maguire, Guy (O'Connor 90), Gibson (Foley-Sheridan 88), Fahey, Paisley, Keane (Mulcahy 63), Quigley.
Odense: Onyszko; Borring, Laursen, Hansen, Christensen A, Helveg, Christensen K (Timm 80), Bechara (Andreasen 69), Jensen, Bolanos, Absalonsen.

FIRST QUALIFYING ROUND SECOND LEG

AIK Stockholm	(2) 4	Glentoran	(0) 0
Almaty	(0) 1	Moravce	(0) 1
Ameri	(2) 2	Belchatow	(0) 0
(aet; Belchatow won 4-2 on penalties.)			
Anorthosis	(0) 1	Vardar	(0) 0
Besa	(0) 0	Bezanija	(0) 0
Brann	(4) 6	Carmarthen Town	(1) 3
Drogheda United	(1) 3	Libertas	(0) 0
Dynamo Brest	(0) 1	Metalurgs	(1) 2
Dynamo Minsk	(0) 2	Skonto Riga	(0) 0
EB/Streymur	(0) 1	MyPa	(0) 1
Ekranas	(0) 3	B36	(0) 2
Etzella	(0) 0	HJK Helsinki	(1) 1
Groclin	(0) 1	MKT Araz	(0) 0
Hajduk Split	(0) 1	Buducnost	(0) 0
Haka	(0) 2	Rhyl	(0) 0
Hibernians	(0) 0	Vojvodina	(1) 2
Honved	(1) 1	Otaci	(0) 1
(aet; Honved won 5-4 on penalties.)			
Kaerjeng	(0) 1	Lillestrom	(0) 0
KR Reykjavik	(0) 0	Hacken	(0) 1
Koper	(1) 2	Siroki	(3) 3
Litex	(1) 4	Sliema Wanderers	(0) 0
Maccabi Tel Aviv	(2) 4	Santa Coloma	(0) 0
Mattersburg	(1) 4	Aktobe	(0) 2
Midtjylland	(0) 2	Keflavik	(1) 1
Mika	(1) 1	MTK Budapest	(0) 0
Neftchi	(2) 2	Ried	(0) 1
Odense	(3) 5	St Patrick's Ath	(0) 0

Partizan Belgrade (3) 5 Zrinjski (0) 0
(Partizan Belgrade expelled from the competition after crowd trouble in the first leg; Zrinjski qualify for next round.)

Rabotnicki	(1) 2	Gorica	(0) 1
Rudar	(0) 0	Omonia	(1) 2
Suduva	(1) 4	Dungannon Swifts	(0) 0
Teuta	(1) 2	Slaven	(0) 2
Trans	(0) 0	Helsingborg	(2) 3
Vaduz	(0) 0	Dynamo Tbilisi	(0) 0
Valerenga	(0) 1	Flora	(0) 0
Young Boys	(3) 4	Banants	(0) 0
Zimbru	(1) 2	Artmedia	(0) 2

Thursday, 2 August 2007

AIK Stockholm (2) 4 *(Ozkan 7, Karlsson 24, Gerndt 88, Johnson 89)*
Glentoran (0) 0 8707

AIK Stockholm: Orlund; Karlsson, Arnefjord, Johansson, Tamandi, Pavey, Stephenson, Ozkan (Gerndt 67), Johnson, Figueiredo (Bengtsson 67), Valdemarin (Mendes 67).
Glentoran: Dougherty; Nixon, Neill, Hill (McMenamin 72), Leeman, Fitzgerald, Ward S, Ward M (Hamill 84), Halliday (Morgan 83), Hamilton, Carson.

Brann (4) 6 *(Vaagan Moen 9, Bjornsson 19, Winters 27, 32, Sigurdsson K 56, Hanstveit 57)*
Carmarthen Town (1) 3 *(Thomas D 36, Hicks 47, 90)* 4597

Brann: Thorbjornsen; Dahl, Hanstveit, Bjarnason, Sigurdsson K, Bjornsson, Vaagan Moen (Guntveit 58), Huseklepp, Jaiteh, Bakke, Winters.
Carmarthen Town: Thomas N; Hancock, Hughes, Warton (Brace 71), Palmer, Thomas C, Thomas D (Davies M 74), Ramasut (Hicks 46), Fowler, Walters, Cotterrall.

Drogheda United (1) 3 *(Keegan 11, 48, Byrne 57)*
Libertas (0) 0 3250

Drogheda United: Connor; Shelley, Webb, Tambouras, Byrne (Bradley 63), Keegan, Gartland, Robinson (Baker 60), Ristila, Zayed, Keddy (O'Keeffe 75).
Libertas: Ceccoli; Sottili, Cevoli, Valentini, Gazzi, Macerata, Tarini, Nanni (Toccaceli 79), Semprini (Pari 58),

Haka (0) 2 *(Innanen 62, Popovich 64)*
Rhyl (0) 0 1565

Haka: Dovbnya; Kangaskorpi, Okkonen, Holopainen, Innanen, Kauppila, Manninen (Strandvall 64), Fowler, Parviainen, Lehtinen (Mahlakaarto 90), Popovich.
Rhyl: Gann; Powell M (Holt 90), Roberts C (Jones 84), Connolly, Horan, Ruffer, Garside (Cameron 75), Kelly, Hunt, Graves, Moran.

Odense (3) 5 *(Andreasen 20, Christensen K 29, 73, Borring 45, Nymann 89)*
St Patrick's Ath (0) 0 5306

Odense: Onyszko; Laursen, Christensen A, Helveg (Troest 46), Sorensen, Andreasen (Nymann 79), Timm, Hansen, Bolanos (Radonjic 70), Borring, Christensen K.
St Patrick's Ath: Ryan; Brennan, Maguire, Quigley (Foley-Sheridan 79), Rogers, Kirby, Fahey, Keane (Paisley 16), Murphy (O'Connor 59), Gibson, Guy.

Suduva (1) 4 *(Grigas 29, Urbsys 50, 55, 84)*
Dungannon Swifts (0) 0 1500

Suduva: Klevinskas S; Grigas, Klevinskas G, Mikuckis, Sobol, Miklinevicius, Maciulevicius (Slavickas G 70), Urbsys (Potapov 84), Viller■, Juska (Jasaitis 46), Braga.
Dungannon Swifts: Nelson; McConkey (Baron 81), Gallagher, McMinn, Fitzpatrick G, Curran, McCabe, Fitzpatrick T (Magennis 64), Campbell, Hegarty (McManus 64), McAllister.

SECOND QUALIFYING ROUND FIRST LEG

Atletico Madrid	(1) 3	Vojvodina	(0) 0
Basle	(1) 2	Mattersburg	(1) 1
Besa	(0) 0	Litex	(3) 3
Brann	(1) 2	Suduva	(0) 1
Cluj	(0) 1	Anorthosis	(1) 3
Dnepr	(0) 1	Belchatow	(1) 1
Drogheda United	(0) 1	Helsingborg	(1) 1
Dunfermline Athletic	(1) 1	Hacken	(0) 1
Dynamo Minsk	(0) 1	Odense	(0) 1
Dynamo Tbilisi	(0) 0	Rapid Vienna	(2) 3
Ekranas	(1) 1	Valerenga	(0) 1
FK Austria	(2) 4	Jablonec	(2) 3
HJK Helsinki	(1) 2	Aalborg	(1) 1
Hajduk Split	(0) 0	Sampdoria	(1) 1
Haka	(0) 1	Midtjylland	(2) 2
Hammarby	(1) 2	Fredrikstad	(0) 1
Honved	(0) 0	Hamburg	(0) 0
Kaerjeng	(0) 0	Standard Liege	(0) 3
Lokomotiv Sofia	(1) 3	Otelul	(0) 1
Maccabi Tel Aviv	(1) 1	Erciyesspor	(1) 1
Metalurgs Liepaja	(2) 3	AIK Stockholm	(0) 2
Mika	(1) 2	Artmedia	(0) 1
Moravce	(0) 0	Zenit	(1) 2
MyPa	(0) 0	Blackburn Rovers	(1) 1
Omonia	(1) 1	CSKA Sofia	(1) 1
Rabotnicki	(0) 0	Zrinjski	(0) 0
Ried	(0) 1	Sion	(0) 1
Siroki	(0) 0	Hapoel Tel Aviv	(2) 3
Slaven	(1) 1	Galatasaray	(1) 2
Tobol	(0) 0	Groclin	(1) 1
Uniao Leiria	(0) 0	Maccabi Netanya	(0) 0
Young Boys	(0) 1	Lens	(0) 1

Thursday, 16 August 2007

Drogheda United (0) 1 *(Zayed 54)*

Helsingborg (1) 1 *(Larsson 34)*   4500

Drogheda United: Connor; Webb, Gavin, Gartland, Shelley, Robinson, Keddy (Cahill 51), Byrne, Ristila (Grant 46), Baker (Keegan 78), Zayed.
Helsingborg: Andersson D; Jakobsson, Andersson C, Ronningberg, Tamboura, Svanback, Dahl, Mariga, Wahlstedt, Omotoyossi, Larsson.

Dunfermline Athletic (1) 1 *(Hamilton 1)*

Hacken (0) 1 *(Henriksson 57)*   6017

Dunfermline Athletic: McKenzie (Murdock 10); Shields, Wilson, Bamba, Young, Thomson S (Morrison S 46), Simmons (Morrison O 77), Harper, Glass, Burchill, Hamilton.
Hacken: Kallqvist; Williams, Lind, Heden, Forsell, Marek, Ze Antonio, Mambo Mumba, Skulason, Henriksson, Larsson (Olofsson 86).

MyPa (0) 0

Blackburn Rovers (1) 1 *(Santa Cruz 6)*   2012

MyPa: Korhonen; Pulkkinen, Huttunen, Miranda, Kansikas, Agboh, Kuparinen (Manso 65), Muinonen (Puhakainen 53), Mustafi, Hyyrynen, Peltonen (Nykanen 79).
Blackburn Rovers: Friedel; Ooijer, Warnock, Dunn (Tugay 72), Nelsen, Samba, Bentley, Savage, Santa Cruz, Roberts (Derbyshire 65), Pedersen (Emerton 72).

SECOND QUALIFYING ROUND SECOND LEG

AIK Stockholm	(1) 2	Metalurgs Liepaja	(0) 0
Aalborg	(3) 3	HJK Helsinki	(0) 0
Anorthosis	(0) 0	Cluj	(0) 0
Artmedia	(1) 2	Mika	(0) 0
Belchatow	(2) 2	Dnepr	(4) 4
Blackburn Rovers	(0) 2	MyPa	(0) 0
CSKA Sofia	(1) 2	Omonia	(1) 1
Erciyesspor	(2) 3	Maccabi Tel Aviv	(1) 1
Fredrikstad	(0) 1	Hammarby	(1) 1
Galatasaray	(2) 2	Slaven	(1) 1
Groclin	(2) 2	Tobol	(0) 0
Hacken	(1) 1	Dunfermline Athletic	(0) 0
Hamburg	(2) 4	Honved	(0) 0
Hapoel Tel Aviv	(1) 3	Siroki	(0) 0
Helsingborg	(0) 3	Drogheda United	(0) 0
Jablonec	(0) 1	FK Austria	(1) 1
Lens	(2) 5	Young Boys	(1) 1
Litex	(1) 3	Besa	(0) 0
Maccabi Netanya	(0) 0	Uniao Leiria	(0) 1
Mattersburg	(0) 0	Basle	(3) 4
Midtjylland	(3) 5	Haka	(1) 2
Odense	(1) 4	Dynamo Minsk	(0) 0
Otelul	(0) 0	Lokomotiv Sofia	(0) 0
Rapid Vienna	(1) 5	Dynamo Tbilisi	(0) 0
Sampdoria	(1) 1	Hajduk Split	(0) 1
Sion	(2) 3	Ried	(0) 0
Standard Liege	(0) 1	Kaerjeng	(0) 0
Suduva	(0) 3	Brann	(2) 4
Valerenga	(3) 6	Ekranas	(0) 0
Vojvodina	(1) 1	Atletico Madrid	(0) 2
Zenit	(1) 3	Moravce	(0) 0
Zrinjski	(1) 1	Rabotnicki	(1) 2

Thursday, 30 August 2007

Blackburn Rovers (0) 2 *(Bentley 48, Roberts 90)*

MyPa (0) 0   13,490

Blackburn Rovers: Friedel; Ooijer, Warnock (Olsson 77), Tugay, Nelsen, Mokoena, Emerton, Bentley, Rigters (Derbyshire 76), Roberts, Pedersen.
MyPa: Korhonen; Pulkkinen, Huttunen, Miranda, Kansikas, Agboh, Kuparinen, Muinonen (Peltonen 73), Leilei (Puhakainen 46), Mustafi, Kangaskolkka (Helenius 60).

Hacken (1) 1 *(Skulason 27)*

Dunfermline Athletic (0) 0   2712

Hacken: Hysen; Lind, Heden, Lucic, Marek, Ljung (Forsell 32), Mambo Mumba, Skulason, Henriksson, Larsson (Olofsson 82), De Oliveira (Holster 90).
Dunfermline Athletic: Gallacher; Shields (Simmons 76), Wilson, Bamba, Morrison S (McManus 52), Young, Harper, Glass, Morrison O (Burchill 67), Crawford, Hamilton[■].

Helsingborg (0) 3 *(Jakobsson 52, Omotoyossi 68, Karekezi 90)*

Drogheda United (0) 0   4767

Helsingborg: Andersson D; Jakobsson, Andersson C, Ronningberg, Tamboura, Svanback, Dahl (Mariga 86), Skulason, Wahlstedt, Omotoyossi (Karekezi 86), Larsson.
Drogheda United: Connor; Byrne, Webb, Gavin, Gartland, Shelley, Robinson (Whelan 79), Keddy (Bates 55), Keegan, Cahill, Zayed (O'Keeffe 74).

FIRST ROUND FIRST LEG

Litex	(0) 0	Hamburg	(0) 1
Lens	(0) 1	FC Copenhagen	(1) 1
AEK Athens	(1) 3	Salzburg	(0) 0
Aberdeen	(0) 0	Dnepr	(0) 0
Anderlecht	(1) 1	Rapid Vienna	(0) 1
Aris Salonika	(1) 1	Zaragoza	(0) 0
Artmedia	(0) 1	Panathinaikos	(0) 2
Atletico Madrid	(2) 4	Erciyesspor	(0) 0
Bayern Munich	(1) 1	Belenenses	(0) 0
Brann	(0) 0	FC Brugge	(0) 1
Dinamo Bucharest	(1) 1	Elfsborg	(2) 2
Dynamo Zagreb	(0) 0	Ajax	(0) 1
Empoli	(1) 2	Zurich	(0) 1
Everton	(1) 1	Metalist Kharkiv	(0) 1
FK Austria	(1) 2	Valerenga	(0) 0
Getafe	(0) 1	Twente	(0) 0
Groclin	(0) 0	Red Star Belgrade	(1) 1
Groningen	(1) 1	Fiorentina	(0) 1
Hammarby	(0) 2	Braga	(0) 1
Hapoel Tel Aviv	(0) 0	AIK Stockholm	(0) 0
Heerenveen	(3) 5	Helsingborg	(0) 3
Larissa	(2) 2	Blackburn Rovers	(0) 0
Leverkusen	(2) 3	Uniao Leiria	(1) 1
Lokomotiv Sofia	(0) 1	Rennes	(1) 3
Midtjylland	(1) 1	Lokomotiv Moscow	(0) 3
Mlada Boleslav	(0) 0	Palermo	(0) 1
Nuremberg	(0) 0	Rapid Bucharest	(0) 0
Pacos Ferreira	(0) 0	AZ	(0) 1
Rabotnicki	(0) 1	Bolton Wanderers	(0) 1
Sampdoria	(1) 2	Aalborg	(1) 2
Sarajevo	(0) 1	Basle	(1) 2
Sion	(3) 3	Galatasaray	(1) 2
Sochaux	(0) 0	Panionios	(1) 2
Sparta Prague	(0) 0	Odense	(0) 0
Spartak Moscow	(3) 5	Hacken	(0) 0
Tampere United	(1) 2	Bordeaux	(0) 3
Tottenham Hotspur	(4) 6	Anorthosis	(0) 1
Toulouse	(0) 0	CSKA Sofia	(0) 0
Villarreal	(2) 4	BATE Borisov	(0) 1
Zenit	(1) 3	Standard Liege	(0) 0

Thursday, 20 September 2007

Aberdeen (0) 0

Dnepr (0) 0   15,431

Aberdeen: Langfield; Hart, Considine, Diamond, McNamara (Foster 62), Severin, Jamie Smith, Nicholson, Young (Lovell 71), Miller, Clark (Mair 90).
Dnepr: Kernozenko; Gritsay, Shershun, Rusol, Denisov, Shelayev, Andrienko, Kravchenko (Lepa 61), Nazarenko, Samodin (Kankava 66), Vorobei (Karnilenka 90).

Everton (1) 1 *(Lescott 24)*

Metalist Kharkiv (0) 1 *(Edmar 78)*   37,120

Everton: Wessels; Hibbert, Baines, Yobo, Lescott, Carsley (Jagielka 79), Osman, Neville, Johnson, Yakubu (Anichebe 65), McFadden.
Metalist Kharkiv: Goryainov; Babych■, Gancarczyk■, Obradovic, Gueye, Bordian, Valyayev, Slyusar, Rykun (Edmar 67), Devic, Nwoga (Antonov 59) (Mahdoufi 77).

244

Larissa (2) 2 *(Bakayoko 33, Cleyton 35)*

Blackburn Rovers (0) 0 8126

Larissa: Kotsolis S; Dabizas, Forster, Katsiaros, Kyriakidis, Galitsios, Cleyton (Kalantzis 85), Sarmiento, Fotakis, Alexandrou (Gikas 77), Bakayoko (Venetis 90).

Blackburn Rovers: Friedel; Emerton, Warnock, Dunn, Nelsen (Khizanishvili 57), Ooijer, Bentley, Savage, Santa Cruz, McCarthy (Tugay 78), Pedersen (Derbyshire 62).

Rabotnicki (0) 1 *(Milisavljevic 53)*

Bolton Wanderers (0) 1 *(Meite 84)* 16,000

Rabotnicki: Madzovski; Demiri, Stanisic, Babatunde, Bozinovski, Vajs, Osmani (Pejcic 65), Gligorov, Milisavljevic (Velkovski 71), Nedzipi, Trickovski (Selim 89).

Bolton Wanderers: Jaaskelainen; Hunt (O'Brien J 75), Gardner, McCann (O'Brien A 63), Cid (Braaten 63), Meite, Nolan, Speed, Anelka, Davies, Diouf.

Tottenham Hotspur (4) 6 *(Kaboul 5, Dawson 40, Keane 42, Bent 43, Defoe 65, 90)*

Anorthosis (0) 1 *(Zlogar 81)* 35,780

Tottenham Hotspur: Cerny; Chimbonda, Assou-Ekotto (Bale 79), Zokora, Kaboul, Dawson, Lennon, Huddlestone, Keane (Defoe 62), Bent, Malbranque (Taarabt 69).

Anorthosis: Beqaj; Katsavakis, Nicolaou (Panagi 58), Loumpoutis, Lambrou, Zlogar (Deanov 81), Poursaitidis, Fabinho (Pahars 64), Skopelitis, Sosin, William.

FIRST ROUND SECOND LEG

Panathinaikos	(2) 3	Artmedia	(0) 0
AIK Stockholm	(0) 0	Hapoel Tel Aviv	(0) 1
AZ	(0) 0	Pacos Ferreira	(0) 0
Aalborg	(0) 0	Sampdoria	(0) 0
Ajax	(0) 2	Dynamo Zagreb*	(1) 3
Anorthosis	(0) 1	Tottenham Hotspur	(0) 1
BATE Borisov	(0) 0	Villarreal	(1) 2
Basle	(4) 6	Sarajevo	(0) 0
Belenenses	(0) 0	Bayern Munich	(0) 2
Blackburn Rovers	(1) 2	Larissa	(1) 1
Bolton Wanderers	(0) 1	Rabotnicki	(0) 0
Bordeaux	(0) 1	Tampere United	(0) 1
Braga	(0) 4	Hammarby	(0) 0
CSKA Sofia	(0) 1	Toulouse	(0) 1
Dnepr	(0) 1	Aberdeen	(1) 1
Elfsborg	(0) 0	Dinamo Bucharest	(1) 1
Erciyesspor	(0) 0	Atletico Madrid	(3) 5
FC Brugge	(0) 1	Brann	(2) 2
FC Copenhagen*	(0) 2	Lens	(1) 1
Fiorentina	(0) 1	Groningen	(0) 1
(aet; Fiorentina won 4-3 on penalties.)			
Galatasaray	(3) 5	Sion	(0) 1
Hacken	(0) 1	Spartak Moscow	(1) 3
Hamburg	(1) 3	Litex	(1) 1
Helsingborg	(3) 5	Heerenveen	(0) 1
Lokomotiv Moscow	(2) 2	Midtjylland	(0) 0
Metalist Kharkiv	(1) 2	Everton	(0) 3
Odense	(0) 0	Sparta Prague	(0) 0
(aet; Sparta Prague won 4-3 on penalties.)			
Palermo	(0) 1	Mlada Boleslav	(0) 1
(aet; Mlada Boleslav won 4-2 on penalties.)			
Panionios	(0) 0	Sochaux	(0) 1

Rapid Bucharest	(1) 2	Nuremberg	(1) 2
Rapid Vienna	(0) 0	Anderlecht	(1) 1
Red Star Belgrade	(1) 1	Groclin	(0) 0
Rennes	(1) 1	Lokomotiv Sofia	(2) 2
Salzburg	(1) 1	AEK Athens	(0) 0
Standard Liege	(1) 1	Zenit	(0) 1
Twente	(1) 3	Getafe*	(0) 2
Uniao Leiria	(2) 3	Leverkusen	(1) 2
Valerenga	(0) 2	FK Austria	(1) 2
Zaragoza	(1) 2	Aris Salonika	(0) 1
Zurich	(1) 3	Empoli	(0) 0

Thursday, 4 October 2007

Anorthosis (0) 1 *(Fabinho 59)*

Tottenham Hotspur (0) 1 *(Keane 78)* 8000

Anorthosis: Nagy; Tripotseris, Nicolaou, Konstantinou, Ndikumana, Zlogar (Skopelitis 46), Fabinho (Pahars 62), Laban (Deanov 83), Panagi, Frousos, William.
Tottenham Hotspur: Robinson; Stalteri, Lee (Keane 75), Zokora, Dawson, Gardner, Boateng (Bale 69), Huddlestone, Bent (Taarabt 85), Defoe, Malbranque.

Blackburn Rovers (1) 2 *(Derbyshire 45 (pen), Warnock 51)*

Larissa (1) 1 *(Cleyton 17)* 20,741

Blackburn Rovers: Friedel; Emerton, Warnock, Tugay, Ooijer, Samba, Bentley, Mokoena (Pedersen 65), Santa Cruz, Derbyshire (McCarthy 68), Dunn (Savage 77).
Larissa: Kotsolis S; Dabizas, Forster, Katsiaros, Kyriakidis, Galitsios (Kalatantzis 77), Cleyton, Sarmiento, Fotakis, Alexandrou (Kotsios 56), Bakayoko (Gikas 90).

Bolton Wanderers (0) 1 *(Anelka 68)*

Rabotnicki (0) 0 18,932

Bolton Wanderers: Jaaskelainen; O'Brien J, Michalik, Alonso (Giannakopoulos 46), O'Brien A, Cid, Guthrie, Wilhelmsson, Braaten (Diouf 75), Davies (Anelka 66), McCann.
Rabotnicki: Pacovski; Demiri, Stanisic, Babatunde (Bozinovski 75), Kovacevic, Vajs, Osmani (Velkovski 46), Gligorov, Milisavljevic, Nedzipi, Trickovski (Pejcic 63).

Dnepr (0) 1 *(Vorobei 75)*

Aberdeen (1) 1 *(Mackie 28)* 26,275

Dnepr: Kernozenko; Shershun, Rusol, Denisov, Shelayev, Kankava (Kravchenko 58), Andrienko, Nazarenko, Lipa, Samodin (Karnilenka 74), Vorobei.
Aberdeen: Langfield; Hart, Nicholson, Diamond, Considine, Severin, Jamie Smith (Mair 46), Clark, Mackie (Lovell 71), Foster, Young.

Metalist Kharkiv (1) 2 *(Edmar 21, Mahdoufi 52)*

Everton (0) 3 *(Lescott 48, McFadden 72, Anichebe 88)*

27,500

Metalist Kharkiv: Goryainov; Obradovic, Gueye, Bordian (Nwoga 85), Valyayev, Edmar, Slyusar, Mahdoufi, Rykun, Devic (Zezeto 90), Jakobia (Danilov 74).
Everton: Howard; Neville, Lescott, Yobo (Baines 76), Stubbs, Jagielka (Anichebe 62), Osman, Pienaar, Yakubu, McFadden (Hibbert 90), Arteta.

GROUP STAGE

GROUP A

Everton	(1) 3	Larissa	(0) 1
Zenit	(1) 1	AZ	(1) 1
Larissa	(0) 2	Zenit	(1) 3
Nuremberg	(0) 0	Everton	(0) 2
AZ	(0) 1	Larissa	(0) 0
Zenit	(0) 2	Nuremberg	(1) 2
Everton	(0) 1	Zenit	(0) 0
Nuremberg	(0) 2	AZ	(1) 1
AZ	(1) 2	Everton	(2) 3
Larissa	(1) 1	Nuremberg	(1) 3

Thursday, 25 October 2007

Everton (1) 3 *(Cahill 14, Osman 50, Anichebe 85)*

Larissa (0) 1 *(Cleyton 65)*   33,777

Everton: Howard; Hibbert, Baines, Yobo, Lescott, Carsley, Osman, Pienaar (Stubbs 87), McFadden (Gravesen 65), Cahill (Anichebe 65), Arteta.
Larissa: Kotsoliss; Venetidis, Dabizas, Forster (Venetis 79), Kyriakidis (Labropoulos 75), Galitsios, Cleyton, Sarmiento, Fotakis, Parra (Kalantzis 58), Bakayoko.

Thursday, 8 November 2007

Nuremberg (0) 0

Everton (0) 2 *(Arteta 83 (pen), Anichebe 88)*   44,000

Nuremberg: Blazek; Glauber (Benko 86), Wolf, Schmidt (Kennedy 77), Reinhardt, Galasek, Misimovic, Mintal, Kluge, Mnari, Saenko (Pagenburg 85).
Everton: Howard; Neville, Nuno Valente, Yobo, Lescott, Carsley, Osman, Pienaar (Hibbert 90), Yakubu (Anichebe 75), Cahill (Jagielka 90), Arteta.

Wednesday, 5 December 2007

Everton (0) 1 *(Cahill 85)*

Zenit (0) 0   38,407

Everton: Howard; Neville, Baines, Jagielka, Lescott, Carsley, Pienaar, Cahill, Johnson (Vaughan 81), McFadden (Anichebe 64), Arteta.
Zenit: Malafeev; Skrtel, Kim, Lombaerts∎, Anyukov (Ho Lee 78), Sirl, Zyryanov, Timoshchuk, Dominguez (Gorshkov 46), Pogrebnyak (Hagen 61), Arshavin.

Thursday, 20 December 2007

AZ (1) 2 *(Pelle 16, Jaliens 65)*

Everton (2) 3 *(Johnson 2, Jagielka 44, Vaughan 79)*   16,578

AZ: Waterman; Jaliens, Opdam, Pocognoli (Agustien 77), De Zeeuw (Jenner 65), Steinsson, Vormer, Mendes da Silva, Cziommer (El Hamdaoui 66), Dembele, Pelle.
Everton: Wessels; Hibbert, Nuno Valente, Gravesen (Rodwell 80), Lescott, Carsley, Jagielka, Pienaar (Vidarsson 69), Johnson (Vaughan 68), Anichebe, McFadden.

Group A Final Table	P	W	D	L	F	A	Pts
Everton	4	4	0	0	9	3	12
Nuremberg	4	2	1	1	7	6	7
Zenit	4	1	2	1	6	6	5
AZ	4	1	1	2	5	6	4
Larissa	4	0	0	4	4	10	0

GROUP B

Lokomotiv Moscow	(1) 3	Atletico Madrid	(1) 3
Panathinaikos	(1) 3	Aberdeen	(0) 0
Aberdeen	(1) 1	Lokomotiv Moscow	(1) 1
FC Copenhagen	(0) 0	Panathinaikos	(1) 1
Atletico Madrid	(1) 2	Aberdeen	(0) 0
Lokomotiv Moscow	(0) 0	FC Copenhagen	(0) 1
FC Copenhagen	(0) 0	Atletico Madrid	(1) 2
Panathinaikos	(0) 2	Lokomotiv Moscow	(0) 0
Aberdeen	(0) 4	FC Copenhagen	(0) 0
Atletico Madrid	(0) 2	Panathinaikos	(1) 1

Thursday, 25 October 2007

Panathinaikos (1) 3 *(Goumas 11, Papadopoulos 73, Salpigidis 77)*

Aberdeen (0) 0 8154

Panathinaikos: Malarz; Morris, Goumas, Fyssas, Marcelo, Tziolis, Ivanschitz (Seric 81), Nilsson, Dimoutsos, Salpigidis (Mantzios 81), N'Doye (Papadopoulos 59).
Aberdeen: Langfield; Hart, McNamara (De Visscher 75), Diamond, Considine (Mair 61), Severin (Aluko 86), Nicholson, Foster, Young, Miller, Clark.

Thursday, 8 November 2007

Aberdeen (1) 1 *(Diamond 27)*

Lokomotiv Moscow (1) 1 *(Ivanovic 45)* 18,843

Aberdeen: Langfield; Hart, Considine, Foster, Diamond, Severin, Nicholson, Clark (Maguire 66), Aluko (De Visscher 81), Miller (Lovell 85), Young.
Lokomotiv Moscow: Pelizzoli; Rodolfo, Spahic, Ivanovic, Sennikov, Gurenko, Asatiani, Bilyaletdinov, Odemwingie, Sychev, Samedov (Cocis 79).

Thursday, 29 November 2007

Atletico Madrid (1) 2 *(Forlan 45 (pen), Simao 61)*

Aberdeen (0) 0 30,000

Atletico Madrid: Abbiati; Antonio Lopez, Pernia, Eller, Pablo Ibanez, Motta, Cleber Santana, Maxi Rodriguez (Maniche 71), Forlan (Mista 70), Luis Garcia, Aguero (Simao 46).
Aberdeen: Langfield; Hart, Byrne, McNamara (Clark 34), Diamond, Severin (Maguire 76), Jamie Smith (De Visscher 44), Foster, Young, Miller, Touzani.

Thursday, 20 December 2007

Aberdeen (0) 4 *(Jamie Smith 47, 55, Antonsson 71 (og), Foster 82)*

FC Copenhagen (0) 0 20,446

Aberdeen: Langfield; Hart, Byrne, Diamond, Considine, Severin, Jamie Smith (Maguire 74), Nicholson, Clark, Aluko (Foster 59), Miller.
FC Copenhagen: Christiansen; Gravgaard, Antonsson, Wendt, Norregaard (Silberbauer 61), Wurtz (Ailton 56), Gronkjaer (Nordstrand 70), Hutchinson, Kvist, Sionko, Allback.

Group B Final Table	P	W	D	L	F	A	Pts
Atletico Madrid	4	3	1	0	9	4	10
Panathinaikos	4	3	0	1	7	2	9
Aberdeen	4	1	1	2	5	6	4
FC Copenhagen	4	1	0	3	1	7	3
Lokomotiv Moscow	4	0	2	2	4	7	2

GROUP C

Elfsborg	(1) 1	AEK Athens	(0) 1
Villarreal	(0) 1	Fiorentina	(0) 1
Fiorentina	(2) 6	Elfsborg	(1) 1
Mlada Boleslav	(0) 1	Villarreal	(1) 2
AEK Athens	(1) 1	Fiorentina	(1) 1
Elfsborg	(1) 1	Mlada Boleslav	(0) 3
Mlada Boleslav	(0) 0	AEK Athens	(0) 1
Villarreal	(1) 2	Elfsborg	(0) 0
AEK Athens	(0) 1	Villarreal	(1) 2
Fiorentina	(1) 2	Mlada Boleslav	(0) 1

Group C Final Table	P	W	D	L	F	A	Pts
Villarreal	4	3	1	0	7	3	10
Fiorentina	4	2	2	0	10	4	8
AEK Athens	4	1	2	1	4	4	5
Mlada Boleslav	4	1	0	3	5	6	3
Elfsborg	4	0	1	3	3	12	1

GROUP D

Basle	(0) 1	Rennes	(0) 0
Brann	(0) 0	Hamburg	(0) 1
Dynamo Zagreb	(0) 0	Basle	(0) 0
Rennes	(0) 1	Brann	(1) 1
Brann	(1) 2	Dynamo Zagreb	(0) 1
Hamburg	(1) 3	Rennes	(0) 0
Basle	(1) 1	Brann	(0) 0
Dynamo Zagreb	(0) 0	Hamburg	(0) 2
Hamburg	(0) 1	Basle	(0) 1
Rennes	(0) 1	Dynamo Zagreb	(0) 1

Group D Final Table	P	W	D	L	F	A	Pts
Hamburg	4	3	1	0	7	1	10
Basle	4	2	2	0	3	1	8
Brann	4	1	1	2	3	4	4
Dynamo Zagreb	4	0	2	2	2	5	2
Rennes	4	0	2	2	2	6	2

GROUP E

Leverkusen	(1) 1	Toulouse	(0) 0
Sparta Prague	(1) 1	Zurich	(1) 2
Spartak Moscow	(0) 2	Leverkusen	(0) 1
Toulouse	(1) 2	Sparta Prague	(0) 3
Sparta Prague	(0) 0	Spartak Moscow	(0) 0
Zurich	(1) 2	Toulouse	(0) 0
Leverkusen	(0) 1	Sparta Prague	(0) 0
Spartak Moscow	(0) 1	Zurich	(0) 0
Toulouse	(1) 2	Spartak Moscow	(0) 1
Zurich	(0) 0	Leverkusen	(2) 5

Group E Final Table	P	W	D	L	F	A	Pts
Leverkusen	4	3	0	1	8	2	9
Spartak Moscow	4	2	1	1	4	3	7
Zurich	4	2	0	2	4	7	6
Sparta Prague	4	1	1	2	4	5	4
Toulouse	4	1	0	3	4	7	3

GROUP F

Bolton Wanderers	(0) 1	Braga	(0) 1
Red Star Belgrade	(1) 2	Bayern Munich	(1) 3
Aris Salonika	(0) 3	Red Star Belgrade	(0) 0
Bayern Munich	(1) 2	Bolton Wanderers	(1) 2
Bolton Wanderers	(0) 1	Aris Salonika	(1) 1
Braga	(0) 1	Bayern Munich	(0) 1
Aris Salonika	(1) 1	Braga	(1) 1
Red Star Belgrade	(0) 0	Bolton Wanderers	(1) 1
Bayern Munich	(2) 6	Aris Salonika	(0) 0
Braga	(1) 2	Red Star Belgrade	(0) 0

Thursday, 25 October 2007

Bolton Wanderers (0) 1 *(Diouf 66)*

Braga (0) 1 *(Jailson 87)*   10,848

Bolton Wanderers: Jaaskelainen; Hunt, Gardner (Teimourian 82), Meite, O'Brien A, Cid, Guthrie (Diouf 61), Speed, Anelka, Davies, McCann.
Braga: Paulo Santos; Rodriguez, Paulo Jorge, Joao Pereira, Castanheira (Stelvio 68), Cesar Peixoto, Andres Madrid (Jailson 76), Vandinho, Jorginho, Wender (Ze Manel 67), Linz.

Thursday, 8 November 2007

Bayern Munich (1) 2 *(Podolski 31, 49)*

Bolton Wanderers (1) 2 *(Gardner 8, Davies 82)*   66,000

Bayern Munich: Kahn; Lucio, Van Buyten, Jansen, Lell, Ribery (Kroos 61), Ottl, Van Bommel, Schweinsteiger (Hamit Altintop 73), Podolski (Toni 58), Klose.
Bolton Wanderers: Al Habsi; Michalik, Gardner, McCann, O'Brien A, Cid, Nolan, Alonso (Giannakopoulos 56), Braaten (Teimourian 77), Davies, Guthrie.

Thursday, 29 November 2007

Bolton Wanderers (0) 1 *(Giannakopoulos 90)*

Aris Salonika (1) 1 *(Toni Calvo 44)*   10,229

Bolton Wanderers: Jaaskelainen; Hunt, Cid, McCann (Alonso 13), O'Brien A, Meite, Nolan, Wilhelmsson (Diouf 65), Davies (Anelka 65), Guthrie, Giannakopoulos.
Aris Salonika: Chalkias; Neto, Ronaldo, Karabelas, Papadopoulos, Nebegleras, Toni Calvo (Javito 61), Ronaldo Garcia (Gogolos 83), Siston, Prittas, Koke (Kyriakos 87).

Thursday, 6 December 2007

Red Star Belgrade (0) 0

Bolton Wanderers (1) 1 *(McCann 45)*   45,000

Red Star Belgrade: Randelovic; Tutoric, Bronowicki (Andelkovic 81), Bajalica, Basta, Milijas (Burzanovic 74), Koroman, Lucas, Molina, Milovanovic, Jestrovic (Djordjevic F 64).
Bolton Wanderers: Al Habsi; Hunt, Samuel, Teimourian, Michalik, Meite, McCann, Speed, Braaten (Sinclair 88), Wilhelmsson, Giannakopoulos.

Group F Final Table	P	W	D	L	F	A	Pts
Bayern Munich	4	2	2	0	12	5	8
Braga	4	1	3	0	5	3	6
Bolton Wanderers	4	1	3	0	5	4	6
Aris Salonika	4	1	2	1	5	8	5
Red Star Belgrade	4	0	0	4	2	9	0

GROUP G

Anderlecht	(1) 2	Hapoel Tel Aviv	(0) 0
Tottenham Hotspur	(1) 1	Getafe	(1) 2
Aalborg	(0) 1	Anderlecht	(0) 1
Hapoel Tel Aviv	(0) 0	Tottenham Hotspur	(2) 2
Getafe	(0) 1	Hapoel Tel Aviv	(2) 2
Tottenham Hotspur	(0) 3	Aalborg	(2) 2
Aalborg	(0) 1	Getafe	(1) 2
Anderlecht	(0) 1	Tottenham Hotspur	(0) 1
Getafe	(1) 2	Anderlecht	(0) 1
Hapoel Tel Aviv	(1) 1	Aalborg	(1) 3

Thursday, 25 October 2007

Tottenham Hotspur (1) 1 *(Defoe 19)*

Getafe (1) 2 *(De la Red 21, Braulio 70)*   36,240

Tottenham Hotspur: Cerny; Chimbonda, Lee, Zokora (Tainio 73), Kaboul, Gardner (Dawson 43), Lennon, Huddlestone, Berbatov, Defoe, Malbranque (Keane 71).
Getafe: Ustari (Abbondanzieri 46); Cata Diaz, Belenguer, Signorino, Cortes, Nacho, Albin, Casquero (Sousa 62), Granero (Mario Cotelo 76), Braulio, De la Red.

Thursday, 8 November 2007

Hapoel Tel Aviv (0) 0

Tottenham Hotspur (2) 2 *(Keane 26, Berbatov 31)*   10,000

Hapoel Tel Aviv: Enyeama; Tai Chen, Dos Santos, Shaish▪, Bakshi (Manzur 46), Natcho, Dego (Antebi 58), Badir, Abutbul (Abedi 46), Mazuwa, Fabio Junior.
Tottenham Hotspur: Robinson; Chimbonda, Lee, Zokora, Stalteri, Dawson, Lennon, Jenas (Boateng 68), Berbatov, Keane (Bent 68), Malbranque (Defoe 56).

Thursday, 29 November 2007

Tottenham Hotspur (0) 3 *(Berbatov 46, Malbranque 51, Bent 66)*

Aalborg (2) 2 *(Enevoldsen 2, Risgard 37)*   29,758

Tottenham Hotspur: Robinson; Chimbonda, Bale, Zokora, Lee (Huddlestone 46), Dawson, Lennon, Jenas (Bent 46), Berbatov (Boateng 74), Keane, Malbranque.
Aalborg: Zaza; Jakobsen M, Pedersen, Califf, Olesen, Johansson, Augustinussen, Risgard, Enevoldsen (Curth 74), Prica, Nomvethe (Lindstrom 61).

Thursday, 6 December 2007

Anderlecht (0) 1 *(Goor 68)*

Tottenham Hotspur (0) 1 *(Berbatov 71 (pen))*   22,500

Anderlecht: Zitka; Deschacht, Van Damme, Juhasz, Wasilewski, Biglia, Polak, Hassan, Goor, Mpenza (Baseggio 72), Frutos (Thereau 55).
Tottenham Hotspur: Robinson; Chimbonda, Lee (Stalteri 81), Zokora, Dawson, Huddlestone, Lennon, Jenas, Keane (Berbatov 59), Bent (Defoe 72), Malbranque.

Group G Final Table	P	W	D	L	F	A	Pts
Getafe	4	3	0	1	7	5	9
Tottenham Hotspur	4	2	1	1	7	5	7
Anderlecht	4	1	2	1	5	4	5
Aalborg	4	1	1	2	7	7	4
Hapoel Tel Aviv	4	1	0	3	3	8	3

GROUP H

Bordeaux	(0) 2	Galatasaray	(1) 1
Helsingborg	(0) 1	Panionios	(1) 1
FK Austria	(1) 1	Bordeaux	(1) 2
Galatasaray	(1) 2	Helsingborg	(2) 3
Helsingborg	(0) 3	FK Austria	(0) 0
Panionios	(0) 0	Galatasaray	(0) 3
Bordeaux	(1) 2	Helsingborg	(1) 1
FK Austria	(0) 0	Panionios	(0) 1
Galatasaray	(0) 0	FK Austria	(0) 0
Panionios	(2) 2	Bordeaux	(1) 3

Group H Final Table	P	W	D	L	F	A	Pts
Bordeaux	4	4	0	0	9	5	12
Helsingborg	4	2	1	1	8	5	7
Galatasaray	4	1	1	2	6	5	4
Panionios	4	1	1	2	4	7	4
FK Austria	4	0	1	3	1	6	1

KNOCK-OUT STAGE

THIRD ROUND FIRST LEG

AEK Athens	(0) 1	Getafe	(0) 1
Anderlecht	(0) 2	Bordeaux	(0) 1
Brann	(0) 0	Everton	(0) 2
Galatasaray	(0) 0	Leverkusen	(0) 0
Marseille	(0) 3	Spartak Moscow	(0) 0
PSV Eindhoven	(2) 2	Helsingborg	(0) 0
Rangers	(0) 0	Panathinaikos	(0) 0
Sporting Lisbon	(1) 2	Basle	(0) 0
Werder Bremen	(2) 3	Braga	(0) 0
Zenit	(0) 1	Villarreal	(0) 0
Aberdeen	(2) 2	Bayern Munich	(1) 2
Benfica	(1) 1	Nuremberg	(0) 0
Bolton Wanderers	(0) 1	Atletico Madrid	(0) 0
Rosenborg	(0) 0	Fiorentina	(1) 1
Slavia Prague	(0) 1	Tottenham Hotspur	(2) 2
Zurich	(0) 1	Hamburg	(0) 3

Wednesday, 13 February 2008

Brann (0) 0

Everton (0) 2 *(Osman 59, Anichebe 88)*   16,207

Brann: Opdal; Dahl (Thwaite 89), Hanstveit, Bjarnason, El-Fakiri (Huseklepp 75), Solli, Vaagan Moen, Bakke, Sigurdsson K, Karadas (Demba-Nyren 69), Helstad.
Everton: Howard; Neville, Lescott, Jagielka, Yobo, Carsley, Osman, Fernandes (Hibbert 89), Johnson (Anichebe 76), Yakubu (Baines 90), Cahill.

Rangers (0) 0

Panathinaikos (0) 0   45,203

Rangers: McGregor; Broadfoot, Papac, Cuellar, Weir, Ferguson, Hemdani, Adam (Cousin 67), Novo (Burke 81), McCulloch, Davis.
Panathinaikos: Galinovic; Morris, Goumas, Simao, Vintra, Mattos, Karagounis, Tziolis, Nilsson, Salpingidis (Helder Postiga 66), N'Doye.

Thursday, 14 February 2008

Aberdeen (2) 2 *(Walker 24, Aluko 41)*

Bayern Munich (1) 2 *(Klose 29, Hamit Altintop 54)*   20,047

Aberdeen: Langfield; Maybury, Mair, Considine, Diamond, Severin, Walker (Touzani 87), Nicholson, Aluko, Miller, Mackie (Lovell 68).
Bayern Munich: Rensing; Lucio, Demichelis, Jansen, Lell (Lahm 46), Hamit Altintop, Ze Roberto (Podolski 66), Ottl, Schweinsteiger, Toni, Klose (Schlaudraff 80).

Bolton Wanderers (0) 1 *(Diouf 74)*

Atletico Madrid (0) 0 26,163

Bolton Wanderers: Jaaskelainen; Hunt, Samuel, Campo, O'Brien A, Cahill, Nolan, Guthrie (Giannakopoulos 59), Taylor, Davies, Diouf.
Atletico Madrid: Abbiati; Antonio Lopez, Pernia, Luis Perea, Pablo Ibanez, Santana, Maxi Rodriguez, Reyes (Aguero■ 59), Simao (Jurado 72), Forlan, Mista (Miguel 88).

Slavia Prague (0) 1 *(Strihavka 69)*

Tottenham Hotspur (2) 2 *(Berbatov 4, Keane 30)* 11,134

Slavia Prague: Vaniak; Brabec, Hubacek, Drizdal, Tavares, Latka, Pudil (Ivana 46), Suchy (Volesak 83), Jarolim (Kalivoda 59), Cerny, Strihavka.
Tottenham Hotspur: Cerny; Chimbonda, Tainio (O'Hara 59), Huddlestone, Woodgate, Zokora, Lennon, Jenas, Berbatov, Keane (Bent 66), Malbranque.

THIRD ROUND SECOND LEG

Atletico Madrid	(0) 0	Bolton Wanderers	(0) 0
Basle	(0) 0	Sporting Lisbon	(2) 3
Bayern Munich	(2) 5	Aberdeen	(0) 1
Bordeaux	(0) 1	Anderlecht	(1) 1
Braga	(0) 0	Werder Bremen	(0) 1
Everton	(2) 6	Brann	(0) 1
Fiorentina	(1) 2	Rosenborg	(0) 1
Getafe	(1) 3	AEK Athens	(0) 0
Hamburg	(0) 0	Zurich	(0) 0
Helsingborg	(0) 1	PSV Eindhoven	(0) 2
Leverkusen	(3) 5	Galatasaray	(0) 1
Nuremberg	(0) 2	Benfica	(0) 2
Panathinaikos	(1) 1	Rangers	(0) 1
Spartak Moscow	(1) 2	Marseille	(0) 0
Tottenham Hotspur	(1) 1	Slavia Prague	(0) 1
Villarreal	(0) 2	Zenit	(1) 1

Thursday, 21 February 2008

Atletico Madrid (0) 0

Bolton Wanderers (0) 0 30,000

Atletico Madrid: Abbiati; Antonio Lopez, Pernia, Luis Perea, Pablo Ibanez (Mista 67), Santana, Luis Garcia (Miguel 54), Maxi Rodriguez, Jurado, Reyes, Forlan.
Bolton Wanderers: Jaaskelainen; Hunt, Samuel, McCann (Campo 58), O'Brien A, Cahill, Nolan, O'Brien J (Meite 85), Taylor, Davies, Giannakopoulos (Diouf 59).

Bayern Munich (2) 5 *(Lucio 12, Van Buyten 36, Podolski 71, 77, Van Bommel 85)*

Aberdeen (0) 1 *(Lovell 83)* 66,000

Bayern Munich: Kahn; Sagnol, Lucio, Van Buyten, Jansen, Hamit Altintop (Schweinsteiger 75), Ottl, Van Bommel, Kroos (Sosa 69), Toni (Klose 65), Podolski.
Aberdeen: Langfield; Maybury, Foster, Considine, Diamond, Severin, Walker (Maguire 62), Nicholson, Aluko (Lovell 79), Miller, Mackie (De Visscher 72).

Everton (2) 6 *(Yakubu 36, 54, 72, Johnson 41, 90, Arteta 70)*

Brann (0) 1 *(Vaagan Moen 60)* 32,834

Everton: Howard; Neville, Nuno Valente, Jagielka, Lescott, Carsley (Fernandes 46), Pienaar, Cahill (Hibbert 46), Johnson, Yakubu (Anichebe 74), Arteta.
Brann: Opdal; Dahl, Hanstveit, Bjarnason (Karadas 65), El-Fakiri (Huseklepp 60), Solli, Vaagan Moen, Bakke, Sigurdsson K, Demba-Nyren (Winters 72), Helstad.

Panathinaikos (1) 1 *(Goumas 12)*

Rangers (0) 1 *(Novo 81)*   14,452

Panathinaikos: Galinovic; Morris, Goumas, Vintra, Mattos, Karagounis, Tziolis (Gonzalez 83), Ivanschitz, Nilsson (Papadopoulos 86), Helder Postiga (N'Doye 62), Salpingidis.
Rangers: McGregor; Broadfoot, Papac (Dailly 66), Cuellar, Weir, Ferguson, Hemdani (Burke 69), Adam (Naismith 66), Boyd, Novo, Davis.

Tottenham Hotspur (1) 1 *(O'Hara 7)*

Slavia Prague (0) 1 *(Krajcik 51)*   34,224

Tottenham Hotspur: Robinson; Chimbonda (Malbranque 61), Tainio, Zokora, Woodgate, Kaboul, Lennon (Jenas 70), Huddlestone, Berbatov (Keane 46), Bent, O'Hara.
Slavia Prague: Vorel; Brabec, Hubacek, Drizdal (Volesak 81), Latka, Pudil, Suchy, Krajcik (Belaid 87), Kalivoda (Ivana 46), Cerny, Strihavka.

FOURTH ROUND FIRST LEG

Anderlecht	(0) 0	Bayern Munich	(2) 5
Benfica	(0) 1	Getafe	(1) 2
Bolton Wanderers	(1) 1	Sporting Lisbon	(0) 1
Fiorentina	(0) 2	Everton	(0) 0
Leverkusen	(0) 1	Hamburg	(0) 0
Marseille	(1) 3	Zenit	(0) 1
Rangers	(1) 2	Werder Bremen	(0) 0
Tottenham Hotspur	(0) 0	PSV Eindhoven	(1) 1

Thursday, 6 March 2008

Bolton Wanderers (1) 1 *(McCann 25)*

Sporting Lisbon (0) 1 *(Vukcevic 69)*   25,664

Bolton Wanderers: Al Habsi; Hunt, Gardner, Campo (Teimourian 84), O'Brien A, Cahill, O'Brien J (Guthrie 66), McCann, Helguson (Giannakopoulos 55), Davies, Taylor.
Sporting Lisbon: Rui Patricio, Anderson Polga, Tonel, Grimi, Miguel Veloso, Abel (Romagnoli 46), Izmailov (Gladstone 84), Vukcevic, Pereirinha, Joao Moutinho, Tiui (Silva 79).

Fiorentina (0) 2 *(Kuzmanovic 70, Montolivo 81)*

Everton (0) 0   32,934

Fiorentina: Frey; Dainelli, Gamberini, Ujfalusi, Pasqual, Donadel, Montolivo, Jorgensen, Kuzmanovic (Gobbi 76), Osvaldo (Santana 74), Vieri (Pazzini 67).
Everton: Howard; Hibbert (Johnson 73), Lescott, Yobo, Jagielka, Carsley, Osman (Arteta 56), Neville, Yakubu, Cahill, Pienaar.

Rangers (1) 2 *(Cousin 45, Davis 48)*

Werder Bremen (0) 0   45,959

Rangers: McGregor; Broadfoot, Papac, Cuellar, Weir, Ferguson, Hemdani, Dailly, Cousin (McCulloch 75), Adam, Davis.
Werder Bremen: Wiese; Pasanen (Boenisch 64), Naldo, Baumann, Fritz, Mertesacker, Vranjes (Hugo Almeida 60), Diego, Jensen, Rosenberg, Hunt.

Tottenham Hotspur (0) 0

PSV Eindhoven (1) 1 *(Farfan 34)*   33,259

Tottenham Hotspur: Robinson; Chimbonda, Gilberto (O'Hara 46), Zokora, Woodgate, King (Taarabt 73), Lennon, Jenas (Huddlestone 64), Berbatov, Keane, Malbranque.
PSV Eindhoven: Gomes; Kromkamp, Salcido, Alcides, Marcellis, Simons, Mendez, Culina, Koevermans (Lazovic 78), Farfan (Dzsudzsak 85), Afellay (Bakkal 90).

FOURTH ROUND SECOND LEG

Bayern Munich	(1) 1	Anderlecht	(2) 2
Everton	(1) 2	Fiorentina	(0) 0
(aet; Fiorentina won 4-2 on penalties.)			
Getafe	(0) 1	Benfica	(0) 0
Hamburg	(0) 3	Leverkusen	(1) 2
PSV Eindhoven	(0) 0	Tottenham Hotspur	(0) 1
(aet; PSV Eindhoven won 6-5 on penalties.)			
Zenit	(1) 2	Marseille	(0) 0
Sporting Lisbon	(0) 1	Bolton Wanderers	(0) 0
Werder Bremen	(0) 1	Rangers	(0) 0

Wednesday, 12 March 2008

Everton (1) 2 *(Johnson 16, Arteta 67)*

Fiorentina (0) 0 38,026

Everton: Howard; Neville, Lescott, Yobo, Jagielka, Carsley, Osman, Pienaar (Anichebe 106), Johnson (Gravesen 119), Yakubu, Arteta.
Fiorentina: Frey; Dainelli, Gamberini, Ujfalusi, Pasqual, Donadel, Montolivo, Jorgensen (Santana 106), Kuzmanovic (Gobbi 90), Osvaldo, Vieri (Pazzini 46).
aet; Fiorentina won 4-2 on penalties.

PSV Eindhoven (0) 0

Tottenham Hotspur (0) 1 *(Berbatov 81)* 33,000

PSV Eindhoven: Gomes; Kromkamp, Salcido, Alcides, Marcellis, Simons, Mendez (Bakkal 112), Culina, Koevermans (Lazovic 72), Farfan, Afellay (Dzsudzsak 82).
Tottenham Hotspur: Robinson; Chimbonda, Lee (Bent 46), Zokora, Woodgate, King (Lennon 61), Huddlestone, Jenas, Berbatov, Keane (O'Hara 86), Malbranque.
aet; PSV Eindhoven won 6-5 on penalties.

Thursday, 13 March 2008

Sporting Lisbon (0) 1 *(Pereirinha 85)*

Bolton Wanderers (0) 0 22,031

Sporting Lisbon: Rui Patricio; Anderson Polga, Tonel, Grimi, Abel, Izmailov (Gladstone 87), Vukcevic (Tiui 66), Pereirinha, Joao Moutinho, Romagnoli (Silva 75), Liedson.
Bolton Wanderers: Al Habsi; Hunt, Samuel, Teimourian (Braaten 71), Cahill, Meite, O'Brien J, Guthrie, Helguson (Woolfe 76), Vaz Te, Giannakopoulos.

Werder Bremen (0) 1 *(Diego 58)*

Rangers (0) 0 33,660

Werder Bremen: Wiese; Boenisch, Naldo, Mertesacker, Diego, Owomoyela (Harnik 78), Jensen, Borowski, Rosenberg, Hunt, Hugo Almeida (Sanogo 66).
Rangers: McGregor; Broadfoot, Papac, Cuellar, Weir, Ferguson, Hemdani, Dailly, Novo (McCulloch 78), Adam (Whittaker 57), Davis.

QUARTER-FINALS FIRST LEG

Bayern Munich	(1) 1	Getafe	(0) 1
Fiorentina	(0) 1	PSV Eindhoven	(0) 1
Leverkusen	(1) 1	Zenit	(1) 4
Rangers	(0) 0	Sporting Lisbon	(0) 0

Thursday, 3 April 2008

Rangers (0) 0

Sporting Lisbon (0) 0 48,923

Rangers: McGregor; Broadfoot, Papac, Cuellar, Weir, Ferguson, Hemdani, Thomson, McCulloch, Darcheville (Novo 72), Davis.
Sporting Lisbon: Rui Patricio; Anderson Polga, Tonel, Grimi, Miguel Veloso, Abel, Izmailov (Pereirinha 70), Vukcevic (Silva 76), Joao Moutinho, Romagnoli, Liedson.

QUARTER-FINALS SECOND LEG

Getafe	(1) 3	Bayern Munich*	(0) 3
PSV Eindhoven	(0) 0	Fiorentina	(1) 2
Sporting Lisbon	(0) 0	Rangers	(0) 2
Zenit	(0) 0	Leverkusen	(1) 1

Thursday, 10 April 2008

Sporting Lisbon (0) 0

Rangers (0) 2 *(Darcheville 60, Whittaker 90)*   31,155

Sporting Lisbon: Rui Patricio; Tonel, Grimi (Tiui 76), Miguel Veloso, Gladstone (Pereirinha 70), Abel, Izmailov (Djalo 62), Vukcevic, Joao Moutinho, Romagnoli, Liedson.
Rangers: McGregor; Broadfoot, Papac, Cuellar, Dailly, Ferguson, Hemdani, Thomson, McCulloch (Whittaker 77), Darcheville (Cousin 72), Davis.

SEMI-FINALS FIRST LEG

| Bayern Munich | (1) 1 | Zenit | (0) 1 |
| Rangers | (0) 0 | Fiorentina | (0) 0 |

Thursday, 24 April 2008

Rangers (0) 0

Fiorentina (0) 0   49,199

Rangers: Alexander; Broadfoot, Papac, Cuellar, Weir, Dailly, Hemdani, Davis, Novo (Buffel 59), Darcheville (Cousin 60), Whittaker.
Fiorentina: Frey; Gamberini, Ujfalusi, Liverani, Montolivo, Gobbi, Jorgensen, Kuzmanovic, Santana, Mutu, Pazzini (Vieri 80).

SEMI-FINALS SECOND LEG

Fiorentina	(0) 0	Rangers	(0) 0
(aet; Rangers won 4-2 on penalties.)			
Zenit	(2) 4	Bayern Munich	(0) 0

Thursday, 1 May 2008

Fiorentina (0) 0

Rangers (0) 0   39,130

Fiorentina: Frey; Gamberini, Ujfalusi, Donadel (Kuzmanovic 42), Liverani, Montolivo, Gobbi, Jorgensen, Santana (Semioli 94), Mutu, Pazzini (Vieri 79).
Rangers: Alexander; Broadfoot, Papac, Cuellar, Weir, Ferguson, Hemdani, Thomson, Davis (Novo 81), Darcheville (Cousin■ 65), Whittaker.
aet; Rangers won 4-2 on penalties.

UEFA CUP FINAL 2008

Wednesday, 14 May 2008
(at City of Manchester Stadium, Manchester, 47,726)

Zenit (0) 2 *(Denisov 72, Zyryanov 90)*   **Rangers (0) 0**

Zenit: Malafeev; Krizanac, Anyukov, Sirl, Shirokov, Zyryanov, Fayzulin (Kim 90), Timoshchuk, Fatih, Arshavin, Denisov.

Rangers: Alexander; Broadfoot, Papac (Novo 77), Cuellar, Weir, Ferguson, Hemdani (McCulloch 80), Thomson, Darcheville, Davis, Whittaker (Boyd 86).

Referee: Frojdfeldt (Sweden).

PAST EUROPEAN CUP FINALS

Year	Winner	Score	Runner-up	Score
1956	Real Madrid	4	Stade de Rheims	3
1957	Real Madrid	2	Fiorentina	0
1958	Real Madrid*	3	AC Milan	2
1959	Real Madrid	2	Stade de Rheims	0
1960	Real Madrid	7	Eintracht Frankfurt	3
1961	Benfica	3	Barcelona	2
1962	Benfica	5	Real Madrid	3
1963	AC Milan	2	Benfica	1
1964	Internazionale	3	Real Madrid	1
1965	Internazionale	1	SL Benfica	0
1966	Real Madrid	2	Partizan Belgrade	1
1967	Celtic	2	Internazionale	1
1968	Manchester U*	4	Benfica	1
1969	AC Milan	4	Ajax	1
1970	Feyenoord*	2	Celtic	1
1971	Ajax	2	Panathinaikos	0
1972	Ajax	2	Internazionale	0
1973	Ajax	1	Juventus	0
1974	Bayern Munich	1 4	Atletico Madrid	1 0
1975	Bayern Munich	2	Leeds U	0
1976	Bayern Munich	1	St Etienne	0
1977	Liverpool	3	Borussia Moenchengladbach	1
1978	Liverpool	1	FC Brugge	0
1979	Nottingham F	1	Malmö	0
1980	Nottingham F	1	Hamburg	0
1981	Liverpool	1	Real Madrid	0
1982	Aston Villa	1	Bayern Munich	0
1983	Hamburg	1	Juventus	0
1984	Liverpool†	1	Roma	1
1985	Juventus	1	Liverpool	0
1986	Steaua Bucharest†	0	Barcelona	0
1987	Porto	2	Bayern Munich	1
1988	PSV Eindhoven†	0	Benfica	0
1989	AC Milan	4	Steaua Bucharest	0
1990	AC Milan	1	Benfica	0
1991	Red Star Belgrade†	0	Marseille	0
1992	Barcelona	1	Sampdoria	0

PAST UEFA CHAMPIONS LEAGUE FINALS

Year	Winner	Score	Runner-up	Score
1993	Marseille	1	AC Milan	0

(Marseille subsequently stripped of title)

Year	Winner	Score	Runner-up	Score
1994	AC Milan	4	Barcelona	0
1995	Ajax	1	AC Milan	0
1996	Juventus†	1	Ajax	1
1997	Borussia Dortmund	3	Juventus	1
1998	Real Madrid	1	Juventus	0
1999	Manchester U	2	Bayern Munich	1
2000	Real Madrid	3	Valencia	0
2001	Bayern Munich†	1	Valencia	1
2002	Real Madrid	2	Leverkusen	1
2003	AC Milan†	0	Juventus	0
2004	Porto	3	Monaco	0
2005	Liverpool†	3	AC Milan	3
2006	Barcelona	2	Arsenal	1
2007	AC Milan	2	Liverpool	1
2008	Manchester U†	1	Chelsea	1

† aet; won on penalties.   * aet.

PAST UEFA CUP FINALS

Year	Team 1			Team 2		
1972	Tottenham H	2	1	Wolverhampton W	1	1
1973	Liverpool	3	0	Borussia Moenchengladbach	0	2
1974	Feyenoord	2	2	Tottenham H	2	0
1975	Borussia Moenchengladbach	0	5	Twente Enschede	0	1
1976	Liverpool	3	1	FC Brugge	2	1
1977	Juventus**	1	1	Athletic Bilbao	0	2
1978	PSV Eindhoven	0	3	SEC Bastia	0	0
1979	Borussia Moenchengladbach	1	1	Red Star Belgrade	1	0
1980	Borussia Moenchengladbach	3	0	Eintracht Frankfurt**	2	1
1981	Ipswich T	3	2	AZ 67 Alkmaar	0	4
1982	IFK Gothenburg	1	3	SV Hamburg	0	0
1983	Anderlecht	1	1	Benfica	0	1
1984	Tottenham H†	1	1	RSC Anderlecht	1	1
1985	Real Madrid	3	0	Videoton	0	1
1986	Real Madrid	5	0	Cologne	1	2
1987	IFK Gothenburg	1	1	Dundee U	0	1
1988	Bayer Leverkusen†	0	3	Espanol	0	3
1989	Napoli	2	3	Stuttgart	1	3
1990	Juventus	3	0	Fiorentina	1	0
1991	Internazionale	2	0	AS Roma	0	1
1992	Ajax**	0	2	Torino	0	2
1993	Juventus	3	3	Borussia Dortmund	1	0
1994	Internazionale	1	1	Salzburg	0	0
1995	Parma	1	1	Juventus	0	1
1996	Bayern Munich	2	3	Bordeaux	0	1
1997	Schalke*†	1	0	Internazionale	0	1
1998	Internazionale		3	Lazio		0
1999	Parma		3	Marseille		0
2000	Galatasaray†		0	Arsenal		0
2001	Liverpool§		5	Alaves		4
2002	Feyenoord		3	Borussia Dortmund		2
2003	Porto*		3	Celtic		2
2004	Valencia		2	Marseille		0
2005	CSKA Moscow		3	Sporting Lisbon		1
2006	Sevilla		4	Middlesbrough		0
2007	Sevilla*†		2	Espanyol		2
2008	Zenit St Petersburg		2	Rangers		0

*After extra time **Won on away goals †Won on penalties §Won on sudden death.*

UEFA CHAMPIONS LEAGUE 2008–2009

PARTICIPATING CLUBS (provisional)

Manchester United FC; Real Madrid CF; Villarreal CF ; FC Barcelona; Club Atlético de Madrid; Chelsea FC; Arsenal FC; Liverpool FC ; FC Internazionale Milano; AS Roma ; Juventus; ACF Fiorentina; Olympique Lyonnais ; FC Girondins de Bordeaux; Olympique de Marseille; FC Bayern München; Werder Bremen; FC Schalke 04; FC Porto; Sporting Clube de Portugal; Vitória SC; CFR 1907 Cluj; FC Steaua Bucureşti; PSV Eindhoven; FC Twente; FC Zenit St. Petersburg; FC Spartak Moskva; Celtic FC; Rangers FC; FC Shakhtar Donetsk; FC Dynamo Kyiv; R. Standard de Liège; RSC Anderlecht; SK Slavia Praha; AC Sparta Praha; Galatasaray AS; Fenerbahçe SK; Olympiacos CFP; Panathinaikos FC; PFC Levski Sofia; FC Basel 1893; SK Brann; Beitar Jerusalem FC; FK Partizan; Aalborg BK; SK Rapid Wien; Wisła Kraków; MTK Budapest; FC Artmedia Petržalka; NK Dinamo Zagreb; Anorthosis Famagusta FC; IFK Göteborg ; NK Domžale ; FK Modriča ; FK Ventspils; FBK Kaunas ; Tampere United; FC Sheriff; Drogheda United FC; FC Dinamo Tbilisi; FK Rabotnicki; Valur Reykjavík; FC BATE Borisov; KS Dinamo Tirana; FC Levadia Tallinn; FC Pyunik; FC İnter Bakı; FK Aktobe; Linfield FC; Llanelli AFC; NSÍ Runavík; F91 Dudelange; Valetta FC; FK Budućnost Podgorica; FC Santa Coloma; S.S. Murata.

UEFA CUP 2008–2009

PARTICIPATING CLUBS

Valencia CF[1]; Sevilla FC; Real Racing Club Santander; Portsmouth FC[1]; Everton FC; Tottenham Hotspur FC[3]; Manchester City FC[4]; AC Milan ; UC Sampdoria; Udinese Calcio; AS Nancy-Lorraine; AS Saint-Etienne; FRAParis Saint-Germain FC[3]; Hamburger SV; VfL Wolfsburg; BV Borussia Dortmund[2]; Hertha BSC Berlin[4]; SL Benfica; S Marítimo; Vitória FC ; FC Rapid Bucureşti; FC Dinamo 1848 Bucureşti; AFC Unirea Valahorum Urziceni; FCU Politehnica Timisoara; Feyenoord[1]; AFC Ajax; SC Heerenveen; NEC Nijmegen; PFC CSKA Moskva[1]; FC Moskva; Motherwell FC; Queen of the South FC[2]; FC Metalist Kharkiv; FC Dnipro Dnipropetrovsk; Club Brugge KV[1]; KAA Gent[2]; FC Baník Ostrava ; FC Slovan Liberec[2]; Kayserispor; Beşiktaş JK; AEK Athens FC; Aris Thessaloniki FC[2]; PFC Litex Lovech[1]; PFC Lokomotiv Sofia; PFC Cherno More Varna; BSC Young Boys; FC Zürich; AC Bellinzona[2]; Lillestrøm SK[1]; Stabæk IF; Viking FC; Maccabi Netanya FC; Hapoel Kiryat Shmona FC; Hapoel Tel-Aviv FC[2]; FK Crvena Zvezda; FK Vojvodina; FK Borac; Brøndby IF[1]; FC Midtjylland; FC København; FC Nordsjælland[4]; FC Salzburg; FK Austria Wien; Legia Warszawa[1]; KKS Lech Poznań; Debreceni VSC; Győri ETO FC; MŠK Žilina; FC Spartak Trnava[2]; NK Slaven Koprivnica; HNK Hajduk Split[2]; APOEL FC[1]; AC Omonia; Kalmar FC[1]; Djurgårdens IF FF; NK IB Ljubljana[1]; FC Koper; NK Zrinjski[1]; NK Široki Brijeg; SK Liepājas Metalurgs; JFK Olimps[2]; FK Suduva; FK Vetra[2]; FC Haka; FC Honko Espoo[2]; FC Dacia Chisinau; FC Nistru Otaci[2]; Cork City FC[1]; Saint Patrick's Athletic FC; FC Zestafoni[1]; FC WIT Georgia; FC Vaduz[1] ; FK Milano; FK Pelister; FH Hafnarfjördur[1]; ÍA Akranes; FC MTZ-RIPO Minsk[1]; FC Gomel; KS Vllaznia[1]; FK Partizani; FC Flora[1]; FC TVMK Tallinn; FC Ararat Yerevan[1]; FC Banants; FK Khazar Lenkoran[1]; FK Olimpik Baku; FC Tobol Kostanay[1]; FC Shakhtyor Karagandy; Glentoran FC; Cliftonville FC; Bangor City FC; The New Saints FC ; EB Streymur; B36 Tórshavn; CS Grevenmacher[1]; FC Racing Union Luxembourg; Birkirkara FC[1]; Marsaxlokk FC; FK Mogren[1]; FK Zeta; UE Sant Julià[1]; AC Juvenes-Dogana[2]; 11 Teams as winners of UEFA Intertoto Cup.

[1] domestic cup winners, [2] losing domestic cup finalists, [3] domestic league cup winners, [4] Fair Play winners

EUROPEAN CHAMPIONSHIP 2008 REVIEW

One goal is often not considered comfortable for the winners. But for the final, the gulf between the two teams was more of an ocean. Spain attacking in droves like bees in search of their hive, swarm all round the Germans, making them at times seem incredibly awkward and out of touch with play surrounding them. But the Spaniards had to be satisfied with a superb effort from Fernando Torres who first undertook, then overtook Phillip Lahm before skipping over Jens Lehmann to clip the ball in for the 33rd minute winner. Overall the best team won Euro 2008.

Statistically, they scored 12 goals in the tournament, had 117 shots and contributed 3,415 passes. Midfield player Xavi Hernandez was considered the player of the finals, too. Yet any firm conclusion drawn from the opening group matches would have been highly misleading. Turkey looked anything but knock-out stage material in losing to Portugal, Italy looked fortunate to get nil against a rampant Holland and Russia were run ragged by a fluent Spanish team. However, Greece the holders were well beaten by Sweden. In addition to all this both hosts lost their opening fixtures, the Swiss to the Czech Republic, Austria to Croatia.

The Portuguese again caught the attention with a 3-1 win over the Czech Republic, but Turkey had to battle hard and late before edging the Swiss. Croatia gave a clever exhibition to make the Germans look much less than the team which had beaten Poland in their opener. At least Austria at the death salvaged a draw against the Poles to give them a chance against their near neighbours. Once again the Dutch produced a fluid performance to make the French look decidedly weak, though the victims were denied an obvious penalty. Italy, the reigning World Cup holders, were only saved when Romania missed a penalty in the dying moments. Russia piled on the agony for Greece and Spain were unable to repeat the dynamism of their first match in beating the Swedes.

But the last group games produced the fireworks. Turkey, two goals down to the Czechs and seemingly preparing to pack their bags, found stamina and spirit and not a little football to win through, the Germans nervously beat target-missing Austria, but Holland resting key players still found space against Romania. Then there was the repeat of the 2006 World Cup final, but it was Italy who prevailed as the French finished with ten players.

Taking stock before the last eight carried on, it is interesting to note that Holland produced the finest goal thus far and the most blatantly off-side one – in the same match. And despite the efforts of the authorities to say differently, a player off the field of play is in no position to play an opponent onside. However, Wesley Sneijder, the finisher of a classic move provided easily the most thrilling goal of the group stage.

To underline the situation, three of the teams who topped their group did not survive the quarter-finals. The draw for the semi-finals could have been better handled by a group of eleven-plus examination sitting school children, since the entire tournament is mapped out before a ball is kicked. So we had a repeat of the Spain v Russia opener! Perhaps UEFA had too much to think about with organising the Intertoto Cup at the same time as Euro 2008 was under way.

But there was the same kind of walkover for the Spaniards as in the previous match, though on this occasion, the Russians hardly had a kick. The day before the Germans played the late, late scoring Turks at their own game. Having gone behind, Germany levelled but when Turkey snatched the lead with a few minutes to spare, at least extra time appeared inevitable. But Phillip Lahm, who only minutes before had been skinned for the equaliser, atoned with the winner.

Overall the standard of play was pleasingly high. Most favoured the solo, isolated striker but the variations on a theme of 4-5-1 did not curtail the attacking intentions, though often the spearhead found himself overwhelmed by numbers and when chances arose, his finishing left much to be desired. Those teams with a more fluid approach to forward movement looked far more at ease. Discipline was reasonable, too, with three dismissals. True, there was plenty of simulated "death" from the briefest of tackles, but no bouts of fisticuffs.

One match might easily have been called off at half-time because of a water-logged pitch. Interesting to note that had it been abandoned what would have happened. Yes, you guessed it – a penalty shoot-out!

EUROPEAN CHAMPIONSHIP 2008 QUALIFYING COMPETION

■ *Denotes player sent off.*

GROUP A

Belgium	(0) 0	Kazakhstan	(0) 0
Poland	(0) 1	Finland	(0) 3
Serbia	(0) 1	Azerbaijan	(0) 0
Armenia	(0) 0	Belgium	(1) 1
Azerbaijan	(1) 1	Kazakhstan	(1) 1
Finland	(1) 1	Portugal	(1) 1
Poland	(1) 1	Serbia	(0) 1
Armenia	(0) 0	Finland	(0) 0
Kazakhstan	(0) 0	Poland	(0) 1
Portugal	(2) 3	Azerbaijan	(0) 0
Serbia	(0) 1	Belgium	(0) 0
Belgium	(1) 3	Azerbaijan	(0) 0
Kazakhstan	(0) 0	Finland	(1) 2
Poland	(2) 2	Portugal	(0) 1
Serbia	(0) 3	Armenia	(0) 0
Belgium	(0) 0	Poland	(1) 1
Finland	(1) 1	Armenia	(0) 0
Portugal	(2) 3	Kazakhstan	(0) 0
Kazakhstan	(0) 2	Serbia	(0) 1
Poland	(3) 5	Azerbaijan	(0) 0
Portugal	(0) 4	Belgium	(0) 0
Azerbaijan	(0) 1	Finland	(0) 0
Poland	(1) 1	Armenia	(0) 0
Serbia	(1) 1	Portugal	(1) 1
Azerbaijan	(1) 1	Poland	(0) 3
Belgium	(0) 1	Portugal	(1) 2
Finland	(0) 0	Serbia	(1) 2
Kazakhstan	(0) 1	Armenia	(2) 2
Armenia	(0) 1	Poland	(0) 0
Finland	(1) 2	Belgium	(0) 0
Kazakhstan	(0) 1	Azerbaijan	(1) 1
Armenia	(1) 1	Portugal	(1) 1
Belgium	(2) 3	Serbia	(0) 2
Finland	(1) 2	Kazakhstan	(1) 1
Portugal	(0) 2	Poland	(1) 2
Serbia	(0) 0	Finland	(0) 0
Finland	(0) 0	Poland	(0) 0
Kazakhstan	(1) 2	Belgium	(2) 2
Portugal	(1) 1	Serbia	(0) 1
Armenia	(0) 0	Serbia	(0) 0
Azerbaijan	(0) 0	Portugal	(2) 2
Belgium	(0) 0	Finland	(0) 0
Poland	(1) 3	Kazakhstan	(1) 1
Azerbaijan	(1) 1	Serbia	(4) 6
Belgium	(0) 3	Armenia	(0) 0
Kazakhstan	(0) 1	Portugal	(0) 2
Finland	(0) 2	Azerbaijan	(0) 1
Poland	(1) 2	Belgium	(0) 0
Portugal	(1) 1	Armenia	(0) 0
Armenia	(0) 0	Kazakhstan	(0) 1
Azerbaijan	(0) 0	Belgium	(0) 1
Portugal	(0) 0	Finland	(0) 0

| Serbia | (0) 2 | Poland | (1) 2 |
| Serbia | (0) 1 | Kazakhstan | (0) 0 |

Group A Table	P	W	D	L	F	A	Pts
Poland	14	8	4	2	24	12	28
Portugal	14	7	6	1	24	10	27
Serbia	14	6	6	2	22	11	24
Finland	14	6	6	2	13	7	24
Belgium	14	5	3	6	14	16	18
Kazakhstan	14	2	4	8	11	21	10
Armenia	12	2	3	7	4	13	9
Azerbaijan	12	1	2	9	6	28	5

Armenia v Azerbaijan and return match not played.

GROUP B

Faeroes	(0) 0	Georgia	(3) 6
Georgia	(0) 0	France	(2) 3
Italy	(1) 1	Lithuania	(1) 1
Scotland	(5) 6	Faeroes	(0) 0
France	(2) 3	Italy	(1) 1
Lithuania	(0) 1	Scotland	(0) 2
Ukraine	(1) 3	Georgia	(1) 2
Faeroes	(0) 0	Lithuania	(0) 1
Italy	(0) 2	Ukraine	(0) 0
Scotland	(0) 1	France	(0) 0
France	(2) 5	Faeroes	(0) 0
Georgia	(1) 1	Italy	(1) 3
Ukraine	(0) 2	Scotland	(0) 0
Faeroes	(0) 0	Ukraine	(1) 2
Lithuania	(0) 0	France	(0) 1
Scotland	(1) 2	Georgia	(1) 1
Georgia	(2) 3	Faeroes	(0) 1
Italy	(1) 2	Scotland	(0) 0
Ukraine	(0) 1	Lithuania	(0) 0
Faeroes	(0) 1	Italy	(1) 2
France	(0) 2	Ukraine	(0) 0
Lithuania	(0) 1	Georgia	(0) 0
Faeroes	(0) 0	Scotland	(2) 2
France	(1) 1	Georgia	(0) 0
Lithuania	(0) 0	Italy	(2) 2
Georgia	(0) 1	Ukraine	(1) 1
Italy	(0) 0	France	(0) 0
Scotland	(1) 3	Lithuania	(0) 1
France	(0) 0	Scotland	(0) 1
Lithuania	(1) 2	Faeroes	(0) 1
Ukraine	(0) 1	Italy	(1) 2
Faeroes	(0) 0	France	(2) 6
Italy	(1) 2	Georgia	(0) 0
Scotland	(2) 3	Ukraine	(1) 1
France	(0) 2	Lithuania	(0) 0
Georgia	(1) 2	Scotland	(0) 0
Ukraine	(3) 5	Faeroes	(0) 0
Lithuania	(1) 2	Ukraine	(0) 0
Scotland	(0) 1	Italy	(1) 2
Georgia	(0) 0	Lithuania	(0) 2
Italy	(3) 3	Faeroes	(0) 1
Ukraine	(1) 2	France	(2) 2

Celtic Park, 2 September 2006, 50,059

Scotland (5) 6 *(Fletcher D 7, McFadden 10, Boyd 24 (pen), 38, Miller 30 (pen), O'Connor 85)*

Faeroes (0) 0

Scotland: Gordon; Dailly, Weir, Pressley, Naysmith, Fletcher D (Teale 46), Hartley, Quashie (Severin 84), Miller (O'Connor 61), Boyd, McFadden.
Faeroes: Mikkelsen; Hansen P, Johannesen O, Danielsen, Joensen J, Benjaminsen, Johnsson (Samuelsen S 76), Borg, Fredriksberg (Thorleifson 60), Jacobsen C, Jacobsen R (Nielsen 84).
Referee: Yegorov (Russia).

Kaunas, 6 September 2006, 6500

Lithuania (0) 1 *(Miceika 85)*   **Scotland (0) 2** *(Dailly 46, Miller 62)*

Lithuania: Karcemarskas; Stankevicius, Dziaukstas, Skerla, Zvirgzdauskas, Savenas (Tamosauskas 50), Kalonas, Mikoliunas (Labukas 66), Preiksaitis (Miceika 81), Poskus, Danilevicius.
Scotland: Gordon; Dailly, Weir, Caldwell G, Naysmith, Pressley, Fletcher D, Quashie (Boyd 43), McFadden (Alexander G 21), Hartley (Severin 88), Miller.
Referee: Hrinek (Slovakia).

Glasgow, 7 October 2006, 57,000

Scotland (0) 1 *(Caldwell G 67)*   **France (0) 0**

Scotland: Gordon; Dailly, Alexander G, Pressley, Weir, Ferguson B, Fletcher D, Caldwell G, McFadden (O'Connor 72), Hartley, McCulloch (Teale 58).
France: Coupet; Abidal, Thuram, Boumsong, Sagnol, Ribery (Wiltord 74), Vieira, Makelele, Malouda, Trezeguet (Saha 62), Henry.
Referee: Busacca (Switzerland).

Kiev, 11 October 2006, 55,000

Ukraine (0) 2 *(Kucher 60, Shevchenko 90 (pen))*   **Scotland (0) 0**

Ukraine: Shovkovskyi; Nesmachni, Sviderskyi, Kucher, Rusol, Tymoschuk, Shelayev, Gusev (Milevski 62), Kalynychenko (Vorobei 76), Shevchenko, Voronin (Shershun 90).
Scotland: Gordon; Neilson (McManus 89), Alexander G, Ferguson B, Weir, Pressley*, Fletcher D, Caldwell G, Miller, Hartley, McFadden (Boyd 73).
Referee: Hansson (Sweden).

Glasgow, 24 March 2007, 50,850

Scotland (1) 2 *(Boyd 11, Beattie 89)*   **Georgia (1) 1** *(Arveladze 41)*

Scotland: Gordon; Alexander G, Naysmith, Ferguson B, Weir, McManus, Teale (Brown 60), Hartley, Boyd (Beattie 76), Miller (Maloney 90), McCulloch.
Georgia: Lomaia; Shashiashvili, Khizanishvili, Sulukvadze, Eliava, Burduli (Siradze 57), Tskitishvili (Mujiri 90), Menteshashvili (Gogua 46), Kobiashvili, Demetradze, Arveladze.
Referee: Vollquartz (Denmark).

Bari, 28 March 2007, 37,500

Italy (1) 2 *(Toni 12, 70)*   **Scotland (0) 0**

Italy: Buffon; Oddo, Cannavaro, Materazzi, Zambrotta, Gattuso, De Rossi, Camoranesi, Perrotta (Pirlo 77), Di Natale (Del Piero 66), Toni (Quagliarella 87).
Scotland: Gordon; Alexander G, Naysmith, Weir, McManus, Ferguson B, Teale (Maloney 66), Hartley, Brown (Beattie 86), McCulloch (Boyd 81), Miller.
Referee: De Bleeckere (Belgium).

Toftir, 6 June 2007, 4100

Faeroes (0) 0   Scotland (2) 2 *(Maloney 31, O'Connor 35)*

Faeroes: Mikkelsen; Danielsen, Jacobsen J, Johannesen O (Djurhuss 36) (Samuelsen S 77), Benjaminsen, Thomassen, Borg (Flotum 82), Olsen, Jacobsen R, Jacobsen C, Holst.
Scotland: Gordon; Alexander G, Weir, McManus, Naysmith, Hartley, Ferguson B, Fletcher D (Teale 68), Maloney (Adam 77), O'Connor, Boyd (Naismith 83).
Referee: Germanakos (Greece).

Hampden Park, 8 September 2007, 51,349

Scotland (1) 3 *(Boyd 31, McManus 77, McFadden 83)*

Lithuania (0) 1 *(Danilevicius 61 (pen))*

Scotland: Gordon; Hutton, McEveley, Brown, Weir, McManus, Teale (McFadden 69), Fletcher D, Boyd, McCulloch (Maloney 76), O'Connor (Beattie 76).
Lithuania: Karcemarskas; Klimavicius, Stankevicius (Jankauskas 56), Skerla, Zvirgzdauskas, Semberas, Kalonas, Cesnauskis, Velicka (Ksanavicius 46), Danilevicius, Morinas (Mikoliunas 46).
Referee: Skomina (Slovenia).

Paris, 12 September 2007, 42,000

France (0) 0   Scotland (0) 1 *(McFadden 64)*

France: Landreau; Abidal (Benzema 77), Thuram, Escude, Ribery, Diarra, Malouda, Vieira (Nasri 69), Makelele, Trezeguet, Anelka.
Scotland: Gordon; Alexander G, Hutton, Ferguson B, Weir, McManus, Hartley, Brown, McFadden (O'Connor 76), McCulloch, Fletcher D (Pearson 26).
Referee: Plautz (Austria).

Hampden Park, 13 October 2007, 51,366

Scotland (2) 3 *(Miller 4, McCulloch 10, McFadden 68)*

Ukraine (1) 1 *(Shevchenko 24)*

Scotland: Gordon; Hutton, Naysmith, Ferguson, Weir, McManus, Pearson, Brown (Maloney 76), McFadden (O'Connor 80), Miller, McCulloch (Dailly 60).
Ukraine: Shovkovskiy; Chigrinskiy, Nesmachny, Kucher, Yezerskiy, Timoshchuk (Shelayev 73), Gusev (Rotan 46), Voronin, Vorobei (Nazarenko 62), Gladkiy, Shevchenko.
Referee: Vink (Holland).

Tbilisi, 17 October 2007, 55,500

Georgia (1) 2 *(Mchedlidze 16, Siradze 64)*   **Scotland (0) 0**

Georgia: Makaridze; Kvirkvelia, Shashiashvili, Khizanishvili, Salukvadze, Menteshashvili, Kankava, Asatiani, Siradze (Jakobia 89), Kenia (Kandelaki 79), Mchedlidze (Kvakhadze 85).
Scotland: Gordon; Alexander G, Murty, Ferguson B, Weir, McManus, Pearson (Boyd 66), Fletcher D, Maloney, Miller (Beattie 66), McFadden.
Referee: Kircher (Germany).

Hampden Park, 17 November 2007, 53,301

Scotland (0) 1 *(Ferguson B 65)*   **Italy (1) 2** *(Toni 2, Panucci 90)*

Scotland: Gordon; Hutton, Naysmith, Ferguson B, Weir, McManus, Hartley, Brown (Miller 74), McFadden, McCulloch (Boyd 90), Fletcher D.
Italy: Buffon; Cannavaro, Barzagli, Panucci, Ambrosini, Pirlo, Camoranesi (Chiellini 83), Gattuso (De Rossi 87), Zambrotta, Toni, Di Natale (Iaquinta 68).
Referee: Gonzalez (Spain).

Group B Table	P	W	D	L	F	A	Pts
Italy	12	9	2	1	22	9	29
France	12	8	2	2	25	5	26
Scotland	12	8	0	4	21	12	24
Ukraine	12	5	2	5	18	16	17
Lithuania	12	5	1	6	11	13	16
Georgia	12	3	1	8	16	19	10
Faeroes	12	0	0	12	4	43	0

GROUP C

Hungary	(0) 1	Norway	(3) 4
Malta	(1) 2	Bosnia	(3) 5
Moldova	(0) 0	Greece	(0) 1
Bosnia	(0) 1	Hungary	(1) 3
Norway	(0) 2	Moldova	(0) 0
Turkey	(0) 2	Malta	(0) 0

(Played behind closed doors in Frankfurt.)

Greece	(1) 1	Norway	(0) 0
Hungary	(0) 0	Turkey	(1) 1
Moldova	(2) 2	Bosnia	(0) 2
Bosnia	(0) 0	Greece	(1) 4
Malta	(1) 2	Hungary	(1) 1
Turkey	(3) 5	Moldova	(0) 0

(Played behind closed doors in Frankfurt.)

Greece	(1) 1	Turkey	(1) 4
Moldova	(0) 1	Malta	(0) 1
Norway	(0) 1	Bosnia	(2) 2
Hungary	(1) 2	Moldova	(0) 0
Malta	(0) 0	Greece	(0) 1
Turkey	(0) 2	Norway	(2) 2

(Played behind closed doors in Frankfurt.)

Bosnia	(2) 3	Turkey	(2) 2
Greece	(2) 2	Hungary	(0) 0
Norway	(1) 4	Malta	(0) 0
Bosnia	(1) 1	Malta	(0) 0
Greece	(1) 2	Moldova	(0) 1
Norway	(1) 4	Hungary	(0) 0
Hungary	(1) 1	Bosnia	(0) 0
Malta	(1) 2	Turkey	(1) 2
Moldova	(0) 0	Norway	(0) 1
Bosnia	(0) 0	Moldova	(1) 1
Norway	(2) 2	Greece	(2) 2
Turkey	(0) 3	Hungary	(0) 0
Greece	(1) 3	Bosnia	(0) 2
Hungary	(1) 2	Malta	(0) 0
Moldova	(1) 1	Turkey	(0) 1
Bosnia	(0) 0	Norway	(1) 2
Malta	(0) 2	Moldova	(3) 3
Turkey	(0) 0	Greece	(0) 1
Greece	(1) 5	Malta	(0) 0
Moldova	(2) 3	Hungary	(0) 0
Norway	(1) 1	Turkey	(1) 2
Hungary	(1) 1	Greece	(1) 2
Malta	(0) 1	Norway	(3) 4
Turkey	(1) 1	Bosnia	(0) 0

Group C Table	P	W	D	L	F	A	Pts
Greece	12	10	1	1	25	10	31
Turkey	12	7	3	2	25	11	24
Norway	12	7	2	3	27	11	23
Bosnia	12	4	1	7	16	22	13
Moldova	12	3	3	6	12	19	12
Hungary	12	4	0	8	11	22	12
Malta	12	1	2	9	10	31	5

GROUP D

Czech Republic	(0) 2	Wales	(0) 1
Germany	(0) 1	Republic of Ireland	(0) 0
Slovakia	(3) 6	Cyprus	(0) 1
San Marino	(0) 0	Germany	(6) 13
Slovakia	(0) 0	Czech Republic	(2) 3
Cyprus	(2) 5	Republic of Ireland	(2) 2
Czech Republic	(4) 7	San Marino	(0) 0
Wales	(1) 1	Slovakia	(3) 5
Republic of Ireland	(0) 1	Czech Republic	(0) 0
Slovakia	(0) 1	Germany	(3) 4
Wales	(2) 3	Cyprus	(0) 1
Cyprus	(1) 1	Germany	(1) 1
Republic of Ireland	(3) 5	San Marino	(0) 0
San Marino	(0) 1	Republic of Ireland	(0) 2
Cyprus	(1) 1	Slovakia	(0) 3
Czech Republic	(0) 1	Germany	(1) 2
Republic of Ireland	(1) 1	Wales	(0) 0
Czech Republic	(1) 1	Cyprus	(0) 0
Republic of Ireland	(1) 1	Slovakia	(0) 0
Wales	(2) 3	San Marino	(0) 0
Germany	(1) 6	San Marino	(0) 0
Wales	(0) 0	Czech Republic	(0) 0
Germany	(2) 2	Slovakia	(1) 1
San Marino	(0) 0	Cyprus	(0) 1
San Marino	(0) 0	Czech Republic	(1) 3
Slovakia	(1) 2	Republic of Ireland	(1) 2
Wales	(0) 0	Germany	(1) 2
Cyprus	(2) 3	San Marino	(0) 0
Czech Republic	(1) 1	Republic of Ireland	(0) 0
Slovakia	(1) 2	Wales	(3) 5
Cyprus	(0) 3	Wales	(1) 1
Republic of Ireland	(0) 0	Germany	(0) 0
Slovakia	(3) 7	San Marino	(0) 0
Germany	(0) 0	Czech Republic	(2) 3
Republic of Ireland	(0) 1	Cyprus	(0) 1
San Marino	(0) 1	Wales	(2) 2
Czech Republic	(1) 3	Slovakia	(0) 1
Germany	(2) 4	Cyprus	(0) 0
Wales	(1) 2	Republic of Ireland	(1) 2
Cyprus	(0) 0	Czech Republic	(1) 2
Germany	(0) 0	Wales	(0) 0
San Marino	(0) 0	Slovakia	(1) 5

Teplice, 2 September 2006, 16,204

Czech Republic (0) 2 *(Lafata 76, 89)*   **Wales (0) 1** *(Jiranek 85 (og))*

Czech Republic: Cech; Ujfalusi, Jiranek, Rozehnal, Jankulovski, Stajner (Sionko 46), Galasek (Kovac R 87), Rosicky, Plasil, Kulic (Lafata 75), Koller.
Wales: Jones P; Delaney (Cotterill 78), Ricketts (Earnshaw 79), Robinson, Gabbidon, Collins J, Davies S, Fletcher (Ledley 47), Bellamy, Nyatanga, Giggs.
Referee: Eriksson (Sweden).

Stuttgart, 2 September 2006, 53,198

Germany (0) 1 *(Podolski 57)*   **Republic of Ireland (0) 0**

Germany: Lehmann; Lahm, Friedrich A, Friedrich M, Jansen, Schneider (Borowski 83), Frings, Ballack, Schweinsteiger, Podolski (Neuville 76), Klose.
Republic of Ireland: Given; Carr, Finnan, Andy O'Brien, Dunne, O'Shea, Duff (McGeady 77), Reid S, Keane, Doyle K (Elliott 79), Kilbane (Alan O'Brien 83).
Referee: Kantalejo (Spain).

Nicosia, 7 October 2006, 12,000
Cyprus (2) 5 *(Konstantinou M 10, 50 (pen), Garpozis 16, Charalambides 60, 75)*
Republic of Ireland (2) 2 *(Ireland 8, Dunne 44)*

Cyprus: Morfis; Satsias, Lambrou, Louka, Theodotou, Michael (Charalambides 46), Garpozis (Charalambous 77), Makrides, Okkas (Yiasoumis 86), Konstantinou M, Aloneftis.
Republic of Ireland: Kenny; Finnan, O'Shea, Andy O'Brien (Lee 71), Dunne■, Kilbane, McGeady (Alan O'Brien 80), Ireland (Douglas 83), Morrison, Keane, Duff.
Referee: Batista (Portugal).

Cardiff, 7 October 2006, 28,493
Wales (1) 1 *(Bale 37)*
Slovakia (3) 5 *(Svento 14, Mintal 32, 38, Karhan 51, Vittek 59)*

Wales: Jones P; Duffy, Bale, Gabbidon, Nyatanga, Robinson, Edwards (Ledley 58), Koumas, Davies S (Cotterill 88), Bellamy, Earnshaw (Parry 46).
Slovakia: Contofalsky; Kozak, Kratochvil, Petras M, Varga, Karhan (Krajcik 67), Mintal (Hodur 71), Vittek (Holosko 77), Petras P, Svento, Durica.
Referee: Egmond (Holland).

Dublin, 11 October 2006, 35,500
Republic of Ireland (0) 1 *(Kilbane 62)*   **Czech Republic (0) 0**

Republic of Ireland: Henderson; Kelly, Finnan, O'Shea, McShane, Carsley, Reid A (Quinn A 72), Douglas, Keane, Kilbane (Alan O'Brien 79), Duff.
Czech Republic: Cech; Polak, Ujfalusi, Kovac R, Jankulovski, Jiranek, Rosicky, Plasil (Grygera 85), Rozehnal, Koller, Baros (Jarolim 82).
Referee: Layec (France).

Cardiff, 11 October 2006, 20,456
Wales (2) 3 *(Koumas 33, Earnshaw 39, Bellamy 72)*   **Cyprus (0) 1** *(Okkas 83)*

Wales: Price; Duffy (Edwards 78), Bale, Gabbidon, Nyatanga, Robinson, Morgan, Koumas (Ledley 76), Earnshaw, Bellamy (Parry 90), Davies S.
Cyprus: Morfis; Theodotou, Lambrou, Louka, Satsias (Yiasoumis 84), Michael (Charalambides 46), Garpozis (Charalambous 46), Makrides, Aloneftis, Konstantinou M, Okkas.
Referee: Granat (Poland).

Dublin, 15 November 2006, 34,018
Republic of Ireland (3) 5 *(Simoncini D 7 (og), Doyle K 24, Keane 31, 58 (pen), 85)*
San Marino (0) 0

Republic of Ireland: Given; Finnan, O'Shea, Dunne, McShane, Carsley (Douglas 50), Reid A, Doyle K (McGeady 63), Keane, Duff, Kilbane (Lee 79).
San Marino: Valentini F; Bugli, Albani, Bacciocchi, Simoncini D (Bonini 81), Vannucci (Crescentini 72), Valentini C, Andreini, Mariotti (Michele Marani 59), Manuel Marani, Selva A.
Referee: Isaksen (Faeroes).

Serravalle, 7 February 2007, 3294
San Marino (0) 1 *(Manuel Marani 86)*
Republic of Ireland (0) 2 *(Kilbane 49, Ireland 90)*

San Marino: Simoncini A; Valentini C, Manuel Marani, Albani, Simoncini D, Muccioli, Bonini (Vannucci 76), Domeniconi (Bugli 88), Michele Marani, Selva A, Gasperoni A (Andreini 66).
Republic of Ireland: Henderson; Finnan, Harte (Hunt 74), Dunne, O'Shea (McShane 46), Carsley, Duff, Ireland, Keane, Long (Stokes 80), Kilbane.
Referee: Rasmussen (Denmark).

Dublin, 24 March 2007, 72,539

Republic of Ireland (1) 1 *(Ireland 39)*   **Wales (0) 0**

Republic of Ireland: Given; Finnan, O'Shea, Dunne, McShane, Carsley, Douglas (Hunt 80), Ireland (Doyle K 59), Keane (McGeady 89), Kilbane, Duff.
Wales: Coyne; Ricketts, Bale (Collins D 74), Collins J, Evans S, Nyatanga, Ledley (Fletcher 46), Robinson (Easter 90), Davies S, Bellamy, Giggs.
Referee: Hauge (Norway).

Dublin, 28 March 2007, 71,297

Republic of Ireland (1) 1 *(Doyle K 12)*   **Slovakia (0) 0**

Republic of Ireland: Given; O'Shea, Finnan, McShane, Dunne, Carsley, Ireland (Hunt 70), McGeady (Quinn A 87), Kilbane, Duff, Doyle K (Long 74).
Slovakia: Contofalsky; Singlar (Sestak 80), Skrtel, Klimpl, Gresko, Svento (Michalik 86), Zofcak, Borbely, Sapara (Holosko 72), Vittek, Jakubko.
Referee: Baskakov (Russia).

Cardiff, 28 March 2007, 18,752

Wales (2) 3 *(Giggs 3, Bale 20, Koumas 63 (pen))*   **San Marino (0) 0**

Wales: Coyne; Ricketts, Evans S (Nyatanga 63), Collins J, Bale, Fletcher, Koumas, Davies S, Giggs (Parry 73), Bellamy, Easter (Cotterill 46).
San Marino: Simoncini A; Valentini C (Toccaceli 85), Andreini, Albani, Muccioli, Bacciocchi, Negri (Nanni 79), Domeniconi (Bugli 67), Manuel Marani, Selva A, Gasperoni A.
Referee: Tchagharyan (Armenia).

Cardiff, 2 June 2007, 30,714

Wales (0) 0   Czech Republic (0) 0

Wales: Hennessey; Ricketts, Nyatanga, Gabbidon, Collins J, Robinson, Ledley, Koumas, Davies S, Giggs (Earnshaw 89), Bellamy.
Czech Republic: Cech; Ujfalusi, Kovac R, Rozehnal, Jankulovski, Polak (Jarolim 65), Sivok (Matejovsky 83), Rosicky, Plasil, Koller, Baros (Kulic 46).
Referee: Allaerts (Belgium).

Bratislava, 8 September 2007, 12,360

Slovakia (1) 2 *(Klimpl 37, Cech 90)*   **Republic of Ireland (1) 2** *(Ireland 7, Doyle K 57)*

Slovakia: Senecky; Durica, Cech, Klimpl, Mintal, Hamsyk, Krajcik, Sapara (Sebo 71), Gresko, Sestak (Obzera 65), Holosko.
Republic of Ireland: Given; Kelly, O'Shea, Dunne, McShane, Carsley, Kilbane, Ireland (Douglas 76), Doyle K (Murphy 89), McGeady (Gibson 61), Keane.
Referee: Farina (Italy).

Millennium Stadium, 8 September 2007, 31,000

Wales (0) 0   Germany (1) 2 *(Klose 5, 60)*

Wales: Hennessey; Ricketts, Gabbidon, Bale, Nyatanga, Robinson, Ledley (Earnshaw 46), Davies S (Crofts 79), Koumas (Fletcher 67), Collins J, Eastwood.
Germany: Lehmann; Metzelder, Mertesacker, Jansen, Friedrich A, Hitzlsperger, Hilbert, Pander (Trochowski 46), Schweinsteiger, Kuranyi (Podolski 73), Klose (Helmes 87).
Referee: Gonzalez (Spain).

Prague, 12 September 2007, 16,648

Czech Republic (1) 1 *(Jankulovski 15)*   **Republic of Ireland (0) 0**

Czech Republic: Cech; Ujfalusi, Rozehnal, Jankulovski, Polak, Plasil, Sionko (Vlcek 74), Kovac, Rosicky, Galasek (Sivok 46), Baros (Jarolim 89).

Republic of Ireland: Given; Kelly, O'Shea (Hunt■ 38), Dunne, McShane, Kilbane, Duff, Reid A, Carsley (Keogh A 82), Keane, McGeady (Long 62).
Referee: Vassaras (Greece).

Trnava, 12 September 2007, 5486

Slovakia (1) 2 *(Mintal 12, 57)*
Wales (3) 5 *(Eastwood 22, Bellamy 34, 41, Durica 78 (og), Davies S 90)*

Slovakia: Senecky; Durica, Klimpl, Cech, Petras, Mintal, Sapara, Hamsyk, Gresko (Zofcak 64), Sestak (Obzera 46), Holosko.
Wales: Hennessey; Bale, Ricketts, Collins J, Gabbidon, Morgan, Ledley (Vaughan 85), Robinson, Bellamy, Eastwood (Fletcher 73), Davies S.
Referee: Duhamel (France).

Nicosia, 13 October 2007, 8500

Cyprus (0) 3 *(Okkas 59, 68, Charalambides 79)*   **Wales (1) 1** *(Collins J 21)*

Cyprus: Georgallides; Okkarides, Elia (Charalambides 63), Christou, Michael (Yiasoumi 46), Satsias (Marangos 71), Makrides, Aloneftis, Okkas, Garpozis, Nicolaou.
Wales: Coyne; Gabbidon, Bale, Ricketts (Easter 73), Nyatanga, Robinson, Davies S, Ledley, Collins J (Morgan 44), Bellamy, Eastwood (Earnshaw 58).
Referee: Bertolini (Switzerland).

Dublin, 13 October 2007, 67,495

Republic of Ireland (0) 0   Germany (0) 0

Republic of Ireland: Given; Kelly, O'Brien J, Dunne, Finnan, Carsley, Kilbane (Murphy 90), Reid A, Doyle K (Long 70), Keane, Keogh A (McGeady 80).
Germany: Lehmann; Mertesacker, Jansen, Friedrich A, Metzelder, Fritz, Trochowski (Castro 90), Schweinsteiger (Rolfes 18), Frings, Kuranyi, Gomez (Podolski 64).
Referee: Hansson (Sweden).

Dublin, 17 October 2007, 45,500

Republic of Ireland (0) 1 *(Finnan 90)*   **Cyprus (0) 1** *(Okkarides 80)*

Republic of Ireland: Given; Finnan, O'Shea, McShane, O'Brien J (Miller 46), Kilbane, Reid A, Doyle K, Keane, Hunt (Murphy 73), Keogh A (McGeady 63).
Cyprus: Georgallides; Okkarides, Elia■, Christou, Makrides (Theofilou 86), Charalambides, Satsias (Marangos 69), Nicolaou, Yiasoumi (Michael 73), Okkas, Garpozis.
Referee: Vuorela (Finland).

Serravalle, 17 October 2007, 1182

San Marino (0) 1 *(Selva A 73)*   **Wales (2) 2** *(Earnshaw 13, Ledley 36)*

San Marino: Šimoncini A; Andreini, Albani■, Vannucci (Bugli 76), Valentini C, Della Valle, Simoncini D, Bonifazi (Bonini 62), Muccioli, Selva A, De Luigi (Vitaioli 80).
Wales: Price; Gabbidon, Bale, Eardley, Nyatanga, Robinson, Ledley, Earnshaw, Bellamy, Davies S, Vaughan (Ricketts 62).
Referee: Zammit (Malta).

Millennium Stadium, 17 November 2007, 24,619

Wales (1) 2 *(Koumas 23, 89 (pen))*   **Republic of Ireland (1) 2** *(Keane 31, Doyle K 60)*

Wales: Hennessey; Gunter, Gabbidon, Eardley (Cotterill 81), Collins J, Robinson (Edwards 37), Fletcher, Ledley, Koumas, Eastwood (Easter 59), Davies S.
Republic of Ireland: Given; O'Shea, Finnan, McShane, Carsley, Kilbane, Reid A (Potter 87), Miller (Hunt 59), Doyle K, Keane, McGeady.
Referee: Oriekhov (Ukraine).

Frankfurt, 21 November 2007, 49,292

Germany (0) 0   Wales (0) 0

Germany: Lehmann; Lahm, Metzelder, Mertesacker, Fritz, Castro (Hilbert 57), Borowski, Hitzlsperger (Rolfes 46), Podolski, Klose, Gomez (Neuville 71).
Wales: Hennessey; Gunter, Ricketts, Gabbidon, Nyatanga, Collins J, Fletcher, Davies S, Edwards (Crofts 90), Earnshaw (Easter 56), Ledley.
Referee: Balaj (Romania).

Group D Table	P	W	D	L	F	A	Pts
Czech Republic	12	9	2	1	27	5	29
Germany	12	8	3	1	35	7	27
Republic of Ireland	12	4	5	3	17	14	17
Slovakia	12	5	1	6	33	23	16
Wales	12	4	3	5	18	19	15
Cyprus	12	4	2	6	17	24	14
San Marino	12	0	0	12	2	57	0

GROUP E

Estonia	(0) 0	Macedonia	(0) 1
England	(3) 5	Andorra	(0) 0
Estonia	(0) 0	Israel	(1) 1
Israel	(3) 4	Andorra	(0) 1
Macedonia	(0) 0	England	(0) 1
Russia	(0) 0	Croatia	(0) 0
Croatia	(2) 7	Andorra	(0) 0
England	(0) 0	Macedonia	(0) 0
Russia	(1) 1	Israel	(0) 1
Andorra	(0) 0	Macedonia	(3) 3
Croatia	(0) 2	England	(0) 0
Russia	(0) 2	Estonia	(0) 0
Israel	(1) 3	Croatia	(2) 4
Macedonia	(0) 0	Russia	(2) 2
Croatia	(0) 2	Macedonia	(1) 1
Estonia	(0) 0	Russia	(0) 2
Israel	(0) 0	England	(0) 0
Andorra	(0) 0	England	(0) 3
Israel	(2) 4	Estonia	(0) 0
Estonia	(0) 0	Croatia	(1) 1
Macedonia	(1) 1	Israel	(2) 2
Russia	(2) 4	Andorra	(0) 0
Andorra	(0) 0	Israel	(1) 2
Croatia	(0) 0	Russia	(0) 0
Estonia	(0) 0	England	(1) 3
Estonia	(1) 2	Andorra	(0) 1
Croatia	(2) 2	Estonia	(0) 0
England	(1) 3	Israel	(0) 0
Russia	(1) 3	Macedonia	(0) 0
Andorra	(0) 0	Croatia	(3) 6
England	(2) 3	Russia	(0) 0
Macedonia	(1) 1	Estonia	(1) 1
Croatia	(0) 1	Israel	(0) 0
England	(3) 3	Estonia	(0) 0
Macedonia	(2) 3	Andorra	(0) 0
Russia	(0) 2	England	(1) 1
Andorra	(0) 0	Estonia	(1) 2
Israel	(1) 2	Russia	(0) 1
Macedonia	(0) 2	Croatia	(0) 0
Andorra	(0) 0	Russia	(1) 1
England	(0) 2	Croatia	(2) 3
Israel	(1) 1	Macedonia	(0) 0

270

Old Trafford, 2 September 2006, 56,290

England (3) 5 *(Crouch 5, 66, Gerrard 13, Defoe 38, 47)*   **Andorra (0) 0**
England: Robinson; Neville P (Lennon 65), Cole A, Hargreaves, Terry, Brown, Gerrard, Lampard, Crouch, Defoe (Johnson A 71), Downing (Richardson 64).
Andorra: Koldo; Lima A, Txema, Ayala, Sonejee, Javi Sanchez (Juli Sanchez 46), Sivera (Garcia 77), Vieira, Silva, Pujol (Jimenez 49), Ruiz.
Referee: Brugger (Austria).

Skopje, 6 September 2006, 16,500

Macedonia (0) 0   England (0) 1 *(Crouch 46)*
Macedonia: Nikolovski; Noveski, Petrov, Sedloski, Mitreski I, Lazarevski, Jancevski (Tasevski 52), Sumulikoski, Naumoski (Sakiri 74), Maznov (Stojkov 56), Pandev.
England: Robinson; Neville P, Cole A, Hargreaves, Terry, Ferdinand, Gerrard, Lampard (Carrick 84), Crouch (Johnson A 87), Defoe (Lennon 76), Downing.
Referee: Layec (France).

Old Trafford, 7 October 2006, 72,062

England (0) 0   Macedonia (0) 0
England: Robinson; Neville G, Cole A, Carrick, Terry, King, Gerrard, Lampard, Crouch, Rooney (Defoe 74), Downing (Wright-Phillips 70).
Macedonia: Nikolovski; Noveski, Petrov, Sedloski, Lazarevski, Mitreski I, Mitreski A, Sumulikoski, Maznov, Naumoski (Stojkov 46), Pandev (Tasevski 83).
Referee: Merk (Germany).

Zagreb, 11 October 2006, 38,000

Croatia (0) 2 *(Eduardo 61, Neville G 69 (og))*   **England (0) 0**
Croatia: Pletikosa; Simic, Simunic, Kovac R, Corluka, Rapaic (Olic 76), Kovac N, Modric, Kranjcar (Babic 89), Eduardo (Leko J 81), Petric.
England: Robinson; Neville G, Cole A, Ferdinand, Terry, Carragher (Wright-Phillips 73), Carrick, Lampard, Crouch (Richardson 72), Rooney, Parker (Defoe 72).
Referee: Rosetti (Italy).

Tel Aviv, 24 March 2007, 35,000

Israel (0) 0   England (0) 0
Israel: Awat; Ben Haim, Gershon, Ziv, Benado, Shpungin, Badir, Benayoun, Ben Shushan (Alberman 87), Tamuz Temile (Barda 75), Balali (Sahar 69).
England: Robinson; Neville P (Richards 72), Carragher, Gerrard, Ferdinand, Terry, Hargreaves, Lampard, Johnson A (Defoe 80), Rooney, Lennon (Downing 83).
Referee: Ovrebo (Norway).

Barcelona, 28 March 2007, 12,800

Andorra (0) 0   England (0) 3 *(Gerrard 54, 76, Nugent 90)*
Andorra: Koldo; Sonejee, Lima A, Ayala, Bernaus, Escura, Vieira, Garcia, Ruiz (Fernandez 88), Jimenez (Martinez 69), Toscano (Moreno 90).
England: Robinson; Richards (Dyer 61), Cole A, Hargreaves, Terry, Ferdinand, Lennon, Gerrard, Johnson A (Nugent 79), Rooney (Defoe 61), Downing.
Referee: Paixao (Portugal).

Tallinn, 6 June 2007, 11,000

Estonia (0) 0   England (1) 3 *(Cole J 37, Crouch 54, Owen 62)*
Estonia: Poom; Jaager, Stepanov, Kruglov, Klavan, Dmitrijev, Lindpere, Vassilijev, Konsa (Neemelo 46), Voskoboinikov, Terehhov (Kink 64).
England: Robinson; Brown, Bridge, Gerrard, Terry, King, Beckham (Dyer 68), Lampard, Crouch, Owen (Jenas 88), Cole J (Downing 75).
Referee: Gilewski (Poland).

Wembley, 8 September 2007, 85,372

England (1) 3 *(Wright-Phillips 20, Owen 49, Richards 66)*   **Israel (0) 0**

England: Robinson; Richards, Cole A, Gerrard (Neville P 71), Terry, Ferdinand, Wright-Phillips (Bentley 83), Barry, Heskey (Johnson A 71), Owen, Cole J.
Israel: Awat; Gershon, Shpungin, Benado (Golan 58), Ben Haim, Badir, Tal, Benayoun, Itzhaki (Tamuz 46), Ziv, Katan (Zandberg 73).
Referee: Vink (Holland).

Wembley, 12 September 2007, 86,106

England (2) 3 *(Owen 7, 31, Ferdinand 84)*   **Russia (0) 0**

England: Robinson; Richards, Cole A, Gerrard, Terry, Ferdinand, Wright-Phillips, Barry, Heskey (Crouch 80), Owen (Downing 90), Cole J (Neville P 88).
Russia: Malafeev; Ignashevich, Anyukov (Kerzhakov A 80), Berezutski V, Berezutski A, Zyryanov, Zhirkov, Bilyaletdinov, Semshov (Bistrov 40), Arshavin, Sychev (Pavlyuchenko 63).
Referee: Hansson (Sweden).

Wembley, 13 October 2007, 86,655

England (3) 3 *(Wright-Phillips 11, Rooney 32, Rahn 33 (og))*   **Estonia (0) 0**

England: Robinson; Richards, Cole A (Neville P 49), Gerrard, Campbell, Ferdinand (Lescott 46), Wright-Phillips, Barry, Rooney, Owen (Lampard 70), Cole J.
Estonia: Poom; Piiroja, Jaager, Stepanov, Kruglov, Rahn, Klavan, Dmitrijev, Lindpere, Saag, Kink (Viikmae 62).
Referee: Vollquartz (Denmark).

Moscow, 17 October 2007, 84,700

Russia (0) 2 *(Pavlyuchenko 70 (pen), 73)*   **England (1) 1** *(Rooney 29)*

Russia: Gabulov; Ignashevich, Anyukov, Berezutski V (Torbinskiy 46), Berezutski A, Zyryanov, Zhirkov, Bilyaletdinov, Semshov, Arshavin (Kolodin 90), Kerzhakov A (Pavlyuchenko 58).
England: Robinson; Richards, Lescott (Lampard 79), Gerrard, Campbell, Ferdinand, Wright-Phillips (Crouch 80), Barry, Rooney, Owen, Cole J (Downing 81).
Referee: Cantalejo (Spain).

Wembley, 21 November 2007, 88,091

England (0) 2 *(Lampard 56 (pen), Crouch 65)*   **Croatia (2) 3** *(Kranjcar 8, Olic 14, Petric 77)*

England: Carson; Lescott, Bridge, Gerrard, Campbell, Richards, Wright-Phillips (Beckham 46), Barry (Defoe 46), Crouch, Lampard, Cole J (Bent D 80).
Croatia: Pletikosa; Corluka, Simunic, Simic, Kovac R, Srna, Modric, Kranjcar (Pranjic 75), Kovac N, Olic (Rakitic 84), Eduardo (Petric 69).
Referee: Frojdfeldt (Sweden).

Group E Table	P	W	D	L	F	A	Pts
Croatia	12	9	2	1	28	8	29
Russia	12	7	3	2	18	7	24
England	12	7	2	3	24	7	23
Israel	12	7	2	3	20	12	23
Macedonia	12	4	2	6	12	12	14
Estonia	12	2	1	9	5	21	7
Andorra	12	0	0	12	2	42	0

GROUP F

Latvia	(0) 0	Sweden	(1) 1
Northern Ireland	(0) 0	Iceland	(3) 3
Spain	(2) 4	Liechtenstein	(0) 0
Iceland	(0) 0	Denmark	(2) 2
Northern Ireland	(1) 3	Spain	(1) 2
Sweden	(1) 3	Liechtenstein	(1) 1
Denmark	(0) 0	Northern Ireland	(0) 0
Latvia	(3) 4	Iceland	(0) 0
Sweden	(1) 2	Spain	(0) 0
Iceland	(1) 1	Sweden	(1) 2
Liechtenstein	(0) 0	Denmark	(2) 4
Northern Ireland	(1) 1	Latvia	(0) 0
Liechtenstein	(0) 1	Northern Ireland	(0) 4
Spain	(2) 2	Denmark	(0) 1
Liechtenstein	(1) 1	Latvia	(0) 0
Northern Ireland	(1) 2	Sweden	(1) 1
Spain	(0) 1	Iceland	(0) 0
Denmark	(1) 3	Sweden	(3) 3

(Match abandoned 89 minutes; match awarded to Sweden 3-0.)

Iceland	(1) 1	Liechtenstein	(0) 1
Latvia	(0) 0	Spain	(1) 2
Latvia	(0) 0	Denmark	(2) 2
Liechtenstein	(0) 0	Spain	(2) 2
Sweden	(3) 5	Iceland	(0) 0
Northern Ireland	(2) 3	Liechtenstein	(0) 1
Iceland	(1) 1	Spain	(0) 1
Latvia	(0) 1	Northern Ireland	(0) 0
Sweden	(0) 0	Denmark	(0) 0
Denmark	(4) 4	Liechtenstein	(0) 0
Iceland	(1) 2	Northern Ireland	(0) 1
Spain	(1) 2	Latvia	(0) 0
Denmark	(0) 1	Spain	(2) 3
Iceland	(1) 2	Latvia	(3) 4
Liechtenstein	(0) 0	Sweden	(2) 3
Denmark	(2) 3	Latvia	(0) 1
Liechtenstein	(1) 3	Iceland	(0) 0
Sweden	(1) 1	Northern Ireland	(0) 1
Latvia	(2) 4	Liechtenstein	(1) 1
Northern Ireland	(0) 2	Denmark	(0) 1
Spain	(2) 3	Sweden	(0) 0
Denmark	(2) 3	Iceland	(0) 0
Spain	(0) 1	Northern Ireland	(0) 0
Sweden	(1) 2	Latvia	(1) 1

Belfast, 2 September 2006, 14,500

Northern Ireland (0) 0

Iceland (3) 3 *(Thorvaldsson 13, Hreidarsson 20, Gudjohnsen E 37)*

Northern Ireland: Taylor; Baird, Capaldi (Duff 76), Davis, Hughes, Craigan, Gillespie, Clingan, Quinn (Feeney 83), Healy, Elliott (Lafferty 63).
Iceland: Arason; Steinsson, Sigurdsson I, Ingimarsson, Hreidarsson, Gunnarsson B (Gislason 75), Arnason (Danielsson 55), Gudjonsson J, Gudjohnsen E, Sigurdsson H (Jonsson H 64), Thorvaldsson.
Referee: Skjerven (Norway).

Belfast, 6 September 2006, 14,500

Northern Ireland (1) 3 *(Healy 20, 64, 80)*   **Spain (1) 2** *(Xavi 14, David Villa 52)*

Northern Ireland: Carroll (Taylor 12); Duff, Hughes, Craigan, Evans, Gillespie, Clingan, Davis, Baird, Healy (Feeney 85), Lafferty (Quinn 54).
Spain: Casillas; Sergio Ramos (Michel Salgado 46), Puyol, Pablo, Antonio Lopez, Albelda (Fabregas 29), Xavi, Xabi Alonso, Fernando Torres (Luis Garcia 63), David Villa, Raul.
Referee: De Bleeckere (Belgium).

Copenhagen, 7 October 2006, 41,482

Denmark (0) 0   Northern Ireland (0) 0

Denmark: Sorensen T (Christiansen 68); Jacobsen, Gravgaard, Agger, Jensen N (Bendtner 73), Jensen D, Poulsen, Kahlenberg, Tomasson, Jorgensen, Lovenkrands (Jensen C 55).
Northern Ireland: Maik Taylor; Duff, Hughes A, Craigan, Baird, Clingan (Johnson 56), Davis, Evans, Gillespie, Lafferty (Jones 63), Healy (Feeney 84).
Referee: Plautz (Austria).

Belfast, 11 October 2006, 14,500

Northern Ireland (1) 1 *(Healy 35)*   **Latvia (0) 0**

Northern Ireland: Maik Taylor; Baird, Evans, Craigan, Hughes A, Davis, Gillespie, Johnson, Lafferty (Quinn 88), Healy (Feeney 90), Clingan.
Latvia: Kolinko; Stepanovs, Astafjevs, Zirnis, Laizans, Kacanovs, Solonicins (Visnakovs 85), Smirnovs (Gorkss 46), Verpakovskis (Kalnins 78), Karlsons, Pahars.
Referee: Fleischer (Germany).

Vaduz, 24 March 2007, 4340

Liechtenstein (0) 1 *(Burgmeier 89)*
Northern Ireland (0) 4 *(Healy 52, 75, 83, McCann 90)*

Liechtenstein: Jehle; Oehri (Telser 68), Martin Stocklasa, Ritter, Michael Stocklasa, Buchel M, Buchel R (Frick D 88), Burgmeier, Beck T, Frick M, Rohrer (Buchel S 84).
Northern Ireland: Maik Taylor; Duff, Johnson, Evans, Hughes A, Craigan, Brunt (McCann 68), Davis, Lafferty (Feeney 56), Healy (Jones 84), Gillespie.
Referee: Oriekhov (Ukraine).

Belfast, 28 March 2007, 14,500

Northern Ireland (1) 2 *(Healy 31, 58)*   **Sweden (1) 1** *(Elmander 26)*

Northern Ireland: Maik Taylor; Duff, Hughes A, Craigan, Evans, Johnson, McCann, Davis, Brunt (Sproule 90), Healy (Webb 89), Feeney (Lafferty 79).
Sweden: Isaksson; Nilsson, Mellberg (Majstorovic 69), Hansson, Edman, Alexandersson (Wilhelmsson 61), Andersson D, Anders Svensson (Kallstrom 46), Ljungberg, Ibrahimovic, Elmander.
Referee: Braamhaar (Holland).

Windsor Park, 22 August 2007, 20,322

Northern Ireland (2) 3 *(Healy 5, 35, Lafferty 56)*   **Liechtenstein (0) 1** *(Frick M 89)*

Northern Ireland: Taylor; McCartney, Duff, Baird, Craigan, Brunt (Elliott 62), Davis, Clingan, Gillespie (Jones 85), Lafferty (Feeney 75), Healy.
Liechtenstein: Jehle; Michael Stocklasa (Oehri 39), Martin Stocklasa, Telser, Biedermann (Buchel S 62), Rohrer (Beck R 74), Buchel R, Frick M, Frick D, D'Elia, Polverino.
Referee: Matejek (Czech Republic).

Riga, 8 September 2007, 7500

Latvia (0) 1 *(Baird 56 (og))* **Northern Ireland (0) 0**

Latvia: Vanins; Zirnis, Klava, Ivanovs, Gorkss, Laizans, Bleidelis, Astafjevs, Rubins, Verpakovskis (Blanks 90), Karlsons (Rimkus 72).
Northern Ireland: Taylor; Evans, Baird, McCartney, Duff, Clingan, Elliott (Brunt 66), Davis, Gillespie, Lafferty (Feeney 72), Healy.
Referee: Proenca (Portugal).

Reykjavik, 12 September 2007, 2500

Iceland (1) 2 *(Bjornsson 6, Gillespie 90 (og))* **Northern Ireland (0) 1** *(Healy 72)*

Iceland: Arason; Hreidarsson, Steinsson, Bjornsson (Gudjohnsen E 53), Sigurdsson R, Hallfredsson, Sigurdsson K, Arnason (Asgeirsson 88), Vidarsson, Ingimarsson, Thorvaldsson (Skulason 79).
Northern Ireland: Taylor; Baird, McCartney, Duff, Evans, Davis (McCann 79), Clingan, Brunt (Jones 83), Healy, Gillespie, Feeney.
Referee: Baskakov (Russia).

Stockholm, 17 October 2007, 33,112

Sweden (1) 1 *(Mellberg 15)* **Northern Ireland (0) 1** *(Lafferty 72)*

Sweden: Isaksson; Edman, Concha, Hansson, Mellberg, Linderoth, Kallstrom (Johansson 85), Wilhelmsson (Nilsson 42), Anders Svensson, Ibrahimovic, Elmander (Allback 73).
Northern Ireland: Taylor; Hughes, McCartney (Capaldi 87), McAuley, Craigan, Clingan, Brunt, Sproule, Davis, Lafferty, Healy.
Referee: Layec (France).

Windsor Park, 17 November 2007, 14,500

Northern Ireland (0) 2 *(Feeney 62, Healy 80)* **Denmark (0) 1** *(Bendtner 51)*

Northern Ireland: Taylor; McAuley, Evans, Hughes, Craigan, Clingan, Brunt, Davis, Gillespie (Sproule 74), Feeney (Baird 85), Healy.
Denmark: Sorensen T; Laursen M, Andreasen, Sorensen C, Kroldrup, Priske (Wurtz 72), Poulsen C, Kahlenberg (Sorensen D 46), Jorgensen (Poulsen S 79), Bendtner, Rommedahl.
Referee: Vink (Holland).

Gran Canaria, 21 November 2007, 30,000

Spain (0) 1 *(Xavi 52)* **Northern Ireland (0) 0**

Spain: Reina; Sergio Ramos, Pernia, Pablo Ibanez, Raul Albiol, Xavi (Villa 67), Iniesta, Marcos Senna, Silva, Fabregas (Joaquin 47), Guiza (Tamudo 57).
Northern Ireland: Taylor; McAuley, Baird, Hughes, Craigan, Clingan, Sproule (Robinson 61), Brunt (Lafferty 59), Davis, Feeney (Paterson 72), Healy.
Referee: Fandel (Germany).

Group F Table	P	W	D	L	F	A	Pts
Spain	12	9	1	2	23	8	28
Sweden	12	8	2	2	23	9	26
Northern Ireland	12	6	2	4	17	14	20
Denmark	12	6	2	4	21	11	20
Latvia	12	4	0	8	15	17	12
Iceland	12	2	2	8	10	27	8
Liechtenstein	12	2	1	9	9	32	7

GROUP G

Belarus	(2) 2	Albania	(1) 2
Luxembourg	(0) 0	Holland	(1) 1
Romania	(1) 2	Bulgaria	(0) 2
Albania	(0) 0	Romania	(0) 2
Bulgaria	(0) 3	Slovenia	(0) 0
Holland	(1) 3	Belarus	(0) 0
Bulgaria	(1) 1	Holland	(0) 1
Romania	(2) 3	Belarus	(1) 1
Slovenia	(2) 2	Luxembourg	(0) 0
Belarus	(1) 4	Slovenia	(2) 2
Holland	(2) 2	Albania	(0) 1
Luxembourg	(0) 0	Bulgaria	(1) 1
Albania	(0) 0	Slovenia	(0) 0
Holland	(0) 0	Romania	(0) 0
Luxembourg	(0) 1	Belarus	(1) 2
Bulgaria	(0) 0	Albania	(0) 0
Romania	(1) 3	Luxembourg	(0) 0
Slovenia	(0) 0	Holland	(0) 1
Albania	(1) 2	Luxembourg	(0) 0
Belarus	(0) 0	Bulgaria	(1) 2
Slovenia	(0) 1	Romania	(0) 2
Bulgaria	(2) 2	Belarus	(1) 1
Luxembourg	(0) 0	Albania	(2) 3
Romania	(1) 2	Slovenia	(0) 0
Belarus	(1) 1	Romania	(2) 3
Holland	(1) 2	Bulgaria	(0) 0
Luxembourg	(0) 0	Slovenia	(2) 3
Albania	(0) 0	Holland	(0) 1
Bulgaria	(2) 3	Luxembourg	(0) 0
Slovenia	(1) 1	Belarus	(0) 0
Belarus	(0) 0	Luxembourg	(0) 1
Romania	(0) 1	Holland	(0) 0
Slovenia	(0) 0	Albania	(0) 0
Albania	(1) 1	Bulgaria	(0) 1
Holland	(1) 2	Slovenia	(0) 0
Luxembourg	(0) 0	Romania	(1) 2
Albania	(2) 2	Belarus	(2) 4
Bulgaria	(1) 1	Romania	(0) 0
Holland	(1) 1	Luxembourg	(0) 0
Belarus	(0) 2	Holland	(0) 1
Romania	(1) 6	Albania	(0) 1
Slovenia	(0) 0	Bulgaria	(0) 2

Group G Table	P	W	D	L	F	A	Pts
Romania	12	9	2	1	26	7	29
Holland	12	8	2	2	15	5	26
Bulgaria	12	7	4	1	18	7	25
Belarus	12	4	1	7	17	23	13
Albania	12	2	5	5	12	18	11
Slovenia	12	3	2	7	9	16	11
Luxembourg	12	1	0	11	2	23	3

EUROPEAN CHAMPIONSHIP 2008 FINALS

■ *Denotes player sent off.*

GROUP A

Geneva, 7 June 2008, 29,106

Portugal (0) 2 *(Pepe 61, Raul Meireles 90)*   **Turkey (0) 0**

Portugal: Ricardo; Bosingwa, Paulo Ferreira, Joao Moutinho, Pepe, Ricardo Carvalho, Ronaldo, Petit, Nuno Gomes (Nani 69), Deco (Fernando Meira 90), Simao (Raul Meireles 83).
Turkey: Volkan; Hamit Altintop (Semih 75), Hakan Balta, Mehmet Aurelio, Gokhan Z (Emre A 55), Servet, Kazim-Richards, Erding (Sabri 46), Emre B, Nihat, Tuncay.
Referee: H. Fandel (Germany).

Basle, 7 June 2008, 39,730

Switzerland (0) 0   Czech Republic (0) 1 *(Sverkos 70)*

Switzerland: Benaglio; Lichtsteiner (Vonlanthen 75), Magnin, Inler, Muller, Senderos, Behrami (Derdiyok 83), Fernandes, Frei (Yakin 46), Streller, Barnetta.
Czech Republic: Cech; Grygera, Sionko (Vlcek 83), Galasek, Ujfalusi, Rozehnal, Jankulovski, Polak, Jarolim (Kovac 87), Koller (Sverkos 56), Plasil.
Referee: R. Rosetti (Italy).

Geneva, 11 June 2008, 29,016

Czech Republic (1) 1 *(Sionko 17)* **Portugal (1) 3** *(Deco 8, Ronaldo 63, Quaresma 90)*

Czech Republic: Cech; Grygera, Jankulovski, Polak, Ujfalusi, Rozehnal, Galasek (Koller 73), Sionko, Matejovsky (Vlcek 68), Baros, Plasil (Jarolim 85).
Portugal: Ricardo; Bosingwa, Paulo Ferreira, Petit, Pepe, Ricardo Carvalho, Joao Moutinho (Fernando Meira 75), Ronaldo, Deco, Nuno Gomes (Hugo Almeida 79), Simao (Quaresma 80).
Referee: K. Vassaras (Greece).

Basle, 11 June 2008, 39,730

Switzerland (1) 1 *(Yakin 32)*   **Turkey (0) 2** *(Semih 57, Arda 90)*

Switzerland: Benaglio; Lichtsteiner, Magnin, Inler, Muller, Senderos, Behrami, Fernandes (Cabanas 76), Yakin (Gygax 85), Barnetta (Vonlanthen 66), Derdiyok.
Turkey: Volkan; Hamit Altintop, Emre A, Servet, Hakan Balta, Mehmet Aurelio, Tumer (Mehmet T 46), Gokdeniz (Semih 46), Tuncay, Arda, Nihat (Kazim-Richards 85).
Referee: L. Michel (Slovakia).

Basle, 15 June 2008, 39,730

Switzerland (0) 2 *(Yakin 71, 83 (pen))*   **Portugal (0) 0**

Switzerland: Zuberbuhler; Lichtsteiner (Grichting 85), Magnin, Fernandes, Muller, Senderos, Behrami, Inler, Yakin, Derdiyok, Vonlanthen.
Portugal: Ricardo; Miguel, Paulo Ferreira (Ribeiro 41), Raul Meireles, Bruno Alves, Pepe, Fernando Meira, Miguel Veloso (Joao Moutinho 70), Quaresma, Helder Postiga (Hugo Almeida 74), Nani.
Referee: K. Plautz (Austria).

Geneva, 15 June 2008, 29,016

Turkey (0) 3 *(Arda 75, Nihat 87, 89)*   **Czech Republic (1) 2** *(Koller 34, Plasil 62)*

Turkey: Volkan■; Hamit Altintop, Hakan Balta, Mehmet Aurelio, Servet, Emre G (Emre A 62), Mehmet T (Kazim-Richards 57), Arda, Semih (Sabri 46), Tuncay, Nihat.
Czech Republic: Cech; Grygera, Jankulovski, Sionko (Vlcek 84), Ujfalusi, Rozehnal, Galasek, Matejovsky (Jarolim 39), Koller, Plasil, Kadlec 80), Polak.
Referee: P. Frojdfeldt (Sweden).

Group A Table	P	W	D	L	F	A	Pts
Portugal	3	2	0	1	5	3	6
Turkey	3	2	0	1	5	5	6
Switzerland	3	1	0	2	3	3	3
Czech Republic	3	1	0	2	4	6	3

GROUP B

Vienna, 8 June 2008, 51,428

Austria (0) 0   Croatia (1) 1 *(Modric 4 (pen))*

Austria: Macho; Prodl, Pogatetz, Aufhauser, Stranzl, Saumel (Vastic 61), Standfest, Ivanschitz, Harnik, Linz (Kienast 74), Gercaliu (Korkmaz 69).
Croatia: Pletikosa; Corluka, Pranjic, Kovac N, Kovac R, Simunic, Srna, Modric, Olic (Vukojevic 83), Petric (Budan 72), Kranjcar (Knezevic 61).
Referee: P. Vink (Holland).

Klagenfurt, 8 June 2008, 30,461

Germany (1) 2 *(Podolski 20, 72)*   **Poland (0) 0**

Germany: Lehmann; Lahm, Jansen, Frings, Metzelder, Mertesacker, Fritz (Schweinsteiger 56), Ballack, Gomez (Hitzlsperger 74), Klose (Kuryani 90), Podolski.
Poland: Boruc; Wasilewski, Golanski (Saganowski 74), Dudka, Michal Zewlakow, Bak, Lobodzinski (Piszczek 66), Uralsk (Guerreiro 46), Lewandowski, Smolarek, Krzynowek.
Referee: T. Ovrebo (Norway).

Vienna, 12 June 2008, 51,428

Austria (0) 1 *(Vastic 90 (pen))*   **Poland (1) 1** *(Guerreiro 30)*

Austria: Macho; Garics, Pogatetz, Aufhauser (Saumel 74), Prodl, Stranzl, Leitgeb, Ivanschitz (Vastic 64), Harnik, Linz (Kienast 64), Korkmaz.
Poland: Boruc; Wasilewski, Michal Zewlakow, Lewandowski, Jop (Golanski 46), Bak, Dudka, Guerreiro (Murawski 85), Smolarek, Saganowski (Lobodzinski 83), Krzynowek.
Referee: H. Webb (England).

Klagenfurt, 12 June 2008, 30,461

Croatia (1) 2 *(Srna 24, Olic 63)*   **Germany (0) 1** *(Podolski 79)*

Croatia: Pletikosa; Corluka, Pranjic, Kovac N, Kovac R, Simunic, Srna (Leko J 80), Rakitic, Modric, Olic (Petric 72), Kranjcar.
Germany: Lehmann; Lahm, Jansen (Odonkor 46), Frings, Metzelder, Mertesacker, Fritz (Kuranyi 82), Ballack, Gomez (Schweinsteiger■ 65), Klose, Podolski.
Referee: F. De Bleeckere (Belgium).

Vienna, 16 June 2008, 51,428

Austria (0) 0   Germany (0) 1 *(Ballack 49)*

Austria: Macho; Garics, Pogatetz, Aufhauser (Saumel 64), Hiden (Leitgeb 55), Stranzl, Fuchs, Harnik (Kienast 67), Ivanschitz, Hoffer, Korkmaz.
Germany: Lehmann; Friedrich A, Lahm, Frings, Mertesacker, Metzelder, Fritz (Borowski 90), Ballack, Gomez (Hitzlsperger 60), Klose, Podolski (Neuville 83).
Referee: M. Gonzalez (Spain).

Klagenfurt, 16 June 2008, 30,461

Poland (0) 0   Croatia (0) 1 *(Klasnic 53)*

Poland: Boruc; Wasilewski, Wawrzyniak, Lobodzinski (Smolarek 55), Michal Zewlakow, Dudka, Murawski, Guerreiro, Lewandowski (Kokoszka 46), Saganowski (Zahorski 68), Krzynowek.
Croatia: Runje; Simic, Pranjic, Vukojevic, Vejic, Knezevic (Corluka 27), Leko J, Pokrivac, Klasnic (Kalinic 74), Petric (Kranjcar 75), Rakitic.
Referee: K. Vassaras (Greece).

Group B Table	P	W	D	L	F	A	Pts
Croatia	3	3	0	0	4	1	9
Germany	3	2	0	1	4	2	6
Austria	3	0	1	2	1	3	1
Poland	3	0	1	2	1	4	1

GROUP C

Berne, 9 June 2008, 30,777

Holland (2) 3 *(Van Nistelrooy 26, Sneijder 31, Van Bronckhorst 80)* **Italy (0) 0**
Holland: Van der Sar; Mathijsen, Van Bronckhorst, De Jong, Engelaar, Boulahrouz (Heitinga 77), Ooijer, Van der Vaart, Sneijder, Van Nistelrooy (Van Persie 70), Kuyt (Afellay 81).
Italy: Buffon; Panucci, Zambrotta, Pirlo, Barzagli, Materazzi (Grosso 55), Gattuso, Camoranesi (Cassano 75), Di Natale (Del Piero 64), Toni, Ambrosini.
Referee: P. Frojdfeldt (Sweden).

Zurich, 9 June 2008, 30,585

Romania (0) 0   France (0) 0
Romania: Lobont; Contra, Rat, Radoi (Dica 90), Tamas, Goian, Cocis (Codrea 63), Chivu, Nicolita, Niculae D, Mutu (Niculae M 79).
France: Coupet; Sagnol, Abidal, Makelele, Thuram, Gallas, Ribery, Toulalan, Anelka (Gomis 72), Benzema (Nasri 77), Malouda.
Referee: M. Gonzalez (Spain).

Berne, 13 June 2008, 30,777

Holland (1) 4 *(Kuyt 10, Van Persie 59, Robben 72, Sneijder 90)*
France (0) 1 *(Henry 71)*
Holland: Van der Sar; Boulahrouz, Van Bronckhorst, Engelaar (Robben 46), Ooijer, Mathijsen, De Jong, Kuyt (Van Persie 55), Van Nistelrooy, Sneijder, Van der Vaart (Bouma 78).
France: Coupet; Sagnol, Evra, Makelele, Thuram, Gallas, Ribery, Toulalan, Govou (Anelka 75), Henry, Malouda (Gomis 60).
Referee: H. Fandel (Germany).

Zurich, 13 June 2008, 30,585

Italy (0) 1 *(Panucci 56)* **Romania (0) 1** *(Mutu 55)*
Italy: Buffon; Zambrotta, Grosso, Pirlo, Panucci, Chiellini, De Rossi, Camoranesi (Ambrosini 84), Del Piero (Quagliarella 77), Toni, Perrotta (Cassano 58).
Romania: Lobont; Contra, Rat, Petre F (Nicolita 60), Tamas, Goian, Radoi (Dica 26), Codrea, Chivu, Niculae D, Mutu (Cocis 87).
Referee: T. Henning (Norway).

Zurich, 17 June 2008, 30,585

France (0) 0   Italy (1) 2 *(Pirlo 25 (pen), De Rossi 82)*
France: Coupet; Clerc, Evra, Makelele, Abidal■, Gallas, Ribery (Nasri 10) (Boumsong 26), Toulalan, Govou (Anelka 66), Benzema, Henry.
Italy: Buffon; Zambrotta, Grosso, Pirlo (Ambrosini 55), Panucci, Chiellini, Gattuso (Aquilani 82), De Rossi, Toni, Cassano, Perrotta (Camoranesi 64).
Referee: L. Michel (Slovakia).

Berne, 17 June 2008, 30,777

Holland (0) 2 *(Huntelaar 54, Van Persie 87)* **Romania (0) 0**
Holland: Stekelenburg; Boulahrouz (Melchiot 58), De Cler, Engelaar, Heitinga, Bouma, Afellay, De Zeeuw, Huntelaar (Vennegoor of Hesselink 82), Van Persie, Robben (Kuyt 62).
Romania: Lobont; Contra, Rat, Codrea (Dica 72), Tamas, Ghionea, Cocis, Chivu, Nicolita (Petre F 82), Niculae M (Niculae D 59), Mutu.
Referee: M. Busacca (Switzerland).

Group C Table	P	W	D	L	F	A	Pts
Holland	3	3	0	0	9	1	9
Italy	3	1	1	1	3	4	4
Romania	3	0	2	1	1	3	2
France	3	0	1	2	1	6	1

GROUP D

Salzburg, 10 June 2008, 31,063

Greece (0) 0   Sweden (0) 2 *(Ibrahimovic 67, Hansson 72)*
Greece: Nikopolidis; Seitaridis, Torosidis, Kyrgiakos, Dellas (Spiropoulos 69), Antzas, Katsouranis, Basinas, Charisteas, Karagounis, Gekas (Samaras 46).
Sweden: Isaksson; Alexandersson (Stoor 74), Nilsson, Andersson D, Mellberg, Hansson, Wilhelmsson (Rosenberg 78), Anders Svensson, Ibrahimovic (Elmander 71), Larsson H, Ljungberg.
Referee: M. Busacca (Switzerland).

Innsbruck, 10 June 2008, 30,772

Spain (2) 4 *(Villa 20, 45, 75, Fabregas 90)*   **Russia (0) 1** *(Pavlyuchenko 86)*
Spain: Casillas; Sergio Ramos, Capdevila, Marcos Senna, Puyol, Marchena, Silva (Xabi Alonso 76), Xavi, Villa, Torres (Fabregas 53), Iniesta (Cazorla 62).
Russia: Akinfeev; Anyukov, Zhirkov, Semak, Shirokov, Kolodin, Sychev (Bystrov 46) (Adamov 70), Bilyaletdinov, Zyryanov, Semshov (Torbinski 57), Pavlyuchenko.
Referee: K. Plautz (Austria).

Salzburg, 14 June 2008, 31,063

Greece (0) 0   Russia (1) 1 *(Zyryanov 34)*
Greece: Nikopolidis; Petridis (Karagounis 39), Torosidis, Basinas, Dellas, Krygiakos, Katsouranis, Patsatzoglou, Amanatidis (Giannakopoulos 79), Liberopoulos (Gekas 60), Charisteas.
Russia: Akinfeev; Anyukov, Zhirkov (Berezutski V 87), Kolodin, Ignashevich, Semak, Torbinsky, Semshov, Bilyaletdinov (Saenko 69), Pavlyuchenko, Zyryanov.
Referee: R. Rosetti (Italy).

Innsbruck, 14 June 2008, 30,772

Sweden (1) 1 *(Ibrahimovic 34)*   **Spain (1) 2** *(Torres 15, Villa 90)*
Sweden: Isaksson; Stoor, Nilsson, Andersson D, Mellberg, Hansson, Elmander (Larsson S 79), Anders Svensson, Ibrahimovic (Rosenberg 46), Larsson H (Kallstrom 86), Ljungberg.
Spain: Casillas; Sergio Ramos, Capdevila, Xavi (Fabregas 59), Puyol (Albiol 24), Marchena, Marcos Senna, Iniesta (Santi Cazorla 59), Torres, Villa, Silva.
Referee: P. Vink (Holland).

Salzburg, 18 June 2008, 30,883

Greece (1) 1 *(Charisteas 42)*   **Spain (0) 2** *(De la Red 61, Guiza 88)*
Greece: Nikopolidis; Vintra, Spiropoulos, Katsouranis, Dellas, Kyrgiakos (Antzas 62), Basinas, Salpigidis (Giannakopoulos 86), Amanatidis, Charisteas, Karagounis (Tziolis 74).
Spain: Reina; Arbeloa, Fernando Navarro, Xabi Alonso, Albiol, Juanito, Sergio Garcia, De la Red, Guiza, Fabregas, Iniesta (Santi Cazorla 58).
Referee: H. Webb (England).

Innsbruck, 18 June 2008, 30,772

Russia (1) 2 *(Pavlychenko 24, Arshavin 50)*   **Sweden (0) 0**
Russia: Akinfeev; Anyukov, Zhirkov, Semshov, Ignashevich, Kolodin, Semak, Bilyaletdinov (Saenko 66), Arshavin, Pavlyuchenko (Bystrov 90), Syryanov.
Sweden: Isaksson; Stoor, Nilsson (Allback 79), Andersson D (Kallstrom 56), Mellberg, Hansson, Elmander, Anders Svensson, Larsson H, Ibrahimovic, Ljungberg.
Referee: F. De Bleeckere (Belgium).

Group D Table	P	W	D	L	F	A	Pts
Spain	3	3	0	0	8	3	9
Russia	3	2	0	1	4	4	6
Sweden	3	1	0	2	3	4	3
Greece	3	0	0	3	1	5	0

QUARTER-FINALS

Basle, 19 June 2008, 39,374

Portugal (1) 2 *(Nuno Gomes 40, Helder Postiga 86)*
Germany (2) 3 *(Schweinsteiger 22, Klose 26, Ballack 62)*
Portugal: Ricardo; Bosingwa, Paulo Ferreira, Joao Moutinho (Raul Meireles 31), Pepe, Ricardo Carvalho, Petit (Helder Postiga 73), Deco, Nuno Gomes (Nani 67), Ronaldo, Simao.
Germany: Lehmann; Friedrich A, Lahm, Rolfes, Metzelder, Mertesacker, Hitzlsperger (Borowski 73), Ballack, Schweinsteiger (Fritz 83), Klose, Podolski.
Referee: P. Frojdfeldt (Sweden).

Vienna, 20 June 2008, 51,428

Croatia (0) 1 *(Klasnik 119)*   **Turkey (0) 1** *(Semih 120)*
Croatia: Pletikosa; Corluka, Pranjic, Kovac N, Kovac R, Simunic, Srna, Modric, Olic (Klasnik 97), Kranjcar (Petric 64), Ratitic.
Turkey: Rustu; Hamit Altintop, Hakan Balta, Sabri, Emre A, Gokhan Z, Arda, Kazim-Richards (Ugur 61), Mehmet T (Semih 76), Nihat (Gokdeniz 117), Tuncay.
aet; Turkey won 3-1 on penalties: Modric missed; Arda scored; Srna scored; Semih scored; Ratitic missed; Hamit Altintop scored; Petric saved.
Referee: R. Rosetti (Italy).

Basle, 21 June 2008, 38,374

Holland (0) 1 *(Van Nistelrooy 86)*
Russia (0) 3 *(Pavlyuchenko 56, Torbinski 112, Arshavin 116)*
Holland: Van der Sar; Boulahrouz (Heitinga 54), Van Bronckhorst, Engelaar (Afellay 61), Ooijer, Mathijsen, De Jong, Kuyt (Van Persie 46), Van Nistelrooy, Sneijder, Van der Vaart.
Russia: Akinfeev; Anyukov, Zhirkov, Semchov (Bilyaletdinov 69), Ignashevich, Kolodin, Semak, Zyryanov, Saenko (Torbinski 81), Pavlyuchenko (Sychev 115), Arshavin.
aet.
Referee: L. Michel (Slovakia).

Vienna, 22 June 2008, 51,178

Spain (0) 0   Italy (0) 0
Spain: Casillas; Sergio Ramos, Capdevila, Xavi (Fabregas 59), Puyol, Marchena, Senna, Iniesta (Santi Cazorla 59), Silva, Torres, Villa.
Italy: Buffon; Zambrotta, Grosso, Di Rossi, Panucci, Chiellini, Aquilani, Ambrosini, Toni, Cassano (Di Natale 75), Perrotta (Camoranesi 58).
aet; Spain won 4-2 on penalties: Villa scored; Grosso scored; Santi Cazorla scored; Di Rossi saved; Senna scored; Camoranesi scored; Guiza saved; Di Natale saved; Fabregas scored.
Referee: H. Fandel (Germany).

SEMI-FINALS

Basle, 25 June 2008, 39,374

Germany (1) 3 *(Schweinsteiger 27, Klose 79, Lahm 90)*
Turkey (1) 2 *(Ugur 22, Semih 86)*
Germany: Lehmann; Friedrich A, Lahm, Rolfes (Frings 46), Metzelder, Mertesacker, Schweinsteiger, Hitzlsperger, Klose (Jansen 90), Ballack, Podolski.
Turkey: Rustu; Sabri, Hakan Balta, Ugur (Gokdeniz 84), Gokhan Z, Mehmet, T Mehmet Aurelio, Ayhan (Erdinc 81), Semih, Hamit Altintop, Kazim-Richards (Tumer 90).
Referee: M. Bussaca (Switzerland).

Vienna, 26 June 2008, 51,428

Russia (0) 0   Spain (0) 3 *(Xavi 50, Guiza 73, Silva 82)*
Russia: Akinfeev; Anyukov, Zhirkov, Semchov (Bilyaletdinov 56), Ignashevich, Berezutski V, Semak, Zyryanov, Pavlyuchenko, Arshavin, Saenko (Sychev 57).
Spain: Casillas; Sergio Ramos, Capdevila, Xavi (Xabi Alonso 69), Puyol, Marchena, Senna, Iniesta, Torres (Guiza 69), Villa (Fabregas 34), Silva.
Referee: F. De Bleeckere (Belgium).

EURO 2008 FINAL

Vienna, 29 June 2008, 51,428

Germany (0) 0   Spain (1) 1 (*Torres 33*)

Germany: Lehmann; Friedrich A, Lahm (Jansen 46), Frings, Metzelder, Mertesacker, Hitzlsperger (Kuranyi 58), Ballack, Klose (Gomes 79), Schweinsteiger, Podolski.

Spain: Casillas; Sergio Ramos, Capdevila, Senna, Puyol, Marchena, Iniesta, Xavi, Torres (Guiza 78), Fabregas (Xabi Alonso 63), Silva (Santi Cazorla 66).

Referee: R. Rossetti (Italy).

PAST EUROPEAN CHAMPIONSHIP FINALS

Year	Winners		Runners-up		Venue	Attendance
1960	USSR	2	Yugoslavia	1	Paris	17,966
1964	Spain	2	USSR	1	Madrid	120,000
1968	Italy	2	Yugoslavia	0	Rome	60,000
	(After 1-1 draw)					75,000
1972	West Germany	3	USSR	0	Brussels	43,437
1976	Czechoslovakia	2	West Germany	2	Belgrade	45,000
	(Czechoslovakia won on penalties)					
1980	West Germany	2	Belgium	1	Rome	47,864
1984	France	2	Spain	0	Paris	48,000
1988	Holland	2	USSR	0	Munich	72,308
1992	Denmark	2	Germany	0	Gothenburg	37,800
1996	Germany	2	Czech Republic	1	Wembley	73,611
	(Germany won on sudden death)					
2000	France	2	Italy	1	Rotterdam	50,000
	(France won on sudden death)					
2004	Greece	1	Portugal	0	Lisbon	62,865
2008	Spain	1	Germany	0	Vienna	51,428

PAST WORLD CUP FINALS

Year	Winners		Runners-up		Venue	Att.	Referee
1930	Uruguay	4	Argentina	2	Montevideo	90,000	Langenus (B)
1934	Italy*	2	Czechoslovakia	1	Rome	50,000	Eklind (Se)
1938	Italy	4	Hungary	2	Paris	45,000	Capdeville (F)
1950	Uruguay	2	Brazil	1	Rio de Janeiro	199,854	Reader (E)
1954	West Germany	3	Hungary	2	Berne	60,000	Ling (E)
1958	Brazil	5	Sweden	2	Stockholm	49,737	Guigue (F)
1962	Brazil	3	Czechoslovakia	1	Santiago	68,679	Latychev (USSR)
1966	England*	4	West Germany	2	Wembley	93,802	Dienst (Sw)
1970	Brazil	4	Italy	1	Mexico City	107,412	Glockner (EG)
1974	West Germany	2	Holland	1	Munich	77,833	Taylor (E)
1978	Argentina*	3	Holland	1	Buenos Aires	77,000	Gonella (I)
1982	Italy	3	West Germany	1	Madrid	90,080	Coelho (Br)
1986	Argentina	3	West Germany	2	Mexico City	114,580	Filho (Br)
1990	West Germany	1	Argentina	0	Rome	73,603	Mendez (Mex)
1994	Brazil*	0	Italy	0	Los Angeles	94,194	Puhl (H)
	(Brazil won 3-2 on penalties)						
1998	France	3	Brazil	0	St-Denis	75,000	Belqola (Mor)
2002	Brazil	2	Germany	0	Yokohama	69,029	Collina (I)
2006	Italy*	1	France	1	Berlin	69,000	Elizondo (Arg)
	(Italy won 5-3 on penalties)						

*After extra time.

WORLD CUP 2010 QUALIFYING RESULTS

SOUTH AMERICA

Argentina 2, Chile 0; Uruguay, 5, Bolivia 0; Colombia 0, Brazil 0; Ecuador 0, Venezuela 1; Peru 0, Paraguay 0; Bolivia 0, Colombia 0; Venezuela 0, Argentina 2; Brazil 5, Ecuador 0; Chile 2, Peru 0; Paraguay 1, Uruguay 0; Argentina 3, Bolivia 0; Colombia 1, Venezuela 0; Paraguay 5, Ecuador 1; Peru 1, Brazil 1; Uruguay 2, Chile 2; Venezuela 5, Bolivia 3; Colombia 2, Argentina 1; Ecuador 5, Peru 1; Brazil 2, Uruguay 1; Chile 0, Paraguay 3; Uruguay 1, Venezuela 1; Argentina 1, Ecuador 1; Bolivia 0, Chile 2; Paraguay 2, Brazil 0; Peru 1, Colombia 1; Bolivia 4, Paraguay 2; Ecuador 0, Colombia 0; Uruguay 6, Peru 0; Brazil 0, Argentina 0; Venezuela 2, Chile 3

OCEANIA

GROUP A
Tahiti 0, New Caledonia 1; Fiji 16, Tuvalu 0; New Caledonia 1, Tuvalu 0; Fiji 4, Cook Islands 0; Tahiti 1, Tuvalu 1; New Caledonia 3, Cook Islands 0; Cook Islands 4, Tuvalu 1; Fiji 4, Tahiti 0; Fiji 1, New Caledonia 1; Tahiti 1, Cook Islands 0.
Fiji and New Caledonia qualify.

GROUP B
Solomon Islands 12, American Samoa 1; Samoa 0, Vanuatu 4; Solomon Islands 4, Tonga 0; Samoa 7, American Samoa 0; Vanuatu 15, American Samoa 0; Samoa 2, Tonga 1; Tonga 1, American Samoa 0; Solomon Islands 2, Vanuatu 0; Samoa 0, Solomon Islands 3; Vanuatu 4, Tonga 1.
Solomon Islands and Vanuatu qualify.

SEMI-FINALS
Solomon Islands 2, New Caledonia 3; Fiji 3, Vanuatu 0.

THIRD PLACE
Vanuatu 2, Solomon Islands 0.

FINAL
Fiji 0, New Caledonia 1.

FINAL ROUND
Fiji 0, New Zealand 2; Vanuatu 1, New Zealand 2; Fiji 3, New Caledonia 3; New Zealand 4, Vanuatu 1; New Caledonia 4, Fiji 0; Vanuatu 1, New Caledonia 1; New Caledonia 3, Vanuatu 0; New Caledonia v Fiji; Fiji v Vanuatu; New Zealand v New Caledonia; Vanuatu v Fiji; New Zealand v Fiji.

ASIA

FIRST ROUND
Bangladesh 1, Tajikistan 1; Tajikistan 5, Bangladesh 0; Thailand 6, Macao 1; Macao 1, Thailand 7; Vietnam 0, UAE 1; UAE 5, Vietnam 0; Oman 2, Nepal 0; Nepal 0, Oman 2; Syria 3, Afganistan 0; Afganistan 1, Syria 2; Palestine 0, Singapore 4; Singapore v Palestine awarded to Singapore 3-0; Lebanon 4, India 1; India 2, Lebanon 2; Yemen 3, Maldives 0; Maldives 2, Yemen 0; Cambodia 0, Turkmenistan 1; Turkmenistan 4, Cambodia 1; Uzbekistan 9, Taiwan 0; Taiwan 0, Uzbekistan 2; Kyrgyzstan 2, Jordan 0; Jordan 2, Kyrgyzstan 0 – Jordan won 6-5 on penalties; Mongolia 1, North Korea 4; North Korea 5, Mongolia 1; Timor-Leste 2, Hong Kong 3; Hong Kong 8, Timor-Leste 1; Sri Lanka 0, Qatar 1; Qatar 5, Sri Lanka 0; China 1, Myanmar 0; Myanmar 0, China 4; Bahrain 4, Malaysia 1; Malaysia 0, Bahrain 0; Pakistan 0, Iraq 7; Iraq 0, Pakistan 0.

SECOND ROUND
Singapore 2, Tajikistan 0; Tajikistan 1, Singapore 1; Indonesia 1, Syria 4; Syria 7, Indonesia 0; Yemen 1, Thailand 1; Thailand 1, Yemen 0; Hong Kong 0, Turkmenistan 0; Turkmenistan 3, Hong Kong 0.

GROUP 1
Australia 3, Qatar 0; Iraq 1, China 1; China 0, Australia 0; Qatar 2, Iraq 0; Australia 1, Iraq 0; Qatar 0, China 0; China 0, Qatar 1; Iraq 1, Australia 0. China 1, Iraq 2; Qatar1, Australia 3; Australia 0, China 1; Iraq 0, Qatar 1.

GROUP 2
Japan 4, Thailand 1; Oman 0, Bahrain 1; Thailand 0, Oman 1; Bahrain 1, Japan 0; Japan 3, Oman 0; Thailand 2, Bahrain 3; Oman 1, Japan 1; Bahrain 1, Thailand 1. Thailand 0, Japan 3; Bahrain 1, Oman 1; Japan 1, Bahrain 0; Oman 2, Thailand 1.

GROUP 3
South Korea 4, Turkmenistan 0; Jordan 0, North Korea 1; North Korea 0, South Korea 0; Turkmenistan 0, Jordan 2; South Korea 2, Turkmenistan 0; North Korea 0; North Korea 1, Turkmenistan 0; Jordan 0, South Korea 1; North Korea 2, Jordan 0; Turkmenistan 1, South Korea 3; South Korea 0, North Korea 0; Jordan 2, Turkmenistan 0.

GROUP 4
Lebanon 0, Uzbekistan 1; Saudi Arabia 2, Singapore 0; Uzbekistan 3, Saudi Arabia 0; Singapore 2, Lebanon 0; Singapore 3, Uzbekistan 7; Saudi Arabia 4, Lebanon 1; Uzbekistan 1, Singapore 0; Lebanon 1, Saudi Arabia 2; Singapore 0, Saudi Arabia 2; Uzbekistan 3, Lebanon 0; Lebanon 1, Singapore 2; Saudi Arabia 4, Uzbekistan 0.

GROUP 5
Iran 0, Syria 0; UAE 2, Kuwait 0; Syria 1, UAE 1; Kuwait 2, Iran 2; Iran 0, UAE 0; Syria 1, Kuwait 0; UAE 0, Iran 1; Kuwait 4, Syria 2; Kuwait 2, UAE 3; Syria 0, Iran 2; Iran 2, Kuwait 0; UAE 1, Syria 3.

CONCACAF

FIRST ROUND
Dominican Republic v Puerto Rico not played; Puerto Rico 1, Dominican Republic 0; US Virgin Islands v Grenada not played; Grenada 10, US Virgin Islands 0; Surinam v Monserrat not played; Monserrat 1, Surinam 7; Bermuda 1, Cayman Islands 1; Cayman Islands 1, Bermuda 3; Belize 3, St Kitts & Nevis 1; St Kitts & Nevis 1, Belize 1; Nicaragua 0, Netherlands Antilles 1; Netherlands Antilles 2, Nicaragua 0; Dominica 1, Barbados 1; Barbados 1, Dominica 0; Aruba 0, Antigua & Barbuda 3; Antigua & Barbuda 1, Aruba 0; Turks & Caicos 2, St Lucia 1; St Lucia 2, Turks & Caicos 0; El Salvador 12, Anguilla 0; Anguilla 0, El Salvador 4; Bahamas 1, British Virgin Islands 1; British Virgin Islands 2, Bahamas 2.

SECOND ROUND
Honduras 4, Puerto Rico 0; Puerto Rico 2, Honduras 2; Belize 0, Mexico 2; Mexico 7, Belize 0; Surinam 1, Guyana 0; Guyana 1, Surinam 2; Grenada 2, Costa Rica 2; Costa Rica 3, Grenada 0; Guatemala 6, St Lucia 0; St Lucia 1, Guatemala 3; St Vincent & the Grenadines 0, Canada 3; Canada 4, St Vincent & the Grenadines 1; Trinidad & Tobago 1, Bermuda 2; Bermuda 0, Trinidad & Tobago 2; Haiti 0, Netherlands Antilles 0; Netherlands Antilles 0, Haiti 1; USA 8, Barbados 0; Barbados 0, USA 1; Panama 1, El Salvador 0; El Salvador 3, Panama 1; Antigua & Barbuda 3, Cuba 0; Cuba 4, Antigua & Barbuda 0; Jamaica 7, Bahamas 0; Bahamas 0, Jamaica 6.

AFRICA

FIRST ROUND
Madagascar 6, Comoros 2; Comoros 0, Madagascar 4; Sierra Leone 1, Guinea-Bissau 0; Guinea-Bissau 0, Sierra Leone 0; Djibouti 1, Somalia 0; Somalia v Djibouti not played.

GROUP 1
Tanzania 1, Mauritius 1; Cameroon 2, Cape Verde Islands 0; Cape Verde Islands 1, Tanzania 0; Mauritius 0, Cameroon 3; Tanzania 0, Cameroon 0; Mauritius 0, Cape Verde Islands 1; Cameroon 2, Tanzania 1; Cape Verde Islands 3, Mauritius 1.

GROUP 2
Namibia 2, Kenya 1; Guinea 0, Zimbabwe 0; Kenya 2, Guinea 0; Zimbabwe 2, Namibia 0; Kenya 2, Zimbabwe 0; Namibia 1, Guinea 2; Guinea 4, Namibia 0; Zimbabwe 0, Kenya 0.

GROUP 3
Uganda 1, Niger 0; Angola 3, Benin 0; Niger 1, Angola 2; Benin 4, Uganda 1; Uganda 3, Angola 1; Niger 0, Benin 2; Angola 0, Uganda 0; Benin 2, Niger 0.

GROUP 4
Equatorial Guinea 2, Sierra Leone 0; Nigeria 2, South Africa 0; South Africa 4, Equatorial Guinea 1; Sierra Leone 0, Nigeria 1; Sierra Leone 1, South Africa 0; Equatorial Guinea 0, Nigeria 1; Nigeria 2, Equatorial Guinea 0; South Africa 0, Sierra Leone 0.

GROUP 5
Gabon v Lesotho not played; Ghana 3, Libya 0; Libya 1, Gabon 0; Lesotho 2, Ghana 3; Gabon 2, Ghana 0; Lesotho 0, Libya 1; Ghana 2, Gabon 0; Libya 4, Lesotho 0.

GROUP 6
Senegal 1, Algeria 0; Liberia 1, Gambia 1; Algeria 3, Liberia 0; Gambia 0, Senegal 0; Gambia 1, Algeria 1; Liberia 2, Senegal 2; Algeria 1, Gambia 1; Senegal 3, Liberia 1.

GROUP 7
Botswana 0, Madagascar 0; Ivory Coast 1, Mozambique 0; Madagascar 0, Ivory Coast 0; Mozambique 1, Botswana 2; Botswana 1, Ivory Coast 1; Madagascar 1, Mozambique 1; Ivory Coast 4, Botswana 0; Mozambique 3, Madagascar 0.

GROUP 8
Rwanda 3, Mauritania 0; Morocco 3, Ethiopia 0; Mauritania 1, Morocco 4; Ethiopia 1, Rwanda 2; Mauritania 0, Ethiopia 1; Rwanda 3, Morocco 1; Ethiopia 6, Mauritania 1; Morocco 2, Rwanda 0.

GROUP 9
Burundi 1, Seychelles 0; Tunisia 1, Burkina Faso 2; Seychelles 0, Tunisia 2; Burkina Faso 2, Burundi 0; Seychelles 2, Burkina Faso 3; Burundi 0, Tunisia 1; Burkina Faso 4, Seychelles 1; Tunisia 2, Burundi 1.

GROUP 10
Sudan v Chad not played; Mali 4, Congo 2; Chad 1, Mali 2; Congo 1, Sudan 0; Chad 2, Congo 1; Sudan 3, Mali 2; Congo 2, Chad 0; Mali 3, Sudan 0.

GROUP 11
Togo 1, Zambia 0; Swaziland 2, Togo 1; Swaziland 0, Zambia 0; Zambia 1, Swaziland 0.

GROUP 12
Malawi 8, Djibouti 1; Egypt 2, Congo DR 1; Djibouti 0, Egypt 4; Congo DR 1, Malawi 0; Djibouti 0, Congo DR 6; Malawi 1, Egypt 0; Egypt 2, Malawi 0; Congo DR 5, Djibouti 1.

REMAINING FIXTURES

EUROPE

GROUP 1
06.09.08 Albania v Sweden; Hungary v Denmark; Malta v Portugal.
10.09.08 Albania v Malta; Portugal v Denmark; Sweden v Hungary.
11.10.08 Hungary v Albania; Denmark v Malta; Sweden v Portugal.
15.10.08 Portugal v Albania; Malta v Hungary.
11.02.09 Malta v Albania.

28.03.09 Albania v Hungary; Malta v Denmark; Portugal v Sweden.
01.04.09 Denmark v Albania; Hungary v Malta.
06.06.09 Albania v Portugal; Sweden v Denmark.
10.06.09 Sweden v Malta.
05.09.09 Denmark v Portugal; Hungary v Sweden.
09.09.09 Albania v Denmark; Malta v Sweden; Hungary v Portugal.

10.10.09 Denmark v Sweden; Portugal v Hungary.
14.10.09 Sweden v Albania; Denmark v Hungary; Portugal v Malta.

GROUP 2
06.09.08 Luxembourg v Greece; Israel v Switzerland; Moldova v Latvia.
10.09.08 Latvia v Greece; Moldova v Israel; Switzerland v Luxembourg.
11.10.08 Greece v Moldova; Luxembourg v Israel; Switzerland v Latvia.
15.10.08 Greece v Switzerland; Latvia v Israel; Luxembourg v Moldova.
28.03.09 Israel v Greece; Luxembourg v Latvia; Moldova v Switzerland.
01.04.09 Greece v Israel; Latvia v Luxembourg; Switzerland v Moldova.
05.09.09 Switzerland v Greece; Israel v Latvia; Moldova v Luxembourg.
09.09.09 Moldova v Greece; Israel v Luxembourg; Latvia v Switzerland.
10.10.09 Greece v Latvia; Israel v Moldova; Luxembourg v Switzerland.
14.10.09 Greece v Luxembourg; Switzerland v Israel; Latvia v Moldova.

GROUP 3
06.09.08 Slovakia v Northern Ireland; Poland v Slovenia.
10.09.08 Northern Ireland v Czech Republic; San Marino v Poland; Slovenia v Slovakia.
11.10.08 Slovenia v Northern Ireland; Poland v Czech Republic; San Marino v Slovakia.
15.10.08 Northern Ireland v San Marino; Slovakia v Poland; Czech Republic v Slovenia.
19.11.08 San Marino v Czech Republic.
11.02.09 San Marino v Northern Ireland.
28.03.09 Northern Ireland v Poland; Slovenia v Czech Republic.
01.04.09 Northern Ireland v Slovenia; Poland v San Marino; Czech Republic v Slovakia.
06.06.09 Slovakia v San Marino.
19.08.09 Slovenia v San Marino.
05.09.09 Poland v Northern Ireland; Slovakia v Czech Republic.
09.09.09 Northern Ireland v Slovakia; Slovenia v Poland; Czech Republic v San Marino.
10.10.09 Czech Republic v Poland; Slovakia v Slovenia.
14.10.09 San Marino v Slovenia; Czech Republic v Northern Ireland; Poland v Slovakia.

GROUP 4
06.09.08 Liechtenstein v Germany; Wales v Azerbaijan.
10.09.08 Azerbaijan v Liechtenstein; Russia v Wales; Finland v Germany.
11.10.08 Germany v Russia; Wales v Liechtenstein; Finland v Azerbaijan.
15.10.08 Germany v Wales; Russia v Finland.
28.03.09 Germany v Liechtenstein; Wales v Finland; Russia v Azerbaijan.
01.04.09 Liechtenstein v Russia; Wales v Germany.
06.06.09 Azerbaijan v Wales; Finland v Liechtenstein.
10.06.09 Finland v Russia.
19.08.09 Azerbaijan v Germany.
05.09.09 Azerbaijan v Finland; Russia v Liechtenstein.
09.09.09 Wales v Russia; Germany v Azerbaijan; Liechtenstein v Finland.
10.10.09 Liechtenstein v Azerbaijan; Finland v Wales; Russia v Germany.
14.10.09 Azerbaijan v Russia; Germany v Finland; Liechtenstein v Wales.

GROUP 5
06.09.08 Armenia v Turkey; Belgium v Estonia; Spain v Bosnia.
10.09.08 Spain v Armenia; Turkey v Belgium; Bosnia v Estonia.
11.10.08 Belgium v Armenia; Turkey v Bosnia; Estonia v Spain.
15.10.08 Bosnia v Armenia; Belgium v Spain; Estonia v Turkey.
28.03.09 Armenia v Estonia; Belgium v Bosnia; Spain v Turkey.
01.04.09 Estonia v Armenia; Bosnia v Belgium; Turkey v Spain.
05.09.09 Armenia v Bosnia; Spain v Belgium; Turkey v Estonia.
09.09.09 Armenia v Belgium; Bosnia v Turkey; Spain v Estonia.
10.10.09 Armenia v Spain; Belgium v Turkey; Estonia v Bosnia.
14.10.09 Turkey v Armenia; Estonia v Belgium; Bosnia v Spain.

GROUP 6
20.08.08 Kazakhstan v Andorra.
06.09.08 Andorra v England; Ukraine v Belarus; Croatia v Kazakhstan.
10.09.08 Andorra v Belarus; Croatia v England; Kazakhstan v Ukraine.
11.10.08 England v Kazakhstan; Ukraine v Croatia.
15.10.08 Croatia v Andorra; Belarus v England.
01.04.09 Andorra v Croatia; Kazakhstan v Belarus; England v Ukraine.
06.06.09 Belarus v Andorra; Kazakhstan v England; Croatia v Ukraine.

10.06.09 England v Andorra.
19.08.09 Belarus v Croatia.
05.09.09 Ukraine v Andorra; Croatia v Belarus.
09.09.09 Andorra v Kazakhstan; Belarus v Ukraine; England v Croatia.
10.09.09 Ukraine v Kazakhstan.
10.10.09 Belarus v Kazakhstan; Ukraine v England.
14.10.09 Andorra v Ukraine; England v Belarus; Kazakhstan v Croatia.

GROUP 7
06.09.08 Serbia v Faeroes; Austria v France; Romania v Lithuania.
10.09.08 Faeroes v Romania; France v Serbia; Lithuania v Austria.
11.10.08 Faeroes v Austria; Romania v France; Serbia v Lithuania.
15.10.08 Lithuania v Faeroes; Austria v Serbia.
28.03.09 Lithuania v France; Romania v Serbia.
01.04.09 France v Lithuania; Austria v Romania.
06.06.09 Lithuania v Romania; Serbia v Austria.
10.06.09 Faeroes v Serbia.
19.08.09 Faeroes v France.
05.09.09 Austria v Faeroes; France v Romania.
09.09.09 Faeroes v Lithuania; Serbia v France; Romania v Austria.
10.10.09 France v Faeroes; Austria v Lithuania; Serbia v Romania.
14.10.09 Romania v Faeroes; France v Austria; Lithuania v Serbia.

GROUP 8
06.09.08 Montenegro v Bulgaria; Georgia v Eire; Cyprus v Italy.
10.09.08 Italy v Georgia; Montenegro v Eire.
11.10.08 Bulgaria v Italy; Georgia v Cyprus.
15.10.08 Georgia v Bulgaria; Eire v Cyprus; Italy v Montenegro.
11.02.09 Eire v Georgia.
28.03.09 Eire v Bulgaria; Cyprus v Georgia; Montenegro v Italy.
01.04.09 Georgia v Montenegro; Bulgaria v Cyprus; Italy v Eire.
06.06.09 Bulgaria v Eire; Cyprus v Montenegro.
05.09.09 Bulgaria v Montenegro; Georgia v Italy; Cyprus v Eire.
09.09.09 Italy v Bulgaria; Montenegro v Cyprus.
10.10.09 Montenegro v Georgia; Cyprus v Bulgaria; Eire v Italy.
14.10.09 Bulgaria v Georgia; Eire v Montenegro; Italy v Cyprus.

GROUP 9
06.09.08 Norway v Iceland; Macedonia v Scotland.
10.09.08 Iceland v Scotland; Macedonia v Holland.
11.10.08 Holland v Iceland; Scotland v Norway.
15.10.08 Iceland v Macedonia; Norway v Holland.
28.03.09 Holland v Scotland.
01.04.09 Scotland v Iceland; Holland v Macedonia.
06.06.09 Iceland v Holland; Macedonia v Norway.
10.06.09 Macedonia v Iceland; Holland v Norway.
19.08.09 Norway v Scotland.
05.09.09 Iceland v Norway; Scotland v Macedonia.
09.09.09 Norway v Macedonia; Scotland v Holland.

SOUTH AMERICA
06.09.08 Argentina v Paraguay; Chile v Brazil; Colombia v Uruguay; Ecuador v Bolivia; Peru v Venezuela.
10.09.08 Brazil v Bolivia; Chile v Colombia; Paraguay v Venezuela; Peru v Argentina; Uruguay v Ecuador.
11.10.08 Argentina v Uruguay; Bolivia v Peru; Colombia v Paraguay; Ecuador v Chile; Venezuela v Brazil.
15.10.08 Chile v Argentina; Brazil v Colombia; Venezuela v Ecuador; Paraguay v Peru; Bolivia v Uruguay.
28.03.09 Colombia v Bolivia; Ecuador v Brazil; Peru v Chile; Uruguay v Paraguay; Argentina v Venezuela.
01.04.09 Bolivia v Argentina; Venezuela v Colombia; Ecuador v Paraguay; Brazil v Peru; Chile v Uruguay.
06.06.09 Uruguay v Brazil; Paraguay v Chile; Argentina v Colombia; Peru v Ecuador; Bolivia v Venezuela.
10.06.09 Ecuador v Argentina; Chile v Bolivia; Brazil v Paraguay; Colombia v Peru; Venezuela v Uruguay.
05.09.09 Paraguay v Bolivia; Argentina v Brazil; Colombia v Ecuador; Peru v Uruguay; Chile v Venezuela.
09.09.09 Paraguay v Argentina; Brazil v Chile; Uruguay v Colombia; Bolivia v Ecuador; Venezuela v Peru.
10.10.09 Bolivia v Brazil; Colombia v Chile; Venezuela v Paraguay; Argentina v Peru; Ecuador v Uruguay.
14.10.09 Uruguay v Argentina; Peru v Bolivia; Paraguay v Colombia; Chile v Ecuador; Brazil v Venezuela.

EUROPEAN SUPER CUP

Played annually between the winners of the European Champions' Cup and the European Cup-Winners' Cup (UEFA Cup from 2000). AC Milan replaced Marseille in 1993–94.

EUROPEAN SUPER CUP 2007

31 August 2007, Monaco (attendance 18,000)

AC Milan (0) 3 *(Inzaghi 55, Jankulovski 62, Kaka 87)*

Sevilla (1) 1 *(Renato 14)*

AC Milan: Dida; Oddo, Kaladze, Nesta, Jankulovski, Ambrosini, Pirlo, Gattuso (Emerson 73), Kaka, Seedorf (Brocchi 89), Inzaghi (Gilardino 88).

Sevilla: Palop; Daniel Alves, Escude (Luis Fabiano 84), Marti (Kerzhakov 65), Dragutinovic, Jesus Navas, Poulsen, Duda (Maresca 74), Renato, Keita, Kanoute.

Referee: K. Plautz (Austria).

Previous Matches

1972	Ajax beat Rangers 3-1, 3-2
1973	Ajax beat AC Milan 0-1, 6-0
1974	Not contested
1975	Dynamo Kiev beat Bayern Munich 1-0, 2-0
1976	Anderlecht beat Bayern Munich 4-1, 1-2
1977	Liverpool beat Hamburg 1-1, 6-0
1978	Anderlecht beat Liverpool 3-1, 1-2
1979	Nottingham F beat Barcelona 1-0, 1-1
1980	Valencia beat Nottingham F 1-0, 1-2
1981	Not contested
1982	Aston Villa beat Barcelona 0-1, 3-0
1983	Aberdeen beat Hamburg 0-0, 2-0
1984	Juventus beat Liverpool 2-0
1985	Juventus v Everton not contested due to UEFA ban on English clubs
1986	Steaua Bucharest beat Dynamo Kiev 1-0
1987	FC Porto beat Ajax 1-0, 1-0
1988	KV Mechelen beat PSV Eindhoven 3-0, 0-1
1989	AC Milan beat Barcelona 1-1, 1-0
1990	AC Milan beat Sampdoria 1-1, 2-0
1991	Manchester U beat Red Star Belgrade 1-0
1992	Barcelona beat Werder Bremen 1-1, 2-1
1993	Parma beat AC Milan 0-1, 2-0
1994	AC Milan beat Arsenal 0-0, 2-0
1995	Ajax beat Zaragoza 1-1, 4-0
1996	Juventus beat Paris St Germain 6-1, 3-1
1997	Barcelona beat Borussia Dortmund 2-0, 1-1
1998	Chelsea beat Real Madrid 1-0
1999	Lazio beat Manchester U 1-0
2000	Galatasaray beat Real Madrid 2-1
	(aet; Galatasaray won on sudden death.)
2001	Liverpool beat Bayern Munich 3-2
2002	Real Madrid beat Feyenoord 3-1
2003	AC Milan beat Porto 1-0
2004	Valencia beat Porto 2-1
2005	Liverpool beat CSKA Moscow 3-1
2006	Sevilla beat Barcelona 3-0
2007	AC Milan beat Sevilla 3-1

FIFA CLUB WORLD CUP 2007–2008

Formerly known as the FIFA Club World Championship, this tournament is played annually between the champion clubs from all 6 continental confederations, although since 2007 the champions of Oceania must play a qualifying play-off against the champion club of the permanent host country Japan.

SEMI-FINALS
Urawa Red Diamonds (0) 0,
AC Milan (0) 1 *(Seedorf 68)*
att: 67,005 in Yokohama.
Etoile Sportive Du Sahel (0) 0,
Boca Juniors (1) 1 *(Cardozo 37)*
att: 37,255 in Tokyo.

MATCH FOR 3RD PLACE
Etoil Sportive Du Sahel (1) 2 *(Frej 5 (pen)*,
Chermiti 75), **Urawa Red Diamonds (1) 2**
(Washington 35, 70)
att: 53,363 in Yokohama.
Urawa Red Diamonds won 4-2 on penalties.

FIFA CLUB WORLD CUP FINAL 2007

Sunday 16 December, Yokohama, Japan (attendance 68,263)

Boca Juniors (1) 2 *(Palacio 22, Ledesma 36)*

AC Milan (1) 4 *(Inzaghi 21, 71, Nesta 50, Kaka 61)*

Boca Juniors: Caranta; Morel Rodriguez, Ibarra, Battaglia, Palermo, Palacio, Gonzalez (Ledesma■ 67), Cardozo (Gracian 68), Maidana, Banega, Battata.
AC Milan: Dida; Maldini, Kaladze■, Gattuso (Emerson 65), Inzaghi (Cafu 76), Seedorf (Brocchi 83), Nesta, Pirlo, Kaka, Ambrosini, Bonera.
Referee: Rodriguez (Mexico).

Previous Matches
2000   Corinthians beat Vaso de Gama 4-3 on penalties after 0-0 draw
2005   Sao Paulo beat Liverpool 1-0
2006   Internacional beat Barcelona 1-0
2007   AC Milan beat Boca Juniors 4-2

WORLD CLUB CHAMPIONSHIP

Played annually up to 1974 and intermittently since then between the winners of the European Cup and the winners of the South American Champions Cup — known as the Copa Libertadores. In 1980 the winners were decided by one match arranged in Tokyo in February 1981 which remained the venue until 2004, after which the match was superseded by the FIFA World Club Championship. AC Milan replaced Marseille who had been stripped of their European Cup title in 1993.

1960 Real Madrid beat Penarol 0-0, 5-1; 1961 Penarol beat Benfica 0-1, 5-0, 2-1; 1962 Santos beat Benfica 3-2, 5-2; 1963 Santos beat AC Milan 2-4, 4-2, 1-0; 1964 Inter-Milan beat Independiente 0-1, 2-0, 1-0; 1965 Inter-Milan beat Independiente 3-0, 0-0; 1966 Penarol beat Real Madrid 2-0, 2-0; 1967 Racing Club beat Celtic 0-1, 2-1, 1-0; 1968 Estudiantes beat Manchester United 1-0, 1-1; 1969 AC Milan beat Estudiantes 3-0, 1-2; 1970 Feyenoord beat Estudiantes 2-2, 1-0; 1971 Nacional beat Panathinaikos* 1-1, 2-1; 1972 Ajax beat Independiente 1-1, 3-0; 1973 Independiente beat Juventus* 1-0; 1974 Atlético Madrid* beat Independiente 0-1, 2-0; 1975 Independiente and Bayern Munich could not agree dates; no matches.; 1976 Bayern Munich beat Cruzeiro 2-0, 0-0; 1977 Boca Juniors beat Borussia Moenchengladbach* 2-2, 3-0; 1978 Not contested; 1979 Olimpia beat Malmö* 1-0, 2-1; 1980 Nacional beat Nottingham Forest 1-0; 1981 Flamengo beat Liverpool 3-0; 1982 Penarol beat Aston Villa 2-0; 1983 Gremio Porto Alegre beat SV Hamburg 2-1; 1984 Independiente beat Liverpool 1-0; 1985 Juventus beat Argentinos Juniors 4-2 on penalties after a 2-2 draw; 1986 River Plate beat Steaua Bucharest 1-0; 1987 FC Porto beat Penarol 2-1 after extra time; 1988 Nacional (Uru) beat PSV Eindhoven 7-6 on penalties after 1-1 draw; 1989 AC Milan beat Atletico Nacional (Col) 1-0 after extra time; 1990 AC Milan beat Olimpia 3-0; 1991 Red Star Belgrade beat Colo Colo 3-0; 1992 Sao Paulo beat Barcelona 2-1; 1993 Sao Paulo beat AC Milan 3-2; 1994 Velez Sarsfield beat AC Milan 2-0; 1995 Ajax beat Gremio Porto Alegre 4-3 on penalties after 0-0 draw; 1996 Juventus beat River Plate 1-0; 1997 Borussia Dortmund beat Cruzeiro 2-0; 1998 Real Madrid beat Vasco da Gama 2-1; 1999 Manchester U beat Palmeiras 1-0; 2000 Boca Juniors beat Real Madrid 2-1; 2001 Bayern Munich beat Boca Juniors 1-0 after extra time; 2002 Real Madrid beat Olimpia 2-0; 2003 Boca Juniors beat AC Milan 3-1 on penalties after 1-1 draw; 2004 Porto beat Once Caldas 8-7 on penalties afer 0-0 draw; *European Cup runners-up; winners declined to take part.*

OTHER BRITISH AND IRISH INTERNATIONAL MATCHES 2007–2008

Wembley, 22 August 2007, 86,133

England (1) 1 *(Lampard 9)*   **Germany (2) 2** *(Kuranyi 26, Pander 40)*

England: Robinson (James 46); Richards, Shorey, Carrick (Barry 55), Ferdinand (Brown 46), Terry, Beckham, Lampard, Smith (Crouch 57), Owen (Dyer 57), Cole J (Wright-Phillips 70).
Germany: Lehmann; Friedrich A, Mertesacker, Metzelder, Lahm, Odonkor (Hilbert 54), Schneider (Castro 90), Hitzlsperger, Pander, Trochowski (Rolfes 72), Kuranyi.
Referee: M. Puscaba (Switzerland).

Vienna, 16 November 2007, 39,432

Austria (0) 0   **England (1) 1** *(Crouch 44)*

Austria: Macho (Manninger 26); Garics, Stanzl (Hiden 86), Schiemer, Gercaliu, Standfest (Kavlak 78), Aufhauser, Sariyar (Harnik 65), Weissenberger (Kienast 46), Ivanschitz, Kuljic (Leitgeb 46).
England: Carson; Richards, Bridge, Gerrard (Barry 46), Lescott, Campbell (Brown 46), Beckham (Bentley 62), Lampard, Crouch (Smith 76), Owen (Defoe 34), Cole J (Young 46).
Referee: N. Vollquartz (Denmark).

Wembley, 6 February 2008, 86,857

England (1) 2 *(Jenas 40, Wright-Phillips 62)*   **Switzerland (0) 1** *(Derdiyok 58)*

England: James; Brown, Cole A (Bridge 74), Barry (Hargreaves 74), Ferdinand, Upson, Bentley, Jenas (Wright-Phillips 57), Rooney (Young 87), Gerrard, Cole J (Crouch 57).
Switzerland: Benaglio; Senderos (Grichting 55), Gygax (Derdiyok 46), Barnetta, Spycher, Yakin H (Margairaz 64), Inler, Lichsteiner (Behrami 46), Nkufo (Vonlanthen 46), Fernandes (Huggel 84), Eggimann.
Referee: F. Bryche (Germany).

Paris, 26 March 2008, 78,500

France (1) 1 *(Ribery 32 (pen))*   **England (0) 0**

France: Coupet; Abidal, Gallas, Makelele, Toulalan, Clerc, Thuram, Ribery, Trezeguet (Gouvou 64), Anelka (Cisse 80), Malouda.
England: James; Brown (Johnson G 63), Cole A, Hargreaves, Ferdinand, Terry (Lescott 46), Beckham (Bentley 63), Barry, Rooney (Owen 46), Gerrard (Crouch 46), Cole J (Downing 46).
Referee: F. Meyer (Germany).

Wembley, 28 May 2008, 71,233

England (1) 2 *(Terry 38, Gerrard 59)*   **USA (0) 0**

England: James; Brown (Johnson G 57), Cole A (Bridge 82), Hargreaves, Ferdinand, Terry, Beckham (Bentley 46), Lampard (Barry 57), Rooney (Cole J 78), Defoe (Crouch 68), Gerrard.
USA: Howard (Guzan 46); Cherundolo (Hejduk 46), Onyewu, Bocanegra, Pearce, Dempsey, Bradley, Clark (Edu 78), Beasley (Lewis 68), Johnson (Jaqua 89), Wolff (Adu 68).
Referee: K. Vassaras (Greece).

Port of Spain, 2 June 2008, 25,001

Trinidad & Tobago (0) 0   England (2) 3 *(Barry 12, Defoe 16, 49)*

Trinidad & Tobago: Ince; Cupid (Smith 46), Lawrence, Hislop, Farrier, Edwards, Hyland (Yorke 76), Whitley, Daniel (Connell 76), John (Forbes 74), Jones K (Roberts D 11) (Telesford 46).
England: James (Hart 46); Johnson G, Bridge (Warnock 84), Gerrard, Ferdinand (Jagielka 46), Woodgate, Beckham (Bentley 46), Barry, Ashton (Crouch 46), Defoe (Walcott 69), Downing (Young A 57).
Referee: E. Wijngaarde (Surinam).

Aberdeen, 22 August 2007, 13,723

Scotland (0) 1 *(Boyd 71)*   **South Africa (0) 0**

Scotland: Gordon; Hutton, Anderson, McManus, McEveley, Brown (Teale 72), Caldwell (Robson 56), Fletcher D, McFadden (Pearson 46), O'Connor (Beattie 68), Miller (Boyd 68).
South Africa: Fernandez; Nzama (Mere 83), Mokoena, Mhlongo, Carnell, Pienaar (Modise 76), Zothwane, Sibaya, Buckley (Sheppard 76), Nkosi (Fanteni 75), Zuma (Nomvethe 14).
Referee: M. Atkinson (England).

Glasgow, 26 March 2008, 28,821

Scotland (1) 1 *(Miller 30)*   **Croatia (1) 1** *(Kranjcar 10)*

Scotland: Gordon; Hutton, Naysmith (McEveley 62), Caldwell (Anderson 70), McManus, Fletcher D (Alexander 90), Hartley, Brown (Teale 66), Maloney (Boyd 72), Miller, Fletcher S (Rae 46).
Croatia: Pletikosa; Kovac R (Knezevic 73), Corluka (Simic 85), Simunic, Srna (Leko 63), Kovac N (Vukojevic 46), Modric, Kranjcar, Pranjic, Petric (Klasnic 58), Olic (Budan 57).
Referee: T. Hauge (Norway).

Prague, 30 May 2008, 11,314

Czech Republic (0) 3 *(Sionko 60, 90, Kadlec 84)*   **Scotland (0) 1** *(Clarkson 85)*

Czech Republic: Cech; Pospech (Sivok 74), Ujfalusi (Rozehnal 46), Kovac, Jankulovski (Kadlec 46), Sionko, Polak, Matejovsky (Jarolim 46), Galasek, Skacel (Plasil 46), Koller (Sverkos 46).
Scotland: Gordon; McNaughton (Berra 90), McManus (Dailly 57), Caldwell G, Naysmith, Robson (McCormack 82), Hartley, Fletcher D, Rae (Clarkson 71), Morrison (Maloney 68), Miller.
Referee: E. Braamhaar (Holland).

Burgas, 22 August 2007, 15,000

Bulgaria (0) 0   Wales (1) 1 *(Eastwood 45)*

Bulgaria: Ivankov; Kishishev (Yankov 52), Wagner (Zanev 54), Tomasic, Angelov S, Petrov S, Tunchev, Telkiyski (Popov I 46), Yovov (Genkov 66), Chillikov (Dimitrov 46), Petrov M.
Wales: Hennessey; Bale (Eardley 46), Ricketts (Collins D 46), Gabbidon, Morgan (Evans S 46), Nyatanga, Crofts, Davies S (Nardiello 66), Eastwood (Earnshaw 46), Vaughan, Ledley (Jones M 61).
Referee: M. Germanakos (Greece).

Wrexham, 6 February 2008, 7000

Wales (1) 3 *(Fletcher 15, Koumas 62, 89)* **Norway (0) 0**

Wales: Hennessey (Price 46); Gunter, Ricketts (Eardley 59), Fletcher, Morgan, Nyatanga, Robinson (Crofts 66), Eastwood (Cotterill 59), Koumas, Davies S (Davies C 59), Ledley (Edwards D 46).
Norway: Opdal; Kah, Hangeland (Kippe 61), Riise, Stromstad (Grindheim 46), Andresen, Carew (Haestad 46), Pedersen, Braaten, Storbaek, Nevland (Bjorkoy 77).
Referee: D. McKeon (Republic of Ireland).

Luxembourg, 26 March 2008, 3000

Luxembourg (0) 0 **Wales (1) 2** *(Eastwood 37, 46)*

Luxembourg: Joubert; Kintziger, Hoffmann, Wagner, Strasser, Leweck (Da Mota 66), Gerson (Lukic 90), Joachim (Kitenge 53), Remy, Mutsch, Lang (Peters 46).
Wales: Price (Myhill 46); Eardley (Duffy 65), Ricketts, Williams A, Morgan, Nyatanga, Eastwood, Fletcher (Cotterill 75), Koumas (Nardiello 84), Davies S, Easter (Tudur-Jones 46).
Referee: B. Kuipers (Holland).

Reykjavik, 28 May 2008, 5322

Iceland (0) 0 **Wales (1) 1** *(Evans C 44)*

Iceland: Sturuson (Torgeirsson 46); Saevarsson B, Thorarinsson, Gunnarsson A (Saevarsson J 76), Sigurdsson J, Palmason, Sigurdsson K, Jonsson (Sigurdsson H 60), Hallfredsson (Bjarnason 70), Thordarson (Danielsson 61), Thorvaldsson (Smarason 81).
Wales: Hennessey; Gunter, Williams A, Morgan, Nyatanga, Collison (Tudur-Jones 60), Fletcher (Evans C 41), Koumas (Crofts 89), Edwards D (Bellamy 62), Ledley (Eardley 49), Eastwood (Vokes 49).
Referee: A. McCourt (Northern Ireland).

Rotterdam, 1 June 2008, 49,000

Holland (1) 2 *(Robben 35, Sneijder 54)* **Wales (0) 0**

Holland: Van der Sar; Ooijer, Mathijsen (Vennegoor of Hesselink 80), Heitinga (Melchiot 46), Van Bronckhorst (De Cler 46), De Zeeuw (Kuyt 46), Englelaar (De Jong 46), Van der Vaart (Afellay 67), Sneijder, Van Nistelrooy, Robben.
Wales: Hennessey; Gunter, Williams A, Morgan, Nyatanga (Collison 47), Ricketts (Crofts 78), Robinson, Edwards D (Evans C 57), Ledley (Eardley 88), Koumas (Vokes 73), Eastwood (Bellamy 57).
Referee: F. Brych (Germany).

Copenhagen, 22 August 2007, 30,000

Denmark (0) 0 **Republic of Ireland (2) 4** *(Keane 29, 40, Long 54, 66)*

Denmark: Christiansen; Bogelund (Kahlenberg 46), Gravgaard (Kristiansen 46), Agger, Jensen N (Kvist 46), Wurtz (Lovenkrands 68), Rommedahl, Jensen D (Laursen 46), Gronkjaer, Bendtner, Tomasson (Nordstrand 59).
Republic of Ireland: Henderson; Carr, Finnan (Kilbane 62), Potter (Kelly 67), O'Shea, Dunne, Reid A (Gibson 46), Hunt (Keogh A 46), Keane (Murphy 58), Doyle K (Long 46), McGeady.
Referee: T. Einwaller (Austria).

Dublin, 6 February 2008, 30,000

Republic of Ireland (0) 0 **Brazil (0) 1** *(Robinho 67)*

Republic of Ireland: Given; Kelly, Kilbane, Miller (Potter 46), O'Shea, Dunne, Duff, Carsley, Keane, Doyle (Hunt 72), McGeady.

Brazil: Julio Cesar; Leonardo, Anderson Silva, Alex, Richarlyson, Josue (Lucas 83), Gilberto Silva, Diego (Anderson 78), Robinho, Luis Fabiano (Rafael Sobis 84), Baptista.
Referee: R. Rogalla (Switzerland).

Croke Park, 24 May 2008, 42,500

Republic of Ireland (0) 1 *(Keogh A 90)*   **Serbia (0) 1** *(Pantelic 75)*

Republic of Ireland: Kiely; Kelly, McShane, Dunne, Delaney, Duff, Whelan, Miller, Hunt (Keogh A 80), Keane (Murphy D 69), Doyle (Long 86).
Serbia: Stojkovic; Rukavina, Ivanovic, Rajkovic, Dragutinovic, Babovic (Markovic 80), Smiljanic, Kuzmanovic, Jankovic, Ilic (Kacar 86), Lazovic (Pantelic 69).
Referee: L. Evans (Wales).

Fulham, 29 May 2008, 15,000

Republic of Ireland (1) 1 *(Keane 3)*   **Colombia (0) 0**

Republic of Ireland: Kiely; O'Shea, Dunne, McShane, Delaney, Miller, Whelan, McGeady, Keogh A (Hoolahan 90), Doyle (Murphy D 85), Keane.
Colombia: Zapata R; Zapata C, Bustos (Vallejo 46), Perea L (Morena 66), Gonzalez (Armero 70), Guarin, Sanchez, Escobar (Sota 63), Torres (Hernandez 73), Perea E, Garcia (Polo 65).
Referee: M. Clattenburg (England).

Belfast, 6 February 2008, 11,000

Northern Ireland (0) 0   Bulgaria (1) 1 *(Evans 38 (og))*

Northern Ireland: Taylor (Mannus 83); McAuley, McCartney (Baird 46), Hughes, Evans (Craigan 46), Clingan, Gillespie (Thompson 78), Johnson (Davis 46), Healy, Lafferty (Paterson 60), Brunt.
Bulgaria: Petkov G (Ivankov 46); Angelov S, Venkov (Zanev 73), Tunchev (Karaslavov 66), Tomasic, Milanov, Petrov M, Yanchev (Dimitrov 46), Georgiev, Berbatov (Domovchiyski 82), Lazarov (Popov I 66).
Referee: D. McDonald (Scotland).

Belfast, 26 March 2008, 15,000

Northern Ireland (3) 4 *(Lafferty 25, 36, Healy 33, Kobiashvili 87 (og))*

Georgia (0) 1 *(Healy 55 (og))*

Northern Ireland: Taylor (Mannus 80); Baird, Hughes, Craigan (McAuley 57), Evans, Gillespie, Johnson (O'Connor 46), Davis (Gault 70), Elliott, Healy (Thompson 70), Lafferty (Feeney 46).
Georgia: Makaridze; Salukvadze, Kaladze, Kenia (Khidasheli 81), Shashiashvili (Jakobia 81), Kobiashvili, Tskitishvili (Eliava 90), Kankava, Kvakhadze, Kvirkevlia, Iashvili.
Referee: L. Wilmes (Luxembourg).

ENGLAND UNDER-21 TEAMS 2007–2008

*Denotes player sent off.

Bristol City, 21 August 2007, 18,640

England (1) 1 *(Derbyshire 8)*   **Romania (1) 1** *(Hart 25 (og)) Scutaru*▪

England: Hart (Alnwick 46); Gardner (Mancienne 46), Onuoha, Wheater, Cranie, Kightly (Johnson A 46), Johnson M (Huddlestone 65), Noble (Muamba 65), Walcott, Derbyshire (Milner 78), Agbonlahor (Moore 78).

Podgorica, 7 September 2007

Montenegro (0) 0   England (2) 3 *(Onuoha 6, Agbonlahor 10, Surman 90)*

England: Hart; Cranie, Taylor A, Noble, Taylor S, Onuoha, Milner, Gardner (Surman 80), Derbyshire (Blackstock 90), Agbonlahor, Walcott (Muamba 63).

Sofia, 11 September 2007, 1000

Bulgaria (0) 0   England (2) 2 *(Huddlestone 25, Noble 32)*

England: Hart; Cranie, Taylor A, Noble, Taylor S, Onuoha, Milner, Huddlestone, Derbyshire (Moore 81), Agbonlahor (Kightly 70), Walcott (Muamba 55).

Leicester, 12 October 2007, 20,022

England (1) 1 *(Derbyshire 20)*   **Montenegro (0) 0**

England: Hart; Cranie, Taylor A, Surman (Muamba 30), Taylor S, Onuoha, Milner, Huddlestone, Derbyshire (Jerome 79), Agbonlahor (Kightly 83), Walcott.

Cork, 16 October 2007

Republic of Ireland (0) 0   England (3) 3 *(Noble 10, 17, Milner 26)*

Republic of Ireland: Randolph; Nolan, O'Halloran, Keogh R, O'Dea, Garvan, O'Brien J, Quinn S, Rooney (Powell 66), Stokes, Clarke (Gleeson 88).
England: Hart; Cranie, Taylor A, Noble, Taylor S, Onuoha (Wheater 77), Milner, Huddlestone, Derbyshire (Moore 66), Agbonlahor (Johnson A 75), Walcott.

Milton Keynes, 16 November 2007, 20,222

England (1) 2 *(Agbonlahor 40, Milner 81 (pen))*   **Bulgaria (0) 0**

England: Hart; Gardner, Mattock, Cattermole, Taylor S, Wheater, Milner, Huddlestone (Johnson A 85), Derbyshire (Muamba 46), Abgonlahor (Leadbitter 79), Walcott.

Agueda, 20 November 2007, 5468

Portugal (1) 1 *(Vieirinha 3 (pen))*   **England (0) 1** *(Johnson A 49)*

England: Hart; Gardner, Mattock, Cattermole, Taylor S (Mancienne 46), Wheater, Milner, Huddlestone, Johnson A, Muamba, Walcott.

Southampton, 5 February 2008, 31,473

England (0) 3 *(O'Halloran 59 (og), Milner 68, Walcott 78)*
Republic of Ireland (0) 0

England: Hart; Gardner, Mattock, Noble (Surman 86), Taylor S, Wheater, Milner, Huddlestone (Jerome 79) Lennon, Muamba, Walcott (Johnson A 86).
Republic of Ireland: Randolph; Nolan, O'Halloran, O'Cearuill, O'Dea, Quinn S (Morris 83), Garvan, O'Toole, Keogh A, Stokes (O'Brien J 87), Clarke (Rooney 65).

Wolverhampton, 25 March 2008, 28,178

England (0) 0   Poland (0) 0

England: Hart (Heaton 46); Mancienne, Fox, Surman (Mattock 88), Onuoha, Shawcross (Dann 65), Gardner (Leadbitter 46), O'Hara, Jerome (Campbell 65), Moore (Derbyshire 65), Johnson A.

POST-WAR INTERNATIONAL APPEARANCES

As at July 2008 *(Season of first cap given)*

ENGLAND

A'Court, A. (5) 1957/8 Liverpool

Adams, T. A. (66) 1986/7 Arsenal

Allen, C. (5) 1983/4 QPR, Tottenham H

Allen, R. (5) 1951/2 WBA

Allen, T. (3) 1959/60 Stoke C

Anderson, S. (2) 1961/2 Sunderland

Anderson, V. (30) 1978/9 Nottingham F, Arsenal, Manchester U

Anderton, D. R. (30) 1993/4 Tottenham H

Angus, J. (1) 1960/1 Burnley

Armfield, J. (43) 1958/9 Blackpool

Armstrong, D. (3) 1979/80 Middlesbrough, Southampton

Armstrong, K. (1) 1954/5 Chelsea

Ashton, D. (1) 2007/08 West Ham U

Astall, G. (2) 1955/6 Birmingham C

Astle, J. (5) 1968/9 WBA

Aston, J. (17) 1948/9 Manchester U

Atyeo, J. (6) 1955/6 Bristol C

Bailey, G. R. (2) 1984/5 Manchester U

Bailey, M. (2) 1963/4 Charlton

Baily, E. (9) 1949/50 Tottenham H

Baker, J. (8) 1959/60 Hibernian, Arsenal

Ball, A. (72) 1964/5 Blackpool, Everton, Arsenal

Ball, M. J. (1) 2000/01 Everton

Banks, G. (73) 1962/3 Leicester C, Stoke C

Banks, T. (6) 1957/8 Bolton W

Bardsley, D. (2) 1992/3 QPR

Barham, M. (2) 1982/3 Norwich C

Barlow, R. (1) 1954/5 WBA

Barmby, N. J. (23) 1994/5 Tottenham H, Middlesbrough, Everton, Liverpool

Barnes, J. (79) 1982/3 Watford, Liverpool

Barnes, P. (22) 1977/8 Manchester C, WBA, Leeds U

Barrass, M. (3) 1951/2 Bolton W

Barrett, E. D. (3) 1990/1 Oldham Ath, Aston Villa

Barry, G. (20) 1999/00 Aston Villa

Barton, J. (1) 2006/07 Manchester C

Barton, W. D. (3) 1994/5 Wimbledon, Newcastle U

Batty, D. (42) 1990/1 Leeds U, Blackburn R, Newcastle U, Leeds U

Baynham, R. (3) 1955/6 Luton T

Beardsley, P. A. (59) 1985/6 Newcastle U, Liverpool, Newcastle U

Beasant, D. J. (2) 1989/90 Chelsea

Beattie, J. S. (5) 2002/03 Southampton

Beattie, T. K. (9) 1974/5 Ipswich T

Beckham, D. R. J. (102) 1996/7 Manchester U, Real Madrid, LA Galaxy

Bell, C. (48) 1967/8 Manchester C

Bent, D. A. (3) 2005/06 Charlton Ath, Tottenham H

Bentley, D. M. (6) 2007/08 Blackburn R

Bentley, R. (12) 1948/9 Chelsea

Berry, J. (4) 1952/3 Manchester U

Birtles, G. (3) 1979/80 Nottingham F

Blissett, L. (14) 1982/3 Watford, AC Milan

Blockley, J. (1) 1972/3 Arsenal

Blunstone, F. (5) 1954/5 Chelsea

Bonetti, P. (7) 1965/6 Chelsea

Bould, S. A. (2) 1993/4 Arsenal

Bowles, S. (5) 1973/4 QPR

Bowyer, L. D. (1) 2002/03 Leeds U

Boyer, P. (1) 1975/6 Norwich C

Brabrook, P. (3) 1957/8 Chelsea

Bracewell, P. W. (3) 1984/5 Everton

Bradford, G. (1) 1955/6 Bristol R

Bradley, W. (3) 1958/9 Manchester U

Bridge, W. M. (30) 2001/02 Southampton, Chelsea

Bridges, B. (4) 1964/5 Chelsea

Broadbent, P. (7) 1957/8 Wolverhampton W

Broadis, I. (14) 1951/2 Manchester C, Newcastle U

Brooking, T. (47) 1973/4 West Ham U

Brooks, J. (3) 1956/7 Tottenham H

Brown, A. (1) 1970/1 WBA

Brown, K. (1) 1959/60 West Ham U

Brown, W. M. (17) 1998/9 Manchester U

Bull, S. G. (13) 1988/9 Wolverhampton W

Butcher, T. (77) 1979/80 Ipswich T, Rangers

Butt, N. (39) 1996/7 Manchester U, Newcastle U

Byrne, G. (2) 1962/3 Liverpool

Byrne, J. (11) 1961/2 Crystal P, West Ham U

Byrne, R. (33) 1953/4 Manchester U

Callaghan, I. (4) 1965/6 Liverpool
Campbell, S. (73) 1995/6 Tottenham H, Arsenal, Portsmouth
Carragher, J. L. (34) 1998/9 Liverpool
Carrick, M. (2) 2000/01 West Ham U, Tottenham H, Manchester U
Carson, S. P. (2) 2007/08 Liverpool
Carter, H. (7) 1946/7 Derby Co
Chamberlain, M. (8) 1982/3 Stoke C
Channon, M. (46) 1972/3 Southampton, Manchester C
Charles, G. A. (2) 1990/1 Nottingham F
Charlton, J. (35) 1964/5 Leeds U
Charlton, R. (106) 1957/8 Manchester U
Charnley, R. (1) 1962/3 Blackpool
Cherry, T. (27) 1975/6 Leeds U
Chilton, A. (2) 1950/1 Manchester U
Chivers, M. (24) 1970/1 Tottenham H
Clamp, E. (4) 1957/8 Wolverhampton W
Clapton, D. (1) 1958/9 Arsenal
Clarke, A. (19) 1969/70 Leeds U
Clarke, H. (1) 1953/4 Tottenham H
Clayton, R. (35) 1955/6 Blackburn R
Clemence, R (61) 1972/3 Liverpool, Tottenham H
Clement, D. (5) 1975/6 QPR
Clough, B. (2) 1959/60 Middlesbrough
Clough, N. H. (14) 1988/9 Nottingham F
Coates, R. (4) 1969/70 Burnley, Tottenham H
Cockburn, H. (13) 1946/7 Manchester U
Cohen, G. (37) 1963/4 Fulham
Cole, Andy (15) 1994/5 Manchester U
Cole, Ashley (64) 2000/01 Arsenal, Chelsea
Cole, J. J. (50) 2000/01 West Ham U, Chelsea
Collymore, S. V. (3) 1994/5 Nottingham F, Aston Villa
Compton, L. (2) 1950/1 Arsenal
Connelly, J. (20) 1959/60 Burnley, Manchester U
Cooper, C. T. (2) 1994/5 Nottingham F
Cooper, T. (20) 1968/9 Leeds U
Coppell, S. (42) 1977/8 Manchester U
Corrigan, J. (9) 1975/6 Manchester C
Cottee, A. R. (7) 1986/7 West Ham U, Everton
Cowans, G. (10) 1982/3 Aston Villa, Bari, Aston Villa
Crawford, R. (2) 1961/2 Ipswich T
Crouch, P. J. (28) 2004/05 Southampton, Liverpool

Crowe, C. (1) 1962/3 Wolverhampton W
Cunningham, L. (6) 1978/9 WBA, Real Madrid
Curle, K. (3) 1991/2 Manchester C
Currie, A. (17) 1971/2 Sheffield U, Leeds U

Daley, A. M. (7) 1991/2 Aston Villa
Davenport, P. (1) 1984/5 Nottingham F
Deane, B. C. (3) 1990/1 Sheffield U
Deeley, N. (2) 1958/9 Wolverhampton W
Defoe, J. C. (28) 2003/04 Tottenham H, Portsmouth
Devonshire, A. (8) 1979/80 West Ham U
Dickinson, J. (48) 1948/9 Portsmouth
Ditchburn, E. (6) 1948/9 Tottenham H
Dixon, K. M. (8) 1984/5 Chelsea
Dixon, L. M. (22) 1989/90 Arsenal
Dobson, M. (5) 1973/4 Burnley, Everton
Dorigo, A. R. (15) 1989/90 Chelsea, Leeds U
Douglas, B. (36) 1957/8 Blackburn R
Downing, S. (18) 2004/05 Middlesbrough
Doyle, M. (5) 1975/6 Manchester C
Dublin, D. (4) 1997/8 Coventry C, Aston Villa
Dunn, D. J. I. (1) 2002/03 Blackburn R
Duxbury, M. (10) 1983/4 Manchester U
Dyer, K. C. (33) 1999/00 Newcastle U, West Ham U

Eastham, G. (19) 1962/3 Arsenal
Eckersley, W. (17) 1949/50 Blackburn R
Edwards, D. (18) 1954/5 Manchester U
Ehiogu, U. (4) 1995/6 Aston Villa, Middlesbrough
Ellerington, W. (2) 1948/9 Southampton
Elliott, W. H. (5) 1951/2 Burnley

Fantham, J. (1) 1961/2 Sheffield W
Fashanu, J. (2) 1988/9 Wimbledon
Fenwick, T. (20) 1983/4 QPR, Tottenham H
Ferdinand, L. (17) 1992/3 QPR, Newcastle U, Tottenham H
Ferdinand, R. G. (68) 1997/8 West Ham U, Leeds U, Manchester U
Finney, T. (76) 1946/7 Preston NE
Flowers, R. (49) 1954/5 Wolverhampton W

Flowers, T. (11) 1992/3 Southampton, Blackburn R
Foster, B. (1) 2006/07 Manchester U
Foster, S. (3) 1981/2 Brighton
Foulkes, W. (1) 1954/5 Manchester U
Fowler, R. B. (26) 1995/6 Liverpool, Leeds U
Francis, G. (12) 1974/5 QPR
Francis, T. (52) 1976/7 Birmingham C, Nottingham F, Manchester C, Sampdoria
Franklin, N. (27) 1946/7 Stoke C
Froggatt, J. (13) 1949/50 Portsmouth
Froggatt, R. (4) 1952/3 Sheffield W

Gardner, A. (1) 2003/04 Tottenham H
Garrett, T. (3) 1951/2 Blackpool
Gascoigne, P. J. (57) 1988/9 Tottenham H, Lazio, Rangers, Middlesbrough
Gates, E. (2) 1980/1 Ipswich T
George, F. C. (1) 1976/7 Derby Co
Gerrard, S. G. (67) 1999/00 Liverpool
Gidman, J. (1) 1976/7 Aston Villa
Gillard, I. (3) 1974/5 QPR
Goddard, P. (1) 1981/2 West Ham U
Grainger, C. (7) 1955/6 Sheffield U, Sunderland
Gray, A. A. (1) 1991/2 Crystal P
Gray, M. (3) 1998/9 Sunderland
Greaves, J. (57) 1958/9 Chelsea, Tottenham H
Green, R. P. (1) 2004/05 Norwich C
Greenhoff, B. (18) 1975/6 Manchester U, Leeds U
Gregory, J. (6) 1982/3 QPR
Guppy, S. (1) 1999/00 Leicester C

Hagan, J. (1) 1948/9 Sheffield U
Haines, J. (1) 1948/9 WBA
Hall, J. (17) 1955/6 Birmingham C
Hancocks, J. (3) 1948/9 Wolverhampton W
Hardwick, G. (13) 1946/7 Middlesbrough
Harford, M. G. (2) 1987/8 Luton T
Hargreaves, O. (42) 2001/02 Bayern Munich, Manchester U
Harris, G. (1) 1965/6 Burnley
Harris, P. (2) 1949/50 Portsmouth
Hart, C. (1) 2007/08 Manchester C
Harvey, C. (1) 1970/1 Everton
Hassall, H. (5) 1950/1 Huddersfield T, Bolton W
Hateley, M. (32) 1983/4 Portsmouth, AC Milan, Monaco, Rangers
Haynes, J. (56) 1954/5 Fulham
Hector, K. (2) 1973/4 Derby Co

Hellawell, M. (2) 1962/3 Birmingham C
Hendrie, L. A. (1) 1998/9 Aston Villa
Henry, R. (1) 1962/3 Tottenham H
Heskey, E. W. (45) 1998/9 Leicester C, Liverpool, Birmingham C, Wigan Ath
Hill, F. (2) 1962/3 Bolton W
Hill, G. (6) 1975/6 Manchester U
Hill, R. (3) 1982/3 Luton T
Hinchcliffe, A. G. (7) 1996/7 Everton, Sheffield W
Hinton, A. (3) 1962/3 Wolverhampton W, Nottingham F
Hirst, D. E. (3) 1990/1 Sheffield W
Hitchens, G. (7) 1960/1 Aston Villa, Internazionale
Hoddle, G. (53) 1979/80 Tottenham H, Monaco
Hodge, S. B. (24) 1985/6 Aston Villa, Tottenham H, Nottingham F
Hodgkinson, A. (5) 1956/7 Sheffield U
Holden, D. (5) 1958/9 Bolton W
Holliday, E. (3) 1959/60 Middlesbrough
Hollins, J. (1) 1966/7 Chelsea
Hopkinson, E. (14) 1957/8 Bolton W
Howe, D. (23) 1957/8 WBA
Howe, J. (3) 1947/8 Derby Co
Howey, S. N. (4) 1994/5 Newcastle U
Hudson, A. (2) 1974/5 Stoke C
Hughes, E. (62) 1969/70 Liverpool, Wolverhampton W
Hughes, L. (3) 1949/50 Liverpool
Hunt, R. (34) 1961/2 Liverpool
Hunt, S. (2) 1983/4 WBA
Hunter, N. (28) 1965/6 Leeds U
Hurst, G. (49) 1965/6 West Ham U

Ince, P. (53) 1992/3 Manchester U, Internazionale, Liverpool, Middlesbrough

Jagielka, P. N. (1) 2007/08 Everton
James, D. B. (39) 1996/7 Liverpool, Aston Villa, West Ham U, Manchester C, Portsmouth
Jeffers, F. (1) 2002/03 Arsenal
Jenas, J. A. (18) 2002/03 Newcastle U, Tottenham H
Jezzard, B. (2) 1953/4 Fulham
Johnson, A. (8) 2004/05 Crystal P, Everton
Johnson, D. (8) 1974/5 Ipswich T, Liverpool
Johnson, G. M. C. (8) 2003/04 Chelsea, Portsmouth
Johnson, S. A. M. (1) 2000/01 Derby Co

Johnston, H. (10) 1946/7 Blackpool
Jones, M. (3) 1964/5 Sheffield U, Leeds U
Jones, R. (8) 1991/2 Liverpool
Jones, W. H. (2) 1949/50 Liverpool

Kay, A. (1) 1962/3 Everton
Keegan, K. (63) 1972/3 Liverpool, SV Hamburg, Southampton
Kennedy, A. (2) 1983/4 Liverpool
Kennedy, R. (17) 1975/6 Liverpool
Keown, M. R. (43) 1991/2 Everton, Arsenal
Kevan, D. (14) 1956/7 WBA
Kidd, B. (2) 1969/70 Manchester U
King, L. B. (19) 2001/02 Tottenham H
Kirkland, C. E. (1) 2006/07 Liverpool
Knight, Z. (2) 2004/05 Fulham
Knowles, C. (4) 1967/8 Tottenham H
Konchesky, P. M. (2) 2002/03 Charlton Ath, West Ham U

Labone, B. (26) 1962/3 Everton
Lampard, F. J. (61) 1999/00 West Ham U, Chelsea
Lampard, F. R. G. (2) 1972/3 West Ham U
Langley, J. (3) 1957/8 Fulham
Langton, R. (11) 1946/7 Blackburn R, Preston NE, Bolton W
Latchford, R. (12) 1977/8 Everton
Lawler, C. (4) 1970/1 Liverpool
Lawton, T. (15) 1946/7 Chelsea, Notts Co
Lee, F. (27) 1968/9 Manchester C
Lee, J. (1) 1950/1 Derby C
Lee, R. M. (21) 1994/5 Newcastle U
Lee, S. (14) 1982/3 Liverpool
Lennon, A. J. (9) 2005/06 Tottenham H
Lescott, J. P. (5) 2007/08 Everton
Le Saux, G. P. (36) 1993/4 Blackburn R, Chelsea
Le Tissier, M. P. (8) 1993/4 Southampton
Lindsay, A. (4) 1973/4 Liverpool
Lineker, G. (80) 1983/4 Leicester C, Everton, Barcelona, Tottenham H
Little, B. (1) 1974/5 Aston Villa
Lloyd, L. (4) 1970/1 Liverpool, Nottingham F
Lofthouse, N. (33) 1950/1 Bolton W
Lowe, E. (3) 1946/7 Aston Villa

Mabbutt, G. (16) 1982/3 Tottenham H
Macdonald, M. (14) 1971/2 Newcastle U
Madeley, P. (24) 1970/1 Leeds U

Mannion, W. (26) 1946/7 Middlesbrough
Mariner, P. (35) 1976/7 Ipswich T, Arsenal
Marsh, R. (9) 1971/2 QPR, Manchester C
Martin, A. (17) 1980/1 West Ham U
Martyn, A. N. (23) 1991/2 Crystal P, Leeds U
Marwood, B. (1) 1988/9 Arsenal
Matthews, R. (5) 1955/6 Coventry C
Matthews, S. (37) 1946/7 Stoke C, Blackpool
McCann, G. P. (1) 2000/01 Sunderland
McDermott, T. (25) 1977/8 Liverpool
McDonald, C. (8) 1957/8 Burnley
McFarland, R. (28) 1970/1 Derby C
McGarry, W. (4) 1953/4 Huddersfield T
McGuinness, W. (2) 1958/9 Manchester U
McMahon, S. (17) 1987/8 Liverpool
McManaman, S. (37) 1994/5 Liverpool, Real Madrid
McNab, R. (4) 1968/9 Arsenal
McNeil, M. (9) 1960/1 Middlesbrough
Meadows, J. (1) 1954/5 Manchester C
Medley, L. (6) 1950/1 Tottenham H
Melia, J. (2) 1962/3 Liverpool
Merrick, G. (23) 1951/2 Birmingham C
Merson, P. C. (21) 1991/2 Arsenal, Middlesbrough, Aston Villa
Metcalfe, V. (2) 1950/1 Huddersfield T
Milburn, J. (13) 1948/9 Newcastle U
Miller, B. (1) 1960/1 Burnley
Mills, D. J. (19) 2000/01 Leeds U
Mills, M. (42) 1972/3 Ipswich T
Milne, G. (14) 1962/3 Liverpool
Milton, C. A. (1) 1951/2 Arsenal
Moore, R. (108) 1961/2 West Ham U
Morley, A. (6) 1981/2 Aston Villa
Morris, J. (3) 1948/9 Derby Co
Mortensen, S. (25) 1946/7 Blackpool
Mozley, B. (3) 1949/50 Derby Co
Mullen, J. (12) 1946/7 Wolverhampton W
Mullery, A. (35) 1964/5 Tottenham H
Murphy, D. B. (9) 2001/02 Liverpool

Neal, P. (50) 1975/6 Liverpool
Neville, G. A. (85) 1994/5 Manchester U
Neville, P. J. (59) 1995/6 Manchester U, Everton
Newton, K. (27) 1965/6 Blackburn R, Everton
Nicholls, J. (2) 1953/4 WBA
Nicholson, W. (1) 1950/1 Tottenham H
Nish, D. (5) 1972/3 Derby Co

Norman, M. (23) 1961/2 Tottenham H
Nugent, D. J. (1) 2006/07 Preston NE

O'Grady, M. (2) 1962/3 Huddersfield T, Leeds U
Osgood, P. (4) 1969/70 Chelsea
Osman, R. (11) 1979/80 Ipswich T
Owen, M. J. (89) 1997/8 Liverpool, Real Madrid, Newcastle U
Owen, S. (3) 1953/4 Luton T

Paine, T. (19) 1962/3 Southampton
Pallister, G. (22) 1987/8 Middlesbrough, Manchester U
Palmer, C. L. (18) 1991/2 Sheffield W
Parker, P. A. (19) 1988/9 QPR, Manchester U
Parker, S. M. (3) 2003/04 Charlton Ath, Chelsea, Newcastle U
Parkes, P. (1) 1973/4 QPR
Parlour, R. (10) 1998/9 Arsenal
Parry, R. (2) 1959/60 Bolton W
Peacock, A. (6) 1961/2 Middlesbrough, Leeds U
Pearce, S. (78) 1986/7 Nottingham F, West Ham U
Pearson, Stan (8) 1947/8 Manchester U
Pearson, Stuart (15) 1975/6 Manchester U
Pegg, D. (1) 1956/7 Manchester U
Pejic, M. (4) 1973/4 Stoke C
Perry, W. (3) 1955/6 Blackpool
Perryman, S. (1) 1981/2 Tottenham H
Peters, M. (67) 1965/6 West Ham U, Tottenham H
Phelan, M. C. (1) 1989/90 Manchester U
Phillips, K. (8) 1998/9 Sunderland
Phillips, L. (3) 1951/2 Portsmouth
Pickering, F. (3) 1963/4 Everton
Pickering, N. (1) 1982/3 Sunderland
Pilkington, B. (1) 1954/5 Burnley
Platt, D. (62) 1989/90 Aston Villa, Bari, Juventus, Sampdoria, Arsenal
Pointer, R. (3) 1961/2 Burnley
Powell, C. G. (5) 2000/01 Charlton Ath
Pye, J. (1) 1949/50 Wolverhampton W

Quixall, A. (5) 1953/4 Sheffield W

Radford, J. (2) 1968/9 Arsenal
Ramsey, A. (32) 1948/9 Southampton, Tottenham H
Reaney, P. (3) 1968/9 Leeds U
Redknapp, J. F. (17) 1995/6 Liverpool
Reeves, K. (2) 1979/80 Norwich C, Manchester C
Regis, C. (5) 1981/2 WBA, Coventry C
Reid, P. (13) 1984/5 Everton

Revie, D. (6) 1954/5 Manchester C
Richards, J. (1) 1972/3 Wolverhampton W
Richards, M. (11) 2006/07 Manchester C
Richardson, K. (1) 1993/4 Aston Villa
Richardson, K. E. (8) 2004/05 Manchester U
Rickaby, S. (1) 1953/4 WBA
Ricketts, M. B. (1) 2001/02 Bolton W
Rimmer, J. (1) 1975/6 Arsenal
Ripley, S. E. (2) 1993/4 Blackburn R
Rix, G. (17) 1980/1 Arsenal
Robb, G. (1) 1953/4 Tottenham H
Roberts, G. (6) 1982/3 Tottenham H
Robinson, P. W. (41) 2002/03 Leeds U, Tottenham H
Robson, B. (90) 1979/80 WBA, Manchester U
Robson, R. (20) 1957/8 WBA
Rocastle, D. (14) 1988/9 Arsenal
Rooney, W. (43) 2002/03 Everton, Manchester U
Rowley, J. (6) 1948/9 Manchester U
Royle, J. (6) 1970/1 Everton, Manchester C
Ruddock, N. (1) 1994/5 Liverpool

Sadler, D. (4) 1967/8 Manchester U
Salako, J. A. (5) 1990/1 Crystal P
Sansom, K. (86) 1978/9 Crystal P, Arsenal
Scales, J. R. (3) 1994/5 Liverpool
Scholes, P. (66) 1996/7 Manchester U
Scott, L. (17) 1946/7 Arsenal
Seaman, D. A. (75) 1988/9 QPR, Arsenal
Sewell, J. (6) 1951/2 Sheffield W
Shackleton, L. (5) 1948/9 Sunderland
Sharpe, L. S. (8) 1990/1 Manchester U
Shaw, G. (5) 1958/9 Sheffield U
Shearer, A. (63) 1991/2 Southampton, Blackburn R, Newcastle U
Shellito, K. (1) 1962/3 Chelsea
Sheringham, E. (51) 1992/3 Tottenham H, Manchester U, Tottenham H
Sherwood, T. A. (3) 1998/9 Tottenham H
Shilton, P. (125) 1970/1 Leicester C, Stoke C, Nottingham F, Southampton, Derby Co
Shimwell, E. (1) 1948/9 Blackpool
Shorey, N, (2) 2006/07 Reading
Sillett, P. (3) 1954/5 Chelsea
Sinclair, T. (12) 2001/02 West Ham U, Manchester C
Sinton, A. (12) 1991/2 QPR, Sheffield W

Slater, W. (12) 1954/5 Wolverhampton W

Smith, A. (19) 2000/01 Leeds U, Manchester U, Newcastle U

Smith, A. M. (13) 1988/9 Arsenal

Smith, L. (6) 1950/1 Arsenal

Smith, R. (15) 1960/1 Tottenham H

Smith, Tom (1) 1970/1 Liverpool

Smith, Trevor (2) 1959/60 Birmingham C

Southgate, G. (57) 1995/6 Aston Villa, Middlesbrough

Spink, N. (1) 1982/3 Aston Villa

Springett, R. (33) 1959/60 Sheffield W

Staniforth, R. (8) 1953/4 Huddersfield T

Statham, D. (3) 1982/3 WBA

Stein, B. (1) 1983/4 Luton T

Stepney, A. (1) 1967/8 Manchester U

Sterland, M. (1) 1988/9 Sheffield W

Steven, T. M. (36) 1984/5 Everton, Rangers, Marseille

Stevens, G. A. (7) 1984/5 Tottenham H

Stevens, M. G. (46) 1984/5 Everton, Rangers

Stewart, P. A. (3) 1991/2 Tottenham H

Stiles, N. (28) 1964/5 Manchester U

Stone, S. B. (9) 1995/6 Nottingham F

Storey-Moore, I. (1) 1969/70 Nottingham F

Storey, P. (19) 1970/1 Arsenal

Streten, B. (1) 1949/50 Luton T

Summerbee, M. (8) 1967/8 Manchester C

Sunderland, A. (1) 1979/80 Arsenal

Sutton, C. R. (1) 1997/8 Blackburn R

Swan, P. (19) 1959/60 Sheffield W

Swift, F. (19) 1946/7 Manchester C

Talbot, B. (6) 1976/7 Ipswich T, Arsenal

Tambling, R. (3) 1962/3 Chelsea

Taylor, E. (1) 1953/4 Blackpool

Taylor, J. (2) 1950/1 Fulham

Taylor, P. H. (3) 1947/8 Liverpool

Taylor, P. J. (4) 1975/6 Crystal P

Taylor, T. (19) 1952/3 Manchester U

Temple, D. (1) 1964/5 Everton

Terry, J. G. (44) 2002/03 Chelsea

Thomas, Danny (2) 1982/3 Coventry C

Thomas, Dave (8) 1974/5 QPR

Thomas, G. R. (9) 1990/1 Crystal P

Thomas, M. L. (2) 1988/9 Arsenal

Thompson, A. (1) 2003/04 Celtic

Thompson, P. (16) 1963/4 Liverpool

Thompson, P. B. (42) 1975/6 Liverpool

Thompson, T. (2) 1951/2 Aston Villa, Preston NE

Thomson, R. (8) 1963/4 Wolverhampton W

Todd, C. (27) 1971/2 Derby Co

Towers, T. (3) 1975/6 Sunderland

Tueart, D. (6) 1974/5 Manchester C

Ufton, D. (1) 1953/4 Charlton Ath

Unsworth, D. G. (1) 1994/5 Everton

Upson, M. J. (8) 2002/03 Birmingham C, West Ham U

Vassell, D. (22) 2001/02 Aston Villa

Venables, T. (2) 1964/5 Chelsea

Venison, B. (2) 1994/5 Newcastle U

Viljoen, C. (2) 1974/5 Ipswich T

Viollet, D. (2) 1959/60 Manchester U

Waddle, C. R. (62) 1984/5 Newcastle U, Tottenham H, Marseille

Waiters, A. (5) 1963/4 Blackpool

Walcott, T. J. (2) 2005/06 Arsenal

Walker, D. S. (59) 1988/9 Nottingham F, Sampdoria, Sheffield W

Walker, I. M. (4) 1995/6 Tottenham H, Leicester C

Wallace, D. L. (1) 1985/6 Southampton

Walsh, P. (5) 1982/3 Luton T

Walters, K. M. (1) 1990/1 Rangers

Ward, P. (1) 1979/80 Brighton

Ward, T. (2) 1947/8 Derby Co

Warnock, S. (2) 2007/08 Blackburn R

Watson, D. (12) 1983/4 Norwich C, Everton

Watson, D. V. (65) 1973/4 Sunderland, Manchester C, Werder Bremen, Southampton, Stoke C

Watson, W. (4) 1949/50 Sunderland

Webb, N. (26) 1987/8 Nottingham F, Manchester U

Weller, K. (4) 1973/4 Leicester C

West, G. (3) 1968/9 Everton

Wheeler, J. (1) 1954/5 Bolton W

White, D. (1) 1992/3 Manchester C

Whitworth, S. (7) 1974/5 Leicester C

Whymark, T. (1) 1977/8 Ipswich T

Wignall, F. (2) 1964/5 Nottingham F

Wilcox, J. M. (3) 1995/6 Blackburn R, Leeds U

Wilkins, R. (84) 1975/6 Chelsea, Manchester U, AC Milan

Williams, B. (24) 1948/9 Wolverhampton W

Williams, S. (6) 1982/3 Southampton

Willis, A. (1) 1951/2 Tottenham H

Wilshaw, D. (12) 1953/4 Wolverhampton W

Wilson, R. (63) 1959/60 Huddersfield T, Everton

Winterburn, N. (2) 1989/90 Arsenal

Wise, D. F. (21) 1990/1 Chelsea
Withe, P. (11) 1980/1 Aston Villa
Wood, R. (3) 1954/5 Manchester U
Woodcock, A. (42) 1977/8 Nottingham
F, FC Cologne, Arsenal
Woodgate, J. S. (7) 1998/9 Leeds U,
Newcastle U, Real Madrid,
Tottenham H
Woods, C. C. E. (43) 1984/5 Norwich
C, Rangers, Sheffield W
Worthington, F. (8) 1973/4 Leicester C
Wright, I. E. (33) 1990/1 Crystal P,
Arsenal, West Ham U

Wright, M. (45) 1983/4 Southampton,
Derby C, Liverpool
Wright, R. I. (2) 1999/00 Ipswich T,
Arsenal
Wright, T. (11) 1967/8 Everton
Wright, W. (105) 1946/7
Wolverhampton W
Wright-Phillips, S. C. (19) 2004/05
Manchester C, Chelsea

Young, A. S. (3) 2007/08 Aston Villa
Young, G. (1) 1964/5 Sheffield W
Young, L. P. (7) 2004/05 Charlton Ath

NORTHERN IRELAND

Aherne, T. (4) 1946/7 Belfast Celtic,
Luton T
Anderson, T. (22) 1972/3 Manchester
U, Swindon T, Peterborough U
Armstrong, G. (63) 1976/7 Tottenham
H, Watford, Real Mallorca, WBA,
Chesterfield

Baird, C. P. (32) 2002/03
Southampton, Fulham
Barr, H. (3) 1961/2 Linfield, Coventry
C
Best, G. (37) 1963/4 Manchester U,
Fulham
Bingham, W. (56) 1950/1 Sunderland,
Luton T, Everton, Port Vale
Black, K. (30) 1987/8 Luton T,
Nottingham F
Blair, R. (5) 1974/5 Oldham Ath
Blanchflower, D. (54) 1949/50
Barnsley, Aston Villa, Tottenham H
Blanchflower, J. (12) 1953/4
Manchester U
Blayney, A. (1) 2005/06 Doncaster R
Bowler, G. (3) 1949/50 Hull C
Braithwaite, R. (10) 1961/2 Linfield,
Middlesbrough
Brennan, R. (5) 1948/9 Luton T,
Birmingham C, Fulham
Briggs, R. (2) 1961/2 Manchester U,
Swansea
Brotherston, N. (27) 1979/80
Blackburn R
Bruce, W. (2) 1960/1 Glentoran
Brunt, C. (17) 2004/05 Sheffield W,
WBA

Campbell, A. (2) 1962/3 Crusaders
Campbell, D. A. (10) 1985/6
Nottingham F, Charlton Ath
Campbell, J. (2) 1950/1 Fulham
Campbell, R. M. (2) 1981/2 Bradford C

Campbell, W. (6) 1967/8 Dundee
Capaldi, A. C. (22) 2003/04 Plymouth
Arg, Cardiff C
Carey, J. (7) 1946/7 Manchester U
Carroll, R. E. (19) 1996/7 Wigan Ath,
Manchester U, West Ham U
Casey, T. (12) 1954/5 Newcastle U,
Portsmouth
Caskey, A. (8) 1978/9 Derby C, Tulsa
Roughnecks
Cassidy, T. (24) 1970/1 Newcastle U,
Burnley
Caughey, M. (2) 1985/6 Linfield
Clarke, C. J. (38) 1985/6
Bournemouth, Southampton,
Portsmouth
Cleary, J. (5) 1981/2 Glentoran
Clements, D. (48) 1964/5 Coventry C,
Sheffield W, Everton, New York
Cosmos
Clingan, S. G. (15) 2005/06
Nottingham F
Clyde, M.G. (3) 2004/05
Wolverhampon W
Cochrane, D. (10) 1946/7 Leeds U
Cochrane, T. (26) 1975/6 Coleraine,
Burnley, Middlesbrough,
Gillingham
Connell, T. E. (1) 1977/8 Coleraine
Coote, A. (6) 1998/9 Norwich C
Cowan, J. (1) 1969/70 Newcastle U
Coyle, F. (4) 1955/6 Coleraine,
Nottingham F
Coyle, L. (1) 1988/9 Derry C
Coyle, R. (5) 1972/3 Sheffield W
Craig, D. (25) 1966/7 Newcastle U
Craigan, S. (35) 2002/03 Partick T,
Motherwell
Crossan, E. (3) 1949/50 Blackburn R
Crossan, J. (24) 1959/60 Sparta
Rotterdam, Sunderland, Manchester
C, Middlesbrough

Cunningham, W. (30) 1950/1 St Mirren, Leicester C, Dunfermline Ath

Cush, W. (26) 1950/1 Glentoran, Leeds U, Portadown

D'Arcy, S. (5) 1951/2 Chelsea, Brentford

Davis, S. (28) 2004/05 Aston Villa, Fulham

Davison, A. J. (3) 1995/6 Bolton W, Bradford C, Grimsby T

Dennison, R. (18) 1987/8 Wolverhampton W

Devine, J. (1) 1989/90 Glentoran

Dickson, D. (4) 1969/70 Coleraine

Dickson, T. (1) 1956/7 Linfield

Dickson, W. (12) 1950/1 Chelsea, Arsenal

Doherty, L. (2) 1984/5 Linfield

Doherty, P. (6) 1946/7 Derby Co, Huddersfield T, Doncaster R

Doherty, T. E. (9) 2002/03 Bristol C

Donaghy, M. (91) 1979/80 Luton T, Manchester U, Chelsea

Dougan, D. (43) 1957/8 Portsmouth, Blackburn R, Aston Villa, Leicester C, Wolverhampton W

Douglas, J. P. (1) 1946/7 Belfast Celtic

Dowd, H. (3) 1973/4 Glenavon, Sheffield W

Dowie, I. (59) 1989/90 Luton T, West Ham U, Southampton, Crystal P, West Ham U, QPR

Duff, M. J. (20) 2001/02 Cheltenham T, Burnley

Dunlop, G. (4) 1984/5 Linfield

Eglington, T. (6) 1946/7 Everton

Elder, A. (40) 1959/60 Burnley, Stoke C

Elliott, S. (39) 2000/01 Motherwell, Hull C

Evans, J. G. (10) 2006/07 Manchester U

Farrell, P. (7) 1946/7 Everton

Feeney, J. (2) 1946/7 Linfield, Swansea T

Feeney, W. (1) 1975/6 Glentoran

Feeney, W. J. (24) 2001/02 Bournemouth, Luton T, Cardiff C

Ferguson, G. (5) 1998/9 Linfield

Ferguson, W. (2) 1965/6 Linfield

Ferris, R. (3) 1949/50 Birmingham C

Fettis, A. (25) 1991/2 Hull C, Nottingham F, Blackburn R

Finney, T. (14) 1974/5 Sunderland, Cambridge U

Fleming, J. G. (31) 1986/7 Nottingham F, Manchester C, Barnsley

Forde, T. (4) 1958/9 Ards

Gallogly, C. (2) 1950/1 Huddersfield T

Garton, R. (1) 1968/9 Oxford U

Gault, M. (1) 2007/08 Linfield

Gillespie, K. R. (81) 1994/5 Manchester U, Newcastle U, Blackburn R, Leicester C, Sheffield U

Gorman, W. (4) 1946/7 Brentford

Graham, W. (14) 1950/1 Doncaster R

Gray, P. (26) 1992/3 Luton T, Sunderland, Nancy, Luton T, Burnley, Oxford U

Gregg, H. (25) 1953/4 Doncaster R, Manchester U

Griffin, D. J. (29) 1995/6 St Johnstone, Dundee U, Stockport Co

Hamill, R. (1) 1998/9 Glentoran

Hamilton, B. (50) 1968/9 Linfield, Ipswich T, Everton, Millwall, Swindon T

Hamilton, G. (5) 2002/03 Portadown

Hamilton, W. (41) 1977/8 QPR, Burnley, Oxford U

Harkin, T. (5) 1967/8 Southport, Shrewsbury T

Harvey, M. (34) 1960/1 Sunderland

Hatton, S. (2) 1962/3 Linfield

Healy, D. J. (64) 1999/00 Manchester U, Preston NE, Leeds U, Fulham

Healy, P. J. (4) 1981/2 Coleraine, Glentoran

Hegan, D. (7) 1969/70 WBA, Wolverhampton W

Hill, C. F. (27) 1989/90 Sheffield U, Leicester C, Trelleborg, Northampton T

Hill, J. (7) 1958/9 Norwich C, Everton

Hinton, E. (7) 1946/7 Fulham, Millwall

Holmes, S. P. (1) 2001/02 Wrexham

Horlock, K. (32) 1994/5 Swindon T, Manchester C

Hughes, A. W. (59) 1997/8 Newcastle U, Aston Villa, Fulham

Hughes, J, (2) 2005/06 Lincoln C

Hughes, M. A. (2) 2005/06 Oldham Ath

Hughes, M. E. (71) 1991/2 Manchester C, Strasbourg, West Ham U, Wimbledon, Crystal P

Hughes, P. (3) 1986/7 Bury

Hughes, W. (1) 1950/1 Bolton W

Humphries, W. (14) 1961/2 Ards, Coventry C, Swansea T

Hunter, A. (53) 1969/70 Blackburn R, Ipswich T
Hunter, B. V. (15) 1994/5 Wrexham, Reading
Hunter, V. (2) 1961/2 Coleraine

Ingham, M. G. (3) 2004/05 Sunderland, Wrexham
Irvine, R. (8) 1961/2 Linfield, Stoke C
Irvine, W. (23) 1962/3 Burnley, Preston NE, Brighton & HA

Jackson, T. (35) 1968/9 Everton, Nottingham F, Manchester U
Jamison, A. (1) 1975/6 Glentoran
Jenkins, I. (6) 1996/7 Chester C, Dundee U
Jennings, P. (119) 1963/4 Watford, Tottenham H, Arsenal, Tottenham H
Johnson, D. M. (48) 1998/9 Blackburn R, Birmingham C
Johnston, W. (2) 1961/2 Glenavon, Oldham Ath
Jones, J. (3) 1955/6 Glenavon
Jones, S. G. (29) 2002/03 Crewe Alex, Burnley

Keane, T. (1) 1948/9 Swansea T
Kee, P. V. (9) 1989/90 Oxford U, Ards
Keith, R. (23) 1957/8 Newcastle U
Kelly, H. (4) 1949/50 Fulham, Southampton
Kelly, P. (1) 1949/50 Barnsley
Kennedy, P. H. (20) 1998/9 Watford, Wigan Ath
Kirk, A. R. (8) 1999/00 Heart of Midlothian, Boston U, Northampton T

Lafferty, K. (16) 2005/06 Burnley
Lawther, I. (4) 1959/60 Sunderland, Blackburn R
Lennon, N. F. (40) 1993/4 Crewe Alex, Leicester C, Celtic
Lockhart, N. (8) 1946/7 Linfield, Coventry C, Aston Villa
Lomas, S. M. (45) 1993/4 Manchester C, West Ham U
Lutton, B. (6) 1969/70 Wolverhampton W, West Ham U

Magill, E. (26) 1961/2 Arsenal, Brighton & HA
Magilton, J. (52) 1990/1 Oxford U, Southampton, Sheffield W, Ipswich T
Mannus, A. (3) 2003/04 Linfield
Martin, C. (6) 1946/7 Glentoran, Leeds U, Aston Villa

McAdams, W. (15) 1953/4 Manchester C, Bolton W, Leeds U
McAlinden, J. (2) 1946/7 Portsmouth, Southend U
McAuley, G. (10) 2004/05 Lincoln C, Leicester C
McBride, S. (4) 1990/1 Glenavon
McCabe, J. (6) 1948/9 Leeds U
McCann, G. S. (16) 2001/02 West Ham U, Cheltenham T, Barnsley, Scunthorpe U
McCarthy, J. D. (18) 1995/6 Port Vale, Birmingham C
McCartney, G. (25) 2001/02 Sunderland, West Ham U
McCavana, T. (3) 1954/5 Coleraine
McCleary, J. W. (1) 1954/5 Cliftonville
McClelland, J. (6) 1960/1 Arsenal, Fulham
McClelland, J. (53) 1979/80 Mansfield T, Rangers, Watford, Leeds U
McCourt, F. (6) 1951/2 Manchester C
McCourt, P. J. (1) 2001/02 Rochdale
McCoy, R. (1) 1986/7 Coleraine
McCreery, D. (67) 1975/6 Manchester U, QPR, Tulsa Roughnecks, Newcastle U, Heart of Midlothian
McCrory, S. (1) 1957/8 Southend U
McCullough, W. (10) 1960/1 Arsenal, Millwall
McCurdy, C. (1) 1979/80 Linfield
McDonald, A. (52) 1985/6 QPR
McElhinney, G. (6) 1983/4 Bolton W
McEvilly, L. R. (1) 2001/02 Rochdale
McFaul, I. (6) 1966/7 Linfield, Newcastle U
McGarry, J. K. (3) 1950/1 Cliftonville
McGaughey, M. (1) 1984/5 Linfield
McGibbon, P. C. G. (7) 1994/5 Manchester U, Wigan Ath
McGrath, R. (21) 1973/4 Tottenham H, Manchester U
McIlroy, J. (55) 1951/2 Burnley, Stoke C
McIlroy, S. B. (88) 1971/2 Manchester U, Stoke C, Manchester C
McKeag, W. (2) 1967/8 Glentoran
McKenna, J. (7) 1949/50 Huddersfield T
McKenzie, R. (1) 1966/7 Airdrieonians
McKinney, W. (1) 1965/6 Falkirk
McKnight, A. (10) 1987/8 Celtic, West Ham U
McLaughlin, J. (12) 1961/2 Shrewsbury T, Swansea T
McLean, B. S. (1) 2005/06 Rangers
McMahon, G. J. (17) 1994/5 Tottenham H, Stoke C
McMichael, A. (39) 1949/50 Newcastle U

303

McMillan, S. (2) 1962/3 Manchester U
McMordie, E. (21) 1968/9 Middlesbrough
McMorran, E. (15) 1946/7 Belfast Celtic, Barnsley, Doncaster R
McNally, B. A. (5) 1985/6 Shrewsbury T
McParland, P. (34) 1953/4 Aston Villa, Wolverhampton W
McVeigh, P. (20) 1998/9 Tottenham H, Norwich C
Montgomery, F. J. (1) 1954/5 Coleraine
Moore, C. (1) 1948/9 Glentoran
Moreland, V. (6) 1978/9 Derby Co
Morgan, S. (18) 1971/2 Port Vale, Aston Villa, Brighton & HA, Sparta Rotterdam
Morrow, S. J. (39) 1989/90 Arsenal, QPR
Mullan, G. (4) 1982/3 Glentoran
Mulryne, P. P. (27) 1996/7 Manchester U, Norwich C, Cardiff C
Murdock, C. J. (34) 1999/00 Preston NE, Hibernian, Crewe Alex, Rotherham U

Napier, R. (1) 1965/6 Bolton W
Neill, T. (59) 1960/1 Arsenal, Hull C
Nelson, S. (51) 1969/70 Arsenal, Brighton & HA
Nicholl, C. (51) 1974/5 Aston Villa, Southampton, Grimsby T
Nicholl, J. M. (73) 1975/6 Manchester U, Toronto Blizzard, Sunderland, Rangers, WBA
Nicholson, J. (41) 1960/1 Manchester U, Huddersfield T
Nolan, I. R. (18) 1996/7 Sheffield W, Bradford C, Wigan Ath

O'Boyle, G. (13) 1993/4 Dunfermline Ath, St Johnstone
O'Connor, M. J. (1) 2007/08 Crewe Alex
O'Doherty, A. (2) 1969/70 Coleraine
O'Driscoll, J. (3) 1948/9 Swansea T
O'Kane, L. (20) 1969/70 Nottingham F
O'Neill, C. (3) 1988/9 Motherwell
O'Neill, H. M. (64) 1971/2 Distillery, Nottingham F, Norwich C, Manchester C, Norwich C, Notts Co
O'Neill, J. (1) 1961/2 Sunderland
O'Neill, J. P. (39) 1979/80 Leicester C
O'Neill, M. A. (31) 1987/8 Newcastle U, Dundee U, Hibernian, Coventry C

Parke, J. (13) 1963/4 Linfield, Hibernian, Sunderland

Paterson, M. A. (2) 2007/08 Scunthorpe U
Patterson, D. J. (17) 1993/4 Crystal P, Luton T, Dundee U
Peacock, R. (31) 1951/2 Celtic, Coleraine
Penney, S. (17) 1984/5 Brighton & HA
Platt, J. A. (23) 1975/6 Middlesbrough, Ballymena U, Coleraine

Quinn, J. M. (46) 1984/5 Blackburn R, Swindon T, Leicester, Bradford C, West Ham U, Bournemouth, Reading
Quinn, S. J. (50) 1995/6 Blackpool, WBA, Willem II, Sheffield W, Peterborough U, Northampton T

Rafferty, P. (1) 1979/80 Linfield
Ramsey, P. (14) 1983/4 Leicester C
Rice, P. (49) 1968/9 Arsenal
Robinson, S. (7) 1996/7 Bournemouth, Luton T
Rogan, A. (18) 1987/8 Celtic, Sunderland, Millwall
Ross, E. (1) 1968/9 Newcastle U
Rowland, K. (19) 1994/5 West Ham U, QPR
Russell, A. (1) 1946/7 Linfield
Ryan, R. (1) 1949/50 WBA

Sanchez, L. P. (3) 1986/7 Wimbledon
Scott, J. (2) 1957/8 Grimsby T
Scott, P. (10) 1974/5 Everton, York C, Aldershot
Sharkey, P. (1) 1975/6 Ipswich T
Shields, J. (1) 1956/7 Southampton
Shiels, D. (4) 2005/06 Hibernian
Simpson, W. (12) 1950/1 Rangers
Sloan, D. (2) 1968/9 Oxford
Sloan, T. (3) 1978/9 Manchester U
Sloan, W. (1) 1946/7 Arsenal
Smith, A. W. (18) 2002/03 Glentoran, Preston NE
Smyth, S. (9) 1947/8 Wolverhampton W, Stoke C
Smyth, W. (4) 1948/9 Distillery
Sonner, D. J. (13) 1997/8 Ipswich T, Sheffield W, Birmingham C, Nottingham F, Peterborough U
Spence, D. (29) 1974/5 Bury, Blackpool, Southend U
Sproule, I. (11) 2005/06 Hibernian, Bristol C
Stevenson, A. (3) 1946/7 Everton
Stewart, A. (7) 1966/7 Glentoran, Derby
Stewart, D. (1) 1977/8 Hull C

Stewart, I. (31) 1981/2 QPR, Newcastle U
Stewart, T. (1) 1960/1 Linfield

Taggart, G. P. (51) 1989/90 Barnsley, Bolton W, Leicester C
Taylor, M. S. (68) 1998/9 Fulham, Birmingham C
Thompson, P. (7) 2005/06 Linfield
Todd, S. (11) 1965/6 Burnley, Sheffield W
Toner, C. (2) 2002/03 Leyton Orient
Trainor, D. (1) 1966/7 Crusaders
Tully, C. (10) 1948/9 Celtic

Uprichard, N. (18) 1951/2 Swindon T, Portsmouth

Vernon, J. (17) 1946/7 Belfast Celtic, WBA

Walker, J. (1) 1954/5 Doncaster R
Walsh, D. (9) 1946/7 WBA
Walsh, W. (5) 1947/8 Manchester C

Watson, P. (1) 1970/1 Distillery
Webb, S. M. (4) 2005/06 Ross Co
Welsh, S. (4) 1965/6 Carlisle U
Whiteside, N. (38) 1981/2 Manchester U, Everton
Whitley, Jeff (20) 1996/7 Manchester C, Sunderland, Cardiff C
Whitley, Jim (3) 1997/8 Manchester C
Williams, M. S. (36) 1998/9 Chesterfield, Watford, Wimbledon, Stoke C, Wimbledon, Milton Keynes D
Williams, P. (1) 1990/1 WBA
Wilson, D. J. (24) 1986/7 Brighton & HA, Luton, Sheffield W
Wilson, K. J. (42) 1986/7 Ipswich T, Chelsea, Notts C, Walsall
Wilson, S. (12) 1961/2 Glenavon, Falkirk, Dundee
Wood, T. J. (1) 1995/6 Walsall
Worthington, N. (66) 1983/4 Sheffield W, Leeds U, Stoke C
Wright, T. J. (31) 1988/9 Newcastle U, Nottingham F, Manchester C

SCOTLAND

Adam, C. G. (2) 2006/07 Rangers
Aird, J. (4) 1953/4 Burnley
Aitken, G. G. (8) 1948/9 East Fife, Sunderland
Aitken, R. (57) 1979/80 Celtic, Newcastle U, St Mirren
Albiston, A. (14) 1981/2 Manchester U
Alexander, G. (33) 2001/02 Preston NE, Burnley
Alexander, N. (3) 2005/06 Cardiff C
Allan, T. (2) 1973/4 Dundee
Anderson, J. (1) 1953/4 Leicester C
Anderson, R. (11) 2002/03 Aberdeen, Sunderland
Archibald, S. (27) 1979/80 Aberdeen, Tottenham H, Barcelona
Auld, B. (3) 1958/9 Celtic

Baird, H. (1) 1955/6 Airdrieonians
Baird, S. (7) 1956/7 Rangers
Bannon, E. (11) 1979/80 Dundee U
Bauld, W. (3) 1949/50 Heart of Midlothian
Baxter, J. (34) 1960/1 Rangers, Sunderland
Beattie, C. (7) 2005/06 Celtic, WBA
Bell, W. (2) 1965/6 Leeds U
Bernard, P. R. (2) 1994/5 Oldham Ath
Berra, C. (1) 2007/08 Heart of Midlothian

Bett, J. (25) 1981/2 Rangers, Lokeren, Aberdeen
Black, E. (2) 1987/8 Metz
Black, I. (1) 1947/8 Southampton
Blacklaw, A. (3) 1962/3 Burnley
Blackley, J. (7) 1973/4 Hibernian
Blair, J. (1) 1946/7 Blackpool
Blyth, J. (2) 1977/8 Coventry C
Bone, J. (2) 1971/2 Norwich C
Booth, S. (21) 1992/3 Aberdeen, Borussia Dortmund, Twente
Bowman, D. (6) 1991/2 Dundee U
Boyd, K. (14) 2005/06 Rangers
Boyd, T. (72) 1990/1 Motherwell, Chelsea, Celtic
Brand, R. (8) 1960/1 Rangers
Brazil, A. (13) 1979/80 Ipswich T, Tottenham H
Bremner, D. (1) 1975/6 Hibernian
Bremner, W. (54) 1964/5 Leeds U
Brennan, F. (7) 1946/7 Newcastle U
Brogan, J. (4) 1970/1 Celtic
Brown, A. (14) 1949/50 East Fife, Blackpool
Brown, H. (3) 1946/7 Partick Th
Brown, J. (1) 1974/5 Sheffield U
Brown, R. (3) 1946/7 Rangers
Brown, S. (9) 2005/06 Hibernian, Celtic
Brown, W. (28) 1957/8 Dundee, Tottenham H

Brownlie, J. (7) 1970/1 Hibernian
Buchan, M. (34) 1971/2 Aberdeen, Manchester U
Buckley, P. (3) 1953/4 Aberdeen
Burchill, M. J. (6) 1999/00 Celtic
Burke, C. (2) 2005/06 Rangers
Burley, C. W. (46) 1994/5 Chelsea, Celtic, Derby Co
Burley, G. (11) 1978/9 Ipswich T
Burns, F. (1) 1969/70 Manchester U
Burns, K. (20) 1973/4 Birmingham C, Nottingham F
Burns, T. (8) 1980/1 Celtic

Calderwood, C. (36) 1994/5 Tottenham H, Aston Villa
Caldow, E. (40) 1956/7 Rangers
Caldwell, G. (27) 2001/02 Newcastle U, Hibernian, Celtic
Caldwell, S. (9) 2000/01 Newcastle U, Sunderland
Callaghan, W. (2) 1969/70 Dunfermline
Cameron, C. (28) 1998/9 Heart of Midlothian, Wolverhampton W
Campbell, R. (5) 1946/7 Falkirk, Chelsea
Campbell, W. (5) 1946/7 Morton
Canero, P. (1) 2003/04 Leicester C
Carr, W. (6) 1969/70 Coventry C
Chalmers, S. (5) 1964/5 Celtic
Clark, J. (4) 1965/6 Celtic
Clark, R. (17) 1967/8 Aberdeen
Clarke, S. (6) 1987/8 Chelsea
Clarkson, D. (1) 2007/08 Motherwell
Collins, J. (58) 1987/8 Hibernian, Celtic, Monaco, Everton
Collins, R. (31) 1950/1 Celtic, Everton, Leeds U
Colquhoun, E. (9) 1971/2 Sheffield U
Colquhoun, J. (2) 1987/8 Heart of Midlothian
Combe, R. (3) 1947/8 Hibernian
Conn, A. (1) 1955/6 Heart of Midlothian
Conn, A. (2) 1974/5 Tottenham H
Connachan, E. (2) 1961/2 Dunfermline Ath
Connelly, G. (2) 1973/4 Celtic
Connolly, J. (1) 1972/3 Everton
Connor, R. (4) 1985/6 Dundee, Aberdeen
Cooke, C. (16) 1965/6 Dundee, Chelsea
Cooper, D. (22) 1979/80 Rangers, Motherwell
Cormack, P. (9) 1965/6 Hibernian, Nottingham F
Cowan, J. (25) 1947/8 Morton

Cowie, D. (20) 1952/3 Dundee
Cox, C. (1) 1947/8 Heart of Midlothian
Cox, S. (24) 1947/8 Rangers
Craig, J. (1) 1976/7 Celtic
Craig, J. P. (1) 1967/8 Celtic
Craig, T. (1) 1975/6 Newcastle U
Crainey, S. (6) 2001/02 Celtic, Southampton
Crawford, S. (25) 1994/5 Raith R, Dunfermline Ath, Plymouth Arg
Crerand, P. (16) 1960/1 Celtic, Manchester U
Cropley, A. (2) 1971/2 Hibernian
Cruickshank, J. (6) 1963/4 Heart of Midlothian
Cullen, M. (1) 1955/6 Luton T
Cumming, J. (9) 1954/5 Heart of Midlothian
Cummings. W. (1) 2001/02 Chelsea
Cunningham, W. (8) 1953/4 Preston NE
Curran, H. (5) 1969/70 Wolverhampton W

Dailly, C. (67) 1996/7 Derby Co, Blackburn R, West Ham U, Rangers
Dalglish, K. (102) 1971/2 Celtic, Liverpool
Davidson, C. I. (17) 1998/9 Blackburn R, Leicester C
Davidson, J. (8) 1953/4 Partick Th
Dawson, A. (5) 1979/80 Rangers
Deans, D. (2) 1974/5 Celtic
Delaney, J. (4) 1946/7 Manchester U
Devlin, P. J. (10) 2002/03 Birmingham C
Dick, J. (1) 1958/9 West Ham U
Dickov, P. (10) 2000/01 Manchester C, Leicester C, Blackburn R
Dickson, W. (5) 1969/70 Kilmarnock
Dobie, R. S. (6) 2001/02 WBA
Docherty, T. (25) 1951/2 Preston NE, Arsenal
Dodds, D. (2) 1983/4 Dundee U
Dodds, W. (26) 1996/7 Aberdeen, Dundee U, Rangers
Donachie, W. (35) 1971/2 Manchester C
Donnelly, S. (10) 1996/7 Celtic
Dougall, C. (1) 1946/7 Birmingham C
Dougan, R. (1) 1949/50 Heart of Midlothian
Douglas, R. (19) 2001/02 Celtic, Leicester C
Doyle, J. (1) 1975/6 Ayr U
Duncan, A. (6) 1974/5 Hibernian
Duncan, D. (3) 1947/8 East Fife
Duncanson, J. (1) 1946/7 Rangers

306

Durie, G. S. (43) 1987/8 Chelsea, Tottenham H, Rangers
Durrant, I. (20) 1987/8 Rangers, Kilmarnock

Elliott, M. S. (18) 1997/8 Leicester C
Evans, A. (4) 1981/2 Aston Villa
Evans, R. (48) 1948/9 Celtic, Chelsea
Ewing, T. (2) 1957/8 Partick Th

Farm, G. (10) 1952/3 Blackpool
Ferguson, B. (43) 1998/9 Rangers, Blackburn R, Rangers
Ferguson, Derek (2) 1987/8 Rangers
Ferguson, Duncan (7) 1991/2 Dundee U, Everton
Ferguson, I. (9) 1988/9 Rangers
Ferguson, R. (7) 1965/6 Kilmarnock
Fernie, W. (12) 1953/4 Celtic
Flavell, R. (2) 1946/7 Airdrieonians
Fleck, R. (4) 1989/90 Norwich C
Fleming, C. (1) 1953/4 East Fife
Fletcher, D. B. (36) 2003/04 Manchester U
Fletcher, S. (1) 2007/08 Hibernian
Forbes, A. (14) 1946/7 Sheffield U, Arsenal
Ford, D. (3) 1973/4 Heart of Midlothian
Forrest, J. (1) 1957/8 Motherwell
Forrest, J. (5) 1965/6 Rangers, Aberdeen
Forsyth, A. (10) 1971/2 Partick Th, Manchester U
Forsyth, C. (4) 1963/4 Kilmarnock
Forsyth, T. (22) 1970/1 Motherwell, Rangers
Fraser, D. (2) 1967/8 WBA
Fraser, W. (2) 1954/5 Sunderland
Freedman, D. A. (2) 2001/02 Crystal P

Gabriel, J. (2) 1960/1 Everton
Gallacher, K. W. (53) 1987/8 Dundee U, Coventry C, Blackburn R, Newcastle U
Gallacher, P. (8) 2001/02 Dundee U
Gallagher, P. (1) 2003/04 Blackburn R
Galloway, M. (1) 1991/2 Celtic
Gardiner, W. (1) 1957/8 Motherwell
Gemmell, T. (2) 1954/5 St Mirren
Gemmell, T. (18) 1965/6 Celtic
Gemmill, A. (43) 1970/1 Derby Co, Nottingham F, Birmingham C
Gemmill, S. (26) 1994/5 Nottingham F, Everton
Gibson, D. (7) 1962/3 Leicester C
Gillespie, G. T. (13) 1987/8 Liverpool
Gilzean, A. (22) 1963/4 Dundee, Tottenham H

Glass, S. (1) 1998/9 Newcastle U
Glavin, R. (1) 1976/7 Celtic
Glen, A. (2) 1955/6 Aberdeen
Goram, A. L. (43) 1985/6 Oldham Ath, Hibernian, Rangers
Gordon, C. S. (31) 2003/04 Heart of Midlothian, Sunderland
Gough, C. R. (61) 1982/3 Dundee U, Tottenham H, Rangers
Gould, J. (2) 1999/00 Celtic
Govan, J. (6) 1947/8 Hibernian
Graham, A. (11) 1977/8 Leeds U
Graham, G. (12) 1971/2 Arsenal, Manchester U
Grant, J. (2) 1958/9 Hibernian
Grant, P. (2) 1988/9 Celtic
Gray, A. (20) 1975/6 Aston Villa, Wolverhampton W, Everton
Gray, A. D. (2) 2002/03 Bradford C
Gray, E. (12) 1968/9 Leeds U
Gray F. (32) 1975/6 Leeds U, Nottingham F, Leeds U
Green, A. (6) 1970/1 Blackpool, Newcastle U
Greig, J. (44) 1963/4 Rangers
Gunn, B. (6) 1989/90 Norwich C

Haddock, H. (6) 1954/5 Clyde
Haffey, F. (2) 1959/60 Celtic
Hamilton, A. (24) 1961/2 Dundee
Hamilton, G. (5) 1946/7 Aberdeen
Hamilton, W. (1) 1964/5 Hibernian
Hammell, S. (1) 2004/05 Motherwell
Hansen, A. (26) 1978/9 Liverpool
Hansen, J. (2) 1971/2 Partick Th
Harper, J. (4) 1972/3 Aberdeen, Hibernian, Aberdeen
Hartford, A. (50) 1971/2 WBA, Manchester C, Everton, Manchester C
Hartley, P. J. (19) 2004/05 Heart of Midlothian, Celtic
Harvey, D. (16) 1972/3 Leeds U
Haughney, M. (1) 1953/4 Celtic
Hay, D. (27) 1969/70 Celtic
Hegarty, P. (8) 1978/9 Dundee U
Henderson, J. (7) 1952/3 Portsmouth, Arsenal
Henderson, W. (29) 1962/3 Rangers
Hendry, E. C. J. (51) 1992/3 Blackburn R, Rangers, Coventry C, Bolton W
Herd, D. (5) 1958/9 Arsenal
Herd, G. (5) 1957/8 Clyde
Herriot, J. (8) 1968/9 Birmingham C
Hewie, J. (19) 1955/6 Charlton Ath
Holt, D. D. (5) 1962/3 Heart of Midlothian
Holt, G. J. (10) 2000/01 Kilmarnock, Norwich C

Holton, J. (15) 1972/3 Manchester U
Hope, R. (2) 1967/8 WBA
Hopkin, D. (7) 1996/7 Crystal P, Leeds U
Houliston, W. (3) 1948/9 Queen of the South
Houston, S. (1) 1975/6 Manchester U
Howie, H. (1) 1948/9 Hibernian
Hughes, J. (8) 1964/5 Celtic
Hughes, R. D. (5) 2003/04 Portsmouth
Hughes, W. (1) 1974/5 Sunderland
Humphries, W. (1) 1951/2 Motherwell
Hunter, A. (4) 1971/2 Kilmarnock, Celtic
Hunter, W. (3) 1959/60 Motherwell
Husband, J. (1) 1946/7 Partick Th
Hutchison, D. (26) 1998/9 Everton, Sunderland, West Ham U
Hutchison, T. (17) 1973/4 Coventry C
Hutton, A. (7) 2006/07 Rangers, Tottenham H

Imlach, S. (4) 1957/8 Nottingham F
Irvine, B. (9) 1990/1 Aberdeen

Jackson, C. (8) 1974/5 Rangers
Jackson, D. (28) 1994/5 Hibernian, Celtic
Jardine, A. (38) 1970/1 Rangers
Jarvie, A. (3) 1970/1 Airdrieonians
Jess, E. (18) 1992/3 Aberdeen, Coventry C, Aberdeen
Johnston, A. (18) 1998/9 Sunderland, Rangers, Middlesbrough
Johnston, M. (38) 1983/4 Watford, Celtic, Nantes, Rangers
Johnston, L. (2) 1947/8 Clyde
Johnston, W. (22) 1965/6 Rangers, WBA
Johnstone, D. (14) 1972/3 Rangers
Johnstone, J. (23) 1964/5 Celtic
Johnstone, R. (17) 1950/1 Hibernian, Manchester C
Jordan, J. (52) 1972/3 Leeds U, Manchester U, AC Milan

Kelly, H. (1) 1951/2 Blackpool
Kelly, J. (2) 1948/9 Barnsley
Kennedy, Jim (6) 1963/4 Celtic
Kennedy, John (1) 2003/04 Celtic
Kennedy, S. (5) 1974/5 Rangers
Kennedy, S. (8) 1977/8 Aberdeen
Kerr, A. (2) 1954/5 Partick Th
Kerr, B. (3) 2002/03 Newcastle U
Kyle, K. (9) 2001/02 Sunderland

Lambert, P. (40) 1994/5 Motherwell, Borussia Dortmund, Celtic

Law, D. (55) 1958/9 Huddersfield T, Manchester C, Torino, Manchester U, Manchester C
Lawrence, T. (3) 1962/3 Liverpool
Leggat, G. (18) 1955/6 Aberdeen, Fulham
Leighton, J. (91) 1982/3 Aberdeen, Manchester U, Hibernian, Aberdeen
Lennox, R. (10) 1966/7 Celtic
Leslie, L. (5) 1960/1 Airdrieonians
Levein, C. (16) 1989/90 Heart of Midlothian
Liddell, W. (28) 1946/7 Liverpool
Linwood, A. (1) 1949/50 Clyde
Little, R. J. (1) 1952/3 Rangers
Logie, J. (1) 1952/3 Arsenal
Long, H. (1) 1946/7 Clyde
Lorimer, P. (21) 1969/70 Leeds U

Macari, L. (24) 1971/2 Celtic, Manchester U
Macaulay, A. (7) 1946/7 Brentford, Arsenal
MacDougall, E. (7) 1974/5 Norwich C
Mackay, D. (22) 1956/7 Heart of Midlothian, Tottenham H
Mackay, G. (4) 1987/8 Heart of Midlothian
Mackay, M. (5) 2003/04 Norwich C
Maloney, S. R. (11) 2005/06 Celtic, Aston Villa
Malpas, M. (55) 1983/4 Dundee U
Marshall, D. J. (2) 2004/05 Celtic
Marshall, G. (1) 1991/2 Celtic
Martin, B. (2) 1994/5 Motherwell
Martin, F. (6) 1953/4 Aberdeen
Martin, N. (3) 1964/5 Hibernian, Sunderland
Martis, J. (1) 1960/1 Motherwell
Mason, J. (7) 1948/9 Third Lanark
Masson, D. (17) 1975/6 QPR, Derby C
Mathers, D. (1) 1953/4 Partick Th
Matteo, D. (6) 2000/01 Leeds U
McAllister, B. (3) 1996/7 Wimbledon
McAllister, G. (57) 1989/90 Leicester C, Leeds U, Coventry C
McAllister, J. R. (1) 2003/04 Livingston
McAvennie, F. (5) 1985/6 West Ham U, Celtic
McBride, J. (2) 1966/7 Celtic
McCall, S. M. (40) 1989/90 Everton, Rangers
McCalliog, J. (5) 1966/7 Sheffield W, Wolverhampton W
McCann, N. D. (26) 1998/9 Heart of Midlothian, Rangers, Southampton
McCann, R. (5) 1958/9 Motherwell

McClair, B. (30) 1986/7 Celtic,
Manchester U
McCloy, P. (4) 1972/3 Rangers
McCoist, A. (61) 1985/6 Rangers,
Kilmarnock
McColl, I. (14) 1949/50 Rangers
McCormack, R. (1) 20007/08
Motherwell
McCreadie, E. (23) 1964/5 Chelsea
McCulloch, L. (15) 2004/05 Wigan
Ath, Rangers
MacDonald, A. (1) 1975/6 Rangers
McDonald, J. (2) 1955/6 Sunderland
McEveley, J. (3) 2007/08 Derby Co
McFadden, J. (37) 2001/02
Motherwell, Everton
McFarlane, W. (1) 1946/7 Heart of
Midlothian
McGarr, E. (2) 1969/70 Aberdeen
McGarvey, F. (7) 1978/9 Liverpool,
Celtic
McGhee, M. (4) 1982/3 Aberdeen
McGinlay, J. (13) 1993/4 Bolton W
McGrain, D. (62) 1972/3 Celtic
McGregor, A. (1) 2006/07 Rangers
McGrory, J. (3) 1964/5 Kilmarnock
McInally, A. (8) 1988/9 Aston Villa,
Bayern Munich
McInally, J. (10) 1986/7 Dundee U
McInnes, D. (2) 2002/03 WBA
MacKay, D. (14) 1958/9 Celtic
McKean, R. (1) 1975/6 Rangers
MacKenzie, J. (9) 1953/4 Partick Th
McKimmie, S. (40) 1988/9 Aberdeen
McKinlay, T. (22) 1995/6 Celtic
McKinlay, W. (29) 1993/4 Dundee U,
Blackburn R
McKinnon, Rob (3) 1993/4 Motherwell
McKinnon, Ronnie (28) 1965/6
Rangers
McLaren, Alan (24) 1991/2 Heart of
Midlothian, Rangers
McLaren, Andy (4) 1946/7 Preston NE
McLaren, Andy (1) 2000/01
Kilmarnock
McLean, G. (1) 1967/8 Dundee
McLean, T. (6) 1968/9 Kilmarnock
McLeish, A. (77) 1979/80 Aberdeen
McLeod, J. (4) 1960/1 Hibernian
MacLeod, M. (20) 1984/5 Celtic,
Borussia Dortmund, Hibernian
McLintock, F. (9) 1962/3 Leicester C,
Arsenal
McManus, S. (13) 2006/07 Celtic
McMillan, I. (6) 1951/2 Airdrieonians,
Rangers
McNamara, J. (33) 1996/7 Celtic,
Wolverhampton W
McNamee, D. (4) 2003/04 Livingston

McNaught, W. (5) 1950/1 Raith R
McNaughton, K. (4) 2001/02
Aberdeen, Cardiff C
McNeill, W. (29) 1960/1 Celtic
McPhail, J. (5) 1949/50 Celtic
McPherson, D. (27) 1988/9 Heart of
Midlothian, Rangers
McQueen, G. (30) 1973/4 Leeds U,
Manchester U
McStay, P. (76) 1983/4 Celtic
McSwegan, G. (2) 1999/00 Heart of
Midlothian
Millar, J. (2) 1962/3 Rangers
Miller, C. (1) 2000/01 Dundee U
Miller, K. (37) 2000/01 Rangers,
Wolverhampton W, Celtic, Derby
Co
Miller, L. (1) 2005/06 Dundee U
Miller, W. (6) 1946/7 Celtic
Miller, W. (65) 1974/5 Aberdeen
Mitchell, R. (2) 1950/1 Newcastle U
Mochan, N. (3) 1953/4 Celtic
Moir, W. (1) 1949/50 Bolton W
Moncur, R. (16) 1967/8 Newcastle U
Morgan, W. (21) 1967/8 Burnley,
Manchester U
Morris, H. (1) 1949/50 East Fife
Morrison, J. C. (1) 2007/08 WBA
Mudie, J. (17) 1956/7 Blackpool
Mulhall, G. (3) 1959/60 Aberdeen,
Sunderland
Munro, F. (9) 1970/1 Wolverhampton
W
Munro, I. (7) 1978/9 St Mirren
Murdoch, R. (12) 1965/6 Celtic
Murray, I. (6) 2002/03 Hibernian,
Rangers
Murray, J. (5) 1957/8 Heart of
Midlothian
Murray, S. (1) 1971/2 Aberdeen
Murty, G. S. (4) 2003/04 Reading

Naismith, S. J. (2) 2006/07 Kilmarnock,
Rangers
Narey, D. (35) 1976/7 Dundee U
Naysmith, G. A. (40) 1999/00 Heart of
Midlothian, Everton, Sheffield U
Neilson, R. (1) 2006/07 Heart of
Midlothian
Nevin, P. K. F. (28) 1985/6 Chelsea,
Everton, Tranmere R
Nicholas, C. (20) 1982/3 Celtic,
Arsenal, Aberdeen
Nicholson, B. (3) 2000/01 Dunfermline
Ath
Nicol, S. (27) 1984/5 Liverpool

O'Connor, G. (15) 2001/02 Hibernian,
Lokomotiv Moscow, Birmingham C

O'Donnell, P. (1) 1993/4 Motherwell
O'Hare, J. (13) 1969/70 Derby Co
O'Neil, B. (7) 1995/6 Celtic,
  Wolfsburg, Derby Co, Preston NE
O'Neil, J. (1) 2000/01 Hibernian
Ormond, W. (6) 1953/4 Hibernian
Orr, T. (2) 1951/2 Morton

Parker, A. (15) 1954/5 Falkirk,
  Everton
Parlane, D. (12) 1972/3 Rangers
Paton, A. (2) 1951/2 Motherwell
Pearson, S. P. (10) 2003/04
  Motherwell, Celtic, Derby Co
Pearson, T. (2) 1946/7 Newcastle U
Penman, A. (1) 1965/6 Dundee
Pettigrew, W. (5) 1975/6 Motherwell
Plenderleith, J. (1) 1960/1 Manchester C
Pressley, S. J. (32) 1999/00 Heart of
  Midlothian
Provan, David (10) 1979/80 Celtic
Provan, Davie (5) 1963/4 Rangers

Quashie, N. F. (14) 2003/04
  Portsmouth, Southampton, WBA
Quinn, P. (4) 1960/1 Motherwell

Rae, G. P. (13) 2000/01 Dundee,
  Rangers, Cardiff C
Redpath, W. (9) 1948/9 Motherwell
Reilly, L. (38) 1948/9 Hibernian
Ring, T. (12) 1952/3 Clyde
Rioch, B. (24) 1974/5 Derby Co,
  Everton, Derby Co
Riordan, D. G. (1) 2005/06 Hibernian
Ritchie, P. S. (7) 1998/9 Heart of
  Midlothian, Bolton W, Walsall
Ritchie, W. (1) 1961/2 Rangers
Robb, D. (5) 1970/1 Aberdeen
Robertson, A. (5) 1954/5 Clyde
Robertson, D. (3) 1991/2 Rangers
Robertson, H. (1) 1961/2 Dundee
Robertson, J. (16) 1990/1 Heart of
  Midlothian
Robertson, J. G. (1) 1964/5 Tottenham
  H
Robertson, J. N. (28) 1977/8
  Nottingham F, Derby Co
Robinson, B. (4) 1973/4 Dundee
Robson, B. (2) 2007/08 Dundee U
Ross, M. (13) 2001/02 Rangers
Rough, A. (53) 1975/6 Partick Th,
  Hibernian
Rougvie, D. (1) 1983/4 Aberdeen
Rutherford, E. (1) 1947/8 Rangers

St John, I. (21) 1958/9 Motherwell,
  Liverpool
Schaedler, E. (1) 1973/4 Hibernian

Scott, A. (16) 1956/7 Rangers, Everton
Scott, Jimmy (1) 1965/6 Hibernian
Scott, Jocky (2) 1970/1 Dundee
Scoular, J. (9) 1950/1 Portsmouth
Severin, S. D. (15) 2001/02 Heart of
  Midlothian, Aberdeen
Sharp, G. M. (12) 1984/5 Everton
Shaw, D. (8) 1946/7 Hibernian
Shaw, J. (4) 1946/7 Rangers
Shearer, D. (7) 1993/4 Aberdeen
Shearer, R. (4) 1960/1 Rangers
Simpson, N. (4) 1982/3 Aberdeen
Simpson, R. (5) 1966/7 Celtic
Sinclair, J. (1) 1965/6 Leicester C
Smith, D. (2) 1965/6 Aberdeen,
  Rangers
Smith, E. (2) 1958/9 Celtic
Smith, G. (18) 1946/7 Hibernian
Smith, H. G. (3) 1987/8 Heart of
  Midlothian
Smith, J. (4) 1967/8 Aberdeen,
  Newcastle U
Smith, J. (2) 2002/03 Celtic
Souness, G. (54) 1974/5
  Middlesbrough, Liverpool,
  Sampdoria
Speedie, D. R. (10) 1984/5 Chelsea,
  Coventry C
Spencer, J. (14) 1994/5 Chelsea, QPR
Stanton, P. (16) 1965/6 Hibernian
Steel, W. (30) 1946/7 Morton, Derby
  C, Dundee
Stein, C. (21) 1968/9 Rangers,
  Coventry C
Stephen, J. (2) 1946/7 Bradford PA
Stewart, D. (1) 1977/8 Leeds U
Stewart, J. (2) 1976/7 Kilmarnock,
  Middlesbrough
Stewart, M. J. (3) 2001/02 Manchester
  U
Stewart, R. (10) 1980/1 West Ham U
Stockdale, R. K. (5) 2001/02
  Middlesbrough
Strachan, G. (50) 1979/80 Aberdeen,
  Manchester U, Leeds U
Sturrock, P. (20) 1980/1 Dundee U
Sullivan, N. (28) 1996/7 Wimbledon,
  Tottenham H

Teale, G. (11) 2005/06 Wigan Ath,
  Derby Co
Telfer, P. N. (1) 1999/00 Coventry C
Telfer, W. (1) 1953/4 St Mirren
Thompson, S. (16) 2001/02 Dundee U,
  Rangers
Thomson, W. (7) 1979/80 St Mirren
Thornton, W. (7) 1946/7 Rangers
Toner, W. (2) 1958/9 Kilmarnock
Turnbull, E. (8) 1947/8 Hibernian

Ure, I. (11) 1961/2 Dundee, Arsenal

Waddell, W. (17) 1946/7 Rangers
Walker, A. (3) 1987/8 Celtic
Walker, J. N. (2) 1992/3 Heart of Midlothian, Partick Th
Wallace, I. A. (3) 1977/8 Coventry C
Wallace, W. S. B. (7) 1964/5 Heart of Midlothian, Celtic
Wardhaugh, J. (2) 1954/5 Heart of Midlothian
Wark, J. (29) 1978/9 Ipswich T, Liverpool
Watson, J. (2) 1947/8 Motherwell, Huddersfield T
Watson, R. (1) 1970/1 Motherwell
Webster, A. (22) 2002/03 Heart of Midlothian
Weir, A. (6) 1958/9 Motherwell
Weir, D. G. (61) 1996/7 Heart of Midlothian, Everton, Rangers
Weir, P. (6) 1979/80 St Mirren, Aberdeen
White, J. (22) 1958/9 Falkirk, Tottenham H

Whyte, D. (12) 1987/8 Celtic, Middlesbrough, Aberdeen
Wilkie, L. (11) 2001/02 Dundee
Williams, G. (5) 2001/02 Nottingham F
Wilson, A. (1) 1953/4 Portsmouth
Wilson, D. (22) 1960/1 Rangers
Wilson, I. A. (5) 1986/7 Leicester C, Everton
Wilson, P. (1) 1974/5 Celtic
Wilson, R. (2) 1971/2 Arsenal
Winters, R. (1) 1998/9 Aberdeen
Wood, G. (4) 1978/9 Everton, Arsenal
Woodburn, W. (24) 1946/7 Rangers
Wright, K. (1) 1991/2 Hibernian
Wright, S. (2) 1992/3 Aberdeen
Wright, T. (3) 1952/3 Sunderland

Yeats, R. (2) 1964/5 Liverpool
Yorston, H. (1) 1954/5 Aberdeen
Young, A. (8) 1959/60 Heart of Midlothian, Everton
Young, G. (53) 1946/7 Rangers
Younger, T. (24) 1954/5 Hibernian, Liverpool

WALES

Aizlewood, M. (39) 1985/6 Charlton Ath, Leeds U, Bradford C, Bristol C, Cardiff C
Allchurch, I. (68) 1950/1 Swansea T, Newcastle U, Cardiff C, Swansea T
Allchurch, L. (11) 1954/5 Swansea T, Sheffield U
Allen, B. (2) 1950/1 Coventry C
Allen, M. (14) 1985/6 Watford, Norwich C, Millwall, Newcastle U

Baker, C. (7) 1957/8 Cardiff C
Baker, W. (1) 1947/8 Cardiff C
Bale, G. (11) 2005/06 Southampton, Tottenham H
Barnard, D. S. (22) 1997/8 Barnsley, Grimsby T
Barnes, W. (22) 1947/8 Arsenal
Bellamy, C. D. (51) 1997/8 Norwich C, Coventry C, Newcastle U, Blackburn R, Liverpool, West Ham U
Berry, G. (5) 1978/9 Wolverhampton W, Stoke C
Blackmore, C. G. (39) 1984/5 Manchester U, Middlesbrough
Blake, N. (29) 1993/4 Sheffield U, Bolton W, Blackburn R, Wolverhampton W

Bodin, P. J. (23) 1989/90 Swindon T, Crystal P, Swindon T
Bowen, D. (19) 1954/5 Arsenal
Bowen, J. P. (2) 1993/4 Swansea C, Birmingham C
Bowen, M. R. (41) 1985/6 Tottenham H, Norwich C, West Ham U
Boyle, T. (2) 1980/1 Crystal P
Brown, J. R. (2) 2005/06 Gillingham, Blackburn R
Browning, M. T. (5) 1995/6 Bristol R, Huddersfield T
Burgess, R. (32) 1946/7 Tottenham H
Burton, O. (9) 1962/3 Norwich C, Newcastle U

Cartwright, L. (7) 1973/4 Coventry C, Wrexham
Charles, J. (38) 1949/50 Leeds U, Juventus, Leeds U, Cardiff C
Charles, J. M. (19) 1980/1 Swansea C, QPR, Oxford U
Charles, M. (31) 1954/5 Swansea T, Arsenal, Cardiff C
Clarke, R. (22) 1948/9 Manchester C
Coleman, C. (32) 1991/2 Crystal P, Blackburn R, Fulham
Collins, D. L. (7) 2004/05 Sunderland
Collins, J. M. (24) 2003/04 Cardiff C, West Ham U

Collison, J. D. (2) 2007/08 West Ham U

Cornforth, J. M. (2) 1994/5 Swansea C

Cotterill, D. R. G. B. (11) 2005/06 Bristol C, Wigan Ath

Coyne, D. (16) 1995/6 Tranmere R, Grimsby T, Leicester C, Burnley, Tranmere R

Crofts, A. L. (12) 2005/06 Gillingham

Crossley, M. G. (8) 1996/7 Nottingham F, Middlesbrough, Fulham

Crowe, V. (16) 1958/9 Aston Villa

Curtis, A. (35) 1975/6 Swansea C, Leeds U, Swansea C, Southampton, Cardiff C

Daniel, R. (21) 1950/1 Arsenal, Sunderland

Davies, A. (13) 1982/3 Manchester U, Newcastle U, Swansea C, Bradford C

Davies. A. R. (1) 2005/06 Yeovil T

Davies, C. (1) 1971/2 Charlton Ath

Davies, C. M. (5) 2005/06 Oxford U, Verona, Oldham Ath

Davies, D. (52) 1974/5 Everton, Wrexham, Swansea C

Davies, G. (16) 1979/80 Fulham, Manchester C

Davies, R. Wyn (34) 1963/4 Bolton W, Newcastle U, Manchester C, Manchester U, Blackpool

Davies, Reg (6) 1952/3 Newcastle U

Davies, Ron (29) 1963/4 Norwich C, Southampton, Portsmouth

Davies, S. (50) 2000/01 Tottenham H, Everton, Fulham

Davies, S. I. (1) 1995/6 Manchester U

Davis, G. (3) 1977/8 Wrexham

Deacy, N. (12) 1976/7 PSV Eindhoven, Beringen

Delaney, M. A. (36) 1999/00 Aston Villa

Derrett, S. (4) 1968/9 Cardiff C

Dibble, A. (3) 1985/6 Luton T, Manchester C

Duffy, R. M. (13) 2005/06 Portsmouth

Durban, A. (27) 1965/6 Derby C

Dwyer, P. (10) 1977/8 Cardiff C

Eardley, N. (7) 2007/08 Oldham Ath

Earnshaw, R. (38) 2001/02 Cardiff C, WBA, Norwich C, Derby Co

Easter, J. M. (7) 2006/07 Wycombe W, Plymouth Arg

Eastwood, F. (9) 2007/08 Wolverhampton W

Edwards, C. N. H. (1) 1995/6 Swansea C

Edwards, D. (5) 2007/08 Luton T, Wolverhampton W

Edwards, G. (12) 1946/7 Birmingham C, Cardiff C

Edwards, I. (4) 1977/8 Chester, Wrexham

Edwards, R. O. (15) 2002/03 Aston Villa, Wolverhampton W

Edwards, R. W. (4) 1997/8 Bristol C

Edwards, T. (2) 1956/7 Charlton Ath

Emanuel, J. (2) 1972/3 Bristol C

England, M. (44) 1961/2 Blackburn R, Tottenham H

Evans, B. (7) 1971/2 Swansea C, Hereford U

Evans, C. M. (2) 2007/08 Manchester C

Evans, I. (13) 1975/6 Crystal P

Evans, P. S. (2) 2001/02 Brentford, Bradford C

Evans, R. (1) 1963/4 Swansea T

Evans, S. J. (6) 2006/07 Wrexham

Felgate, D. (1) 1983/4 Lincoln C

Fletcher, C. N. (29) 2003/04 Bournemouth, West Ham U, Crystal P

Flynn, B. (66) 1974/5 Burnley, Leeds U, Burnley

Ford, T. (38) 1946/7 Swansea T, Aston Villa, Sunderland, Cardiff C

Foulkes, W. (11) 1951/2 Newcastle U

Freestone, R. (1) 1999/00 Swansea C

Gabbidon, D. L. (40) 2001/02 Cardiff C, West Ham U

Garner, G. (1) 2005/06 Leyton Orient

Giggs, R. J. (64) 1991/2 Manchester U

Giles, D. (12) 1979/80 Swansea C, Crystal P

Godfrey, B. (3) 1963/4 Preston NE

Goss, J. (9) 1990/1 Norwich C

Green, C. (15) 1964/5 Birmingham C

Green, R. M. (2) 1997/8 Wolverhampton W

Griffiths, A. (17) 1970/1 Wrexham

Griffiths, H. (1) 1952/3 Swansea T

Griffiths, M. (11) 1946/7 Leicester C

Gunter, C. R. (6) 2006/07 Cardiff C, Tottenham H

Hall, G. D. (9) 1987/8 Chelsea

Harrington, A. (11) 1955/6 Cardiff C

Harris, C. (24) 1975/6 Leeds U

Harris, W. (6) 1953/4 Middlesbrough

Hartson, J. (51) 1994/5 Arsenal, West Ham U, Wimbledon, Coventry C, Celtic

Haworth, S. O. (5) 1996/7 Cardiff C, Coventry C

Hennessey, T. (39) 1961/2 Birmingham C, Nottingham F, Derby Co
Hennessey, W. R. (10) 2006/07 Wolverhampton W
Hewitt, R. (5) 1957/8 Cardiff C
Hill, M. (2) 1971/2 Ipswich T
Hockey, T. (9) 1971/2 Sheffield U, Norwich C, Aston Villa
Hodges, G. (18) 1983/4 Wimbledon, Newcastle U, Watford, Sheffield U
Holden, A. (1) 1983/4 Chester C
Hole, B. (30) 1962/3 Cardiff C, Blackburn R, Aston Villa, Swansea C
Hollins, D. (11) 1961/2 Newcastle U
Hopkins, J. (16) 1982/3 Fulham, Crystal P
Hopkins, M. (34) 1955/6 Tottenham H
Horne, B. (59) 1987/8 Portsmouth, Southampton, Everton, Birmingham C
Howells, R. (2) 1953/4 Cardiff C
Hughes, C. M. (8) 1991/2 Luton T, Wimbledon
Hughes, I. (4) 1950/1 Luton T
Hughes, L. M. (72) 1983/4 Manchester U, Barcelona, Manchester U, Chelsea, Southampton
Hughes, W. (3) 1946/7 Birmingham C
Hughes, W. A. (5) 1948/9 Blackburn R
Humphreys, J. (1) 1946/7 Everton

Jackett, K. (31) 1982/3 Watford
James, G. (9) 1965/6 Blackpool
James, L. (54) 1971/2 Burnley, Derby C, QPR, Burnley, Swansea C, Sunderland
James, R. M. (47) 1978/9 Swansea C, Stoke C, QPR, Leicester C, Swansea C
Jarvis, A. (3) 1966/7 Hull C
Jenkins, S. R. (16) 1995/6 Swansea C, Huddersfield T
Johnson, A. J. (15) 1998/9 Nottingham F, WBA
Johnson, M. (1) 1963/4 Swansea T
Jones, A. (6) 1986/7 Port Vale, Charlton Ath
Jones, Barrie (15) 1962/3 Swansea T, Plymouth Argyle, Cardiff C
Jones, Bryn (4) 1946/7 Arsenal
Jones, C. (59) 1953/4 Swansea T, Tottenham H, Fulham
Jones, D. (8) 1975/6 Norwich C
Jones, E. (4) 1947/8 Swansea T, Tottenham H
Jones, J. (72) 1975/6 Liverpool, Wrexham, Chelsea, Huddersfield T
Jones, K. (1) 1949/50 Aston Villa

Jones, M. A. (2) 2006/07 Wrexham
Jones, M. G. (13) 1999/00 Leeds U, Leicester C
Jones, P. L. (2) 1996/7 Liverpool, Tranmere R
Jones, P. S. (50) 1996/7 Stockport Co, Southampton, Wolverhampton W, QPR
Jones, R. (1) 1993/4 Sheffield W
Jones, T. G. (13) 1946/7 Everton
Jones, V. P. (9) 1994/5 Wimbledon
Jones, W. (1) 1970/1 Bristol R

Kelsey, J. (41) 1953/4 Arsenal
King, J. (1) 1954/5 Swansea T
Kinsey, N. (7) 1950/1 Norwich C, Birmingham C
Knill, A. R. (1) 1988/9 Swansea C
Koumas, J. (29) 2000/01 Tranmere R, WBA, Wigan Ath
Krzywicki, R. (8) 1969/70 WBA, Huddersfield T

Lambert, R. (5) 1946/7 Liverpool
Law, B. J. (1) 1989/90 QPR
Lea, C. (2) 1964/5 Ipswich T
Ledley, J. C. (22) 2005/06 Cardiff C
Leek, K. (13) 1960/1 Leicester C, Newcastle U, Birmingham C, Northampton T
Legg, A. (6) 1995/6 Birmingham C, Cardiff C
Lever, A. (1) 1952/3 Leicester C
Lewis, D. (1) 1982/3 Swansea C
Llewellyn, C. M. (6) 1997/8 Norwich C, Wrexham
Lloyd, B. (3) 1975/6 Wrexham
Lovell, S. (6) 1981/2 Crystal P, Millwall
Lowndes, S. (10) 1982/3 Newport Co, Millwall, Barnsley
Lowrie, G. (4) 1947/8 Coventry C, Newcastle U
Lucas, M. (4) 1961/2 Leyton Orient
Lucas, W. (7) 1948/9 Swansea T

Maguire, G. T. (7) 1989/90 Portsmouth
Mahoney, J. (51) 1967/8 Stoke C, Middlesbrough, Swansea C
Mardon, P. J. (1) 1995/6 WBA
Margetson, M. W. (1) 2003/04 Cardiff C
Marriott, A. (5) 1995/6 Wrexham
Marustik, C. (6) 1981/2 Swansea C
Medwin, T. (30) 1952/3 Swansea T, Tottenham H
Melville, A. K. (65) 1989/90 Swansea C, Oxford U, Sunderland, Fulham, West Ham U
Mielczarek, R. (1) 1970/1 Rotherham U

313

Millington, A. (21) 1962/3 WBA, Crystal P, Peterborough U, Swansea C

Moore, G. (21) 1959/60 Cardiff C, Chelsea, Manchester U, Northampton T, Charlton Ath

Morgan, C. (8) 2006/07 Milton Keynes D, Peterborough U

Morris, W. (5) 1946/7 Burnley

Myhill, G. O. (1) 2007/08 Hull C

Nardiello, D. (2) 1977/8 Coventry C

Nardiello, D. A. (3) 2006/07 Barnsley, QPR

Neilson, A. B. (5) 1991/2 Newcastle U, Southampton

Nicholas, P. (73) 1978/9 Crystal P, Arsenal, Crystal P, Luton T, Aberdeen, Chelsea, Watford

Niedzwiecki, E. A. (2) 1984/5 Chelsea

Nogan, L. M. (2) 1991/2 Watford, Reading

Norman, A. J. (5) 1985/6 Hull C

Nurse, M. T. G. (12) 1959/60 Swansea T, Middlesbrough

Nyatanga, L. J. (21) 2005/06 Derby Co

O'Sullivan, P. (3) 1972/3 Brighton & HA

Oster, J. M. (13) 1997/8 Everton, Sunderland

Page, M. (28) 1970/1 Birmingham C

Page, R. J. (41) 1996/7 Watford, Sheffield U, Cardiff C, Coventry C

Palmer, D. (3) 1956/7 Swansea T

Parry, J. (1) 1950/1 Swansea T

Parry, P. I. (11) 2003/04 Cardiff C

Partridge, D. W. (7) 2004/05 Motherwell, Bristol C

Pascoe, C. (10) 1983/4 Swansea C, Sunderland

Paul, R. (33) 1948/9 Swansea T, Manchester C

Pembridge, M. A. (54) 1991/2 Luton T, Derby C, Sheffield W, Benfica, Everton, Fulham

Perry, J. (1) 1993/4 Cardiff C

Phillips, D. (62) 1983/4 Plymouth Argyle, Manchester C, Coventry C, Norwich C, Nottingham F

Phillips, J. (4) 1972/3 Chelsea

Phillips, L. (58) 1970/1 Cardff C, Aston Villa, Swansea C, Charlton Ath

Pipe, D. R. (1) 2002/03 Coventry C

Pontin, K. (2) 1979/80 Cardiff C

Powell, A. (8) 1946/7 Leeds U, Everton, Birmingham C

Powell, D. (11) 1967/8 Wrexham, Sheffield U

Powell, I. (8) 1946/7 QPR, Aston Villa

Price, L. P. (6) 2005/06 Ipswich T, Derby Co

Price, P. (25) 1979/80 Luton T, Tottenham H

Pring, K. (3) 1965/6 Rotherham U

Pritchard, H. K. (1) 1984/5 Bristol C

Rankmore, F. (l) 1965/6 Peterborough U

Ratcliffe, K. (59) 1980/1 Everton, Cardiff C

Ready, K. (5) 1996/7 QPR

Reece, G. (29) 1965/6 Sheffield U, Cardiff C

Reed, W. (2) 1954/5 Ipswich T

Rees, A. (1) 1983/4 Birmingham C

Rees, J. M. (1) 1991/2 Luton T

Rees, R. (39) 1964/5 Coventry C, WBA, Nottingham F

Rees, W. (4) 1948/9 Cardiff C, Tottenham H

Richards, S. (1) 1946/7 Cardiff C

Ricketts, S. (28) 2004/05 Swansea C, Hull C

Roberts, A. M. (2) 1992/3 QPR

Roberts, D. (17) 1972/3 Oxford U, Hull C

Roberts, G. W. (9) 1999/00 Tranmere R

Roberts, I. W. (15) 1989/90 Watford, Huddersfield T, Leicester C, Norwich C

Roberts, J. G. (22) 1970/1 Arsenal, Birmingham C

Roberts, J. H. (1) 1948/9 Bolton W

Roberts, N. W. (4) 1999/00 Wrexham, Wigan Ath

Roberts, P. (4) 1973/4 Portsmouth

Roberts, S. W. (1) 2004/05 Wrexham

Robinson, C. P. (46) 1999/00 Wolverhampton W, Portsmouth, Sunderland, Norwich C, Toronto Lynx

Robinson, J. R. C. (30) 1995/6 Charlton Ath

Rodrigues, P. (40) 1964/5 Cardiff C, Leicester C, Sheffield W

Rouse, V. (1) 1958/9 Crystal P

Rowley, T. (1) 1958/9 Tranmere R

Rush, I. (73) 1979/80 Liverpool, Juventus, Liverpool

314

Saunders, D. (75) 1985/6 Brighton & HA, Oxford U, Derby C, Liverpool, Aston Villa, Galatasaray, Nottingham F, Sheffield U, Benfica, Bradford C

Savage, R. W. (39) 1995/6 Crewe Alexandra, Leicester C, Birmingham C

Sayer, P. (7) 1976/7 Cardiff C

Scrine, F. (2) 1949/50 Swansea T

Sear, C. (1) 1962/3 Manchester C

Sherwood, A. (41) 1946/7 Cardiff C, Newport C

Shortt, W. (12) 1946/7 Plymouth Argyle

Showers, D. (2) 1974/5 Cardiff C

Sidlow, C. (7) 1946/7 Liverpool

Slatter, N. (22) 1982/3 Bristol R, Oxford U

Smallman, D. (7) 1973/4 Wrexham, Everton

Southall, N. (92) 1981/2 Everton

Speed, G. A. (85) 1989/90 Leeds U, Everton, Newcastle U, Bolton W

Sprake, G. (37) 1963/4 Leeds U, Birmingham C

Stansfield, F. (1) 1948/9 Cardiff C

Stevenson, B. (15) 1977/8 Leeds U, Birmingham C

Stevenson, N. (4) 1981/2 Swansea C

Stitfall, R. (2) 1952/3 Cardiff C

Sullivan, D. (17) 1952/3 Cardiff C

Symons, C. J. (37) 1991/2 Portsmouth, Manchester C, Fulham, Crystal P

Tapscott, D. (14) 1953/4 Arsenal, Cardiff C

Taylor, G. K. (15) 1995/6 Crystal P, Sheffield U, Burnley, Nottingham F

Thatcher, B. D. (7) 2003/04 Leicester C, Manchester C

Thomas, D. (2) 1956/7 Swansea T

Thomas, M. (51) 1976/7 Wrexham, Manchester U, Everton, Brighton & HA, Stoke C, Chelsea, WBA

Thomas, M. R. (1) 1986/7 Newcastle U

Thomas, R. (50) 1966/7 Swindon T, Derby C, Cardiff C

Thomas, S. (4) 1947/8 Fulham

Toshack, J. (40) 1968/9 Cardiff C, Liverpool, Swansea C

Trollope, P. J. (9) 1996/7 Derby Co, Fulham, Coventry C, Northampton T

Van Den Hauwe, P. W. R. (13) 1984/5 Everton

Vaughan, D. O. (13) 2002/03 Crewe Alex, Real Sociedad

Vaughan, N. (10) 1982/3 Newport Co, Cardiff C

Vearncombe, G. (2) 1957/8 Cardiff C

Vernon, R. (32) 1956/7 Blackburn R, Everton, Stoke C

Villars, A. (3) 1973/4 Cardiff C

Vokes, S. (2) 2007/8 AFC Bournemouth

Walley, T. (1) 1970/1 Watford

Walsh, I. (18) 1979/80 Crystal P, Swansea C

Ward, D. (2) 1958/9 Bristol R, Cardiff C

Ward, D. (5) 1999/00 Notts Co, Nottingham F

Webster, C. (4) 1956/7 Manchester U

Weston, R. D. (7) 1999/00 Arsenal, Cardiff C

Williams, A. (13) 1993/4 Reading, Wolverhampton W, Reading

Williams, A. E. (3) 2007/08 Stockport Co

Williams, A. P. (2) 1997/8 Southampton

Williams, D. G. (13) 1987/8 Derby Co, Ipswich T

Williams, D. M. (5) 1985/6 Norwich C

Williams, G. (1) 1950/1 Cardiff C

Williams, G. E. (26) 1959/60 WBA

Williams, G. G. (5) 1960/1 Swansea T

Williams, G. J. (2) 2005/06 West Ham U, Ipswich T

Williams, H. (4) 1948/9 Newport Co, Leeds U

Williams, Herbert (3) 1064/5 Swansea T

Williams, S. (43) 1953/4 WBA, Southampton

Witcomb, D. (3) 1946/7 WBA, Sheffield W

Woosnam, P. (17) 1958/9 Leyton Orient, West Ham U, Aston Villa

Yorath, T. (59) 1969/70 Leeds U, Coventry C, Tottenham H, Vancouver Whitecaps

Young, E. (21) 1989/90 Wimbledon, Crystal P, Wolverhampton W

REPUBLIC OF IRELAND

Aherne, T. (16) 1945/6 Belfast Celtic, Luton T
Aldridge, J. W. (69) 1985/6 Oxford U, Liverpool, Real Sociedad, Tranmere R
Ambrose, P. (5) 1954/5 Shamrock R
Anderson, J. (16) 1979/80 Preston NE, Newcastle U

Babb, P. (35) 1993/4 Coventry C, Liverpool, Sunderland
Bailham, E. (1) 1963/4 Shamrock R
Barber, E. (2) 1965/6 Shelbourne, Birmingham C
Barrett, G. (6) 2002/03 Arsenal, Coventry C
Beglin, J. (15) 1983/4 Liverpool
Bennett, A. J. (2) 2006/07 Reading
Bonner, P. (80) 1980/1 Celtic
Braddish, S. (1) 1977/8 Dundalk
Brady, T. R. (6) 1963/4 QPR
Brady, W. L. (72) 1974/5 Arsenal, Juventus, Sampdoria, Internazionale, Ascoli, West Ham U
Branagan, K. G. (1) 1996/7 Bolton W
Breen, G. (63) 1995/6 Birmingham C, Coventry C, West Ham U, Sunderland
Breen, T. (3) 1946/7 Shamrock R
Brennan, F. (1) 1964/5 Drumcondra
Brennan, S. A. (19) 1964/5 Manchester U, Waterford
Browne, W. (3) 1963/4 Bohemians
Bruce, A. (1) 2006/07 Ipswich T
Buckley, L. (2) 1983/4 Shamrock R, Waregem
Burke, F. (1) 1951/2 Cork Ath
Butler, P. J. (1) 1999/00 Sunderland
Butler, T. (2) 2002/03 Sunderland
Byrne, A. B. (14) 1969/70 Southampton
Byrne, J. (23) 1984/5 QPR, Le Havre, Brighton & HA, Sunderland, Millwall
Byrne, J. (2) 2003/04 Shelbourne
Byrne, P. (8) 1983/4 Shamrock R

Campbell, A. (3) 1984/5 Santander
Campbell, N. (11) 1970/1 St Patrick's Ath, Fortuna Cologne
Cantwell, N. (36) 1953/4 West Ham U, Manchester U
Carey, B. P. (3) 1991/2 Manchester U, Leicester C
Carey, J. J. (21) 1945/6 Manchester U
Carolan, J. (2) 1959/60 Manchester U
Carr, S. (44) 1998/9 Tottenham H, Newcastle U

Carroll, B. (2) 1948/9 Shelbourne
Carroll, T. R. (17) 1967/8 Ipswich T, Birmingham C
Carsley, L. K. (39) 1997/8 Derby Co, Blackburn R, Coventry C, Everton
Cascarino, A. G. (88) 1985/6 Gillingham, Millwall, Aston Villa, Celtic, Chelsea, Marseille, Nancy
Chandler, J. (2) 1979/80 Leeds U
Clarke, C. R. (2) 2003/04 Stoke C
Clarke, J. (1) 1977/8 Drogheda U
Clarke, K. (2) 1947/8 Drumcondra
Clarke, M. (1) 1949/50 Shamrock R
Clinton, T. J. (3) 1950/1 Everton
Coad, P. (11) 1946/7 Shamrock R
Coffey, T. (1) 1949/50 Drumcondra
Colfer, M. D. (2) 1949/50 Shelbourne
Colgan, N. (9) 2001/02 Hibernian, Barnsley
Conmy, O. M. (5) 1964/5 Peterborough U
Connolly, D. J. (41) 1995/6 Watford, Feyenoord, Wolverhampton W, Excelsior, Wimbledon, West Ham U, Wigan Ath
Conroy, G. A. (27) 1969/70 Stoke C
Conway, J. P. (20) 1966/7 Fulham, Manchester C
Corr, P. J. (4) 1948/9 Everton
Courtney, E. (1) 1945/6 Cork U
Coyle, O. (1) 1993/4 Bolton W
Coyne, T. (22) 1991/2 Celtic, Tranmere R, Motherwell
Crowe, G. (2) 2002/03 Bohemians
Cummins, G. P. (19) 1953/4 Luton T
Cuneen, T. (1) 1950/1 Limerick
Cunningham, K. (72) 1995/6 Wimbledon, Birmingham C
Curtis, D. P. (17) 1956/7 Shelbourne, Bristol C, Ipswich T, Exeter C
Cusack, S. (1) 1952/3 Limerick

Daish, L. S. (5) 1991/2 Cambridge U, Coventry C
Daly, G. A. (48) 1972/3 Manchester U, Derby C, Coventry C, Birmingham C, Shrewsbury T
Daly, M. (2) 1977/8 Wolverhampton W
Daly, P. (1) 1949/50 Shamrock R
Deacy, E. (4) 1981/2 Aston Villa
Delaney, D. F. (2) 2007/08 QPR
Delap, R. J. (11) 1997/8 Derby Co, Southampton
De Mange, K. J. P. P. (2) 1986/7 Liverpool, Hull C
Dempsey, J. T. (19) 1966/7 Fulham, Chelsea

Dennehy, J. (11) 1971/2 Cork Hibernian, Nottingham F, Walsall
Desmond, P. (4) 1949/50 Middlesbrough
Devine, J. (13) 1979/80 Arsenal, Norwich C
Doherty, G. M. T. (34) 1999/00 Luton T, Tottenham H, Norwich C
Donovan, D. C. (5) 1954/5 Everton
Donovan, T. (1) 1979/80 Aston Villa
Douglas, J. (8) 2003/04 Blackburn R, Leeds U
Doyle, C. (1) 1958/9 Shelbourne
Doyle, Colin (1) 2006/07 Birmingham C
Doyle, K. E. (18) 2005/06 Reading
Doyle, M. P. (1) 2003/04 Coventry C
Duff, D. A. (68) 1997/8 Blackburn R, Chelsea, Newcastle U
Duffy, B. (1) 1949/50 Shamrock R
Dunne, A. P. (33) 1961/2 Manchester U, Bolton W
Dunne, J. C. (1) 1970/1 Fulham
Dunne, P. A. J. (5) 1964/5 Manchester U
Dunne, R. P. (42) 1999/00 Everton, Manchester C
Dunne, S. (15) 1952/3 Luton T
Dunne, T. (3) 1955/6 St Patrick's Ath
Dunning, P. (2) 1970/1 Shelbourne
Dunphy, E. M. (23) 1965/6 York C, Millwall
Dwyer, N. M. (14) 1959/60 West Ham U, Swansea T

Eccles, P. (1) 1985/6 Shamrock R
Eglington, T. J. (24) 1945/6 Shamrock R, Everton
Elliott, S. W. (9) 2004/05 Sunderland
Evans, M. J. (1) 1997/8 Southampton

Fagan, E. (1) 1972/3 Shamrock R
Fagan, F. (8) 1954/5 Manchester C, Derby C
Fairclough, M. (2) 1981/2 Dundalk
Fallon, S. (8) 1950/1 Celtic
Farrell, P. D. (28) 1945/6 Shamrock R, Everton
Farrelly, G. (6) 1995/6 Aston Villa, Everton, Bolton W
Finnan, S. (50) 1999/00 Fulham, Liverpool
Finucane, A. (11) 1966/7 Limerick
Fitzgerald, F. J. (2) 1954/5 Waterford
Fitzgerald, P. J. (5) 1960/1 Leeds U, Chester
Fitzpatrick, K. (1) 1969/70 Limerick
Fitzsimons, A. G. (26) 1949/50 Middlesbrough, Lincoln C
Fleming, C. (10) 1995/6 Middlesbrough

Fogarty, A. (11) 1959/60 Sunderland, Hartlepool U
Foley, D. J. (6) 1999/00 Watford
Foley, T. C. (9) 1963/4 Northampton T
Fullam, J. (1960/1 Preston NE, Shamrock R

Gallagher, C. (2) 1966/7 Celtic
Gallagher, M. (1) 1953/4 Hibernian
Galvin, A. (29) 1982/3 Tottenham H, Sheffield W, Swindon T
Gamble, J. (2) 2006/07 Cork C
Gannon, E. (14) 1948/9 Notts Co, Sheffield W, Shelbourne K
Gannon, M. (1) 1971/2 Shelbourne
Gavin, J. T. (7) 1949/50 Norwich C, Tottenham H, Norwich C
Gibbons, A. (4) 1951/2 St Patrick's Ath
Gibson, D. T. D. (2) 2007/08 Manchester U
Gilbert, R. (1) 1965/6 Shamrock R
Giles, C. (1) 1950/1 Doncaster R
Giles, M. J. (59) 1959/60 Manchester U, Leeds U, WBA, Shamrock R
Given, S. J. J. (86) 1995/6 Blackburn R, Newcastle U
Givens, D. J. (56) 1968/9 Manchester U, Luton T, QPR, Birmingham C, Neuchatel Xamax
Gleeson, S. M. (2) 2006/07 Wolverhampton W
Glynn, D. (2) 1951/2 Drumcondra
Godwin, T. F. (13) 1948/9 Shamrock R, Leicester C, Bournemouth & BA
Goodman, J. (4) 1996/7 Wimbledon
Goodwin, J. (1) 2002/03 Stockport Co
Gorman, W. C. (2) 1946/7 Brentford
Grealish, A. (45) 1975/6 Orient, Luton T, Brighton & HA, WBA
Gregg, E. (8) 1977/8 Bohemians
Grimes, A. A. (18) 1977/8 Manchester U, Coventry C, Luton T

Hale, A. (13) 1961/2 Aston Villa, Doncaster R, Waterford
Hamilton, T. (2) 1958/9 Shamrock R
Hand, E. K. (20) 1968/9 Portsmouth
Harte, I. P. (64) 1995/6 Leeds U, Levante
Hartnett, J. B. (2) 1948/9 Middlesbrough
Haverty, J. (32) 1955/6 Arsenal, Blackburn R, Millwall, Celtic, Bristol R, Shelbourne
Hayes, A. W. P. (1) 1978/9 Southampton
Hayes, W. E. (2) 1946/7 Huddersfield T
Hayes, W. J. (1) 1948/9 Limerick

Healey, R. (2) 1976/7 Cardiff C
Healy, C. (13) 2001/02 Celtic,
Sunderland
Heighway, S. D. (34) 1970/1 Liverpool,
Minnesota Kicks
Henderson, B. (2) 1947/8 Drumcondra
Henderson, W. C. P. (6) 2005/06
Brighton & HA, Preston NE
Hennessy, J. (5) 1964/5 Shelbourne, St
Patrick's Ath
Herrick, J. (3) 1971/2 Cork
Hibernians, Shamrock R
Higgins, J. (1) 1950/1 Birmingham C
Holland, M. R. (49) 1999/00 Ipswich T,
Charlton Ath
Holmes, J. (30) 1970/1 Coventry C,
Tottenham H, Vancouver Whitecaps
Hoolahan, W. (1) 2007/08 Blackpool
Houghton, R. J. (73) 1985/6 Oxford U,
Liverpool, Aston Villa, Crystal P,
Reading
Howlett, G. (1) 1983/4 Brighton & HA
Hughton, C. (53) 1979/80 Tottenham
H, West Ham U
Hunt, S. P. (11) 2006/07 Reading
Hurley, C. J. (40) 1956/7 Millwall,
Sunderland, Bolton W

Ireland, S. J. (6) 2005/06 Manchester C
Irwin, D. J. (56) 1990/1 Manchester U

Kavanagh, G. A. (16) 1997/8 Stoke C,
Cardiff C, Wigan Ath
Keane, R. D. (81) 1997/8
Wolverhampton W, Coventry C,
Internazionale, Leeds U, Tottenham
H
Keane, R. M. (67) 1990/1 Nottingham
F, Manchester U
Keane, T. R. (4) 1948/9 Swansea T
Kearin, M. (1) 1971/2 Shamrock R
Kearns, F. T. (1) 1953/4 West Ham U
Kearns, M. (18) 1969/70 Oxford U,
Walsall, Wolverhampton W
Kelly, A. T. (34) 1992/3 Sheffield U,
Blackburn R
Kelly, D. T. (26) 1987/8 Walsall, West
Ham U, Leicester C, Newcastle U,
Wolverhampton W, Sunderland,
Tranmere R
Kelly, G. (52) 1993/4 Leeds U
Kelly, J. A. (48) 1956/7 Drumcondra,
Preston NE
Kelly, J. P. V. (5) 1960/1
Wolverhampton W
Kelly, M. J. (4) 1987/8 Portsmouth
Kelly, N. (1) 1953/4 Nottingham F
Kelly, S. M. (11) 2005/06 Tottenham
H, Birmingham C
Kenna, J. J. (27) 1994/5 Blackburn R

Kennedy, M. (34) 1995/6 Liverpool,
Wimbledon, Manchester C,
Wolverhampton W
Kennedy, M. F. (2) 1985/6 Portsmouth
Kenny, P. (7) 2003/04 Sheffield U
Keogh, A. D. (7) 2006/07
Wolverhampton W
Keogh, J. (1) 1965/6 Shamrock R
Keogh, S. (1) 1958/9 Shamrock R
Kernaghan, A. N. (22) 1992/3
Middlesbrough, Manchester C
Kiely, D. L. (10) 1999/00 Charlton
Ath, WBA
Kiernan, F. W. (5) 1950/1 Shamrock R,
Southampton
Kilbane, K. D. (87) 1997/8 WBA,
Sunderland, Everton, Wigan Ath
Kinnear, J. P. (26) 1966/7 Tottenham
H, Brighton & HA
Kinsella, M. A. (48) 1997/8 Charlton
Ath, Aston Villa, WBA

Langan, D. (26) 1977/8 Derby Co,
Birmingham C, Oxford U
Lapira, J. (1) 2006/07 Notre Dame
Lawler, J. F. (8) 1952/3 Fulham
Lawlor, J. C. (3) 1948/9 Drumcondra,
Doncaster R
Lawlor, M. (5) 1970/1 Shamrock R
Lawrenson, M. (39) 1976/7 Preston
NE, Brighton & HA, Liverpool
Lee, A. L. (10) 2002/03 Rotherham U,
Cardiff C, Ipswich T
Leech, M. (8) 1968/9 Shamrock R
Long, S. P. (8) 2006/07 Reading
Lowry, D. (1) 1961/2 St Patrick's Ath

McAlinden, J. (2) 1945/6 Portsmouth
McAteer, J. W. (52) 1993/4 Bolton W,
Liverpool, Blackburn R, Sunderland
McCann, J. (1) 1956/7 Shamrock R
McCarthy, M. (57) 1983/4 Manchester
C, Celtic, Lyon, Millwall
McConville, T. (6) 1971/2 Dundalk,
Waterford
McDonagh, Jim (25) 1980/1 Everton,
Bolton W, Notts C
McDonagh, Jacko (3) 1983/4
Shamrock R
McEvoy, M. A. (17) 1960/1 Blackburn
R
McGeady, A. (18) 2003/04 Celtic
McGee, P. (15) 1977/8 QPR, Preston
NE
McGoldrick, E. J. (15) 1991/2 Crystal
P, Arsenal
McGovan, D. (3) 1948/9 West Ham U
McGowan, J. (1) 1946/7 Cork U
McGrath, M. (22) 1957/8 Blackburn R,
Bradford PA

McGrath, P. (83) 1984/5 Manchester U, Aston Villa, Derby C

McLoughlin, A. F. (42) 1989/90 Swindon T, Southampton, Portsmouth

McMillan, W. (2) 1945/6 Belfast Celtic

McNally, J. B. (3) 1958/9 Luton T

McPhail, S. (10) 1999/00 Leeds U

McShane, P. D. (11) 2006/07 WBA, Sunderland

Macken, A. (1) 1976/7 Derby Co

Macken, J. P. (1) 2004/05 Manchester C

Mackey, G. (3) 1956/7 Shamrock R

Mahon, A. J. (2) 1999/00 Tranmere R

Malone, G. (1) 1948/9 Shelbourne

Mancini, T. J. (5) 1973/4 QPR, Arsenal

Martin, C. J. (30) 1945/6 Glentoran, Leeds U, Aston Villa

Martin, M. P. (52) 1971/2 Bohemians, Manchester U, WBA, Newcastle U

Maybury, A. (10) 1997/8 Leeds U, Heart of Midlothian, Leicester C

Meagan, M. K. (17) 1960/1 Everton, Huddersfield T, Drogheda

Miller, L. W. P. (18) 2003/04 Celtic, Manchester U, Sunderland

Milligan, M. J. (1) 1991/2 Oldham Ath

Mooney, J. (2) 1964/5 Shamrock R

Moore, A. (8) 1995/6 Middlesbrough

Moran, K. (71) 1979/80 Manchester U, Sporting Gijon, Blackburn R

Moroney, T. (12) 1947/8 West Ham U, Evergreen U

Morris, B. (35) 1987/8 Celtic, Middlesbrough

Morrison, C. H. (36) 2001/02 Crystal P, Birmingham C, Crystal P

Moulson, G. B. (3) 1947/8 Lincoln C

Mucklan, C. (1) 1977/8 Drogheda

Mulligan, P. M. (50) 1968/9 Shamrock R, Chelsea, Crystal P, WBA, Shamrock R

Munroe, L. (1) 1953/4 Shamrock R

Murphy, A. (1) 1955/6 Clyde

Murphy, B. (1) 1985/6 Bohemians

Murphy, D. (8) 2006/07 Sunderland

Murphy, Jerry (1) 1979/80 Crystal P

Murphy, Joe (1) 2003/04 WBA

Murphy, P. M. (1) 2006/07 Carlisle U

Murray, T. (1) 1949/50 Dundalk

Newman, W. (1) 1968/9 Shelbourne

Nolan, R. (10) 1956/7 Shamrock R

O'Brien, A. (5) 2006/07 Newcastle U

O'Brien, A. J. (26) 2000/01 Newcastle U, Portsmouth

O'Brien, F. (3) 1979/80 Philadelphia Fury

O'Brien, J. M. (3) 2005/06 Bolto.

O'Brien, L. (16) 1985/6 Shamrock ., Manchester U, Newcastle U, Tranmere R

O'Brien, R. (5) 1975/6 Notts Co

O'Byrne, L. B. (1) 1948/9 Shamrock R

O'Callaghan, B. R. (6) 1978/9 Stoke C

O'Callaghan, K. (21) 1980/1 Ipswich T, Portsmouth

O'Cearuill, J. (2) 2006/07 Arsenal

O'Connnell, A. (2) 1966/7 Dundalk, Bohemians

O'Connor, T. (4) 1949/50 Shamrock R

O'Connor, T. (7) 1967/8 Fulham, Dundalk, Bohemians

O'Driscoll, J. F. (3) 1948/9 Swansea T

O'Driscoll, S. (3) 1981/2 Fulham

O'Farrell, F. (9) 1951/2 West Ham U, Preston NE

O'Flanagan, K. P. (3) 1946/7 Arsenal

O'Flanagan, M. (1) 1946/7 Bohemians

O'Halloran, S. E. (2) 2006/07 Aston Villa

O'Hanlon, K. G. (1) 1987/8 Rotherham U

O'Keefe, E. (5) 1980/1 Everton, Port Vale

O'Leary, D. (68) 1976/7 Arsenal

O'Leary, P. (7) 1979/80 Shamrock R

O'Neill, F. S. (20) 1961/2 Shamrock R

O'Neill, J. (17) 1951/2 Everton

O'Neill, J. (1) 1960/1 Preston NE

O'Neill, K. P. (13) 1995/6 Norwich C, Middlesbrough

O'Regan, K. (4) 1983/4 Brighton & HA

O'Reilly, J. (2) 1945/6 Cork U

O'Shea, J. F. (45) 2001/02 Manchester U

Peyton, G. (33) 1976/7 Fulham, Bournemouth, Everton

Peyton, N. (6) 1956/7 Shamrock R, Leeds U

Phelan, T. (42) 1991/2 Wimbledon, Manchester C, Chelsea, Everton, Fulham

Potter, D. M. (5) 2006/07 Wolverhampton W

Quinn, A. (8) 2002/03 Sheffield W, Sheffield U

Quinn, B. S. (4) 1999/00 Coventry C

Quinn, N. J. (91) 1985/6 Arsenal, Manchester C, Sunderland

Reid, A. M. (27) 2003/04 Nottingham F, Tottenham H, Charlton Ath, Sunderland

Reid, S. J. (20) 2001/02 Millwall, Blackburn R
Richardson, D. J. (3) 1971/2 Shamrock R, Gillingham
Ringstead, A. (20) 1950/1 Sheffield U
Robinson, M. (24) 1980/1 Brighton & HA, Liverpool, QPR
Roche, P. J. (8) 1971/2 Shelbourne, Manchester U
Rogers, E. (19) 1967/8 Blackburn R, Charlton Ath
Rowlands, M. C. (3) 2003/04 QPR
Ryan, G. (18) 1977/8 Derby Co, Brighton & HA
Ryan, R. A. (16) 1949/50 WBA, Derby C

Sadlier, R. T. (1) 2001/02 Millwall
Savage, D. P. T. (5) 1995/6 Millwall
Saward, P. (18) 1953/4 Millwall, Aston Villa, Huddersfield T
Scannell, T. (1) 1953/4 Southend U
Scully, P. J. (1) 1988/9 Arsenal
Sheedy, K. (46) 1983/4 Everton, Newcastle U
Sheridan, J. J. (34) 1987/8 Leeds U, Sheffield W
Slaven, B. (7) 1989/90 Middlesbrough
Sloan, J. W. (2) 1945/6 Arsenal
Smyth, M. (1) 1968/9 Shamrock R
Stapleton, F. (71) 1976/7 Arsenal, Manchester U, Ajax, Le Havre, Blackburn R
Staunton, S. (102) 1988/9 Liverpool, Aston Villa, Liverpool, Aston Villa
Stevenson, A. E. (6) 1946/7 Everton
Stokes, A. (3) 2006/07 Sunderland
Strahan, F. (5) 1963/4 Shelbourne

Swan, M. M. G. (1) 1959/60 Drumcondra
Synott, N. (3) 1977/8 Shamrock R

Taylor T. (1) 1958/9 Waterford
Thomas, P. (2) 1973/4 Waterford
Thompson, J. (1) 2003/04 Nottingham F
Townsend, A. D. (70) 1988/9 Norwich C, Chelsea, Aston Villa, Middlesbrough
Traynor, T. J. (8) 1953/4 Southampton
Treacy, R. C. P. (42) 1965/6 WBA, Charlton Ath, Swindon T, Preston NE, WBA, Shamrock R
Tuohy, L. (8) 1955/6 Shamrock R, Newcastle U, Shamrock R
Turner, P. (2) 1962/3 Celtic

Vernon, J. (2) 1945/6 Belfast Celtic

Waddock, G. (21) 1979/80 QPR, Millwall
Walsh, D. J. (20) 1945/6 Linfield, WBA, Aston Villa
Walsh, J. (1) 1981/2 Limerick
Walsh, M. (21) 1975/6 Blackpool, Everton, QPR, Porto
Walsh, M. (4) 1981/2 Everton
Walsh, W. (9) 1946/7 Manchester C
Waters, J. (2) 1976/7 Grimsby T
Whelan, G. D. (2) 2007/08 Stoke C
Whelan, R. (2) 1963/4 St Patrick's Ath
Whelan, R. (53) 1980/1 Liverpool, Southend U
Whelan, W. (4) 1955/6 Manchester U
Whittaker, R. (1) 1958/9 Chelsea

REPUBLIC OF IRELAND LEAGUE 2007

	P	W	D	L	F	A	Pts
Drogheda United	33	19	11	3	48	24	68
St Patrick's Athletic	33	18	7	8	54	29	61
Bohemians	33	16	10	7	35	17	58
Cork City	33	15	10	8	44	32	55
Shamrock Rovers	33	14	9	10	36	26	51
Sligo Rovers	33	12	5	16	34	45	41
Derry City	33	8	13	12	30	31	37
Galway United	33	7	14	12	28	35	35
Bray Wanderers	33	8	10	15	30	48	34
UCD	33	7	10	16	31	44	31
Waterford United	33	7	9	17	23	47	30
Longford Town*	33	9	8	16	34	49	29

Longford Town six points deducted for breach of licence.
Top scorer: Mooney (Longford Town) 19.

BRITISH ISLES INTERNATIONAL GOALSCORERS SINCE 1946

ENGLAND

A'Court, A.	1	Crouch, P.J.	14	Kevan, D.T.	8
Adams, T.A.	5	Currie, A.W.	3	Kidd, B.	1
Allen, R.	2			King, L.B.	1
Anderson, V.	2	Defoe, J.C.	5		
Anderton, D.R.	7	Dixon, L.M.	1	Lampard, F.J.	14
Astall, G.	1	Dixon, K.M.	4	Langton, R.	1
Atyeo, P.J.W.	5	Douglas, B.	11	Latchford, R.D.	5
				Lawler, C.	1
Baily, E.F.	5	Eastham, G.	2	Lawton, T.	16
Baker, J.H.	3	Edwards, D.	5	Lee, F.	10
Ball, A.J.	8	Ehiogu, U.	1	Lee, J.	1
Barmby, N.J.	4	Elliott, W.H.	3	Lee, R.M.	2
Barnes, J.	11			Lee, S.	2
Barnes, P.S.	4	Ferdinand, L.	5	Le Saux, G.P.	1
Barry, G.	1	Ferdinand, R.G.	2	Lineker, G.	48
Beardsley, P.A.	9	Finney, T.	30	Lofthouse, N.	30
Beattie, J.K.	1	Flowers, R.	10		
Beckham, D.R.J.	17	Fowler, R.B.	7	Mabbutt, G.	1
Bell, C.	9	Francis, G.C.J.	3	McDermott, T.	3
Bentley, R.T.F.	9	Francis, T.	12	Macdonald, M.	6
Blissett, L.	3	Froggatt, J.	2	McManaman, S.	3
Bowles, S.	1	Froggatt, R.	2	Mannion, W.J.	11
Bradford, G.R.W.	1			Mariner, P.	13
Bradley, W.	2	Gascoigne, P.J.	10	Marsh, R.W.	1
Bridge, W.M.	1	Gerrard, S.G.	13	Matthews, S.	3
Bridges, B.J.	1	Goddard, P.	1	Medley, L.D.	1
Broadbent, P.F.	2	Grainger, C.	3	Melia, J.	1
Broadis, I.A.	8	Greaves, J.	44	Merson, P.C.	3
Brooking, T.D.	5			Milburn, J.E.T.	10
Brooks, J.	2	Haines, J.T.W.	2	Moore, R.F.	2
Bull, S.G.	4	Hancocks, J.	2	Morris, J.	3
Butcher, T.	3	Hassall, H.W.	4	Mortensen, S.H.	23
Byrne, J.J.	8	Hateley, M.	9	Mullen, J.	6
		Haynes, J.N.	18	Mullery, A.P.	1
Campbell, S.J.	1	Heskey, E.W.	5	Murphy, D.B.	1
Carter, H.S.	5	Hirst, D.E.	1		
Chamberlain, M.	1	Hitchens, G.A.	5	Neal, P.G.	5
Channon, M.R.	21	Hoddle, G.	8	Nicholls, J.	1
Charlton, J.	6	Hughes, E.W.	1	Nicholson, W.E.	1
Charlton, R.	49	Hunt, R.	18	Nugent, D.J.	1
Chivers, M.	13	Hunter, N.	2		
Clarke, A.J.	10	Hurst, G.C.	24	O'Grady, M.	3
Cole, A.	1			Owen, M.J.	40
Cole, J.J.	7	Ince P.E.C.	2	Own goals	21
Connelly, J.M.	7				
Coppell, S.J.	7	Jeffers, F.	1	Paine, T.L.	7
Cowans, G.	2	Jenas, J.A.	1	Palmer, C.L.	1
Crawford, R.	1	Johnson, D.E.	6	Parry, R.A.	1
				Peacock, A.	3
		Kay, A.H.	1	Pearce, S.	5
		Keegan, J.K.	21	Pearson, J.S.	5
		Kennedy, R.	3	Pearson, S.C.	5
		Keown, M.R.	2	Perry, W.	2

Peters, M.	20	**SCOTLAND**		Fletcher, D.	4
Pickering, F.	5	Aitken, R.	1	Freedman, D.A.	1
Platt, D.	27	Archibald, S.	4		
Pointer, R.	2			Gallacher, K.W.	9
		Baird, S.	2	Gemmell, T.K	
Ramsay, A.E.	3	Bannon, E.	1	(St Mirren)	1
Redknapp, J.F.	1	Bauld, W.	2	Gemmell, T.K	
Revie, D.G.	4	Baxter, J.C.	3	(Celtic)	1
Richards, M.	1	Beattie, C.	1	Gemmill, A.	8
Richardson, K.E.	2	Bett, J.	1	Gemmill, S.	1
Robson, B.	26	Bone, J.	1	Gibson, D.W.	3
Robson, R.	4	Booth, S.	6	Gilzean, A.J.	12
Rooney, W.	14	Boyd, K.	7	Gough, C.R.	6
Rowley, J.F.	6	Boyd, T.	1	Graham, A.	2
Royle, J.	2	Brand, R.	8	Graham, G.	3
		Brazil, A.	1	Gray, A.	7
Sansom, K.	1	Bremner, W.J.	3	Gray, E.	3
Scholes, P.	14	Brown, A.D.	6	Gray, F.	1
Sewell, J.	3	Buckley, P.	1	Greig, J.	3
Shackleton, L.F.	1	Burke, C.	2		
Shearer, A.	30	Burley, C.W.	3	Hamilton, G.	4
Sheringham, E.P.	11	Burns, K.	1	Harper, J.M.	2
Smith, A.	1			Hartford, R.A.	4
Smith, A.M.	2			Hartley, P.J.	1
Smith, R.	13	Caldwell, G.	2	Henderson, J.G.	1
Southgate, G.	2	Calderwood, C.	1	Henderson, W.	5
Steven, T.M.	4	Caldow, E.	4	Hendry, E.C.J.	3
Stiles, N.P.	1	Cameron, C.	2	Herd, D.G.	3
Stone, S.B.	2	Campbell, R.	1	Herd, G.	1
Summerbee, M.G.	1	Chalmers, S.	3	Hewie, J.D.	2
		Clarkson, D.	1	Holt, G.J.	1
Tambling, R.V.	1	Collins, J.	12	Holton, J.A.	2
Taylor, P.J.	2	Collins, R.V.	10	Hopkin, D.	2
Taylor, T.	16	Combe, J.R.	1	Houliston, W.	2
Terry, J.G.	4	Conn, A.	1	Howie, H.	1
Thompson, P.B.	1	Cooper, D.	6	Hughes, J.	1
Tueart, D.	2	Craig, J.	1	Hunter, W.	1
		Crawford, S.	4	Hutchison, D.	6
Vassell, D.	6	Curran, H.P.	1	Hutchison, T.	1
Viollet, D.S.	1				
		Dailly, C.	6	Jackson, C.	1
Waddle, C.R.	6	Dalglish, K.	30	Jackson, D.	4
Wallace, D.L.	1	Davidson, J.A.	1	Jardine, A.	1
Walsh, P.	1	Dickov, P.	1	Jess, E.	2
Watson, D.V.	4	Dobie, R.S.	1	Johnston, A.	2
Webb, N.	4	Docherty, T.H.	1	Johnston, L.H.	1
Weller, K.	1	Dodds, D.	1	Johnston, M.	14
Wignall, F.	2	Dodds, W.	7	Johnstone, D.	2
Wilkins, R.G.	3	Duncan, D.M.	1	Johnstone, J.	4
Wilshaw, D.J.	10	Durie, G.S.	7	Johnstone, R.	10
Wise, D.F.	1			Jordan, J.	11
Withe, P.	1	Elliott, M.S.	1		
Woodcock, T.	16			Kyle, K.	1
Worthington, F.S.	2	Ferguson, B.	3		
Wright, I.E.	9	Fernie, W.	1	Lambert, P.	1
Wright, M.	1	Flavell, R.	2	Law, D.	30
Wright, W.A.	3	Fleming, C.	2	Leggat, G.	8
Wright-Phillips, S.C.	4			Lennox, R.	3

Liddell, W.	6	Parlane, D.	1	Charles, J.	1
Linwood, A.B.	1	Pettigrew, W.	2	Charles, M.	6
Lorimer, P.	4	Provan, D.	1	Charles, W.J.	15
				Clarke, R.J.	5
Macari, L.	5	Quashie, N.F.	1	Coleman, C.	4
MacDougall, E.J.	3	Quinn, J.	7	Collins, J.	1
MacKay, D.C.	4	Quinn, P.	1	Curtis, A.	6
Mackay, G.	1				
MacKenzie, J.A.	1	Reilly, L.	22	Davies, G.	2
MacLeod, M.	1	Ring, T.	2	Davies, R.T.	9
McAllister, G.	5	Rioch, B.D.	6	Davies, R.W.	6
McAvennie, F.	1	Ritchie, P.S.	1	Davies, Simon	6
McCall, S.M.	1	Robertson, A.	2	Deacy, N.	4
McCalliog, J.	1	Robertson, J.	3	Durban, A.	2
McCann, N.	3	Robertson, J.N.	8	Dwyer, P.	2
McClair, B.	2				
McCoist, A.	19	St John, I.	9	Earnshaw, R.	13
McCulloch, L.	1	Scott, A.S.	5	Eastwood, F.	4
McFadden, J.	13	Sharp, G.	1	Edwards, G.	2
McGhee, M.	2	Shearer, D.	2	Edwards, R.I.	4
McGinlay, J.	3	Smith, G.	4	England, H.M.	4
McInally, A.	3	Souness, G.J.	4	Evans, C.	1
McKimmie, S.I.	1	Steel, W.	12	Evans, I.	1
McKinlay, W.	4	Stein, C.	10		
McKinnon, R.	1	Stewart, R.	1	Fletcher, C.	1
McLaren, A.	4	Strachan, G.	5	Flynn, B.	7
McLean, T.	1	Sturrock, P.	3	Ford, T.	23
McLintock, F.	1			Foulkes, W.J.	1
McManus S.	1	Thompson, S.	3		
McMillan, I.L.	2	Thornton, W.	1	Giggs, R.J.	12
McNeill, W.	3			Giles, D.	2
McPhail, J.	3	Waddell, W.	6	Godfrey, B.C.	2
McQueen, G.	5	Wallace, I.A.	1	Griffiths, A.T.	6
McStay, P.	9	Wark, J.	7	Griffiths, M.W.	2
McSwegan, G.J.	1	Webster, A.	1		
Maloney, S.	1	Weir, A.	1	Harris, C.S.	1
Mason, J.	4	Weir, D.	1	Hartson, J.	14
Masson, D.S.	5	White, J.A.	3	Hewitt, R.	1
Miller, K.	11	Wilkie, L.	1	Hockey, T.	1
Miller, W.	1	Wilson, D.	9	Hodges, G.	2
Mitchell, R.C.	1			Horne, B.	2
Morgan, W.	1	Young, A.	2	Hughes, L.M.	16
Morris, H.	3				
Mudie, J.K.	9	**WALES**		James, L.	10
Mulhall, G.	1	Allchurch, I.J.	23	James, R.	7
Murdoch, R.	5	Allen, M.	3	Jones, A.	1
Murray, J.	1	Bale, G.	2	Jones, B.S.	2
		Barnes, W.	1	Jones, Cliff	16
Narey, D.	1	Bellamy, C.D.	15	Jones, D.E.	1
Naysmith, G.A.	1	Blackmore, C.G.	1	Jones, J.P.	1
Nevin, P.K.F.	5	Blake, N.A.	4		
Nicholas, C.	5	Bodin, P.J.	3	Koumas, J.	9
		Bowen, D.I.	3	Kryzwicki, R.I.	1
O'Connor, G.	4	Bowen, M.	2		
O'Hare, J.	5	Boyle, T.	1	Ledley, J.	1
Ormond, W.E.	2	Burgess, W.A.R.	1	Leek, K.	5
Orr, T.	1			Llewelyn, C.M	1
Own goals	9				

Lovell, S. 1
Lowrie, G. 2

Mahoney, J.F. 1
Medwin, T.C. 6
Melville, A.K. 3
Moore, G. 1

Nicholas, P. 2

O'Sullivan, P.A. 1
Own goals 8

Palmer, D. 1
Parry, P.I. 1
Paul, R. 1
Pembridge, M.A. 6
Phillips, D. 2
Powell, A. 1
Powell, D. 1
Price, P. 1

Reece, G.I. 2
Rees, R.R. 3
Roberts, P.S. 1
Robinson, C.P. 1
Robinson, J.R.C. 3
Rush, I. 28

Saunders, D. 22
Savage R.W. 2
Slatter, N. 2
Smallman, D.P. 1
Speed, G.A. 7
Symons, C.J. 2

Tapscott, D.R. 4
Taylor, G.J. 1
Thomas, M. 4
Toshack, J.B. 12

Vernon, T.R. 8

Walsh, I. 7
Williams, A. 1
Williams, G.E. 1
Williams, G.G. 1
Woosnam, A.P. 3

Yorath, T.C. 2
Young, E. 1

NORTHERN IRELAND

Anderson, T. 4
Armstrong, G. 12

Barr, H.H. 1
Best, G. 9
Bingham, W.L. 10
Black, K. 1
Blanchflower, D. 2
Blanchflower, J. 1
Brennan, R.A. 1
Brotherston, N. 3

Campbell, W.G. 1
Casey, T. 2
Caskey, W. 1
Cassidy, T. 1
Clarke, C.J. 13
Clements, D. 2
Cochrane, T. 1
Crossan, E. 1
Crossan, J.A. 10
Cush, W.W. 5

Davis, S. 1
D'Arcy, S.D. 1
Doherty, I. 1
Doherty, P.D. 2
Dougan, A.D. 8
Dowie, I. 12

Elder, A.R. 1
Elliott, S. 4

Feeney, W. 1
Feeney, W.J. 3
Ferguson, W. 1
Ferris, R.O. 1
Finney, T. 2

Gibson, W. 1
Gillespie, K.R. 2
Gray, P. 6
Griffin, D.J. 1

Hamilton, B. 4
Hamilton, W. 5
Harkin, J.T. 2
Harvey, M. 3
Healy, D.J. 34
Hill, C.F. 1
Humphries, W. 1
Hughes, M.E. 5
Hunter, A. 1
Hunter, B.V. 1

Irvine, W.J. 8

Johnston, W.C. 1
Jones, J. 1
Jones, S. 1

Lafferty, K. 5
Lennon, N.F. 2
Lockhart, N. 3
Lomas, S.M. 3

Magilton, J. 5
McAdams, W.J. 7
McCann, G.S. 1
McCartney, G. 1
McClelland, J. 1
McCrory, S. 1
McCurdy, C. 1
McDonald, A. 3
McGarry, J.K. 1
McGrath, R.C. 4
McIlroy, J. 10
McIlroy, S.B. 5
McLaughlin, J.C. 6
McMahon, G.J. 2
McMordie, A.S. 3
McMorran, E.J. 4
McParland, P.J. 10
Moreland, V. 1
Morgan, S. 3
Morrow, S.J. 1
Mulryne, P.P. 3
Murdoch, C.J. 1

Neill, W.J.T. 2
Nelson, S. 1
Nicholl, C.J. 3
Nicholl, J.M. 1
Nicholson, J.J. 6

O'Boyle, G. 1
O'Kane, W.J. 1
O'Neill, J. 2
O'Neill, M.A. 4
O'Neill, M.H. 8
Own goals 7

Patterson, D.J. 1
Peacock, R. 2
Penney, S. 2

Quinn, J.M. 12
Quinn, S.J. 4

Rowland, K. 1

Simpson, W.J. 5
Smyth, S. 5
Spence, D.W. 3
Sproule, I. 1
Stewart, I. 2

Taggart, G.P. 7
Tully, C.P. 3

Walker, J. 1
Walsh, D.J. 5
Welsh, E. 1
Whiteside, N. 9
Whitley, Jeff 2
Williams, M.S. 1
Wilson, D.J. 1
Wilson, K.J. 6
Wilson, S.J. 7

EIRE

Aldridge, J. 19
Ambrose, P. 1
Anderson, J. 1

Barrett, G. 2
Brady, L. 9
Breen, G. 7
Byrne, J. 4

Cantwell, J. 14
Carey, J. 3
Carroll, T. 1
Cascarino, A. 19
Coad, P. 3
Connolly, D.J. 9
Conroy, T. 2
Conway, J. 3
Coyne, T. 6
Cummins, G. 5
Curtis, D. 8

Daly, G. 13
Dempsey, J. 1
Dennehy, M. 2
Doherty, G.M.T. 4
Doyle, K.E. 5
Duff, D.A. 7
Duffy, B. 1
Dunne, R.P. 5

Eglinton, T. 2
Elliott, S.W. 1

Fagan, F. 5
Fallon, S. 2
Farrell, P. 3
Finnan, S. 2
Fitzgerald, J. 1

Fitzgerald, P. 2
Fitzsimons, A. 7
Fogarty, A. 3
Foley, D. 2
Fullam, J. 1

Galvin, A. 1
Gavin, J. 2
Giles, J. 5
Givens, D. 19
Glynn, D. 1
Grealish, T. 8
Grimes, A.A. 1

Hale, A. 2
Hand, E. 2
Harte, I.P. 11
Haverty, J. 3
Healy, C. 1
Holland, M.R. 5
Holmes, J. 1
Houghton, R. 6
Hughton, C. 1
Hurley, C. 2

Ireland, S.J. 4
Irwin, D. 4

Kavanagh, G.A. 1
Keane, R.D. 33
Keane, R.M. 9
Kelly, D. 9
Kelly, G. 2
Kennedy, M. 4
Keogh, A. 1
Kernaghan, A. 1
Kilbane, K.D. 7
Kinsella, M.A. 3

Lawrenson, M. 5
Leech, M. 2
Long, S.P. 3

McAteer, J.W. 3
McCann, J. 1
McCarthy, M. 2
McEvoy, A. 6
McGee, P. 1
McGrath, P. 8
McLoughlin, A. 2
McPhail, S. 1

Mancini, T. 1
Martin, C. 6
Martin, M. 4
Miller, L.W.P. 1
Mooney, J. 1
Moran, K. 6
Moroney, T. 1
Morrison, C.H. 9
Mulligan, P. 1

O'Brien, A.J. 1
O'Callaghan, K. 1
O'Connor, T. 2
O'Farrell, F. 2
O'Keefe, E. 1
O'Leary, D.A. 1
O'Neill, F. 1
O'Neill, K.P. 4
O'Reilly, J. 1
O'Shea, J.F. 1
Own goals 10

Quinn, N. 21

Reid, A.M. 4
Reid, S.J. 2
Ringstead, A. 7
Robinson, M. 4
Rogers, E. 5
Ryan, G. 1
Ryan, R. 3

Sheedy, K. 9
Sheridan, J. 5
Slaven, B. 1
Sloan, J. 1
Stapleton, F. 20
Staunton, S. 7
Strahan, F. 1

Townsend, A.D. 7
Treacy, R. 5
Tuohy, L. 4

Waddock, G. 3
Walsh, D. 5
Walsh, M. 3
Waters, J. 1
Whelan, R. 3

UEFA UNDER-21 CHAMPIONSHIP 2007–08

Qualifying competition

GROUP 1
Italy 4, Albania 0
Greece 4, Azerbaijan 1
Croatia 2, Faeroes 0
Croatia 3, Greece 2
Albania 1, Faeroes 0
Azerbaijan 0, Greece 2
Italy 2, Faeroes 1
Albania 1, Croatia 0
Albania 0, Italy 1
Croatia 3, Azerbaijan 2
Faeroes 0, Greece 2
Italy 2, Croatia 0
Faeroes 1, Azerbaijan 0
Greece 2, Italy 2
Azerbaijan 1, Albania 1
Faeroes 1, Croatia 2
Italy 5, Azerbaijan 0
Faeroes 0, Albania 5
Greece 3, Croatia 4
Azerbaijan 0, Croatia 1
Faeroes 0, Italy 1
Greece 2, Albania 1
Azerbaijan 0, Italy 2

GROUP 2
Armenia 1, Liechtenstein 0
Ukraine 1, Turkey 2
Ukraine 4, Armenia 0
Armenia 1, Czech Republic 1
Liechtenstein 2, Turkey 3
Czech Republic 8, Liechtenstein 0
Armenia 0, Ukraine 2
Liechtenstein 0, Czech Republic 4
Turkey 2, Ukraine 0
Liechtenstein 1, Armenia 4
Turkey 3, Liechtenstein 0

GROUP 3
Bulgaria 1, Montenegro 2
Republic of Ireland 0, Portugal 2
Montenegro 0, England 3
Bulgaria 0, England 2
Portugal 4, Montenegro 0
Bulgaria 1, Portugal 0
England 1, Montenegro 0
Montenegro 1, Portugal 2
Republic of Ireland 0, England 3
Montenegro 1, Republic of Ireland 0
England 2, Bulgaria 0
Republic of Ireland 1, Bulgaria 0
England 3, Republic of Ireland 0
Republic of Ireland 1, Montenegro 1
Portugal 2, Bulgaria 0

GROUP 4
Georgia 0, Spain 1
Kazakhstan 0, Russia 3

Poland 3, Georgia 1
Georgia 2, Kazakhstan 1
Russia 1, Poland 0
Poland 1, Kazakhstan 0
Spain 4, Georgia 0
Russia 4, Kazakhstan 0
Poland 0, Spain 2
Kazakhstan 4, Georgia 1
Poland 0, Russia 1
Spain 3, Poland 0
Georgia 2, Russia 0
Spain 5, Kazakhstan 0

GROUP 5
Estonia 0, Norway 1
Macedonia 0, Holland 1
Norway 0, Holland 1
Switzerland 1, Macedonia 1
Macedonia 1, Estonia 0
Norway 2, Switzerland 1
Macedonia 1, Norway 1
Estonia 0, Switzerland 4
Holland 1, Macedonia 0
Switzerland 5, Estonia 0
Norway 2, Estonia 0
Macedonia 2, Switzerland 1
Holland 3, Estonia 0
Holland 0, Switzerland 1

GROUP 6
Slovenia 2, Lithuania 1
Denmark 0, Finland 1
Denmark 4, Lithuania 0
Finland 3, Scotland 2
Lithuania 0, Slovenia 0
Scotland 0, Denmark 0
Scotland 3, Lithuania 0
Finland 1, Slovenia 0
Slovenia 1, Denmark 3
Lithuania 0, Finland 1
Lithuania 0, Denmark 3
Slovenia 0, Scotland 4
Denmark 1, Slovenia 0
Finland 2, Lithuania 1
Scotland 2, Finland 1

GROUP 7
Iceland 0, Cyprus 1
Slovakia 2, Iceland 2
Belgium 0, Austria 1
Slovakia 1, Austria 1
Iceland 0, Belgium 0
Austria 2, Cyprus 1
Belgium 4, Slovakia 2
Iceland 1, Austria 1
Slovakia 4, Cyprus 1
Cyprus 1, Slovakia 2
Austria 3, Belgium 2
Cyprus 1, Austria 2

Belgium 1, Iceland 2
Cyprus 2, Iceland 0
Cyprus 0, Belgium 2
Austria 1, Slovakia 0

GROUP 8
Serbia 1, Latvia 1
Belarus 1, Hungary 0
Hungary 1, Latvia 0
San Marino 0, Belarus 3
Belarus 2, Latvia 1
San Marino 1, Hungary 6
Serbia 3, Belarus 1
Latvia 2, San Marino 0
Hungary 2, Serbia 1
Serbia 3, San Marino 0
Hungary 0, Belarus 1
Belarus 6, San Marino 0
Latvia 1, Hungary 0
Belarus 1, Serbia 1
San Marino 0, Serbia 5

GROUP 9
Moldova 0, Northern Ireland 1
Israel 3, Luxembourg 0
Northern Ireland 0, Germany 3
Moldova 1, Israel 0
Luxembourg 1, Northern Ireland 2

Israel 2, Germany 2
Luxembourg 0, Moldova 2
Germany 3, Moldova 0
Northern Ireland 1, Israel 3
Northern Ireland 5, Luxembourg 0
Northern Ireland 3, Moldova 0
Israel 2, Northern Ireland 1
Germany 6, Luxembourg 0
Israel 1, Moldova 0

GROUP 10
France 1, Romania 1
Malta 0, Romania 1
France 1, Wales 0
Bosnia 4, Malta 0
Romania 3, Bosnia 0
Malta 0, France 2
France 4, Bosnia 0
Romania 0, France 0
Wales 3, Malta 0
Romania 4, Malta 0
Wales 4, Bosnia 0
Malta 2, Bosnia 1
Wales 4, France 2
Malta 0, Wales 4
Bosnia 1, Wales 2

Competition still being played.

UEFA UNDER-17 CHAMPIONSHIP 2008

Finals in Turkey

GROUP A
Scotland 0, Serbia 2
Turkey 3, Holland 0
Turkey 1, Scotland 0
Holland 1, Serbia 0
Serbia 0, Turkey 0
Holland 2, Scotland 0

GROUP B
France 2, Republic of Ireland 1
Spain 2, Switzerland 0

Republic of Ireland 0, Switzerland 1
France 3, Spain 3
Switzerland 0, France 2
Republic of Ireland 1, Spain 3

SEMI-FINALS
Spain 2, Holland 1
Turkey 1, France 1
(France won 4-3 on penalties).

FINAL
France 0, Spain 4

FIFA UNDER-17 WORLD CUP 2007

Finals in South Korea

GROUP A	P	W	D	L	F	A	Pts
Peru	3	2	1	0	2	0	7
Costa Rica	3	1	1	1	3	2	4
South Korea	3	1	0	2	2	4	3
Togo	3	0	2	1	2	3	2

GROUP B	P	W	D	L	F	A	Pts
England	3	2	1	0	8	2	7
Brazil	3	2	0	1	14	3	6
North Korea	3	1	1	1	3	7	4
New Zealand	3	0	0	3	0	13	0

GROUP C	P	W	D	L	F	A	Pts
Spain	3	2	1	0	7	4	7
Argentina	3	1	2	0	5	2	5
Syria	3	1	1	1	3	2	4
Honduras	3	0	0	3	3	10	0

GROUP D	P	W	D	L	F	A	Pts
Nigeria	3	3	0	0	9	2	9
France	3	1	1	1	4	4	4
Japan	3	1	0	2	4	6	3
Haiti	3	0	1	2	3	8	1

GROUP E	P	W	D	L	F	A	Pts
Tunisia	3	3	0	0	8	3	9
USA	3	1	0	2	6	7	3
Tajikistan	3	1	0	2	4	5	3
Belgium	3	1	0	2	3	6	3

GROUP F	P	W	D	L	F	A	Pts
Germany	3	2	1	0	11	5	7
Ghana	3	2	0	1	8	5	6
Colombia	3	1	1	1	9	5	4
Trinidad & Tobago	3	0	0	3	1	14	0

FIRST ROUND

Tunisia 1, France 3
Spain 3, North Korea 0
Ghana 1, Brazil 0
Peru 1, Tajikistan 1
Peru won 5-4 on penalties.
Argentina 2, Costa Rica 0
Nigeria 2, Colombia 1

England 3, Syria 1
Germany 2, USA 1

QUARTER-FINALS

France 1, Spain 1
Spain won 5-4 on penalties.
Ghana 2, Peru 0
Argentina 0, Nigeria 2
England 1, Germany 4

SEMI-FINALS

Spain 2, Ghana 1
Nigeria 3, Germany 1

MATCH FOR THIRD PLACE

Ghana 1, Germany 2

FINAL

Spain 0, Nigeria 0
Nigeria won 3-0 on penalties.

FIFA UNDER-20 WORLD CUP 2007

Finals in Canada

GROUP A	P	W	D	L	F	A	Pts
Chile	3	2	1	0	6	0	7
Austria	3	1	2	0	2	1	5
Congo	3	1	1	1	3	4	4
Canada	3	0	0	3	0	6	0

GROUP B	P	W	D	L	F	A	Pts
Spain	3	2	1	0	8	5	7
Zambia	3	1	1	1	4	3	4
Uruguay	3	1	1	1	3	4	4
Jordan	3	0	1	2	3	6	1

GROUP C	P	W	D	L	F	A	Pts
Mexico	3	3	0	0	7	2	9
Gambia	3	2	0	1	3	4	6
Portugal	3	1	0	2	4	4	3
New Zealand	3	0	0	3	1	5	0

GROUP D	P	W	D	L	F	A	Pts
USA	3	2	1	0	9	3	7
Poland	3	1	1	1	3	7	4
Brazil	3	1	0	2	4	5	3
South Korea	3	0	2	1	4	5	2

GROUP E	P	W	D	L	F	A	Pts
Argentina	3	2	1	0	7	0	7
Czech Republic	3	1	2	0	4	3	5
North Korea	3	0	2	1	2	3	2
Panama	3	0	1	2	1	8	1

GROUP F	P	W	D	L	F	A	Pts
Japan	3	2	1	0	4	1	7
Nigeria	3	2	1	0	3	0	7
Costa Rica	3	1	0	2	2	3	3
Scotland	3	0	0	3	2	7	0

FIRST ROUND

Austria 2, Gambia 1
USA 2, Uruguay 1
Spain 4, Brazil 2
Japan 2, Czech Republic 2
Czech Republic won 4-3 on penalties.
Chile 1, Portugal 0
Zambia 1, Nigeria 2
Argentina 3, Poland 1
Mexico 3, Congo 0

QUARTER-FINALS

Austria 2, USA 1
Spain 1, Czech Republic 1
Czech Republic won 4-3 on penalties.
Chile 4, Nigeria 0
Argentina 1, Mexico 0

SEMI-FINALS

Austria 0, Czech Republic 2
Chile 0, Argentina 3

MATCH FOR THIRD PLACE

Austria 0, Chile 1

FINAL

Czech Republic 1, Argentina 2

BLUE SQUARE PREMIER 2007–2008

		Home						Away					Total						
	P	W	D	L	F	A	W	D	L	F	A	W	D	L	F	A	GD	Pts
1 Aldershot T	46	18	2	3	44	21	13	6	4	38	27	31	8	7	82	48	34	101
2 Cambridge U	46	14	6	3	36	17	11	5	7	32	24	25	11	10	68	41	27	86
3 Torquay U	46	15	3	5	39	21	11	5	7	44	36	26	8	12	83	57	26	86
4 Exeter C	46	13	9	1	44	26	9	8	6	39	32	22	17	7	83	58	25	83
5 Burton Alb	46	15	3	5	48	31	8	9	6	31	25	23	12	11	79	56	23	81
6 Stevenage B	46	13	5	5	47	25	11	2	10	35	30	24	7	15	82	55	27	79
7 Histon	46	10	7	6	42	36	10	5	8	34	31	20	12	14	76	67	9	72
8 Forest Green R	46	11	6	6	45	34	8	8	7	31	25	19	14	13	76	59	17	71
9 Oxford U	46	10	8	5	32	21	10	3	10	24	27	20	11	15	56	48	8	71
10 Grays Ath	46	11	6	6	35	23	8	7	8	23	24	19	13	14	58	47	11	70
11 Ebbsfleet U	46	14	3	6	40	29	5	9	9	25	32	19	12	15	65	61	4	69
12 Salisbury C	46	12	7	4	35	22	6	7	10	35	38	18	14	14	70	60	10	68
13 Kidderminster H	46	12	5	6	38	23	7	5	11	36	34	19	10	17	74	57	17	67
14 York C	46	8	5	10	33	34	9	6	8	38	40	17	11	18	71	74	-3	62
15 Crawley T*	46	12	5	6	47	31	7	4	12	26	36	19	9	18	73	67	6	60
16 Rushden & D	46	7	10	6	26	22	8	4	11	29	33	15	14	17	55	55	0	59
17 Woking	46	7	9	7	28	27	5	8	10	25	34	12	17	17	53	61	-8	53
18 Weymouth	46	7	5	11	24	34	4	8	11	29	39	11	13	22	53	73	-20	44
19 Northwich Vic	46	6	7	10	30	36	5	4	14	22	42	11	11	24	52	78	-26	44
20 Halifax T†	46	8	10	5	30	29	4	6	13	31	41	12	16	18	61	70	-9	42
21 Altrincham	46	6	6	11	32	44	3	8	12	24	38	9	14	23	56	82	-26	41
22 Farsley Celtic	46	6	5	12	27	38	4	4	15	21	48	10	9	27	48	86	-38	39
23 Stafford R	46	2	4	17	16	48	3	6	14	26	51	5	10	31	42	99	-57	25
24 Droylsden	46	4	5	14	27	45	1	4	18	19	58	5	9	32	46	103	-57	24

* Crawley Town deducted 6 points; † Halifax Town deducted 10 points.

Leading Goalscorers 2007–08

	League	FA Cup	Trophy	Total
Stuart Fleetwood (Forest Green Rovers)	28	6	2	36
Steve Morison (Stevenage Borough)	22	0	1	23
Colin Little (Altrincham)	21	1	1	23
John Grant (Aldershot Town)	20	0	5	25
Jon Shaw (Halifax Town)	20	1	4	25
Daryl Clare (Burton Albion)	19	2	3	24
Tim Sills (Torquay United)	19	0	2	21
Richard Logan (Exeter City)	18	0	0	18
Chris Zebroski (Torquay United loan)	18	0	0	18
Scott Rendell (Cambridge United)	17	4	2	23
Mark Beesley (Cambridge United)	17	2	0	19
(Includes 10 League and 2 FA Cup goals for Forest Green Rovers).				
Iyseden Christie (Kidderminster Harriers)	17	0	0	17

BLUE SQUARE PREMIER RESULTS 2007–2008

	Aldershot T	Altrincham	Burton Alb	Cambridge U	Crawley T	Droylsden	Ebbsfleet U	Exeter C	Farsley Celtic	Forest Green R	Grays Ath	Halifax T	Histon	Kidderminster H	Northwich Vic	Oxford U	Rushden & D	Salisbury C	Stafford R	Stevenage B	Torquay U	Weymouth	Woking	York C
Aldershot T	—	2-1	1-2	2-0	0-3	3-1	2-0	2-0	4-3	0-1	3-2	1-0	3-1	2-1	5-0	1-0	2-1	2-1	4-3	3-1	0-3	0-0	2-1	2-0
Altrincham	1-2	—	0-3	1-2	0-1	2-0	2-1	1-1	3-1	3-1	2-1	1-1	1-1	1-0	4-1	0-3	2-2	2-2	3-1	1-1	2-2	2-1	1-1	2-2
Burton Alb	2-0	1-1	—	1-2	1-0	5-0	2-0	4-4	1-0	1-1	2-3	2-1	1-3	0-2	4-1	1-2	1-0	4-3	2-1	3-0	1-1	2-1	2-0	2-1
Cambridge U	1-1	1-2	0-0	—	2-1	5-0	1-1	4-2	2-1	1-1	3-2	2-1	2-1	0-2	1-0	1-0	1-0	0-3	6-0	0-2	0-0	2-1	2-0	4-3
Crawley T	0-1	2-3	1-0	1-2	—	2-0	1-1	2-2	1-5	3-1	1-0	3-0	1-0	0-4	1-1	2-0	3-2	1-1	1-2	1-4	1-2	2-2	5-3	1-2
Droylsden	2-2	0-2	0-0	2-1	5-0	—	3-3	0-3	3-1	5-3	1-0	0-4	2-1	1-0	1-0	0-3	2-1	4-1	0-2	1-0	2-3	1-3	2-1	3-4
Ebbsfleet U	2-2	2-1	2-0	1-1	1-1	3-3	—	2-1	2-2	2-2	0-0	1-0	2-0	0-1	0-0	0-1	2-2	1-1	1-0	1-2	2-0	0-0	1-1	1-1
Exeter C	1-1	1-1	0-2	1-2	2-2	3-0	2-1	—	2-1	5-3	1-2	0-2	2-1	1-0	1-3	2-1	1-1	0-3	1-1	1-0	1-0	2-1	1-1	3-0
Farsley Celtic	1-3	2-1	2-1	2-1	1-5	1-2	1-1	2-1	—	3-1	1-2	3-0	0-1	2-2	2-1	0-1	0-3	4-0	1-0	1-2	4-3	0-0	2-1	1-4
Forest Green R	0-1	3-1	1-1	1-1	3-0	5-3	1-0	5-3	3-0	—	2-1	3-2	1-2	1-0	1-0	0-0	2-2	1-0	1-3	0-6	1-3	1-0	3-2	0-2
Grays Ath	3-2	0-1	2-3	1-2	2-1	4-1	0-0	2-1	1-3	1-2	—	1-0	0-0	1-0	1-0	0-0	1-0	0-1	1-0	1-2	1-0	0-1	1-1	3-1
Halifax T	1-0	3-3	2-1	1-0	0-4	1-0	1-0	0-1	3-0	1-1	3-3	—	1-3	2-2	1-1	2-3	2-1	3-1	3-1	1-0	2-3	2-0	1-0	3-0
Histon	3-1	2-1	1-3	1-0	1-0	0-1	0-1	5-4	1-3	1-1	0-1	0-0	—	1-1	1-3	3-0	2-1	2-1	0-1	1-0	3-3	2-1	1-1	0-1
Kidderminster H	2-1	2-1	0-2	0-3	0-4	1-0	0-1	5-0	2-2	5-1	1-6	2-1	0-0	—	1-1	1-3	0-0	3-1	6-0	4-3	2-0	1-1	1-1	1-3
Northwich Vic	5-0	4-1	2-1	2-1	1-3	1-0	1-3	4-1	1-3	1-1	3-1	1-1	0-1	2-1	—	0-2	1-0	2-1	0-0	0-0	2-0	2-3	1-1	3-0
Oxford U	1-0	1-3	1-2	1-2	2-0	4-1	1-0	1-3	0-1	0-0	0-0	0-3	0-1	2-0	0-2	—	1-0	5-0	3-2	3-0	1-2	0-1	1-1	0-1
Rushden & D	2-1	2-1	1-0	4-1	0-3	2-2	0-2	1-4	2-1	3-0	1-1	2-0	1-0	1-0	1-0	1-0	—	1-1	0-1	3-2	3-2	1-1	2-3	2-1
Salisbury C	2-1	2-0	4-3	1-1	0-0	4-2	2-2	0-3	0-3	1-1	1-0	1-1	1-1	2-2	2-1	0-1	1-5	—	4-0	1-0	2-1	3-2	4-0	1-3
Stafford R	4-3	2-0	2-1	1-2	1-2	0-1	2-1	4-1	0-2	5-1	6-0	4-3	1-1	1-0	1-0	0-3	1-1	0-1	—	1-2	1-0	0-3	1-1	2-0
Stevenage B	3-1	2-0	2-1	1-2	2-3	0-2	1-0	4-0	4-1	0-2	1-2	0-2	0-1	2-1	1-0	1-0	1-2	4-2	0-4	—	1-1	1-0	0-2	3-2
Torquay U	0-1	2-2	1-1	0-0	1-2	2-3	2-3	1-2	4-3	4-3	1-2	4-5	3-3	2-0	0-3	3-2	2-0	1-3	1-3	1-3	—	1-3	2-1	0-1
Weymouth	0-0	2-1	0-1	1-2	1-3	2-0	0-0	1-3	0-2	3-2	2-2	2-0	1-3	2-0	1-1	3-2	1-0	3-0	3-2	1-1	3-0	—	1-1	1-1
Woking	2-1	2-2	2-0	2-1	5-3	1-1	1-1	1-1	2-1	1-1	2-0	0-1	1-1	1-1	0-1	1-1	2-1	0-1	1-1	0-1	1-3	0-1	—	2-3
York C	2-0	2-2	4-3	1-2	6-1	3-4	1-1	1-4	1-2	0-2	3-1	3-0	0-1	1-3	3-0	0-1	1-1	1-2	0-2	3-2	0-1	1-1	2-3	—

BLUE SQUARE PREMIER PLAY-OFFS 2007–2008

BLUE SQUARE PREMIER SEMI-FINALS FIRST LEG

| Exeter C | (0) 1 | Torquay U | (1) 2 |
| Burton Alb | (0) 2 | Cambridge U | (0) 2 |

BLUE SQUARE PREMIER SEMI-FINALS SECOND LEG

| Torquay U | (0) 1 | Exeter C | (0) 4 |
| Cambridge U | (1) 2 | Burton Alb | (1) 1 |

BLUE SQUARE PREMIER FINAL (at Wembley)

Sunday, 18 May 2008

Exeter C (1) 1 *(Edwards 22)*

Cambridge U (0) 0   42,511

Exeter C: Jones; Friend, Tully, Seaborne, Edwards, Taylor M, Harley, Gill, Stansfield (Watson), Logan, Moxey.
Cambridge U: Potter; Gleeson (Fortune-West), Pitt, Albrighton, Peters, Hatswell, Carden, Wolleaston, Boylan (Vieira), McEvilly, Brown (Reed).
Referee: C. Pawson (Sheffield).

ATTENDANCES BY CLUB 2007–2008

	Aggregate 2007–08	Average 2007–08	Highest Attendance 2007–08
Oxford United	108,750	4,728	5,900 v Crawley Town
Exeter City	85,206	3,705	7,839 v Torquay United
Cambridge United	81,675	3,551	7,125 v Histon
Torquay United	71,879	3,125	6,021 v Exeter City
Aldershot Town	69,710	3,031	5,980 v Weymouth
York City	51,940	2,258	3,136 v Cambridge United
Stevenage Borough	51,166	2,225	4,533 v Cambridge United
Burton Albion	41,079	1,786	2,881 v Exeter City
Woking	40,353	1,754	4,356 v Aldershot Town
Rushden & Diamonds	36,487	1,586	2,405 v Stevenage Borough
Kidderminster Harriers	35,786	1,556	2,027 v Torquay United
Salisbury City	35,488	1,543	2,633 v Torquay United
Weymouth	32,463	1,411	2,995 v Exeter City
Halifax Town	31,011	1,348	2,875 v York City
Forest Green Rovers	27,104	1,178	2,382 v Torquay United
Altrincham	27,053	1,176	4,154 v Farsley Celtic
Ebbsfleet United	25,002	1,087	1,852 v Oxford United
Histon	24,454	1,063	3,721 v Cambridge United
Crawley Town	23,955	1,042	1,940 v Aldershot Town
Grays Athletic	21,144	919	1,460 v Stevenage Borough
Northwich Victoria	20,888	908	1,875 v Droylsden
Stafford Rangers	19,394	843	1,853 v Farsley Celtic
Farsley Celtic	16,187	704	1,603 v York City
Droylsden	14,800	643	1,178 v Altrincham

APPEARANCES AND GOALSCORERS 2007–2008

ALDERSHOT TOWN
Goals: *League (82):* John Grant 20 (3 pens), Davies 10, Dixon 7, Elvins 7, Hudson 7, Harding 5, Hylton 5, Joel Grant 4, Soares 4, Chalmers 3, Day 3 (2 pens), Newman 2, Charles 1, Donnelly 1, Mendes 1, Winfield 1, own goal 1.
FA Cup (3): Dixon 2, Soares 1.
Trophy (16): John Grant 5, Dixon 2, Hudson 2, Mendes 2, Charles 1, Davies 1, Harding 1, Soares 1, Winfield 1.
League Appearances: Bull, 44; Chalmers, 41+1; Charles, 35; Davies, 24+5; Day, 32+4; Dixon, 18+3; Donnelly, 2+6; Elvins, 29+8; Gier, 38; Joel Grant 20+10; John Grant 32+2; Harding, 46; Hudson, 18+17; Hylton, 9+14; Jaimez-Ruiz, 2+1; Mendes, 3+3; Newman, 14+13; Scott, 1; Simmons, 0+1; Smith, 6+2; Soares, 30+7; Straker, 43; Williams, 1; Winfield, 18+6.

ALTRINCHAM TOWN
Goals: *League (56):* Little 21 (2 pens), Senior 8, Shotton 5, O'Neill 4, Peyton 3 (1 pen), Sedgemore 3 (1 pen), Lawton 2, Tinson 2, Battersby 1, Cahill 1, Dean 1, Lane 1, Munroe 1, Young 1, own goals 2.
FA Cup (2): Little 1, Senior 1.
Trophy (1): Little 1.
League Appearances: Acton, 8; Aspinall, 8+4; Battersby, 4+7; Berkeley, 0+2; Cahill, 6+5; Clancy, 1+3; Coburn, 37; Coo, 0+1; Dean, 3; Jennings, 9; King, 16; Lane, 32+7; Lawton, 45; Little, 34+5; Logan, 9+10; Lynch, 8; McFadden, 4+3; Munroe, 12+4; O'Neill, 23+19; Owen, 11+2; Peyton, 41+2; Potts, 0+13; Roca, 0+7; Rose, 1+1; Saunders, 1; Scott, 14+5; Sedgemore, 18+4; Senior, 28+10; Shotton, 34; Tansey, 5; Thornley, 0+1; Tinson, 45; Toulson, 13+2; Turnbull, 6; Whalley, 9+5; Young, 21+1.

BURTON ALBION
Goals: *League (79):* Clare 19 (3 pens), Harrad 16, Gilroy 6, Webster 6, Brayford 5, Greaves 5, Edwards 4, Goodfellow 4, McGrath 4, Williams 3, Corbett 2, Holmes 2, Gooding 1, Taylor 1, own goal 1.
FA Cup (7): Clare 2, McGrath 2, Harrad 1, Stride 1, own goal 1.
Trophy (8): Clare 3 (1 pen), Edwards 2, McGrath 2, Brayford 1.
Play-Offs (3): Clare 2 (1 pen), Stride 1.
League Appearances: Aiston, 4+1; Austin, 5+6; Brayford, 45; Clare, 33+6;

Clough, 0+1; Corbett, 33+3; Deeney, 13+1; Edwards, 23+9; Farrell, 17+4; Gilroy, 32+3; Goodfellow, 15+20; Gooding, 11+1; Greaves, 30+5; Hall, 0+2; Harrad, 26+20; Holmes, 10+11; Hurst, 16; James, 29+1; McGrath, 46; Poole, 32; Shaw, 2+3; Simpson, 25; Stride, 16+8; Taylor, 3+2; Tomlinson, 1; Webster, 33+4; Williams, 6+3.

CAMBRIDGE UNITED
Goals: *League (68):* Rendell 17, Boylan 11 (2 pens), Beesley 7, Fortune-West 6, Wolleaston 5, McEvilly 3, Pitt 3, Albrighton 2, Convery 2, Farrell 2, Hatswell 2, Vieira 2, Gleeson 1, Hoyte 1, Jeffrey 1, Reed 1, Robinson 1, own goal 1.
FA Cup (10): Rendell 4 (3 pens), Boylan 2, Knight 2, Fortune-West 1, Wolleaston 1.
Trophy (5): Rendell 2, Boylan 1, Fortune-West 1, Hoyte 1.
Play-Offs (4): McEvilly 2 (1 pen), Wolleaston 2.
League Appearances: Albrighton, 37+1; Beesley, 13+4; Boylan, 24+8; Brown, 13+1; Carden, 17; Collins, 0+1; Convery, 13+9; Coulson, 9+4; Farrell, 7+6; Fortune-West, 17+6; Gleeson, 40; Hatswell, 18; Hoyte, 11; Hyem, 0+5; Jeffrey, 4+6; Knights, 4; McCarthy, 1; McEvilly, 13+1; McShane, 1; Morrison, 39+1; Peters, 26+7; Pitt, 40+6; Potter, 44; Quinton, 12+3; Reed, 28+10; Rendell, 23+6; Robinson, 2+2; Smith, 1+13; Vieira, 4+6; Willmott, 1+14; Wolleaston, 44.

CRAWLEY TOWN
Goals: *League (73):* Cook 16 (3 pens), Pittman 12 (1 pen), Madjo 11 (3 pens), Vieira 5, Joseph-Dubois 4, Pinault 4, Thompson 4, Allen 2 (1 pen), Bulman 2, Carayol 2, Hall 2, James 2, Stevens 2, Blackburn 1, Evans 1, Mills 1, Murphy 1, own goal 1.
FA Cup (1): Carayol 1.
Trophy (12): Cook 4 (1 pen), Vieira 4, Bulman 2, Pitman 2.
League Appearances: Allen, 2; Bayes, 45; Blackburn, 15+9; Bull, 20; Bulman, 42+2; Carayol, 13+13; Carter, 0+3; Cook, 36+4; Dutton-Black, 1+2; Evans, 2+11; Hall, 14+2; James, 10+2; Joseph-Dubois, 9+22; Judge, 1+1; Knowles, 1; Krause, 24+3; Lovegrove, 1+1; Madjo, 17+1; Mills, 14; Murphy, 20+3; Nlome-Ndebi, 1+1; Pinault, 38+3; Pittman, 32+4;

Raynor, 0+1; Scully, 3; Shimmin, 2; Stevens, 43; Thomas, 12+6; Thompson, 42+2; Ujah, 2; Vieira, 11+11; Watson, 11; Wilson, 31+4.

DROYLSDEN

Goals: *League (46):* Banim 10 (4 pens), Fearns 8, McGuire 7, Denham 6, Daly 4 (1 pen), Burberry 2, Lynch 2, Cryan 1, Johnson 1, Mackin 1, Newton 1, Talbot 1, own goals 2.

FA Cup (2): Banim 1 (pen), Fearns 1.

Trophy (3): Banim 2 (1 pen), Fearns 1.

League Appearances: Banim, 27+4; Burberry, 22+4; Burke, 5; Cryan, 37+3; Daly, 24+2; Denham, 35+2; Dugdale, 8+6; Ellis, 3+9; Fearns, 30+9; Gibson, 5+6; Halford, 33+2; Hotte, 3; Johnson, 3; Lynch, 21+10; Mackin, 12; Marsh-Evans, 2+1; McGuire, 36; Morris, 18+3; Munroe, 7+4; Murphy, 17+13; Murray, 19; Murtagh, 6; Newton, 14+1; Norton, 0+1; Phillips, 44; Robinson, 4; Roche, 20+1; Salmon, 2+15; Senior, 2; Smith, 1+1; Stephens, 5+2; Strong, 13+1; Talbot, 4+14; Tandy, 9+11; Taylforth, 1+1; Vaughan, 2; Warner, 12+3; Williams, 0+1; Wilson, 0+1; Woods, 0+1.

EBBSFLEET UNITED

Goals: *League (65):* Long 14, Eribenne 9, Moore 7, Akinde 6, McPhee 5 (2 pens), Bostwick 4, Nade 4, Purcell 4, Debolla 3 (1 pen), Barrett 2, Hearn 2, Smith 2, Coleman Luke 1, own goals 2.

FA Cup (1): Moore 1.

Trophy (13): McPhee 6, Akinde 1, Barrett 1, Bostwick 1, Long 1, McCarthy 1, Moore 1, Opinel 1.

League Appearances: Akinde, 15+4; Barrett, 26+8; Bostwick, 40+3; Bull, 6+3; Charles, 8+1; Coleman, Liam 2+12; Coleman, Luke 0+4; Cronin, 38; Debolla, 13+3; Eribenne, 17+12; Goodhind, 7+1; Hastings, 5+2; Hawkins, 37+1; Hearn, 6+7; Long, 43+1; MacDonald, 5+2; Maskell, 0+1; McCarthy, 27+1; McPhee, 43+1; Moore, 39+5; Mott, 1; Nade, 20+13; Opinel, 32+2; Purcell, 21+11; Ricketts, 22+7; Slatter, 4+2; Smith, 21+2; Starkey, 1+1; Tynan, 7.

EXETER CITY

Goals: *League (83):* Logan 18 (4 pens), Mackie 11, Stansfield 10, Moxey 9, Taylor M 9, Basham 5 (1 pen), Carlisle 4, Elam 3, Gill 3, Seaborne 2, Edwards 1, Friend 1, Harley 1, Watson 1, own goals 4.

FA Cup (7): Mackie 2, Taylor M 2, Basham 1 (pen), Carlisle 1, own goal 1.

Trophy (3): Basham 1, Mackie 1, Moxey 1.

Play-Offs (6): Carlisle 2, Edwards 1, Harley 1, Logan 1, Watson 1 (pen).

League Appearances: Artus, 8+2; Basham, 15+17; Carlisle, 24+8; Cozic, 10+5; Edwards, 46; Elam, 9+14; Friend, 27+3; Gill, 43; Harley, 9+3; Jones, 7; Logan, 28+13; Mackie, 21+3; Marriott, 39; Moxey, 43+2; Richardson, 15+4; Seaborne, 24; Sercombe, 4+3; Stansfield, 36+5; Taylor, A. 19+1; Taylor, M. 40; Tully, 38+1; Watson, 1+8.

FARSLEY CELTIC

Goals: *League (48):* Reeves 11, Bambrook 5, Downes 4 (4 pens), Grant 4, Stamer 4, Knowles 3, McNiven D 3, Torpey 3, Heath 2 (1 pen), Iqbal 2, Krief 2 (1 pen), Whitman 2, Bentham 1, Jackson 1, own goal 1.

FA Cup (2): Reeves 2.

Trophy (6): Tuck 2, Bambrook 1, Billy 1, Knowles 1, own goal 1.

League Appearances: Allanson, 7+14; Aspden, 21; Bambrook, 30+9; Bentham, 16; Billy, 12+3; Camfield, 0+5; Crossley, 20; Cuss, 4; Downes, 35+1; Dunne, 1+3; Gardner, 3; Grant, 12+8; Heath, 4+9; Hotte, 2; Iqbal, 40; Jackson, 26+5; Knowles, 28+8; Krief, 17+2; Law, 2; Lawlor, 1; Lloyd, 3; McNiven, D. 6+6; McNiven, S. 28+3; Morgan, 15; Pearson, 7; Prendergast, 16+1; Reeves, 43+1; Santos, 17; Serrant, C. 7; Serrant, R. 10+2; Smith, 0+1; Stamer, 21+8; Sugden, 2+1; Sutcliffe, 2; Torpey, 17+5; Tuck, 7+9; Watson, 17+10; Whitman, 3+10; Wilberforce, 4+1.

FOREST GREEN ROVERS

Goals: *League (76):* Fleetwood 28 (1 pen), Beesley 10, Carey-Bertram 7, Rigoglioso 6, Jones 5, Clist 3, Dodgson 3, Giles 3, Afful 2, Lawless 2, Smith 2, Stonehouse 2, Brough 1, Preece 1, own goal 1.

FA Cup (14): Fleetwood 6, Beesley 2, Carey-Bertram 2, Clist 1, Dodgson 1, Forbes 1, Giles 1, Lawless 1.

Trophy (5): Fleetwood 2 (1 pen), Giles 1, Lawless 1, Stonehouse 1.

League Appearances: Afful, 20+22; Beesley, 19+4; Brough, 31+2; Burton, 14+1; Carey-Bertram, 13+11; Clist, 39; Dodgson, 16+12; Fleetwood, 41; Giles, 30+3; Hardiker, 31+3; James, 4+3; Jones, 37+2; Lawless, 32; Pitman, 29+2; Preece, 17+18; Rigoglioso, 18+9; Robinson, 32+1; Smith, 11+14; Stonehouse, 24+11; Tonkin, 37+1; Welsh, 11+5.

GRAYS ATHLETIC
Goals: *League (58):* Kedwell 13 (4 pens), Taylor J 9, Cogan 5, Watson 5, O'Connor 4, Murray 3, Taylor S 3, Ashton 2, Cumbers 2, Goulding 2, Grant 2, Hearn 2, Standing 2, Day 1, McAllister 1, Obersteller 1, Power 1.
FA Cup (1): O'Connor 1.
Trophy (5): O'Connor 3 (1 pen), Kedwell 2.
League Appearances: Ashton, 39+1; Barnard, 4; Barnes, 0+1; Button, 1; Cogan, 10+3; Cooksey, 18+1; Cumbers, 1+4; Daniel, 0+1; Day, 8+9; Downer, 29; Eyre, 10+1; Flitney, 30; Gaia, 8; Goulding, 2+7; Grant, 9+6; Gross, 25+2; Haverson, 2+1; Hearn, 12+3; Kamara, 0+1; Kedwell, 35+7; Knowles, 5; Lawson, 5+4; Marshall, 3+8; Mawer, 4+1; McAllister, 5+4; McCafferty, 10+6; Murray, 23; O'Connor, 34+12; Obersteller, 9+3; Oli, 16+1; Patterson, 7+2; Potter, 0+1; Power, 4+1; Sambrook, 22+1; Saunders, 1+1; Selley, 3+1; Standing, 9+6; Stuart, 43; Taylor, J. 13+4; Taylor, S. 11+7; Thurgood, 24+1; Watson, 12+12; Whincup, 0+1.

HALIFAX TOWN
Goals: *League (61):* Shaw 20 (6 pens), Campbell 8 (2 pens), Heslop 5, Griffith 4, Killeen 3, Stamp 3, Belle 2, Forrest 2, Nelthorpe 2, Torpey 2 (1 pen), Clarke 1, Davies 1, Doughty 1, Joynes 1, Kearney 1, Taylor 1, Whitehouse 1, own goals 3.
FA Cup (2): Shaw 1, Heslop 1.
Trophy (8): Shaw 4, Heslop 1, Nelthorpe 1, Quinn 1, Sharpe 1.
League Appearances: Ainge, 11+1; Atherton, 1; Bailey, 2+2; Belle, 16+3; Bushell, 8+6; Campbell, 15+15; Clarke, 7; Dadson, 0+2; Davies, 10+1; Doughty, 31+7; Forrest, 22+6; Gaia, 6+3; Gray, 0+7; Griffith, 35+2; Harban, 4+2; Heslop, 28+2; Joynes, 5; Kearney, 38+3; Killeen, 33+7; Legzdins, 30; Mawson, 16; Nelthorpe, 6+1; O'Callaghan, 1; Oliver, 2; Quinn, 32+1; Scott, 11+1; Sharpe, 1; Shaw, 36+1; Stamp, 13+10; Taylor, 10+14; Torpey, 16+6; Toulson, 16+3; Whitehouse, 0+4; Wright, 34+3; Young, 10+1.

HISTON
Goals: *League (76):* Wright 15, Murray 13, Akurang 10 (3 pens), Knight-Percival 8, Midson 5, Gwillim 4 (2 pens), Kennedy J 4, Langston 4, Mitchell-King 3, Andrews 2, Barker 2, Nightingale 2, Okay 2, Dillon 1, own goal 1.
FA Cup (4): Barker 1, Knight-Percival 1,

Murray 1, Wright 1.
Trophy (8): Knight-Percival 3, Wright 2, Kennedy J 1, Murray 1, Nightingale 1.
League Appearances: Ada, 32+4; Akurang, 19; Andrews, 0+3; Barker, 11+25; Cambridge, 36+5; Dillon, 1+2; Gwillim, 42+2; Haniver, 5+5; Hipperson, 4+2; Kennedy, J. 45; Kennedy, N. 1+10; Knight-Percival, 43+1; Langston, 16+8; Midson, 17+2; Mitchell-King, 40; Murray, 39+2; Naisbitt, 36; Nightingale, 10+8; Okay, 41+2; Osborn, 10; Pope, 28; Wright, 30+11.

KIDDERMINSTER HARRIERS
Goals: *League (74):* Christie 17 (4 pens), Constable 11, Penn 11, Barnes-Homer 6 (1 pen), Richards 6 (2 pens), Russell 6, Knights 4, Creighton 3, Hurren 2, Bennett 1, Bignot 1, Blackwood 1, Ferrell 1 (pen), Harkness 1, McGrath 1, own goals 2.
FA Cup (6): Barnes-Homer 1, Blackwood 1, Constable 1, Creighton 1, McGrath 1, Richards 1.
Trophy (4): Constable 1, Harkness 1, Kenna 1, Russell 1 (pen).
League Appearances: Bailey, 2+1; Barnes-Homer, 17+17; Bennett, 33+2; Bevan, 17; Bignot, 25+3; Blackwood, 27; Christie, 24+14; Coleman, 8+2; Constable, 24; Creighton, 44; Ferrell, 31+7; Harkness, 15+3; Hurren, 31+3; Jeannin, 17+1; Jones, 6; Kenna, 26+2; Knights, 12+5; MacKenzie, 21; McGrath, 10+21; Munday, 3; Penn, 42; Richards, 22+4; Russell, 24+6; Smikle, 8+20; Whitehead, 16+1; Wylde, 1+1.

NORTHWICH VICTORIA
Goals: *League (52):* Steele 13, Byrom 5, Welch 4, Burns 3, Byrne 3 (1 pen), Tait 3, Stamp 3, Brown R 2, Carr 2, Coulson 2, Rusk 2, Williams C 2, Williams D 2 (2 pens), Akins 1, Belle 1, Roberts 1, Crowell 1, Brown D 1, own goal 1.
FA Cup (4): Tait 1, Townson 1, Williams D 1, own goal 1.
Trophy (1): Steele 1.
League Appearances: Akins, 10; Barker, 0+4; Battersby, 18+2; Belle, 16; Birch Roberts, 18+2; Bowler, 5; Brown, R. 38; Burns, 7+12; Byrne, 17+11; Byrom, 21; Carr, 33+8; Connett, 19+1; Coulson, 6; Coward, 0+1; Crowell, 14+1; Edge, 4; Evans Brown, D. 9+1; Farquharson, 2+1; Hanley, 1+6; Heslop, 6; Horrocks, 9+6; Johnson, 0+1; Kerr, 13; Maamria, 6+5; Maylett, 11+5; Meadowcroft, 8+1; Morning, 3+3; Mullan, 15+4; Murphy, 2; Roddy, 0+1; Rusk, 15+1; Scales, 0+1;

334

Sharp, 7; Speight Allan, 1+5; Steele, 23+6; Strong, 16+2; Tait, 13+3; Taylor, 1; Townson Stamp, 13+6; Tunnicliffe, 2+1; Tynan, 21; Warhurst, 2; Welch, 33+2; Williams, C. 12+2; Williams, D. 15+2; Wilson, 21+5.

OXFORD UNITED

Goals: *League (56):* Green 10, Odubade 10, Trainer 9, Duffy 6 (4 pens), Murray 3 (3 pens), Twigg 3 (1 pen), McAllister 2, Shaw 2, Anaclet 1, Barnes 1, Corcoran 1, Day 1, Fisher 1, Howard 1, Hutchinson 1, Jeannin 1, Quinn 1, Richards 1, own goal 1.
FA Cup (5): Rhodes 2, Anaclet 1, Jeannin 1, Odubade 1 (pen).
Trophy (0).
League Appearances: Anaclet, 30+2; Bailey, 3; Barnes, 1+2; Benjamin, 0+2; Blackwood, 5+2; Clarke, 13+5; Collins, 1; Corcoran, 14+2; Day, 36+3; Duffy, 14+6; Fisher, 1+9; Foster, 30+2; Gilchrist, 3; Gnohere, 7+1; Green, 16+4; Hand, 13; Howard, 17; Hutchinson, 22+6; Jeannin, 27+1; Ledgister, 6+3; McAllister, 9+8; Murray, 21; Odubade, 28+13; Pettefer, 15+8; Quinn, 42; Rhodes, 3+1; Richards, 10+5; Robinson, 2+7; Rose, 4+15; Semple, 0+1; Shaw, 10; St Aimie, 2; Standing, 3+3; Tardif, 1+1; Taylor, 0+3; Trainer, 41; Turley, 45; Twigg, 5+5; Weedon, 1+1; Willmott, 5+2.

RUSHDEN & DIAMONDS

Goals: *League (55):* Jackson 16 (2 pens), Rankine 12 (1 pen), Challinor 5, Burgess 3, Hatswell 3, Shaw 3 (1 pen), Hope 2, Ademeno 1, Gulliver 1, Howell 1 (pen), Malcolm 1, McAllister 1, Smith 1, Tomlin 1, Woodhouse 1, own goals 3.
FA Cup (9): Jackson 2, Kelly 2, Burgess 1, Challinor 1, Gulliver 1, Rankine 1, own goal 1.
Trophy (8): Tomlin 3, Brown 1, Burgess 1, Gulliver 1, Hales 1, Kelly 1.
League Appearances: Ademeno, 4+3; Andersen, 3; Bastock, 19; Beecroft, 0+3; Brown, 2+; Burgess, 35+4; Challinor, 35+10; Corcoran, 14; El Kholti, 9+4; Foster, 20; Gooding, 10+3; Gulliver, 31+3; Hales, 4+3; Hatswell, 22+1; Hope, 36+1; Howell, 40+3; Jackson, 32; Kelly, 19+6; Lambley, 0+3; Malcolm, 2+6; Margarson, 3; McAllister, 7+2; Nicholls, 8; Nunn, 0+1; Osano, 42; Platt, 7+3; Rankine, 27+15; Roberts, 13; Rusk, 6; Semple, 2+2; Shaw, 15+17; Smith, 3+5; Tomlin, 15+19; Watson, 3+1; Woodhouse, 28+1.

SALISBURY CITY

Goals: *League (70):* Tubbs 16 (4 pens), Brown 11, Feeney 9, Matthews 8, Turk 5, Clarke D 4, Cook 3, Sandell 3, Bond 2, Fowler 2, Oliver 2, Barnes 1, Sinclair 1, own goals 3.
FA Cup (0).
Trophy (0).
League Appearances: Assau-Adjaye, 14; Barnes, 7+3; Barron, 0+2; Bartlett, 31+4; Bass, 36; Beswetherick, 1+1; Bond, 17+2; Brown, 12+22; Clarke, D. 30+3; Clarke, R. 46; Clay, 5+6; Cook, 42; Feeney, 23+19; Fowler, 25+5; Herring, 11+2; Knight, 0+1; Matthews, 26+6; Oliver, 9+1; Prince, 3+7; Richards, 2+4; Robinson, 43; Sales, 0+2; Sandell, 32+1; Sinclair, 15+1; Tubbs, 33+9; Turk, 43; Widdrington, 0+1.

STAFFORD RANGERS

Goals: *League (42):* Grayson 11 (1 pen), Adaggio 6 (1 pen), McNiven 5, Wellecomm 4, Arnolin 2 (1 pen), Flynn 2, Jarrett 2 (1 pen), Smith 2, Street 2, Djoumin 1, McAughtrie 1, Reid 1, Richards 1, Sangare 1, Shaw 1.
FA Cup (2): Grayson 1 (pen), Street 1.
Trophy (8): McNiven 3 (1 pen), Draper 1, Flynn 1, Sangare 1, Jarrett 1, Street 1.
League Appearances: Adaggio, 16+8; Alcock, 32; Arnolin, 12+5; Avinel, 8; Daniel, 42+2; Djoumin, 7+1; Dodd, 3+1; Draper, 26+6; Duggan, 2; Flynn, 38+3; Gibson, 13; Grayson, 34+8; Hamilton, 1+4; Hazley, 11+4; Hopkinson, 9+6; Hughes, 3; Humphrey, 4; Ingram, 6+3; Jarrett, 10+6; Loach, 11; Loukes, 7+2; Lynch, 2; Manak, 0+3; Mawene, 16+2; McAughtrie, 6; McNiven, 20+3; Meakin-Richards, 1; Murray, 16; Olaoye, 5+3; Oldfield, 7+3; Potter, 6; Puddy, 1; Reid, 9+3; Richards, 6+3; Robinson, 0+2; Sangare, 24+2; Shaw, 1+5; Smith, 8+9; Stones, 9+1; Street, 25+6; Sutton, 39+1; Wellecomm, 9+2; Youngs, 1+2.

STEVENAGE BOROUGH

Goals: *League (82):* Morison 22 (2 pens), Dobson 10, Grant 7 (1 pen), McMahon 7, Arber 5 (3 pens), Miller 5 (1 pen), Lewis S 3, Berry 2, Cole 2, Martin 2, Nutter 2 (1 pen), Oliver 2, Westwood 2, Allen 1, Bramble 1, Burke 1, Gaia 1, Henry 1, Laird 1, Moore 1, Stokes 1, Vincenti 1, Willock 1, own goal 1.
FA Cup (1): Molesley 1.
Trophy (1): Morison 1.
League Appearances: Allen, 1+12; Anderson, 1+5; Arber, 27; Batt, 0+2; Berry, 8+6; Bramble, 4+7; Buchanan,

0+1; Burke, 0+2; Cole, 22+5; Dobson, 24+2; Eames, 0+1; Fuller, 22+2; Gaia, 6+3; Grant, 12+2; Hakim, 1+2; Henry, 33+3; John, 0+5; Julian, 43; Laird, 11+4; Lewis, J. 8; Lewis, S. 21+1; Liptak, 2; Martin, 33; Masters, 3; McMahon, 27+10; Miller, 16; Mitchell, 5+1; Molesley, 5+6; Moore, 11+1; Morison, 43; Murray, 12+1; Nutter, 13+1; O'Sullivan, 1+6; Oliver, 14+2; Rankin, 2+4; Smith, 15; Stokes, 2+1; Vincenti, 11+1; Westwood, 20; White, 4; Willock, 6+3; Wilson, 17+7.

TORQUAY UNITED
Goals: *League (83):* Sills 19 (3 pens), Zebroski 18 (1 pen), Phillips 12 (2 pens), Benyon 5, Todd 5, D'Sane 3 (1 pen), Ellis 3, Hargreaves 3, Hill 2, Mohamed 2, Robertson 2, Stevens 2, Hinshelwood 1, Hockley 1, Mansell 1, Mullings 1, Nicholson 1, Welsh 1, own goal 1.
FA Cup (6): Stevens 3, Todd 2, Phillips 1.
Trophy (11): Phillips 3, D'Sane 2 (1 pen), Hargreaves 2, Mohamed 2, Sills 2.
Play-Offs (3): Hill 1, Sills 1, Zebroski 1.
League Appearances: Adams, 11+1; Andersen, 3; Banim, 3+5; Bedeau, 13+10; Benyon, 5+17; D'Sane, 14+5; Ellis, 22; Hargreaves, 38; Hill, 4+9; Hinshelwood, 7; Hockley, 23+6; Laird, 2; Mansell, 34; Mohamed, 5+5; Mullings, 3+3; Nicholson, 46; Phillips, 35+7; Poke, 4; Rayner, 30; Rice, 9; Robertson, 23; Sills, 43+1; Stevens, 18+11; Thompson, 0+1; Todd, 41; Welsh, 5+13; Woods, 21; Wring, 0+7; Zebroski, 43+3.

WEYMOUTH
Goals: *League (53):* Louis 7, Coutts 6, McCallum 6, Robinson 5, Weatherstone 5 (1 pen), Crittenden 4, Beavon 3, Malcolm 3, Blackburn 2, Platt 2, Vickers 2, Bedeau 1, Doe 1, Douglas 1, Hyde 1, Jombarti 1, Vernazza 1, own goals 2.
FA Cup (6): Beavon 3, Louis 1, Roberts J 1, Robinson 1.
Trophy (3): Malcolm 2, Louis 1.
League Appearances: Anzite, 3+1; Bailey, 9; Beavon, 31+8; Bedeau, 1; Bernard, 9; Blackburn, 12+1; Browning, 16+3; Challis, 16+2; Compton, 1; Convery, 4+1; Coutts, 33+8; Critchell, 34+1; Crittenden, 25+12; Doe, 30+4; Domoraud, 4; Douglas, 2+14; Gross,

2+1; Hart, 1; Henderson, 16; Hyde, 3+2; Jombarti, 11+1; Kitamirike, 18; Louis, 16+5; Malcolm, 8+11; Matthews, 22; McCallum, 10+14; Ngala, 2; Okuonghae, 5; Phillips, 4+11; Platt, 13+7; Roberts, D. 0+1; Roberts, J. 20+2; Robinson, 42+1; Stewart, 8; Swaibu, 1; Vernazza, 27+2; Vickers, 10+2; Weatherstone, 24+3; Young, 3.

WOKING
Goals: *League (53):* Sole 14 (6 pens), Morgan 10, Pattison 9, Norville 4, Quamina 3, Gatting 2 (1 pen), Hakin 2, Hutchinson 2, Marum 2, Ruby 2, Batt 1, Bunce 1, own goal 1.
FA Cup (0).
Trophy (3): James 1, Morgan 1, Norville 1.
League Appearances: Batt, 10+3; Bunce, 41; Charles, 1+4; Christon, 1+1; Gasson, 42+1; Gatting, 13+2; Gibbs, 3+1; Gindre, 30; Gray, 21+8; Green, 18+3; Hakin, 3+4; Harusha, 1+1; Hutchinson, 33; James, 18; Lambu, 30+11; Lorraine, 34; Maledon, 8+10; Marum, 8+18; McCarthy, 1; Morgan, 39+3; Norville, 13+3; Pattison, 40+2; Quamina, 37+1; Ruby, 22+4; Shin, 0+1; Sole, 24+16; Warner, 15+1; Yorkie, 0+1.

YORK CITY
Goals: *League (71):* Sodje 14, Woolford 14, Brodie 10, Farrell 8 (3 pens), Wroe 6 (3 pens), Brayson 4, Elliott 3, Fortune-West 2, Kelly 2, McBreen 2, Robinson 2, McGurk 1, Meechan 1, Panther 1, Parslow 1.
FA Cup (6): Farrell 3, Sodje 2, Wroe 1.
Trophy (12): Farrell 3 (1 pen), Wroe 3, Brodie 2 (1 pen), Lloyd 1, Parslow 1, Woolford 1, own goal 1.
League Appearances: Beadle, 4; Beardsley, 4+4; Boyes, 0+3; Brayson, 16+6; Brodie, 21+18; Craddock, 25+5; Duncum, 1+1; Elliott, 32+4; Evans, 36; Farrell, 13+7; Fortune-West, 7+6; Fry, 0+4; Greenwood, 4+3; Hall, 1+1; Hegarty, 2; Henderson, 7; Hutchinson, 2+1; Jones, 2; Kelly, 25+2; Lloyd, 11+4; McBreen, 5; McGurk, 46; McWilliams, 4+1; Meechan, 3+4; Mimms, 3+1; Panther, 36+4; Parslow, 30+1; Purkiss, 33+4; Robinson, 28+3; Rusk, 10+4; Shepherd, 0+3; Sodje, 29+16; Woolford, 45+1; Wroe, 21+8.

BLUE SQUARE NORTH 2007–2008

FINAL LEAGUE TABLE

			Home					Away					Total					
	P	W	D	L	F	A	W	D	L	F	A	W	D	L	F	A	GD	Pts
1 Kettering T	42	17	1	3	57	19	13	6	2	36	15	30	7	5	93	34	59	97
2 AFC Telford U	42	14	4	3	45	21	10	4	7	25	22	24	8	10	70	43	27	80
3 Stalybridge Celtic	42	12	4	5	47	24	13	0	8	41	27	25	4	13	88	51	37	79
4 Southport	42	10	8	3	38	21	12	3	6	39	29	22	11	9	77	50	27	77
5 Barrow	42	13	4	4	40	18	8	9	4	30	21	21	13	8	70	39	31	76
6 Harrogate T	42	10	6	5	25	16	11	5	5	30	25	21	11	10	55	41	14	74
7 Nuneaton B	42	12	6	3	32	17	7	8	6	26	23	19	14	9	58	40	18	71
8 Burscough	42	8	8	5	33	30	11	0	10	29	28	19	8	15	62	58	4	65
9 Hyde U	42	12	2	7	45	32	8	1	12	39	34	20	3	19	84	66	18	63
10 Boston U	42	12	3	6	39	22	5	5	11	26	35	17	8	17	65	57	8	59
11 Gainsborough Tr	42	8	8	5	35	26	7	4	10	27	39	15	12	15	62	65	–3	57
12 Worcester C	42	8	7	6	27	30	6	5	10	21	38	14	12	16	48	68	–20	54
13 Redditch U	42	10	4	7	28	24	5	4	12	13	34	15	8	19	41	58	–17	53
14 Workington	42	8	4	9	25	20	5	7	9	27	36	13	11	18	52	56	–4	50
15 Tamworth	42	9	6	6	31	20	4	5	12	22	39	13	11	18	53	59	–6	50
16 Alfreton T	42	7	5	9	27	26	5	6	10	22	28	12	11	19	49	54	–5	47
17 Solihull Moors	42	7	5	9	29	36	5	6	10	21	40	12	11	19	50	76	–26	47
18 Blyth Spartans	42	7	2	12	27	31	5	8	8	25	31	12	10	20	52	62	–10	46
19 Hinckley U	42	7	4	10	24	28	4	8	9	24	41	11	12	19	48	69	–21	45
20 Hucknall T	42	4	4	13	25	36	7	2	12	28	39	11	6	25	53	75	–22	39
21 Vauxhall Motors	42	5	4	12	26	47	2	3	16	16	53	7	7	28	42	100	–58	28
22 Leigh	42	5	4	12	21	38	1	4	16	15	49	6	8	28	36	87	–51	26

BLUE SQUARE SETANTA SHIELD FINAL 2007–08

at Aldershot

Attendance 3174

Aldershot Town (0) 3 *(Mendes 71, Hudson 95, Donnelly 107)*
Rushden & Diamonds (0) 3 *(Burgess 73, 109 (pen), Rankine 120)*
aet; Aldershot Town won 4-3 on penalties.

Aldershot: Jaimez-Ruiz; Smith, Straker, Donnelly, Newman, Winfield (Gier), Hudson, Chalmers (Harding), John Grant (Hylton), Mendes, Joel Grant.

Rushden & Diamonds: Roberts; Osano (El Kholti), Howell, Hope, Gulliver, Shaw (Gooding), Challinor, Woodhouse, Kelly (Tomlin), Rankine, Burgess.

Penalties: Gooding missed; Donnelly scored; Howell scored; Harding scored; Burgess scored; Newman scored; Woodhouse scored; Hudson scored; Hope saved.

Referee: S. Hooper (Wiltshire).

BLUE SQUARE NORTH RESULTS 2007–2008

	Alfreton T	AFC Telford U	Barrow	Blyth Spartans	Boston U	Burscough	Gainsborough Trinity	Harrogate T	Hinckley U	Hucknall T	Hyde U	Kettering T	Leigh RMI	Nuneaton B	Redditch U	Solihull Moors	Southport	Stalybridge C	Tamworth	Vauxhall M	Worcester C	Workington
Alfreton T	—	1-0	0-0	1-1	1-1	1-2	3-1	1-2	2-1	1-0	0-3	1-1	1-0	1-3	0-0	0-0	0-0	3-4	1-2	4-0	3-1	2-0
AFC Telford U	3-0	—	0-2	3-1	1-1	1-0	4-1	1-1	3-0	2-1	2-1	0-1	6-1	0-0	1-0	4-0	1-5	3-0	4-1	3-2	0-1	3-3
Barrow	2-1	4-0	—	1-1	2-1	4-1	4-1	2-2	1-1	1-0	1-2	2-0	1-2	0-1	0-0	5-1	1-0	1-3	1-0	4-1	6-0	1-1
Blyth Spartans	2-0	0-2	2-3	—	2-1	1-4	1-1	0-1	0-1	1-2	0-2	2-0	2-0	2-1	2-4	1-0	1-0	0-1	1-1	0-2	2-2	2-0
Boston U	2-1	2-1	2-1	3-2	—	2-1	0-1	0-1	1-1	2-3	3-2	1-1	5-1	2-0	0-2	2-2	1-1	3-1	0-1	5-1	1-1	2-0
Burscough	1-1	1-3	2-1	0-1	1-3	—	2-2	0-1	1-1	2-1	3-3	1-1	5-2	1-0	2-0	0-2	2-1	2-1	2-3	0-0	1-1	1-1
Gainsborough Trinity	2-2	1-0	0-1	0-1	0-1	0-1	—	1-0	2-2	4-1	3-3	0-0	2-1	0-0	3-0	0-2	0-3	2-1	1-0	3-0	0-2	1-1
Harrogate T	0-1	1-0	2-2	4-0	1-3	2-3	2-3	—	1-1	0-0	1-4	0-2	0-1	2-1	2-0	0-1	1-3	0-3	3-2	2-0	2-4	2-1
Hinckley U	1-0	0-2	1-0	0-3	0-1	0-1	1-2	5-2	—	2-1	1-2	0-3	3-1	1-1	1-2	0-1	2-3	2-1	3-1	1-0	5-0	2-1
Hucknall T	2-2	1-2	1-2	0-3	1-2	1-2	0-1	2-2	5-2	—	2-1	0-3	0-0	3-3	4-0	3-0	1-3	1-3	3-1	2-0	3-1	1-2
Hyde U	0-2	1-0	1-2	0-2	0-2	0-1	3-0	1-1	5-2	4-2	—	1-0	3-0	3-2	0-1	6-1	1-1	1-3	1-2	6-3	0-1	3-1
Kettering T	1-1	0-3	3-1	2-4	3-0	1-0	1-3	0-2	4-0	3-2	3-0	—	1-0	3-0	2-1	2-1	2-3	1-3	0-0	3-1	1-1	3-1
Leigh RMI	1-0	2-0	1-0	2-1	2-2	5-1	2-1	2-0	4-2	3-0	2-0	3-0	—	1-0	0-1	0-1	0-2	1-3	1-1	0-1	1-0	3-0
Nuneaton B	1-0	1-1	1-2	3-0	3-1	2-1	3-2	1-2	2-0	0-1	2-1	2-1	2-0	—	0-0	2-1	3-1	0-2	3-1	3-0	2-3	2-2
Redditch U	1-1	2-0	2-0	2-1	3-1	2-3	1-3	0-2	4-0	3-0	2-1	2-0	1-0	0-0	—	0-1	0-2	1-3	2-1	2-0	0-2	2-0
Solihull Moors	0-3	2-0	0-5	2-2	1-0	3-1	0-1	1-3	5-2	5-0	1-4	6-1	1-0	3-1	2-1	—	4-1	0-4	0-2	1-1	1-2	3-0
Southport	1-0	1-1	3-1	2-2	2-2	1-3	5-1	1-2	3-0	0-3	2-1	5-2	2-0	0-2	0-1	4-1	—	2-1	2-2	3-2	0-2	2-5
Stalybridge C	3-1	1-2	1-2	0-0	3-1	1-0	3-2	3-2	3-4	2-1	3-1	1-3	2-0	0-1	1-0	3-2	2-2	—	0-0	4-1	2-0	2-2
Tamworth	0-1	1-0	2-3	3-0	1-0	2-5	0-3	2-0	3-1	0-3	1-1	1-4	2-2	1-2	2-0	4-0	1-2	2-0	—	0-1	2-5	2-0
Vauxhall M	3-2	1-3	0-1	2-2	2-1	3-0	0-3	0-1	0-1	0-3	2-0	3-1	3-1	0-0	2-0	3-2	1-1	2-5	1-3	—	1-1	2-5
Worcester C	1-1	0-3	1-3	2-2	2-1	2-1	0-3	1-1	0-1	1-0	2-0	0-6	2-2	0-4	0-0	3-2	2-3	1-0	1-3	1-0	—	2-2
Workington	1-2	0-1	0-1	2-0	0-1	0-1	1-2	0-1	2-0	1-3	1-0	0-3	2-1	2-0	1-1	1-1	1-1	5-0	5-0	1-0	1-0	—

BLUE SQUARE SOUTH 2007–2008

FINAL LEAGUE TABLE

			Home					Away					Total					
		P	W	D	L	F	A	W	D	L	F	A	W	D	L	F	A	GD	Pts
1	Lewes	42	14	4	3	37	13	13	4	4	44	26	27	8	7	81	39	42	89
2	Eastbourne B	42	12	6	3	42	15	11	5	5	41	23	23	11	8	83	38	45	80
3	Hampton & R	42	10	8	3	49	23	11	6	4	38	26	21	14	7	87	49	38	77
4	Fisher Ath	42	10	3	8	35	36	12	2	7	30	25	22	5	15	65	61	4	71
5	Braintree T	42	13	4	4	30	14	6	8	7	22	28	19	12	11	52	42	10	69
6	Eastleigh	42	9	7	5	34	29	10	3	8	42	33	19	10	13	76	62	14	67
7	Havant & W	42	14	3	4	33	16	5	7	9	26	37	19	10	13	59	53	6	67
8	Bath C	42	10	8	3	30	12	7	7	7	29	24	17	15	10	59	36	23	66
9	Newport Co	42	9	5	7	37	27	9	7	5	27	22	18	12	12	64	49	15	66
10	Bishop's Stortford	42	9	6	6	43	32	9	4	8	29	28	18	10	14	72	60	12	64
11	Bromley	42	11	3	7	44	29	8	4	9	33	37	19	7	16	77	66	11	64
12	Thurrock	42	13	4	4	39	26	5	5	11	24	38	18	9	15	63	64	−1	63
13	Hayes & Yeading U	42	7	9	5	40	35	7	3	11	27	38	14	12	16	67	73	−6	54
14	Cambridge C	42	8	7	6	43	32	6	3	12	28	40	14	10	18	71	72	−1	52
15	Basingstoke	42	8	6	7	33	34	4	8	9	21	41	12	14	16	54	75	−21	50
16	Welling U	42	6	5	10	23	34	7	2	12	18	30	13	7	22	41	64	−23	46
17	Maidenhead U	42	2	6	13	24	34	9	6	6	32	25	11	12	19	56	59	−3	45
18	Bognor Regis T	42	6	5	10	21	31	5	6	10	28	36	11	11	20	49	67	−18	44
19	St Albans C	42	5	5	11	21	35	5	7	9	22	34	10	12	20	43	69	−26	42
20	Weston Super Mare	42	6	4	11	28	38	3	6	12	24	47	9	10	23	52	85	−33	37
21	Dorchester T	42	5	4	12	17	33	3	6	12	19	37	8	10	24	36	70	−34	34
22	Sutton U	42	2	3	16	13	45	3	6	12	19	41	5	9	28	32	86	−54	24

BLUE SQUARE SOUTH RESULTS 2007–2008

	Basingstoke T	Bath C	Bishop's Stortford	Bognor Regis T	Braintree T	Bromley	Cambridge C	Dorchester T	Eastbourne B	Eastleigh	Fisher Ath	Hampton & Richmond B	Havant & Waterlooville	Hayes & Yeading U	Lewes	Maidenhead U	Newport Co	St Albans C	Sutton U	Thurrock	Welling U	Weston Super Mare
Basingstoke T	—	0-4	1-2	3-2	1-1	2-0	3-0	1-0	0-0	3-4	1-5	2-3	2-3	1-1	1-1	1-1	3-1	1-3	1-0	3-0	2-1	0-0
Bath C	0-1	—	4-0	0-2	2-0	1-2	2-0	2-1	0-1	2-2	0-1	2-1	1-1	1-2	1-2	2-0	1-0	3-0	2-3	3-1	2-0	1-0
Bishop's Stortford	0-0	1-1	—	0-2	2-1	1-2	4-0	1-0	0-1	2-2	1-2	1-1	1-0	1-1	1-5	2-0	0-0	3-4	1-1	1-0	1-2	2-2
Bognor Regis T	1-1	1-3	5-3	—	2-1	1-2	2-0	0-0	0-0	0-2	1-2	2-4	1-1	3-0	0-5	1-2	0-2	0-2	1-0	3-1	2-0	2-0
Braintree T	2-1	2-0	3-4	2-1	—	4-0	2-0	0-0	1-3	0-3	2-3	3-0	2-1	0-1	3-2	1-1	0-1	3-4	1-1	3-0	2-1	4-0
Bromley	3-2	3-1	1-2	1-2	2-1	—	3-1	1-0	1-3	1-2	1-2	0-2	2-3	1-0	1-0	3-0	2-2	2-4	1-0	8-1	2-0	3-1
Cambridge C	3-0	1-1	2-4	2-0	2-0	1-2	—	2-2	0-4	1-2	3-2	1-2	0-1	1-4	1-3	3-0	2-3	0-4	4-1	2-2	3-1	5-1
Dorchester T	1-0	2-1	1-1	4-1	0-0	3-2	3-2	—	0-4	3-2	4-0	0-1	2-2	1-0	3-0	1-1	1-0	0-0	3-0	1-0	1-1	2-2
Eastbourne B	6-0	0-4	3-0	1-0	3-3	1-2	2-0	4-1	—	1-1	3-0	1-1	4-2	3-1	1-3	3-2	1-3	4-0	3-0	1-0	1-0	1-2
Eastleigh	1-1	4-4	0-0	3-1	0-3	1-4	2-1	1-2	1-2	—	3-0	4-2	3-3	4-2	0-0	0-2	0-0	1-2	4-2	2-3	1-3	3-2
Fisher Ath	4-1	0-0	1-1	3-0	0-1	1-4	3-2	2-0	1-2	3-0	—	4-1	1-0	4-1	6-1	0-1	1-3	4-1	3-3	4-0	3-2	3-1
Hampton & Richmond B	2-2	0-1	1-0	3-3	1-2	0-3	1-2	4-0	0-4	3-1	1-0	—	0-3	2-1	1-2	0-1	4-2	0-0	4-0	3-1	1-1	5-1
Havant & Waterlooville	1-1	1-0	2-2	0-2	2-1	1-1	1-2	4-0	2-2	1-0	2-1	0-3	—	2-1	0-3	1-4	1-3	2-1	0-5	1-0	2-0	1-1
Hayes & Yeading U	1-1	2-2	1-2	2-0	3-0	4-1	1-0	1-1	2-1	2-4	0-0	4-1	4-0	—	0-0	0-0	0-0	3-1	1-1	1-2	1-0	2-2
Lewes	4-0	1-0	1-1	1-0	6-1	1-2	2-0	3-1	0-3	3-2	2-3	3-3	3-3	2-1	—	0-3	1-2	0-1	2-0	0-1	2-0	3-0
Maidenhead U	1-2	1-0	5-0	2-2	2-2	0-1	2-3	3-2	1-1	0-5	2-3	1-2	1-3	1-1	1-3	—	2-3	2-0	1-1	1-4	0-1	0-3
Newport Co	2-0	2-3	1-0	1-1	0-1	1-3	0-0	1-1	2-3	1-2	0-2	2-0	1-3	1-0	0-3	1-1	—	2-0	2-3	0-5	1-2	3-2
St Albans C	4-1	0-4	1-2	1-0	2-1	4-0	1-3	3-1	1-2	1-2	0-2	0-5	2-1	2-0	2-1	0-3	0-0	—	3-3	1-2	0-1	2-1
Sutton U	2-0	1-2	0-4	2-0	1-3	3-0	5-2	1-1	1-5	4-1	2-3	1-1	1-2	1-2	0-3	2-3	3-0	2-0	—	0-5	2-1	1-2
Thurrock	1-1	0-4	1-0	1-0	3-2	1-0	3-1	1-1	3-2	3-1	0-1	1-3	1-1	2-0	0-4	3-0	1-0	0-0	1-2	—	1-2	0-3
Welling U	0-1	1-0	2-1	2-3	1-0	2-0	1-2	1-0	2-6	3-1	1-3	1-1	3-1	1-2	0-2	1-2	2-2	1-1	0-1	1-0	—	2-1
Weston Super Mare	3-3	0-2	0-4	3-2	0-1	2-2	0-1	1-0	1-2	0-3	1-1	2-1	3-1	3-1	1-2	1-2	3-2	0-3	3-0	3-1	0-3	—

340

UNIBOND LEAGUE 2007–2008

Premier Division

		Home					Away					Total						
	P	W	D	L	F	A	W	D	L	F	A	W	D	L	F	A	GD	Pts
1 Fleetwood Town	40	14	4	2	43	23	14	3	3	38	16	28	7	5	81	39	42	91
2 Witton Albion	40	17	1	2	54	15	10	7	3	30	13	27	8	5	84	28	56	89
3 Gateshead	40	14	2	4	43	16	12	5	3	50	26	26	7	7	93	42	51	85
4 Eastwood Town	40	13	4	3	40	24	7	5	8	21	21	20	9	11	61	45	16	69
5 Buxton	40	10	3	7	36	27	10	5	5	24	23	20	8	12	60	50	10	68
6 Guiseley	40	9	6	5	29	21	10	4	6	36	22	19	10	11	65	43	22	67
7 Marine	40	11	0	9	37	30	8	4	8	33	35	19	4	17	70	65	5	61
8 Hednesford Town	40	9	4	7	36	32	6	4	10	26	33	15	8	17	62	65	-3	53
9 Worksop Town	40	6	8	6	31	32	7	4	9	28	30	13	12	15	59	62	-3	51
10 Ashton United	40	8	6	6	31	31	3	9	8	32	42	11	15	14	63	73	-10	48
11 Kendal Town	40	7	8	5	36	27	5	3	12	25	43	12	11	17	61	70	-9	47
12 Whitby Town	40	9	2	9	41	37	4	5	11	27	38	13	7	20	68	75	-7	46
13 Prescot Cables	40	8	4	8	21	24	5	4	11	27	38	13	8	19	48	62	-14	46
14 Frickley Athletic	40	8	6	6	29	22	3	7	10	21	46	11	13	16	50	68	-18	46
15 North Ferriby U	40	7	3	10	26	40	6	4	10	27	36	13	7	20	53	76	-23	46
16 Matlock Town	40	9	6	5	34	24	3	3	14	21	44	12	9	19	55	68	-13	45
17 Ilkeston Town	40	6	6	8	40	39	4	8	8	24	33	10	14	16	64	72	-8	44
18 Ossett Town	40	6	4	10	21	28	6	4	10	27	32	12	8	20	48	60	-12	44
19 Leek Town	40	5	8	7	27	30	6	3	11	27	38	11	11	18	54	68	-14	44
20 Stamford	40	6	6	8	30	38	5	4	11	29	48	11	10	19	59	86	-27	43
21 Lincoln United	40	2	4	14	18	39	5	4	11	26	46	7	8	25	44	85	-41	29

Gateshead promoted via play-offs; Prescot Cables deducted 1 point for playing ineligible player.

SOUTHERN LEAGUE DIVISION 2007–2008

Premier Division

		Home			Away			Total						
	P	W	D	L	W	D	L	W	D	L	F	A	GD	Pts
1 King's Lynn	42	14	6	1	10	7	4	24	13	5	91	36	55	85
2 Team Bath	42	12	4	5	13	4	4	25	8	9	71	41	30	83
3 Halesowen Town	42	13	4	4	9	9	3	22	13	7	80	46	34	79
4 Chippenham Town	42	11	8	2	9	5	7	20	13	9	73	44	29	73
5 Bashley	42	12	7	2	7	5	9	19	12	11	60	46	14	69
6 Gloucester City	42	10	5	6	9	6	6	19	11	12	81	50	31	68
7 Hemel Hempstead Town	42	8	6	7	11	5	5	19	11	12	67	50	17	68
8 Brackley Town	42	9	5	7	7	7	7	16	12	14	57	53	4	60
9 Banbury United	42	7	8	6	7	8	6	14	16	12	55	57	-2	58
10 Yate Town	42	9	3	9	7	7	7	16	10	16	71	76	-5	58
11 Clevedon Town	42	7	9	5	6	9	6	13	18	11	49	46	3	57
12 Swindon Supermarine	42	7	8	6	7	4	10	14	12	16	51	67	-16	54
13 Merthyr Tydfil	42	10	5	6	3	9	9	13	14	15	65	70	-5	53
14 Mangotsfield United	42	8	9	4	4	7	10	12	16	14	38	42	-4	52
15 Rugby Town	42	7	5	9	6	7	8	13	12	17	55	66	-11	51
16 Corby Town	42	8	3	10	6	5	10	14	8	20	60	67	-7	50
17 Tiverton Town	42	8	8	5	5	3	13	13	11	18	45	60	-15	50
18 Hitchin Town	42	8	5	8	4	6	11	12	11	19	46	61	-15	47
19 Bedford Town	42	7	6	8	5	3	13	12	9	21	54	73	-19	45
20 Bromsgrove Rovers	42	5	9	7	5	3	13	10	12	20	46	61	-15	42
21 Cirencester Town	42	6	3	12	2	5	14	8	8	26	44	80	-36	32
22 Cheshunt	42	3	5	13	2	3	16	5	8	29	42	103	-61	23

RYMAN LEAGUE 2007–2008

Premier Division			Home					Away					Total				
	P	W	D	L	F	A	W	D	L	F	A	W	D	L	F	A	GD	Pts
1 Chelmsford City	42	15	5	1	53	16	11	4	6	31	23	26	9	7	84	39	45	87
2 Staines Town	42	12	6	3	50	23	10	6	5	35	31	22	12	8	85	54	31	78
3 AFC Wimbledon	42	12	3	6	40	21	10	6	5	41	26	22	9	11	81	47	34	75
4 AFC Hornchurch	42	13	2	6	38	20	7	8	6	30	24	20	10	12	68	44	24	70
5 Ramsgate	42	13	5	3	43	21	6	6	9	24	32	19	11	12	67	53	14	68
6 Ashford Town	42	14	3	4	51	29	6	3	12	28	36	20	6	16	79	65	14	66
7 Hendon	42	9	8	4	32	28	9	3	9	47	39	18	11	13	79	67	12	65
8 Tonbridge Angels	42	11	6	4	40	24	6	6	9	37	33	17	12	13	77	57	20	63
9 Margate	42	11	5	5	46	35	6	6	9	25	33	17	11	14	71	68	3	62
10 Billericay Town	42	10	6	5	40	26	6	6	9	26	31	16	12	14	66	57	9	60
11 Horsham	42	12	1	8	37	26	6	4	11	26	37	18	5	19	63	63	0	59
12 Heybridge Swifts	42	10	6	5	38	27	4	7	10	26	37	14	13	15	64	64	0	55
13 Wealdstone	42	8	5	8	37	37	7	4	10	31	38	15	9	18	68	75	–7	54
14 Hastings United	42	11	2	8	35	26	4	6	11	23	41	15	8	19	58	67	–9	53
15 Harlow Town	42	6	8	7	31	28	7	5	9	25	24	13	13	16	56	52	4	52
16 Harrow Borough	42	11	0	10	38	37	4	7	10	23	37	15	7	20	61	74	–13	52
17 Maidstone United	42	7	4	10	30	33	9	0	12	26	46	16	4	22	56	79	–23	52
18 Carshalton Ath	42	7	7	7	21	21	7	1	13	31	44	14	8	20	52	65	–13	50
19 Boreham Wood	42	9	4	8	30	27	6	1	14	26	46	15	5	22	56	73	–17	50
20 East Thurrock U	42	9	3	9	24	29	5	6	10	24	38	14	9	19	48	67	–19	50
21 Folkestone Invicta	42	7	7	7	24	31	6	3	12	25	39	13	10	19	49	70	–21	49
22 Leyton	42	2	3	16	20	60	2	1	18	15	63	4	4	34	35	123	–88	16

East Thurrock United deducted 1 point.

CUP FINALS AND PLAY-OFFS 2007–2008

UNIBOND LEAGUE

CHALLENGE CUP FINAL 2007–00
Eastwood Town 3, Skelmersdale United 0

PRESIDENT'S CUP FINAL
FC United of Manchester 2,
Radcliffe Borough 0

PLAY-OFF FINALS
Premier Division
Gateshead 2, Buxton 0

First Division North
FC United of Manchester 4,
Skelmersdale United 1

First Division South
Nantwich Town 2,
Sheffield 2
Nantwich Town won 4-1 on penalties.

SOUTHERN LEAGUE

ERREA SOUTHERN LEAGUE CUP

Final First Leg
Hillingdon Borough 1, Clevedon Town 1

Final Second Leg
Clevedon Town 0, Hillingdon Borough 3

PLAY-OFF FINALS
Premier Division
Team Bath 2, Halesown Town 1

Division One Midlands
Stourbridge 2, Leamington 1

Division One South & West
Oxford City 1, Uxbridge 0

RYMAN LEAGUE

ISTHMIAN LEAGUE CUP
AFC Sudbury 0, Ramsgate 0
aet; Ramsgate won 5-4 on penalties.

PLAY-OFF FINALS
Premier Division
Staines Town 1, AFC Wimbledon 2

Division One North
Redbridge 1, Canvey Island 1
Canvey Island won 5-4 on penalties.

Division One South
Tooting & Mitcham United 1, Cray
Wanderers 0

PONTIN'S HOLIDAYS LEAGUE 2007–2008

DIVISION ONE CENTRAL

	P	W	D	L	F	A	GD	Pts
Nottingham F	22	19	2	1	67	21	46	59
Port Vale	22	11	4	7	38	30	8	37
Coventry C	22	10	6	6	42	27	15	36
Leicester C	22	10	4	8	49	39	10	34
WBA	22	9	6	7	51	45	6	33
Wolverhampton W	22	9	5	8	41	34	7	32
Walsall	22	10	2	10	35	36	–1	32
Shrewsbury T	22	9	4	9	35	39	–4	31
Stoke C	22	9	3	10	25	36	–11	30
Bradford C	22	7	2	13	30	43	–13	23
Huddersfield T	22	5	5	12	21	34	–13	20
Oldham Ath	22	1	3	18	20	70	–50	6

DIVISION ONE WEST

	P	W	D	L	F	A	GD	Pts
Morecambe	22	14	4	4	43	31	12	46
Manchester C	22	13	3	6	61	35	26	42
Carlisle U	22	11	5	6	43	30	13	38
Preston NE	22	11	2	9	41	39	2	35
Wrexham	22	11	2	9	46	45	1	35
Burnley	22	10	4	8	37	33	4	34
Blackpool	22	9	4	9	43	33	10	31
Tranmere R	22	9	2	11	23	31	–8	29
Bury	22	6	6	10	30	40	–10	24
Chester C	22	6	5	11	23	44	–21	23
Rochdale	22	6	3	13	41	46	–5	21
Accrington S	22	5	2	15	29	53	–24	17

DIVISION ONE EAST

	P	W	D	L	F	A	GD	Pts
Hartlepool U	22	13	3	6	53	31	22	42
Sheffield U	22	11	5	6	35	28	7	38
Sheffield W	22	11	4	7	37	23	14	37
Hull C	22	11	4	7	30	26	4	37
Rotherham U	22	10	2	10	33	39	–6	32
Leeds U	22	8	6	8	33	29	4	30
Scunthorpe U	22	7	8	7	35	40	–5	39
Grimsby T	22	8	3	11	34	43	–9	27
Darlington	22	8	3	11	21	31	–10	27
York C	22	8	2	12	30	31	–1	26
Barnsley	22	7	5	10	29	44	–15	26
Lincoln C	22	7	1	14	37	42	–5	22

PONTIN'S HOLIDAYS COMBINATION 2007–2008

CENTRAL DIVISION

	P	W	D	L	GD	Pts
Southampton	18	12	3	3	20	39
Charlton Ath	18	11	4	3	22	37
Watford	18	9	4	5	5	31
Crystal Palace	18	5	8	5	–2	23
Leyton Orient	18	7	2	9	–5	23
Wycombe W	18	7	2	9	–5	23
Brighton & HA	18	6	3	9	3	21
Millwall	18	5	5	8	–14	20
Aldershot T	18	5	4	9	–12	19
QPR	18	3	5	10	–12	14

EAST DIVISION

	P	W	D	L	GD	Pts
Ipswich T	18	16	1	1	49	49
Norwich C	18	9	5	4	19	32
Southend U	18	9	3	6	12	30
Colchester U	18	5	10	3	3	25
Peterborough U	18	6	5	7	–4	23
Luton T	18	6	3	9	–11	21
Milton Keynes D	18	6	2	10	–13	20
Northampton T	18	5	4	9	–13	19
Stevenage B	18	3	6	9	–20	15
Grays Ath	18	3	5	10	–22	14

WALES AND WEST DIVISION

	P	W	D	L	GD	Pts
Bristol C	18	14	1	3	33	43
Yeovil T	18	11	4	3	20	37
Plymouth Arg	18	10	3	5	16	33
Swindon T	18	8	6	4	6	30
Exeter C	18	6	5	7	–7	23
Swansea C	18	6	2	10	–13	20
Bournemouth	18	6	2	10	–14	20
Bristol R	18	5	4	9	–9	19
Forest Green R	18	4	2	12	–8	14
Cheltenham T	18	3	5	10	–24	14

FA ACADEMY UNDER-18 LEAGUE
2007–2008

GROUP A	P	W	D	L	F	A	GD	Pts
Arsenal	28	17	5	6	74	31	43	56
West Ham U	28	16	3	9	63	38	25	51
Fulham	28	14	7	7	39	28	11	49
Portsmouth	28	15	4	9	44	44	0	49
Crystal Palace	28	14	5	9	59	41	18	47
Southampton	28	13	4	11	43	52	–9	43
Chelsea	28	11	6	11	58	52	6	39
Charlton Ath	28	9	8	11	47	51	–4	35
Ipswich T	28	9	5	14	39	53	–14	32
Norwich C	28	6	9	13	45	56	–11	27
Millwall	28	4	6	18	30	64	–34	18

GROUP B	P	W	D	L	F	A	GD	Pts
Aston Villa	28	22	2	4	84	33	51	68
Tottenham H	28	18	5	5	69	35	34	59
Leicester City	28	18	4	6	70	41	29	58
Reading	28	13	5	10	40	42	–2	44
Bristol C	28	11	5	12	50	51	–1	38
Milton Keynes D	28	9	2	17	33	54	–21	29
Watford	28	7	6	15	30	54	–24	27
Birmingham C	28	5	8	14	31	54	–23	23
Coventry C	28	4	6	18	31	58	–27	18
Cardiff C	28	3	7	18	30	68	–38	16

GROUP C	P	W	D	L	F	A	GD	Pts
Manchester C	28	21	4	3	75	22	53	67
Everton	28	17	7	4	56	24	32	58
Manchester U	28	14	6	8	47	44	3	48
Crewe Alex	28	14	6	8	50	51	–1	48
Liverpool	28	11	10	7	49	34	15	43
Blackburn R	28	10	5	13	36	38	–2	35
WBA	28	8	7	13	44	66	–22	31
Wolverhampton W	28	7	8	13	29	37	–8	29
Bolton W	28	6	9	13	42	47	–5	27
Stoke C	28	6	7	15	28	42	–14	25

GROUP D	P	W	D	L	F	A	GD	Pts
Sunderland	28	20	3	5	68	31	37	63
Nottingham F	28	16	5	7	58	42	16	53
Leeds U	28	13	6	9	53	38	15	45
Middlesbrough	28	11	9	8	39	37	2	42
Sheffield U	28	10	6	12	33	34	–1	36
Huddersfield T	28	9	7	12	30	42	–12	34
Derby Co	28	10	2	16	26	53	–27	32
Newcastle U	28	7	6	15	41	49	–8	27
Sheffield W	28	5	7	16	24	53	–29	22
Barnsley	28	3	4	21	20	73	–53	13

FA PREMIER RESERVE LEAGUES
2007–2008
NORTH SECTION

	P	W	D	L	F	A	GD	Pts
Liverpool	18	13	4	1	31	8	23	43
Manchester C	18	8	6	4	34	29	5	30
Manchester U	18	8	5	5	25	19	6	29
Sunderland	18	9	2	7	28	24	4	29
Blackburn R	18	8	4	6	32	25	7	28
Newcastle U	18	5	7	6	31	27	4	22
Middlesbrough	18	5	7	6	23	26	–3	22
Everton	18	4	4	10	21	31	–10	16
Wigan Ath	18	4	3	11	19	36	–17	15
Bolton W	18	3	4	11	13	32	–19	13

Leading Goalscorers

Nemeth K	Liverpool	9
Brouwer J	Liverpool	8
Judge A	Blackburn R	7
Grimes A	Manchester C	7
Carroll A	Newcastle U	7
Clarke A	Blackburn R	6
Craddock T	Middlesbrough	6
Hutchinson B	Middlesbrough	6
Godsmark J	Newcastle U	6
Stokes A	Sunderland	6

SOUTH SECTION

	P	W	D	L	F	A	GD	Pts
Aston Villa	18	10	5	3	38	17	21	35
West Ham U	18	9	4	5	32	21	11	31
Reading	18	8	7	3	32	16	16	31
Arsenal	18	8	6	4	26	17	9	30
Fulham	18	8	4	6	27	25	2	28
Chelsea	18	5	7	6	23	21	2	22
Birmingham C	18	6	4	8	25	33	–8	22
Tottenham H	18	5	6	7	22	24	–2	21
Portsmouth	18	5	4	9	12	25	–13	19
Derby Co	18	1	3	14	13	51	–38	6

Leading Goalscorers

Mikaelsson T	Aston Villa	8
Lita L	Reading	8
Di Santo F	Chelsea	7
Barazite N	Arsenal	6
Danns N	Birmingham C	6
Forssell M	Birmingham C	5
Brown W	Fulham	5
Henry J	Reading	5
Pekhart T	Tottenham H	5

WOMEN'S FOOTBALL 2007–2008

PREMIER LEAGUE
NATIONAL DIVISION

	P	W	D	L	F	A	GD	Pts
Arsenal	22	20	2	0	85	15	70	62
Everton	22	18	3	1	69	14	55	57
Leeds U	22	12	4	6	45	33	12	40
Bristol Academy	22	10	4	8	45	35	10	34
Chelsea	22	9	5	8	40	35	5	32
Doncaster R Belles	22	8	5	9	44	42	2	29
Watford	22	9	2	11	53	52	1	29
Blackburn R	22	8	4	10	50	45	5	28
Birmingham C	22	7	4	11	34	39	–5	25
Liverpool	22	6	4	12	31	51	–20	22
Cardiff C	22	3	3	16	19	69	–50	12
Charlton Ath	22	0	4	18	6	91	–85	4

NORTHERN DIVISION

	P	W	D	L	F	A	GD	Pts
Nottingham F	22	18	4	0	80	26	54	58
Lincoln C	22	18	1	3	66	16	50	55
Sunderland	22	16	2	4	52	30	22	50
Newcastle U	22	10	3	9	58	46	12	33
Preston NE	22	10	1	11	39	39	0	31
Sheffield W	22	8	2	12	38	48	–10	26
Manchester C	22	7	4	11	29	41	–12	25
Tranmere R	22	7	3	12	36	57	–21	24
Rotherham U	22	7	1	14	41	62	–21	22
Aston Villa	22	6	3	13	49	59	–10	21
Stockport Co	22	6	1	15	21	54	–33	19
Crewe Alex	22	5	4	14	30	61	–31	18

SOUTHERN DIVISION

	P	W	D	L	F	A	GD	Pts
WFC Fulham	22	15	5	2	70	19	51	50
Millwall Lionesses	22	13	5	4	50	21	29	44
Barnet	22	13	4	5	61	21	40	43
Portsmouth	22	13	3	6	63	26	37	42
West Ham U	22	12	0	10	63	46	17	36
Crystal Palace	22	10	4	8	45	30	15	34
Colchester U	22	10	1	11	51	54	–3	31
Keynsham T	22	8	6	8	51	31	20	30
Newquay	22	9	2	11	50	45	5	29
Brighton & HA	22	6	2	14	35	57	–22	20
AFC Team Bath	22	5	4	13	39	53	–14	19
Reading Royals	22	0	0	22	8	183	–175	0

FA WOMEN'S CUP FINAL 2007–2008

Monday, 5 May 2008

(at Nottingham Forest)

Arsenal 4 *(Smith K 53, 83, Ludlow 59, Sanderson 60)*

Leeds U 1 *(Clarke 69)* 24,582

Arsenal: Byrne; Scott, Ludlow, White, Grant (Tracy 74), Smith K, Sanderson (Fleeting 74), Yankey (Davison 74), Carney, Asante, Phillip.

Leeds U: Telford; Bradley, Wright (Bonner 86), Holtham, Smith S, Houghton, Clarke, Moore (Sutcliffe 60), Barr, Culvin (Thackray 86), Walton.

ENGLAND WOMEN'S INTERNATIONAL MATCHES 2007–2008

WORLD CUP

11 September 2007 *(in Shanghai)*   27,146
Japan 2 *(Miyama 55, 90)*   **England 2** *(Smith K 81, 83)*
England: Brown; Scott A (Johnson 89), Stoney, Chapman, White, Phillip, Carney, Williams, Aluko (Scott J 74), Smith K, Yankey.

14 September 2007 *(in Shanghai)*   27,730
England 0   Germany 0
England: Brown; Scott A, Stoney, Chapman, White, Phillip, Carney (Yankey 56), Williams, Smith K, Asante, Scott J.

17 September 2007 *(in Chengdu)*   30,730
England 6 *(Gonzalez 9 (og), Scott J 10, Williams 51 (pen), Smith K 64, 77, Exley 90 (pen))*   **Argentina 1** *(Gonzalez 60)*
England: Brown; Scott A (Smith S 68), Stoney, White, Phillip, Williams, Aluko (Handley 79), Smith K (Exley 79), Yankey, Asante, Scott J.

22 September 2007 *(in Tianjin)*   29,586
England 0   USA 3 *(Wambach 48, Boxx 57, Lilly 60)*
England: Brown; Scott A, Stoney, Chapman, White, Phillip (Sanderson 81), Carney, Aluko (Yankey 46), Smith K, Asante, Scott J.

27 October 2007 *(at Walsall)*   8632
England 4 *(Scott A 11, 64, Smith K 33, Aluko 49)*   **Belarus 0**
England: Brown; Scott A, Stoney, Chapman (Scott J), Phillip, Asante, Carney (Smith S 46), Williams, Aluko, Smith K (Sanderson 55), Yankey.

25 November 2007 *(at Shrewsbury)*   8753
England 1 *(Carney 65)*   **Spain 0**
England: Brown; Scott A, Stoney, Scott J, White, Asante, Carney, Williams, Aluko (Sanderson 55), Smith K, Yankey.

12 February 2008 *(in Larnaca)*
England 0   Sweden 2 *(Schelin 44, 81)*
England: Chamberlain; Scott A (Handley 80), White (Bassett 80), Phillip, Stoney (Unitt 62), Asante, Scott J (Aluko 40), Williams, Carney (Smith S 40) (Johnson 69), Smith K (Westwood 62), Yankey.

14 February 2008 *(in Larnaca)*
Norway 1 *(Stensland 53)*   **England 2** *(Williams 47, Smith K 64 (pen)*
England: Chamberlain (Hawke 73); Scott A, White, Phillip, Stoney, Asante, Williams, Smith K, Carney, Sanderson (Aluko 73), Yankey.

6 March 2008 *(in Lurgan)*
Northern Ireland 0   England 2 *(Williams 18, White 84)*
England: Chamberlain; Scott A (Johnson 71), Stoney, Asante, White, Phillip, Carney, Scott J, Smith K, Williams, Yankey.

20 March 2008 *(at Doncaster)*   5975
England 0   Czech Republic 0
England: Chamberlain; Scott A, Stoney, Asante, White, Phillip (Johnson 46), Carney, Williams, Sanderson (Aluko 46), Westwood, Yankey.

8 May 2008 *(in Minsk)*
Belarus 1 *(Ryzhevich 30)*   **England 6** *(Scott J 1, Williams 6, 25, 86, Sanderson 43, White 90).*
England: Chamberlain; Scott A (Johnson 46), Stoney, Scott J, White, Asante, Carney (Handley 46), Williams, Sanderson, Smith K (Bassett 59), Yankey.

UEFA WOMEN'S CHAMPIONSHIP 2006–2008

QUALIFYING ROUND

GROUP 1
England 4, Northern Ireland 0
Northern Ireland 1, Czech Republic 3
Belarus 0, Spain 3
Belarus 5, Northern Ireland 0
Belarus 1, Czech Republic 4
Czech Republic 2, Spain 2
England 4, Belarus 0
England 1, Spain 0
Spain 4, Northern Ireland 0
Northern Ireland 0, England 2
England 0, Czech Republic 0
Czech Republic 4, Northern Ireland 0
Spain 6, Belarus 1
Spain 4, Czech Republic 1
Belarus 1, England 6
Northern Ireland 0, Spain 3

GROUP 2
Republic of Ireland 2, Hungary 1
Hungary 3, Romania 3
Italy 0, Sweden 2
Republic of Ireland 1, Italy 2
Romania 0, Sweden 7
Sweden 7, Hungary 0
Romania 0, Republic of Ireland 2
Hungary 1, Italy 3
Italy 5, Romania 0
Republic of Ireland 2, Romania 1
Italy 4, Republic of Ireland 1
Hungary 0, Republic of Ireland 2
Hungary 0, Sweden 6
Sweden 1, Italy 0
Romania 1, Italy 6
Romania 3, Hungary 1

GROUP 3
France 6, Greece 0
Slovenia 0, Serbia 5
France 6, Slovenia 0
Greece 0, Iceland 3
Iceland 1, France 0
Iceland 5, Serbia 0
Slovenia 2, Iceland 1
Serbia 0, France 8
Slovenia 0, France 2
Serbia 1, Greece 2
Greece 0, France 5
Serbia 0, Slovenia 3
France 2, Serbia 0
Slovenia 3, Greece 1
Serbia 0, Iceland 4

GROUP 4
Germany 5, Holland 1
Switzerland 1, Belgium 0
Switzerland 2, Holland 2
Wales 0, Germany 6
Germany 7, Switzerland 0
Holland 2, Wales 1
Wales 0, Switzerland 2
Germany 3, Belgium 0
Belgium 1, Wales 0
Holland 0, Germany 1
Wales 0, Belgium 1
Wales 0, Holland 1
Belgium 2, Holland 2
Belgium 3, Switzerland 1
Belgium 0, Germany 5
Switzerland 2, Wales 0 .
Germany 4, Wales 0

GROUP 5
Slovakia 2, Portugal 1
Scotland 0, Portugal 0
Slovakia 0, Ukraine 4
Ukraine 0, Scotland 1
Ukraine 5, Slovakia 0
Denmark 5, Portugal 1
Slovakia 0, Scotland 3
Portugal 0, Slovakia 1
Portugal 0, Ukraine 1
Scotland 0, Denmark 1
Slovakia 1, Denmark 4
Denmark 2, Scotland 0
Portugal 1, Scotland 4
Portugal 0, Denmark 4
Scotland 0, Ukraine 1
Denmark 6, Slovakia 1

GROUP 6
Austria 0, Poland 1
Israel 2, Poland 2
Israel 0, Russia 6
Israel 1, Norway 3
Poland 4, Israel 1
Austria 1, Russia 5
Austria 5, Israel 0
Norway 3, Russia 0
Russia 3, Poland 1
Norway 3, Austria 0
Norway 7, Israel 0
Norway 3, Poland 0
Poland 2, Austria 4
Russia 4, Israel 0
Competition still being played.

349

THE FA TROPHY 2007–2008

FINAL (at Wembley) – Saturday, 10 May 2008

Ebbsfleet United (1) 1 *(McPhee 45)*

Torquay United (0) 0   40,186

Ebbsfleet United: Cronin; Hawkins, Opinel, Bostwick, Smith, McCarthy, McPhee, Barrett, Moore, Akinde, Long (MacDonald).
Torquay United: Rice; Adams, Nicholson, Mansell, Woods, Todd, Phillips (Stevens), Hargreaves, D'Sane (Benyon), Sills (Hill), Zebroski.
Referee: M. Atkinson (West Riding).

THE FA VASE 2007–2008

FINAL (at Wembley) – Sunday, 11 May 2008

Kirkham & Wesham (0) 2 *(Walwyn 84, 90)*

Lowestoft Town (1) 1 *(Thompson 10)*   19,537

Kirkham & Wesham: Summerfield; Jackson (Walwyn 80), Keefe (Allen 54), Thompson, Shaw, Eastwood, Clark, Blackwell, Wane, Paterson (Sheppard 90), Smith.
Lowestoft Town: Reynolds; Poppy, Potter, Woodrow, Saunders, Plaskett (McGee 79), Godbould, Darren Cockrill (Dale Cockrill 46), Stock, King (Hunn 54).
Referee: A. D'Urso (Essex).

THE FA YOUTH CUP 2007–2008

FINAL (First Leg) – Thursday, 3 April 2008

Chelsea (0) 1 *(Kakuta 66)*

Manchester City (0) 1 *(Sturridge 49)*   11,890

Chelsea: Taylor; Ofori-Twumasi, Gordon, Woods, Bruma, Van Aanholt, Stoch, Mellis, Nielsen (Phillip 62), Kakuta, Tejera Rodriguez.
Manchester City: Hartley; Trippier, McGivern, Tutte, Boyata, Mee, Weiss, Kay, Ball (Ibrahim 86), Sturridge, McDermott (Tsiaklis 71).
Referee: P. Walton (Northamptonshire).

FINAL (Second Leg) – Wednesday, 16 April 2008

Manchester City (2) 3 *(Mee 24, Weiss 35, Ball 87 (pen))*

Chelsea (1) 1 *(McGivern 6 (og))*   19,780

Manchester City: Hartley; Trippier (Ibrahim 90), Boyata (Tsiaklis 82), Kay, Mee, McGivern, Tutte, Weiss, Mak, Ball, McDermott.
Chelsea: Taylor; Ofori-Twumasi, Gordon (Nouble 73), Woods, Bruma, Van Aanholt, Stoch, Mellis, Tejera, Kakuta, Nielsen (Phillip 54).
Referee: P. Walton (Northamptonshire).

THE FA SUNDAY CUP 2007–2008

FINAL (at Liverpool FC)

Coundon Conservative 2 *(Thompson 2, Houlahan 24)*

Hetton Lyons Cricket Club 3 *(Clarke 12, Irvine 55, Pearson 84 (pen))*   1052

THE FA COUNTY YOUTH CUP 2007–2008

FINAL (at Ipwich Town FC)

Suffolk (2) 2 *(Read 4, Garnham 16)*

Cambridgeshire (1) 1 *(Marriott 18)*   948

NATIONAL LIST OF REFEREES FOR SEASON 2008–2009

List 2007–08 season

Armstrong, P (Paul) – Berkshire
Atkinson, M (Martin) – W. Yorkshire
Attwell, SB (Stuart) – Warwickshire
Bates, A (Tony) – Staffordshire
Beeby, RJ (Richard) – Northamptonshire
Bennett, SG (Steve) – Kent
Booth, RJ (Russell) – Nottinghamshire
Boyeson, C (Carl) – E. Yorkshire
Bratt, SJ (Steve) – West Midlands
Clattenburg, M (Mark) – Tyne & Wear
Cook, SD (Steven) – Surrey
Crossley, PT (Phil) – Kent
Deadman, D (Darren) – Cambridgeshire
Dean, ML (Mike) – Wirral
Dorr, SJ (Steve) – Worcestershire
Dowd, P (Phil) – Staffordshire
Drysdale, D (Darren) – Lincolnshire
D'Urso, AP (Andy) – Essex
East, R (Roger) – Wiltshire
Evans, KG (Karl) – Gtr Manchester
Foster, D (David) – Tyne & Wear
Foy, CJ (Chris) – Merseyside
Friend, KA (Kevin) – Leicestershire
Graham F (Fred) – Essex
Haines, A (Andy) – Tyne & Wear
Hall, AR (Andy) – W. Midlands
Halsey, MR (Mark) – Lancashire
Haywood, M (Mark) – W. Yorkshire
Hegley, GK (Grant) – Hertfordshire
Hill, KD (Keith) – Hertfordshire
Horwood, GD (Graham) – Bedfordshire
Ilderton, EL (Eddie) – Tyne & Wear
Jones, MJ (Michael) – Cheshire
Joslin, PJ (Phil) – Nottinghamshire
Kettle, TM (Trevor) – Rutland
Knight, B (Barry) – Kent
Laws, G (Graham) – Tyne & Wear
Lee, R (Ray) – Essex

Lewis, GJ (Gary) – Cambridgeshire
Lewis, RL (Rob) – Shropshire
McDermid, D (Danny) – London
Marriner, AM (Andre) – W. Midlands
Mason, LS (Lee) – Lancashire
Mathieson, SW (Scott) – Cheshire
Mellin, PW (Paul) – Surrey
Miller, NS (Nigel) – Durham
Miller, P (Pat) – Bedfordshire
Moss, J (Jon) – W. Yorkshire
Oliver, CW (Clive) – Northumberland
Oliver, M (Michael) – Northumberland
Penn, AM (Andy) – W. Midlands
Penton, C (Clive) – Sussex
Pike, MS (Mike) – Cumbria
Probert, LW (Lee) – Wiltshire
Rennie, UD (Uriah) – S. Yorkshire
Riley, MA (Mike) – W. Yorkshire
Russell, MP (Mike) – Hertfordshire
Salisbury, G (Graham) – Lancashire
Shoebridge, RL (Rob) – Derbyshire
Singh, J (Jarnail) – Middlesex
Stroud, KP (Keith) – Hampshire
Styles, R (Rob) – Hampshire
Swarbrick, ND (Neil) – Lancashire
Tanner, SJ (Steve) – Somerset
Taylor, A (Anthony) – Gtr Manchester
Taylor, P (Paul) – Hertfordshire
Thorpe, M (Mike) – Suffolk
Walton, P (Peter) – Northamptonshire
Ward, GL (Gavin) – Surrey
Webb, HM (Howard) – S. Yorkshire
Webster, CH (Colin) – Tyne & Wear
Whitestone, D (Dean) – Northamptonshire
Wiley, AG (Alan) – Staffordshire
Williamson, IG (Iain) – Berkshire
Woolmer, KA (Andy) – Northamptonshire
Wright, KK (Kevin) – Cambridgeshire

Promoted to National List for 2008–09

Gibbs, P (Phil) – Midlands
Hooper, S (Simon) – Wiltshire
Langford, O (Oliver) – West Midlands
Linington, J (James) – Isle of Wight
Pawson, C (Craig) – Yorkshire

Phillips, D (David) – West Sussex
Sarginson, C (Chris) – Staffordshire
Scott, G (Graham) – Oxfordshire
Webb, D (David) – Co Durham

ENGLISH LEAGUE FIXTURES 2008–2009

Reproduced under licence from Football DataCo Limited. All rights reserved. Licence number PRINT/PLAFANNU/166136a

*Sky Sports

Saturday, 9 August 2008
Coca-Cola Football League Championship
Birmingham C v Sheffield U* (12.45)
Blackpool v Bristol C
Cardiff C v Southampton
Charlton Ath v Swansea C
Coventry C v Norwich C
Crystal Palace v Watford
Derby Co v Doncaster R
Ipswich T v Preston NE
Plymouth Arg v Wolverhampton W
QPR v Barnsley
Sheffield W v Burnley

Coca-Cola Football League One
Bristol R v Carlisle U
Crewe Alex v Brighton & HA
Hartlepool U v Colchester U
Huddersfield T v Stockport Co
Leicester C v Milton Keynes D
Leyton Orient v Hereford U
Northampton T v Cheltenham T
Oldham Ath v Millwall
Scunthorpe U v Leeds U
Southend U v Peterborough U
Swindon T v Tranmere R
Yeovil T v Walsall

Coca-Cola Football League Two
Accrington S v Aldershot T
Barnet v Chesterfield
Bournemouth v Gillingham
Bradford C v Notts Co
Bury v Brentford
Dagenham & R v Chester C
Darlington v Exeter C
Grimsby T v Rochdale
Luton T v Port Vale
Rotherham U v Lincoln C
Shrewsbury T v Macclesfield T
Wycombe W v Morecambe

Sunday, 10 August 2008
Coca-Cola Football League Championship
Nottingham F v Reading* (1.15)

Saturday, 16 August 2008
Barclays Premier League
Arsenal v WBA* (12.45)
Aston Villa v Manchester C
Bolton W v Stoke C
Everton v Blackburn R
Hull C v Fulham
Middlesbrough v Tottenham H
Sunderland v Liverpool
West Ham U v Wigan Ath

Coca-Cola Football League Championship
Barnsley v Coventry C
Bristol C v Derby Co* (5.20)
Burnley v Ipswich T
Doncaster R v Cardiff C
Norwich C v Blackpool
Preston NE v Crystal Palace
Reading v Plymouth Arg
Sheffield U v QPR
Southampton v Birmingham C
Swansea C v Nottingham F
Watford v Charlton Ath
Wolverhampton W v Sheffield W

Coca-Cola Football League One
Brighton & HA v Bristol R
Carlisle U v Crewe Alex
Cheltenham T v Swindon T
Colchester U v Huddersfield T
Hereford U v Yeovil T
Leeds U v Oldham Ath
Millwall v Southend U
Milton Keynes D v Northampton T
Peterborough U v Leyton Orient
Stockport Co v Leicester C
Tranmere R v Hartlepool U
Walsall v Scunthorpe U

Coca-Cola Football League Two
Aldershot T v Bournemouth
Brentford v Grimsby T
Chester C v Wycombe W
Chesterfield v Bury
Exeter C v Shrewsbury T
Gillingham v Luton T
Lincoln C v Dagenham & R
Macclesfield T v Bradford C
Morecambe v Rotherham U
Notts Co v Darlington
Port Vale v Accrington S
Rochdale v Barnet

Sunday, 17 August 2008
Barclays Premier League
Chelsea v Portsmouth* (1.30)
Manchester U v Newcastle U* (4.00)

Saturday, 23 August 2008
Barclays Premier League
Blackburn R v Hull C
Fulham v Arsenal
Liverpool v Middlesbrough
Newcastle U v Bolton W
Stoke C v Aston Villa
Tottenham H v Sunderland
WBA v Everton
Wigan Ath v Chelsea

Coca-Cola Football League Championship
Birmingham C v Barnsley
Blackpool v Sheffield U
Cardiff C v Norwich C
Charlton Ath v Reading
Coventry C v Bristol C
Crystal Palace v Burnley
Derby Co v Southampton
Ipswich T v Wolverhampton W
Nottingham F v Watford
Plymouth Arg v Swansea C
QPR v Doncaster R
Sheffield W v Preston NE

Coca-Cola Football League One
Bristol R v Hereford U
Crewe Alex v Walsall
Hartlepool U v Stockport Co
Huddersfield T v Milton Keynes D
Leicester C v Tranmere R
Leyton Orient v Carlisle U
Northampton T v Millwall
Oldham Ath v Cheltenham T
Scunthorpe U v Peterborough U
Southend U v Brighton & HA
Swindon T v Colchester U
Yeovil T v Leeds U

Coca-Cola Football League Two
Accrington S v Macclesfield T
Barnet v Brentford
Bournemouth v Exeter C
Bradford C v Rochdale
Bury v Morecambe
Dagenham & R v Port Vale
Darlington v Gillingham
Grimsby T v Chesterfield
Luton T v Notts Co
Rotherham U v Chester C
Shrewsbury T v Aldershot T
Wycombe W v Lincoln C

Sunday, 24 August 2008
Barclays Premier League
Manchester C v West Ham U* (4.00)

Monday, 25 August 2008
Barclays Premier League
Portsmouth v Manchester U* (8.00)

Saturday, 30 August 2008
Barclays Premier League
Arsenal v Newcastle U
Bolton W v WBA
Everton v Portsmouth
Hull C v Wigan Ath
Manchester U v Fulham
Middlesbrough v Stoke C
Sunderland v Manchester C
West Ham U v Blackburn R

Coca-Cola Football League Championship
Barnsley v Derby Co
Bristol C v QPR
Burnley v Plymouth Arg
Doncaster R v Coventry C
Norwich C v Birmingham C
Preston NE v Charlton Ath
Reading v Crystal Palace
Sheffield U v Cardiff C
Southampton v Blackpool
Swansea C v Sheffield W
Watford v Ipswich T* (5.20)
Wolverhampton W v Nottingham F

Coca-Cola Football League One
Brighton & HA v Leyton Orient
Carlisle U v Yeovil T
Cheltenham T v Leicester C
Colchester U v Oldham Ath
Hereford U v Crewe Alex
Leeds U v Bristol R
Millwall v Huddersfield T
Milton Keynes D v Swindon T
Peterborough U v Hartlepool U
Stockport Co v Scunthorpe U

Tranmere R v Northampton T
Walsall v Southend U

Coca-Cola Football League Two
Aldershot T v Bradford C
Brentford v Rotherham U
Chester C v Barnet
Chesterfield v Wycombe W
Exeter C v Luton T
Gillingham v Accrington S
Lincoln C v Grimsby T
Macclesfield T v Darlington
Morecambe v Dagenham & R
Notts Co v Shrewsbury T
Port Vale v Bournemouth
Rochdale v Bury

Sunday, 31 August 2008
Barclays Premier League
Aston Villa v Liverpool* (4.00)
Chelsea v Tottenham H* (1.30)

Saturday, 6 September 2008
Coca-Cola Football League One
Brighton & HA v Scunthorpe U
Carlisle U v Southend U
Cheltenham T v Huddersfield T
Colchester U v Leicester C
Hereford U v Swindon T
Leeds U v Crewe Alex
Millwall v Hartlepool U
Milton Keynes D v Yeovil T
Peterborough U v Bristol R
Stockport Co v Northampton T
Tranmere R v Oldham Ath
Walsall v Leyton Orient

Coca-Cola Football League Two
Aldershot T v Darlington
Brentford v Dagenham & R
Chester C v Bury
Chesterfield v Rotherham U
Exeter C v Accrington S
Gillingham v Grimsby T
Lincoln C v Barnet
Macclesfield T v Luton T
Morecambe v Shrewsbury T
Notts Co v Bournemouth
Port Vale v Bradford C
Rochdale v Wycombe W

Saturday, 13 September 2008
Barclays Premier League
Blackburn R v Arsenal
Fulham v Bolton W
Liverpool v Manchester U* (12.45)
Manchester C v Chelsea
Newcastle U v Hull C
Portsmouth v Middlesbrough

Tottenham H v Aston Villa
WBA v West Ham U
Wigan Ath v Sunderland

Coca-Cola Football League Championship
Birmingham C v Doncaster R
Blackpool v Barnsley
Cardiff C v Bristol C
Charlton Ath v Wolverhampton W
Coventry C v Preston NE
Crystal Palace v Swansea C
Derby Co v Sheffield U
Ipswich T v Reading
Nottingham F v Burnley
Plymouth Arg v Norwich C
QPR v Southampton
Sheffield W v Watford

Coca-Cola Football League One
Bristol R v Walsall
Crewe Alex v Colchester U
Hartlepool U v Cheltenham T
Huddersfield T v Tranmere R
Leicester C v Millwall
Leyton Orient v Stockport Co
Northampton T v Peterborough U
Oldham Ath v Milton Keynes D
Scunthorpe U v Carlisle U
Southend U v Hereford U
Swindon T v Leeds U
Yeovil T v Brighton & HA

Coca-Cola Football League Two
Accrington S v Notts Co
Barnet v Morecambe
Bournemouth v Macclesfield T
Bradford C v Exeter C
Bury v Lincoln C
Dagenham & R v Chesterfield
Darlington v Port Vale
Grimsby T v Chester C
Luton T v Aldershot T
Rotherham U v Rochdale
Shrewsbury T v Gillingham
Wycombe W v Brentford

Sunday, 14 September 2008
Barclays Premier League
Stoke C v Everton* (1.30)

Tuesday, 16 September 2008
Coca-Cola Football League Championship
Barnsley v Cardiff C
Bristol C v Birmingham C
Burnley v Blackpool
Doncaster R v Charlton Ath
Norwich C v QPR

Preston NE v Nottingham F
Reading v Sheffield W
Sheffield U v Coventry C
Southampton v Ipswich T
Swansea C v Derby Co
Watford v Plymouth Arg
Wolverhampton W v Crystal Palace

Saturday, 20 September 2008
Barclays Premier League
Blackburn R v Fulham
Bolton W v Arsenal
Hull C v Everton
Liverpool v Stoke C
Manchester C v Portsmouth
Sunderland v Middlesbrough
Tottenham H v Wigan Ath
West Ham U v Newcastle U

Coca-Cola Football League Championship
Birmingham C v Blackpool
Bristol C v Doncaster R
Coventry C v QPR
Crystal Palace v Plymouth Arg
Derby Co v Cardiff C
Norwich C v Sheffield U
Nottingham F v Charlton Ath
Preston NE v Wolverhampton W
Sheffield W v Ipswich T
Southampton v Barnsley
Swansea C v Burnley
Watford v Reading

Coca-Cola Football League One
Brighton & HA v Walsall
Carlisle U v Leeds U
Colchester U v Milton Keynes D
Crewe Alex v Southend U
Hartlepool U v Oldham Ath
Hereford U v Scunthorpe U
Huddersfield T v Northampton T
Leyton Orient v Leicester C
Millwall v Cheltenham T
Peterborough U v Tranmere R
Stockport Co v Swindon T
Yeovil T v Bristol R

Coca-Cola Football League Two
Aldershot T v Gillingham
Barnet v Bury
Bradford C v Bournemouth
Brentford v Lincoln C
Chester C v Shrewsbury T
Darlington v Accrington S
Exeter C v Notts Co
Morecambe v Grimsby T
Port Vale v Macclesfield T
Rochdale v Chesterfield

Rotherham U v Luton T
Wycombe W v Dagenham & R

Sunday, 21 September 2008
Barclays Premier League
Chelsea v Manchester U* (2.00)
WBA v Aston Villa* (12.00)

Saturday, 27 September 2008
Barclays Premier League
Arsenal v Hull C
Aston Villa v Sunderland
Everton v Liverpool* (12.45)
Fulham v West Ham U
Manchester U v Bolton W
Middlesbrough v WBA
Newcastle U v Blackburn R
Stoke C v Chelsea

Coca-Cola Football League Championship
Barnsley v Norwich C
Blackpool v Coventry C
Burnley v Preston NE
Cardiff C v Birmingham C
Charlton Ath v Sheffield W
Doncaster R v Southampton
Ipswich T v Crystal Palace
Plymouth Arg v Nottingham F
QPR v Derby Co
Reading v Swansea C
Sheffield U v Watford
Wolverhampton W v Bristol C

Coca-Cola Football League One
Bristol R v Crewe Alex
Cheltenham T v Stockport Co
Leeds U v Hereford U
Leicester C v Hartlepool U
Milton Keynes D v Peterborough U
Northampton T v Brighton & HA
Oldham Ath v Huddersfield T
Scunthorpe U v Yeovil T
Southend U v Leyton Orient
Swindon T v Millwall
Tranmere R v Colchester U
Walsall v Carlisle U

Coca-Cola Football League Two
Accrington S v Rochdale
Bournemouth v Darlington
Bury v Wycombe W
Chesterfield v Brentford
Dagenham & R v Rotherham U
Gillingham v Port Vale
Grimsby T v Barnet
Lincoln C v Morecambe
Luton T v Chester C
Macclesfield T v Exeter C

Notts Co v Aldershot T
Shrewsbury T v Bradford C

Sunday, 28 September 2008
Barclays Premier League
Portsmouth v Tottenham H* (1.30)
Wigan Ath v Manchester C* (4.00)

Tuesday, 30 September 2008
Coca-Cola Football League
Championship
Bristol C v Plymouth Arg
Burnley v Watford
Cardiff C v Coventry C
Crystal Palace v Charlton Ath
Derby Co v Birmingham C
Doncaster R v Sheffield U
Ipswich T v Barnsley
Preston NE v Swansea C
QPR v Blackpool
Sheffield W v Nottingham F
Southampton v Norwich C
Wolverhampton W v Reading

Saturday, 4 October 2008
Barclays Premier League
Blackburn R v Manchester U
Chelsea v Aston Villa
Manchester C v Liverpool
Portsmouth v Stoke C
Sunderland v Arsenal
Tottenham H v Hull C
WBA v Fulham
Wigan Ath v Middlesbrough

Coca-Cola Football League
Championship
Barnsley v Doncaster R
Birmingham C v QPR
Blackpool v Cardiff C
Charlton Ath v Ipswich T
Coventry C v Southampton* (5.20)
Norwich C v Derby Co
Nottingham F v Crystal Palace
Plymouth Arg v Sheffield W
Reading v Burnley
Sheffield U v Bristol C
Swansea C v Wolverhampton W
Watford v Preston NE

Coca-Cola Football League One
Brighton & HA v Cheltenham T
Carlisle U v Tranmere R
Colchester U v Bristol R
Crewe Alex v Northampton T
Hartlepool U v Swindon T
Hereford U v Walsall
Huddersfield T v Leicester C
Leyton Orient v Scunthorpe U

Millwall v Milton Keynes D
Peterborough U v Leeds U
Stockport Co v Oldham Ath
Yeovil T v Southend U

Coca-Cola Football League Two
Aldershot T v Bury
Barnet v Accrington S
Bradford C v Luton T
Brentford v Macclesfield T
Chester C v Lincoln C
Darlington v Shrewsbury T
Exeter C v Gillingham
Morecambe v Chesterfield
Port Vale v Notts Co
Rochdale v Dagenham & R
Rotherham U v Grimsby T
Wycombe W v Bournemouth

Sunday, 5 October 2008
Barclays Premier League
Everton v Newcastle U* (4.00)
West Ham U v Bolton W* (1.30)

Saturday, 11 October 2008
Coca-Cola Football League One
Bristol R v Leyton Orient
Cheltenham T v Colchester U
Leeds U v Brighton & HA
Leicester C v Yeovil T
Milton Keynes D v Carlisle U
Northampton T v Hartlepool U
Oldham Ath v Hereford U
Scunthorpe U v Crewe Alex
Southend U v Stockport Co
Swindon T v Huddersfield T
Tranmere R v Millwall
Walsall v Peterborough U

Coca-Cola Football League Two
Accrington S v Bradford C
Bournemouth v Rotherham U
Bury v Exeter C
Chesterfield v Chester C
Dagenham & R v Barnet
Gillingham v Morecambe
Grimsby T v Wycombe W
Lincoln C v Rochdale
Luton T v Darlington
Macclesfield T v Aldershot T
Notts Co v Brentford
Shrewsbury T v Port Vale

Saturday, 18 October 2008
Barclays Premier League
Arsenal v Everton
Aston Villa v Portsmouth
Bolton W v Blackburn R
Fulham v Sunderland

Hull C v West Ham U
Liverpool v Wigan Ath
Manchester U v WBA
Middlesbrough v Chelsea* (12.45)
Newcastle U v Manchester C

Coca-Cola Football League Championship
Bristol C v Norwich C
Burnley v Birmingham C
Cardiff C v Charlton Ath
Crystal Palace v Barnsley
Derby Co v Plymouth Arg
Doncaster R v Blackpool
Ipswich T v Swansea C
Preston NE v Reading
QPR v Nottingham F
Sheffield W v Sheffield U
Southampton v Watford
Wolverhampton W v Coventry C

Coca-Cola Football League One
Brighton & HA v Hereford U
Carlisle U v Peterborough U
Cheltenham T v Scunthorpe U
Crewe Alex v Milton Keynes D
Huddersfield T v Bristol R
Leyton Orient v Tranmere R
Millwall v Leeds U
Northampton T v Yeovil T
Oldham Ath v Leicester C
Southend U v Swindon T
Stockport Co v Colchester U
Walsall v Hartlepool U

Coca-Cola Football League Two
Aldershot T v Brentford
Bradford C v Gillingham
Chester C v Port Vale
Dagenham & R v Bury
Exeter C v Grimsby T
Lincoln C v Chesterfield
Luton T v Accrington S
Morecambe v Rochdale
Notts Co v Macclesfield T
Rotherham U v Barnet
Shrewsbury T v Bournemouth
Wycombe W v Darlington

Sunday, 19 October 2008
Barclays Premier League
Stoke C v Tottenham H* (4.00)

Tuesday, 21 October 2008
Coca-Cola Football League Championship
Barnsley v Sheffield W
Birmingham C v Crystal Palace
Blackpool v Derby Co

Charlton Ath v Bristol C
Coventry C v Burnley
Norwich C v Wolverhampton W
Nottingham F v Ipswich T
Plymouth Arg v Preston NE
Reading v Doncaster R
Sheffield U v Southampton
Swansea C v QPR
Watford v Cardiff C

Coca-Cola Football League One
Bristol R v Oldham Ath
Colchester U v Millwall
Hartlepool U v Huddersfield T
Hereford U v Carlisle U
Leeds U v Leyton Orient
Leicester C v Walsall
Milton Keynes D v Stockport Co
Peterborough U v Brighton & HA
Scunthorpe U v Southend U
Swindon T v Northampton T
Tranmere R v Cheltenham T
Yeovil T v Crewe Alex

Coca-Cola Football League Two
Accrington S v Shrewsbury T
Barnet v Wycombe W
Bournemouth v Dagenham & R
Brentford v Morecambe
Bury v Rotherham U
Darlington v Bradford C
Gillingham v Notts Co
Grimsby T v Luton T
Macclesfield T v Lincoln C
Port Vale v Exeter C
Rochdale v Chester C

Wednesday, 22 October 2008
Coca-Cola Football League Two
Chesterfield v Aldershot T

Saturday, 25 October 2008
Barclays Premier League
Blackburn R v Middlesbrough
Everton v Manchester U
Manchester C v Stoke C
Portsmouth v Fulham
Sunderland v Newcastle U* (12.45)
Tottenham H v Bolton W
WBA v Hull C
Wigan Ath v Aston Villa

Coca-Cola Football League Championship
Barnsley v Bristol C
Birmingham C v Sheffield W
Blackpool v Crystal Palace
Charlton Ath v Burnley
Coventry C v Derby Co

Norwich C v Doncaster R
Nottingham F v Cardiff C
Plymouth Arg v Ipswich T
Reading v QPR* (5.20)
Sheffield U v Preston NE
Swansea C v Southampton
Watford v Wolverhampton W

Coca-Cola Football League One
Bristol R v Southend U
Colchester U v Carlisle U
Hartlepool U v Brighton & HA
Hereford U v Stockport Co
Leeds U v Walsall
Leicester C v Northampton T
Milton Keynes D v Cheltenham T
Peterborough U v Huddersfield T
Scunthorpe U v Millwall
Swindon T v Oldham Ath
Tranmere R v Crewe Alex
Yeovil T v Leyton Orient

Coca-Cola Football League Two
Accrington S v Wycombe W
Barnet v Exeter C
Bournemouth v Lincoln C
Brentford v Shrewsbury T
Bury v Luton T
Chesterfield v Notts Co
Darlington v Dagenham & R
Gillingham v Chester C
Grimsby T v Bradford C
Macclesfield T v Rotherham U
Port Vale v Morecambe
Rochdale v Aldershot T

Sunday, 26 October 2008
Barclays Premier League
Chelsea v Liverpool* (1.30)
West Ham U v Arsenal* (4.00)

Tuesday, 28 October 2008
Barclays Premier League
Bolton W v Everton
Hull C v Chelsea
Manchester U v West Ham U
Middlesbrough v Manchester C
Stoke C v Sunderland* (8.00)

Coca-Cola Football League Championship
Bristol C v Sheffield U
Burnley v Reading
Cardiff C v Blackpool
Crystal Palace v Nottingham F
Derby Co v Norwich C
Doncaster R v Barnsley
Ipswich T v Charlton Ath
Preston NE v Watford

QPR v Birmingham C
Sheffield W v Plymouth Arg
Southampton v Coventry C
Wolverhampton W v Swansea C

Coca-Cola Football League One
Brighton & HA v Leicester C
Carlisle U v Hartlepool U
Cheltenham T v Bristol R
Crewe Alex v Peterborough U
Huddersfield T v Yeovil T
Leyton Orient v Milton Keynes D
Millwall v Hereford U
Northampton T v Colchester U
Oldham Ath v Scunthorpe U
Southend U v Leeds U
Stockport Co v Tranmere R
Walsall v Swindon T

Coca-Cola Football League Two
Aldershot T v Port Vale
Bradford C v Bury
Chester C v Brentford
Dagenham & R v Grimsby T
Exeter C v Chesterfield
Lincoln C v Gillingham
Luton T v Bournemouth
Morecambe v Accrington S
Notts Co v Rochdale
Rotherham U v Darlington
Shrewsbury T v Barnet
Wycombe W v Macclesfield T

Wednesday, 29 October 2008
Barclays Premier League
Arsenal v Tottenham H* (8.00)
Aston Villa v Blackburn R
Fulham v Wigan Ath
Liverpool v Portsmouth
Newcastle U v WBA

Saturday, 1 November 2008
Barclays Premier League
Chelsea v Sunderland
Everton v Fulham* (12.45)
Manchester U v Hull C
Middlesbrough v West Ham U
Newcastle U v Aston Villa
Portsmouth v Wigan Ath
Stoke C v Arsenal
Tottenham H v Liverpool
WBA v Blackburn R

Coca-Cola Football League Championship
Birmingham C v Coventry C
Bristol C v Reading
Burnley v Norwich C
Cardiff C v Wolverhampton W

Charlton Ath v Barnsley
Crystal Palace v Sheffield W
Derby Co v Nottingham F
Doncaster R v Swansea C
Ipswich T v QPR
Preston NE v Southampton
Sheffield U v Plymouth Arg
Watford v Blackpool

Coca-Cola Football League One
Brighton & HA v Millwall
Cheltenham T v Leeds U
Huddersfield T v Crewe Alex
Leicester C v Bristol R
Leyton Orient v Hartlepool U
Milton Keynes D v Tranmere R
Oldham Ath v Yeovil T
Peterborough U v Hereford U
Scunthorpe U v Swindon T
Southend U v Colchester U
Stockport Co v Carlisle U
Walsall v Northampton T

Coca-Cola Football League Two
Bournemouth v Chesterfield
Bradford C v Barnet
Brentford v Rochdale
Dagenham & R v Accrington S
Exeter C v Chester C
Grimsby T v Darlington
Lincoln C v Port Vale
Macclesfield T v Gillingham
Morecambe v Aldershot T
Notts Co v Bury
Rotherham U v Wycombe W
Shrewsbury T v Luton T

Sunday, 2 November 2008
Barclays Premier League
Bolton W v Manchester C* (4.00)

Saturday, 8 November 2008
Barclays Premier League
Arsenal v Manchester U* (12.45)
Aston Villa v Middlesbrough
Hull C v Bolton W
Liverpool v WBA
Manchester C v Tottenham H
Sunderland v Portsmouth
West Ham U v Everton
Wigan Ath v Stoke C

Coca-Cola Football League Championship
Barnsley v Sheffield U
Blackpool v Ipswich T
Coventry C v Crystal Palace
Norwich C v Preston NE
Nottingham F v Birmingham C

Plymouth Arg v Charlton Ath
QPR v Cardiff C
Reading v Derby Co
Sheffield W v Doncaster R
Southampton v Bristol C* (5.20)
Swansea C v Watford
Wolverhampton W v Burnley

Sunday, 9 November 2008
Barclays Premier League
Blackburn R v Chelsea* (1.30)
Fulham v Newcastle U* (4.00)

Saturday, 15 November 2008
Barclays Premier League
Arsenal v Aston Villa
Blackburn R v Sunderland
Bolton W v Liverpool* (12.45)
Fulham v Tottenham H
Manchester U v Stoke C
Newcastle U v Wigan Ath
WBA v Chelsea
West Ham U v Portsmouth

Coca-Cola Football League Championship
Barnsley v Watford
Birmingham C v Charlton Ath
Blackpool v Preston NE
Bristol C v Nottingham F
Cardiff C v Crystal Palace
Coventry C v Plymouth Arg
Derby Co v Sheffield W
Doncaster R v Ipswich T
Norwich C v Swansea C
QPR v Burnley
Sheffield U v Reading
Southampton v Wolverhampton W

Coca-Cola Football League One
Bristol R v Scunthorpe U
Carlisle U v Brighton & HA
Colchester U v Walsall
Crewe Alex v Leyton Orient
Hartlepool U v Milton Keynes D
Hereford U v Cheltenham T
Leeds U v Huddersfield T
Millwall v Stockport Co
Northampton T v Oldham Ath
Swindon T v Leicester C
Tranmere R v Southend U
Yeovil T v Peterborough U

Coca-Cola Football League Two
Accrington S v Bournemouth
Aldershot T v Exeter C
Barnet v Notts Co
Bury v Grimsby T
Chester C v Morecambe

Chesterfield v Shrewsbury T
Darlington v Lincoln C
Gillingham v Rotherham U
Luton T v Dagenham & R
Port Vale v Brentford
Rochdale v Macclesfield T
Wycombe W v Bradford C

Sunday, 16 November 2008
Barclays Premier League
Everton v Middlesbrough* (1.30)
Hull C v Manchester C* (4.00)

Saturday, 22 November 2008
Barclays Premier League
Aston Villa v Manchester U
Chelsea v Newcastle U
Liverpool v Fulham
Manchester C v Arsenal
Middlesbrough v Bolton W
Portsmouth v Hull C
Stoke C v WBA
Wigan Ath v Everton

Coca-Cola Football League
Championship
Burnley v Doncaster R
Charlton Ath v Sheffield U
Crystal Palace v Bristol C
Ipswich T v Derby Co
Nottingham F v Norwich C* (5.20)
Plymouth Arg v Cardiff C
Preston NE v Barnsley
Reading v Southampton
Sheffield W v Coventry C
Swansea C v Birmingham C
Watford v QPR
Wolverhampton W v Blackpool

Coca-Cola Football League One
Brighton & HA v Huddersfield T
Bristol R v Swindon T
Carlisle U v Cheltenham T
Crewe Alex v Stockport Co
Hereford U v Northampton T
Leeds U v Hartlepool U
Leyton Orient v Millwall
Peterborough U v Colchester U
Scunthorpe U v Leicester C
Southend U v Oldham Ath
Walsall v Milton Keynes D
Yeovil T v Tranmere R

Coca-Cola Football League Two
Barnet v Macclesfield T
Brentford v Darlington
Bury v Gillingham
Chester C v Aldershot T
Chesterfield v Accrington S

Dagenham & R v Notts Co
Grimsby T v Bournemouth
Lincoln C v Shrewsbury T
Morecambe v Exeter C
Rochdale v Luton T
Rotherham U v Bradford C
Wycombe W v Port Vale

Sunday, 23 November 2008
Barclays Premier League
Sunderland v West Ham U* (4.00)
Tottenham H v Blackburn R* (1.30)

Tuesday, 25 November 2008
Coca-Cola Football League
Championship
Barnsley v Burnley
Birmingham C v Ipswich T
Blackpool v Sheffield W
Bristol C v Watford
Cardiff C v Reading
Coventry C v Swansea C
Derby Co v Preston NE
Doncaster R v Nottingham F
Norwich C v Crystal Palace
QPR v Charlton Ath
Sheffield U v Wolverhampton W
Southampton v Plymouth Arg

Coca-Cola Football League One
Cheltenham T v Southend U
Colchester U v Yeovil T
Hartlepool U v Bristol R
Huddersfield T v Leyton Orient
Leicester C v Crewe Alex
Millwall v Carlisle U
Milton Keynes D v Hereford U
Northampton T v Leeds U
Oldham Ath v Walsall
Stockport Co v Brighton & HA
Swindon T v Peterborough U
Tranmere R v Scunthorpe U

Coca-Cola Football League Two
Accrington S v Bury
Aldershot T v Lincoln C
Bournemouth v Morecambe
Bradford C v Chesterfield
Darlington v Chester C
Exeter C v Rotherham U
Gillingham v Rochdale
Luton T v Brentford
Macclesfield T v Grimsby T
Notts Co v Wycombe W
Port Vale v Barnet
Shrewsbury T v Dagenham & R

Saturday, 29 November 2008
Barclays Premier League
Aston Villa v Fulham
Liverpool v West Ham U
Middlesbrough v Newcastle U
Portsmouth v Blackburn R
Stoke C v Hull C
Sunderland v Bolton W
Tottenham H v Everton
Wigan Ath v WBA

Coca-Cola Football League Championship
Burnley v Derby Co
Charlton Ath v Southampton
Crystal Palace v QPR
Ipswich T v Sheffield U
Nottingham F v Barnsley
Plymouth Arg v Blackpool
Preston NE v Bristol C
Reading v Coventry C
Sheffield W v Norwich C
Watford v Doncaster R
Wolverhampton W v Birmingham C

Sunday, 30 November 2008
Barclays Premier League
Chelsea v Arsenal* (4.00)
Manchester C v Manchester U* (1.30)

Coca-Cola Football League Championship
Swansea C v Cardiff C* (11.30)

Saturday, 6 December 2008
Barclays Premier League
Arsenal v Wigan Ath
Blackburn R v Liverpool
Bolton W v Chelsea
Everton v Aston Villa
Fulham v Manchester C
Hull C v Middlesbrough
Manchester U v Sunderland
Newcastle U v Stoke C
WBA v Portsmouth
West Ham U v Tottenham H

Coca-Cola Football League Championship
Barnsley v Reading
Birmingham C v Watford
Blackpool v Charlton Ath
Bristol C v Swansea C
Cardiff C v Preston NE
Coventry C v Nottingham F
Derby Co v Crystal Palace
Doncaster R v Plymouth Arg
Norwich C v Ipswich T
QPR v Wolverhampton W

Sheffield U v Burnley
Southampton v Sheffield W

Coca-Cola Football League One
Cheltenham T v Crewe Alex
Colchester U v Hereford U
Hartlepool U v Yeovil T
Huddersfield T v Walsall
Leicester C v Southend U
Millwall v Bristol R
Milton Keynes D v Scunthorpe U
Northampton T v Leyton Orient
Oldham Ath v Brighton & HA
Stockport Co v Peterborough U
Swindon T v Carlisle U
Tranmere R v Leeds U

Coca-Cola Football League Two
Accrington S v Brentford
Aldershot T v Wycombe W
Bournemouth v Chester C
Bradford C v Dagenham & R
Darlington v Rochdale
Exeter C v Lincoln C
Gillingham v Chesterfield
Luton T v Barnet
Macclesfield T v Bury
Notts Co v Morecambe
Port Vale v Grimsby T
Shrewsbury T v Rotherham U

Tuesday, 9 December 2008
Coca-Cola Football League Championship
Burnley v Cardiff C
Charlton Ath v Coventry C
Crystal Palace v Southampton
Ipswich T v Bristol C
Nottingham F v Sheffield U
Plymouth Arg v Birmingham C
Preston NE v Doncaster R
Reading v Blackpool
Sheffield W v QPR
Swansea C v Barnsley
Watford v Norwich C
Wolverhampton W v Derby Co

Saturday, 13 December 2008
Barclays Premier League
Aston Villa v Bolton W
Chelsea v West Ham U
Liverpool v Hull C
Manchester C v Everton
Middlesbrough v Arsenal
Portsmouth v Newcastle U
Stoke C v Fulham
Sunderland v WBA
Tottenham H v Manchester U
Wigan Ath v Blackburn R

**Coca-Cola Football League
Championship**
Burnley v Southampton
Charlton Ath v Derby Co
Crystal Palace v Doncaster R
Ipswich T v Cardiff C
Nottingham F v Blackpool
Plymouth Arg v QPR
Preston NE v Birmingham C
Reading v Norwich C
Sheffield W v Bristol C
Swansea C v Sheffield U
Watford v Coventry C
Wolverhampton W v Barnsley

Coca-Cola Football League One
Brighton & HA v Milton Keynes D
Bristol R v Tranmere R
Carlisle U v Leicester C
Crewe Alex v Swindon T
Hereford U v Hartlepool U
Leeds U v Colchester U
Leyton Orient v Cheltenham T
Peterborough U v Oldham Ath
Scunthorpe U v Northampton T
Southend U v Huddersfield T
Walsall v Millwall
Yeovil T v Stockport Co

Coca-Cola Football League Two
Barnet v Gillingham
Brentford v Bradford C
Bury v Port Vale
Chester C v Notts Co
Chesterfield v Macclesfield T
Dagenham & R v Exeter C
Grimsby T v Shrewsbury T
Lincoln C v Accrington S
Morecambe v Darlington
Rochdale v Bournemouth
Rotherham U v Aldershot T
Wycombe W v Luton T

Saturday, 20 December 2008
Barclays Premier League
Arsenal v Liverpool
Blackburn R v Stoke C
Bolton W v Portsmouth
Everton v Chelsea
Fulham v Middlesbrough
Hull C v Sunderland
Manchester U v Wigan Ath
Newcastle U v Tottenham H
WBA v Manchester C
West Ham U v Aston Villa

**Coca-Cola Football League
Championship**
Barnsley v Plymouth Arg

Birmingham C v Reading
Blackpool v Swansea C
Bristol C v Burnley
Cardiff C v Sheffield W
Coventry C v Ipswich T
Derby Co v Watford
Doncaster R v Wolverhampton W
Norwich C v Charlton Ath
QPR v Preston NE
Sheffield U v Crystal Palace
Southampton v Nottingham F

Coca-Cola Football League One
Cheltenham T v Walsall
Colchester U v Scunthorpe U
Hartlepool U v Southend U
Huddersfield T v Hereford U
Leicester C v Peterborough U
Millwall v Crewe Alex
Milton Keynes D v Leeds U
Northampton T v Carlisle U
Oldham Ath v Leyton Orient
Stockport Co v Bristol R
Swindon T v Yeovil T
Tranmere R v Brighton & HA

Coca-Cola Football League Two
Accrington S v Rotherham U
Aldershot T v Grimsby T
Bournemouth v Bury
Bradford C v Chester C
Darlington v Barnet
Exeter C v Rochdale
Gillingham v Brentford
Luton T v Morecambe
Macclesfield T v Dagenham & R
Notts Co v Lincoln C
Port Vale v Chesterfield
Shrewsbury T v Wycombe W

Friday, 26 December 2008
Barclays Premier League
Aston Villa v Arsenal
Chelsea v WBA
Liverpool v Bolton W
Manchester C v Hull C
Middlesbrough v Everton
Portsmouth v West Ham U
Stoke C v Manchester U
Sunderland v Blackburn R
Tottenham H v Fulham
Wigan Ath v Newcastle U

**Coca-Cola Football League
Championship**
Burnley v Barnsley
Charlton Ath v QPR
Crystal Palace v Norwich C
Ipswich T v Birmingham C

Nottingham F v Doncaster R
Plymouth Arg v Southampton
Preston NE v Derby Co
Reading v Cardiff C
Sheffield W v Blackpool
Swansea C v Coventry C
Watford v Bristol C
Wolverhampton W v Sheffield U

Coca-Cola Football League One
Brighton & HA v Colchester U
Bristol R v Milton Keynes D
Carlisle U v Huddersfield T
Crewe Alex v Oldham Ath
Hereford U v Tranmere R
Leeds U v Leicester C
Leyton Orient v Swindon T
Peterborough U v Millwall
Scunthorpe U v Hartlepool U
Southend U v Northampton T
Walsall v Stockport Co
Yeovil T v Cheltenham T

Coca-Cola Football League Two
Barnet v Aldershot T
Brentford v Bournemouth
Bury v Darlington
Chester C v Accrington S
Chesterfield v Luton T
Dagenham & R v Gillingham
Grimsby T v Notts Co
Lincoln C v Bradford C
Morecambe v Macclesfield T
Rochdale v Shrewsbury T
Rotherham U v Port Vale
Wycombe W v Exeter C

Sunday, 28 December 2008
Barclays Premier League
Arsenal v Portsmouth
Blackburn R v Manchester C
Bolton W v Wigan Ath
Everton v Sunderland
Fulham v Chelsea
Hull C v Aston Villa
Manchester U v Middlesbrough
Newcastle U v Liverpool
WBA v Tottenham H
West Ham U v Stoke C

Coca-Cola Football League Championship
Barnsley v Preston NE
Birmingham C v Swansea C
Blackpool v Wolverhampton W
Bristol C v Crystal Palace
Cardiff C v Plymouth Arg
Coventry C v Sheffield W
Derby Co v Ipswich T
Doncaster R v Burnley

Norwich C v Nottingham F
QPR v Watford
Sheffield U v Charlton Ath
Southampton v Reading

Coca-Cola Football League One
Cheltenham T v Peterborough U
Colchester U v Leyton Orient
Hartlepool U v Crewe Alex
Huddersfield T v Scunthorpe U
Leicester C v Hereford U
Millwall v Yeovil T
Milton Keynes D v Southend U
Northampton T v Bristol R
Oldham Ath v Carlisle U
Stockport Co v Leeds U
Swindon T v Brighton & HA
Tranmere R v Walsall

Coca-Cola Football League Two
Accrington S v Grimsby T
Aldershot T v Dagenham & R
Bournemouth v Barnet
Bradford C v Morecambe
Darlington v Chesterfield
Exeter C v Brentford
Gillingham v Wycombe W
Luton T v Lincoln C
Macclesfield T v Chester C
Notts Co v Rotherham U
Port Vale v Rochdale
Shrewsbury T v Bury

Saturday, 3 January 2009
Coca-Cola Football League One
Brighton & HA v Northampton T
Carlisle U v Walsall
Colchester U v Tranmere R
Crewe Alex v Bristol R
Hartlepool U v Leicester C
Hereford U v Leeds U
Huddersfield T v Oldham Ath
Leyton Orient v Southend U
Millwall v Swindon T
Peterborough U v Milton Keynes D
Stockport Co v Cheltenham T
Yeovil T v Scunthorpe U

Coca-Cola Football League Two
Aldershot T v Notts Co
Barnet v Grimsby T
Bradford C v Shrewsbury T
Brentford v Chesterfield
Chester C v Luton T
Darlington v Bournemouth
Exeter C v Macclesfield T
Morecambe v Lincoln C
Port Vale v Gillingham
Rochdale v Accrington S
Rotherham U v Dagenham & R
Wycombe W v Bury

Saturday, 10 January 2009
Barclays Premier League
Arsenal v Bolton W
Aston Villa v WBA
Everton v Hull C
Fulham v Blackburn R
Manchester U v Chelsea
Middlesbrough v Sunderland
Newcastle U v West Ham U
Portsmouth v Manchester C
Stoke C v Liverpool
Wigan Ath v Tottenham H

Coca-Cola Football League Championship
Barnsley v Southampton
Blackpool v Birmingham C
Burnley v Swansea C
Cardiff C v Derby Co
Charlton Ath v Nottingham F
Doncaster R v Bristol C
Ipswich T v Sheffield W
Plymouth Arg v Crystal Palace
QPR v Coventry C
Reading v Watford
Sheffield U v Norwich C
Wolverhampton W v Preston NE

Coca-Cola Football League One
Bristol R v Yeovil T
Cheltenham T v Millwall
Leeds U v Carlisle U
Leicester C v Leyton Orient
Milton Keynes D v Colchester U
Northampton T v Huddersfield T
Oldham Ath v Hartlepool U
Scunthorpe U v Hereford U
Southend U v Crewe Alex
Swindon T v Stockport Co
Tranmere R v Peterborough U
Walsall v Brighton & HA

Coca-Cola Football League Two
Accrington S v Darlington
Bournemouth v Bradford C
Bury v Barnet
Chesterfield v Rochdale
Dagenham & R v Wycombe W
Gillingham v Aldershot T
Grimsby T v Morecambe
Lincoln C v Brentford
Luton T v Rotherham U
Macclesfield T v Port Vale
Notts Co v Exeter C
Shrewsbury T v Chester C

Saturday, 17 January 2009
Barclays Premier League
Blackburn R v Newcastle U

Bolton W v Manchester U
Chelsea v Stoke C
Hull C v Arsenal
Liverpool v Everton
Manchester C v Wigan Ath
Sunderland v Aston Villa
Tottenham H v Portsmouth
WBA v Middlesbrough
West Ham U v Fulham

Coca-Cola Football League Championship
Birmingham C v Cardiff C
Bristol C v Wolverhampton W
Coventry C v Blackpool
Crystal Palace v Ipswich T
Derby Co v QPR
Norwich C v Barnsley
Nottingham F v Plymouth Arg
Preston NE v Burnley
Sheffield W v Charlton Ath
Southampton v Doncaster R
Swansea C v Reading
Watford v Sheffield U

Coca-Cola Football League One
Brighton & HA v Leeds U
Carlisle U v Milton Keynes D
Colchester U v Cheltenham T
Crewe Alex v Scunthorpe U
Hartlepool U v Northampton T
Hereford U v Oldham Ath
Huddersfield T v Swindon T
Leyton Orient v Bristol R
Millwall v Tranmere R
Peterborough U v Walsall
Stockport Co v Southend U
Yeovil T v Leicester C

Coca-Cola Football League Two
Aldershot T v Macclesfield T
Barnet v Dagenham & R
Bradford C v Accrington S
Brentford v Notts Co
Chester C v Chesterfield
Darlington v Luton T
Exeter C v Bury
Morecambe v Gillingham
Port Vale v Shrewsbury T
Rochdale v Lincoln C
Rotherham U v Bournemouth
Wycombe W v Grimsby T

Saturday, 24 January 2009
Coca-Cola Football League One
Bristol R v Colchester U
Cheltenham T v Brighton & HA
Leeds U v Peterborough U
Leicester C v Huddersfield T

364

Milton Keynes D v Millwall
Northampton T v Crewe Alex
Oldham Ath v Stockport Co
Scunthorpe U v Leyton Orient
Southend U v Yeovil T
Swindon T v Hartlepool U
Tranmere R v Carlisle U
Walsall v Hereford U

Coca-Cola Football League Two
Accrington S v Barnet
Bournemouth v Wycombe W
Bury v Aldershot T
Chesterfield v Morecambe
Dagenham & R v Rochdale
Gillingham v Exeter C
Grimsby T v Rotherham U
Lincoln C v Chester C
Luton T v Bradford C
Macclesfield T v Brentford
Notts Co v Port Vale
Shrewsbury T v Darlington

Tuesday, 27 January 2009
Barclays Premier League
Portsmouth v Aston Villa
Sunderland v Fulham
Tottenham H v Stoke C
WBA v Manchester U
West Ham U v Hull C
Wigan Ath v Liverpool

Coca-Cola Football League Championship
Barnsley v Ipswich T
Birmingham C v Derby Co
Blackpool v QPR
Charlton Ath v Crystal Palace
Coventry C v Cardiff C
Norwich C v Southampton
Nottingham F v Sheffield W
Plymouth Arg v Bristol C
Reading v Wolverhampton W
Sheffield U v Doncaster R
Swansea C v Preston NE
Watford v Burnley

Coca-Cola Football League One
Bristol R v Cheltenham T
Colchester U v Northampton T
Hartlepool U v Carlisle U
Hereford U v Millwall
Leeds U v Southend U
Leicester C v Brighton & HA
Milton Keynes D v Leyton Orient
Peterborough v Crewe Alex
Scunthorpe U v Oldham Ath
Swindon T v Walsall

Tranmere R v Stockport Co
Yeovil T v Huddersfield T

Coca-Cola Football League Two
Accrington S v Morecambe
Barnet v Shrewsbury T
Bournemouth v Luton T
Brentford v Aldershot T
Bury v Bradford C
Darlington v Rotherham U
Gillingham v Lincoln C
Grimsby T v Dagenham & R
Macclesfield T v Wycombe W
Port Vale v Chester C
Rochdale v Notts Co

Wednesday, 28 January 2009
Barclays Premier League
Blackburn R v Bolton W
Chelsea v Middlesbrough
Everton v Arsenal
Manchester C v Newcastle U

Coca-Cola Football League Two
Chesterfield v Exeter C

Saturday, 31 January 2009
Barclays Premier League
Arsenal v West Ham U
Aston Villa v Wigan Ath
Bolton W v Tottenham H
Fulham v Portsmouth
Hull C v WBA
Liverpool v Chelsea
Manchester U v Everton
Middlesbrough v Blackburn R
Newcastle U v Sunderland
Stoke C v Manchester C

Coca-Cola Football League Championship
Bristol C v Barnsley
Burnley v Charlton Ath
Cardiff C v Nottingham F
Crystal Palace v Blackpool
Derby Co v Coventry C
Doncaster R v Norwich C
Ipswich T v Plymouth Arg
Preston NE v Sheffield U
QPR v Reading
Sheffield W v Birmingham C
Southampton v Swansea C
Wolverhampton W v Watford

Coca-Cola Football League One
Brighton & HA v Hartlepool U
Carlisle U v Colchester U
Cheltenham T v Milton Keynes D
Crewe Alex v Tranmere R

Huddersfield T v Peterborough U
Leyton Orient v Yeovil T
Millwall v Scunthorpe U
Northampton T v Leicester C
Oldham Ath v Swindon T
Southend U v Bristol R
Stockport Co v Hereford U
Walsall v Leeds U

Coca-Cola Football League Two
Aldershot T v Rochdale
Bradford C v Grimsby T
Chester C v Gillingham
Dagenham & R v Darlington
Exeter C v Barnet
Lincoln C v Bournemouth
Luton T v Bury
Morecambe v Port Vale
Notts Co v Chesterfield
Rotherham U v Macclesfield T
Shrewsbury T v Brentford
Wycombe W v Accrington S

Tuesday, 3 February 2009
Coca-Cola Football League Championship
Bristol C v Charlton Ath
Burnley v Coventry C
Cardiff C v Watford
Crystal Palace v Birmingham C
Derby Co v Blackpool
Doncaster R v Reading
Ipswich T v Nottingham F
Preston NE v Plymouth Arg
QPR v Swansea C
Sheffield W v Barnsley
Southampton v Sheffield U
Wolverhampton W v Norwich C

Coca-Cola Football League One
Brighton & HA v Peterborough U
Carlisle U v Hereford U
Cheltenham T v Tranmere R
Crewe Alex v Yeovil T
Huddersfield T v Hartlepool U
Leyton Orient v Leeds U
Millwall v Colchester U
Northampton T v Swindon T
Oldham Ath v Bristol R
Southend U v Scunthorpe U
Stockport Co v Milton Keynes D
Walsall v Leicester C

Coca-Cola Football League Two
Aldershot T v Chesterfield
Bradford C v Darlington
Chester C v Rochdale
Dagenham & R v Bournemouth
Exeter C v Port Vale

Lincoln C v Macclesfield T
Luton T v Grimsby T
Morecambe v Brentford
Notts Co v Gillingham
Rotherham U v Bury
Shrewsbury T v Accrington S
Wycombe W v Barnet

Saturday, 7 February 2009
Barclays Premier League
Blackburn R v Aston Villa
Chelsea v Hull C
Everton v Bolton W
Manchester C v Middlesbrough
Portsmouth v Liverpool
Sunderland v Stoke C
Tottenham H v Arsenal
WBA v Newcastle U
West Ham U v Manchester U
Wigan Ath v Fulham

Coca-Cola Football League Championship
Barnsley v Crystal Palace
Birmingham C v Burnley
Blackpool v Doncaster R
Charlton Ath v Cardiff C
Coventry C v Wolverhampton W
Norwich C v Bristol C
Nottingham F v QPR
Plymouth Arg v Derby Co
Reading v Preston NE
Sheffield U v Sheffield W
Swansea C v Ipswich T
Watford v Southampton

Coca-Cola Football League One
Bristol R v Huddersfield T
Colchester U v Stockport Co
Hartlepool U v Walsall
Hereford U v Brighton & HA
Leeds U v Millwall
Leicester C v Oldham Ath
Milton Keynes D v Crewe Alex
Peterborough U v Carlisle U
Scunthorpe U v Cheltenham T
Swindon T v Southend U
Tranmere R v Leyton Orient
Yeovil T v Northampton T

Coca-Cola Football League Two
Accrington S v Luton T
Barnet v Rotherham U
Bournemouth v Shrewsbury T
Brentford v Chester C
Bury v Dagenham & R
Chesterfield v Lincoln C
Darlington v Wycombe W
Gillingham v Bradford C

Grimsby T v Exeter C
Macclesfield T v Notts Co
Port Vale v Aldershot T
Rochdale v Morecambe

Saturday, 14 February 2009
Coca-Cola Football League
Championship
Birmingham C v Nottingham F
Bristol C v Southampton
Burnley v Wolverhampton W
Cardiff C v QPR
Charlton Ath v Plymouth Arg
Crystal Palace v Coventry C
Derby Co v Reading
Doncaster R v Sheffield W
Ipswich T v Blackpool
Preston NE v Norwich C
Sheffield U v Barnsley
Watford v Swansea C

Coca-Cola Football League One
Brighton & HA v Carlisle U
Cheltenham T v Hereford U
Huddersfield T v Leeds U
Leicester C v Swindon T
Leyton Orient v Crewe Alex
Milton Keynes D v Hartlepool U
Oldham Ath v Northampton T
Peterborough U v Yeovil T
Scunthorpe U v Bristol R
Southend U v Tranmere R
Stockport Co v Millwall
Walsall v Colchester U

Coca-Cola Football League Two
Bournemouth v Accrington S
Bradford C v Wycombe W
Brentford v Port Vale
Dagenham & R v Luton T
Exeter C v Aldershot T
Grimsby T v Bury
Lincoln C v Darlington
Macclesfield T v Rochdale
Morecambe v Chester C
Notts Co v Barnet
Rotherham U v Gillingham
Shrewsbury T v Chesterfield

Saturday, 21 February 2009
Barclays Premier League
Arsenal v Sunderland
Aston Villa v Chelsea
Bolton W v West Ham U
Fulham v WBA
Hull C v Tottenham H
Liverpool v Manchester C
Manchester U v Blackburn R
Middlesbrough v Wigan Ath

Newcastle U v Everton
Stoke C v Portsmouth

Coca-Cola Football League
Championship
Barnsley v Charlton Ath
Blackpool v Watford
Coventry C v Birmingham C
Norwich C v Burnley
Nottingham F v Derby Co
Plymouth Arg v Sheffield U
QPR v Ipswich T
Reading v Bristol C
Sheffield W v Crystal Palace
Southampton v Preston NE
Swansea C v Doncaster R
Wolverhampton W v Cardiff C

Coca-Cola Football League One
Bristol R v Leicester C
Carlisle U v Stockport Co
Colchester U v Southend U
Crewe Alex v Huddersfield T
Hartlepool U v Leyton Orient
Hereford U v Peterborough U
Leeds U v Cheltenham T
Millwall v Brighton & HA
Northampton T v Walsall
Swindon T v Scunthorpe U
Tranmere R v Milton Keynes D
Yeovil T v Oldham Ath

Coca-Cola Football League Two
Accrington S v Dagenham & R
Aldershot T v Morecambe
Barnet v Bradford C
Bury v Notts Co
Chester C v Exeter C
Chesterfield v Bournemouth
Darlington v Grimsby T
Gillingham v Macclesfield T
Luton T v Shrewsbury T
Port Vale v Lincoln C
Rochdale v Brentford
Wycombe W v Rotherham U

Saturday, 28 February 2009
Barclays Premier League
Arsenal v Fulham
Aston Villa v Stoke C
Bolton W v Newcastle U
Chelsea v Wigan Ath
Everton v WBA
Hull C v Blackburn R
Manchester U v Portsmouth
Middlesbrough v Liverpool
Sunderland v Tottenham H
West Ham U v Manchester C

**Coca-Cola Football League
Championship**
Barnsley v QPR
Bristol C v Blackpool
Burnley v Sheffield W
Doncaster R v Derby Co
Norwich C v Coventry C
Preston NE v Ipswich T
Reading v Nottingham F
Sheffield U v Birmingham C
Southampton v Cardiff C
Swansea C v Charlton Ath
Watford v Crystal Palace
Wolverhampton W v Plymouth Arg

Coca-Cola Football League One
Brighton & HA v Crewe Alex
Carlisle U v Bristol R
Cheltenham T v Northampton T
Colchester U v Hartlepool U
Hereford U v Leyton Orient
Leeds U v Scunthorpe U
Millwall v Oldham Ath
Milton Keynes D v Leicester C
Peterborough U v Southend U
Stockport Co v Huddersfield T
Tranmere R v Swindon T
Walsall v Yeovil T

Coca-Cola Football League Two
Aldershot T v Accrington S
Brentford v Bury
Chester C v Dagenham & R
Chesterfield v Barnet
Exeter C v Darlington
Gillingham v Bournemouth
Lincoln C v Rotherham U
Macclesfield T v Shrewsbury T
Morecambe v Wycombe W
Notts Co v Bradford C
Port Vale v Luton T
Rochdale v Grimsby T

Tuesday, 3 March 2009
Barclays Premier League
Portsmouth v Chelsea
Stoke C v Bolton W
Tottenham H v Middlesbrough
WBA v Arsenal
Wigan Ath v West Ham U

**Coca-Cola Football League
Championship**
Birmingham C v Bristol C
Blackpool v Burnley
Cardiff C v Barnsley
Charlton Ath v Doncaster R
Coventry C v Sheffield U
Crystal Palace v Wolverhampton W

Derby Co v Swansea C
Ipswich T v Southampton
Nottingham F v Preston NE
Plymouth Arg v Watford
QPR v Norwich C
Sheffield W v Reading

Coca-Cola Football League One
Bristol R v Brighton & HA
Crewe Alex v Carlisle U
Hartlepool U v Tranmere R
Huddersfield T v Colchester U
Leicester C v Stockport Co
Leyton Orient v Peterborough U
Northampton T v Milton Keynes D
Oldham Ath v Leeds U
Scunthorpe U v Walsall
Southend U v Millwall
Swindon T v Cheltenham T
Yeovil T v Hereford U

Coca-Cola Football League Two
Accrington S v Port Vale
Barnet v Rochdale
Bournemouth v Aldershot T
Bradford C v Macclesfield T
Bury v Chesterfield
Dagenham & R v Lincoln C
Darlington v Notts Co
Grimsby T v Brentford
Luton T v Gillingham
Rotherham U v Morecambe
Shrewsbury T v Exeter C
Wycombe W v Chester C

Wednesday, 4 March 2009
Barclays Premier League
Blackburn R v Everton
Fulham v Hull C
Liverpool v Sunderland
Manchester C v Aston Villa
Newcastle U v Manchester U

Saturday, 7 March 2009
**Coca-Cola Football League
Championship**
Birmingham C v Southampton
Blackpool v Norwich C
Cardiff C v Doncaster R
Charlton Ath v Watford
Coventry C v Barnsley
Crystal Palace v Preston NE
Derby Co v Bristol C
Ipswich T v Burnley
Nottingham F v Swansea C
Plymouth Arg v Reading
QPR v Sheffield U
Sheffield W v Wolverhampton W

Coca-Cola Football League One
Bristol R v Leeds U
Crewe Alex v Hereford U
Hartlepool U v Peterborough U
Huddersfield T v Millwall
Leicester C v Cheltenham T
Leyton Orient v Brighton & HA
Northampton T v Tranmere R
Oldham Ath v Colchester U
Scunthorpe U v Stockport Co
Southend U v Walsall
Swindon T v Milton Keynes D
Yeovil T v Carlisle U

Coca-Cola Football League Two
Accrington S v Gillingham
Barnet v Chester C
Bournemouth v Port Vale
Bradford C v Aldershot T
Bury v Rochdale
Dagenham & R v Morecambe
Darlington v Macclesfield T
Grimsby T v Lincoln C
Luton T v Exeter C
Rotherham U v Brentford
Shrewsbury T v Notts Co
Wycombe W v Chesterfield

Tuesday, 10 March 2009
Coca-Cola Football League
Championship
Barnsley v Birmingham C
Bristol C v Coventry C
Burnley v Crystal Palace
Doncaster R v QPR
Norwich C v Cardiff C
Preston NE v Sheffield W
Reading v Charlton Ath
Sheffield U v Blackpool
Southampton v Derby Co
Swansea C v Plymouth Arg
Watford v Nottingham F
Wolverhampton W v Ipswich T

Coca-Cola Football League One
Brighton & HA v Southend U
Carlisle U v Leyton Orient
Cheltenham T v Oldham Ath
Colchester U v Swindon T
Hereford U v Bristol R
Leeds U v Yeovil T
Millwall v Northampton T
Milton Keynes D v Huddersfield T
Peterborough U v Scunthorpe U
Stockport Co v Hartlepool U
Tranmere R v Leicester C
Walsall v Crewe Alex

Coca-Cola Football League Two
Aldershot T v Shrewsbury T
Brentford v Barnet
Chester C v Rotherham U
Exeter C v Bournemouth
Gillingham v Darlington
Lincoln C v Wycombe W
Macclesfield T v Accrington S
Morecambe v Bury
Notts Co v Luton T
Port Vale v Dagenham & R
Rochdale v Bradford C

Wednesday, 11 March 2009
Coca-Cola Football League Two
Chesterfield v Grimsby T

Saturday, 14 March 2009
Barclays Premier League
Arsenal v Blackburn R
Aston Villa v Tottenham H
Bolton W v Fulham
Chelsea v Manchester C
Everton v Stoke C
Hull C v Newcastle U
Manchester U v Liverpool
Middlesbrough v Portsmouth
Sunderland v Wigan Ath
West Ham U v WBA

Coca-Cola Football League
Championship
Barnsley v Blackpool
Bristol C v Cardiff C
Burnley v Nottingham F
Doncaster R v Birmingham C
Norwich C v Plymouth Arg
Preston NE v Coventry C
Reading v Ipswich T
Sheffield U v Derby Co
Southampton v QPR
Swansea C v Crystal Palace
Watford v Sheffield W
Wolverhampton W v Charlton Ath

Coca-Cola Football League One
Brighton & HA v Yeovil T
Carlisle U v Scunthorpe U
Cheltenham T v Hartlepool U
Colchester U v Crewe Alex
Hereford U v Southend U
Leeds U v Swindon T
Millwall v Leicester C
Milton Keynes D v Oldham Ath
Peterborough U v Northampton T
Stockport Co v Leyton Orient
Tranmere R v Huddersfield T
Walsall v Bristol R

Coca-Cola Football League Two
Aldershot T v Luton T
Brentford v Wycombe W
Chester C v Grimsby T
Chesterfield v Dagenham & R
Exeter C v Bradford C
Gillingham v Shrewsbury T
Lincoln C v Bury
Macclesfield T v Bournemouth
Morecambe v Barnet
Notts Co v Accrington S
Port Vale v Darlington
Rochdale v Rotherham U

Saturday, 21 March 2009
Barclays Premier League
Blackburn R v West Ham U
Fulham v Manchester U
Liverpool v Aston Villa
Manchester C v Sunderland
Newcastle U v Arsenal
Portsmouth v Everton
Stoke C v Middlesbrough
Tottenham H v Chelsea
WBA v Bolton W
Wigan Ath v Hull C

Coca-Cola Football League Championship
Birmingham C v Norwich C
Blackpool v Southampton
Cardiff C v Sheffield U
Charlton Ath v Preston NE
Coventry C v Doncaster R
Crystal Palace v Reading
Derby Co v Barnsley
Ipswich T v Watford
Nottingham F v Wolverhampton W
Plymouth Arg v Burnley
QPR v Bristol C
Sheffield W v Swansea C

Coca-Cola Football League One
Bristol R v Peterborough U
Crewe Alex v Leeds U
Hartlepool U v Millwall
Huddersfield T v Cheltenham T
Leicester C v Colchester U
Leyton Orient v Walsall
Northampton T v Stockport Co
Oldham Ath v Tranmere R
Scunthorpe U v Brighton & HA
Southend U v Carlisle U
Swindon T v Hereford U
Yeovil T v Milton Keynes D

Coca-Cola Football League Two
Accrington S v Exeter C
Barnet v Lincoln C

Bournemouth v Notts Co
Bradford C v Port Vale
Bury v Chester C
Dagenham & R v Brentford
Darlington v Aldershot T
Grimsby T v Gillingham
Luton T v Macclesfield T
Rotherham U v Chesterfield
Shrewsbury T v Morecambe
Wycombe W v Rochdale

Saturday, 28 March 2009
Coca-Cola Football League One
Brighton & HA v Tranmere R
Bristol R v Stockport Co
Carlisle U v Northampton T
Crewe Alex v Millwall
Hereford U v Huddersfield T
Leeds U v Milton Keynes D
Leyton Orient v Oldham Ath
Peterborough U v Leicester C
Scunthorpe U v Colchester U
Southend U v Hartlepool U
Walsall v Cheltenham T
Yeovil T v Swindon T

Coca-Cola Football League Two
Barnet v Darlington
Brentford v Gillingham
Bury v Bournemouth
Chester C v Bradford C
Chesterfield v Port Vale
Dagenham & R v Macclesfield T
Grimsby T v Aldershot T
Lincoln C v Notts Co
Morecambe v Luton T
Rochdale v Exeter C
Rotherham U v Accrington S
Wycombe W v Shrewsbury T

Saturday, 4 April 2009
Barclays Premier League
Arsenal v Manchester C
Blackburn R v Tottenham H
Bolton W v Middlesbrough
Everton v Wigan Ath
Fulham v Liverpool
Hull C v Portsmouth
Manchester U v Aston Villa
Newcastle U v Chelsea
WBA v Stoke C
West Ham U v Sunderland

Coca-Cola Football League Championship
Barnsley v Nottingham F
Birmingham C v Wolverhampton W
Blackpool v Plymouth Arg
Bristol C v Preston NE

370

Cardiff C v Swansea C
Coventry C v Reading
Derby Co v Burnley
Doncaster R v Watford
Norwich C v Sheffield W
QPR v Crystal Palace
Sheffield U v Ipswich T
Southampton v Charlton Ath

Coca-Cola Football League One
Cheltenham T v Leyton Orient
Colchester U v Leeds U
Hartlepool U v Hereford U
Huddersfield T v Southend U
Leicester C v Carlisle U
Millwall v Walsall
Milton Keynes D v Brighton & HA
Northampton T v Scunthorpe U
Oldham Ath v Peterborough U
Stockport Co v Yeovil T
Swindon T v Crewe Alex
Tranmere R v Bristol R

Coca-Cola Football League Two
Accrington S v Lincoln C
Aldershot T v Rotherham U
Bournemouth v Rochdale
Bradford C v Brentford
Darlington v Morecambe
Exeter C v Dagenham & R
Gillingham v Barnet
Luton T v Wycombe W
Macclesfield T v Chesterfield
Notts Co v Chester C
Port Vale v Bury
Shrewsbury T v Grimsby T

Saturday, 11 April 2009
Barclays Premier League
Aston Villa v Everton
Chelsea v Bolton W
Liverpool v Blackburn R
Manchester C v Fulham
Middlesbrough v Hull C
Portsmouth v WBA
Stoke C v Newcastle U
Sunderland v Manchester U
Tottenham H v West Ham U
Wigan Ath v Arsenal

Coca-Cola Football League Championship
Burnley v QPR
Charlton Ath v Birmingham C
Crystal Palace v Cardiff C
Ipswich T v Doncaster R
Nottingham F v Bristol C
Plymouth Arg v Coventry C
Preston NE v Blackpool

Reading v Sheffield U
Sheffield W v Derby Co
Swansea C v Norwich C
Watford v Barnsley
Wolverhampton W v Southampton

Coca-Cola Football League One
Brighton & HA v Swindon T
Bristol R v Northampton T
Carlisle U v Oldham Ath
Crewe Alex v Hartlepool U
Hereford U v Leicester C
Leeds U v Stockport Co
Leyton Orient v Colchester U
Peterborough U v Cheltenham T
Scunthorpe U v Huddersfield T
Southend U v Milton Keynes D
Walsall v Tranmere R
Yeovil T v Millwall

Coca-Cola Football League Two
Barnet v Bournemouth
Brentford v Exeter C
Bury v Shrewsbury T
Chester C v Macclesfield T
Chesterfield v Darlington
Dagenham & R v Aldershot T
Grimsby T v Accrington S
Lincoln C v Luton T
Morecambe v Bradford C
Rochdale v Port Vale
Rotherham U v Notts Co
Wycombe W v Gillingham

Monday, 13 April 2009
Coca-Cola Football League Championship
Barnsley v Swansea C
Birmingham C v Plymouth Arg
Blackpool v Reading
Bristol C v Ipswich T
Cardiff C v Burnley
Coventry C v Charlton Ath
Derby Co v Wolverhampton W
Doncaster R v Preston NE
Norwich C v Watford
QPR v Sheffield W
Sheffield U v Nottingham F
Southampton v Crystal Palace

Coca-Cola Football League One
Cheltenham T v Yeovil T
Colchester U v Brighton & HA
Hartlepool U v Scunthorpe U
Huddersfield T v Carlisle U
Leicester C v Leeds U
Millwall v Peterborough U
Milton Keynes D v Bristol R
Northampton T v Southend U

Oldham Ath v Crewe Alex
Stockport Co v Walsall
Swindon T v Leyton Orient
Tranmere R v Hereford U

Coca-Cola Football League Two
Accrington S v Chester C
Aldershot T v Barnet
Bournemouth v Brentford
Bradford C v Lincoln C
Darlington v Bury
Exeter C v Wycombe W
Gillingham v Dagenham & R
Luton T v Chesterfield
Macclesfield T v Morecambe
Notts Co v Grimsby T
Port Vale v Rotherham U
Shrewsbury T v Rochdale

Saturday, 18 April 2009
Barclays Premier League
Aston Villa v West Ham U
Chelsea v Everton
Liverpool v Arsenal
Manchester C v WBA
Middlesbrough v Fulham
Portsmouth v Bolton W
Stoke C v Blackburn R
Sunderland v Hull C
Tottenham H v Newcastle U
Wigan Ath v Manchester U

Coca-Cola Football League Championship
Burnley v Sheffield U
Charlton Ath v Blackpool
Crystal Palace v Derby Co
Ipswich T v Norwich C
Nottingham F v Coventry C
Plymouth Arg v Doncaster R
Preston NE v Cardiff C
Reading v Barnsley
Sheffield W v Southampton
Swansea C v Bristol C
Watford v Birmingham C
Wolverhampton W v QPR

Coca-Cola Football League One
Brighton & HA v Oldham Ath
Bristol R v Millwall
Carlisle U v Swindon T
Crewe Alex v Cheltenham T
Hereford U v Colchester U
Leeds U v Tranmere R
Leyton Orient v Northampton T
Peterborough U v Stockport Co
Scunthorpe U v Milton Keynes D
Southend U v Leicester C

Walsall v Huddersfield T
Yeovil T v Hartlepool U

Coca-Cola Football League Two
Barnet v Luton T
Brentford v Accrington S
Bury v Macclesfield T
Chester C v Bournemouth
Chesterfield v Gillingham
Dagenham & R v Bradford C
Grimsby T v Port Vale
Lincoln C v Exeter C
Morecambe v Notts Co
Rochdale v Darlington
Rotherham U v Shrewsbury T
Wycombe W v Aldershot T

Saturday, 25 April 2009
Barclays Premier League
Arsenal v Middlesbrough
Blackburn R v Wigan Ath
Bolton W v Aston Villa
Everton v Manchester C
Fulham v Stoke C
Hull C v Liverpool
Manchester U v Tottenham H
Newcastle U v Portsmouth
WBA v Sunderland
West Ham U v Chelsea

Coca-Cola Football League Championship
Barnsley v Wolverhampton W
Birmingham C v Preston NE
Blackpool v Nottingham F
Bristol C v Sheffield W
Cardiff C v Ipswich T
Coventry C v Watford
Derby Co v Charlton Ath
Doncaster R v Crystal Palace
Norwich C v Reading
QPR v Plymouth Arg
Sheffield U v Swansea C
Southampton v Burnley

Coca-Cola Football League One
Cheltenham T v Carlisle U
Colchester U v Peterborough U
Hartlepool U v Leeds U
Huddersfield T v Brighton & HA
Leicester C v Scunthorpe U
Millwall v Leyton Orient
Milton Keynes D v Walsall
Northampton T v Hereford U
Oldham Ath v Southend U
Stockport Co v Crewe Alex
Swindon T v Bristol R
Tranmere R v Yeovil T

Coca-Cola Football League Two
Accrington S v Chesterfield
Aldershot T v Chester C
Bournemouth v Grimsby T
Bradford C v Rotherham U
Darlington v Brentford
Exeter C v Morecambe
Gillingham v Bury
Luton T v Rochdale
Macclesfield T v Barnet
Notts Co v Dagenham & R
Port Vale v Wycombe W
Shrewsbury T v Lincoln C

Saturday, 2 May 2009
Barclays Premier League
Aston Villa v Hull C
Chelsea v Fulham
Liverpool v Newcastle U
Manchester C v Blackburn R
Middlesbrough v Manchester U
Portsmouth v Arsenal
Stoke C v West Ham U
Sunderland v Everton
Tottenham H v WBA
Wigan Ath v Bolton W

Coca-Cola Football League One
Brighton & HA v Stockport Co
Bristol R v Hartlepool U
Carlisle U v Millwall
Crewe Alex v Leicester C
Hereford U v Milton Keynes D
Leeds U v Northampton T
Leyton Orient v Huddersfield T
Peterborough U v Swindon T
Scunthorpe U v Tranmere R
Southend U v Cheltenham T
Walsall v Oldham Ath
Yeovil T v Colchester U

Coca-Cola Football League Two
Barnet v Port Vale
Brentford v Luton T
Bury v Accrington S
Chester C v Darlington
Chesterfield v Bradford C
Dagenham & R v Shrewsbury T
Grimsby T v Macclesfield T
Lincoln C v Aldershot T
Morecambe v Bournemouth
Rochdale v Gillingham
Rotherham U v Exeter C
Wycombe W v Notts Co

Sunday, 3 May 2009
Coca-Cola Football League Championship
Burnley v Bristol C
Charlton Ath v Norwich C
Crystal Palace v Sheffield U
Ipswich T v Coventry C
Nottingham F v Southampton
Plymouth Arg v Barnsley
Preston NE v QPR
Reading v Birmingham C
Sheffield W v Cardiff C
Swansea C v Blackpool
Watford v Derby Co
Wolverhampton W v Doncaster R

Saturday, 9 May 2009
Barclays Premier League
Arsenal v Chelsea
Blackburn R v Portsmouth
Bolton W v Sunderland
Everton v Tottenham H
Fulham v Aston Villa
Hull C v Stoke C
Manchester U v Manchester C
Newcastle U v Middlesbrough
WBA v Wigan Ath
West Ham U v Liverpool

Saturday, 16 May 2009
Barclays Premier League
Bolton W v Hull C
Chelsea v Blackburn R
Everton v West Ham U
Manchester U v Arsenal
Middlesbrough v Aston Villa
Newcastle U v Fulham
Portsmouth v Sunderland
Stoke C v Wigan Ath
Tottenham H v Manchester C
WBA v Liverpool

Sunday, 24 May 2009
Barclays Premier League
Arsenal v Stoke C
Aston Villa v Newcastle U
Blackburn R v WBA
Fulham v Everton
Hull C v Manchester U
Liverpool v Tottenham H
Manchester C v Bolton W
Sunderland v Chelsea
West Ham U v Middlesbrough
Wigan Ath v Portsmouth

BLUE SQUARE PREMIER FIXTURES 2008–2009

Friday, 8 August 2008
Barrow v Oxford U

Saturday, 9 August 2008
Crawley T v York C
Eastbourne B v Rushden & D'monds
Ebbsfleet U v Mansfield T
Histon v Torquay U
Kettering T v Forest Green R
Kidderminster H v Lewes
Northwich Vic v Cambridge U
Salisbury C v Burton Alb
Weymouth v Grays Ath
Woking v Altrincham T
Wrexham v Stevenage B

Tuesday, 12 August 2008
Altrincham T v Barrow
Burton Alb v Northwich Vic
Cambridge U v Kidderminster H
Forest Green R v Salisbury C
Grays Ath v Kettering T
Lewes v Crawley T
Mansfield T v Histon
Oxford U v Weymouth
Rushden & D'monds v Ebbsfleet U
Stevenage B v Eastbourne B
Torquay U v Woking

Thursday, 14 August 2008
York C v Wrexham

Saturday, 16 August 2008
Altrincham T v Kettering T
Burton Alb v Woking
Cambridge U v Barrow
Forest Green R v Crawley T
Grays Ath v Northwich Vic
Lewes v Salisbury C
Mansfield T v Kidderminster H
Oxford U v Eastbourne B
Rushden & D'monds v Wrexham
Stevenage B v Weymouth
York C v Histon

Monday, 18 August 2008
Torquay U v Ebbsfleet U

Thursday, 21 August 2008
Wrexham v Oxford U

Saturday, 23 August 2008
Barrow v Mansfield T
Crawley T v Torquay U
Eastbourne B v Cambridge U
Ebbsfleet U v Stevenage B
Histon v Burton Alb

Kettering T v Rushden & D'monds
Kidderminster H v Altrincham T
Northwich Vic v York C
Salisbury C v Grays Ath
Weymouth v Lewes
Woking v Forest Green R

Monday, 25 August 2008
Altrincham T v Wrexham
Burton Alb v Kidderminster H
Cambridge U v Kettering T
Forest Green R v Weymouth
Grays Ath v Eastbourne B
Lewes v Ebbsfleet U
Mansfield T v Northwich Vic
Oxford U v Woking
Rushden & D'monds v Histon
Stevenage B v Crawley T
Torquay U v Salisbury C
York C v Barrow

Thursday, 28 August 2008
Torquay U v York C

Saturday, 30 August 2008
Barrow v Stevenage B
Burton Alb v Lewes
Crawley T v Northwich Vic
Eastbourne B v Altrincham T
Ebbsfleet U v Oxford U
Histon v Forest Green R
Kettering T v Woking
Kidderminster H v Rushden & D'monds
Mansfield T v Grays Ath
Salisbury C v Wrexham
Weymouth v Cambridge U

Tuesday, 2 September 2008
Barrow v Rushden & D'monds
Crawley T v Grays Ath
Eastbourne B v Forest Green R
Ebbsfleet U v Cambridge U
Histon v Altrincham T
Kettering T v Stevenage B
Kidderminster H v Torquay U
Northwich Vic v Oxford U
Salisbury C v Weymouth
Woking v Lewes
Wrexham v Burton Alb
York C v Mansfield T

Saturday, 6 September 2008
Altrincham T v Salisbury C
Cambridge U v Wrexham
Forest Green R v Ebbsfleet U
Grays Ath v Kidderminster H

374

Lewes v Barrow
Mansfield T v Eastbourne B
Oxford U v Kettering T
Rushden & D'monds v Crawley T
Stevenage B v Burton Alb
Torquay U v Northwich Vic
Weymouth v Histon
York C v Woking

Saturday, 13 September 2008
Burton Alb v Weymouth
Cambridge U v Torquay U
Crawley T v Mansfield T
Eastbourne B v Histon
Kettering T v York C
Kidderminster H v Oxford U
Lewes v Rushden & D'monds
Northwich Vic v Forest Green R
Salisbury C v Barrow
Stevenage B v Altrincham T
Woking v Grays Ath
Wrexham v Ebbsfleet U

Saturday, 20 September 2008
Altrincham T v Lewes
Barrow v Kettering T
Ebbsfleet U v Woking
Forest Green R v Stevenage B
Grays Ath v Wrexham
Histon v Northwich Vic
Mansfield T v Cambridge U
Oxford U v Crawley T
Rushden & D'monds v Burton Alb
Torquay U v Eastbourne B
Weymouth v Kidderminster H
York C v Salisbury C

Tuesday, 23 September 2008
Altrincham T v Mansfield T
Ebbsfleet U v Eastbourne B
Forest Green R v Torquay U
Grays Ath v Stevenage B
Histon v Lewes
Kettering T v Burton Alb
Kidderminster H v York C
Northwich Vic v Barrow
Oxford U v Cambridge U
Weymouth v Crawley T
Woking v Salisbury C
Wrexham v Rushden & D'monds

Saturday, 27 September 2008
Barrow v Ebbsfleet U
Burton Alb v Forest Green R
Cambridge U v Grays Ath
Crawley T v Kettering T
Eastbourne B v Kidderminster H
Lewes v Oxford U
Northwich Vic v Weymouth
Rushden & D'monds v Altrincham T

Salisbury C v Mansfield T
Stevenage B v York C
Woking v Histon
Wrexham v Torquay U

Saturday, 4 October 2008
Altrincham T v Ebbsfleet U
Burton Alb v Crawley T
Forest Green R v Wrexham
Grays Ath v Lewes
Histon v Salisbury C
Kettering T v Northwich Vic
Kidderminster H v Barrow
Mansfield T v Woking
Oxford U v Rushden & D'monds
Torquay U v Stevenage B
Weymouth v Eastbourne B
York C v Cambridge U

Tuesday, 7 October 2008
Barrow v Burton Alb
Cambridge U v Lewes
Crawley T v Forest Green R
Eastbourne B v Kettering T
Ebbsfleet U v Histon
Northwich Vic v Kidderminster H
Rushden & D'monds v Grays Ath
Salisbury C v Altrincham T
Stevenage B v Mansfield T
Torquay U v Oxford U
Woking v Weymouth
Wrexham v York C

Saturday, 11 October 2008
Altrincham T v Oxford U
Burton Alb v Mansfield T
Cambridge U v Weymouth
Crawley T v Barrow
Eastbourne B v Stevenage B
Kidderminster H v Ebbsfleet U
Lewes v Forest Green R
Northwich Vic v Grays Ath
Rushden & D'monds v Torquay U
Salisbury C v Kettering T
Woking v York C
Wrexham v Histon

Saturday, 18 October 2008
Barrow v Eastbourne B
Ebbsfleet U v Torquay U
Forest Green R v Cambridge U
Grays Ath v Woking
Histon v Crawley T
Kettering T v Kidderminster H
Lewes v Northwich Vic
Mansfield T v Wrexham
Oxford U v Burton Alb
Stevenage B v Salisbury C
Weymouth v Altrincham T
York C v Rushden & D'monds

Saturday, 1 November 2008
Altrincham T v Histon
Barrow v Forest Green R
Burton Alb v Ebbsfleet U
Cambridge U v Rushden & D'monds
Kettering T v Weymouth
Kidderminster H v Grays Ath
Northwich Vic v Eastbourne B
Oxford U v York C
Salisbury C v Crawley T
Torquay U v Mansfield T
Woking v Stevenage B
Wrexham v Lewes

Saturday, 15 November 2008
Crawley T v Cambridge U
Eastbourne B v Woking
Ebbsfleet U v Barrow
Forest Green R v Altrincham T
Grays Ath v Oxford U
Histon v Kettering T
Lewes v Burton Alb
Mansfield T v Salisbury C
Rushden & D'monds v
  Kidderminster H
Stevenage B v Northwich Vic
Weymouth v Wrexham
York C v Torquay U

Tuesday, 18 November 2008
Cambridge U v York C
Crawley T v Ebbsfleet U
Eastbourne B v Salisbury C
Grays Ath v Rushden & D'monds
Kettering T v Barrow
Mansfield T v Altrincham T
Northwich Vic v Burton Alb
Oxford U v Kidderminster H
Stevenage B v Histon
Torquay U v Lewes
Weymouth v Woking
Wrexham v Forest Green R

Saturday, 22 November 2008
Altrincham T v Cambridge U
Barrow v Weymouth
Burton Alb v Stevenage B
Ebbsfleet U v Kettering T
Forest Green R v Mansfield T
Histon v Oxford U
Kidderminster H v Wrexham
Lewes v Grays Ath
Rushden & D'monds v Eastbourne B
Salisbury C v Northwich Vic
Woking v Torquay U
York C v Crawley T

Saturday, 29 November 2008
Altrincham T v Rushden & D'monds
Barrow v Histon

Burton Alb v Eastbourne B
Burton Alb v Eastbourne B
Cambridge U v Ebbsfleet U
Grays Ath v Torquay U
Kettering T v Lewes
Northwich Vic v Crawley T
Oxford U v Forest Green R
Salisbury C v York C
Stevenage B v Wrexham
Weymouth v Mansfield T
Woking v Kidderminster H

Saturday, 6 December 2008
Crawley T v Altrincham T
Eastbourne B v Northwich Vic
Ebbsfleet U v Weymouth
Forest Green R v Burton Alb
Histon v Woking
Kidderminster H v Salisbury C
Lewes v Stevenage B
Mansfield T v Oxford U
Rushden & D'monds v Barrow
Torquay U v Cambridge U
Wrexham v Kettering T
York C v Grays Ath

Tuesday, 9 December 2008
Barrow v Altrincham T
Burton Alb v Cambridge U
Eastbourne B v Torquay U
Ebbsfleet U v Forest Green R
Histon v York C
Kettering T v Crawley T
Kidderminster H v Mansfield T
Northwich Vic v Wrexham
Salisbury C v Lewes
Stevenage B v Grays Ath
Weymouth v Oxford U
Woking v Rushden & D'monds

Saturday, 20 December 2008
Altrincham T v Burton Alb
Cambridge U v Salisbury C
Crawley T v Kidderminster H
Forest Green R v Kettering T
Grays Ath v Barrow
Lewes v Woking
Mansfield T v Weymouth
Oxford U v Stevenage B
Rushden & D'monds v Northwich Vic
Torquay U v Histon
Wrexham v Eastbourne B
York C v Ebbsfleet U

Friday, 26 December 2008
Barrow v Wrexham
Burton Alb v York C
Eastbourne B v Lewes
Ebbsfleet U v Grays Ath
Histon v Cambridge U
Kettering T v Mansfield T

Kidderminster H v Forest Green R
Northwich Vic v Altrincham T
Salisbury C v Oxford U
Stevenage B v Rushden & D'monds
Weymouth v Torquay U
Woking v Crawley T

Sunday, 28 December 2008
Cambridge U v Stevenage B
Crawley T v Eastbourne B
Forest Green R v Barrow
Grays Ath v Histon
Lewes v Kettering T
Mansfield T v Burton Alb
Northwich Vic v Salisbury C
Oxford U v Ebbsfleet U
Rushden & D'monds v Weymouth
Torquay U v Kidderminster H
Wrexham v Woking
York C v Altrincham T

Thursday, 1 January 2009
Altrincham T v Northwich Vic
Cambridge U v Histon
Crawley T v Woking
Forest Green R v Kidderminster H
Grays Ath v Ebbsfleet U
Lewes v Eastbourne B
Mansfield T v Kettering T
Oxford U v Salisbury C
Rushden & D'monds v Stevenage B
Torquay U v Weymouth
Wrexham v Barrow
York C v Burton Alb

Saturday, 3 January 2009
Altrincham T v Forest Green R
Barrow v Cambridge U
Burton Alb v Torquay U
Eastbourne B v Oxford U
Ebbsfleet U v Wrexham
Histon v Mansfield T
Kettering T v Grays Ath
Kidderminster H v Crawley T
Salisbury C v Rushden & D'monds
Stevenage B v Lewes
Weymouth v York C
Woking v Northwich Vic

Saturday, 17 January 2009
Cambridge U v Woking
Ebbsfleet U v Rushden & D'monds
Forest Green R v Eastbourne B
Grays Ath v Burton Alb
Kettering T v Salisbury C
Kidderminster H v Weymouth
Mansfield T v Crawley T
Northwich Vic v Histon
Oxford U v Altrincham T
Stevenage B v Barrow

Torquay U v Wrexham
York C v Lewes

Saturday, 24 January 2009
Altrincham T v Torquay U
Barrow v Kidderminster H
Burton Alb v Kettering T
Crawley T v Oxford U
Eastbourne B v York C
Histon v Grays Ath
Lewes v Mansfield T
Rushden & D'monds v Forest Green R
Salisbury C v Stevenage B
Weymouth v Northwich Vic
Woking v Ebbsfleet U
Wrexham v Cambridge U

Tuesday, 27 January 2009
Altrincham T v York C
Burton Alb v Barrow
Cambridge U v Oxford U
Ebbsfleet U v Crawley T
Grays Ath v Weymouth
Kidderminster H v Histon
Lewes v Torquay U
Mansfield T v Rushden & D'monds
Salisbury C v Forest Green R
Stevenage B v Kettering T
Woking v Eastbourne B
Wrexham v Northwich Vic

Saturday, 31 January 2009
Barrow v Salisbury C
Crawley T v Wrexham
Eastbourne B v Mansfield T
Ebbsfleet U v Kidderminster H
Forest Green R v Histon
Kettering T v Altrincham T
Northwich Vic v Woking
Oxford U v Lewes
Rushden & D'monds v Cambridge U
Torquay U v Grays Ath
Weymouth v Burton Alb
York C v Stevenage B

Saturday, 7 February 2009
Altrincham T v Eastbourne B
Barrow v Torquay U
Burton Alb v Rushden & D'monds
Grays Ath v Crawley T
Histon v Weymouth
Kettering T v Oxford U
Kidderminster H v Cambridge U
Lewes v Wrexham
Mansfield T v York C
Northwich Vic v Ebbsfleet U
Salisbury C v Woking
Stevenage B v Forest Green R

Saturday, 14 February 2009
Cambridge U v Mansfield T
Eastbourne B v Crawley T
Ebbsfleet U v Burton Alb
Kidderminster H v Northwich Vic
Oxford U v Barrow
Rushden & D'monds v Lewes
Salisbury C v Histon
Torquay U v Altrincham T
Weymouth v Stevenage B
Woking v Kettering T
Wrexham v Grays Ath
York C v Forest Green R

Saturday, 21 February 2009
Altrincham T v Woking
Barrow v Grays Ath
Burton Alb v Wrexham
Crawley T v Salisbury C
Forest Green R v Northwich Vic
Histon v Eastbourne B
Kettering T v Torquay U
Lewes v Cambridge U
Mansfield T v Ebbsfleet U
Stevenage B v Kidderminster H
Weymouth v Rushden & D'monds
York C v Oxford U

Tuesday, 24 February 2009
Burton Alb v Altrincham T
Crawley T v Lewes
Eastbourne B v Ebbsfleet U
Grays Ath v Cambridge U
Histon v Barrow
Northwich Vic v Kettering T
Oxford U v Mansfield T
Rushden & D'monds v York C
Stevenage B v Woking
Torquay U v Forest Green R
Wrexham v Kidderminster H

Saturday, 28 February 2009
Altrincham T v Stevenage B
Barrow v Northwich Vic
Cambridge U v Crawley T
Forest Green R v Grays Ath
Kidderminster H v Eastbourne B
Lewes v Histon
Oxford U v Torquay U
Rushden & D'monds v Mansfield T
Woking v Burton Alb
Wrexham v Salisbury C
York C v Weymouth

Saturday, 7 March 2009
Cambridge U v Burton Alb
Crawley T v Weymouth
Eastbourne B v Wrexham
Ebbsfleet U v York C
Forest Green R v Oxford U

Grays Ath v Altrincham T
Kettering T v Histon
Mansfield T v Lewes
Northwich Vic v Stevenage B
Salisbury C v Kidderminster H
Torquay U v Rushden & D'monds
Woking v Barrow

Tuesday, 10 March 2009
Weymouth v Salisbury C

Saturday, 14 March 2009
Altrincham T v Weymouth
Burton Alb v Salisbury C
Crawley T v Rushden & D'monds
Histon v Ebbsfleet U
Lewes v Kidderminster H
Mansfield T v Forest Green R
Oxford U v Grays Ath
Stevenage B v Cambridge U
Torquay U v Barrow
Woking v Wrexham
York C v Kettering T

Saturday, 21 March 2009
Barrow v Lewes
Eastbourne B v Burton Alb
Ebbsfleet U v Altrincham T
Forest Green R v York C
Grays Ath v Mansfield T
Histon v Stevenage B
Kidderminster H v Woking
Northwich Vic v Torquay U
Rushden & D'monds v Oxford U
Weymouth v Kettering T
Wrexham v Crawley T

Tuesday, 24 March 2009
Cambridge U v Northwich Vic
Kettering T v Eastbourne B
Salisbury C v Ebbsfleet U

Saturday, 28 March 2009
Altrincham T v Crawley T
Burton Alb v Grays Ath
Forest Green R v Lewes
Histon v Wrexham
Kettering T v Ebbsfleet U
Mansfield T v Torquay U
Northwich Vic v Rushden & D'monds
Salisbury C v Eastbourne B
Stevenage B v Oxford U
Weymouth v Barrow
Woking v Cambridge U
York C v Kidderminster H

Saturday, 4 April 2009
Barrow v Woking
Cambridge U v Forest Green R
Crawley T v Burton Alb

Eastbourne B v Weymouth
Ebbsfleet U v Northwich Vic
Grays'Ath v York C
Kidderminster H v Stevenage B
Lewes v Altrincham T
Oxford U v Histon
Rushden & D'monds v Salisbury C
Torquay U v Kettering T
Wrexham v Mansfield T

Saturday, 11 April 2009
Altrincham T v Kidderminster H
Burton Alb v Histon
Cambridge U v Eastbourne B
Forest Green R v Woking
Grays Ath v Salisbury C
Lewes v Weymouth
Mansfield T v Barrow
Oxford U v Wrexham
Rushden & D'monds v Kettering T
Stevenage B v Ebbsfleet U
Torquay U v Crawley T
York C v Northwich Vic

Monday, 13 April 2009
Barrow v York C
Crawley T v Stevenage B
Eastbourne B v Grays Ath
Ebbsfleet U v Lewes
Histon v Rushden & D'monds
Kettering T v Cambridge U
Kidderminster H v Burton Alb
Northwich Vic v Mansfield T

Salisbury C v Torquay U
Weymouth v Forest Green R
Woking v Oxford U
Wrexham v Altrincham T

Saturday, 18 April 2009
Altrincham T v Grays Ath
Barrow v Crawley T
Burton Alb v Oxford U
Forest Green R v Rushden & D'monds
Histon v Kidderminster H
Kettering T v Wrexham
Northwich Vic v Lewes
Salisbury C v Cambridge U
Stevenage B v Torquay U
Weymouth v Ebbsfleet U
Woking v Mansfield T
York C v Eastbourne B

Saturday, 25 April 2009
Cambridge U v Altrincham T
Crawley T v Histon
Eastbourne B v Barrow
Ebbsfleet U v Salisbury C
Grays Ath v Forest Green R
Kidderminster H v Kettering T
Lewes v York C
Mansfield T v Stevenage B
Oxford U v Northwich Vic
Rushden & D'monds v Woking
Torquay U v Burton Alb
Wrexham v Weymouth

OTHER FIXTURES — SEASON 2008–2009

AUGUST 2008

Tue 5	UEFA Champions League 2Q (2)
Wed 6	UEFA Champions League 2Q (2)
Sat 9	FL Season starts
Sun 10	FA Community Shield
Tue 12	UEFA Champions League 3Q (1)
Wed 13	UEFA Champions League 3Q (1)
Thu 14	UEFA Cup 2Q (1)
Sat 16	FA Cup EP
	PL Season starts
Wed 20	England v Czech Republic (F)
Mon 25	Bank Holiday

Tue 26	UEFA Champions League 3Q (2)
Wed 27	UEFA Champions League 3Q (2)
Thu 28	UEFA Cup 2Q (2)
Fri 29	UEFA Super Cup Final
Sat 30	FA Cup P

SEPTEMBER 2008

Sat 6	Andorra v England (WCQ)
	FA Vase 1Q
Sun 7	FA Women's Cup P
Mon 8	FA Youth Cup P**
Wed 10	Croatia v England (WCQ)
Sat 13	FA Cup 1Q
Tue 16	UEFA Champions League MD 1
Wed 17	UEFA Champions League MD 1

Thu 18	UEFA Cup 1 (1)
Sat 20	FA Vase 2Q
Sun 21	FA Sunday Cup P
Mon 22	FA Youth Cup 1Q**
Sat 27	FA Cup 2Q
Sun 28	Czech Republic v England (Women's ECQ)
	FA Women's Cup 1Q
Tue 30	UEFA Champions League MD 2

OCTOBER 2008

Wed 1	UEFA Champions League MD 2
Thu 2	UEFA Cup 1 (2)
	Spain v England (Women's ECQ)
Sat 4	FA Trophy P
	FA Vase 1P
Mon 6	FA Youth Cup 2Q**
Sat 11	England v Kazakhstan (WCQ)
	FA Cup 3Q
Sun 12	FA Women's Cup 2Q
Wed 15	Belarus v England (WCQ)
Sat 18	FA Trophy 1Q
Sun 19	FA Sunday Cup 1
	FA County Youth Cup 1*
Mon 20	FA Youth Cup 3Q**
Tue 21	UEFA Champions League MD 3
Wed 22	UEFA Champions League MD 3
Thu 23	UEFA Cup MD 1
Sat 25	FA Cup 4Q
Sun 26	FA Women's Cup 3Q

NOVEMBER 2008

Sat 1	FA Trophy 2Q
Tue 4	UEFA Champions League MD 4
Wed 5	UEFA Champions League MD 4
Thu 6	UEFA Cup MD 2
Sat 8	FA Cup 1P
	FA Youth Cup 1P*
Sun 9	FA Women's Cup 1P
Sat 15	FA Vase 2P
Sun 16	FA Sunday Cup 2
	FA County Youth Cup 2*

Wed 19	Germany v England (F)
Sat 22	FA Trophy 3Q
	FA Youth Cup 2P*
Sun 23	FA Women's Cup 2P
Tue 25	UEFA Champions League MD 5
Wed 26	UEFA Champions League MD 5
Thu 27	UEFA Cup MD 3
Sat 29	FA Cup 2P

DECEMBER 2008

Wed 3	UEFA Cup MD 4
Thu 4	UEFA Cup MD 4
Sat 6	FA Vase 3P
Sun 7	FA Sunday Cup 3
Tue 9	UEFA Champions League MD 6
Wed 10	UEFA Champions League MD 6
Sat 13	FA Trophy 1P
	FA Youth Cup 3P*
Sun 14	FA Women's Cup 3P
Wed 17	UEFA Cup MD 5
Thu 18	UEFA Cup MD 5
Sun 21	FA County Youth Cup 3*

JANUARY 2009

Sat 3	FA Cup 3P
Sun 4	FA Women's Cup 4P
Sat 10	FA Trophy 2P
Sun 11	FA Sunday Cup 4
Sat 17	FA Vase 4P
	FA Youth Cup 4P*
Sat 24	FA Cup 4P
Sun 25	FA County Youth Cup 4*
	FA Women's Cup 5P
Sat 31	FA Trophy 3P
	FA Youth Cup 5P*

FEBRUARY 2009

Sat 7	FA Vase 5P
Wed 11	International Friendly
Sat 14	FA Cup 5P
	FA Youth Cup 6P*
Wed 18	UEFA Cup 32 (1)
Thu 19	UEFA Cup 32 (1)
Sat 21	FA Trophy 4P
Sun 22	FA Sunday Cup 5
	FA Women's Cup 6P

Tue 24	UEFA Champions League 16 (1)
Wed 25	UEFA Champions League 16 (1)
Thu 26	UEFA Cup 32 (2)
Sat 28	FA Vase 6P

MARCH 2009

Sun 1	FA County Youth Cup SF*
Sat 7	FA Cup 6P
	FA Youth Cup SF1*
Tue 10	UEFA Champions League 16 (2)
Wed 11	UEFA Champions League 16 (2)
Thu 12	UEFA Cup 16 (1)
Sat 14	FA Trophy SF1
Wed 18	UEFA Cup 16 (2)
Thu 19	UEFA Cup 16 (2)
Sat 21	FA Trophy SF2
	FA Youth Cup SF2*
Sun 22	FA Sunday Cup SF
	FA Women's Cup SF
Sat 28	FA Vase SF1

APRIL 2009

Wed 1	England v Ukraine (WCQ)
Sat 4	FA Vase SF2
Tue 7	UEFA Champions League QF (1)
Wed 8	UEFA Champions League QF (1)
Thu 9	UEFA Cup QF (1)
Fri 10	Good Friday
Mon 13	Easter Monday
Tue 14	UEFA Champions League QF (2)
Wed 15	UEFA Champions League QF (2)
Thu 16	UEFA Cup QF (2)

Sat 18	FA Cup SF
Sun 19	FA Cup SF
Sat 25	FA County Youth Cup Final (prov)
Sun 26	FA Sunday Cup Final (prov)
Tue 28	UEFA Champions League SF (1)
Wed 29	UEFA Champions League SF (1)
Thu 30	UEFA Cup SF (1)

MAY 2009

Sat 2	FL Season ends
	FA County Youth Cup Final (prov)
Sun 3	FA Sunday Cup Final (prov)
Mon 4	Bank Holiday
	FA Women's Cup Final
Tue 5	UEFA Champions League SF (2)
Wed 6	UEFA Champions League SF (2)
Thu 7	UEFA Cup SF (2)
Sat 9	FA Trophy Final
Sun 10	FA Vase Final
Wed 20	UEFA Cup Final
Sat 23	PL Season ends
	FL Play-Off Final League 2
Sun 24	FL Play-Off Final League 1
Mon 25	Bank Holiday
	FL Play-Off Final Championship
Wed 27	UEFA Champions League Final
Sat 30	FA Cup Final

JUNE 2009

| Sat 6 | Kazakhstan v England (WCQ) |
| Wed 10 | England v Andorra (WCQ) |

* closing date of round
** ties to be played in the week commencing
FA Youth Cup Final 1st & 2nd Legs – dates to be confirmed

STOP PRESS

Summer transfers completed and pending:

Premier League: Arsenal: Aaron Ramsey (Cardiff C) undisclosed; Samir Nasri (Marseille). **Aston Villa:** Steve Sidwell (Chelsea) undisclosed; Curtis Davies (WBA) undisclosed. **Bolton W:** Johan Elmander (Toulouse) undisclosed; Fabrice Muamba (Birmingham C) undisclosed. **Chelsea:** Jose Bosingwa (Porto) £16.2m; Deco (Barcelona) £7.9m. **Fulham:** Andranik Teimourian (Bolton W) Free; Zoltan Gera (WBA) Free; David Stockdale (Darlington) undisclosed; Mark Schwarzer (Middlesbrough) Free; Toni Kallio (Young Boys) undisclosed. **Hull C:** Craig Fagan (Derby Co) £750,000; Bernard Mendy (Paris St Germain); Geovanni (Manchester C) Free. **Liverpool:** Philip Degen (Borussia Dortmund) Free; Diego Cavalieri (Palmeiras) undisclosed; Andrea Dossena (Udinese) undisclosed. **Manchester C:** Jo (CSKA Moscow) £19m. **Middlesbrough:** Didier Digard (Paris St Germain) £4m; Marvin Emnes (Sparta Rotterdam) £3.2m. **Newcastle U:** Jonas Gutierrez (Mallorca) undisclosed; Danny Guthrie (Liverpool) undisclosed. **Portsmouth:** Ben Sahar (Chelsea) Loan; Glen Little (Reading) undisclosed; Peter Crouch (Liverpool) £11m. **Tottenham H:** Heurelho Gomes (PSV Eindhoven) undisclosed; Giovanni (Barcelona) undisclosed; Luka Modric (Dinamo Zagreb) £16.5m. **WBA:** Gianni Zuiverloon (Heerenveen) undisclosed; Luke Moore (Aston Villa) £3m; Graham Dorrans (Livingston) undisclosed. **Wigan Ath:** Daniel De Ridder (Birmingham C) Free.

Football League Championship: Barnsley: Darren Moore (Derby Co) Free; Iain Hume (Leicester C) £1.2m. **Birmingham C:** Lee Carsley (Everton) Free; Kevin Phillips (WBA) Free. **Blackpool:** Alex John-Baptiste (Mansfield T); Matthew Gilks (Norwich C) Free; Marlon Broomes (Stoke C) Free; Joe Martin (Tottenham H); Steven Kabba (Watford) Loan; Jermaine Wright (Southampton) Free. **Bristol C:** Gavin Williams (Ipswich T). **Burnley:** Kevin McDonald (Dundee) £500,000; Martin Paterson (Scunthorpe U) £1m; Remco Van der Schaaf (Vitesse) Free. **Cardiff C:** Tom Heaton (Manchester U) Loan. **Charlton Ath:** Mark Hudson (Crystal Palace) Free. **Coventry C:** Guillaume Beuzelin (Hibernian) Free; Kieren Westwood (Carlisle U) Free; Freddy Eastwood (Wolverhampton W). **Crystal Palace:** Johannes Ertl (FK Austria); Nick Carle (Bristol C). **Derby Co:** Martin Albrechtsen (WBA) Free; Kris Commons (Nottingham F) Free; Paul Green (Doncaster R) Free; Nathan Ellington (Watford) Loan; Jordan Stewart (Watford) Free. **Doncaster R:** John Spicer (Burnley) Free. **Norwich C:** Wes Hoolahan (Blackpool); Ryan Bertrand (Chelsea) Loan. **Nottingham F:** Paul Anderson (Swansea C) Loan; Guy Moussi (Angers); Robert Earnshaw (Derby Co) £2.65m; Andy Cole (Sunderland) Free. **Preston NE:** Barry Nicholson (Aberdeen) Free. **QPR:** Radek Cerny (Slavia Prague) Free; Peter Ramage (Newcastle U) Free. **Sheffield U:** Greg Halford (Sunderland) Loan; Sun Jihai (Manchester C) Free. **Sheffield W:** James O'Connor (Burnley) Free. **Southampton:** Lee Holmes (Derby Co) Free; Tommy Forecast (Tottenham H). **Swansea C:** Mark Gower (Southend U) Free; Alberto Serran (Espanyol). **Wolverhampton W:** David Jones (Derby Co); Sam Vokes (Bournemouth).

Football League 1: Brighton & HA: Adam Virgo (Celtic) Free; Colin Hawkins (Chesterfield) Free. **Bristol R:** Jeff Hughes (Crystal Palace); Darryl Duffy (Swansea C) £100,000. **Carlisle U:** Ben Williams (Crewe Alex) Free; Josh Gowling (Bournemouth) Free. **Colchester U:** Paul Reid (Barnsley) Free; Matt Lockwood (Nottingham F); David Perkins (Rochdale) Free. **Crewe Alex:** Steve Collis (Southend U) Free; Joel Grant (Aldershot T) £130,000; Jake Livermore (MK Dons) Loan. **Hartlepool U:** Ritchie Jones (Yeovil T) Free; Alan Power (Nottingham F) Free. **Hereford U:** Matt Done (Wrexham); Darren Randolph (Charlton Ath) Loan; Toumani Diagouraga (Watford). **Huddersfield T:** Jim Goodwin (Scunthorpe U) Free; Chris Lucketti (Southampton) Free. **Leeds U:** Enoch Showunmi (Bristol C) Free; Alan Sheehan (Leicester C) Free; Andy Robinson (Swansea C) Free. **Leicester C:** Michael Morrison (Cambridge U); Lloyd Dyer (MK Dons) Free; Kelvin Etuhu (Manchester C) Loan; Kerrea Gilbert (Arsenal) Loan. **Leyton Orient:**

Simon Dawkins (Tottenham H) Loan; Danny Granville (Colchester U) Free. **Millwall:** Nadjim Abdou (Plymouth Arg) Free. **Northampton T:** Leon Constantine (Leeds U) Free; Liam Davis (Coventry C); Mark Haines (Grays Ath) Free. **Oldham Ath:** Danny Whitaker (Port Vale) Free; Greg Fleming (Gretna) Free. **Peterborough U:** Russell Martin (Wycombe W). **Scunthorpe U:** Kenny Milne (Falkirk) Free. **Southend U:** Paul Furlong (Luton T) Free; Osei Sankofa (Charlton Ath) Free; Steve Mildenhall (Yeovil T) Free; Ian Joyce (Watford) Free. **Stockport Co:** Johnny Mullins (Mansfield T); Owain fon Williams (Crewe Alex) Free. **Tranmere R:** George O'Callaghan (Cork C); Bas Savage (Millwall) Free; Edrissa Sonko (Walsall) Free. **Walsall:** Dwayne Mattis (Barnsley) Free; Stephen Roberts (Doncaster R) Free; Jabo Ibehre (Leyton Orient) Free. **Yeovil T:** Kieran Murtagh (Fisher Ath); Danny Schofield (Huddersfield T) Free; Darren Way (Swansea C) £50,000.

Football League 2: Aldershot T: Dean Howell (Rushden & D) Free; Chris Blackburn (Swindon T); Marvin Morgan (Woking). **Barnet:** Luke Medley (Bradford C) Free. **Bradford C:** Paul McLaren (Tranmere R) Free; Graeme Lee (Shrewsbury T); Chris Brandon (Huddersfield T) Free. **Brentford:** Marvin Williams (Yeovil T); Marcus Bean (Blackpool) Free; Charlie MacDonald (Southend U). **Bury:** Efetobor Sodje (Bury) Free; Wayne Brown (Hereford U) Free; Ryan Cresswell (Sheffield U) Free. **Chester C:** Ryan Lowe (Crewe Alex) Free; David Mannix (Accrington S) Free; James Harris (Accrington S) Free. **Chesterfield:** Zavon Hines (West Ham U) Loan; Paul Harsley (Port Vale) Free; Robert Page (Huddersfield T) Free. **Darlington:** David Poole (Stockport Co) Free; Adam Griffin (Stockport Co) Free; Adam Proudlock (Stockport Co) Free. **Gillingham:** Mark McCammon (Doncaster R) Free. **Grimsby:** Robbie Stockdale (Tranmere R); Matthew Heywood (Brentford); Richard Hope (Wrexham) Free; Chris Llewellyn (Wrexham) Free. **Lincoln C:** Robert Burch (Sheffield U) Free; Aaron Brown (Gillingham) Free; Janos Kovacs (Chesterfield) Free; Stefan Oakes (Wycombe W) Free. **Macclesfield T:** Paul Morgan (Bury) Loan. **Morecambe:** Michael Carr (Northwich Vic) Free. **Notts Co:** Matt Hamshaw (Mansfield T) Free; Michael Johnson (Derby Co) Free; Jason Beardsley (Derby Co) Loan. **Port Vale:** John McCombe (Hereford U) Free; David Howland (Birmingham C) Free; Steve Thompson (Middlesbrough). **Rochdale:** Scott Wiseman (Darlington) Free; Clark Keltie (Darlington) Free; Ciaran Toner (Grimsby T) Free; Jon Shaw (Halifax T) Free. **Shrewsbury T:** Shane Cansdell-Sherriff (Tranmere R) Free; Grant Holt (Nottingham F) £170,000; Stephen Hindmarch (Carlisle U); Paul Murray (Gretna) Free. **Wycombe W:** Lewis Spence (Crystal Palace) Free.

Scottish Premier League: Aberdeen: Bertrand Bossu (Walsall) Free; Stuart Duff (Dundee U) Free. **Dundee U:** Warren Feeney (Cardiff C) Loan; Paul Dixon (Dundee) Nominal; Michael McGovern (Celtic) Free. **Falkirk:** Neil McCann (Hearts) Free. **Hibernian:** David van Zanten (St Mirren) Free. **Kilmarnock:** Allan Russell (Airdrie U) Free. **Rangers:** Kyle Lafferty (Burnley) £3m; Kenny Miller (Derby Co) £2m. **St Mirren:** Tom Brighton (Millwall) Free.

Leaving the country: Mathieu Flamini Arsenal to AC Milan; Patrik Berger Aston Villa to Sparta Prague; Daniel Braaten Bolton W to Toulouse; Slobodan Rajkovic Chelsea to Twente; Brian McBride Fulham to Toronto; Harry Kewell Liverpool to Galatasaray; Anthony Le Tallec Liverpool to Le Mans; John Arne Riise Liverpool to Roma £3.96m; Andreas Isaksson Manchester City to PSV Eindhoven; Fabio Rochemback Middlesbrough to Sporting Lisbon; Emre Newcastle U to Fenerbahce £2m; Andreas Granqvist Wigan Ath to Groningen £600,000; Julius Aghahowa Wigan Ath to Kayseri; Mikael Forssell Birmingham C to Hannover 96; Ellery Cairo Coventry C to NAC Breda; Junior Agogo Nottingham F to Zanzibar £565,000; Emerse Fae Reading to Nice Loan.

Colin Kazim-Richards was transferred to Fenerbahce in June 2007, but still appears on Sheffield United's retained list.

Now you can buy any of these other bestselling sports titles
from your bookshop or *direct from the publisher.*

Sky Sports Football Yearbook 2008–2009	Glenda Rollin and Jack Rollin	£20.00
1966 and All That	Geoff Hurst	£7.99
Psycho	Stuart Pearce	£7.99
Vinnie	Vinnie Jones	£7.99
Left Foot Forward	Garry Nelson	£6.99
The Doc	Tommy Docherty	£8.99
The Autobiography	Niall Quinn	£7.99
Fathers, Sons and Football	Colin Shindler	£6.99
Cloughie	Brian Clough	£7.99
True Grit	Frank McLintock	£7.99
Gazza: My Story	Paul Gascoigne	£7.99
Right Back to the Beginning	Jimmy Armfield	£7.99
My Defence	Ashley Cole	£7.99
Fallen Idle	Peter Marinello	£6.99
Being Gazza	Paul Gascoigne	£6.99
The Beatles, Football and Me	Hunter Davies	£7.99
The Autobiography	Alan Mullery	£7.99

TO ORDER SIMPLY CALL THIS NUMBER

01235 400 414

or visit our website:
www.headline.co.uk
Prices and availability subject to change without notice.